THE INTERNATIONAL FILM INDUSTRY

RESEARCH ASSOCIATE

Patricia Coward

SPECIAL CONTRIBUTORS

Val Almendarez: France
Alan Gevinson: Denmark, Finland, Japan, Norway, and Sweden
Kevin Hagopian: Canada and the United Kingdom
Andrew Horton: Yugoslavia
Ana Lopez: Argentina, Bolivia, Brazil, Central America, Chile, Colombia, Cuba, Mexico, Nicaragua, Peru, Uruguay, and Venezuela
Lindsay Shelton: New Zealand

THE INTERNATIONAL FILM INDUSTRY

A HISTORICAL DICTIONARY

Anthony Slide

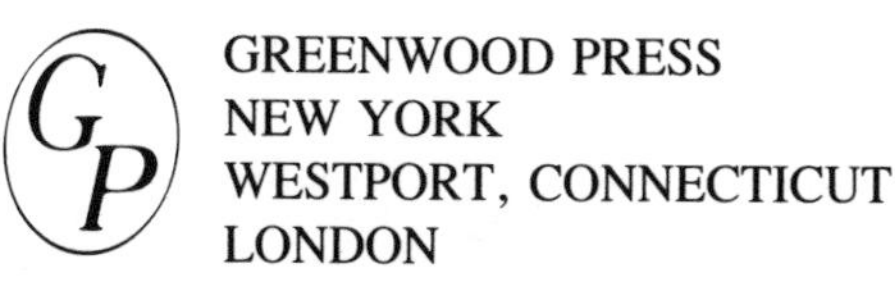
GREENWOOD PRESS
NEW YORK
WESTPORT, CONNECTICUT
LONDON

Library of Congress Cataloging-in-Publication Data

Slide, Anthony.
The international film industry : a historical dictionary / Anthony Slide.
p. cm.
Bibliography: p.
Includes index.
ISBN 0–313–25635–7 (lib. bdg. : alk. paper)
1. Motion picture industry—Dictionaries. I. Title.
PN1993.45.S57 1989
384′.8′0973—dc19 88–25103

British Library Cataloguing in Publication Data is available.

Library of Congress Catalog Card Number: 88–25103
ISBN: 0–313–25635–7

First published in 1989

Greenwood Press, Inc.
88 Post Road West, Westport, Connecticut 06881

Printed in the United States of America

The paper used in this book complies with the Permanent Paper Standard issued by the National Information Standards Organization (Z39.48–1984).

10 9 8 7 6 5 4 3 2 1

Contents

Introduction vii

Entries 1

General Bibliography 401

Index 403

Introduction

The International Film Industry: A Historical Dictionary attempts to provide the same type of reference information for world cinema as was provided for the United States with the author's earlier *The American Film Industry: A Historical Dictionary* (Greenwood Press, 1986). The present volume, like its predecessor, is basically a what's what, rather than a who's who. It offers entries on international production companies, studios, distributors, technical innovations, organizations, and other items. Additionally, the book provides brief historical essays on the cinema in virtually every country of the world, certainly all countries that have any pretense at a film industry. These entries vary in length according to the importance of the film industry in the country concerned and whether there are supplemental entries appropriate to that country. Perhaps naturally, the largest amount of space is devoted to British cinema, which, after the American film industry, has the greatest influence and popularity in the United States.

If a particular company or studio is not the subject of a separate entry but is mentioned in a country entry, immediate access to the information is available through the index. The index provides quick access to a company entry where the names of those associated are all the information a researcher has. Similarly, the index provides access to all entries relating to a specific country. Entries are under the most familiar name of the entity (not necessarily its correct or current one), but both the popular and the correct names can be found in the index.

Whenever a film is mentioned in the text, the original language title is given first, followed by an English translation or the U.S. release title, together with the date of release in the country of origin. Similarly, where the name of an organization is given in its original language, an English translation follows. An asterisk following a name indicates that the entity is the subject of a separate entry.

Quite obviously, it would be impossible to include all companies and organizations, but certainly every major entity dating back to the turn of the century as well as the more important recent subjects are to be found here. The book also provides entries on international genres, with information on films utilizing foreign locations, foreign wars, and foreign characters of international renown, such as Jack the Ripper or Robin Hood. Where appropriate, series are also included; thus, the James Bond films will be found here, because the series is produced by a British rather than an American company.

Some countries that no longer have legal existence have entries, as do the League of Nations and the United Nations and certain regions such as Antarctica and the South Pacific. It has not always been possible—indeed, sometimes it is totally impossible—to keep international politics out of the entries, but an attempt has been made to remain politically neutral in this volume. At the same time, the editor has made an effort to include headings that might offer opportunities for reading enjoyment or browsing pleasure, as well as those on the more obvious and serious topics. More than 650 entries are included, ranging from London's Academy Cinema to an optical toy named the Zoetrope.

This present volume should serve as an essential reference tool for the film scholar, student, and librarian. Additional reference value is provided by the inclusion of a brief bibliography, where appropriate, after most entries. Wherever feasible, birth and death years are noted for key figures mentioned in the entries. A general bibliography of books on world cinema is included at the end of the book.

Acknowledgment is made to the following individuals and organizations for their help in the preparation of this volume: AB Svensk Filmindustri; Margaret Herrick Library of the Academy of Motion Picture Arts and Sciences; Association of Cinematograph, Television and Allied Technicians (Peter Avis); Association of Independent Producers Ltd. (Shelly Bancroft); Australian Film Commission (Peta Spear); Beverly Hills Public Library; British Academy of Film and Television Arts (Kit Greveson); British Federation of Film Societies (Peter Cargin); British Film Institute (F. Margaret Binnie); British Kinematograph, Sound and Television Society (Bill Pay); Cinematograph Exhibitors' Association (Mrs. K. Wheeler); Cineplex Odeon Corporation (Linda Friendly); The Danish Film Institute; Det Danske Filmmuseum (Ellen Grønberg); Geoffrey N. Donaldson; Berit Engen; Allen Eyles; Filmoteca Española (Dolores Devesa); Finnish Film Archive (Irmeli Aronen); Instituto Angolano de Cinema (Arnaldo Santos); International Federation of Film Archives (Brigitte van der Elst); Kristine L. Krueger; Lisa Mosher; The National Film and Television School; National Film Board of Canada (Ron Jones); New South Wales Film Corporation (Jenny Woods); New Zealand Film Commission; New Zealand National Film Unit (Linda McGregor); Nordisk Film Distribution AS; Norsk Film A/S; Norsk Filminstitutt (Øivind Hanche); The Ontario Film Institute (Gerald Pratley); David and Sydney Samuelson; Sandrew Film & Teater AB (Kerstin von Sivers); The Scottish Film Council (John Brown); Clive Sowry; W. Steenbeck & Co. (Winifried Bass); Studio City Public Library; Suomi-Filmi Oy (Kare Orko); and Transit-Film-Gesellschaft MBH (Karl A. Wörner). Special thanks to Linda Wood, for allowing the use of her research for some of the British entries, and to Marilyn Brownstein, who has always been a supportive and helpful editor at Greenwood Press.

A

THE ACADEMY CINEMA, situated on London's Oxford Street, opened in 1913 as the Picture House, changing its name to the Academy in 1928. At that time it was faring badly, but was saved by the arrival of a new proprietor named Elsie Cohen. Cohen had worked on the trade periodical *Kinematograph Weekly** and had organized Britain's first art movie theatre at the Windmill Theatre. Her initial success at the Academy was with a backlog of notable silent films, starting with *Earth,* which had not been publicly screened in the United Kingdom. The screening of new sound films from the Continent, such as *Westfront 1918, Kameradschaft/Comradeship*, and *The Blue Express,* established the importance of the Academy in catering for an intelligent film public. In 1937, George Hoellering came to assist Elsie Cohen and took over as managing director in 1944, when she was in bad health. A filmmaker in his own right, Hoellering shared the same enthusiasms as Elsie Cohen, but he also admired the French film, *Les Enfants du Paradis/The Children of Paradise,* and the Academy has always been associated with screenings of the film, although it was not the first or only theatre to show it. During the Second World War, the Academy suffered bomb damage and was closed for four years. Hoellering was interned as an "enemy alien," and in the internment camp he met emigré artist Peter Strausfeld. The latter was to design every poster, initially using a linoblock based on a still from the film, for the Academy until his death in 1981, and his distinctive linocut style became a hallmark of the Academy Cinema. In March 1965, a second theatre, Academy Two opened in the basement of what had been a ballroom, and, in 1967, the Academy Cinema Club (which had opened in the upper part of the building in 1964) became Academy Three.

Hoellering had been assisted for a number of years by his stepson, Ivo Jarosy, who took over when Hoellering died in 1980. The Academy theatres were the first to screen the films of Ingmar Bergman, Satyajit Ray, Andrzej Wajda, and Miklós Jancsó in the United Kingdom. Many of Michelangelo Antonioni's films were shown there, as were the films of the French New Wave. In 1984, the Film Section of the British Critics Circle gave the Academy a special award for its high standard of programming. However, in 1986 Jarosy received a substantial offer for the building housing the theatres, and on April 2 of that year the three Academy theatres closed. The final films screened there were the Swiss *Dangerous Moves,* the Japanese *The Empty Table,* and the French *The Wanderer.*

BIBLIOGRAPHY

Coxhead, Elizabeth, "Towards a Co-operative Cinema, the Work of the Academy, Oxford Street," *Close Up,* vol. X, no. 2, June 1933, pp. 133–137.

Slide, Anthony, "Elsie Cohen Talks to Anthony Slide about the Academy Cinema, Political Censorship and the British Cinema Scene in the Thirties," *The Silent Picture,* no. 11/12, Summer-Autumn 1971, unpaged.

Taylor, John Russell, "Academic Distinctions," *Sight & Sound,* vol. LV, no. 3, Summer 1986, pp. 184–186.

THE ACADEMY OF CANADIAN CINEMA AND TELEVISION is similar in many respects to its American counterpart, the Academy of Motion Picture Arts and Sciences. Founded in 1979, it sponsors an annual awards presentation; provides a training program for young, would-be filmmakers; and showcases new Canadian cinema. It has also published a number of useful books, including *The Shape of Rage: The Films of David Cronenberg* (1983) and *Who's Who in Canadian Film and Television* (1985). Founded through a grant from the Ontario government, the Academy is now funded by Telefilm Canada* and the Ontario Film Development Corporation.

The most important aspect of its work is the awards program. Genies are presented for work in film, Geminis for work in English language television, and Gemeaux for work in French language television. The presentation of the television awards was taken over from the Alliance of Canadian Cinema, Television, and Radio Artists in 1986. The film awards date back to 1947, when they were first presented by the Canadian Association for Adult Education. Awards for feature films were not presented between 1951 and 1964. The presentation was first televised, by the Canadian Broadcasting Corporation in 1968. With the creation of the Academy, the former method of jury selection of the awards was abolished, and a peer group voting process instituted. At the same time, the awards were named the Genies.

As of 1988, membership in the Academy was 1,500.

Address: 653 Yonge Street, Toronto, Ontario, M4Y I29, Canada.

BIBLIOGRAPHY

Martin, Donald, "The Academy of Canadian Cinema and Television: Taking a Look Inside," *Faces International,* vol. VIII, no. 1, Winter 1988, pp. 450–455.

ACE FILMS was a British distributor of the thirties, specializing in entertainment shorts. It also released the 1935, four-reel documentary on *Lawrence of Arabia.*

ACT FILMS LTD. See ASSOCIATION OF CINEMATOGRAPH, TELEVISION, AND ALLIED TECHNICIANS

THE ADANAC PRODUCING COMPANY was a Canadian concern—the name is "Canada" spelled backwards—founded by George Brownridge and active from 1918 to 1920. Utilizing studios at Trenton, Ontario, the company's films include *Power* (1918), *The Marriage Trap* (1918), and *The Great Shadow* (1919).

BIBLIOGRAPHY

Morris, Peter. *Embattled Shadows: A History of Canadian Cinema 1895–1939*. Montreal: McGill-Queen's University Press, 1978.

AFGHANISTAN has a small film industry, which does not thrive, but at least survives, despite the continuing civil unrest in the country. By 1983, only six features had been produced in Afghanistan, the majority by the government-owned Afghan Films, whose studios were financed in part by American aid. The first feature film to be shot in the country was Columbia's *The Horsemen* (1971), directed by John Frankenheimer, and made with the cooperation of Afghan Films. Aside from Afghan Films, other producers in Afghanistan are Shafaq Films, founded by director Toryali Shafaq in 1979, whose first film was *Janayat Karan/Thieves* (1981); Gulistan Films, founded in 1980; Aparsin Films; and Aryana Films. Nazir Films died in 1981, with its founder, director Mohamed Nazir, who directed Afghanistan's first and only historical drama, *Rabhie Bhalkie,* in 1975.

AFRICA. The African Continent has served as a backdrop for many features. Among the more important are *West of Zanzibar* (1928), *A Dangerous Woman* (1929), *Sanders of the River* (1935), *Song of Freedom* (1936), *Rhodes of Africa* (U.S. *Rhodes,* 1936), *King Solomon's Mines* (1937), *Stanley and Livingstone* (1939), *Africa Screams* (1949), *The African Queen* (1951), *The Snows of Kilimanjaro* (1952), *Mogambo* (1953), *Call Me Bwana* (1963), *Guns at Batasi* (1964), *White Hunter* (1965), *Noir et Blanc en Couleur/Black and White in Color* (1976), *Raid on Entebbe* (1977), *Victory at Entebbe* (1977), *The Gods Must Be Crazy* (1980), *Raiders of the Lost Ark* (1982), *Greystoke* (1985), *King Solomon's Mines* (1986), and *Out of Africa* (1986). The many features in the "Tarzan" series have also been set in Africa.

Two early adventurers-cum-cinematographers Martin E. and Osa Johnson made a number of features set in Africa, including *Trailing African Wild Animals* (1923), *Congorilla* (1932), and *Baboona* (1935). After the death of her husband in 1937, Osa Johnson worked solo, with later films including *I Married Adventure* (1940) and *African Paradise* (1942). Osa Johnson published a volume on the careers of herself and her husband, *I Married Adventure* (Philadelphia: J.B. Lippincott), in 1940.

The Bantu Educational Cinema Experiment was introduced in March 1935, through the efforts of Major L.A. Notcutt and J. Merle Davis. This somewhat patronizing project involved the production and exhibition of special films for the black natives of various British colonies in Africa, in an effort to combat the distorted presentation of the lives of the white races as depicted in commercial films. The project was conducted under the auspices of the British Department of Social and Industrial Research, in cooperation with the British Colonial Office and the British Film Institute*. It is discussed in detail in *The African and the Cinema: An Account of the Work of the Bantu Educational Cinema Experiment during the Period March 1935 to May 1937* by L.A. Notcutt and G.C. Latham (London: Edinburgh House Press, 1937).

See also ALGERIA; ANGOLA; CAMEROON; CONGO, PEOPLE'S REPUBLIC OF; EGYPT; GABON; IVORY COAST; MALI; MOROCCO; NIGER; NIGERIA; SENEGAL; SOUTH AFRICA; TUNISIA; and UPPER VOLTA.

BIBLIOGRAPHY

Kamphausen, Hannes, "Cinema in Africa: A Survey," *Cineaste,* vol. V, no. 3, Summer 1972, pp. 29–41.

Maynard, Richard A. *Africa on Film: Myth and Reality*. Rochelle Park, N.J.: Hayden Book Co., 1974.

Pfaff, Françoise. *Twenty-Five Black African Filmmakers: A Critical Study, with Filmography and Bio-Bibliography*. Westport, Conn.: Greenwood Press, 1988.

AGENCE GÉNÉRALE CINÉMATOGRAPHIQUE (AGC) was an important French film distributor during the silent era, handling the releases of Eclair*, The Eclipse Company*, Film d'Art*, and others.

AGFACOLOR was introduced as a multilayer color process for use with 16mm film by the German company, Agfa Filmfabrik, in 1936. The system utilized color-forming substances in three emulsion layers rather than being carried in the color developers, and thus a single development could produce three color images in all three layers simultaneously. Professional 35mm use of the process was developed in 1939 and came into use in Germany in 1940 with the feature *Frauen sind doch bessere diplomaten/Women Are the Best Diplomats*. Agfacolor was utilized by the German film industry throughout the Second World War, with the best known example of its use being in Josef von Baky's *Münchhausen* (1943) and Veit Harlan's *Kolberg* (1945).

At the close of the Second World War, the Agfacolor patents were seized by the Russians and used as the basis for Sovcolor* and for the East German color process, Orwocolor. An American subsidiary of Agfa continued with the process in the United States, where it was renamed Ansco Color. In 1964, the German Agfa AG merged with the Belgian company, Gevaert Photo-Producten N.V., and the new company, and its color process, became Agfa-Gevaert.

Address: Agfa-Gevaert N.V., Septestraat 27, B-2510 Mortsel, Antwerp, Belgium.

AGITAKI. See AGIT-PROP

AGIT-PROP. A Russian term meaning the information and education of the masses in the theory and practice of communism, Agit-Prop has been an important part of the Soviet film industry since the Revolution. The newsreels, documentaries, and features created to this end are known as Agitaki.

AJYM was formed as a production company by French film director Claude Chabrol (born 1930), with an inheritance from his first wife. He later married Stéphane Audran, who appears in many of his films. AJYM produced Chabrol's first two features, both released in 1958, *Le Beau Serge/Handsome Serge* and *Les Cousins/The Cousins.*

ALBANIA. From the first film production in Albania in 1947, the number of features has risen slowly, with an average of one a year through the late sixties, two in 1969, four in 1970, and fourteen in 1985. The first Albanian film studio, Shaipëria e re (New Albanian Film Studio) opened in 1952, under government control—all theatres were nationalized in 1947. Albania's first feature, *Velikii voin Albanii Skanderbeg/The Great Warrior Skanderbeg,* was directed by the Soviet filmmaker, Sergei Yutkevich, in 1954. The first major Albanian feature was *Tana,* directed by Kristaq Dhamo in 1958, and the next Albanian feature, *Debatik,* directed by Hysen Hakanin, was not released until 1961.

Films are made exclusively for home consumption, and no effort is made to export Albanian features. Major directors include Dhimitër Anagosti, Endri Keko, and Piro Milkani.

BIBLIOGRAPHY

Bachmann, Gideon, "Albania: Films Surprisingly Good, but Heavies Are Always Italian," *Variety,* May 2, 1979, pp. 5, 36.

———, "Albanian Attitudes," *Sight & Sound,* vol. XLVIII, no. 3, Summer 1979, pp. 156–157.

"Rare Glimpses of Albanian Cinema at Giffoni Event," *Variety,* August 14, 1985, pp. 5, 22.

Velissariou, Rena, "Albania Was Once 85% Illiterate, Uses Screen To Exhort 'Education,' " *Variety,* October 10, 1979, p. 112.

ALGERIA. Prior to Algeria's independence in 1962, one studio and film laboratory, Africa Film, was in operation (it later moved to Tunisia), and in 1954 the French had installed three regional television stations. The Algerian National Liberation Front set up a short-lived film school in 1957. A similar organization, the Algerian National Cinema Institute, was created in 1964, and here almost sixty filmmakers and technicians were trained prior to its closure.

In the same year as Algeria's independence, Yacef Saadi founded Casbah Films, which was involved in the co-production and co-financing of a number of major productions. A year later, the Algerian Current Affairs Office was established, and it produced a number of shorts and one feature, *Le vent des Aurès/Winds of the Aures*. In 1964, the government nationalized the entire Algerian film industry, and established the Office National pour le Commerce et l'Industrie Cinématographiques (ONCIC, Immeuble les Asphodeles, Ben-Aknoun, Alger, Algeria). As a result, American film companies refused to "sell" their product to Algeria, and it was not until the mid-seventies that the situation became more normalized, with both the United States and France once more distributing features in the country.

Following the war of independence, Algerian filmmakers created the *Cinéma Maudjahid* (The Cinema of the Freedom Fighter), which consisted of features, directed by Lakhdar-Hamina, Slid Riad, Mustapha Badie, Achmed Rachedi, and others, that glorified the fight against colonialism. In the early seventies, a new genre, *Cinéma Djidid* (New Cinema) was created by Mohamed Boumari, Ahmed Lallem, Moussa Haddad, and others, that dealt more with social realism. One of the first major films in this genre was Abdelaziz Tolbi's *Nous* (1972).

The role of women in Algeria was discussed in *La Nouba des femmes du Mt. Chenoua/The Nouba of the Women of Mt. Chenoua* (1978), directed by female novelist Assia Djebar. The meeting of different cultures, Arab and American, is the subject of Ibrahim Tsaki's *Histoire d'une rencontre/Story of an Encounter* (1983). Other important Algerian features of the eighties include Abdelkrim Bahloul's *Thé à la menthe/Mint Tea* (1984) and Ali Ghalem's *Une femme pour mon fils/A Wife for My Son* (1983). Algerian filmmaking received a major boost in 1975 when Mohamed Lakhdar-Hamina's *Chronique des Années de Braise/Chronicle of the Years of Embers* won the Grand Prix at the Cannes Film Festival*.

There are approximately 350 film theatres in Algeria, and a typical Algerian production is budgeted at between $100,000 and $150,000 (all that it could possibly earn through a domestic release). As of 1985, the state monopoly on film production and distribution ceased.

BIBLIOGRAPHY

Brossard, Jean Pierre, editor. *L'Algérie vue par son Cinéma*. Locarno: Festival du Film, 1981.

Maherzi, Lotfi. *Le cinéma Algérien*. Alger: Société Nationale d'Edition et de Diffusion, 1980.

Malkmus, Lizbeth, "Algeria," in *International Film Guide 1986,* editor Peter Cowie. London: Tantivy Press, 1985, pp. 36–38.

Salmane, Hala, Simon Hartog, and David Wilson, editors. *Algerian Cinema*. London: British Film Institute, 1976.

Samak, Qussai, "The Arab Cinema and the National Question: From the Trivial to the Sacrosanct," *Cineaste,* vol. IX, no. 3, Spring 1979, pp. 32–34.

ALLIANCE ENTERTAINMENT CORPORATION claims to be the largest independent producer in Canada. Co-founded by Robert Lantos, Denis Heroux, and John Kemeny, Alliance is involved in television production (with two series, *Night Heat* and *Diamonds,* seen on late-night television in the United States) and various features and movies-made-for-television. According to *Variety* (November 24, 1987), Alliance claimed a 1987 production budget of $70 million, Canadian.

Address: 92 Isabella Street, Toronto, Ontario M4Y 1N4, Canada.

THE ALL-RED FEATURE COMPANY was founded in Windsor, Canada, in the summer of 1914 by American cinematographer Frederic Colburn Clarke. It produced a three-reel drama, *The War Pigeon* (1914) and a newsreel, *All-Red Weekly,* before ceasing operations.

BIBLIOGRAPHY

Morris, Peter. *Embattled Shadows: A History of Canadian Cinema 1895–1939*. Montreal: McGill-Queen's University Press, 1978.

AMANDA AWARDS. The most important of all Norwegian film awards, the Amanda Awards are presented annually in August at the same time as the Norwegian Film Festival. They are broadcast live over the Norwegian Broadcasting Corporation.

Norsk kino- og filmfond/The Norwegian Cinema and Film Foundation and the township of Haugesund established A/S Filmfestivalen/The Norwegian Film Festival. The Amanda—den norske film og TV-prisen/The Amanda Award for Television and Cinematography Merit was first presented at the festival on August 17, 1985, for films and television programs first seen between June 1984 and June 1985. That first year ten categories were included: Best Norwegian Feature, Best TV Play, Best Short, Best Children's Film or TV Production, Best Actor, Best Actress, Best Cinematography, Best Original Music Score, Best Foreign Film, and a Honorary Award. The categories vary slightly from year to year.

The Amanda Awards are intended to create a greater interest in Norwegian production. The winner is selected by a three-person jury, headed by Jan Erik Holst. There are three nominees in each category. Films must be entered by their producers, and must have 50 percent Norwegian capitalization, except, of course, for the foreign film entrants, which must be submitted by the Norwegian distributor.

The name of the award is taken from a well-known sailor's ballad, ''Amanda fra Haugesund,'' the heroine of which is from Haugesund. The award is a bronze statuette of Amanda, created by sculptor Kristian Kvakland.

ANCINEX is a French production company, active since 1962, whose features include *Mourir à Madrid/To Die in Madrid* (1962), *Les Animaux/The Animals* (1963), and *Phèdre* (1968).

Address: 36 rue de Colisee, 75008 Paris, France.

ANGLIA FILMS LTD. was a British production company of the thirties, specializing in cartoon shorts in the Dunning color process. The chief animator was Anson Dyer, and the films featured a working-class character from the north of England named Sam, with the voice of Stanley Holloway.

ANGLO-AMALGAMATED FILM DISTRIBUTORS LTD. The British production and distribution company, Anglo-Amalgamated Film Distributors Ltd., was formed in 1942 by Nat Cohen and Stuart Levy. The two men remained partners until Levy's death in 1968.

Cohen was born in the East End of London, the son of a butcher who was also a silent partner in a small chain of movie theatres. The younger Cohen entered the film industry in 1930 as an exhibitor, but he always wanted to be involved in production and distribution, and this he was able to do by selling the theatre chain and using the capital to form Anglo-Amalgamated Film Distributors Ltd. Likewise, Levy started on the exhibition side of the business, working with his uncle in Liverpool. He went into distribution with the Liverpool branch of Ideal Films, later representing RKO and becoming general manager of International Film Renters.

Initially, Anglo-Amalgamated specialized in ''B'' films, including some fifty titles based on the works of Edgar Wallace. Its first major success came in 1957 with *The Tommy Steele Story*. In the same year, it launched the first ''Carry On''* feature, *Carry On Sergeant,* and was to distribute the next twelve films in the series. Directors John Schlesinger and Ken Loach were given their first chances by Anglo-Amalgamated; Schlesinger with *A Kind of Loving* (1962) and Loach with *Poor Cow* (1967). Stars, such as Julie Christie and Alan Bates, also owe their early successes to Anglo-Amalgamated; Julie Christie with *Billy Liar, Darling,* and *Far from the Madding Crowd* and Bates with *A Kind of Loving, Darling,* and *Far from the Madding Crowd*. Cohen prided himself on his financial skills and once boasted, ''Lawrence Harvey got his lowest salary ever for *Darling,* but came out with the most money he ever made. Same with Terence Stamp and *Poor Cow*.''

In 1962, half the company was purchased by Associated British Picture Corporation, and in 1969 Cohen sold his last 25 percent of Anglo-Amalgamated to EMI for a reported £500,000. In May 1970, he became chairman and chief executive officer of the newly created Anglo-EMI. His proud boast was that ''90 percent of the films I've been involved with have made money.''

THE ANGLO-AMERICAN FILM AGREEMENT followed the 1947 imposition by a British Socialist government of a 75 percent ad valorem tax on American films released in the United Kingdom. When the Americans responded with a boycott of the British market, an agreement was worked out whereby a limit was placed on the profits that American producers/distributors could take out of Britian, and required the remainder be used to promote film production in the United Kingdom.

ANGOLA. Following its independence from Portugal in 1975, the African nation of Angola began actively to produce revolutionary documentaries. It established the Instituto Angolano de Cinema (Caixa Postal No. 3512, Luanda, People's Republic of Angola), headed by Angolan novelist, Luandino Vieira. The earliest Angolan films, including *Acontecimentos de Luanda, Aghostinho Neto em Cabinda,* and *Caxito 1,* were directed in 1975 by Carlos Sousa e Costa. An important group of ten documentaries was directed in 1975 by Raúl de Almeida, António Ole, Rui Duarte, Aúrea de Carvalho, Carlos António, and Jorge Gouveia, under the collective title of *Sou Angolano, Trabalho com força/I Am Angolan, I Work Hard*. The first fictional Angolan feature-length film was *Nelisita,* directed by Rui Duarte in 16mm in 1982. It was filmed in black-and-white. Feature-length documentary films had been made in Angola prior to 1982, as had a forty-three minute "featurette," titled *Kiala Mukanga,* released in 1981.

All films released in Angola, which come from both Western nations and Eastern European countries, are imported by the state-owned ENCINE, which also controls all theatres in the country.

BIBLIOGRAPHY

Abrantes, José Mena. *Cinema Angolano: Um Passado a Merecer Melhor Presente*. Luanda: Cinemateca Nacional, 1986.

Armes, Roy, "Angola," in *International Film Guide 1986,* editor Peter Cowie. London: Tantivy Press, 1985, pp. 39–40.

10 Anos Cinema Angolano. Luanda: Cinemateca Nacional, 1985.

ANGRY YOUNG MEN was a term used to describe the directors of the British Free Cinema* movement who emerged in the late fifties. It was first used in relationship to the theatre in describing the exponents of so-called "Kitchen Sink Drama," which dates from the 1956 production of John Osborne's *Look Back in Anger*. The latter was filmed in 1959 by one of the cinema's angry young men, Tony Richardson. Other directors to whom the term was applied are Lindsay Anderson, Karel Reisz, and Albert Finney.

ANICA (Associazone Nazionale Industrie Cinematografiche Affini) is the Italian equivalent of the Motion Picture Association of America. Under its umbrella title are various subgroups: the Union of Producers, the Union of Distributors, the Union of Film Importers, and the Union of Technical Industries. Carmine Cianfarani has been president of the organization since 1973.

Address: 286 Viale R. Margherita, 286 00198 Rome, Italy.

ANOUCHKA FILMS was founded by French director Jean-Luc Godard (born December 3, 1930) and his then-wife, Anna Karina, in 1964. It has produced or co-produced almost all of the director's films: *Bande à part/Band of Outsiders* (1964), *Le femme mariée/The Married Woman* (1964), *Masculin-Féminin/Masculine Feminine* (1965), *Made in USA* (1966), *Deux ou trois choses que je sais d'elle/Two or Three Things That I Know about Her* (1966), *La Chinoise* (1967),

Le gai savoir/The Joy of Learning (1968), *Vent d'est/Wind from the East* (1970), *Lotte in Italia/Struggles in Italy* (1970), and *Tout va bien/Just Great* (1972).

ANTARCTICA has been the setting for a number of features, including *With Byrd at the South Pole* (1930), *Scott of the Antarctic* (1948), *Antarctic Crossing* (1959), *Never Cry Wolf* (1984), *Antarctica* (1985), and *White Nights* (1986). On a sillier note, it has also served as a backdrop for *The Thing* (1951), *The Navy vs. the Night Monsters* (1966), and *Iceman* (1985).

THE ARCHERS was a production company established by director Michael Powell and screenwriter Emeric Pressburger in 1943 to produce the two men's films for the "Independent Producers"* program of The Rank Organization*. The two decided upon a target with an arrow hitting center as their trademark, with the words "A Production of The Archers" superimposed upon it. It was agreed that the final credit should not take into account what each man had contributed to the film, but read simply "Written, Produced and Directed by Michael Powell and Emeric Pressburger."

The following are Archers productions or co-productions: *The Silver Fleet* (1943), *The Life and Death of Colonel Blimp* (U.S. *Colonel Blimp,* 1943), *The Volunteer* (1943), *A Canterbury Tale* (1944), *I Know Where I'm Going* (1945), *A Matter of Life and Death* (U.S. *Stairway to Heaven,* 1946), *Black Narcissus* (1947), *The End of the River* (1947), *The Red Shoes* (1948), *The Small Back Room* (1949), *The Elusive Pimpernel* (1950), *The Tales of Hoffmann* (1951), *Oh Rosalinda!* (1955), *The Battle of the River Plate* (1956), and *Ill Met by Moonlight* (1956).

BIBLIOGRAPHY

Christie, Ian, editor. *Powell, Pressburger and Others*. London: British Film Institute, 1978.

Powell, Michael. *A Life in Movies*. London: Heinemann, 1986.

ARDMORE STUDIOS was opened by Emmet Dalton and Louis Elliman in 1958. It is located some twelve miles outside of Dublin, near the town of Bray, County Wicklow, and covers approximately forty acres. It is Ireland's only film studio, and the first production to be shot there was *Home Is the Hero* (1959), based on the play by Walter Macken. The studio has never been financially successful. It went into receivership in 1962; was sold to the New Brighton Tower Company in 1967; was purchased by the Irish government in 1973; closed down in 1982; purchased by Pakistani shipping magnate Mahmound Sipra in 1984; and acquired by the American MTM Enterprises in 1985.

Address: Bray, County Wicklow, Ireland.

ARGENTINA. A group of European immigrants was responsible for the first cinématographe screening in Buenos Aires in July 1896. They included Henri Lepage (Belgium), Max Glucksmann (Austria), and Eugene Py (France, also responsible for the first Argentine film, *La Bandera Argentina/The Argentine Flag,* 1897). This group was typical of the individuals who developed the Argentine silent cinema, all recent immigrants from northern Europe who invested, first, in foreign films and projection equipment and spaces for theatrical exhibition, and only later in production technology and studio facilities. By 1908–1909, many local distributors were handling foreign films and also producing short features and documentaries. Further national investment in the young industry was spurred by the remarkable commercial success of *Nobleza Gaucha* (1915), which grossed six hundred thousand pesos (on an investment of only twenty). Then, with the interruption of European film imports caused by the First World War in 1916–1919, national production boomed.

Among the most important silent films were *El Ultimo Malón* (Alcides Greco, 1916) and *Juan Sin Ropa* (Juan Quiroga, 1919). A new director, Roberto Guidi, demonstrated an interest in cultural and theoretical issues in his *Mala Yerba* (1920) and *Escándalo a Medianoche* (1923). However, José Agustin Ferreyra was the first truly nationalist filmmaker, the first to produce a cinema that celebrated national authenticity without folkloricism. As the titles of his silent filmography indicate, Ferreyra was fascinated by tangos and his films explored the Buenos Aires tango environment and its popular types: *Corazón de Criolla* (1923), *Mientras Buenos Aires Duerme* (1924), *Mi Último Tango* (1925), *La Cancion del Gaucho* (1930).

It was the coming of sound that finally defined the Argentine film industry and propelled it to Latin American prominence. The schism in the international film market produced by the sudden untranslateablity of the Hollywood cinema, opened a space for Argentine films throughout Latin America. Other national film industries (in Mexico and Brazil, for example) withered when confronted with the challenge of sound technology, but the Argentine flourished because it transformed the tango into a vehicle for cinematic expansion. Although Carlos Gardel, tango's premier star, was whisked off to Joinville (Paris) in 1931 to make films for Paramount, a new breed of Argentine producers quickly followed the lead.

Angel Mentasti, for instance, nicknamed the "czar of the Argentine cinema," founded Argentina Sono Films and cast his first production, *Tango!* (1933), with every well-known tango orchestra and singer as well as the stars of the silent cinema and the stage. The film was so successful that its "review" formula (minimal script/maximum music) was consecrated in dozens of subsequent Sono Film features. Meanwhile, the pioneers of Argentine radio founded a rival company, Lumiton, and built extensive studios in the style of the Hollywood majors. Lumiton's first feature, *Los Tres Berretines* (1933) also dealt with the tango (together with soccer and the cinema, the "three" popular obsessions) and was extremely successful, transforming popular actor Luis Sandrini into a major star.

Not content merely to link together a series of musical numbers like his peers in the silent era, director José Agustin Ferreyra developed a unique cinematic form inspired by tangos. His realist, populist tendencies flourished in this period with films like *Calles de Buenos Aires* (1933). His subsequent films, always musicals with a melodramatic plot, created singer Libertad Lamarque as the principal figure of the nascent Argentine star-system: *Ayudame a Vivir* (1936), *Besos Brujos* (1937), and *La Ley Que Olvidaron* (1937). In tandem with these successes, annual feature production between 1932 and 1942 increased from two to fifty-six films, a record that would never be bettered. In its heyday, four thousand actors and technicians were employed by over thirty studios in Buenos Aires. Yet, Ferreyra was swallowed whole by the transformation he himself sparked, and, unable to adapt his improvisational, anarchic style to the strictures of industrialized studio filmmaking, he ended his days, like a tango protagonist, destitute and forgotten.

The industry, however, continued to exploit the links between the cinema and the tango tradition for several years, until, having exhausted its public, it sought more middle-class audiences with sophisticated and urbane productions. For example, director Francisco Mugica specialized in the Argentine equivalent of Italian white telephone films* (*Margarita, Armando y su Padre,* 1939), and Luis Cesar Amadori and Luis Saaslavsky were diligent calligraphists in the service of the studios. The most interesting directors, however, were linked to a realist cinematic strain. Mario Soffici explored the poverty of the countryside in his *Prisioneros de la Tierra* (1939) while Leopoldo Torres Rios focused on urban problems in his *La Vuelta al Nido* (1938) and *Pelota de Trapo* (1948).

The prosperity of the Argentine industry lasted less than a dozen years, and after the Second World War, Mexico became dominant in the Latin American market. The national industry declined because of aesthetic as well as economic problems. A wartime export embargo by the United States cut off Argentina's access to celluloid and crippled production during the war. After the war, the industry sought international status by underplaying the national characteristics that had originally promoted its success—the typical *lufardo* slang of inner-city Buenos Aires, the tango, the urban melodrama, and the Strindberg, Tolstoy, and Ibsen adaptations that took their place did not generate much interest.

Once production declined, it became apparent that the Argentine studios were and had always been dependent upon distributors and exhibitors, sectors closely affiliated with foreign concerns uninterested in developing the national cinema. Furthermore, Juan Perón's government, although based on state protectionism, did not have a policy for the development of the national cinematic industry. Some protectionist measures were implemented in the mid to late forties (screen quotas and a limit on imports), but they were mere palliatives that did not address the deeper contradictions of the system.

Perón's protectionist measures were not successful, but their sudden abolishment by the military government that deposed Perón in 1955 gave the coup de grace to an already-weakened industry and essentially ended studio-system production in Argentina. After a postwar high of fifty-six films in 1950, the annual number of productions declined steadily and reached a postwar low of fifteen films in 1957.

New protectionist measures—the "Cinema Law" and the creation of the Instituto Nacional de Cinematografía—were put into effect in 1957, but the impetus for the "New" Argentine cinema of the late fifties and early sixties arose, not from changes in the commercial sector, but from changes in the relationship between filmmakers and the cinema.

One early spark of change in an otherwise moribund industry was the emergence of two new directors in the early fifties—Leopoldo Torre-Nilsson and Fernando Ayala. Both found the inspiration for their films in Argentine fiction and were able to capitalize upon the success of their films to set up their own independent production companies (respectively, Producciones Angel and Aries Cinematografíca), but the trajectory of their careers differed significantly. Torre-Nilsson went on to become the best-known auteur of the Argentine cinema, while Ayala, with Aries Cinematografíca, made increasingly more commercial and less ambitious films.

Together with this auteurist impulse, the emergence of cinema culture—especially cine clubs, university education, and specialized film journals—was crucial for the development of a group of young, new directors who began their careers with shorts and premiered their first features in 1959–1961. The principal filmmakers of the *Joven Cine* (Young Cinema) movement were Simón Feldman, José A. Martínez Suárez, Manuel Antín, David José Kohon, Rodolfo Kuhn, and Lautaro Murúa. With the exception of Murua, these young cineastes, trained in cinématheques and cine-clubs rather than in studios, adopted the cinema as a vehicle of self-expression. Their films were narratively experimental, personal, and cosmopolitan, exploiting the streets of Buenos Aires as locales for *intimiste,* almost autobiographical expression. Although at first promising, this Argentine "New Wave" withered quickly because of economic problems, social limitations, and the political instability of Argentina.

Simultaneous with *Joven Cine,* however, filmmaker Fernando Birri was developing a different kind of national cinema in the northeastern city of Santa Fe. Through the auspices of the Universidad del Litoral, Birri and his students prepared the groundwork for a realist, popular national cinema that spoke with the Argentines rather than to them and, above all, that served a social function. With films like *Tire Dié/Throw a Dime* (1956), Birri (known as the "father" of the New Latin American Cinema) addressed issues that echoed throughout Latin America in the late fifties and sixties and that had a decisive impact on filmmaking throughout the continent.

In Argentina, this pan–Latin American force was most noticeable in the work of clandestine filmmakers who took up the cinema on the margins of the still struggling commercial industry, as an active agent for political change in the late sixties and seventies. The best known of these groups was the pro-Perón *Grupo Cine Liberacion/Liberation Cinema Group* (Fernando Solanas, Octavio Getino, and Gerardo Vallejo). Their film *La Hora de los Hornos/The Hour of the Furnaces* (1968–1969) remains one of the most significant achievements of international political filmmaking and their manifesto, "Hacia un Tercer Cine," a crucial document for the development of the New Latin American Cinema.

When a Perónist, Hector José Campora, assumed the presidency in 1973, the political euphoria of the period reinvigorated all filmmaking, even in the weak commercial sector. A number of significant films were produced by "name" directors: Héctor Olivera's *La Patagonia Rebelde/Rebellion in Patagonia* (financed by the largest commercial producer, Aries Cinematografíca), Leopoldo Torre-Nilsson's *Boquitas Pintadas/Painted Lips,* Leonardo Favio's *Juan Moreira,* and Lautaro Murúa's *La Raulito.* Under Perónist rule, film production (fifty-four films in fourteen months) and attendance (40 percent increase) grew dramatically.

After Perón assumed the presidency, political pressures and terrorist activities escalated and filmmakers of all persuasions went into exile in order to not be "disappeared" by paramilitary squads. After 1976—when a military coup deposed Isabel Perón—cinema activities came to an almost complete standstill: only sixteen films were produced in 1976 and seventeen in 1977.

The military junta that ruled Argentina until 1983 imposed a regime of terror that curtailed the development of the national cinema. However, sweeping changes were made following the election of Raul Alfonsin to the presidency: filmmaker Manuel Antin was named director of the Instituto Nacional de Cinematografiá and promised to restore production to thirty films per year, censorship was abolished, and the film critic Jorge Miguel Couselo was appointed head of the film classification board. Although production levels for 1986 and 1987 were not as high as anticipated, and the industry continued to struggle with inflation and decreasing theatrical audiences, the success of films like *La Historia Oficial/The Official Story* (Luis Puenzo, 1986; Best Foreign Film Oscar) and *Tangos: El Exilio de Gardel/Tangos: The Exile of Gardel* (Fernando Solanas, 1986; Special Jury Prize Venice Film Festival) bode well for the future of the Argentine cinema.

BIBLIOGRAPHY

Burton, Julianne, compiler. *The New Latin American Cinema: An Annotated Bibliography of English-Language Sources, 1960–1976.* New York: Cineaste, 1976.

Couselo, Jorge Miguel, editor. *Cine Argentino, 1897–1931.* Buenos Aires: Centro de Investigation de la Historia del Cine Argentino, 1959.

Hurie, William G., "The Argentine Republic and Its Film Industry," *Sight & Sound,* vol. VIII, no. 31, Autumn 1939, pp. 93–96.

Norgate, Matthew, "The Argentine Cinema," *Sight & Sound,* vol. XVII, no. 66, Summer 1948, pp. 45–47.

Tew, H.P., "Cinema in the Argentine," *Close Up,* vol. VI, no. 2, 1930, pp. 140–145.

ARGUI FILMS was a French production company formed by Jacques-Louis Nounez to produce two films directed by Jean Vigo (1883–1934): *Zéro de Conduite/Zero for Conduct* (1933) and *L'Atalante* (1934).

ARIANE FILMS (also known as Les Films Ariane) has been a major French film producer since 1946. Among its features are *Les Enfants Terribles/The Strange Ones* (1948), *Fanfan la Tulipe/Fanfan the Tulip* (1952), *Vivre pour vivre/Live for Life* (1966), *Stavisky* (1973), and *Preparez vos mouchoirs/Get Out Your Handkerchiefs* (1978).

In 1986, the company was acquired by Éditions Mondiales, and a year later announced a gross income of $25 million. Ariane announced plans to enter the distribution field in January 1989, with nine features which it had self-produced and a further three which it had purchased.

Address: 44 Champs-Elysées, 75008 Paris, France.

ARK stands for the Association of Revolutionary Cinematography (Assotsiatsiia Revoliutsionnoi Kinematografii), a professional society, founded in Moscow in February 1924. Its first chairman was Nikolai Lebedev and among its members were Sergei Eisenstein and Lev Kuleshov. It published an important early Soviet critical film journal, *Kino-zhurnal ARK,* from 1925. Largely because of its independence, it was the subject of a number of purges, beginning in 1930, and the association was officially disbanded in 1935.

BIBLIOGRAPHY

Youngblood, Denise J. *Soviet Cinema in the Silent Era, 1918–1935*. Ann Arbor, Mich.: UMI Research Press, 1985.

ARMENIA is remembered today for the massacre of its people by the Turks between 1894 and 1915. The massacre was the subject of an American feature, *Ravished Armenia* (also known as *Auction of Souls*), the story of Aurora Mardiganian, which received its premiere in January 1919. *Ravished Armenia* was produced by William N. Selig for the American Committee for Armenian and Syrian Relief, and directed by Oscar Apfel.

Now part of the USSR, Armenia has a filmmaking tradition dating back to 1906. The most prominent of early Armenian filmmakers was Amo Bek-Nazarov, active as a director in the twenties and thirties, in whose honor the Armenian film studios at Erevan are named. A so-called New Armenian Cinema developed in the sixties, with directors Stepan Kevorkov, Erasm Karamyan, Frunze Dovlatyan, Genrikh Malyan, Khoren Abramyan, and Arkady Ayrapetyan.

Armenia also gave one major filmmaker to the American film industry in the person of Rouben Mamoulian (1898–1988). Perhaps rather fancifully, he claims that the tune, "Isn't It Romantic," from one of his most popular productions, *Love Me Tonight* (1932), is based on an Armenian folk song.

ARNOLD & RICHTER CINE TECHNIK. See ARRIFLEX

ARRIFLEX or Arri is the name by which the German company of Arnold & Richter Cine Technik is known throughout the world. Founded in 1917 by Dr. Robert Richter (died 1971) and Dr. August Arnold (died 1983), Arnold & Richter is the world's largest manufacturer of motion picture equipment, with more than one thousand employees. It introduced its first hand-held 35mm camera in 1936 (a camera utilized by newsreel cameramen for both the Allies and the Axis powers during the Second World War) and its first 16mm camera in 1952. Its American subsidiary, Arriflex Corporation of America, was founded in 1953.

Arnold & Richter has received three Scientific or Technical Awards from the Academy of Motion Picture Arts and Sciences: A Class II Award in 1966 "for the design and development of the Arriflex 35mm Portable Motion Picture Reflex Camera"; a Class II Award in 1973 "for the development and engineering of the Arriflex 35BL Motion Picture Camera"; and an Award of Merit in 1982 "for the concept and engineering of the first operational 35mm, hand-held, spring-mirror reflex, motion picture camera."

Address: 89 Turkenstrasse, 8000 Munich 40, West Germany; 500 Route 300, Blauvelt, NY 10913.

ARTHURIAN CINEMA. The legend of King Arthur dates back in print at least to 1485. On film, the legend has been perpetuated in, among others, *A Connecticut Yankee* (1931), *King Arthur Was a Gentleman* (1942), *A Connecticut Yankee at King Arthur's Court* (1949), *Knights of the Round Table* (1954), *The Black Knight* (1954), *Prince Valiant* (1954), *Lancelot and Guinevere* (1963), *To Parsifal* (1963), *The Sword in the Stone* (1964), *Camelot* (1967), *Lancelot du Lac* (1974), *Perceval* (1978), and *Excalibur* (1981). There was also a popular television series, *Sir Lancelot* (1956–1957), with William Russell in the title role and Ronald Leigh-Hunt as King Arthur.

BIBLIOGRAPHY

"Arthurian Cinema," *Field of Vision,* no. 13, Spring 1985, pp. 2–9.

ARTS COUNCIL OF GREAT BRITAIN. Founded in 1945, the Arts Council of Great Britain has financed a number of important documentaries and also funds the exhibition and distribution of artists' films and video. It is funded by the Office of Arts and Libraries.

Address: 105 Piccadilly, London W1V OAU, United Kingdom.

THE ASKANIA CAMERA, manufactured by Askania Werke A.G. of Berlin, was one of the most popular 35mm cameras in use in Nazi Germany; it was used by Leni Riefenstahl to film both *Triumph des willens/Triumph of the Will* (1935) and *Olympia* (1938).

ASSOCIATED BRITISH PICTURE CORPORATION. See ELSTREE STUDIOS

ASSOCIATED REALIST FILM PRODUCERS was formed in the United Kingdom in 1936 as a society for all involved in documentary film production. Its activities were suspended in 1940 as a result of the Second World War.

ASSOCIATED SCREEN NEWS OF CANADA LTD. was founded in July 1920 by Bernard E. Norrish, who had earlier been responsible for the Canadian government's Film Bureau in Ottawa. Associated Screen News opened a film laboratory, and quickly became the major supplier of newsreel footage on Canada for use in both foreign newsreels and Canadian adaptations of the same. Canadian Pacific Railway (CPR) was a major investor in the company, which produced a considerable number of films promoting travel in Canada by the CPR. It was later to be a major producer of sponsored films for companies such as the Ford Motor Company, Shell, Canadian General Electric, and Sun Life.

Among the films of Associated Screen News in the twenties are *Old French Canada* (1921), *Heap Busy Indians* (1922), *New Homes within the Empire* (1923), *Making New Canadians* (1925), *Rivers of Romance* (1927), *Yukon* (1928), and *From British Home to Canadian Farm* (1929). Many of these films were part of popular series, titled "Kinograms," first produced in 1921, and the mainstay of the company's activities in the twenties. Interestingly, many of the titles for Associated Screen News' silent releases were the work of American Terry Ramsaye, who wrote the classic text on the history of the motion picture industry, *A Million and One Nights* (New York: Simon and Schuster, 1926).

In the early thirties, filmmaker Gordon Sparling joined the company, and he was to direct many of Associated Screen News' "Canadian Cameos" series, which commenced in 1932 and was seen on Canadian screens until 1953. The series depicted all aspects of Canadian life and includes such titles as *Hockey, Canada's National Game* (1932), *Back in '23* (1933), and *Return of the Buffalo* (1934).

Associated Screen News ceased operations in 1958, and was for many years not only Canada's oldest surviving film company but also the only Canadian producer to have been in existence for more than thirty years. Its longevity has since been superseded by the National Film Board of Canada.

BIBLIOGRAPHY

Morris, Peter. *Embattled Shadows: A History of Canadian Cinema 1895–1939*. Montreal: McGill-Queen's University Press, 1978.

L'ASSOCIATION DES AUTEURS DE FILMS was, at one time, the oldest organization of screenwriters in the world. It was founded in 1917 by Colette, Abel Gance, Louis Feuillade, Tristan Bernard, and others in France, as La Société des Auteurs de Films. It changed its name in 1928 and remained active long after the Second World War.

ASSOCIATION OF CINEMATOGRAPH, TELEVISION, AND ALLIED TECHNICIANS. The need for a union of British film technicians came about in the early thirties, as studios demanded that their employees work longer hours without overtime pay and as an influx of refugees from Nazi Germany created an overflow of film technicians willing to work at low wages. First discussions of unionization began at the Gaumont-British* studios at Shepherd's Bush, led by a soundman namd Stanley Jolly. Jolly and others enlisted the aid of Matthew Cope, who operated a cafe in Shepherd's Bush Market, and he contacted sympathetic workers at other studios, collected union subscriptions, and was to serve as the first secretary and organizer of the Association of Studio Workers, as the union was initially called.

A general meeting was held at the Blackamoor's Head in London's Whitcombe Street in May 1933, and in June 1933 the Association of Cine-Technicians (ACT) was registered as a trade union. In January 1934, George Elvin was appointed the ACT's general secretary, a post he was to hold until April 1969, when Alan Sapper was appointed general secretary and Elvin was elected president. Director Anthony Asquith was elected the union's first president in May 1937, a position he held until his death in 1968.

It took a number of years for ACT to make its power felt within the British film industry. It signed its first major agreement with the laboratory section of the Film Production Employers' Federation in February 1939, and its first agreement with the Association of Specialised Film Producers in September 1942. In April 1955, ACT organized a strike of commercial television broadcasting in the United Kingdom, which led to a "closed shop" policy preventing anyone who is not a member of ACT or another appropriate union from working in British commercial television. As a result of this incursion into television, ACT became the Association of Cinematograph, Television, and Allied Technicians (ACTT) in March 1956. The first national television strike, organized by the ACTT took place in July 1964.

Major economic problems within the British film industry of the late forties led to the union's creating its own production company, ACT Films Ltd. in May 1950. It produced its first feature, *Green Grow the Rushes,* with financing from the National Film Finance Corporation* and the Co-operative Wholesale Society Bank. The film, which was released by British Lion in 1950, starred Richard Burton and was directed by Derek Twist for a budget of £96,000. Other ACT films include *Night Was Our Friend* (1951), *The Final Test* (1952), *Dangerous Cargo* (1954), *Second Fiddle* (1957), *The Kitchen* (1961), and *The People's March for Jobs* (1981). The ACTT remains the only union to also operate a film production company.

Since May 1935, the union has published a journal, initially titled *The Journal of the Association of Cine-Technicians* and now called *Film and TV Technician (FTT)*. It published its first book, *A Long Look at Short Films* by Vincent Porter and Derrick Knight, in 1966.

Address: 111 Wardour Street, London W1V 4AY, United Kingdom.

BIBLIOGRAPHY

Avis, Peter, editor. *Action!: Fifty Years in the Life of a Union*. London: Association of Cinematograph, Television, and Allied Technicians, 1983.

THE ASSOCIATION OF INDEPENDENT PRODUCERS LTD. was formed in the United Kingdom in 1976 to promote and encourage the activities of independent filmmakers. It is involved in political lobbying, marketing, and public relations. It publishes a journal titled *Producer,* and also provides workshops, seminars, and legal surgeries for its membership of more than 850.

Address: 17 Great Pulteney Street, London W1R 3DG, United Kingdom.

ASSOCIATION OF WOMEN FILM WORKERS (Verband der Filmarbeiterinnen) was founded in West Germany in the fall of 1970. Its goals are to seek equal rights for women in all aspects of the film industry and to promote films made by women. The most prominent member of the organization is director Margarethe von Trotta.

Address: Apostel-Paulus Strasse 32, 1000 Berlin 62, West Germany.

ATLANTIC-FILM LTD. was a major Swiss producer of the sixties and was founded by Peter and Martin Hellstern. From its headquarters in Zurich, it produced not only Swiss features but also co-productions with Germany and Yugoslavia. It maintained a distribution setup in Switzerland, through Rialto-Film, and also acquired many major foreign-language features for worldwide distribution.

ATLAS FILM CO. LTD. was founded in the United Kingdom in 1928 by Ralph Bond for the purpose of importing Soviet films into the country.

ATLAS INTERNATIONAL FILM GmbH. Atlas Film is perhaps most familiar to Americans through the beautiful film posters of classic German films and "cult" features from other countries which it made available in the late sixties and early seventies. The company was founded on January 11, 1967, by Dieter Menz, who had started his career as a legal counsel with Atlas Filmverleih in Duisberg in 1964. Atlas distributes foreign films in West Germany and, from 1968–1984, also distributed German classic features abroad.

Address: Burgstrasse 7, D-8000 Munich 2, West Germany.

BIBLIOGRAPHY

"West German Pic Importer Atlas Int'l Observes 20th Anniversary," *Daily Variety,* January 30, 1987, p. 24.

ATTICA was the name of the company created in 1955 by Charles Chaplin (1889–1977) in the United Kingdom for the production of *A King in New York* (1957).

AUSTRALIA. The first films were screened in Australia in May 1896 at Rickard's Melbourne Opera House by an American vaudeville entertainer named Carl Hertz. The first theatre designed specifically for motion picture use was not opened until 1909—by T.J. West. Shortly thereafter a number of major exhibition circuits were formed, notably the Greater D.J. Williams Amusement Company, Spencer's Pictures Ltd., and West's Amalgamated Pictures. These companies and others were merged in 1913 to become Greater Union Theatres, which in 1920 claimed some 808 operating cinemas in Australia, the bulk in the New South Wales area.

Contemporary exhibition and distribution is dominated by three companies, Village Theatres (with its distribution arm, Roadshow), Hoyts Theatres and Hoyts Distribution, and Greater Union Theatres and Greater Union Film Distributors. Village Theatres/Roadshow was one of the first to show an interest in the distribution of Australian films when it agreed to handle Tim Burstall's *Alvin Purple* in 1972, and it later established an independent production company, Hexagon, for Burstall and Graham Burke.

Filmmaking in Australia dates back to the 1890s, and two of the first important films to be made there are *Soldiers of the Cross* and *The Early Christian Martyrs,* both produced by the Salvation Army in 1900 and 1901. Between 1906 and 1914, some 90 feature films were produced, the most famous of which is *The Story of the Kelly Gang* (1906), which is claimed as the first feature film to be produced anywhere. During the remainder of the silent era more than 150 features were produced in Australia by directors including Franklyn Barrett, Paulette McDonagh, Charles Chauvel, and Raymond Longford. The last was responsible for *The Sentimental Bloke* (1919), starring Arthur Tauchert and Lottie Lyell, and based on the poems, "Songs of a Sentimental Bloke," by C.J. Dennis. The film was hailed by *The Picture Show* (October 25, 1919) as "Australia's first screen classic," and critics consider it to be the first film to capture the Australian spirit.

The British and American film industries dominated Australia in the thirties, and the work of only two Australian filmmakers, Ken Hall at Cinesound* and Charles Chauvel (1897–1959) had any impact. Among the latter's features in that decade and the next are *In the Wake of the Bounty* (1933, and famous as the first film starring Errol Flynn), *Heritage* (1935), *Uncivilised* (1936), *Forty Thousand Horsemen* (1941), and *The Rats of Tobruk* (1944).

The Second World War put Australian feature filmmaking on hold, but it helped to encourage documentary filmmaking with the government's establishment of what became the Commonwealth Film Unit and is now known as Film Australia*. Additionally, outside producers began making documentaries in the country, beginning with Harry Watt and *The Overlanders* for Ealing Studios* in 1945, and including John Heyer and *The Back of Beyond* for the Shell Film Unit* in 1954.

No indigenous Australian feature films were produced between 1958 and 1968, with the exception of Michael Powell's *They're a Weird Mob* (1966) which received some Australian financing. Indeed the only Australian feature films of any importance made after the Second World War are Charles Chauvel's *Sons of Matthew* (1949) and *Jedda* (1955). It was not until 1969 that the government of then-prime minister John Gorton recognized the importance of an Australian film industry, and, in 1970, the Australian Film Development Corporation (later to become the Australian Film Commission*) was established.

Between 1970 and 1980 more than 150 features were produced, and Australia gradually became recognized for the outstanding quality and entertainment value of its films. Filmmakers who came to prominence in this period include Tim Burstall, Bruce Beresford, George Miller, John D. Murray, and Peter Weir. The release in the United States of Weir's *Picnic at Hanging Rock* and *The Last Wave* in 1977 helped spark America interest in Australian films, as did the 1976 Academy Award for Best Animated Short going to Bruce Petty and Suzanne Baker's *Leisure*. In 1978, seasons of Australian films were held at the Cork Film Festival and at London's National Film Theatre. In 1980, Bruce Beresford's *Breaker Morant* was a major success in the United States, and was entered in competition at the Cannes Film festival. It, along with *Frontline* (1980) and *My Brilliant Career* (1979), also received Academy Award nominations.

In June 1981, the government introduced a tax incentive scheme, through the Income Tax Assessment Act, to help attract private investment in Australian film production. In part thanks to this measure, between 1980 and 1983, eighty-one feature films and eleven mini-series (including the highly acclaimed *A Town Like Alice*) were produced. In 1981, *The Man from Snowy River* became the most successful film, of any nationality, to be released in Australia.

Aside from directors such as Bruce Beresford, Peter Weir and Gillian Armstrong, who have gone on to enjoy international success with non-Australian films, the Australian film industry has also produced a number of actors and actresses of note in recent years. Mel Gibson first came to prominence with the "Mad Max" series* and *Gallipoli* (1980). Judy Davis received the Best Actress award from the British Academy of Film and Television Arts* for her work in *My Brilliant Career* (1979).

In 1986, *Crocodile Dundee*, directed by Peter Faiman and starring Paul Hogan, proved beyond a doubt that the Australian film industry could compete with both the American and British cinemas. Curiously, although he was well known as a television personality, Paul Hogan had not previously been associated with the film industry. The success of *Crocodile Dundee* led to a sequel, *Crocodile Dundee II* (1988), directed by John Cornell.

There are three unions for film and television personnel: the Australian Theatrical & Amusement Employees Association (15 Glebe Point Road, Glebe, NSW 2037), Actors Equity of Australia (32 Orwell Road, Potts Point, NSW 2011), and the Australian Writers Guild (171 New South Head Road, Edgecliff NSW 2027). Producers have two associations—Screen Production Association of Australia (33 Albany Street, Crows Nest, NSW 2056) and Producers & Directors Guild of Australia (P.O. Box 219, St. Leonards, NSW 2065). The two directors' associations are Australia Screen Directors Association (Room 27, Trades Hall, 4 Goulburn Street, Sydney, NSW 2000) and Melbourne Directors Guild (P.O. Box 409G, Melbourne, Victoria 3001). The two major motion picture awards in Australia are the Australian Film Awards and the Greater Union Awards.

Among the best known of foreign features to be shot in Australia are *A Town Like Alice* (1956), *On the Beach* (1959), and *The Sundowners* (1960).

BIBLIOGRAPHY

Baxter, John. *The Australian Cinema*. Sydney: Pacific Books, 1970.

Brand, Simon. *The Australian Film Book*. Sydney: Dreamweaver, 1985.

Chauvel, Elsa. *My Life with Charles Chauvel*. Sydney: Shakespeare Head Press, 1973.

Cooper, Ross, and Andrew Pike. *Australian Film, 1900–1977*. Melbourne: Oxford University Press, 1980.

Hall, Ken. *Australian Film: The Inside Story*. Sydney: Summit Books, 1980.

Hall, Sandra. *Critical Business: The New Australian Cinema in Review*. New York: Rigby, 1985.

Lansell, Ross, and Peter Bielby. *The Documentary Film in Australia*. North Melbourne: Cinema Papers/Film Victoria, 1982.

Lewis, Glen. *Australian Movies and the American Dream*. New York: Praeger, 1987.

Long, Joan and Martin. *The Pictures That Moved*. Melbourne: Hutchinson, 1982.

Mathews, Sue. *35mm Dreams*. New York: Penguin Books, 1984.

Moran, Albert, and Tom O'Regan. *An Australian Film Reader*. Sydney: Currency Press, 1985.

Reade, Eric. *Australian Silent Films*. Melbourne: Lansdowne, 1970.

———. *The Australian Screen: A Pictorial History of Australian Film Making 1896–1974*. Melbourne: Lansdowne, 1975.

Scott, Murray, editor. *The New Australian Cinema*. Melbourne: Nelson, 1980.

Shirley, Graham, and Brian Adams. *Australian Cinema: The First Eighty Years*. Sydney: Angus & Robertson/Currency Press, 1983.

Stratton, David. *The Last New Wave*. Sydney: Angus & Robertson, 1980.

Tulloch, John. *Legends of the Screen: The Narrative Film in Australia, 1919–1929*. Sydney: Currency Press/Australian Film Institute, 1981.

AUSTRALIAN FILM COMMISSION. A federal statutory authority, the Australian Film Commission is primarily responsible for the promotion of the Australian film industry. It provides financial assistance to Australian producers; funds script and project development; helps promote new films throughout the world; offers legal advice; and, for a two-year trial period commencing January 1, 1986, has been involved in an international co-production program.

As early as 1970, the Australian government had established the Australian Film Development Corporation, providing financial assistance for film production. In May 1975, its functions were absorbed by the Australian Film Commission, established by the Australian Film Commission Act of 1975. With headquarters in Sydney, the Australian Film Commission also maintains offices in Melbourne, London, and Los Angeles.

Address: 8 West Street, Box 3984, North Sydney, NSW 2001, Australia.

AUSTRALIAN FILM, TELEVISION, AND RADIO SCHOOL. The idea for a film school in Australia had first been suggested by Lord Ted Willis following a 1968 UNESCO proposal. A year later, the Film Committee of the

Council for the Arts made a similar suggestion and provided $100,000, Australian, for an interim council. Colin Young from Britain's National Film and Television School* and Jersy Töplitz from Poland were invited to visit Australia, and a film school seemed imminent until a change in prime ministers shelved the project.

The Australian Film, Television, and Radio School was eventually established in 1972, with Töplitz as its first director. The school enrolled its first students in a one-year interim program in 1973–1974, with a three-year program commencing the following year. It is one of two major film schools in Australia—the other being the Swinburne Film & Television School in Hawthorn, Victoria—and also maintains a library, accessible to the public, of books, periodicals, and stills.

Address: 13–15 Lyonpark Road, P.O. Box 126, North Ryde, NSW 2113, Australia.

AUSTRIA. Films had first been screened in Vienna in 1895, and the city's first film theatre opened in 1903. However, it was not until 1908 that photographer Anton Kolm directed Austria's first film production, *Von Stufe zu Stufe*. The Austrian film industry may well be said to have been the creation of Graf Alexander "Sascha" Kolowrat-Krakovsky (1886–1927), a wealthy nobleman who founded the Sascha film company circa 1910 and produced Austria's first feature film, *Der Millionenonkel,* in 1913. He founded the first Austrian newsreel company, Sascha Woche, in 1918, and became Paramount's distributor in Austria.

In the twenties and thirties, Austrian cinema specialized in lightweight features, with its two most important films of the period being Max Ophuls' *Liebelei* (1932) and Willi Forst's *Maskerade/Masquerade in Vienna* (1934). Forst is considered the greatest of all Austrian directors. Prior to the 1938 German takeover of the country, Austria boasted some 871 theatres and forty-nine film distributors. In 1933, considered the film industry's most productive year, some twenty-seven Austrian features were released. Among the most important Austrian films from the Nazi occupation (1938–1945) are Gustav Ucicky's *Der Postmeister/The Postmaster* (1940), Willi Forst's *Operette* (1940), and Geza von Bolvary's *Schrammeln* (1944).

Since the war, Austrian cinema has made little impact in the world. Few of its productions are screened outside of the country. Its films are basically lightweight, and the industry remains heavily under German influence. The number of films produced grew from four in 1946 to thirty-seven in 1956, but by 1968, only five Austrian features were released. An average of between twelve and twenty films were produced in the eighties.

In 1980, the Austrian government established the Austrian Film Fund (Österreichischer Filmförderungsfond, Plunkergasse 3–5, A–1150 Vienna), intended to both aid production and promote Austrian culture. Austrian films are promoted during the Vienna Film Week, an annual event since 1961.

In recent years, Austria has gained some reputation for its experimental and avant-garde films, thanks to the efforts of Peter Kubelka.

Austria has been seen as a location in a number of foreign films, notably *The Third Man* (1949) and *The Sound of Music* (1965).

BIBLIOGRAPHY

Brody, Agnes Bleir, "Midwife Role in Cinema's Birth," *Variety,* May 7, 1986, p. 434.

Fritz, Walter. *Die Österreichischen Spielfilme der Stummfilmzeit (1907–1930).* Vienna: Österreichischen Filmarchivs & Osterreichischen Gesellschaft fur Filmwissenschaft, 1967.

Kocian, Billy, "Austrian Cinema: From Wilder to Wolkenstein," *The Hollywood Reporter,* February 11, 1986, pp. A1–A6.

"Sascha-Wien Centerfold of Austrian Breakout from Limited Appeal," *Variety,* May 18, 1977, p. 70.

AUTEUR THEORY. Although it has never been defined to the satisfaction of all, the auteur theory is a basic assumption as to whom is the "author" of the film. The critical argument is that the author or auteur is generally the director, but it can also be the star in certain cases—for example, Mae West, Buster Keaton, and Jerry Lewis—where the star's personality and involvement in the film is such that the director's contribution is secondary. To define a director as an auteur, it is necessary to study his work as a whole, and critics tend to agree that a director cannot be dignified with the title of auteur based upon a single film.

British critic, Alan Lovell, has written (in *Screen,* vol. X, no. 2, 1969), "By the 'auteur' principle I understand a descriptive method which seeks to establish, not whether a director is a great director, but what the basic structure of a director's work is. The assumption behind the principle is that any director creates his films on the basis of a central structure and that all his films can be seen as variations or developments of it."

The auteur theory began life in France as the "politique des auteurs" in the late fifties. It was evinced by a group of young critics (all directors-to-be), including François Truffaut, Eric Rohmer, Claude Chabrol, and Jean-Luc Godard, in the pages of *Cahiers du Cinéma,* and had its theoretical origins in the writings of the distinguished French critic and theorist André Bazin. (In reality, the concept of a director's cinema, as Andrew Tudor has pointed out, dates back at least to 1935.) The French critics eagerly hailed certain American directors as auteurs, especially Alfred Hitchcock, John Ford, Howard Hawks, Nicholas Ray, Joseph Losey, Vincente Minnelli, and Otto Preminger.

The auteur theory was embraced in the United Kingdom in the pages of the magazine, *Movie,* which began publication in June 1962. In the United States, its chief protagonist was Andrew Sarris, writing in *The Village Voice* and later as editor of *Cahiers du Cinema in English* (1966–1967). Sarris and the auteur theory was strongly attacked by Pauline Kael in a 1963 article in *The New Yorker* (reprinted in Kael's *I Lost It at the Movies* [Boston: Little, Brown, 1965]).

BIBLIOGRAPHY

Bazin, André, "On the Politique des Auteurs," *Cahiers du Cinema in English,* no. 1, January 1966, pp. 8–18.

Durgnat, Raymond, "Hawks Isn't Good Enough," *Film Comment,* vol. XIII, no. 4, July-August 1977, pp. 8–19.

Hess, John, "Auteurism and After," *Film Quarterly,* vol. XXVII, no. 2, Winter 1973–1974, pp. 28–37.

———. "La Politique des Auteurs, Part One: World View as Aesthetic," *Jump Cut,* no. 1, May-June 1974, pp. 19–22.

———, "La Politique des Auteurs, Part Two: Truffaut's Manifesto," *Jump Cut,* no. 2, July-August 1974, pp. 20–22.

Lehmam, Peter, "Script/Performance/Text: Performance Theory and Auteur Theory," *Film Reader,* no. 3, 1978, pp. 197–206.

Neale, Steve, "Authors and Genres," *Screen,* vol. XXIII, no. 2, July-August 1982, pp. 84–89.

O'Pray, Michael, "Authorship and Independent Film Exhibition," *Screen,* vol. XXI, no. 2, Summer 1980, pp. 73–78.

Petrie, Graham, "Alternatives to Auteurs," *Film Quarterly,* vol. XXVI, no. 3, Spring 1973, pp. 27–35.

———, "Auteurism: More Aftermatch," *Film Quarterly,* vol. XXVII, no. 3, Spring 1974, pp. 61–63.

Ryan, Tom, "I Like What I Am," *Cinema Papers,* no. 19, January/February 1979, pp. 198–199, 241.

Sarris, Andrew, "Notes on the Auteur Theory in 1962," *Film Culture,* no. 27, Winter 1962/63, pp. 1–8.

———, "Notes on the Auteur Theory in 1970," *Film Comment,* vol. VI, no. 3, Fall 1970, pp. 6–9.

———, "Auteurism Is Alive and Well," *Film Quarterly,* vol. XXVIII, no. 1, Fall 1974, pp. 60–63.

———, "The Auteur Theory Revisited," *American Film,* vol. II, no. 9, July/August 1977, pp. 49–53.

Thomson, David, "Focus on Education: The Obsessive Art," *American Film,* vol. I, no. 9, August 1976, pp. 75–77.

———, "Appraise the Lords," *Film Comment,* vol. XVIII, no. 4, July-August 1982, pp. 42–46.

Tudor, Andrew. *Theories of Film.* New York: Viking Press, 1973.

AWARDS. See THE ACADEMY OF CANADIAN CINEMA AND TELEVISION; AMANDA AWARDS; BODIL AWARDS; THE BRITISH ACADEMY OF FILM AND TELEVISION ARTS; CÉSAR AWARDS; CITRA AWARDS; THE DAVID DI DONATELLO AWARDS; FILM FESTIVALS; THE GEORGES DE BEAUREGARD AWARD; THE GOFTA AWARD; THE GOLD BUG AWARDS; THE GOYA AWARDS; THE JUSSI AWARDS; THE LLOYDS BANK SCREENWRITING COMPETITION; THE LONDON EVENING STANDARD AWARDS; THE NEVILLE WRAN AWARD FOR EXCELLENCE; THE ORSON WELLES MOTION PICTURE DIRECTORIAL

ACHIEVEMENT AWARD; THE OSKAR GISLASON AWARD; THE PRIX FRANCE-CANADA; ROBERT AWARDS; THE ROBERTO ROSSELINI AWARD; and THE WARNER BROS. FUND FOR DEVELOPMENT OF SCRIPT WRITING IN ISRAEL

B

BAHAMAS. The number of theatres on this group of islands has remained constant at three since the thirties. Among the films shot or set here are *The Idol Dancer* (1920), *Bahama Passage* (1941), *20,000 Leagues under the Sea* (1954, shot on New Providence Island), *Flame of the Islands* (1955), *Help* (1965), *Around the World under the Sea* (1965), and *Thunderball* (1965). The last was made by Bramwell Productions, which had its corporate headquarters in the Bahamas. In 1969, International Producers Centre opened in Freeport as a film and television production complex.

BAMFORTH AND CO. LTD., located in the small Yorkshire, England, community of Holmfirth, was founded in 1870 by James Bamforth and was a prominent manufacturer of magic lantern slides and postcards. In 1899, it joined forces with William Riley of Riley Brothers, a Bradford company, to produce films, which it did until 1903. The company returned to production in 1914 and enjoyed some success with a comedy series featuring "Winky," played by Reginald Switz. It ceased production in 1915.

BIBLIOGRAPHY

Low, Rachael, and Roger Manvell. *The History of the British Film: 1896–1906*. London: George Allen & Unwin, 1948.

Sutherland, Allan T., "The Yorkshire Pioneers," *Sight & Sound,* vol. XLVI, no. 1, Winter 1976/77, pp. 48–51.

THE BANCA NAZIONALE DEL LAVORO is the major source of financing for Italian films outside of government subsidies. It has also helped pay print costs for the Italian release of quality, award-winning films from various festivals. When its Film Credit Section celebrated the fiftieth anniversary of its formation in 1985, the Bank announced it had financed 2,986 films.

BIBLIOGRAPHY

Werba, Hank, "Banca Nazionale del Lavoro Credit a Vital Force of Italian Industry," *Variety,* May 12, 1971, p. 41.

BANGLADESH. Although East Pakistan did not declare itself the independent nation of Bangladesh until March 26, 1971, the Bangladesh film industry is generally dated from 1956 when its first film, *Mukh-O-Mukhosh,* was released. The first film studio in the capital of Dacca was established in 1959, and early directors include Nazir Ahmed and Fateh Lohani.

Following the 1971 war of independence, films generally dealt with the conflict, with the most important productions being *Ora Egarojon/Those Eleven Men* (1972), directed by Chashi Nazrul Islan, and *Arunodoyer Agnishakhi/In the Flames of Sunrise* (1972), directed by Subhash Dutta. A major setback to the industry came in 1972 with the murder of actor Raju Aman who was featured in half of all the films in production at that time. Films were produced mainly in black-and-white until 1977. A national film archive and institute was established in 1979.

An average of fifty films a year are produced, with the bulk co-sponsored by the government-controlled Bangladesh Film Development Corporation (Tejgaon, Dhaka-8). The industry is subject to heavy censorship, and each print of each film is subject to taxation. Films are screened in English, Bengali, Urdu, and Hindi, and, despite independence, the country remains dominated by the Indian cinema. Major directors include Subhash Dutta, Abdus Samad, Alamgir Kabir, Rafiqul Bari Chowdhury, and C.B. Jaman.

BARBADOS has no film industry, and the number of theatres here has remained constant at three since 1937.

THE BARCELONA MANIFESTO is the name given to a document signed by seven hundred international directors who insisted that their films be screened only in their original, uncut, and unmutilated forms. It was issued on July 23, 1987, during the Barcelona Film Festival, at which a number of directors, including George Sidney and Fred Zinnemann, had argued for the rights of the director to protect his or her films. The manifesto was brought on, in part, because of the directors' opposition to the "colorization" of black-and-white films.

BIBLIOGRAPHY

Besas, Peter, "Directors' 'Barcelona Manifesto' Demands Pix Be Shown without Exhib 'Mutilation,' " *Daily Variety,* July 24, 1987, p. 2.

THE BARNES MUSEUM OF CINEMATOGRAPHY was founded in the Cornish town of St. Ives in 1963 by John Barnes. It is a private museum, housing more than one thousand exhibition items relating to the history of cinema and precinema. Barnes has authored three important texts relating to early motion pictures: *Precursors of the Cinema* (St. Ives: Barnes Museum of Cinematography, 1967), *Optical Projection* (St. Ives: Barnes Museum of Cinematography,

1970), and *The Beginnings of the Cinema in England* (New York: Barnes & Noble, 1976).

Address: 44 Fore Street, St. Ives, Cornwall TR26 1HE, United Kingdom.

BARRANDOV. The Barrandov Film Studios (Filmové Studio Barrandov) are the largest and oldest studios in Czechoslovakia*. Constructed in 1933 by the A.B. Company, Barrandov was initially utilized as an international production center for films such as Julian Duvivier's *Le Golem* (1935). During the Second World War, the studios were taken over by the German film industry and heavily used for production until 1945, when Barrandov was nationalized by the Czech government. Its first postwar film was *Muži bez křídel/Men without Wings* (1946).

Address: Praha 5, Keizeneckého 322, Czechoslovakia.

BIBLIOGRAPHY

Brach, Stanislav, editor. *Barrandov*. Prague: Československý filmexport and Filmové studio Barrandov, 1965.

THE BEIRUT AGREEMENT is an international treaty dating from 1949, whereby films of an educational, cultural, or scientific nature are exempt from export duties in some sixty countries, including the United States. All film certification operations under this agreement were suspended by the United States Information Agency in August 1988 after the U.S. courts ruled unconstitutional the Agency's rules permitting it to brand certain films as propaganda and thus hamper their export by the imposition of customs duties.

BÉLA BÁLAZS STUDIO. Named after the Hungarian-born and internationally renowned film theorist, the Béla Bálazs Studio was created in 1958 to enable students to gain practical knowledge of filmmaking. It was not until 1961 that the studio established its importance under the leadership of László Beke and Gábor Bódy. Although part of the Hungarian film industry, the Béla Bálazs Studio is semi-autonomous, run by an elected body that selects scripts and projects, but with the appropriate government ministry having the right of veto. The studio is noted for the liberality of its films, with its first important project being István Szabó's *Te/You* (1963).

BIBLIOGRAPHY

Kuttna, Mari, "Hungary: Realism and Renewal," *Sight & Sound,* vol. XLVII, no. 3, Summer 1968, pp. 159–160.

BELFAST. The capital of Northern Ireland is primarily known for the violence of the civil unrest between Protestants and Catholics and so it is with films with a Belfast setting. The first prominent feature to utilize Belfast as a locale was Carol Reed's *Odd Man Out* (1947). The Irish-American co-production *A Terrible Beauty* (1960), directed by Tay Garnett, was, like *Odd Man Out,* concerned with IRA activities in Northern Ireland. A similar and much bloodier picture of Northern Ireland was presented in the Canadian feature, *A Quiet Day in Belfast*

(1974), directed by Milad Bessada. Three recent Irish features have also been set in Northern Ireland, although in reality filmed in the Republic of Ireland: *Maeve* (1981), directed by Pat Murphy; *Angel* (U.S. *Danny Boy,* 1982), directed by Neil Jordan; and *Cal* (1984), directed by Pat O'Connor. Brian Moore's 1955 novel, *The Lonely Passion of Judith Hearne,* was set in Belfast, but the 1987 screen version, written by Peter Nelson, directed by Jack Clayton, and starring Maggie Smith in the title role, took place in Dublin, where it was also filmed.

BIBLIOGRAPHY

Slide, Anthony. *The Cinema and Ireland.* Jefferson, N.C.: McFarland, 1988.

BELGIUM has little filmmaking tradition. Feature film production was almost non-existent prior to the forties, and during that decade and the following only a handful of films were produced. Thanks to Henri Storck (born 1907), the country does have a fine tradition of documentary filmmaking. Some of Storck's later films, such as *Fêtes de Belgique* (1973) are as impressive as his earliest work, such as *Borinage* (1933), co-directed with Joris Ivens. Aside from Storck, the only Belgian filmmaker to have gained international prominence is André Delvaux (born 1906), who began his career in the fifties and gained worldwide recognition with *De man die zijn haar kort liet knippen/The Man Who Had His Hair Cut Short* (1966).

The Belgian film industry survives thanks in no small part to government subsidies through the French and Flemish speaking ministries of culture, Ministère de la Culture Française and Ministerie voor Nederlandse Cultuur, both of which have been active since the mid-sixties. They help encourage the establishment of a film industry through grants for first films by graduates of the country's film schools—a program established in 1966. Among such film schools are the Institut des Arts de Diffusion (at which Henri Storck lectures), the Institut National Supérieur des Arts du Spectacle et Techniques de Diffusion, and the Hoger Rijksinstituut voor Toneel en Cultuurspreidung. Graduates of these film schools who became directors in the Belgian film industry include Jacques Brel, Patrick Ledoux, and Harry Kumel.

In the seventies a major woman director emerged in Belgium in the person of Chantal Akerman (born 1950), who began her career with *Je, tu, il, elle/I, You, He, She* (1974), in which she also starred. Although she is primarily an avant-garde filmmaker, Chantal's films have garnered considerable notice. Her 1983 production, *Les annees 80/Golden Eighties* was a musical comedy. Also worthy of mention among Belgium's filmmakers is animator Raoul Servais.

There were 1,100 theatres in operation in Belgium prior to the Second World War. By the fifties, the number had increased to 1,700, but by the mid-eighties, the number was down to less than 500. The most important of Belgium's theatres is the twenty-seven-screen theatre just outside of Brussels, opened in 1988 by exhibitor Albert Bert. With some seven thousand seats, it is boosted as the world's largest multiplex theatre. American films dominated Belgian screens in the thirties, with some ten distributors releasing an average of 400 films a year.

Foreign films still overshadow native production, and it was considered something of a rarity in 1987 when 4 Belgian films were playing simultaneously in Brussels.

There is no film censorship in Belgium; the constitution forbids any form of censorship.

BIBLIOGRAPHY

Batz, Jean-Claude. *À propos de la crise de l'industrie du cinéma*. Brussels: Les Éditions de l'Institut de Sociologie/Université Libre de Bruxelles, 1963.

"Belgian Round-Up," *Screen International*, May 4, 1985 p. 204.

Davay, Paul, "Cinéma de Belgique, 1965–1972" *Cinéma* 73, no. 174, 1973 pp. 68–79.

Duynslaegher, Pat, "Good Times Ahead Pictured for Belgian Box-Office," *Daily Variety*, May 21, 1982, p. 25.

Maelstaf, R. *Belgian Talent, Foreign Films*. Brussels: Ministry of Foreign Affairs and External Trade, 1966.

———. *The Animated Cartoon Film in Belgium*. Brussels: Ministry of Foreign Affairs and External Trade, 1970.

Mancini, Elaine, "Belgium," in *World Cinema since 1945*, editor William Luhr. New York: Ungar, 1987, pp. 62–69.

Nelissen, Ivo. *Ten Years of Film-Making Policy in Flanders*. Brussels: Ministry of Flemish Culture, undated.

Roanne, Henri, "Le 'Nouveau' Cinéma Belge," *Cinéma Quebec*, vol. III, nos. 9–10, August 1974, pp. 54–58.

BELIZE. See CENTRAL AMERICA

BELOKAPI is France's largest animation studio and was founded in 1968 by Nicole Pichon. It is primarily involved in the production of animated series for French and Canadian television. The company was taken over by Bayard Press, a major French publisher, in 1986 and in January 1988 filed for bankruptcy.

Address: 70 rue de Strasbourg, 94300 Vincennes, France.

BIBLIOGRAPHY

Alderman, Bruce, "France's Largest Animation Firm Bellies Up," *Daily Variety*, January 7, 1988, pp. 21, 45.

THE BENSHI was an "actor" or "photo-interpreter" in Japanese silent films who would sit to the left of the screen and explain or interpret the action to the audience. An article in the August 10, 1915, issue of *Kinema-Record* noted,

> Sometimes they act as dialogists for the players in the picture and some of them make a dialogue so skillfully as if the players in the picture were really speaking. . . . Any photo-play-house in Japan has two or three "interpreters" at least, so the total number reach to above three thousand in all throughout Japan, the number of the photoplay house being more than nine hundred. Most of them are educated and have the knowledge of a foreign language, English at least.

Benshi cinema survived into the thirties with the Benshi interpreting foreign-language films. The last-trained Benshi, still active in Japan in the 1980s, is Shunsui Matsuda.

BIBLIOGRAPHY

Anderson, Joseph L., "In Praise of Benshi," in *The Japanese Film: Art and Industry* by Joseph L. Anderson and Donald Richie. Princeton, N.J.: Princeton University Press, 1982, pp. 439–444.

Kirihara, Donald, "A Reconsideration of the Institution of the Benshi," *Film Reader,* no. 6, 1985, pp. 41–53.

Komatsu, Hiroshi, and Charles Musser, "Benshi Search," *Wide Angle,* vol. IX, no. 2, 1987, pp. 72–90.

BERLIN has been used as a backdrop for many features, the more important of which are *Yankee Doodle in Berlin* (1919), *Isn't Life Wonderful* (1924), *A Foreign Affair* (1948), *I Am a Camera* (1955), *One, Two, Three* (1961), *Escape from East Berlin* (1962), *Escape to Berlin* (1962), *The Spy Who Came in from the Cold* (1965), *The Quiller Memorandum* (1966), and *Funeral in Berlin* (1966). The film which best captures the spirit and life of the city is *Berlin, die symphonie einer grossstadt/Berlin, the Symphony of a Great City* (1927), created by Carl Mayer and Walter Ruttmann. It helped pave the way for a later documentary on Berlin, *Menschen am Sonntag/People on Sunday* (1929), created by Eugen Shuftan, Robert Siodmak, Edgar Ullmer, Billy Wilder, Fred Zinnemann, and Moritz Seeler.

The city is also the site of the Berlin International Film Festival (Budapester Strasse 50, D-1000 Berlin 30, West Germany).

BIANCO E NERO. The most important of Italian film journals, *Bianco e Nero* commenced publication in January 1937 under the auspices of the Centro Sperimentale di Cinematografia*. It ceased publication in September 1943 and was not reestablished until October 1947.

Address: Via Tuscolana, 1524 Rome, Italy.

BIBLIOGRAPHY

Slide, Anthony, editor. *International Film, Radio, and Television Journals.* Westport, Conn.: Greenwood Press, 1985.

BILD-UND FILMAMT (BUFA) was established by the German government in January 1917 to produce propaganda films on the German First World War effort. It was later merged with Ufa*.

THE BILLANCOURT STUDIOS were founded in 1922 by Henri Diamant-Berger in an unused airplane hangar at Niepce, just outside of Paris. Diamant-Berger lost control of the studios in less than a year. They were utilized by Abel Gance for the production of *Napoléon* (1927) and also for the production of *La*

Passion de Jeanne d'Arc/The Passion of Joan of Arc (1928), *Cagliostro* (1929), *Fanny* (1932), and many other features.

Address: 50 quai des Point-du-Jour, 92100 Billancourt, France.

BIOPHON was the name of a sound-on-disc system perfected by Oskar Messter (1886–1944) and first demonstrated as Biophon-Tonbilder der Specht at the Apollo Theatre, Berlin, on August 29, 1903. A vast number of these sound films were produced by Messter until 1914, by which time the public had long grown tired of them.

THE BIOSCOPE. Along with *Kinematograph Weekly**, *The Bioscope* was the most important of early British trade journals, published on a weekly basis from September 18, 1908, through May 4, 1932.

BIBLIOGRAPHY

Slide, Anthony, editor. *International Film, Radio, and Television Journals.* Westport, Conn.: Greenwood Press, 1985.

BIOSKOP was the name of the projection equipment designed by Max Skladanowsky (1863–1939) and first utilized publicly in Germany by Max and his brother Emil at the Wintergarten, Berlin, on November 1, 1895. It consisted of two machines projecting alternate frames of film at eight frames per second.

BLACK INDEPENDENT FILMMAKING IN THE UNITED KINGDOM dates back to the sixties and the work of Lionel Ngakane (*Jemima and Johnnie,* 1964). Other contemporary black filmmakers living and working in the United Kingdom include Horace Ove and Menelik Shabazz. In 1983, the Black Audio Film Collective was established in London, and in 1986 it gained funding from Channel 4*. Black filmmakers in the United Kingdom work outside of the established film industry and, as a group, are comprised of individuals of West Indian origin, rather than Indians and Pakistanis who make up a considerable percentage of Britain's black minority.

BODIL AWARDS. One of Denmark's two film awards—the other is the Robert*—the Bodil Awards were created in 1948 by Filmmedarbejderforeningen (c/o Helle Hellmann, Dagbladet Politiken, Rådhuspladsen, 37, DK 1550 Copenhagen V), an organization of critics from Copenhagen's daily newspapers. The award is named after two of Denmark's most popular actresses, Bodil Kjer (born 1917) and Bodil Ipsen (1889–1974). The former received the Actress Award in 1948, and Bodil Ipsen, who was also active as a director, received the Director Awards in 1949, 1951, and 1952.

The award, which is in the form of a porcelain figure of a woman designed by illustrator Ebbe Sadolin and sculptor Svend Jacobsen, is presented in the following categories: Best Danish Film/Director, Best Actor, Best Actress, Best Supporting Actor, Best Supporting Actress, Best Documentary Film, Best European Film, and Best Non-European/American Film. The Awards have taken place since 1950 at Copenhagen's Dagmar Teatret, and in 1988, director Svend Aage Lorentz was asked to produce a short documentary on their history.

BOLIVIA. In 1909, after traveling through Colombia, Ecuador, and Peru, the cinema arrived in Bolivia in the hands of two Italian producers who held the first screening in a small port town on the shores of Lake Titicaca. The cinema's late arrival to Bolivia, fourteen years after its first introduction in Latin America, is indicative of some of the restrictions faced by the national cinema, even to this day. The Bolivian film market has always been small, not only because of the country's size and its relative disadvantages as a landlocked nation, but also because of low industrialization and urbanization, and the extreme economic and cultural gaps among its social and ethnic groups.

Notwithstanding these limitations, filmmakers emerged quickly after the medium was introduced. Luis G. Castillo produced *Vistas Locales,* a record of life in La Paz, early in 1913 and continued with a series of documentary shorts that were quickly and inexpensively produced. The recognized pioneer of silent filmmaking in Bolivia, Castillo founded a production company in 1918 (Andes Film) and later joined with archeologist Arturo Posnansky to produce *La Gloria de La Raza* (1926).

It is important to note that, from its earliest days, filmmaking in Bolivia has been concerned with the realities of the large (60 percent), marginalized Indian population. The first Bolivian feature-length fiction film, *La Profecía del Lago* (produced in 1923 by Jose Maria Velasco Maidana) was never commercially released because of censorship problems, its interracial interclass love story (white upper-class woman/Indian lower-class man) apparently too scandalous to be tolerated.

The first Bolivian fictional feature to be commercially released was *Corazon Aymara* (1925). Produced by Pedro Sambarino, an Italian immigrant, it was based on a play by Bolivian playwright Angel Sales, and dealt with the problems of a young Aymara Indian girl who was persecuted by her family. *Wara Wara* (1929) and *Hacia la Gloria* (1931) close the brief cycle of Bolivian silent filmmaking. Although both were critically well-received, neither film was commercially successful, their release curtailed by the introduction of foreign sound films in 1931. From that point on, the Bolivian film market would be dominated by the North American and European films preferred by the upper/white classes and the Mexican and Argentine imports consumed by the mestizo and Indian lower classes. Fully sonorized feature-length film production was not undertaken until 1958. The only feature-length film made and released in the thirties and forties (while Bolivia was recuperating from the Chaco War with Paraguay) was *Infierno Verde* (1938) a documentary on that conflict by Luis Bazoberry.

These fallow years ended with the Nationalist Revolution of 1952. One of the most important social revolutions in Latin America, its progressive measures and extensive program of social reforms attempted to integrate the Indian population into Bolivian political life. The new government created the Bolivian Film Institute (Instituto Cinematográfico Boliviano, ICB) to encourage the development of new filmmakers and to use the cinema as an instrument for popular education and consciousness raising. Although it produced only newsreels and documentaries, the ICB was the first step toward a national cinematography and allowed young filmmakers some technical and financial resources.

The most significant Bolivian filmmaker between 1945 and 1960 was Jorge Ruiz. Ruiz and Augusto Roca, with the financial backing of a U.S. citizen living in Bolivia, founded Bolivia Films in 1947 and produced the first sound short and a number of documentaries in later years (most of them financed by U.S. information agencies or by the Alliance for Progress). Their *Vuelve Sebastiana/Come Back Sebastiana* (1953), an independently financed semi-documentary about the almost extinct Chipaya Indian community, was the first Bolivian film to win an award at a foreign film festival.

Ruiz was later appointed director of the ICB, and while there, produced *La Vertiente/The Watershed* (1958), Bolivia's first sound feature length fiction film. Again mixing documentary and fictional modes, this film complicates a love story with a real community's efforts to secure a source of safe drinking water, and clearly presents the ideas of solidarity and self-reliant community development also espoused by the government.

Yet these social concerns were soon buried when, after twelve years of a nationalist government, a coup in 1964 installed a harsh military regime. Ironically, however, in 1965 this government placed the ICB in the hands of a young and fairly inexperienced filmmaker, Jorge Sanjinés, who would go on to become Bolivia's best-known and most revolutionary cineaste and an important contributor to the New Latin American Cinema movement. Shortly before the military coup, Sanjinés, in collaboration with screenwriter Oscar Soria and Ricardo Rama, had produced a short documentary, *Revolución/Revolution,* that, using only images and music, presented a powerful exploration of underdevelopment and the class struggle in Bolivia. While coordinating the production of newsreels and documentaries as technical director of the ICB, Sanjinés also worked on *Ukamau/That's the Way It Is* (1966), the first feature-film spoken in Aymara, the language of the majority Indian population. Eliminating the voice-over narration typical of exhortatory filmmaking, Sanjinés and his group attempted to let the Indian peasants tell their story from their own perspective. The government, although officially compelled to praise the film, closed down the ICB shortly after its release; the defiant Sanjinés group responded by assuming the name Grupo Ukamau.

Yawar Mallku/Blood of The Condor (1969) was their next film. The first film in Quechuan, another majority Indian language, *Yawar Mallku* specifically indicts the sterilizations without consent performed by a Peace Corps–like agency, and emblematically condemns North American intervention in Bolivia. When the government tried to postpone the film's premiere, spontaneous demonstrations nevertheless forced its release. With their next film, *El Coraje del Pueblo/The*

Courage of the People (1971), Grupo Ukamau began to experiment with different narrative forms. This film attempts to recreate the events preceding, during, and subsequent to a famous miner's massacre in 1967 using the entire community of the Siglo XX mine.

A right-wing military coup during Sanjinés postproduction work on the film in Italy effectively split the Ukamau group. Cameraman Antonio Eguino and screenwriter Oscar Soria remained in Bolivia, while Sanjinés, Rama, and Beatriz Palacios began to explore filmmaking opportunities in the other Andean countries. Working semi-clandestinely among the Indian communities, they made *El Enemigo Principal/The Principal Enemy* (1973) in Peru; *¡Fuera de Aquí!/Get Out of Here!* (1976) in Ecuador; and *¡Basta Ya!/That's Enough!* (1979) in Colombia and Venezuela. A change of government finally allowed them to return to Bolivia in 1979.

In the meantime, the other Ukamau group produced two successful features in Bolivia: *Pueblo Chico/Small Town* (1974) and *Chuquiago* (1977). The latter film, an exploration of the social topography of La Paz, was the biggest box-office hit in the history of the Bolivian cinema.

Before the military coup of 1980, a number of Super 8mm workshops had been established in worker and peasant organizations throughout the nation thanks to the efforts of French filmmaker Alain Labrousse and Bolivian historian-critic-filmmaker Alfonso Gumucio Dagron. A return to democratic rule is now necessary to continue this work, which takes the impulse toward a representative, popular, national cinema even further in the effort to create a cinema of/for/by the majority of Bolivian citizens.

BIBLIOGRAPHY

Burton, Julianne, editor. *Cinema and Social Change in Latin America*. Austin: University of Texas Press, 1986.

BORNEO has been presented on film only because of its primitive society and culture. Martin and Osa Johnson made two features there, *Jungle Adventures* (1921) and *Borneo* (1937), and the country was also seen in two silent American feature-length documentaries, both released in 1925, *Wild Men and Beasts of Borneo* and *Wonders of the Wild*. The tattooing of its women was featured in *La donna nel mondo/Women of the World* (1963), and its wedding rituals were seen in *Il pelo nel mondo/Go, Go, Go, World!* (1964), both of which emanated from Italy.

BRAZIL. The first decade of the Brazilian cinema was one of its most glorious. The cinema was heralded, along with electrical power, as a sign of Rio de Janeiro's booming modernity and sophistication. The first individuals responsible for importing Lumière films in 1896—Paschoal and Affonso Segreto—were also the first to film in Brazil. By 1898 they were exhibiting series of "local views" and important events. Especially after Rio was fully electrified by a new hydroelectric power plant in 1907, the cinema became an important business, a profitable source of entertainment for *cariocas* (inhabitants of Rio).

Beginning in 1908 with the runaway success of Antônio Leal's *Os Estranguladores/The Stranglers,* this "Golden Age" of the Brazilian cinema lasted until 1911–1912 and ultimately 650 titles were produced in a wide variety of genres. Supported by a fledgling form of vertical integration created by local exhibitors who simultaneously handled production, distribution of imports, as well as exhibition, the cinema was a successful business as well as the preferred form of entertainment of urban elites. However, this national cinematic euphoria was short-lived. In Europe and North America filmmaking had already become industrialized, and Brazil quickly became a market that, preferring the less artisanal foreign films, could not protect its national cinema. From a high of 45 fiction films in 1909, production dropped steadily until 1914, when only one was produced. And, although limited import possibilities during the First World War restimulated production to some degree (in 1917 production reached a peak for the period of 22 features) filmmaking would remain a marginal activity until the coming of sound.

There were, of course, individual filmmakers who produced even in the face of a hostile market (with an average of twenty fiction films per year through the twenties and thirties). First of all, the influence of the European avant-garde of the twenties was felt in a number of significant films, particularly Mário Peixoto's *Limite/Limit* (1930), a film that has acquired status as *the* Brazilian experimental film. Second, outside the urban centers of Rio and São Paulo, the cinema evolved in regional cycles (with only regional distribution and exhibition) in Rio Grande do Sul, Recife, Manaus, Catagueses, and Campinas. The most important filmmaker of this period, Humberto Mauro, emerged from one such cycle in Catagueses, and went on to become the first fully professional (salaried) Brazilian film director. His *Ganga Bruta/Brutal Gang* (1933) is still considered one of the greatest achievements of the Brazilian cinema.

As in Argentina and Mexico, many Brazilian producers saw the coming of sound as an opportunity to establish a national cinema that could compete with imports. Producer-director Adhemar Gonzaga, for example, set up the Cinédia Studios and hired Humberto Mauro to direct *Lábios sem Beijos/Lips without Kisses* (1930), the first sound feature. Although his Cinédia was not lavishly capitalized, and its first few films were not very successful, Gonzaga perfected a formula for successful sound films—many musical numbers, often using popular carnival sambas (first created at about the same time as sound cinematography), interwoven around a thin plot—and created a Brazilian genre, the *chanchada*. His *Alô, Alô, Brasil* (1935) and *Alô, Alô, Carnaval* (1936) introduced the genre—and the popular radio performer Carmen Miranda (later lured to Hollywood by Fox)—to the screen. Although Cinédia was later unable to sustain this output, other producers took up the genre and made hundreds of *chanchadas* in the forties and fifties, which, although superficial, established an authentic link between Brazilians and their cinema.

Other producers attempted to follow different paths with varying degrees of success. Carmen Santos, for example, a cinema actress in the twenties, set up Brasil Vita Filme in 1933 and lured Humberto Mauro from Gonzaga as her technical director. Her company produced some of Mauro's most significant later films, but her own *Inconfidência Mineira/Conspiracy in Minas* (1948), although ten years in the making, was not successful.

Even as this and other national films foundered against the competition, producers continued to strive for the development of a national industry modeled on Hollywood without creating distribution or exhibition sectors to support it. Although some protective measures (a modest screen quota) were implemented by the populist-nationalist government of Getulio Vargas, nothing was done to restrict the number of imports. Throughout the thirties production declined, reaching almost total paralysis in 1941–1942, when distribution and exhibition bottlenecks coincided with wartime celluloid shortages.

In 1941, however, a new company founded by Moacyr Fenelon—Atlantida Cinematografica—ambitiously set out to produce films with local content and atmosphere but that avoided the *chanchada* stereotypes. Its first release, *Moleque Tiao* (José Carlos Burle, 1943), was a well-received social comedy featuring a young black actor who would become Brazil's most popular star: Grande Otelo. However, after Fenelon joined with the principal national exhibition chain in 1947, Atlantida returned to the production of inexpensive *chanchadas* designed to fulfill quota requirements (eighty-five films between 1943 and 1971).

As Atlantida succumbed to *chanchadas,* a group fueled by the growing industrial power of the São Paulo bourgeoisie set up the Vera Cruz studios precisely as an antidote to what was perceived as that genre's "vulgarity." Brazilian-born avant-garde filmmaker Alberto Cavalcanti returned from Europe to head the extensive Vera Cruz facilities (modeled on the M-G-M studios), contracting actors and directors. Attempting to produce "high quality" films for national and international distribution, the Vera Cruz experiment produced eighteen features in five years, including the biggest box-office success in Brazilian history: Lima Barreto's *O Cangaceiro/The Bandit,* a "western" set in the picturesque Northeast which won first prize at Cannes in 1954. The success of this film should have bolstered the company, but, pressured by large debts, Vera Cruz had previously sold the international distribution rights of all its films to Columbia Pictures at a fixed price, and, in 1954, was finally forced into bankruptcy.

The failure of Vera Cruz (and a number of smaller producers in São Paulo) dispelled the dreams of an industrialized Brazilian cinema and reduced the national cinema to *carioca* producers of *chanchadas* and small, struggling independents. But it was precisely these small independents who, in the wake of the developmentalist euphoria and cultural renovation of Juscelino Kubitschek's newly-elected government of 1955, resuscitated the Brazilian cinema with the *Cinema Novo** movement.

Influenced by Neo-Realism* and seeking to develop a non-industrial base for the national cinema, the *Cinema Novo* movement was inspired by a series of independently produced socially conscious films: Alex Viany's *Agulha no Palheiro/Needle in the Haystack* (1953), Nelson Pereira dos Santos' *Rio 40 Graus* (1955) and *Rio Zona Norte/Rio Northern Zone* (1957), and Roberto Santos' *O Grande Momento/The Great Moment* (1958). By 1960–1964, *Cinema Novo* emerged as a coherent movement with a definite aesthetic (anti-Hollywood), political position (leftist), and production practice (independent). The filmmakers of *Cinema Novo*—politically committed and aesthetically experimental—refused to follow the exploitative tendencies of *chanchadas* or the Europeanized work of Vera Cruz, and sought out in the *favelas* (slums) and *sertao* (the arid northeast) the contradictions of Brazilian social life. The most important films of this first phase of *Cinema novo*—Glauber Rocha's *Barravento* (1962) and *Deus e o Diabo na Terra do Sol/Black God, White Devil* (1964), Ray Guerra's *Os Cafajestes/The Hustler* (1962), and *Os Fuzis/The Guns* (1964), Carlos Diegues' *Ganga Zumba* (1963), and Nelson Pereira dos Santos' *Vidas Secas/Barren Lives* (1963)—dealt with the problems of the rural and/or urban poor and had an often harsh, imperfect, and intentionally underdeveloped style (later dubbed "an aesthetics of hunger" by Glauber Rocha).

The second phase of *Cinema Novo,* delimited by the 1964 military coup d'etat and the 1968 coup within the coup, was deeply marked by the turbulent politics of the period. The military takeover left artists and intellectuals bewildered and self-questioning and their films echoed their state: Paulo César Sareceni's *O Desafio/The Challenge* (1966), Rocha's *Terra em Transe/Land in Anguish* (1967), Gustavo Dahl's *O Bravo Guerreiro/The Brave Warrior* (1968), and Nelson Pereira dos Santos' *Fome de Amor/Hunger for Love* (1968). Of these, Rocha's *Terra em Transe/Earth Entranced* was the angriest, most disillusioned, and most brilliant, ascerbically analyzing the contradictory class alliances of Brazilian populism through an allegorical self-reflexive parody of an intellectual's role in the political system of an imaginary state.

In this second phase of the movement, filmmakers also began to take steps to improve their access to the nation's theatres, establishing a distribution cooperative—Difilm—in 1965, and beginning to make films with more popular appeal (for example, Leon Hirzsman's *Garota de Ipanema/The Girl from Ipanema* (1967), the first *Cinema Novo* film in color).

The first *Cinema Novo* film to be truly popular at the box office and in cultural terms was, however, part of the third and last phase of the movement: Joaquim Pedro de Andrade's *Macunaíma* (1968). Like most films of this "Tropicalist" period, *Macunaíma* adopted an indirect, allegorical form designed to circumvent the strict censorship of the military regime. Other important films were Rocha's *O Dragao da Maldade Contra o Santo Guerreiro/Antonio Das Mortes* (1968), Guerra's *Os Deuses e os Mortos/The Gods and the Dead* (1970), Diegues' *Os Herdeiros/The Heirs* (1969), and dos Santos' *Como Era Gostoso Meu Francês/How Tasty Was My Little Frenchman* (1970). At the end of this phase, the *Cinema Novo* entered into a politically generated crisis that peaked in 1971–1972, when the growing censorship and repression of the military government forced a number of *Cinema Novo* filmmakers into exile and national production was dominated by vapid pseudo-erotic comedies known as *pornochanchadas* (often produced by exhibitors in order to benefit from increases in the national film quota).

Although after 1970 we can no longer speak of a *Cinema Novo* movement, the Brazilian cinema survived the crisis and went on to prosper. As the political situation improved with the *abertura* of the mid-seventies, filmmakers began to return and resume their careers. Most significantly, the state organism for the cinema, Embrafilme, began to take an active role protecting the national cinema. Although founded in 1969, Embrafilme was little more than a bureaucratic agency until filmmaker Roberto Farias was appointed as director in 1974. Farias implemented a significant program of co-productions with independent producers (114 co-productions between 1973 and 1979), developed its domestic distribution activities (headed by another filmmaker, Gustavo Dahl), and vastly improved the distribution of Brazilian films abroad.

Brazilian production in the seventies and eighties was not concentrated in large studios, and has remained dispersed but effective (in 1977, for example, sixty-five different production companies produced seventy-three films, of which twenty-four were co-produced with Embrafilme). Important films were made by *Cinema Novo* directors—dos Santos' *O Amuleto de Ogum/The Amulet of Ogum* (1974) and *Tenda dos Milagres/Tent of Miracles* (1977), Diegues' *Xica da Silva/Xica* (1976) and *Bye, Bye Brasil* (1980), Leon Hirzsman's *Sao Bernardo* (1973)—as well as by newcomers: Eduardo Escorel's *Liçião de Amor/Lesson of Love* (1975), Bruno Barreto's *Dona Flor e Seus Dois Maridos/Dora Flor and Her Two Husbands* (1976), Hector Babenco's *Pixote* (1980), Tizuka Yamasaki's *Gaijin* (1980).

The seventies were exciting years for the Brazilian cinema—with increases in production (up to an average 100 films per year), in attendance, and in the income of national films—but the eighties have been less successful. The number of theaters has declined from 3,276 in 1976 to 1,553 in 1984, attendance has dropped from 61,800,000 in 1978 to 30,637,544 in 1984, and, national production has declined from 102 films in 1980 to 84 in 1983 (of which approximately 70 percent were pornographic "quota quickies"). Partly due to a general economic crisis (high debts and runaway inflation), but also as a result of increased competition with television, the future of the Brazilian cinema depends on a restructuring of the activities of Embrafilme and the state's role in protecting the national cinema. The Sarney Law of 1986—allowing corporations to shelter as much as 2 percent of their income tax by financing cultural projects—was an important step in this direction, increasing investments in film production in one year by approximately $4 million.

BIBLIOGRAPHY

Burton, Julianne, compiler. *The New Latin American Cinema: An Annotated Bibliography of English-Language Sources, 1960–1976*. New York: Cineaste, 1976.

de Almeida, Prado D., "Dramatic Renaissance," *Atlantic*, February 1956, pp. 157–160.

Fenin, George N., "Film Progress in Brazil," *Quarterly of Film, Radio, and Television,* vol. X, no. 3, Spring 1956, pp. 253–256.

"Hollywood Producers Go Rolling Down to Rio," *Business Week,* September 25, 1965, pp. 32–33.

Johnson, Randal. *Cinema Novo × 5: Masters of Contemporary Brazilian Film.* Austin: University of Texas Press, 1984.

Johnson, Randal, and Robert Stam. *Brazilian Cinema.* Teaneck, N.J.: Fairleigh Dickinson University Press, 1982.

Peixoto, Mario, "Limits," *Close Up,* vol. IX, no. 1, March 1932, pp. 47–49.

Viany, Alex, "Production in Brazil," *Films in Review,* February 1951, pp. 28–32.

———, "Old and New in Brazilian Cinema," *Tulane Drama Review,* Winter 1970, pp. 141–144.

"BRIGHTON SCHOOL." One of the places in the United Kingdom that helped to give birth to cinematography was the South Coast seaside resort of Brighton. Here, a small but significant group of film pioneers—A. Esme Collins, G. Albert Smith, James Williamson, and Alfred Darling—were at work during the latter half of the 1890s. A. Esme Collins was a well-known portrait photographer who was one of the first to take up film production. G. Albert Smith was an enthusiastic astronomer giving lectures illustrated by magic lantern slides, which led him, like many others, into an interest in cinematography. He began experimentation with trick photography, taking out a patent for double exposure in 1897, and, in 1900, he started working for the Warwick Trading Company, having had a "film factory" built for himself at St. Ann's Well Garden. He was closely associated with Charles Urban in the color process, Kinemacolor. A close friend of Smith's was James A. Williamson who had a chemist's shop in Hove, just outside of Brighton, where he sold photographic materials. By 1897, he was making his own films, such as *Attack on a Chinese Mission, Fire!,* and *Stop Thief!,* which displayed remarkable progress in narrative style. All three pioneers were given assistance by Alfred Darling, a mechanical engineer who became interested in the requirements of filmmakers. He made particular advances in equipment for perforating and printing films and devised a "claw" mechanism for advancing film in the camera. Among the specialized cameras that he produced was the "Tropical" model, utilized by the first newsreel cameramen covering the Boer War.

The term, "Brighton School" has often been credited to French film historian Georges Sadoul, who is said to have used it, for convenience, in his pamphlet, *British Creators of Film Technique.* A reading of this pamphlet does not reveal any such use of the term.

BIBLIOGRAPHY

Low, Rachael, and Roger Manvell. *The History of the British Film: 1896–1906.* London: George Allen & Unwin, 1948.

THE BRITISH ACADEMY OF FILM AND TELEVISION ARTS. As early as April 24, 1929, British director George Pearson suggested in the pages of the trade paper, *The Bioscope**, that the British film industry create an institution similar to the American Academy of Motion Picture Arts and Sciences. Such an organization, the British Film Academy, was eventually established in March 1947, with a dinner meeting at Claridge's Hotel, London. Among the founders were Alexander Korda, David Lean, Paul Rotha, Michael Balcon, and Alberto Cavalcanti, with Roger Manvell joining the Academy in August 1947 as its first Secretary-General.

In 1953, members of the British television industry founded the Guild of Television Producers and Directors, and, in 1958, the two groups combined to become the Society of Film and Television Arts, which later changed its name to the British Academy of Film and Television Arts. The published objectives of the Academy are "to promote, maintain, improve, and advance original and creative work among persons engaged in film and television production; to create and maintain a high standard of qualification and performance in such persons; and to encourage and promote experiment and research in the arts, sciences, and techniques of film and television production." The most highly visible of the Academy's activities are its awards ceremonies, which have been televized since 1969. The British Academy Award is based on a design by Mitzi Cunliffe. It has also published a quarterly journal from 1948–1974, initially titled *British Film Academy Quarterly* and later renamed *Journal of the Society of Film and Television Arts*.

Address: 195 Piccadilly, London W1V 9LG, United Kingdom.

BIBLIOGRAPHY

Manvell, Roger, "The British Film Academy," *Films in Review*, January 1952, pp. 28–33.

THE BRITISH AMERICAN FILM COMPANY was a Canadian producer, responsible for one film, the country's first native drama, *The Battle of the Long Sault*, a two-reeler, released in 1913. This was the only film produced by the British American Film Company, which was located in Montreal.

BIBLIOGRAPHY

Morris, Peter. *Embattled Shadows: A History of Canadian Cinema 1895–1939*. Montreal: McGill-Queen's University Press, 1978.

BRITISH AND COLONIAL KINEMATOGRAPH COMPANY. Founded in 1909, the British and Colonial Kinematograph Company was usually known simply as B & C. With studios in the London suburb of East Finchley—in 1913 it moved to new studios in Walthamstow—the company produced the popular Lt. Daring series, starring Percy Moran, and, in 1913, made a series of films in the West Indies, as well as what is arguably the first British epic production, *The Battle of Waterloo*. It ceased production in 1918.

BRITISH AND DOMINION FILM CORPORATION. See ELSTREE STUDIOS

BRITISH BOARD OF FILM CENSORS. See BRITISH BOARD OF FILM CLASSIFICATION

BRITISH BOARD OF FILM CLASSIFICATION. The existing system of censorship in the United Kingdom came into being through the Cinematograph Act of 1909. In order to protect audiences from safety hazards, particularly fire, it charged local authorities with licensing buildings where inflammable film was projected for public entertainment, and the authorities used such power widely in order to prevent the showing of films that they judged improper. The film industry, alarmed by the activities of local censors and their unpredictable rulings, agitated for a centralized system of censorship, but the Home Office declined to appoint a censor and so the industry created its own self-censoring board, the British Board of Film Censors (BBFC), which commenced operations on January 1, 1913. The Board depended for its effectiveness upon the cooperation of both the film industry—in submitting its films—and the local authorities—in recognizing and acting upon its classifications. Local authorities gradually came to accept the Board's authority, although they still retain the right to pass for local showings a film which has been refused a certificate by the Board, or to ban a film which it has passed. Films cannot be screened in public in the United Kingdom unless they have the BBFC's certificate or the relevant local authorization.

The Board consists of a president and secretary, appointed by the film industry; examiners; readers of scripts; and clerical staff. The presidents, who have usually no connection with the motion picture, are chosen for their high public reputation, and the appointment is approved by the Home Secretary. The Board's work is financed by viewing fees based on a film's running time. There are no written rules, but in viewing a film, the Board attempts to judge whether it is liable to break the law, for example, by depraving and corrupting a significant proportion of its likely audience. It also assesses whether there is material greatly and gratuitously offensive to a large number of people. The Board attempts to reflect contemporary public attitudes, but has often been accused of being behind the times. It is also the Board's policy not to censor any film on political grounds.

There have been different sets of categories of certificates over the years, but in December 1982, the following five categories came into effect:

U or Universal, suitable for all

PG or Parental Guidance, some scenes may be unsuitable for young children

15, passed only for persons of 15 years and over

18, passed only for persons of 18 years and over

R18, for restricted distribution only, through segregated premises, to which no-one under 18 years is admitted

In May 1985, due to the death of the Board's president, Lord Harlech, in a road accident, Lord Harewood became president. The following month, the

Board was renamed the British Board of Film Classification. A recent additional role of the Board, under the 1985 Video Recording Act, is to be responsible for the certification of videotapes available in the United Kingdom.

Address: 3 Soho Square, London W1V 5DE, United Kingdom.

BIBLIOGRAPHY

Brown, Beverly, "A Curious Arrangement: Interview with Secretary of BBFC James Ferman," *Screen,* vol. XXIII, no. 5, November-December 1982, pp. 2–25.

Hunnings, Neville March. *Film Censorship and the Law*. London: George Allen & Unwin, 1967.

O'Higgins, Paul. *Censorship in Britain*. London: Nelson, 1972.

Phelps, Guy. *Film Censorship*. London: Victor Gollancz, 1975.

Richards, Jeffrey, "The British Board of Film Censors and Content Control in the 1930s: Images of Britain," *Historical Journal of Film, Radio, and Television,* vol. I, no. 2, October 1981, pp. 95–116.

———, "The British Board of Film Censors and Content Control in the 1930s: Foreign Affairs," *Historical Journal of Film, Radio, and Television,* vol. II, no. 1, March 1982, pp. 39–48.

Robertson, James C., "British Film Censorship Goes to War," *Historical Journal of Film, Radio, and Television,* vol. II, no. 1, March 1982, pp. 49–64.

———. *The British Board of Film Censors: Film Censorship in Britain, 1896–1950.* Beckenham, Kent: Croom Helm, 1985.

Trevelyan, John. *What the Censor Saw*. London: Michael Joseph, 1973.

Wistrich, Enid. *I Don't Mind the Sex, It's the Violence: Film Censorship*. London: Marion Boyars, 1978.

Wood, Linda. *British Film Industry*. London: British Film Institute, 1980.

BRITISH COLUMBIA FILM. Funded by the provincial government, British Columbia Film was created in 1987 to help finance local film production. The organization provides low-interest loans for features, script development loans, preproduction loans, promotional loans for marketing purposes, and smaller loans for shorts and non-theatrical films.

Address: 800 Hornby Street, Suite 140, Vancouver, B.C. V6Z ZC5, Canada.

BIBLIOGRAPHY

Tusher, Will, "Fostering Home-Grown Prod'n British Columbia Film Goal," *Daily Variety,* October 12, 1987, p. 18.

THE BRITISH EMPIRE has been glorified as much on film by the Americans as the British. The Empire has also been vilified by Nazi filmmakers, most notably in *Ohm Krüger/Uncle Krüger* (1941). Among the many, many films of empire are *The Four Feathers* (1929), *Tell England* (1930), *Cavalcade* (1932), *Clive of India* (1935), *Lives of a Bengal Lancer* (1935), *Charge of the Light Brigade* (1936), *Rhodes of Africa* (1936), *Wee Willie Winkie* (1937), *King Solomon's Mines* (1937), *Sixty Glorious Years* (1938), *The Four Feathers* (1939), *Gunga Din* (1939), *The Prime Minister* (1940), *King Solomon's Mines* (1950), *Bengal Brigade* (1954), and *Bhowani Junction* (1955). The appeal of films dealing with the British Empire disappeared in the fifties, but was revived in the eighties as a number of filmmakers turned to India under the British as a suitable subject for pageantry and political commentary. Of course, it was left to the Americans, in the form of Universal Pictures and director Rowland V. Lee, to make a film titled *The Sun Never Sets* (1940)—and, in fact, as far as American filmmakers were concerned for a number of years thereafter it never did.

BIBLIOGRAPHY

Richards, Jeffrey. *Visions of Yesterday*. Boston: Routledge & Kegan Paul, 1973.

BRITISH EMPIRE FILMS was a Canadian company, founded in June 1927 by Colonel W.F. Clarke, which collapsed in 1929. Its subsidiary, Canadian International Films, produced the important Canadian feature, *Carry On, Sergeant,* during 1927–1928.

BIBLIOGRAPHY

Morris, Peter. *Embattled Shadows: A History of Canadian Cinema 1895–1939*. Montreal: McGill-Queen's University Press, 1978.

THE BRITISH FEDERATION OF FILM SOCIETIES was founded, with some forty-six member organizations, in 1945. At the same time, the British Film Institute* created a booking agency to provide films for the member societies, with Hannah Lawson serving as first booking secretary of the agency and as assistant to the honorary secretary of the Federation (Oliver Bell, director of the British Film Institute). Later in 1945, Francis Howard-Gwynne was appointed full-time manager of the booking agency and secretary of the Federation. In 1950, when the British Film Institute was unable to continue financial assistance to the Federation, Howard-Gwynne was succeeded by an honorary secretary, Margaret Hancock. Upon her retirement in 1964, she was succeeded by Ronald Shields, who was succeeded in 1966 by Peter Cargin.

An earlier attempt at a British Federation of Film Societies had been made in 1937, with Barbara Frey as secretary. Prior to the creation of the new Federation, there were many major film societies active in the United Kingdom, including The Film Society*, the Film Society of Glasgow (founded 1929), the Leeds Film Society (founded 1929), the Edinburgh Film Guild (founded 1930), the Southampton Film Society (founded 1930), and the Cambridge Film Society (founded in 1941). A Scottish Federation of Film Societies was formed in 1936, with Forsyth Hardy as its honorary secretary, and it remained in existence until 1969, when it merged with the British Federation.

In October 1954, the British Federation of Film Societies began publication of *Film,* which was issued on a triannual and then quarterly basis until 1972, and a monthly basis thereafter.

Address: 21 Stephen Street, London W1P 1PL, United Kingdom.

THE BRITISH FILM AND TELEVISION PRODUCERS' ASSOCIATION is an amalgamation of the British Film Producers' Association (formed 1941) and the Federation of British Filmmakers (formed 1957). It represents the interests of producers in contacts with the government and unions.

Address: Paramount House, 162–170 Wardour Street, London W1V 4LA, United Kingdom.

THE BRITISH FILM DESIGNERS GUILD LTD. began life in 1946 as the Society of British Art Directors and Designers. The latter subsequently became the Guild of Film Art Directors, and the British Film Designers Guild Ltd. was created in 1982. Its membership includes those involved in any branch of the art department, and it actively promotes work for its members within the British film industry.

Address: 26–28 Binney Street, London W1Y 1YN, United Kingdom.

THE BRITISH FILM INSTITUTE (BFI) is a multifaceted organization, responsible, to a great extent, for the cultural and educational aspects of the motion picture in the United Kingdom. It publishes two major journals; operates London's National Film Theatre; is charged with the preservation of the country's film and television heritage; and helps fund many important, low-key British films.

The Institute came into being as a result of a 1932 study of *The Film in National Life,* prepared by the Commission on Educational and Cultural Films of the British Institute of Adult Education. The BFI was incorporated on September 30, 1933, with a board of governors and a grant from the Cinematograph Fund. Initially located at 4 Great Russell Street, almost opposite the British Museum, the Institute established a library and information service—G.K. Hall published the catalog of books in the collection in 1975. In May 1935, the National Film Library was established, later becoming the National Film Archive, under the curatorship of Ernest Lindgren. J.W. Benson was the Institute's first director (then called general manager).

Sight & Sound had commenced publication in the spring of 1932, and it was taken over by the British Film Institute in 1933. It remains the leading British film journal, and, although somewhat archaic in its editorial policy, has tremendous influence throughout the world. Noted for its complete credit information on all films released in the United Kingdom, *Monthly Film Bulletin* has been published by the Institute since February 1934. It also provides synopses and, in recent years, lengthy, sometimes esoteric critical judgments. Between 1961 and 1966, the BFI also published a critical television quarterly, *Contrast,* edited by David Robinson. It has also published monographs, and was copublisher of a series of film books, titled "Cinema One," with Thames and Hudson in the late sixties and seventies. (The first volume in the series was on Jean-Luc Godard, written by Richard Roud, and published in 1967.)

A film distribution library and a central booking agency for use by film societies was established in 1938 and remains active. Although the Institute collected still photographs from its inception, it was not until 1948 that an official stills archive was established under Norah Traylen. The stills archive expanded and prospered in later years thanks to the work of Michele Snapes, who became associate curator of the National Film Archive in 1987, working under longtime curator, David Francis.

The British Film Institute first began making grants for film production in 1951, with the establishment of the Experimental Film Fund, under the chairmanship of Michael Balcon. The Fund was later renamed the Production Board, and Bruce Beresford (who was to become a successful Australian film director) was its first production officer from 1966–1971. In recent years it has helped finance such important British features as Peter Greenaway's *The Draughtsman's Contract* (1982) and Derek Jarman's *Caravaggio* (1986).

The National Film Theatre (NFT), with its daily screenings and its excellent program brochures and notes, was a continuation of the Telekinema at the Festival of Britain, and had first opened under the auspices of the British Film Institute on November 8, 1952. A new theatre complex, on the same site next to the Festival Hall on London's South Bank, was opened by Princess Margaret on October 15, 1957, and a second auditorium NFT2, opened on September 21, 1970. The London Film Festival, sponsored by the Institute, has been held at the NFT since its inception in 1957.

Although it was founded primarily in the interest of film for educational purposes, the Institute did not become actively involved in screen education until 1957, when Stanley Reed (later to become the BFI's director) was appointed its film appreciation officer.

After a number of temporary homes, the Institute moved to 81 Dean Street, in the Soho district, in June 1980. In November 1987, it moved to a new address at 21 Stephen Street, to a building made available to it through a grant from J. Paul Getty, Jr. Getty has donated some $22 million to the BFI between 1981 and 1986. Thanks to his generosity, the J. Paul Getty Conservation Centre opened at Berkhamsted in 1987 for the controlled storage of papers and films and as the world's first conservation project devoted to the motion picture.

A Museum of the Moving Image was opened by the Institute, adjacent to the National Film Theatre in the fall of 1988.

Address: 21 Stephen Street, London W1P 1PL, United Kingdom.

BIBLIOGRAPHY

Butler, Ivan. *"To Encourage the Art of the Film."* London: Robert Hale, 1971.

"Film Institute Is Sitting Pretty," *Variety,* January 14, 1987, pp. 106, 128.

"The National Film Archive," *Journal of the Society of Film and Television Arts,* no. 39, Spring 1970, entire issue.

Robinson, David, "Fifty Years of the British Film Institute," *Times Literary Supplement,* November 18, 1983, p. 1292.

BRITISH FILM YEAR (BFY) ran from March 1985 through May 1986, with its basic aim being to increase movie theatre ticket sales for films produced in the United Kingdom. It was announced by its president, Sir Richard Attenborough, at a press conference at the Cannes Film Festival in May 1984, followed by a press conference, at which confusion reigned, in London in the fall. The idea for BFY came from twenty-eight-year-old Fiona Halton, a successful director of the Association of Independent Producers, described as "a cross between Margaret Thatcher and Mary Poppins." Her wholehearted efforts as executive director of BFY won her a hard-earned award from the Institute of Sales and Marketing Management. Backing came from the British Government (in the amount of £325,000), EMI, Rank*, Cannon-Classic, Goldcrest, and Virgin, bringing the total to £1,250,000. Patrons of British Film Year were the Prince and Princess of Wales.

One of the main features of BFY was the Roadshow, which took films, stars, directors, costume designers, stuntmen, and technicians to twenty-three cities outside of London. Omar Sharif was mobbed in the old-star style in Lincoln, and a Swansea grandmother won lunch with Christopher Cazenove. In London, Leicester Square's Star Pavement (inspired by the legendary forecourt of Grauman's Chinese Theatre in Los Angeles) was inaugurated, with Alan Bates, Charlton Heston, Sir John Mills, Dame Anna Neagle, and Omar Sharif placing their hands in cement. Film festivals were inaugurated, competitions held and there were open days at movie theatres. Thames Television invited three prominent British directors—Lindsay Anderson, Sir Richard Attenborough, and Alan Parker—to present their personal views on the British film industry. There were three major exhibitions of photographs: "The British Film Collection 1896–1984: A History of the British Cinema in Pictures," "Stars of the British Screen: Photographs from the 1930s to the 1980s," and "Take One: British Film Stills." Over four thousand schools received educational publications from BFY and the Post Office issued stamps commemorating five British-born stars and filmmakers, Charlie Chaplin, Alfred Hitchcock, Vivien Leigh, David Niven, and Peter Sellers.

Greeted initially with skepticism from the press and receiving uneven criticism during its life, British Film Year did achieve what it set out to do; theatre attendances went up 35 percent from the previous year's figures.

BIBLIOGRAPHY

"Forward into British Film Year," *Sight & Sound,* vol. LIV, no. 1, Winter 1984/85, pp. 9–15.

Hawkins, John, "British Film Year," *Sight & Sound,* vol. LIV, no. 1, Winter 1984/85, p. 8.

"Heurtebise," "The Distinguished Thingumabob," *Sight & Sound,* vol. LIV, no. 1, Winter 1984/85, pp. 34–35.

"Kockenlocker," "BFY," *Sight & Sound*, vol. LV, no. 2, Spring 1986, p. 95.

BRITISH INSTRUCTIONAL FILMS was founded in 1919 by Henry Bruce Woolfe and quickly gained a reputation for its educational, nature, scientific, and industrial films. Its first production was *The Battle of Jutland* (1921), a precursor of the company's later documentaries of the First World War, directed by Walter Summers: *Ypres* (1925), *Mons* (1926), and *Battles of the Coronel and Falkland Islands* (1927). British Instructional Films gained wide praise for its

"Secrets of Nature" series, released from 1922 onwards. It made its first dramatic feature, *Nelson,* starring Cedric Hardwicke in the title role, in 1926, and was also responsible for launching the career of director Anthony Asquith with *Shooting Stars* (1928) and *Underground* (1928). It was eventually acquired by British International Pictures*.

BRITISH INTERNATIONAL PICTURES (BIP) was founded in March 1927, with a share capital of £50,000, by John Maxwell, a leading distributor, who had commenced his career as an exhibitor in 1912. The company came into being as a response to the concern of the government and the Federation of British Industries that the United States had acquired a monopoly of the film industry. Having established BIP, Maxwell's first step was to take over the newly built studios at Elstree*, with his first feature being *The White Sheik* (1928), starring Lillian Hall Davis and Warwick Ward as the passionate lovers. This was followed by *A Little Bit of Fluff* (U.S. *Skirts,* 1928), starring Betty Balfour, who was known as the English Mary Pickford. Balfour was also the star of the first British musical, BIP's *Raising the Roof* (1930).

One of the first directors signed by Maxwell was Alfred Hitchcock, whose first film for BIP was *The Ring* (1928), followed by *The Farmer's Wife* (1928), *Champagne* (1928), and *The Manxman* (1929). Maxwell's next appointment was Walter Mycroft, who was initially scenario editor and then studio head (and such was his authority that he was nicknamed "Czar of All the Rushes"). Wanting to expand into the European market, Maxwell signed the German director E.A. Dupont to make *Moulin Rouge* (1928), which was followed by *Piccadilly* (1929) and *Atlantic* (1929), the first multilingual talkie, with separate English, French, and German casts.

Maxwell had made quiet preparations for sound, and what is generally accepted as the first British "talkie" Hitchock's *Blackmail* (1929), was a BIP feature. It was a tremendous success, and, within a year, Elstree's four stages were expertly divided to provide nine sound-proof stages. During the thirties, BIP flourished with a wide range of productions, including musicals (BIP's 1931 feature, *Out of the Blue,* gave Jessie Matthews her first starring role), comedies starring music hall personalities such as Stanley Lupino and Lupino Lane, adaptations of stage plays, costume features, modern dramas, and operettas (with Richard Tauber, BIP's biggest celebrity). In 1933, Maxwell formed the Associated British Picture Corporation (ABPC) as a holding company to take over the capital of BIP, British Instructional Films (which BIP had acquired), Wardour Films (which handled the sales and distribution of BIP films), and Maxwell's original ABC circuit of cinemas. The studios continued to be known as BIP until 1939, when, with the outbreak of the Second World War, all production ceased. Maxwell died in 1940.

BIBLIOGRAPHY

Low, Rachael. *The History of the British Film: 1918–1929*. London: George Allen & Unwin, 1971.

———. *Film Making in 1930s Britain*. London: George Allen & Unwin, 1985.
Warren, Patricia. *Elstree: The British Hollywood*. London: Elm Tree Books, 1983.
Wilson, Freddie, "A Museum of Recollection," *The Guild of British Film Editors Journal,* no. 53, December 1979, pp. 8–13.

THE BRITISH KINEMATOGRAPH, SOUND AND TELEVISION SOCIETY (BKSTS) is concerned with the technological aspects of the film and television industries in much the same way as the American Society of Motion Picture and Television Engineers, from which it sprang. A London branch of the Society of Motion Picture Engineers, as it was then called, was established at a meeting at Kingsway House, on October 10, 1928. Because the American parent body failed to publish papers presented at its London meetings, questioned the membership of certain individuals, and refused to cover all the expenses of a formal dinner by the London Section for Sir Oliver Lodge, the London branch decided to disband, and, in January 1931, it was reestablished as the British Kinematograph Society. A new constitution was accepted by the Board of Trade in 1946, and the British Kinematograph Society was incorporated on May 3 of that year. The name was changed to the British Kinematograph, Sound and Television Society when it merged with the British Sound Recording Association in 1964.

The Society is managed by an elected president and council. It has published a journal, first on a quarterly and then monthly basis, since 1931. The BKSTS publishes a wide range of training manuals and organizes training courses, workshops and seminars. Regular meetings are held at which papers are presented. Every two years, the Society organizes an international technology conference and exhibition that attracts delegates from all over the world. The Society has branches outside London in Birmingham, Bristol, Manchester, and Plymouth. It has representatives in most parts of the world and liaises with equivalent organizations in Europe and the United States.

Address: 549 Victoria House, Vernon Place, London WC1B 4DJ, United Kingdom.

BIBLIOGRAPHY

Kimbley, Denis, "How the B.K.S. Began," *The BKSTS Journal,* January 1981, pp. 12–13.
Wratten, I.D., "The Early Years of the Society," *The BKSTS Journal,* January 1981, pp. 14–15.

BRITISH LION was founded in 1927 by Samuel Woolf Smith, who had been in film distribution since 1910, in order to make use of the talents of Edgar Wallace in adapting his crime stories for the screen. A small studio at Beaconsfield, northwest of London, was acquired, and an arrangement made with Michael Balcon to produce a series of Gainsborough-British Lion films, with the first being *The Ringer,* directed in 1931 by Walter Forde. A renting subsidiary was formed, for which British Lion imported films. However, the character of the company changed when Wallace died in February 1932 while on a two-month contract in Hollywood. Output expanded with safe, light features and filmed variety acts, and a boost was given to the company when it signed an agreement with Republic Pictures to distribute all of its films in the United Kingdom. During the Second World War, British Lion financed Noël Coward's *In Which We Serve* (1942).

In 1946, Alexander Korda gained control of the company by acquiring it through London Films*. He had also acquired Shepperton Studios*, and British Lion production moved there. Subsequent years saw high production losses that were further increased when Republic set up its own distribution outfit in the United Kingdom. The National Film Finance Corporation* had made British Lion a £3 million loan which, when the company's financial crisis reached its peak in 1954, was called in. A receiver was appointed and Korda removed.

A new British Lion was formed in January 1955 to take over the assets of its insolvent predecessor, with its main function being the provision of distribution and financial guarantees to independent producers. The managing director was David Kingsley, one of the industry's shrewdest accountants, who persuaded the Boulting Brothers, Frank Launder, and Sidney Gilliat to join the board of directors. In the early sixties, the company's finances were improved with the success of such films as *Only Two Can Play* (1961), *The Wrong Arm of the Law* (1961), and *The L-Shaped Room* (1962). Then, in 1964, the government decided to sell off British Lion—despite considerable opposition from within the film industry—to a group headed by Michael Balcon and including John Schlesinger, Tony Richardson, and Karel Reisz. The consortium failed to work, a disenchanted Balcon departed, and Lord Goodman became chairman. After a period of mixed fortunes, British Lion was taken over in April 1972 by Barclay Securities, headed by John Bentley. Bentley was then himself the subject of a lightning takeover by a financial services group, J.H. Varvasseur, in February 1973. Films made during this unsettled period include Nicholas Roeg's *Don't Look Now* (1973), Joseph Losey's *A Doll's House* (1973), and Peter Snell's *The Wicker Man* (1973). By 1975, cash flow had become such a serious problem that negotiations for a takeover by EMI began, and it was completed in May 1976. Despite securing a promise that the name British Lion would not be allowed to die, it did, in fact, quickly disappear from all EMI films.

BIBLIOGRAPHY

Low, Rachael. *Film Making in 1930s Britain*. London: George Allen & Unwin, 1985.

Walker, Alexander. *Hollywood England: The British Film Industry in the Sixties*. London: Michael Joseph, 1974.

———. *National Heroes: British Cinema in the Seventies and Eighties*. London: Harrap, 1985.

BRITISH MOVIETONE NEWS was, as its name suggests, Britain's version of the American Fox Movietone News. The newsreel was seen in British theatres from 1929-1979. Its best-known commentator was Leslie Mitchell. Its footage is available for commercial use from the British Movietone Library (North Orbital Road, Denham, Uxbridge, Middlesex, United Kingdom).

BIBLIOGRAPHY

Gay, Ken, "The Lone Newsreel," *Films and Filming*, April 1970, p. 88.

Norris, Glen, "A Wide-Open Letter to Mr. Gerald Sanger, Production Chief of British Movietonews [*sic*]", *World Film News*, vol. II, no. 6, September 1937, pp. 32–33.

BRITISH MUSIC HALL, the equivalent of American vaudeville, has provided the American film industry with two of its greatest comedians: Charles Chaplin and Stan Laurel. Other entertainers who made a transition from Music Hall to the British film industry include Bud Flanagan and Chesney Allen, Florence Desmond (also in American films), Sid Field, Gracie Fields (also in American films), George Formby, Will Fyffe (also in American films), Tony Hancock, Will Hay, Arthur Lucan (who appeared as "Old Mother Riley"), Max Miller, Tessie O'Shea (also in American films), Sandy Powell, George Robey, Tommy Steele (also in American films), Tommy Trinder, and Norman Wisdom.

Among the few feature films dealing with life in the British Music Hall are *Raise the Roof* (1930), *Music Hall* (1934), and *Champagne Charlie* (1944), which concerned the rivalry between two Victorian Music Hall personalities, George Leybourne and the Great Vance. Pat Kirkwood, who had also appeared on the Music Hall stage, played the great British male impersonator, Vesta Tilley, in *After the Ball* (1956).

BIBLIOGRAPHY

Busby, Roy. *British Music Hall: An Illustrated Who's Who from 1850 to the Present Day*. London: Paul Elek, 1976.

BRITISH PRODUCTION FUND. See EADY LEVY

BRYANSTON FILMS was the idea of independent producer Maxwell Setton, who wanted to form a filmmakers' cooperative whose members would be producers or producers-directors, and whose established reputation and credit-worthiness would give them easier access to distribution guarantees and possible new sources of finance. The resulting company, Bryanston Films, was launched in April 1959 with Sir Michael Balcon as its chairman and Setton as managing director. Members—of which there were sixteen—included Michael Relph, Charles Frend, and Basil Dearden, all of whom had worked for Balcon at Ealing Studios*; Ronald Neame, director of photography and producer; Julian Winter and Leslie Parkyn, independent producers who released films through the Rank Organization*; and Gerald and Kenneth Shipman, who owned Twickenham Film Studios*. Initial capital was around £1 million, which came from the members themselves and from various investors, including British Lion*, Lloyds Bank, Alliance Film Studios, and Denham Laboratories. Distribution of the films was to be through British Lion.

The first productions—*The Battle of the Sexes* (1959), *The Boy Who Stole a Million* (1960), and *Light Up the Sky* (1960)—were unassuming but successful. Bryanston's first box-office failure came with *The Entertainer* (1960), in which Laurence Olivier repeated his moving stage performances as Archie Rice. It was made by an outside consortium, Woodfall Films*, but that company's next production, *Saturday Night and Sunday Morning* (1960) for which Bryanston provided 70 percent of the budget, became a milestone in British cinema. Subsequent Woodfall productions financed by Bryanston were *A Taste of Honey* (1961) and *The Loneliness of the Long Distance Runner* (1962).

In November 1961, Bryanston announced expansion plans involving its joining forces with the affluent Seven Arts Productions UK. Its aims were to develop, finance, and distribute British films of international significance by arranging 100 percent financing, thus leaving the producer with his entire time to the creative aspects of the production. The first film so produced was *Sammy Going South* (1963). Being heavily committed to this film, Bryanston was unable to finance Woodfall's *Tom Jones* (1963), which was eventually financed by United Artists. When *Tom Jones* became such an unqualified success, Bryanston realized its mistake, as independent producers found they were able to look to American sources of finance rather than to Bryanston. Setton left to become production chief for Columbia Pictures' European operations. Bryanston found itself unable to obtain screenings for its films on the major circuits and a cash flow problem developed. In January 1965, the company, with a library of thirty features, was taken over by Associated Television, an independent television company.

BIBLIOGRAPHY

Walker, Alexander. *Hollywood England: The British Film Industry in the Sixties*. London: Michael Joseph, 1974.

BUDAPEST. The capital of Hungary has been used as a locale for a number of American feature films, including *Silken Shackles* (1926), *The Heart Thief* (1927), *The Yellow Lily* (1928), *The Garden of Eden* (1928), *Is Everybody Happy?* (1929), *Shop around the Corner* (1940), and *The Great White Hope* (1970). Hungarian playwright and novelist Ferenc Molnar (1878–1952) is the author of a number of works set in Budapest and translated to the screen, notably *Liliom* (1930) and *The Good Fairy* (1935). The Hungarian feature filmed in Budapest, *A Pál Utcai Fiúk/The Boys of Paul Street* (1969) is based on a story by Molnar. The American feature, *Zoo in Budapest* (1933) has become a cult favorite, although there is only a small zoo in Budapest.

BULGARIA. The first films were screened in Bulgaria in 1897; the first Bulgarian showman was Vladimir Petkov, who became active in 1897. The first theatre was built in Sofia in 1908. Documentary film production began in Bulgaria in 1910, and some two hundred documentaries were produced up to the Second World War. In 1915, the first Bulgarian feature film, *The Bulgar Is a Gentleman,* was made by Vassil Gendov.

A major production company, Luna Film, was established in the twenties, initially producing short subjects and later features. The country was very late in accepting sound films, with the last silent feature, *Revolt of the Slaves,* directed by V. Guendov, being produced in Bulgaria in 1933. The first sound feature came a year later. Up to the Second World War, the country's film industry had produced some fifty feature films.

Following the Second World War, the film industry was nationalized in April 1948, when the General Department of Cinematography was created; it became the Committee for Cinematography in 1952. The first modern Bulgarian feature is *Kalin Orelat/Kalin the Eagle* (1949), directed by Boris Borozanov.

Films are imported and exported by Filmbulgaria (135 Rakovsky St., Sofia). As of 1987, the Bulgarian Cinematography Corporation has responsibility for all film production, operating under the Council of Ministers and the chairmanship of Lyudmil Staikov, who is a filmmaker in his own right. A number of studios operate under the corporation, the largest of which is the Boyana Feature Film Studio, producing between twenty and twenty-five features a year. The other studios are the Vreme Popular Science and Documentary Film Studio, the Sofia Animated Film Studio, the Globus Film Unit, and the Experimental Film Studio of the Union of Bulgarian Film Workers. Major directors of the eighties include Nikolai Volev, Nikolai Roudarov, Borislav Sharaliev, Lyudmil Kirkov, Zacco Heskia, Roumyana Petkova, and Ivan Andonov.

BIBLIOGRAPHY

Elley, Derek, "Bulgar Baubles," *Films and Filming,* February 1980, pp. 6–7.

Hibbin, Nina. *Eastern Europe: An Illustrated Guide*. New York: A.S. Barnes, 1969.

Liehm, Mira, and Antonin J. Liehm. *The Most Important Art: Eastern Europe Film after 1945*. Berkeley: University of California Press, 1977.

Paul, David W., editor. *Politics, Art and Commitment in East European Cinema*. New York: St. Martin's Press, 1983.

Stoil, Michael Jon. *Cinema beyond the Danube*. Metuchen, N.J.: Scarecrow Press, 1974.

———. *Balkan Cinema*. Ann Arbor, Mich.: UMI Research Press, 1982.

Stoyanovich, Ivan, "Bulgaria," in *International Film Guide 1988,* editor Peter Cowie. New York: New York Zoetrope, 1987, pp. 122–127.

BUNDESMINISTERIUM DES INNERN (West German Ministry of the Interior) has been subsidizing film projects since 1951. As of 1987, it had eight million Deutsche marks available for distribution. It also awards the annual Deutsche Filmpreise (German Film Prize).

Address: Bonn, West Germany.

BURMA. Although its productions are almost totally unknown outside of this socialist republic (and former kingdom), Burma has had an active film industry since 1920, when the first Burmese film, a newsreel of the funeral of politician U Tun Shein was made by U Ohn Maung. The first feature-length talkie was *Shine ein the,* produced by the British Burma Company in 1932. By 1940, the country had 137 theatres, and boasted the production of 63 films, of which 27 were made by non-professionals. The Japanese invasion of the country closed down production, but by 1948, 80 theatres were open, and in that year the industry turned out 46 films, of which forty were still silent productions. The first postwar film was *Bama thit,* directed by Loon Pe, and produced by New Burma Films.

The country presently boasts more than 400 theatres, most of which predate independence. Theatres in all major cities were nationalized in 1968, and the government controls film importation through the Motion Picture Corporation (312–314 Merchant Street, Rangoon), which also handles distribution and exhibition internally, and which is subsidized by the Ministry of Culture. Apart from Hindi-language Indian films, that are the most popular of imported products, films are generally screened in English-dubbed versions. No films are shown with subtitles. Until the eighties, the government policy was not to permit any Burmese films to be screened in festivals outside of the country. This policy changed in 1983, when two films by U Tu Kha were seen, and praised, at the Manilla International Film Festival.

The film industry is subsidized in part, and there are more than one hundred producers in Burma. The most important is A-1 Films, which is responsible for an average of five features a year. Burma's most important director is U Myint Soe, whose features usually star his wife, Daisy Po. Other directors include U Tu Kha, U Khin Soe, Soe Thein, Maung Tin Oo, Kyi Soe Tun, Than Htut, Bo Ba Ko, and Ko Myint. Almost half of all Burmese features continue to be produced in black-and-white, and no color films were made prior to 1984.

C

CAHIERS DU CINÉMA. The best known of French critical journals, *Cahiers du Cinéma* was founded in 1951 by André Bazin and Jacques Doniol-Valcroze. In the mid-fifties, it served as a vehicle for the new ideas of critics such as François Truffaut and helped create the French New Wave*. An English-language edition was published in New York from 1966–1967.

Address: Édition de L'Étoile, 9 Passage de la Boulevard Blanche, 75012 Paris, France.

BIBLIOGRAPHY

Slide, Anthony, editor. *International Film, Radio, and Television Journals*. Westport, Conn.: Greenwood Press, 1985.

CALLIGRAPHISM is the term coined by Guiseppe De Santis to describe the preoccupations with formalism and the past evidenced in the films of his fellow Italian directors during the Second World War. Among such films are Mario Soldati's *Piccolo Mondo Antico/Little Old-Fashioned World* (1940) and *Malombra* (1942), and Renato Castellani's *Un Colpo di Pistola/A Pistol Shot* (1941).

BIBLIOGRAPHY

Armes, Roy. *Patterns of Realism*. South Brunswick, N.J.: A.S. Barnes, 1971.

CAMBODIA. The film industry in Cambodia was dominated by Prince Norodom Sihanouk, who was actively involved as a director and writer until he was removed from power in a 1970 bloodless coup. Sihanouk established an international film festival in Phnom Penh—held in 1968 and 1969—at which his films received the top awards. Sihanouk's most important film is *Shadow over Angkor* (1966), in which he and his wife, Princess Monique, appeared. With the establishment of the bloody Khmer Rouge regime in 1975, filmmaking ceased, and by 1979 all of the country's eighty or so theatres had been closed.

BIBLIOGRAPHY

Hitchens, Gordon, "The Short, Fruitful Film Career of Norodom Sihanouk (A Prince)," *Take One*, vol. II, no. 7, 1970, p. 19.

———, "Cambodia's Ousted Prince Writes, Directs, Stars and Wins His Own Festival's Prizes, But No More," *Variety,* May 27, 1970, p. 6.

CAMEROON. There has been limited filmmaking in Cameroon since its independence in 1959. The country gained minor international recognition with two 1975 features, *Muna Moto,* directed by Jean-Pierre Dikongue-Pipa and *Pousse-Pousse,* directed by Daniel Kamwa. A state agency, Fonds d'Aide à l'Industrie Cinématographique, was established in 1973, but with only twenty-three theatres in the entire country (according to a 1966 USIA report), filmmaking obviously has low priority.

CANADA. No other national cinema has been faced with the triumvirate of problems that Canada has: detrimental proximity to the monolithic Hollywood–New York axis of American filmmaking and financing; the sheer size of its own country, with its far-flung population and inherent distribution problems; and the presence within Canadian borders of a large and vocal ethnic minority, speaking a different language than the rest of the nation, who have consistently recognized and sought to control the cultural power of the motion picture screen and soundtrack. The story of Canadian feature filmmaking is the story of the failure of entrepreneurial capital, until very recently, to triumph over these obstacles, and of the uneasy relationship between American interests, Canadian government policy, and those same entrepreneurs.

The first recorded public screening of motion pictures in Canada occurred on July 21, 1896, at West End Park in Ottawa. Intended originally as a promotion of the Ottawa Electric Railway's expansion plans, the program, with other variety acts, was arranged by George and Andrew Holland, major licensees for the eastern United States and Canada of various Thomas Edison inventions, including the phonograph and the kinetoscope. The Edison Vitascope program of shorts was extended beyond its original planned two-week run, and the show, hosted by traveling magician-showman John C. Green, was hugely successful, attracting audiences of up to 1,600 a night. Within six months, the Hollands and other territorially licensed promoters were showing programs of Vitascope shorts across Lower Canada. Toronto first saw projected motion pictures in September 1896, at the Canadian National Exhibition. In that same month, projected motion pictures were also shown in Montreal, and in early 1897, a showman named H.J. Hill was touring provincial Ontario with a Lumière machine.

John Albert Schuberg opened the first facility exclusively used for the screening of films, Vancouver's Electric Theatre, in February 1903. He followed this with two theatres in Winnipeg in the autumn of that year. Montreal had a legitimate film theatre by 1904, St. Johns and Toronto by 1906, Hamilton by 1907. Schuberg's theatres in Winnipeg provided the basis of the Nash Circuit, with theatres in Manitoba and the American Midwest. John C. Griffin's Toronto Theatorium became the basis of an eleven-house chain. The Americans Jules and Jay Allan, using their Theatorium in Brantford (1907) opened a formal film exchange, the Allan Amusement Corporation, in 1908, and in 1911 built Canada's first "palace" theatre, the Allan in Calgary, which seated 800. The Allans also developed a chain, which was dominant in Canada through the twenties.

Production prior to World War I was sporadic. Actuality films of Canadian subjects recognizable to Americans, often Niagara Falls, appeared as early as 1896. Photographed by William Kennedy Dickson, for Biograph, and by cameramen for both Edison and Lumière, these films initiated the use of Canada-as-locale for American interests. Canadian production before the First World War consisted primarily of industrial subjects and sponsored fiction films encouraging immigration to Canada. These films were sponsored by, among others, the Canadian Pacific Railroad, the Northern Pacific Railroad, and the Grand Trunk Railroad, as well as Massey-Harris, and helped to establish a competitive tradition in the factual film which paralleled the development of the privately produced fiction film—and for many years, dwarfed it.

The first fiction film of Canadian lineage appears to have been *Hiawatha, Messiah of the Ojibways,* directed by Canadian Joe Rosenthal and released by Charles Urban in 1903. But Canada continued to make itself known primarily as a location for New York–based companies, as they entered the field of fiction filmmaking, and producers such as Kalem, Biograph, and Edison sent crews north to shoot films such as *Pierre of the North* and *Sons of the Northland* (both 1913).

Prior to the First World War, a number of independent feature filmmaking companies did spring up in Canada including the British American Film Company of Montreal, the Conness Till Company* of Halifax, Starland Ltd. in Winnipeg, Kinemacolor of Canada, Montreal Motion Pictures, and several other companies in Montreal.

However, as historian Peter Morris has pointed out, Canadians had no geographical center of production and thus could not practice the economies of scale in which competing American majors normally indulged. In addition, the growth of the movies was hampered by a weak native theatrical tradition in Canada; the talent pool of writers, actors, and directors nurtured by such a climate in the United States did not exist in Canada. The result was a trickle of indigenous film production—only three or four fiction films a year were released between 1913 and 1919. Yet, during this time, Canadian theatre circuits continued to grow; by 1919 the Allans owned forty-five theatres, and Nathan Nathanson controlled sixteen theatres by September 1919. Their negotiations for product focused almost exclusively on Europe and America. By 1913, the American share of films imported into Canada had risen to 63 percent, higher than with any other world power with which America traded.

The war saw great interest in newsreel production and marked the beginning of the presence of the government as a force in production. In 1916, Canada joined a consortium of Empire and Dominions topical film producers and began sponsoring a series of war-oriented shorts and feature length documentaries, such as *Canada's Work for Wounded Soldiers* (1918). But even war bond shorts were provided by American companies, chiefly Famous Players–Lasky.

During the period 1914–1922, at least thirty-six film companies established themselves in Canada, but few produced anything. Production inexperience, larceny, and above all a lack of access not only to American markets but often to their own Canadian houses killed all of these ventures, and by 1927, funding sources for any genuinely Canadian undertaking dried up almost completely.

The single exception to this pattern of failure was the work of Canadian-born Ernest Shipman, among whose "Northerns" (an American trade name for Canadian outdoor adventure films) were *Back to God's Country* (1919), *God's Crucible* (1920), and *Cameron of the Mounted* (1921). These films took advantage of a passing taste for Canadiana in the United States nurtured by such writers as James Oliver Curwood, and they were strenuously promoted there by Shipman. In addition, Shipman developed a production method perfectly suited for a decentralized system. Working closely with local authorities, he enlisted the aid of locals as extras, shot as little interior footage as possible, and took full advantage of the beautiful exteriors available to him throughout Canada. His Winnipeg Productions proved very successful, and he set up five regional production companies around Canada in 1921–1922. But the failure of *Blue Water* in 1923 ended Shipman's grandiose scheme when he was not able to find an American distributor who would handle the film either in the United States or in Canada. That same year, after financial difficulties, the Allans sold their theatre chain to N.L. Nathanson. Nathanson gained absolute control of first-run exhibition in Canada, and his Famous Players Canadian Corporation not only dealt exclusively with American producers, but also squeezed out major independents who posed threats in individual markets. Beginning in 1923, Canadian films found a hostile exhibition climate even in their own country.

By 1925, interest in financing Canadian production had virtually ended. Instead, the very features that had attracted Ernest Shipman to Canada—its scenery and the comparatively low cost of production—were appropriated by American producers, who continued the extensive location shooting of their prewar predecessors. Paramount's *The Canadian* (1926) was shot in Alberta, and "Canadian subjects" remained popular throughout the silent and sound era. The stereotypical view of Canadian life that these films presented—particularly their use of stock French-Canadian villains, such as in Cecil B. De Mille's *Royal Canadian Mounted Police* (1940)—produced reactions ranging from mild frustration to anger in Canadians and was the source of protests in the forties.

The production and reception of *Carry On, Sergeant* and an accompanying series of shorts in 1927–1928 by Canadian International Films virtually finished "A" feature production in Canada, reducing Canadian production to a shadow agency of the U.S. majors. *Carry On, Sergeant* was intended as a war film to redress the balance of American depictions of the First World War which ignored Canadians' crucial contribution to the war effort. The film, however, was plagued by huge cost overruns; its final budget was well over $500,000. Embezzlement and payroll-padding among the film's producers caused acrimony among the small community of film financiers in Canada. The film was poorly received by critics and the public, and finally it was unable to secure either an American or British release. The film even lost money on its Canadian bookings. Most significantly, the Trenton Studios, Canada's most sophisticated studio facility since 1917, were repossessed by the Ontario provincial government for use in the making of shorts after the *Carry On, Sergeant* debacle. No event so clearly foretold the position of primacy that documentary, short, and sponsored filmmaking would have for the next twenty years.

The British Quota Act was, coincidentally, enacted in 1927 to protect the British domestic market for native Empire and Dominions filmmakers. Exploitation of its provisos began almost immediately, and the depressed state of Canadian filmmaking made it a locus of such abuse. Canada became, between 1928 and 1938, a center for low-budget production by filmmakers who meant to qualify their productions as technically "British," and thus guarantee themselves quality bookings in England. Cheap features were produced for the British market by Canadian filmmakers, which constituted nearly all the features produced in Canada during this period. Connections with the American majors bankrolled much of the production of these "quota quickies."* Western Canada, with its mountainous scenery, was home to several minor production outfits, such as Commonwealth Productions and Central Films. They produced such films as *Death Goes North, Vengeance,* and *Tugboat Princess,* utilizing failed or untested Hollywood talent as leads and using young Canadian actors as second leads and supporting players. The films featured extensive location shooting, with interior work shot at small facilities such as the Willows Studios and the Lions Gate Studios (said to be a subsidiary of the American First National Organization) located in Vancouver. The low quality of Canadian films was a direct cause of the changing of the Quota Law in 1938 to exclude Dominions films. The Canadians had never adapted the Quota Law for their own except on a difficult-to-enforce provincial level, thus creating an impossible situation for themselves in which there was little self-determination in either production or exhibition. By this time, although the Combines Investigation of 1930 showed him to be in clear restraint of trade, N.L. Nathanson was in control of hundreds of theatres and over 50 percent of Canada's box-office gross. In addition, he owned a large share of Associated Screen News*, which generated most of the Canadian release prints of American films.

In December 1938, coinciding with the almost total darkening of Canadian studios, John Grierson arrived from England to set up the National Film Board of Canada (NFB)*, bringing with him then and in the next few years many top documentary filmmakers and animators from England and around the world.

Nothing that could be called a feature was released in either 1941 or 1942; indeed, only ten features were produced in the entire decade. In England, the war produced a renaissance of filmmaking; Canada saw no such rebirth in the years 1941–1945. The late forties were notable, however, for the first flowering of the French Canadian cinema. French films were shot in Quebec between 1944 and 1953, nearly the entire feature output of the nation. The appropriately named Renaissance Films built a studio in Montreal and put together a rudimentary distribution network in 1945–1946. Québec Productions erected studio facilities shortly after. Previous to this, continental French films had provided entertainment for Canada's French speakers, and the French Canadians discovered a reciprocal market for their films overseas. The Québecois had always had a higher rate of movie attendance per capita than other Canadians, and in addition, filmmaking (and film criticism) became an important forum for debating the issues of culture and society that drew French and English Canada into such often harsh opposition. (A young René Levesque was an outspoken film critic during this time.) The most popular subjects during the immediate postwar years were films which glorified a Catholic, pastoral existence, such as *Le Curé de village/The Village Priest* (1949).

Other events, notably expansionist moves on the part of American and British studios then at the very height of success, caused English-language production in Canada to be the focus of a political and economic debate in these years, a debate which finally did nothing to rejuvenate native production. There was talk of America's Monogram studios arranging to have a program of films made in Canada, a clear return to the production values of the "quota quickies." But the most grandiose plans were those of British mogul J. Arthur Rank, who planned to make Canada part of his English-speaking film empire, which would place studios and theatre holdings in South Africa, Australia, and, most ambitiously, Canada. In 1945, Rank built the Queensway Studios in Toronto and announced a program of thirty-five features budgeted at £8 million. But the wholesale collapse of the Rank interests by 1948 put an end to these plans, quashing plans for four low-budget features which were then the only films on Rank's agenda ready to shoot.

In the wake of the balance of payments crisis that had forced Rank's hand in England, engendering the infamous ad valorem tax and freezing American funds there, American producers were fearful lest similar protectionist sentiment, which certainly represented the direction Canadian industry lobbyists were then taking, would encumber the lucrative Canadian market for American films with tariffs and quotas. Acting to protect their virtual free market situation, in 1948 the Americans pushed through the enactment of the Canadian Cooperation Project (CCP). The CCP was extraordinarily beneficial to its American signatories, the members of the Motion Picture Producers and Directors Association (MPPDA). It stated that, in return for continued free access to Canadian theatres, the MPPDA would show NFB product (as well as shorts that promoted Canadian tourism) in its theatres; provide its extensive promotional operation for the promotion of Canada in other media; and see to it that Canadian sequences were placed in Hollywood films, an informal agreement corollary provided for an increase in location shooting in Canada.

Not only was the $17 million-a-year Canadian market protected for the Americans as a result of this agreement, but the Americans had found a new, low-cost supplier of short films as well. The agreement was regarded in industry circles as a selling-out of Canadian interests by its own government signatories, and its inequitable nature was demonstrated by its abandonment in 1958.

In the meantime, however, American producers *did* come to Canada for location shooting in record numbers. Between 1948 and 1955, thirteen American features were shot there, among them Otto Preminger's *The Thirteenth Letter* (1948) and Alfred Hitchcock's *I Confess* (1950).

There were many reasons why this activity did not help to generate Canadian production, as had been hoped. Most notably, the exhibition situation in Canada exerted a tremendous negative influence on native production. N.L. Nathanson had, on the eve of the Second World War, constructed a second theatre combine to "compete" with his Famous Players Canada chain in the wake of government investigations in the thirties, which were critical of his monopolistic hold over Canadian exhibition. Odeon Theatres now existed in tandem with Regal Films, Nathanson's second distribution arm that held the exclusive franchise to all M-G-M films shown in Canada. Independent exhibitors were signed on to the Odeon circuit with promise of access to "quality" American films. (Famous Players held a similar franchise with Paramount, and the two companies obtained preferred treatment from other American majors as well.) Nathanson's own connections to these two companies are incredibly difficult to sort out, but on his death in 1943, his son Paul Nathanson arranged to sell the Odeon chain to J. Arthur Rank. Odeon then embarked on a program of theatre construction, increasing its holdings in Ontario alone by 36 percent in 1946–1951. At the same time, Famous Players theatres were undergoing a similarly thorough program of refurbishment. Thus, by the early fifties, the two companies had the best theatres in the most populous areas of Ontario.

Although Odeon was the second-largest chain (after Famous Players) in 1948, there were a total of only 1,500 theatres in Canada. While Famous Players and Odeon (and those few other chains which owned more than twenty theatres) controlled only 32 percent of Canada's theatres, they took in at least 60 percent of the country's box office—a far greater total, incidentally, than the U.S. majors, who had been found to be unfairly restricting trade in the landmark Paramount case that same year. Although Famous Players and Odeon appeared to be in competition, in fact they were carefully dividing major markets for themselves, content in leaving more rural areas, where films were much slower to pay off, to the independent exhibitors.

Between 1956 and 1964, only thirty-two features were produced. Several of these were shot on 16mm stock and achieved only informal or limited distribution, such as Claude Jutra's *À tout prendre/Take It All* (1963). Others, such as *Wolf Dog* (1958) were short "B" features, continuing the depressing tradition of the "quota quickies" of the thirties. (These films, while registered as Canadian, used mostly American casts and crews.) Other "features" consisted merely of interlinked short films. Only the French cinema continued to prosper. Although the first producer-releasers such as Renaissance and Québec Productions had folded by 1950, their studios at St. Hyacinthe and elsewhere in Quebec still stood and could be rented by other occupants. Ideologically, films such as *Les 90 jours* (1959) show a clear drift away from the Catholic idylls of the previous decade toward a distinctively urban and secular vision. Virtually an underground cinema, many French films of the period are visually striking and daringly separatist in their politics.

The work of filmmakers like Claude Jutra and NFB filmmakers such as Norman McLaren were by this time attracting notice abroad through festivals and awards and helped to renew interest at the end of the decade in a distinctively national cinema. Still, the exodus continued; actors and directors, exasperated with the lack of opportunity in Canada, continued to take their talents to America. Probably the most celebrated of these expatriates in the sixties and seventies were directors Sidney Furie and Norman Jewison. If the signs of rebirth were few, they were significant. In 1951, for instance, the antecedent of the modern Canadian Film Institute (CFI) was set up. Although intended primarily as an archive and library, leaving the bulk of government funding with the NFB, the CFI nonetheless contributed to a sense of community among filmmakers. That sense of community was given an outlet when, in the wake of the disorganized industry response to the CCP, a trade group named the Association of Motion Picture Producers and Laboratories of Canada was set up in 1948.

Beginning in 1964, a resurgence of filmmaking activity occurred throughout Canada. The frosty local exhibition climate was changing slightly. In 1966, the Canadian Film Development Corporation (CFDC) was formed, with an initial grant of $10 million from government sources to finance genuinely Canadian production. The NFB financed its first feature film, *The Drylanders,* in 1963 and moved from Ottawa to Montreal, bringing many previously disaffected French Canadian filmmakers into a peer group. Television broadcasting via the Canadian Broadcasting Corporation (CBC), which had gone on the air in September 1952, encouraged production throughout Canada, notably in the West. Vancouver filmmakers, including Larry Kent, constituted a major regional movement. And under renewed pressure from many quarters, a movement began in 1968 to generate a "voluntary quota" to which Famous Players and Odeon would be the major parties. In 1971, these companies agreed to show every Canadian film in at least three major markets; more if box-office figures warranted it. Although a compromise, the "voluntary quota" did represent a slight lessening of the Famous Players–Odeon locking-out of Canadian films, and would be refined several times before 1980.

Most remarkably, a film milieu had grown up in Quebec during this period that proved genuinely nourishing to feature filmmakers. Journals, modeled on their argumentative continental counterparts, such as *Objectif* and *Sequences,* carried on and expanded upon a tradition of passionate film and cultural criticism. The film society movement, and the Montreal Film Festival which sprang out of it in 1960, as well as university courses in film, provided a small but articulate group of filmmakers with opportunities for meeting and collaboration. Films such as the group-authored *Seul ou avec d'autres/Alone or with Others* (1961) were the direct result of this atmosphere. The Cinémathèque Québec's founding in 1963 further solidified the identity of provincial filmmaking. In 1964, paralleling the national movement of fifteen years previous, Quebec producers put together their own trade organization, L'Association professionelle des cinéastes du Québec, which began strenuous lobbying on behalf of Quebec cinema. One of the more important early victories for the newly unified industry was the lifting of restrictive censorship regulations and Sunday screening laws in Quebec.

Several productions in the early sixties cracked the American market in a small way; among these was *The Luck of Ginger Coffey* (1964), which was, essentially, a Canadian production using American financing. This period was a time of experiment in both French and English-Canadian films. In Quebec, Pierre Patry's Coopératio* was, as its name suggests, a commercial cooperative. Coopératio produced six films during the years 1964–1967. Other French-Canadian filmmakers, however, found the NFB and its features program more amenable to their goals; Jutra, Denys Arcand, and Gilles Carle were among these. Independents such as Pierre Perrault also had an opportunity to make features for comparatively low budgets.

In English-Canadian cinema, films such as *The Bitter Ash* (1963) and *Nobody Waved Goodbye* (1963–1964), as well as David Cronenberg's remarkable debut film and $8,500 feature *Stereo* (1969), also suggested that the CFDC might create a healthy industry on this base of dedicated young filmmakers. Over one hundred features were released in the period 1964–1969. A corps of Canadian technicians was winning places on American location shoots in Canada, such as Robert Altman's *That Cold Day in the Park* (1969), much of which was shot in Vancouver. Yet the decade also saw a cottage industry in exploitation horror and sex films become prominent.

However, the CFDC's assistance and the liberal application of tax shelter availability to the movie industry through government legislation had an entirely unforeseen effect in the early seventies. Money earned by presales to distributors was only lightly taxed; essentially, producers in this heady atmosphere were only responsible, and only in the very long run, to syndicates of original investors, and there was little attempt to produce responsibly. One hundred percent of a film's production costs were allowed as capital costs. Distributors, such as Harold Greenberg's Bellevue-Pathé, made available large pools of money for production financing. Tax shelter incentives begun in 1974 attracted American investors and new Canadian entrepreneurs, such as lawyer Garth Drabinsky and distributor Pierre David.

The CFDC went from being a clumsy but well-meaning democracy, with various committees overseeing grants, to being a funnel for American investment. Voices of common sense were raised to protest this pyramiding of production monies. These voices included many of the filmmakers who had served on these boards of control, had made up alternative trade groups such as the Council of Canadian Film Makers, and had developed independent distribution channels such as the Canadian Film Makers Distribution Center and the Toronto Film Makers Co-Op.

These opinions were shared by many in the industry, with the result that the industry trade organizations split into two forces, one neutral-to-skeptical, and the other openly allied with American financing and with the distribution networks of the American majors. This second splinter group, finally emerging as the Association of Canadian Motion Picture Production Companies, also dominated the new Academy of Canadian Cinema, an American-allied industry think tank intended to supplant the annual Canadian Cinema Awards, begun in 1948 as a spur to indigenous production.

Production, especially in English-Canada, was up in this period, but notable international successes, such as *The Apprenticeship of Duddy Kravitz,* obscured the backlog of failed and unreleased films. When the tax shelter legislation was withdrawn in the mid-seventies, a huge shortfall of production money was generated—some put the figure as high as $48 million out of a total production budget of $100 to $150 million. The inroads of U.S. distributors in Canada continued, mostly through the aid of the Motion Picture Industry of Canada, a lobbying organization backed by the American majors. Canadian-earned receipts from American films quadrupled from 1963 to 1977. The eight U.S. majors in Canada took in 78 percent of the total box office. Yet, between 1968 and 1978, of 448 Canadian films, only 14 were released in Canada by U.S. majors; 100 more were released by 8 Canadian distributors. Many were released in only a few theatres.

Exhibition in the late sixties and early seventies had changed very little from the bilateral monopoly Nathanson had created in 1941. By 1974, Canada had become the number one "foreign" market for U.S. films, due in large part to the cooperation U.S. majors received from Canadian circuits. In fact, Famous Players is owned by Paramount, USA, which in turn is owned by Gulf + Western, a U.S.-based multinational. Odeon was until 1978 a unit of the Rank Organisation, a British media conglomerate. Those two companies controlled 654 screens (40 percent) of the national total of 1,633 in 1977, a higher figure than ever. They have an even higher concentration in major markets, particularly in Ontario, the richest province for exhibition, which makes up 37 percent of total admissions in 1976. Famous Players and Odeon increased their holdings in Ontario over 14 percent from 1963 to 1976, finishing that year with nearly 50 percent of the theatres in the province and nearly all the first-run houses under their control. As before, these circuits sign exclusive agreements with the American majors and continue to slight Canadian films with poor playdates.

Since 1977, recovery measures have been taken, but the connections with American interests have been hard to sever. Funding tended to go to those films that emulated those that had made money. In addition to low budget horror films, these included such films as *Meatballs* (1979) and *Porky's* (1981). The shakeout from overinvestment in the mid- to late seventies was bound to come, and indeed, the pipeline quickly dried up. In 1982, only seventeen features were made, with budgets totaling $35 million; in 1980, the figures, already depressed, had been fifty films, budgeted at $165 million. The government took steps to revamp the CFDC in order to recentralize funding and retain a more public and responsible decision-making policy. Beginning in 1983, government funding was centralized under a "new" CFDC, Telefilm Canada*. Telefilm Canada was capitalized at $34 million a year; CFDC had had, after an initial grant of $10 million, only $4 million a year to apportion. Telefilm Canada would have, over a five-year period, $175 million to grant. Further, films would be guaranteed exhibition on television.

In the early eighties, Alberta and Manitoba established film development corporations to fund local production. In 1985, the most ambitious of these undertakings, the Ontario Film Development Corporation*, emerged and capitalized at $7 million per year. British Columbia and Nova Scotia have announced plans to add production financing agencies to their provincial governments.

In 1985, the Canadian Cinema Industry Task Force report noted the deep structural problems that the feature industry had and that guaranteed exhibition on television would do nothing to solve: American ownership and influence on exhibition in Canada. Like many issues of friction between the United States and Canada during the eighties, the Reagan administration's commitment to free trade has been a contributing factor to the continuation of unfair trade practices because the U.S. has been in a commanding economic position in a large overseas market. The results have already been positive; production had been considerably up since 1984; in 1987, eighty-one Canadian features were released, while eighteen U.S. features were location shot in Canada. Many of these, such as *Moonstruck* (1987), were shot in Toronto, which has undergone a production boom, making it, after New York and Los Angeles, the third-largest television and motion picture center servicing both American and Canadian film and television.

Perhaps the most dramatic and, at this writing, unresolved change in the industry since 1977 has been the entry of Cineplex into exhibition in 1979 as the country's third major player in the exhibition wars. Garth Drabinsky, CEO of Cineplex, fought the traditional exclusive distribution arrangements with the American majors in court and got the Americans to allow films to be bid on an individual basis. However, the major circuits, having the most financial resources to use in these auctions, continue to control exhibition patterns. This reconcentration of power made Cineplex in 1983 a pivotal operation, and in June 1984, Drabinsky acquired Odeon for Cineplex. Cineplex-Odeon* added the Plitt chain in the United States, fourth largest in the States, and many smaller chains. In April 1987, Cineplex Odeon, with 1,501 houses in 478 cities, was the largest theatre chain in the United States. In addition to arranging the purchase of a large interest in the company by MCA, the American major, Cineplex-Odeon is beginning to underwrite Canadian production and has formed a television subsidiary. Cineplex-Odeon is now a major force in all phases of film distribution, exhibition, and production. Drabinsky has become the first Canadian movie mogul since the death of N.L. Nathanson. And while much is made of the fact that Drabinsky is the most powerful foreign influence in the United States since J. Arthur Rank in the mid-forties, Drabinsky's "foreignness" with relation to the United States is difficult to assess.

During this period of tumult followed by decline and eventual uncertain recovery, the Quebec cinema was less disrupted than the English-Canadian cinema. Perhaps this was due to the relatively insular and stable market French films enjoyed, but clearly, the implications of large-scale production financing were explored better in Quebec than in other provinces. Co-production with continental French firms, and distribution by French firms, has continued since the early sixties. During the funding crisis of the mid- to late seventies, Quebec filmmakers, always less dependent on American connections, used neglected Canadian sources to patch together modest production budgets—money came from the NFB, the Société Generale du Cinéma*, Radio Canada, Radio Québec and some private investors. Since 1983, the Société General du Cinéma (SGC) has become an umbrella production, distribution, and even promotion and lobbying organization. Focusing on theatrical features, it provides up to 60 percent of production money, but works under an arbitrary ceiling—$500,000 for features—that works toward keeping production budgets low in the planning stages. SGC even awards incentive money to theatres that show Quebec films. SGC was also a motivating force behind Bill 109, the Cinema Law, passed in 1983. It was not only the enabling legislation for SGC itself, but also demanded that distributors be 80 percent Quebec owned; the bill worked to rationalize provincial film involvement in many other areas. Because of a change in provincial government, the closing out of U.S. distributors from Quebec—which the 80 percent rule envisioned—has not yet occurred, but the idea has found adherents around the country, as industry figures, sadder but wiser, look again at the American influence.

In 1985–1986 there were moderate returns on many English-Canadian films, among them *My American Cousin* (1985). The same season, however, was one of the best on record for the Quebec cinema, and directors such as Léa Pool and Denys Arcand, and producers such as Rock Demers have proven that the SGC's program is a sound one.

In the late eighties distribution remains the crucial factor in Canada's cinema future. The American majors operate branch offices—not, significantly, "foreign offices"—in Canada, and these are responsible for the bulk of film earnings. Pan-Canadian Distributors is affiliated with Cineplex-Odeon and gives that circuit access to independent features. But other companies, such as Astral-Bellevue-Pathé (with forty years of distribution history), Spectrafilm, and Norstar (two distributorships begun in the eighties) stand to benefit from any "ownership quotas" the provincial governments might apply to distributors. Cinephile and Creative Exposure are two new firms committed to screening Canadian first features, as well as more marginal British and American fare. Astral and Cinema International are the largest French language distributors, and with close ties to the SGC, are optimally situated for further growth. Should a wave of nationalism sweep the Canadian Parliament, it is these companies, working with agencies such as the NFB, the SGC, Telefilm Canada, and the provincial funding agencies that will have the largest responsibilities in any revision of the current system of American-controlled product flow.

The Canadians have shown, since the 1977 debacle, that they can efficiently manage overseas distribution and co-production arrangements. By July 1984, Algeria, France, Italy, Belgium, West Germany, Israel, and Great Britain had signed co-production agreements with Canada; Spain followed in 1985, along with a revised, treaty-level agreement with the continental French. Telefilm Canada has several foreign sales and distribution offices, as well as a festivals coordinating body, that regulate and rationalize Canadian activity on the all-important festival circuit. Telefilm has also promoted festivals across Canada and is working to expand production into the Atlantic Provinces through its offices in Halifax.

Several directors, most notably David Cronenberg, have shown a willingness to return to Canada to work even after success in the United States. Others, such as Norman Jewison, are working to fund activities like archival collections, awards, and scholarships that will help to sponsor long-term growth in the industry. The notable television co-production between the CBC and CBS, *Night Heat,* and the use of Toronto as a generic location for American features, as well as the increase in studio facilities there, make very real the possibility that Canada will soon become a world center of filmmaking—and be able to bank the revenues taken in through rentals, fees, and the box office instead of sending them south.

BIBLIOGRAPHY

Beattie, Eleanor, editor. *A Handbook of Canadian Film*. Toronto: Peter Martin Associates, 1973.

Berton, Pierre. *Hollywood's Canada: The Americanization of Our National Image*. Toronto: McClelland and Stewart, 1975.

Harcourt, Peter. *Cinema Quebec*. Boston: Museum of Fine Arts, 1983.

Hofsess, John. *Inner Views: Ten Canadian Film-Makers*. New York: McGraw-Hill-Ryerson, 1975.

Jaffe, Chapelle, editor. *Who's Who in Canadian Film and Television*. Toronto: Academy of Canadian Cinema and Television, 1985.

Morris, Peter. *Canadian Feature Films, 1913–1969*. Ottawa: Canadian Film Institute, 1970.

———. *Embattled Shadows: A History of Canadian Cinema 1895–1939*. Montreal: McGill-Queen's University Press, 1978.

Reid, Alison. *Canadian Women Film-Makers: An Interim Filmography*. Ottawa: Canadian Film Institute, 1972.

Turner, John D. *Canadian Feature Film Index, 1913–1985*. Ottawa: Public Archives, 1987.

Veronneau, Pierre, editor. *Self-Portrait: Essays on the Canadian and Quebec Cinemas*. Ottawa: Canadian Film Institute, 1980.
Worsnop, Brenda M., and Chris M. Worsnop. *The Film Users' Guide to Canadian Short Films*. Mississauga, Ontario: Wright Communications, 1980.

CANADA CARRIES ON. Similar to *The World in Action**, the "Canada Carries On" series was a newsreel compilation devoted to Canadian achievements. It was produced by the National Film Board of Canada under the supervision of Stuart Legg and was released once a month from 1940–1945.

THE CANADIAN BIOSCOPE COMPANY was founded in the Canadian city of Halifax in 1912 and remained in existence until the start of the First World War. Its president was Captain H.H.B. Holland, with H.T. Oliver serving as general manager, vice-president, and cameraman. The company's first release was a five-reel version of *Evangeline* (1913) starring Laura Lyman and John F. Carleton.

BIBLIOGRAPHY

Morris, Peter. *Embattled Shadows: A History of Canadian Cinema 1895–1939*. Montreal: McGill-Queen's University Press, 1978.

THE CANADIAN COOPERATION PROJECT (CCP) was a joint project between the Canadian and U.S. governments, whereby the American film industry agreed to screen films promoting Canadian tourism and to produce a number of features in Canada. The Project, which was much criticized as working against the Canadian film industry and government support thereof, lasted from 1948 to 1955.

CANADIAN FILM DEVELOPMENT CORPORATION. See TELEFILM CANADA

CANADIAN PHOTOPLAYS LTD. was founded in February 1919 by Ernest Shipman. It produced the important early Canadian feature, *Back to God's Country,* starring Shipman's wife, Nell, and was based on a story by James Oliver Curwood. The company ceased operations in 1920. Other companies with which Shipman was associated from 1920 to 1923 were Ottawa Film Productions, Sault Ste. Marie Films, New Brunswick Films, Newfoundland Films, Halifax Films, and Prince Edward Island Films.

BIBLIOGRAPHY

Morris, Peter. *Embattled Shadows: A History of Canadian Cinema 1895–1939*. Montreal: McGill-Queen's University Press, 1978.

THE CANARY ISLANDS have been used for the location shooting of at least two features, *Moby Dick* (1965) and *Swinger's Paradise* (1965).

CANNES FILM FESTIVAL. The best-known film festival in the world, the Cannes Film Festival is important both as a competitive festival (with the best film receiving the Palme d'or/Golden Palm) and as a trade gathering where films and television programs are bought and sold. It is noted for its hoopla more than its cultural significance, with scantily clad starlets frolicking on the beaches of this South of France city for the benefit of reporters and photographers from throughout the world. The Festival has also gained importance as a showcase for films from countries not usually associated with motion picture production; for example both the Australian and New Zealand film industries received tremendous boosts thanks to the acclaim their films received at Cannes.

The Cannes Film Festival was initially planned for the fall of 1939, but because of the outbreak of the Second World War, it was postponed, and the first festival was not held until the fall of 1946. From 1946 to 1950, it was held in the fall of each year, but in 1951, it was moved to the spring, during which season it has been held ever since. The Festival was not held in 1948 and 1950, and in 1968 it was not held in its entirety following demonstrations against the commercial course that it had chosen to take.

Address: 71 rue de Faubourg St. Honore, 75008 Paris, France.

BIBLIOGRAPHY

Perry, Simon, "Cannes, Festivals and the Movie Business," *Sight & Sound,* vol. L, no. 4, Autumn 1981, pp. 226–232.

Scherer, Kees, Bob Bertina, Jan Blokker, Paul De Casparis, and H. J. Oolbekkink. *Film Festival.* London: Andre Deutsch, 1962.

CAPTAIN KETTLE FILM COMPANY was a small producer active from 1913 to 1914. Founded by Henry Hibbert, it is of interest in that it was located not, like most British companies, in the London area, but in the northern city of Bradford.

BIBLIOGRAPHY

Sutherland, Allan T., "The Yorkshire Pioneers," *Sight & Sound,* vol. XLVI, no. 1, Winter 1976/77, pp. 48–51.

CARLTON COMMUNICATIONS PLC gained international attention in September 1988 with the announcement of its purchase of the American Technicolor Corporation. Previous to this, Carlton Communications was a little-known British company, founded in 1983, with a market capitalization of $15 million. The company has been described by *Daily Variety* (September 12, 1988) as "Britain's largest independent tv facilities and production house." In the United Kingdom, its major subsidiary is The Moving Picture Co., which is, besides a video facility, also involved in production (*The Assam Garden, Parker,* etc.). Aside from Technicolor, Carlton Communications' holdings in the United States include Complete Post, Abekas Video Systems Inc., Modern Video Prods., and Post Perfect.

Address: 25 Noel Street, London W1V 3RD, United Kingdom.

BIBLIOGRAPHY
Gelman, Morris, "Carlton Buying Technicolor," *Daily Variety,* September 12, 1988, pp. 1, 13.

CARRICK FILMS was a British producer of the thirties, specializing in educational, documentary, and industrial films.

"CARRY ON" SERIES. Beginning with *Carry On Sergeant,* twenty-nine "Carry On" features were produced between 1958 and 1979, together with a compilation film, *That's Carry On,* released in 1979. This popular British comedy series has its origins in British Music Hall*. It is noted for its bawdy visual and oral humor and its general vulgarity. All of the films were produced at an average cost of £150,000 by Peter Rogers and were directed by Gerald Thomas. Regular members of the cast were Jim Dale, Kenneth Connor, Charley Hawtrey, Peter Butterworth, Sidney James, Barbara Windsor, and Kenneth Williams. The most successful of the series to be released in the United States was the second, *Carry On Nurse* (1960).

BIBLIOGRAPHY
Eastaugh, Kenneth. *The Carry-On Book.* Pomfret, Vt.: David & Charles, 1978.

CASABLANCA, the largest city in Morocco, has given its name to and was the location for the 1942 Warner Bros. feature, directed by Michael Curtiz and starring Humphrey Bogart, Ingrid Bergman, Paul Henreid, and Claude Rains. The city was also the site for the 1945 United Artists' release, *A Night in Casablanca,* directed by Archie Mayo, and starring the Marx Brothers. Gunrunning in Casablanca was the subject of the 1930 William Fox release, *Women Everywhere,* directed by Alexander Korda, and starring J. Harold Murray and Fifi Dorsay.

CCC (Central Cinema Company) was one of the first companies to be granted a production license by the British occupying forces in West Germany after the Second World War. Its first release was an operetta, *Herzkönig/King of Hearts* (1947), produced by Arthur Brauner.

CELOR FILMS was a French production company founded in 1922 by director Julien Duvivier (1896–1967), and it remained active for three years.

THE CENTRAL AFRICAN FILM UNIT was created by the Federal Government of Rhodesia and Nyasaland and was active through the sixties. It produced many documentaries in 16mm, which were distributed through Rhodesian and Nyasaland embassies abroad.

CENTRAL AMERICA. Belize, Costa Rica, El Salvador, Guatemala, Honduras, Nicaragua, and Panama make up the Central American isthmus that separates Mexico from South America. Of these nations, only Nicaragua*, the largest country; Panama*, the most colonized; and El Salvador, the smallest, have managed to sustain any consistent cinematic production, although in all Central American nations, the cinema, as an imported phenomenom, has been a most popular form of entertainment.

Introduced as early as September 1896 (in Guatemala) and as late as 1908 (in Costa Rica), the cinema settled uneasily in these varied countries. There was little silent film production throughout the region, with only scattered, artisanal productions in the largest countries: Guatemala's first fiction film, *Agente no. 13* (Alberto de la Riva, 1912), Costa Rica's first film, *El Retorno* (Romulo Bertoni, 1926), El Salvador's first feature, *Aguilas Civilizadas* (Alfredo Massi, 1924).

The introduction of sound, and the subsequent development of comparatively strong export industries in Argentina* and Mexico*, coupled with the area's limited economic resources and troubled politics, further limited the possibilities of national cinemas. Only Guatemala, after the triumph of a democratic revolution in 1944, was able to enjoy a brief "golden era" in the late forties and early fifties that peaked with its first sound feature, *El Sombreron* (Guillermo Andreu and Eduardo Fleischmann, 1950).

Throughout Central America, national cinemas existed in the fifties and sixties only as utopian dreams. In Guatemala, some efforts were made to develop commercial forms, but producers dependent on an already-decaying Mexican industry for financing were doomed to failure.

It was not until the seventies that some national efforts began to bear fruit. In Panana, where the cinema (as well as everything else, up to and including the national currency) had always been synonymous with the United States, the strong nationalist tendencies of the late sixties, combined with an influential week-long festival of Cuban films in 1972 organized by the university cine-club, led to the formation of GECU (Experimental Group of University Cinema). Notwithstanding their lack of production experience, this group of young intellectuals and cinephiles managed to produce the first short films of a Panamanian national cinema: *Canto a la Patria que Ahora Nace* (1972), *505* (1973), *Ahora Ya no Estamos Solos* (1973), *Velada, Velada* (1974). Producing ten other documentaries in the next two years with the joint support of the university and the state, GECU's productiveness was cut short by complex economic-political restrictions, although they have retaliated by concentrating on the distribution of their oeuvre via TV, mobile units, and alternative exhibition.

In El Salvador, after some isolated individual efforts in the sixties proved unsuccessful, the national cinema emerged in tandem with the first stirrings of armed struggle in the seventies. In 1980, a theatrical collective called Taller de los Vagos (The Lazy Workshop) produced *La Zona Intertidal,* an aesthetically innovative short dedicated to the memory of the victims of the bloody national political repression. Another collective group was also founded in 1980: Cero a la Izquierda. Their first film was *Morazan,* a documentary about a liberated region in the northeast of the country.

Although the media claimed that the FMLN (Farabundo Marti National Liberation Front) had been finally defeated in early 1981, in fact it slowly continued to make important inroads, liberating an ever expanding area of El Salvador. Similarly, the Salvadoran cinema has also been a guerrilla, clandestine cinema conceived of as an integral weapon in the struggle for liberation. Fragile and beleaguered, these and other collectives (like Sistema Radio Venceremos) function with scarce resources, and their production has therefore been limited (approximately ten films and ten video productions between 1980 and 1985). However, their production and distribution methods are surprisingly sophisticated and effective, differentiating between films and videos destined for international and domestic consumption, for example. Of all the films produced, Cero a Ia Izquierda's *Decisión de Vencer/Decision to Win* (1981) and Radio Venceremos' *Tiempo de Audacia/A Time of Daring* (1983) are the most impressive efforts.

Given the dramatic political tensions of the eighties, the immediate future of these fledgling cinemas is not too promising. Their best hope can only be to survive on the margins, and to promote the political changes that might bring about their long wished-for independence and peace.

There were thirty-four theatres in Guatemala in 1937, rising to thirty-eight in 1941 and forty-three in 1948, before dropping to thirty in 1979. No American films were imported into Guatemala between 1953 and 1954 as a protest against the activities of the pro-Communist government.

In 1973, the Film Department of the Costa Rican Ministry of Culture was founded as the first major film group. In its first four years of operation, it produced some thirty documentaries. It was merged into the Centro Costarricense de Produccion Cinematografica/Costa Rican Centre of Film Production in 1978. In 1988, Mario Sotela was appointed president of the newly formed Costa Rican Film Commission, which tries to persuade American filmmakers to shoot on location in the country. Sotela (who also controls Lago Films with ten theatres in Costa Rica) owns a Hollywood production company, Sotela Pictures Ltd., which shoots in Costa Rica.

CENTRAL FILMS. When producer Kenneth Bishop's Commonwealth Productions collapsed in 1934—it was founded in 1932—he established Central Films in Victoria, British Columbia, Canada. The company made films, usually directed by minor American filmmakers, such as Nick Grinde, Del Lord, and Ford Beebe, and starring minor American performers, such as Lyle Talbot and Charles Starrett, which were released in the United States by Columbia Pictures. Rita Hayworth was featured in two of Central's 1938 productions, *Convicted* and *Special Inspector* (U.S. *Across the Border*). What had chiefly kept the company in business was that Canadian films were considered British films for the purposes of the 1927 Cinematograph Films Act, which had created the quota quickies*. When the Act was repealed in 1938, there was no longer a market for Central's films, and the company collapsed.

BIBLIOGRAPHY
Morris, Peter. *Embattled Shadows: A History of Canadian Cinema 1895–1939*. Montreal: McGill-Queen's University Press, 1978.

THE CENTRAL INFORMATION BUREAU FOR EDUCATIONAL FILMS was created in the United Kingdom in 1932 and was active, under the managing directorship of J. Russell Orr, through the mid-thirties, when most of its functions were taken over by the British Film Institute (of which it was initially a competitor). It published *Guide to Instructional and Educational Films*.

THE CENTRAL OFFICE OF INFORMATION: FILMS AND TELEVISION DIVISION came into being in 1940, when the General Post Office (GPO) and Empire Library was dissolved, and the GPO Film Unit became the Crown Film Unit. It assumed some of the functions of the Ministry of Information in April 1946, and from 1948–1950, John Grierson was its commissioner. It is the central agency for United Kingdom government film production and distribution, and it operates CFL Vision (which began life in 1927 as the Central Film Library), and is believed to be the oldest non-theatrical film library in the world.

Address: Hercules Road, London SE1 7DU, United Kingdom.

CENTRE NATIONAL DE LA CINÉMATOGRAPHIE. Founded in 1947, the Centre National de la Cinématographie is the leading French trade organization, on a par with the Motion Picture Association of America. In addition, it operates the official French film archives at the Bois d'Arcy.

Address: 12 rue de Lubeck, 75116 Paris, France.

THE CENTRO SPERIMENTALE DI CINEMATOGRAFIA (The Experimental Cinema Center) is one of Europe's better-known film schools, founded in Rome in 1935 and government-funded. A frequent site of student unrest, the school has had little impact in recent years, although it can boast of Roberto Rosselini as its one-time head. It is internationally renowned for its journal, *Bianco e Nero**.

Address: via Tuscolana 154, Rome, Italy.

BIBLIOGRAPHY
Rose, Ernest D. *World Film & TV Study Resources*. Bonn-Bad Godesberg: Friedrich-Ebert-Stiftung, 1974.

CÉSAR AWARDS. The French equivalent of the Oscars, the César Awards have been presented annually since 1976 and are named after the sculptor who created the curiously shaped and somewhat ugly statuette. The awards were first conceived of by publicist Georges Cravenne in 1975, and he helped create the organization that presents them, l'Académie des Arts et Techniques du Cinéma. The awards go only to French films and personnel and are presented in the following categories: Film and Director, Actress, Actor, Supporting Actress,

Supporting Actor, Screenplay, Female Newcomer, Male Newcomer, First Fiction Feature, Cinematography, Art Direction, Sound, Editing, Costumes, Animation Short, Documentary Short, Fiction Short, and Film Poster.

CHAMBARA is a genre in Japanese cinema, in which the story is set prior to the nineteenth century and in which sword fights play a prominent part.

CHANNEL 4, as its name implies, is the fourth national television network in the United Kingdom, after the two British Broadcasting Corporation (BBC) services and the advertising-financed Independent Television (ITV). Its program schedule of nearly seventy-five hours a week is networked to the whole country with the exception of Wales, which has its own Welsh Fourth Channel Authority, scheduling some thirty-two hours of Welsh language programming. The Fourth Channel Television Service was authorized by Parliament in the Broadcasting Act 1981 and was launched on November 2, 1982. In the preceding years there had been many prolonged and heated debates on what form a fourth channel should take, mainly divided between those who wanted a duplicate of the existing ITV company, which deals mainly in popular entertainment, and those who wanted a public service type channel operating independently of both the BBC and ITV. Channel 4 is a wholly owned subsidiary of the Independent Broadcasting Authority (IBA), with the responsibility of planning, scheduling, commissioning, and acquiring programs. The Channel is financed by subscriptions from the ITV companies levied by the IBA and passed on to the Channel 4 company.

Two major aims of Channel 4 are to provide for tastes and interests not generally catered to on ITV and to encourage innovation and experiment in the form and content of programs. Apart from a weekly "answerback" program, "Right to Reply," the Channel makes nothing itself, but commissions or buys from a variety of sources, through a team of Commissioning Editors who sift proposals from programs, select them, and follow through on their progress. Channel 4 provides an hour of news each weeknight, which is complemented with such programs as "What the Papers Say" and "A Week in Politics." There have been several weekly slots for ethnic communities in the United Kingdom, such as "Black on Black" and "Eastern Eye." It has its own soap opera, "Brookside," set on a northern housing estate, and shows prestigious American series, such as "Hill Street Blues," "St. Elsewhere," and "Cheers."

However, one of the most significant results of Channel 4's arrival has been its funding of numerous low- and medium-budget films, which have been widely praised on their theatrical release in the United States. *Letter to Brezhnev* (1985) was completed with funding from C4, *My Beautiful Laundrette* (1985) was fully financed by C4, and *Dance with a Stranger* (1985) and *The Draughtsman's Contract* (1982) were made because C4 was prepared to make up the difference between the money raised and required. At the 1987 Cannes Film Festival*,

Channel 4 was awarded the Prix Rossellini for its contribution to British film production.

Address: 60 Charlotte Street, London W1P 2AX, United Kingdom.

BIBLIOGRAPHY

Blanchard, Simon, and David Morley, editors. *What's This Channel Four?: An Alternative Report.* London: Comedia, 1982.

Lambert, Stephen. *Channel Four: Television with a Difference?* London: British Film Institute, 1982.

McRobbie, Angela, editor. *Four on 4: Transcriptions from Four Open Forums on the New Television Channel.* Stafford: Birmingham Film Workshop and West Midlands Arts, 1982.

Wyver, John, "The English Channel 4," *American Film,* vol. XI, no. 9, July/August 1986, pp. 46–49.

CHAPLIN is the largest film periodical in Northern Europe. It was founded in Stockholm, Sweden, in 1959 by Bengt Forslund, and was taken over by the Swedish Film Institute* in 1965. It is primarily concerned with Scandinavian cinema.

Address: Svenska Filminstitutet, Filmhuset Borgvägen, Box 27126, 10252 Stockholm 27, Sweden.

BIBLIOGRAPHY

Slide, Anthony, editor. *International Film, Radio, and Television Journals.* Westport, Conn.: Greenwood Press, 1985.

CHILDREN'S FILM AND TELEVISION FOUNDATION LTD. A nonprofit organization, the Children's Film and Television Foundation Ltd. was established in 1951 by members of the British film industry, to produce features and short subjects for screening at special children's matinees (usually on Saturday mornings) at British theatres. The Foundation is run by a board of directors appointed by the industry, and the subjects for its films are selected by a voluntary committee, with the films being produced by commercial companies at a fixed and small budget. With the demise of children's matinees in recent years, the Foundation has been less than active.

Address: EMI Elstree Studios, Boreham Wood, Herts WD6 1JG, United Kingdom.

CHILE. Like other Latin American nations, Chile had its first film screening shortly after the medium's introduction in Europe. Soon thereafter, in April 1902, an unknown cameraman recorded a military parade in Valparaiso, and the resulting film (advertised as an American Biograph production) premiered a month later. It was not until 1910 that two Chilean filmmakers were identified by name: Julio Chevenay and Arturo Lorrain, who filmed the burial of President Pedro Montt.

An Argentinian, Salvador Giambastiani, was the first to produce feature-length films. His 1916 *La Baraja de la Muerte,* based on a local murder case, was also the first film to be censored. In conjunction with his wife, Gabriella Bussenius, Giambastiani established a film company (Chile Films) and continued to make films until his death in 1921.

Both film production companies and movie theatres proliferated in several Chilean cities in this period, and, by Latin American standards, Chile was an active producer: approximately eighty films were made between 1916 and 1932, almost half of them between 1925 and 1927. Among the most significant productions were Pedro Sienna's *El Grito en el Mar* (1925) and *El Husar de la Muerte* (1925) (the latter is the only Chilean silent film that has survived). Chilean films were successful at home and well-regarded internationally, but the economic basis for production was haphazard and most film producers disappeared after making only one or two films.

While filmmaking was still a relatively artisanal business, Chilean production could continue even with limited resources and restrictions on foreign imports (for example, a photographer used his mechanical gifts to build his own movie camera, piece by piece, in order to make films). When the arrival of sound in 1931 transformed the production sphere, however, national production came to a standstill. Only one feature-length film was produced between 1930 and 1939: *Norte y Sur* (1934), directed by Jorge Delano, a Chilean who had been sent to Hollywood by the Ibanez government to learn the new technology. Although *Norte y Sur* was successful, sound production remained difficult and would not be attempted again until 1939.

In 1938, the advent of a Popular Front government that supported import-substitution industrialization, together with the scarcity of imported European films during the Second World War stimulated national film production. In 1941, the state's Production Development Corporation (CORFO), convinced that film production had the potential to become an important national industry, created Chile Films, a state corporation designed to foment the national cinema by serving the needs of independent producers as a capitalist partner. Although a year later well-appointed studios were built, Chile Films still lacked control of the distribution and exhibition channels and thus could not provide a firm economic base for national production. Furthermore, it contracted an Argentine producer (Argentina Sono Films) as technical and commercial adviser, a decision that resulted in a Hollywood-style studio operation that was untenable given the Chilean market and its limited export possibilities.

Chile Films sponsored a number of productions, but most were critical and box-office failures, especially its co-productions with Argentina. These "national" films—melodramas, staid historical epics, or folkloricist comedies—had little to do with contemporary Chilean life. Chile Films produced its last feature in 1950, and subsequently its studios were leased to independent producers on a film-by-film basis. Between 1950 and 1960, film production was sporadic, with only thirteen national films (five of them produced by foreigners).

In 1960, however, with a different, radicalized, political climate (after the victory of the Christian Democratic party in 1962) and the development of cinema culture, cinematic production found a new momentum. Fueled by the growing cine club movements, university cinema education, and amateur filmmaking activities, the Chilean cinema assumed a new character: non-industrial, responsive to national needs and history, attentive to the needs of broader audiences.

The reopening of Chile Films in 1967 was an important first step. With the directorship in the hands of an experienced filmmaker, Patricio Kaulen, the government agreed to fund the production of a regular newsreel. It also established an advisory Council to promote the interests of the national cinema and enacted a number of protectionist measures. These actions proved largely ineffective—national films such as Helvio Soto's *Erase un niño, un guerrillero y un caballo* (1967) encountered serious obstacles erected by distributors and exhibitors—and yet served to further stimulate the growing concern over the national cinema.

The real catalyst for change in the structures of Chilean filmmaking emerged fully at the 1967 Meeting of Latin American Filmmakers sponsored by the Cine Club Vina del Mar. In 1968–1969 a number of films were released that indicated a change had taken place: instead of following the patterns of the old commercial cinema, filmmakers were using the cinema as a weapon in the development of cultural and political consciousness by criticizing the excesses and organizations of the dominant classes. Miguel Littín's *El Chacal de Nahueltoro* (1969) denounced the abuses of the judicial system; Raúl Ruiz's *Tres Tristes Tigres/Three Sad Tigers* (1968), the decadence of the bourgeoisie; and Helvio Soto's *Caliche Sangriento* (1968), the excesses of the military establishment. Increasingly aligned with the Popular Unity party, Littín and a number of other filmmakers outside the commercial sector joined forces and produced the "Manifesto of the Cineastes of Popular Unity."

After the election of the Popular Unity candidate, Salvador Allende, in 1970, these filmmakers were given control of Chile Films. However, plagued by insufficient technical resources, limited funds for raw film stock purchases, and high payroll expenses, Chile Films was not immediately able to transform the Chilean cinema. Its potential effectiveness was further curtailed by its limited control of distribution (especially after U.S. distributors stopped exporting their films to Chile in 1971) and its inability to alter the existing structure of commercial theatrical exhibition (via nationalizations) until 1973. Under these conditions, Chile Films' greatest achievements in this period were in documentary and newsreel production and in cinematic education (its *talleres* or production seminars trained an entire generation of filmmakers). Nevertheless, several important feature fiction films were produced during the Allende years: Helvio Soto's *Metamorfósis del Jefe de la Policía Política/Metamorphosis of a Political Police Chief* (1972), Aldo Francia's *Ya No Basta con Rezar/Praying Is No Longer Enough* (1971), and Raúl Ruiz's *La Colonia Penal* (1970), *Nadie Dijo Nada/No One Said a Thing* (1971), and *Palomita Blanca* (1973).

As the social and political crisis in Chile deepened toward the end of the Allende years, film production became increasingly more tentative. The 1973 military coup d'etat that overthrew Allende, the bloodiest and most repressive in Latin American history, effectively froze national cinematic production. Although Aldo Francia and Carlos Flores opted to remain in Chile, all the other feature filmmakers and most documentarists left the country: Miguel Littin went to Mexico, Raúl Ruiz and Helvio Soto to France, and Patricio Guzman and Pedro Chaskel to Cuba.

In exile, Chilean filmmakers have managed to sustain their identity as Chileans while producing an impressive body of work totaling two hundred films and videos between 1973 and 1985. Among the most important filmmakers of the Chilean cinema in exile are Miguel Littín (who has filmed all over Latin America) and the prolific and experimental Raúl Ruiz, who remained in France. This Chilean exile cinema is an astonishing phenomenon without precedent in the history of the cinema: the first national cinema to exist outside the borders of its nation-state.

In Chile, the extreme repressive and anticultural policies of the military junta have made cinematic production almost impossible, and only a handful of films have been produced since the coup: an anonymous documentary about "disappeared" people, a couple of documentaries on cultural topics, and an important feature, Silvio Caiozzi's *Julio Comienza en Julio/Julio Begins in July* (1979).

In the eighties, many of the exiled filmmakers have attempted to return to their homeland, but they confront a bleak cultural landscape because, in Chile, the cinema is no longer an important mode of national expression.

BIBLIOGRAPHY

Chanan, Michael, editor. *Chilean Cinema*. London: British Film Institute, 1976.

del Castillo, Ramón, "The Cinema in Chile," *Sight & Sound*, vol. XV, no. 60, Winter 1946/47, pp. 121–124.

CHIMICOLOR is a French three-color subtractive process that was developed by the Syndicat de la Cinématographe des Couleurs in 1931. The German occupation forces refused permission for the company's Paris research laboratories to remain open during the Second World War, but work on the process was resumed in the mid-forties.

BIBLIOGRAPHY

Cornwell-Clyne, Major Adrian. *Colour Cinematography*. London: Chapman & Hall, 1951.

CHINA. Despite the size of the country, Chinese films have never had any impact aboard, and nor has the film industry achieved recognition in proportion to the audience that it serves. There is, however, a major film archive in China, with headquarters in Beijing, but with negatives stored some two thousand miles away under exceptional archival conditions in Xi'an. Only 10 percent of all films made prior to the Second World War are preserved, but films from the Communist takeover of the country onwards are safeguarded, and, surprisingly, no damage was done to the archives' holdings during the Cultural Revolution.

Films were first screened in China, in Shanghai, on August 11, 1896. They were known as "dianying" or electric shadows, and later became popularized as "xingxi" (movies). The first film to be made in China was *Dingjun Mountain,* produced by Ren Jingfeng, in 1905, and starring a leading player with the Beijing Opera. The next major Chinese production was *The Suffering Couple,* directed by Zheng Zhenqiu in 1913. In the late teens and twenties, a number of film companies were established, the most important of which were the China Film Company and the Mingxing Film Company. The latter was directed by Zhang Shichuan, who established the first Chinese film school and also produced the first Chinese serial, *The Burning of Red Lotus Temple* (1928), that is also credited as the first kung fu production.

Mingxing co-produced China's first sound film, *Red Peony, The Singing Girl,* in 1930. In the thirties, Chinese films began dealing with social issues, attacking the feudal system and arguing for women's rights. After an initial influence by American films, Chinese cinema began to imitate the Soviet films from 1933 onwards. Major directors from this decade include Shen Xilin, Sun Yu, Wu Yonggang, Cai Chusheng, and Yuan Muzhi. Many directors and screenwriters were active in left-wing movements—political films were unknown in China until the thirties. Two of the major stars of the period were Hu Die and Ruan Lingyu. The latter has been described by critic/historian Jay Leyda as "one of the great actresses of film history." She committed suicide in 1935.

Even during the civil unrest following the Second World War, the film industry remained active, with important features of these years including Cai Chusheng and Zheng Junli's *Spring River Flows East* (1947), Shi Dunshan's *Eighty Thousand Li of Clouds and the Moon* (1947), and Zhao Ming and Yan Gong's *The Adventures of a Vagabond Waif* (1948).

State control of the film industry began with the "liberation" of the country on October 1, 1949. The National Film Bureau, under the Ministry of Culture, was created and it approves all film projects. A separate film bureau exists in Shanghai, which has been the center of the Chinese film industry since the twenties. The Film Association, to which producers belong, was revived in 1978, following its banishment by the Cultural Revolution. A co-production corporation was established in 1981, and it has worked with producers in Italy, Japan, and Hong Kong.

China's only film school, the Beijing Film Academy, was founded in 1950, and in 1984 a Film Research Center for the academic study of Chinese film history was created. There are thirteen major film studios in China, the oldest and largest of which are located in Beijing, Shanghai, and Manchuria. All filmmakers receive fixed salaries, whether or not they work. Filmgoing is an immensely popular entertainment in China, and the number of theatres has grown from under six hundred in 1949 to forty thousand in the late eighties, with a further 110,000 mobile projection units serving rural areas.

The 1966 Cultural Revolution had a devastating effect on the film industry. Two hundred and twenty-nine films were made in 1958 and 1959, but in the six years from 1966 no films were produced at all. Between 1972 and 1976, only political subjects and newsreels were approved for production. Filmmakers were expected to work in the fields alongside the peasants. As an example of the ruthlessness of the Cultural Revolution, Cheng Jihua, editor-in-chief of the China Film Press was arrested in 1966 and spent eight years in solitary confinement. All copies of his two-volume seminal work, *The History and Development of the Chinese Cinema,* were ordered destroyed, as were his notes for a third volume.

Between 1905 and 1980, a total of five thousand films were produced in China.

Among the many films which have utilized China for an often romantic backdrop are *The Toll of the Sea* (1922), *The Mystery of Dr. Fu Manchu* (1929), *The Return of Dr. Fu Manchu* (1930), *The Mask of Fu Manchu* (1932), *Shanghai Express* (1932), *Too Hot to Handle* (1938), *55 Days at Peking* (1963), *The Sand Pebbles* (1966), *The Vengeance of Fu Manchu* (1968), and *The Last Emperor* (1987).

BIBLIOGRAPHY

Beijing Film Studio. *Beijing Film Studio in the Last 30 Years: 1949–1979*. Beijing: 1979.

Berry, Chris, editor. *Perspectives on Chinese Cinema*. Ithaca, N.Y.: Cornell University Press, 1985.

"Chinese Cinema Section," *On Film,* no. 14, Spring 1985, pp. 2–35.

Leyda, Jay. *Dianying*. Cambridge, Mass.: MIT Press, 1972.

Liu, Alan P.L., "Mass Communication and Media in China's Cultural Revolution," *Journalism Quarterly,* vol. LXVI, 1969, pp. 314–319.

Pickowicz, Paul, "Cinema and Revolution in China," *American Behaviorial Scientist,* vol. XVII, no. 3, January/February 1974, pp. 328–359.

Quiquemelle, Marie-Claire, and Jean-Loup Passek. *Le Cinéma Chinois*. Paris: Centre Georges Pompidou, 1985.

Rayns, Tony, and Scott Meek. *Electric Shadow: 45 Years of Chinese Cinema*. London: British Film Institute, 1980.

Scher, Mark, "Film in China," *Film Comment,* Spring 1969, pp. 8–21.

Semsel, George Stephen, editor. *Chinese Film: The State of the Art in the People's Republic*. New York: Praeger, 1987.

Toroptsez, Sergei, "The Chinese Cinema under the Veil of 'Revival,' " *Asia and Africa Today,* no. 5, 1978, pp. 61–62.

Weakland, John H., "Themes in Chinese Communist Film," *American Anthropologist,* vol. LXVIII, 1966, pp. 477–484.

———, "Conflicts Between Love and Family Relationships in Chinese Films," *Journal of Popular Film,* vol. I, no. 4, Fall 1972, pp. 290–298.

Yau, Esther, "China," in *World Cinema since 1945,* editor William Luhr. New York: Ungar, 1987, pp. 116–139.

THE CHINA CINEMA COMPANY LTD. operated in the teens in Hong Kong, under the general managership of Ben Brodsky. It produced the ten-reel feature, *A Trip through China* (1916) and operated some eighty theatres in China, as well as a studio and a laboratory.

BIBLIOGRAPHY
"Chinese Film Market," *Variety*, August 11, 1916, p. 27.

CHRONOPHOTOGRAPH was the name given to a gun-shaped camera invented by French physiologist Étienne-Jules Marey (1830–1904), to record movement in a series of still photographs. The photographs were first published in 1882 and are similar in concept to the work of Eadweard Muybridge in the United States. The name was also used by Marey's pupil Georges Demeny (1850–1917) for a film camera dating from 1894. Demeny called his camera the Phonoscope.

BIBLIOGRAPHY
Frizot, Michel. *Avant le cinématographe: la chronophotographie*. Beaune: Association des Amis de Marey/Ministère de la Culture, 1984.
Marey, E.J., translated by Eric Pritchard. *Movement*. London: William Heinemann, 1895.

CILECT is the acronym for the Centre International de Liaison des Écoles de Cinéma et de Television, an international organization of film and television schools which was formed in Cannes, France, in 1955. Its aim is to raise the quality of teaching in the world's film and television schools.

Address: rue Theresienne 8, 1000 Brussels, Belgium.

LES CINÉASTES ASSOCIÉS was founded in 1953 by Jacques Forgeot. The French-based company quickly became noted for its production of animated television commercials, not only for French television, but also for television in Germany, the United Kingdom, and Italy. A leading animator there was Polish-born Walerian Borowczyk, and Les Cinéastes Associés produced his first feature-length animated film, *Le Théâtre de M. et Mme. Kabal* (1967).

Address: 12 rue de l'Echiquier, 75010 Paris, France.

BIBLIOGRAPHY
"Les Cinéastes Associés: A Survey," in *International Film Guide 1966*, editor Peter Cowie. London: Tantivy Press, 1965, p. 177.

CINECITTÀ SPA. Known as "Hollywood on the Tiber," the Cinecittà studios in Rome are the best known of all Italian studios. Luigi Freddi, Italy's first fascist director-general for cinema had long planned for a "city of cinema," and when the privately owned Cines-Pittaluga studios on Via Vejo was destroyed by fire in September 1936, he was able to persuade the latter's owner, Carlo Roncoroni, to become involved in his project. The new Cinecittà studios were to be built some five miles from the gates of Rome, and the first stone was laid in January 1936. Benito Mussolini inaugurated the new studios on April 21, 1937, and he watched production of the first feature to be shot there, Goffredo Alessandrini's *Luciano Serra pilota*. Carlo Roncoroni died in 1939, and at that time the studios came under the control of the Italian government, with Luigi Freddi becoming the new president.

Production was suspended at Cinecittà in 1943, when the studio was bombed and the Germans occupied Rome. When the Allies entered the city, the studio was utilized as a center for refugees. The rebuilding of Cinecittà began in 1947, but it was not until 1950 that all twelve stages on the lot were operational. American use of the studio began late in 1949 with the arrival of the cast and crew for M-G-M's *Quo Vadis,* directed by Mervyn LeRoy and starring Robert Taylor and Deborah Kerr. Other American features shot in whole or part at Cinecittà include *Roman Holiday* (1952), *Helen of Troy* (1954), *The Little Hut* (1956), *A Farewell to Arms* (1957), and *Ben-Hur* (1959). Major Italian features filmed at Cinecittà in the last thirty years have included *Umberto D* (1951), *Le Amiche/The Girl Friends* (1955), *Le Notti Bianche/White Nights* (1957), *Il Generale Della Rovere* (1960), *La Dolce Vita* (1960), *Giulietta degli spiriti/Juliet of the Spirits* (1964), *Satyricon* (1969), *Morte a Venezia/Death in Venice* (1970), *Amarcord* (1972), *La cage aux folles* (1978), *La Traviata* (1982), *Le Bal* (1983), and *Good Morning Babylon* (1986).

Cinecittà was restructured in the early seventies, following a period of financial troubles. Some of its land was sold off, and its laboratory, recording studios, and sound stages were refurbished. The studio is operated by a holding company, Ente Autonomo Gestione Cinema, which funnels state funds into Cinecittà.

On the occasion of its fiftieth anniversary, the studio was honored with a tribute by New York's Museum of Modern Art during 1987–1988.

Address: via Tuscolana 1055, 00173 Rome, Italy.

BIBLIOGRAPHY

Bernardini, Aldo, "Cinecitta: The Stuff of Legends," *Variety,* February 25, 1987, pp. 314, 334–335.

"Cinecitta: European Answer to Tinsel Town," *Screen International,* August 30, 1986, p. 48.

"Cinecitta Filmography," *Variety,* February 25, 1987, pp. 346, 350.

Lane, John Francis, "Has Cinecitta Danced Its Last Tango?" *Films and Filming,* September 1973, pp. 27–29.

Young, Deborah, "To Fellini, Home Is Where You Hang Your Dreams, and That Means Cinecitta," *Variety,* February 25, 1987, p. 320.

CINÉGRAPHIC was founded in Paris in 1922 by director Marcel L'Herbier (1890–1979) with financial patronage from the Vicomte de Noialles. L'Herbier utilized the company's offices at 9 rue Boissy d'Anglais as a center for the study of film, and the company produced films by directors other than L'Herbier: Jaque Catelain's *Le marchand de plaisir* (1923), Claude Autant-Lara's *Faits-divers* (1924), and Louis Delluc's *L'innondation* (1924). The company failed in 1925 following the co-production of L'Herbier's *Feu Mathias Pascal/The Late Matthew Pascal.*

CINEGUILD, LTD. was an independent production company created within the Rank Organization*. Nöel Coward and David Lean were the names most closely associated with the company, which produced a number of major British features of the forties: *This Happy Breed* (1944), *Blithe Spirit* (1945), *Brief Encounter* (1945), *Great Expectations* (1946), *Blanche Fury* (1948), *Oliver Twist* (1948), *The Passionate Friends* (U.S. *One Woman's Story,* 1949), and *Madeleine* (1950).

CINÉ LIBERTÉ was a socialistic program in France, whereby a film's audience paid for its production rather than for the later privilege of viewing the film in a theatre. Through Ciné Liberté, Jean Renoir's *La vie est à nous/People of France* (1936) was produced.

CINEMA NOVO is the term used to describe modern Brazilian cinema as an independent, nationalistic force, unaffected by outside influences. The concept of Cinema Novo was first discussed at film industry congresses held in Rio de Janeiro and São Paulo in 1952. In his book, *Cinema Novo × 5,* Randal Johnson divides Cinemo Novo into three phases: the first from 1960 to 1964 was concerned with rural Brazil; the second from 1964 to 1968 produced films with urban settings; and the third from 1968 to 1972 saw filmmakers utilizing allegory as the military dictatorship tightened censorship. Cinema Novo survives to the present, and is sometimes described as *Cinema Novo de novo* (Cinema Novo Anew).

Among the major films of Cinema Novo are Nelson Pereira dos Santos' *Vidas Secas/Barren Lives* (1963), Ruy Guerra's *Os Fuzis/The Guns* (1964), Glauber Rocha's *Deus e Diabo na Terra do Sol/Black God, White Devil* (1964), Glauber Rocha's *Terra em Transe/Land in Anguish* (1967), Gustavo Dahl's *O Bravo Guerreiro/The Brave Warrior* (1968), Nelson Pereira dos Santos' *Azyllo Muito Louco/The Alienist* (1970), and Arnaldo Jabor's *Pindorama* (1971.)

BIBLIOGRAPHY

Proppe, Hans, and Susan Tarr, "Cinema Novo: Pitfalls of Cultural Nationalism," *Jump Cut,* no. 10/11, Summer 1976, pp. 45–48.

Randal, Johnson, "Brazilian Cinema Today," *Film Quarterly,* vol. XXXI, no. 4, Summer 1978, pp. 42–43.

———. *Cinema Novo × 5.* Austin: University of Texas Press, 1984.

Ross, Dasha, "Brazilian Cinema—A Crisis of Direction," *Cinema Papers,* December 1979-January 1980, pp. 608–611.

CINÉMATHÈQUE FRANÇAISE. One of the best known and most controversial of film archives, the Cinémathèque Française, was founded by Henri Langlois (1914–1977) in collaboration with Georges Franju and Jean Mitry in Paris in 1936. Initial funding came from Paul-Auguste Harle, publisher of *La Cinématographie Française,* who put up money for the purchase of prints of various classic films, beginning with *The Fall of the House of Usher* and *The Birth of a Nation.* Harle also persuaded Albatross Films to deposit copies of its films with the Cinémathèque and found and paid for a building to house the new institution.

Langlois was a colorful character who cared more about films than administration. He safeguarded many films, but, at the same time, he was lax in assuring their ultimate preservation. Although he was the head of the organization, he always adopted the title of secretary-general, rather than director. Three women were important in the Cinémathèque's history: the German historian Lotte Eisner, who was with Langlois at the Cinémathèque's founding; Mary Meerson, who joined the Cinémathèque in 1939; and Marie Epstein, who became associated with the institution in 1954.

During the Second World War, Langlois was responsible for hiding a vast quantity of films that might have been seized by the occupying German army. He also hid Lotte Eisner, whose life, as a German Jewess, was in jeopardy.

In 1948, the Cinémathèque opened the Musée Permanent du Cinéma on Paris's Avenue de Messine, and began a regular program of film screenings. That same year, the French government made an abandoned fort at Bois d'Arcy available for film storage. In 1955, the Cinémathèque retained its administrative offices on the rue de Courcelles, but moved its screening facility to the rue d'Ulm. A new auditorium was opened at the Palais de Chaillot in June 1963, and here, eventually, the Cinémathèque established a major exhibit on the history of the motion picture. Aside from the screening facility at the Palais de Chaillot, a second screening room is also operated at the Georges Pompidou Center.

In 1960, Langlois found the International Federation of Film Archives (FIAF*) that he had helped to establish too bureaucratic for his taste, and he resigned from the organization. In 1964, the French government began investigating the running of the Cinémathèque; it renamed Langlois artistic and technical director, and appointed Claude Fabrizio as adminstrative and financial director. The French government of General de Gaulle became increasingly critical of Langlois, and on February 6, 1968, he was dismissed by the Cinémathèque's administrative council. The *affaire Langlois,* as it came to be known, had begun. The press was highly critical of the government's actions, and forty filmmakers, including Abel Gance, François Truffaut, Jean Renoir, and Jean Luc Godard, announced they would not permit their films to be screened at the Cinémathèque. On February 14, rioting broke out near the Palais de Chaillot. Eventually, on April 22, the government gave in; Langlois was restored as head of the Cinémathèque but at the same time government funding was cut off.

Following Langlois' death, the Cinémathèque was reorganized along the lines of most other archives. Preservation, which had never been a major concern with Langlois, was considered top priority. Unfortunately, a disastrous fire on August 3, 1980, destroyed an estimated 40,000 reels of films in the Cinémathèque's holdings.

Although Langlois has both his defenders and his critics, and although there was certainly much wrong in the way in which he managed the Cinémathèque Française, he most certainly played a crucial role in the film archival world. Most of the younger French filmmakers learned of cinema thanks to his screenings, and, as *Cahiers du Cinéma* (April-May 1968) commented, "Without Langlois there would be neither *Cahiers du Cinéma* nor New Wave."

Plans for a New York operation were formulated in the sixties, under the guidance of Eugene Stavis, but despite an initial collaboration with the Metropolitan Museum of Art, nothing came of the idea.

Address: 29 rue du Colisée, F-75008 Paris, France.

BIBLIOGRAPHY

Langlois, Georges P., and Glenn Myrent. *Henri Langlois: Premier Citoyen du Cinéma*. Paris: Editions Denoël, 1987.

Langlois, Henri. *Trois Cents Ans de Cinéma*. Paris: Cahiers du Cinéma and Cinémathèque Française, 1987.

Moskowitz, Gene, "Cinémathèque Fire," *Sight & Sound,* vol. IL, no. 4, Autumn 1980, p. 214.

Roud, Richard. *A Passion for Films*. New York: Viking, 1983.

Turk, Edward Baron, "Film Treasures of the Palais de Chaillot," *American Film,* vol. V, no. 8, June 1980, pp. 18–20, 54–56.

CINEMATOGRAPH EXHIBITORS' ASSOCIATION OF GREAT BRITAIN AND IRELAND. A trade organization concerned with the interests of exhibitors, the Cinematograph Exhibitors' Association of Great Britain and Ireland (CEA) was founded in 1912. Despite its title, it represents only the exhibitors of England, Wales, Scotland, and Northern Ireland, not the Republic of Ireland. By 1922, at which time the CEA began keeping records, it had twenty-four regional branches with some 2,000 members. It reached its membership peak in the late forties and early fifties, when membership rose to more than 4,000. With the decrease of screens in the United Kingdom, membership has fallen in the eighties to approximately 1,200. Individual exhibitors are represented in the CEA together with the major British circuits: Odeon Cinemas Limited, Cannon Cinemas Limited, Granada Theatres Limited, CAC Leisure PLC, and Apollo-Hutchinson Leisure Group Limited.

Address: 22/25 Dean Street, London W1V 6HQ, United Kingdom.

THE CINEMATOGRAPH FILMS COUNCIL was created in 1938 to advise the British Secretary of State on matters affecting the film industry.

Address: Department of Trade and Industry, Bressenden Place, London SW1 5DT, United Kingdom.

CINEMA-YE-AZADE-IRAN (Free Cinema of Iran) was founded in 1969 by Bassir Nassibi to encourage production of Super 8mm films as an art form. Films from the group were shown not only at the Tehran International Film Festival, but also in a number of European countries.

CINEORAMA was a system similar to the later American innovation Circarama, which presented films on a screen that completely encircled the audience. Invented in 1896 by Frenchman Raoul Grimoin-Sanson, Cineorama utilized eight synchronized projectors and was first presented publicly at the 1900 Paris Exposition, where the audience entered what appeared to be a gigantic air balloon, and were presented with views of Brussels, Barcelona, Biarritz, Southampton, and Nice, as if they were standing on the platform of the balloon. Unfortunately, the fire risk from ten projectors was too great, and the presentation was closed down at its fourth performance.

BIBLIOGRAPHY

Deslandes, Jacques, and Jacques Richard. *Histoire Comparée du Cinéma, Tome II.* Brussels: Casterman, 1968.

Grimoin-Sanson, Raoul. *Le Film de ma vie.* Paris: Éditions Henri Parville, 1926.

Sadoul, Georges. *Les Pionniers du Cinéma: 1897–1909.* Paris: Éditions Denoël, 1947.

CINEPLEX ODEON CORPORATION. Founded by entertainment lawyer Garth Drabinsky—he is Chairman, President, and Chairman of the Board—Cineplex Odeon Corporation began operations in 1979 with the opening of its first multi-screen theatre complex at the Eaton Centre in Toronto, Canada. It is now one of the largest exhibitors in North America, with more than 1,500 screens in 500 locations.

Following a July 1983 consent decree with the Canadian Government, whereby distributors were forced to make their films available to all exhibitors, Cineplex was able to break the monopoly of the country's two largest theatre chains, Famous Players and Canadian Odeon Theatres Ltd. In June 1984, Cineplex, with financial backing from the Bronfman family (who owned Seagram), was able to acquire Canadian Odeon Theatres Ltd., making it the largest theatre chain in Canada. In November 1985, the corporation acquired its first major U.S. holdings, Plitt Theatres Inc. and Plitt Theatre Holdings, Inc. In April 1976, it purchased Septum Cinemas of Atlanta, and in May of the same year acquired the Chicago-based Essaness Theatre Circuit. In September 1986, the New York–based RKO Century Warner Theatre chain was added to its holdings, and two months later, Neighborhood Theatres of Richmond, Virginia, became part of Cineplex Odeon. The final 1986 acquisition came in December, when the Corporation purchased the SRO Theatre Circuit in Seattle. On March 19, 1987, the Corporation announced agreement in principle to acquire all of the shares of the Walter Reade Organization, Inc., a New York–based theatre circuit.

In addition to its theatre holdings, Cineplex Odeon Corporation also operates Cineplex Odeon Films (formerly Pan-Canadian Film Distributors), which is involved in film distribution, with its first release in the United States being *The Decline of the American Empire* (1986); Toronto International Studios, Canada's largest studio facility; and the Film House Group, Inc. (acquired in July 1986), Canada's largest film laboratory and postproduction facility.

On May 12, 1986, MCA, Inc. became a 50 percent owner of the Corporation. With MCA, Cineplex Odeon will control and operate Universal Studios Florida, a studio tour and production facility; Steven Spielberg is the venture's creative consultant. On July 1, 1987, Cineplex Odeon opened an eighteen-screen complex on the MCA-Universal backlot in Los Angeles. This is the world's largest theatre complex, dwarfing the Corporation's earlier Beverly Center Cineplex complex in Los Angeles, which opened on July 16, 1982.

In 1988, the company became active in the United Kingdom with an announcement that it would develop some 110 screens there by 1990.

Address: 1303 Yonge Street, Toronto, Ontario M4T 2Y9, Canada.

BIBLIOGRAPHY

Zehr, Leonard, "Garth Drabinsky Jars Movie-House Industry, Sets New Standards," *Wall Street Journal,* March 16, 1987, pp. 1, 20.

CINÉ-ROMAN, which translates as "Film-Novel," is a French term introduced in the early years of this century to describe films that have all the attributes of a popular novel. Post-1950, when theorist and critic André Bazin hailed "the age of the scenario," Ciné-Roman was the name given to scripts written directly for the screen, but only those which work on a high, intellectual level. The most obvious examples of Ciné-Romans are Alain Resnais' *L'Année Dernière à Marienbad/Last Year at Marienbad* (1961) and Alain Robbe-Grillet's *L'immortelle* (1963).

BIBLIOGRAPHY

VanWert, William, "La Jetee," *Cinema,* no. 34, 1974, pp. 56–58.

CINES. A major Italian production company from the silent era, Cines was founded in 1906, with its first important director being Gaston Velle, who specialized in costume dramas. The company was reorganized in 1909 by Carlo Rossi. Spectacular costume epics such as *Les Miserables* (1912) and *Quo Vadis* (1913) enhanced the company's reputation throughout the world, and, in 1912, the great Italian actress Francesca Bertini became a star as a result of her performance in the Cines production of *Rosa di Tebe/Rose of Thebes*. Cines suffered heavy financial losses as a result of the First World War and ceased production in 1921.

A new Cines company was founded in 1929 and prospered under the guidance of Stefano Pittaluga and Emilio Cecchi until 1933, when it declared bankruptcy. It was later revived by the Italian government.

CINESOUND. The best known of all Australian production companies, Cinesound was formed in Sydney in 1931, with a capital of £50,000, and took over the Bondi and St. Kilda studios of Australasian Films Productions. It entered production in February 1931 with short subjects, making its first feature, *On Our Selection,* later that same year. A newsreel, *Cinesound Review,* was introduced in November 1931, and portions of it were incorporated in the British Pathé News and the American Universal News. An industrial film department, under Frank Hurley, was created in April 1936.

The figure most associated with Cinesound is Ken G. Hall (born 1901), who served as both general manager and director of many Cinesound releases. He received an Academy Award for Best Documentary in 1942 for *Kokoda Front Line*.

Feature production ceased at Cinesound during the Second World War, when the studio was taken over by the U.S. Signal Corps. Among Cinesound's features are *The Squatter's Daughter* (1933), *The Silence of Dean Maitland* (1934), *Grandad Rudd* (1935), *Thoroughbred* (1936), *Tall Timbers* (1937), *Broken Melody* (1938), *Ants in His Pants* (1939), and *Dad Rudd MP* (1940).

BIBLIOGRAPHY

Hall, Ken G. *Australian Film: The Inside Story*. Sydney: Summit Books, 1980.

CINETYP is believed to be the oldest extant subtitling company in the world. It was founded in Berne, Switzerland, in 1937 by two brothers, H. and J. Weber. The first film it subtitled was Marcel Pagnol's *Regain*. When the Webers retired in 1969, the company was taken over by George Egger. It now maintains offices outside of Switzerland, in New York and Los Angeles, and provides subtitling as well as captioning for the hearing-impaired on both film and video.
Address: Grunaustrasse 10, 3084 Wabern-Bern, Switzerland.

CITRA AWARDS are presented at the Indonesian Film Festival and are named after the Citra Foundation, which has helped promote film education in Indonesia since 1971.

THE CLARENDON FILM COMPANY was founded in 1904 by H.V. Lawley and Percy Stow and had a studio at 16 Limes Road in the South London suburb of Croydon. It was best known for its series of one-reel films featuring the character of Lt. Rose, first produced in 1909. The company and its studio were taken over in the late teens by Harma & Co. Ltd.

CLASSIC CINEMAS were once a favorite haunt of British film buffs, long noted for their frequent revivals of Marx Brothers and Greta Garbo features, along with occasional British films starring Jessie Matthews and Will Hay. The Classic Cinemas were created in 1935 by Capital and Provincial News Theatres, and the circuit owes much of its success to the work of managing director Eric Rhodes, who sought to maintain an image of the Classic Cinemas as a family business.

From fewer than one hundred theatres, the circuit expanded in 1969, with the acquisition of 7 Cameo theatres and 47 theatres from the Rank Organization*. The circuit was taken over in 1971 by the Tigon Group, a fairly minor production organization, which added the Essoldo circuit and the Jacey circuit of theatres to the Classic Cinemas circuit in 1972. Tigon subsequently disposed of the circuit, and in the spring of 1982, it was acquired by the Cannon Group for a reported £7 million. At that time, with 131 theatres, the Classic Cinemas circuit was the third largest in the United Kingdom.

Address: Cannon Cinemas Ltd., 167–169 Wardour Street, London W1V 3TA, United Kingdom.

BIBLIOGRAPHY

"Fun and Games," *Time Out,* no. 109, March 11–23, pp. 44–45.

COCINOR. Active from 1952 to 1967, Cocinor was a French production company involved primarily in international co-productions. Among its best-known features are *Le tombeur* (1957), *Rocco e i suoi fratelli/Rocco and His Brothers* (1960), *Les Carabiniers/The Riflemen* (1962), *La curée/The Game Is Over* (1965), and *Mon amour, mon amour* (1966).

COLOMBIA. It is perhaps indicative of the importance of the new medium then, that no one has been able to identify how or when the cinema first appeared in Colombia. What is known is that two Italian immigrant brothers who imported historical epics had, by 1915, produced a polemical documentary entitled *El Drama del 15 de Octubre,* Colombia's first motion picture. The cinema, by this time a fledgling commercial enterprise, was in this case quite profitably used to sensationalize the assassination of the head of the national liberal party.

With the exception of the efforts of the Di Domenico brothers, there was little cinematic activity until 1921–1927, a period when twelve feature films were released. The Di Domenicos continued producing, and were joined by a new company, Acevedo and Sons, which began Colombia's first and longest-lived newsreel (enduring for twenty-four years). Both companies capitalized on the national propensity toward the melodramatic, and their films were, for the most part, sterile tear-jerkers: Di Domenico's *Aura o las Violetas* (1923), about a poor girl married to a rich man, and the Acevedo's *La Tragedia del Silencio* (1924), a pathetic melodrama about the life of a leper. These filmmakers created contrived emotional turbulence while ignoring the country's perpetual political turmoil—the silent Colombian cinema refused to witness the innumerable social and political conflicts of the period.

The arrival of sound interrupted these fledgling filmmaking activities—between 1928 and 1938, only the Acevedo's newsreel was produced continuously—and when sound cinematography began it was not particularly successful. After the first sound feature was released in 1938 (*Al Son de las Guitarras*), a number of producing companies were founded but few managed to remain in business for more than two or three films due to inadequate capitalization, technical problems, and the lackluster box-office performance of national films. By the mid-forties, total national production did not exceed forty films and Colombian screens (the third largest Latin American market) were filled with Hollywood, Mexican, and Argentine films.

Although in the fifties a higher degree of professionalism and organization emerged among Colombian producers, national production never exceeded three or four films per year, and rarely addressed national issues or problems (for example, no Colombian film ever analyzed "La Violencia," a ten-year period beginning in 1948 of cataclysmic political turmoil that resulted in more than 300,000 deaths).

Significant changes took place in the sixties, however. First of all, a group of filmmakers who had studied abroad returned and began to attempt to produce a national cinema. Limited by scarce resources, Francisco Nordem, Guillermo Angulo, Jorge Pinto, and Alvaro Gomez (known as the "generation of the masters") procured financing from corporate sponsors (especially Esso) and produced a number of glossy documentaries and features that were "Colombian" only in name. Along with the "generation of the masters," came an increase in co-productions, particularly with Mexico, although these contributed little to the development of a cinema of national consequence, or to develop the cinematic infrastructure in Colombia.

These small steps forward were soon dwarfed by the sudden importance of the growth of alternative cinema culture in cine clubs (over twenty-five), cinema publications (especially the influential *Ojo al Cine*), and amateur production (capped by Diego Leon Giralso's *Camilo Torres* [1967], a much-discussed short documentary about the guerrilla priest's death in combat).

Although rarely exhibited commercially due to the strict censorship exercised by the Junta de Clasificacion, the influence of the radical politics and aesthetics of the New Latin American Cinema was apparent in the work of a number of "amateurs": Carlos Alvarez (*Asalto/Assault* 1968), Julia Alvarez (*Un Dia Yo Pregunté/One Day I Asked,* 1970), Carlos Mayolo (*La Quinta de Bolívar/Bolivar's Country House,* 1970), and Marta Rodríguez and Jorge Silva (*Chircales/Brickmakers,* 1968). With limited personal financing and primitive facilities, and always under the watchful eye of the state's repressive mechanisms, these filmmakers finally began to address the sociopolitical problems of Colombia in their documentaries.

These marginal activities took place in the context of the Colombian government's newly discovered interest in the cinema. In 1971–1972, a new law made the exhibition of Colombian shorts mandatory at first-run houses, raised admission prices, and established a system of rebates to producers and distributors of national films. Known as the *ley de sobreprecio* (the surcharge law), this law gave rise to a *cine de sobreprecio,* a "quickie" cinema designed to capitalize on the fast profits made possible by the law. Under the jurisdiction of the Film Quality Advisory Board, the films approved for "obligatory exhibition" were those that exploited national characteristics touristically. By decree, the board is, furthermore, required to deny classification to any film that criticizes or presents a negative image of the nation. In 1978, the government set up FOCINE, a state-owned commercial enterprise linked to the Ministry of Communication and financed by the Film Development Fund, to implement state policies in the film sector.

Although the statistics are impressive (in 1975 annual production increased to nearly one hundred short films), the *ley de sobreprecio* has divided filmmakers into two camps: those that seek profits and a popular audience at any cost (often producing very low quality films) and those that reject the state cinematic apparatus, continuing to make films on its margins (although this second option became more and more limited in the late seventies, as the state actively attempted to reduce the margins via repression). Some filmmakers have tried to beat the government's game by producing fictional shorts with concealed subversive messages: Carlos Mayolo and Luis Ospina's *Sin Telón/Without Curtain, Asunción,* and *La Hamaca/The Hammock* (all 1975) are early examples of this approach.

After a reorganization and the appointment of Maria Emma Mejias as director in 1983, the tensions among directors have eased up and FOCINE has been actively sponsoring national feature production by direct financing (six films in 1985), participation in foreign festivals and the Latin American common market (MECLA), and a policy of co-productions with Latin American and European countries. Its most successful recent feature was Jorge Ali Triana's *Tiempo de Morir* (1985), a co-production with Cuba based on a Gabriel Garcia Marquez story, which, with excellent performances (Gustavo Angarita) and tight script and direction (including one of the greatest moments of the Western genre when, just before the final shoot-out in the corral, the protagonists asks his adversary to wait a second while he puts on his glasses before taking aim), has won several awards at international festivals.

THE COLONIAL FILM UNIT was founded in October 1939 by William Sellers as part of Britain's wartime information service. Sellers was Propaganda Officer to the Medical Health Service in Nigeria, and, in the early thirties, had realized that, once he could get his native audiences used to film, he could teach them simple matters of health and hygiene far more widely and effectively than ever could be done by word of mouth. Sellers had then gone about learning the elements of his craft—how the simplest techniques of filmmaking were the best for illiterate audiences—and on the strength of these experiences he was asked to form the Unit at the outbreak of the Second World War. The Unit was administered by the Films Division of the Ministry of Information, but an appropriation from the Colonial Development Fund provided finance throughout its existence. Its task was to produce and distribute informational and propaganda films for the British Colonial Territories. Instructional courses were run from a training school in Cyprus, under the guidance of veteran film director George Pearson, to encourage Colonial Territories to make their own films. The films were kept simple, dealing with everyday matters and with the aim of improving the health and well-being of Colonial peoples. Mobile cinema vans catered for an average audience of two thousand, and a quarterly journal, *Colonial Cinema,* was published from 1942 to 1955. The Unit was closed down in March 1955.

BIBLIOGRAPHY

Manvell, Roger, "Colonial Films & Film-Makers: The Colonial Film Unit," *British Film Academy Journal,* Summer 1955, pp. 13, 15.

COMMEDIA BRILLANTE (Light Comedy) is an Italian film genre of the early teens, examples of which are Mario Caserini's *Santarellina* (1911), Eleuterio Rodolfi's *Il cappello di papa* (1914), and Lucio D'Ambra's *Il re, le torri, gli alfieri* (1916). Critic Pierre Leprohon describes the last as "an operetta for the screen."

BIBLIOGRAPHY

Leprohon, Pierre. *The Italian Cinema*. New York: Praeger, 1972.

COMMERCIAL AND EDUCATIONAL FILMS was a British producer of the thirties, specializing, as its name suggests, in educational, documentary, sponsored, and industrial films.

COMMISSION SUPÉRIEURE TECHNIQUE DU CINÉMA FRANÇAISE is the French equivalent of, and of equal importance as, the American Society of Motion Picture and Television Engineers. It was founded in September 1944 by Jean Painlevé, and the majority of French film technicians belong to the organization.

Address: 11 rue Galilee, 75116 Paris, France.

COMMONWEALTH FILM UNIT. See FILM AUSTRALIA

LA COMPAGNIE GÉNÉRALE FRANÇAISE DE CINÉMATOGRAPHIE was formed in Paris in 1921 by the merger of Film d'Art*, Eclair*, Agence Générale Cinématographique,* and others. It lasted less than one year and produced only one film, Jacques de Baroncelli's *La rêve/The Dream* (1921).

CONGO, PEOPLE'S REPUBLIC OF. A minor film producing country, most activity is controlled through the Office National du Cinéma (P.O. Box 1068, Brazzaville, Congo), which supervises theatres (only ten reported in 1966) screening in either 35mm or 16mm. Major Congo directors are Sébastien Kamba and Jean-Michel Tchissoukou.

CONGRÈS DES DUPES was the name coined by the French magazine *Ciné-Journal* for the first meeting of film manufacturers from France, Germany, the United Kingdom, Italy, Denmark, and Russia—Premier Congrès International des Fabricants de Film—in Paris in February 1909, under the presidency of Georges Méliès. The meeting was called to consider the implications of the creation in the United States of the Motion Picture Patents Company and to consider the monopolization of the supply of film stock by George Eastman. The meeting established the concept of renting films to exhibitors rather than selling them outright.

THE CONNESS TILL FILM COMPANY was founded in Toronto, Canada, in April 1914, with financing from an American theatrical entrepreneur named Luke Edwin Conness and a Canadian businessman named Louis A. Till. Its first film, *On the King's Highway,* was released in February 1915, and it continued to produce and release films on a regular basis during 1915 until its studios were destroyed by fire later that year.

BIBLIOGRAPHY

Morris, Peter. *Embattled Shadows: A History of Canadian Cinema 1895–1939.* Montreal: McGill-Queen's University Press, 1978.

CONTINENTAL GESELLSCHAFT. Following the Nazi occupation of Paris, Joseph Goebbels ordered the establishment of Continental Gesellschaft, to produce lightweight films for French audiences. In all, some 30 of the 220 films produced during the Occupation were made by Continental, and 9 of them were also released in Germany. Goebbels was far from happy with these French productions and wrote in his diary on May 13, 1942

> I took a look at another French movie, *Annette et la dame blonde* [directed by Henri Decoin]. It is of the same levity and elegance as the Darrieux movie, *Caprices* [directed by Leo Joanon, 1941]. We shall have to be careful about the French so that they won't build up a new moving-picture art under our leadership which will give us too serious competition in the European market. I shall see to it that especially trained French film actors are gradually engaged for the German movie.

Among the directors who worked for Continental were André Cayatte, Henri Decoin, Christian-Jaque, and Henri-Georges Clouzot. The last directed the most important Continental production, *Le Corbeau/The Raven* (1943), concerning poison pen letters in a small French town. The film was believed to present a negative view of France, and Clouzot was branded a collaborationist and "blacklisted" for a number of years. In fact, the film was considered unsuitable for release in Germany; it was distributed in the United States in 1948.

BIBLIOGRAPHY

Bazin, André. *French Cinema of the Occupation and Resistance.* New York: Ungar, 1981.

Lochner, Louis P., editor. *The Goebbels Diaries.* Garden City, N.Y.: Doubleday and Doran, 1948.

THE COOK ISLANDS has no film industry. The main town of Avarua on the largest island, Rarotonga, has two theatres, and films are also screened on the island of Aitutaki. The 1987 CBS made-for-television movie, *Angel in Green,* directed by Marvin J. Chomsky and starring Bruce Boxleitner and Susan Dey, was shot on Rarotonga.

COOPÉRATIO was the name of a Montreal, Canada, film company, active from 1964 to 1967, whose filmmaker members deferred their salaries against future profits. The most important of the six films produced by Coopératio was Michel Brault's *Entre la mer et l'eau douce/Drifting Upstream* (1967).

COSTA RICA. See CENTRAL AMERICA

THE COUNCIL OF EUROPE is concerned with mutual understanding and the adoption of a united policy concerning cultural matters by the various countries of Europe. Between 1960 and 1970, it maintained a technical committee on film activities which was involved in short films, educational and documentary films, and the translation of film terms into various European languages. It has also organized many conferences on film, including ones on "the Democratic Renewal of Theatrical Arts" (in Athens, 1976) and "Cinema and State" (in Lisbon, 1978).

CRICKET. The English sport of cricket dates back at least to the sixteenth century and is one of the most popular games throughout the former British Empire. On film, the sport has been seen in a number of British features, beginning with *Old College Badge* in 1913, and including *Badger's Green* (1937), *It's Not Cricket* (1937), *Badger's Green* (1949), *It's Not Cricket* (1949), *The Final Test* (1953), *The Go-Between* (1971), *Good and Bad at Games* (1983), and *Maurice* (1987). Perhaps the best-known allusion to cricket in a film, although the game is never seen, occurs in Alfred Hitchcock's *The Lady Vanishes* (1938), in which Basil Radford and Naunton Wayne play two characters more concerned with the latest test match scores than a murder.

BIBLIOGRAPHY

Zucker, Harvey Marc, and Laurence J. Babich. *Sports Films: A Complete Reference.* Jefferson, N.C.: McFarland, 1987.

CRICKS AND MARTIN. Located in the South London suburb of Croydon, the British producer Cricks and Martin had begun life in 1901 as Cricks and Sharp (founded by G.H. Cricks and H.M. Sharp). The name change came in 1908 when J.H. Martin replaced Sharp. The company was one of Britain's major film producers until its demise in 1913.

THE CROWN FILM UNIT, Britain's official government film unit, was in existence under this name from April 1940 through March 1952. Its origins lie in the Empire Marketing Board (EMB) Film Unit created in 1929 by Sir Stephen Tallents and the founder of the British documentary film movement, John Grierson. The first film made by the Empire Marketing Board Film Unit was *Drifters,* a now-classic silent documentary on North Sea herring fishermen. When the EMB was dissolved in 1933, Sir Stephen Tallents moved to the General Post Office (GPO), and the film unit moved with him, with Grierson supervising the talented young directors, such as Paul Rotha, Basil Wright, Harry Watt, and Edgar Anstey, which it had acquired. During this period there were considerable advances in sound recording and new techniques were introduced into the making of such documentary films as *Song of Ceylon, Coalface,* and *Nightmail.* In 1937, Grierson left and Alberto Cavalcanti took over as producer.

With the outbreak of the Second World War in 1939, doubts arose as to the future control of the Film Unit, and a survey of its functions took place, resulting in control being transferred to the Ministry of Information and the adoption of the name, Crown Film Unit. In the meantime, Ian Dalrymple had succeeded Cavalcanti as producer. The Ministry of Information had no recognized propaganda policy at that time but, following reorganization of the Unit, it commenced production of propaganda films, such as Humphrey Jennings' *Fires Were Started, The Silent Village,* and *A Diary for Timothy,* and Harry Watts' *Target for Tonight* and *Squadron 999.* In 1943, a board of management, including J. Arthur Rank, was set up, and the functions of the Unit officially defined. The Unit was based at Pinewood Studios* and continued in production throughout the war. It also supervised the productions of the Army and RAF film units.

From 1947 to 1949, John Grierson resumed control of the Unit as head of the Film Division of the Central Office of Information (COI), which had taken over from the Ministry of Information at war's close. Beaconsfield Studios became the Unit's headquarters, and productions included *Queen o' the Border, The Magic Thread,* and *Daybreak in UDI* (which won both an Academy Award and a British Film Academy Award). When the Conservative Party was returned to power in 1951, the Unit was disbanded as part of the Government's economy measures, and, despite vigorous protests, production ceased in March 1952.

BIBLIOGRAPHY

Sussex, Elizabeth. *The Rise and Fall of British Documentary.* Berkeley: University of California Press, 1975.

CUBA. Although it is often said that the Cuban cinema began with Fidel Castro's 1959 revolution, the cinema has played an important role in Cuban life since the turn of the century. In fact, as early as 1897, Cubans had already welcomed programs of Lumière shorts as well as Thomas Edison's Vitascope. Gabriel Veyre, the Lumière agent responsible for the Cinématographe screenings, was also the first to film in Cuba, a short documentary called *Simulacro de un Incendio* (1898). That same year, Albert E. Smith and J. Stuart Blackton of the Vitagraph Company arrived in Cuba to film battle scenes of Cuba's war of independence from Spain which were subsequently used to promote anti-Spanish sentiment in the United States. Cuba's first indigenous films were shot by Jose E. Casasus *(El Brujo Desaparecido,* 1905) and Enrique Diaz Quesada *(La Habana en agosto, 1906,* and *El Parque de Palatino,* 1906). Both of these pioneers of the Cuban cinema were financed by business concerns; the former by a beer merchant, the latter by an amusement park company attempting to promote tourism.

These early cinematic activities already exhibit the principal characteristics that dominated the Cuban cinema for the next five decades: the exploitation of the Cuban market by foreign concerns, the cinematic interpretation of Cuban sociopolitical life by foreigners for their own interests, and the commercialization of all aspects of national production.

Throughout the silent period, the Cuban cinema market (the most profitable market in Latin America) was controlled first by European firms and, after the First World War, by North American companies. Although several film production companies were established between 1913–1930, none managed to produce more than a few films before declaring bankruptcy or simply disappearing. The most notable silent Cuban production was Ramon Peon's *La Virgen de la Caridad* (1930), a film that historian Georges Sadoul praised as ''almost neo-realist.''

The coming of sound further limited the development of the Cuban cinema. Throughout the thirties, forties, and fifties, the Cuban market was filled with Mexican *rancheras,* Argentine tango and *gaucho* films, as well as North American releases. Cuban productions of this period tended to use sound to highlight the more folkloric and touristy aspects of Cuban life, especially its music (for example, Cuba's first sound film, a short entitled *Maracas y Bongo,* 1934).

Manuel Alonso, the director of Cuba's first sound feature (*La Serpiente Roja,* 1937) was the most commercially successful figure of Cuba's film world in the forties and fifties. Alonso's success was based on the production of newsreels: his ''Noticiario CMQ-Cristal'' was in production for eighteen years. The Alonso formula—mixing hard news with social reporting and outright commercials—filled a gap in the Cuban market and allowed him to gain control of important distribution exchanges as well as the best production facilities available in the island (often leased to North American pornography producers).

Although there was little steady feature film production, a general public fascination with the cinema translated, in the forties and fifties, into an interest in promoting the development of cinema culture. Historian-critic José Manuel Valdes-Rodriguez was responsible for establishing the Cuban cine-club movement, cinema education at the university level, and the Cuban Cinematheque. Cinematic activities were also encouraged by other cultural organizations such as the Cuban Photo Club, the Centro Catolico de Orientacion Cinematica, the Sociedad Cine Vision, and, most significantly, by the highly politicized Sociedad Cultural Nuestro Tiempo.

In 1954, two members of Nuestro Tiempo, Tomás Gutiérrez Alea and Julio García Espinosa, completed a two-year course in filmmaking at the Centro Sperimentale di Cinematografia* in Rome and, upon their return to Cuba, collaborated on a mid-length feature, *El Mégano/The Charcoal Worker*. Although this documentary-style denunciation of the hardships of coal workers in the swampy regions south of Havana was not commercially exhibited, and, in fact, was confiscated by the Batista government, it was the first precursor of the revolutionary cinema. All those who collaborated on this film (Alea, Espinosa, Alfredo Guevara, Jorge Haydu, and Jorge Fraga) would make up the central core of ICAIC (Instituto Cubano de Arte e Industria Cinematográfica).

Immediately after Fidel Castro's successful march to Havana in January 1959, the rebels addressed the nation's and the revolution's cultural needs, setting up a Cultural Department to offer its members (many of whom were illiterate) access to culture. One of the divisions of this department was Cine Rebelde. Under the direction of Julio García Espinosa, Cine Rebelde produced two documentaries in early 1959: *Esta Tierra Nuestra* (Tomás Gutiérrez Alea) and *La Vivienda* (Julio García Espinosa). Cine Rebelde was, however, a short-lived organization, for upon the creation of ICAIC by governmental decree in March 1959, its activities were incorporated into the new organism.

ICAIC was organized to supervise and coordinate all activities relating to the cinema in Cuba. It was the first organization of its kind in Latin America: a government agency entrusted with the national cinema, run primarily by filmmakers and not government bureaucrats. The decree that established the institute recognized the cinema as a crucial medium to promote the cultural and ideological evolution of the Cuban people and the success of the Revolution. ICAIC was set up as an independent agency governed by a director (Alfredo Guevara, 1959–1980; Julio García Espinosa, 1980 to the present) appointed by the First Minister of the government and by a three-member advisory board.

Concerned with pedagogical and didactic uses of the cinema, ICAIC concentrated its first efforts in developing a cadre of documentary filmmakers and, in their hands, the short film became a vibrant and important cinematic form. It was thus a documentarist that first garnered international recognition for the Cuban cinema: Santiago Alvarez. With the production of ICAIC's weekly *Latin American Newsreel* in his hands, Alvarez abandoned the traditional episodic form to create dynamic, essayistic shorts. Alvarez transformed apparently insurmountable material constraints—chronic shortages of funds, footage, and skilled personnel—into aesthetic assets and developed a graphic, montagist style based upon secondhand sources such as news photos and TV footage. In his own documentary work, Alvarez perfected the use of a collagist style for political agitation. *Ciclon* (1963), his first film to receive wide acclaim, was followed by, among many others, *Now* (1965), *Hanoi, Martes 13* (1967), and *79 Primaveras* (1969).

The importance of the Cuban documentary—to this day the training ground for most of ICAIC's filmmakers—cannot be overestimated. Its influence is apparent even in ICAIC's fictional productions. Developed alongside the documentary cinema, ICAIC's fiction films reflect a simultaneous admiration and suspicion of Hollywood and European styles of filmmaking in their search for a new cinematic language appropriate to Cuba's new sociopolitical realities.

Between 1966 and 1979, the best years of Cuban feature production, ICAIC's films were characterized by a plurality of approaches and a rich experimental spirit. Tomás Gutiérrez Alea directed *Memorias del Subdesarrollo/Memories of Underdevelopment* (1968), a film widely regarded as the best Latin America has produced. A very young novice director, Humberto Solás, directed *Lucía* (1968), an epic historical drama that focused on three female heroines named Lucia to depict the key stages of Cuba's struggles for independence. Other important films were Julio García Espinosa's *Las Aventuras de Juan Quin Quin/Adventures of Juan Quin Quin* (1967), a comedic pastiche of cinematic genres, and Manuel

Octavio Gómez's *La Primera Carga al Machete/The First Charge with the Machete* (1969), a highly experimental "documentary" reconstruction of an episode from the Cuban war of independence.

In this early period, ICAIC filmmakers enjoyed an autonomy within the Cuban sociopolitical sphere not shared by other cultural workers. Taking advantage of this freedom, the Cuban cinema did not avoid politically sensitive topics and was both politically committed and revolutionary while freed from populist stereotypes and socialist realist tendencies.

In the late seventies, however, the Cuban cinema began to shy away from contemporary issues and increasingly turned toward historical themes. Many of the best films of the Cuban cinema were nevertheless produced in this period, especially those films dealing with Cuban slavery. The most notable in this genre were Sergio Giral's *El Otro Francisco/The Other Francisco* (1975), an adaption of a classic romantic abolitionist novel that combined the nineteenth-century melodrama of the original with a thoroughly twentieth-century "rereading," and Tomás Gutiérrez Alea's *La Última Cena/The Last Supper* (1977). Although the exception rather than the rule, several important films dealing with contemporary issues were also produced: Manuel Octavio Gómez's *Ustedes Tienen la Palabra/Now It's Up to You* (1973) and *Una Mujer, un Hombre y una Ciudad/A Woman, A Man, A City* (1978), Sara Gómez's *De Cierta Manera/One Way or Another* (1974), and Pastor Vega's *Retrato de Teresa/Portrait of Teresa* (1979).

This latter film is the best example of another tendency that emerged in the late seventies—the return to the unbroken narrative line and seamless transparent style of Hollywood filmmaking. Octavio Cortázar's *El Brigadista/The Teacher* (1977) surprised foreign audiences with its lack of experimentation and utterly conventional style, but, like *Retrato de Teresa,* it was a great popular success with Cuban audiences. In the eighties, stylistic and visual experimentation became the exception rather than the norm, as popular comedies on safe topics replaced the early ambitious attempts to deal with difficult social issues: Juan Carlos Tabio's *Se Permuta* (1984), Rolando Díaz's *Los Pajaros Tirandole a la Escopeta* (1984).

In the eighties ICAIC also attempted to produce a "blockbuster," Humberto Solas' *Cecilia* (1982, in co-production with Spain), based on a nineteenth-century Cuban classic about an illicit interclass, interrace love affair. ICAIC invested almost all of its resources in this two-year production, and the film's subsequent popular and critical failure prompted a reevaluation of the organization's goals and a reorganization of its operations.

Under the leadership of Julio Garcia Espinosa, ICAIC has adopted a strategy of diversification. In the mid- to late eighties, the goal has been to provide minimal financing for as many films as possible. Younger as well as established directors are explicitly encouraged—by monetary incentives—to proceed from treatment to finished film as quickly as possible. This has significantly increased the number of features produced annually, and has made possible a reappearance of more self-reflexive, critical works such as Tomás Gutiérrez Alea's *Hasta Cierto Punto/Up to a Certain Point* (1983) and Jesús Díaz's *Lejania* (1985).

In addition to its responsibility to maintain national cinematic production, ICAIC has also been, since the 1961 nationalization of U.S. interests, in charge of all film distribution and exhibition. Although as many as 97 percent of all the films screened annually are still foreign, they represent a wide variety of nations and interests and are no longer limited to Hollywood imports. Among ICAIC's most famous distribution programs was the innovative "cine-movil" project which, on vans, mules, and motor boats, brought the cinema to inaccessible rural areas throughout the island. Other programs—the cine-club movement and prime-time TV programs dedicated to film history and analysis—were also designed to encourage the development of cinematic culture and critical consciousness.

Since 1979, ICAIC has also been visibly involved in the maintenance and support of the New Latin American Cinema. Its annual "International Festival of New Latin American Cinema" has proven to be a remarkable forum for filmmakers and critics from all over the continent. The establishment of a Latin American Film Market (MECLA) at the 1980 film festival and the inauguration, in 1986, of a Third World Film School in Cuba sponsored by a pan–Latin American Foundation of Latin American Filmmakers indicate that Cuba—and the Cuban cinema—will continue to play an essential role in the development of the cinemas of Latin America.

BIBLIOGRAPHY

Brook, Peter, "The Cuban Enterprise," *Sight & Sound,* Spring 1961, pp. 78–79.

del Castillo, Ramón, "Cuban Cinema," *Sight & Sound,* Spring 1947, p. 8.

Douglas, Maria Eulalia, "The Cuban Cinema," *Take One,* vol. I, no. 12, 1968, pp. 6–9.

Engel, Andi, "Solidarity and Violence," *Sight & Sound,* Autumn 1969, pp. 196–200.

Myerson, Michael, editor. *Memories of Underdevelopment.* New York: Grossman, 1973.

Sutherland, Elizabeth, "Cinema of Revolution—90 Miles from Home," *Film Quarterly,* vol. XV, no. 2, Winter 1961–62, pp. 42–49.

THE CURZON CINEMA, one of London's leading art houses, is situated in the heart of exclusive Mayfair. Opened on March 6, 1934, the building was an outstanding example of thirties architecture. To appease the fierce opposition to a film theatre opening in Mayfair, the frontage had to be less than thirty-five feet high and a design in brick of stark simplicity in the European style was created. The theatre was run by the Marquis de Casa Maury, a decorative artist, who had been much impressed by the Parisian art theatres and who was determined to set new standards in comfort and elegance. The Curzon opened with an Austrian film on the life of Schubert titled *Unfinished Symphony*. The theatre closed for redecoration on September 2, 1939, but, with the declaration of war, it remained closed until it was taken over by the Directorate of Army Cinematography for army screenings.

After the war, the Curzon was purchased by H.H. Wingate's General Cinema Theatres, and reopened on February 14, 1946, with *Love Eternal*. Its reputation as an art house grew, and it was second only in importance to the Academy*. *La Ronde* was an enormous success there, running for seventy-six weeks from April 27, 1951, to October 9, 1952. However, with the increasing property values in London, there came the time when the original building could not provide an adequate return on the prime space that it occupied, and the theatre was closed on August 26, 1963. The site was developed as an office building, but incorporating a new Curzon, which opened in 1966.

In 1984, Chesterfield Properties PLC, the umbrella owner of the Curzon bought back the lease on the Premiere Cinema on Shaftesbury Avenue. This theatre, on its completion in 1958, had been leased to Columbia Pictures, which used it initially as a first-run theatre. Columbia sold the lease in 1982 to the Cannon Classic Group, who, by 1984, felt that the theatre was superfluous to its needs and offered the lease back to Chesterfield. After extensive refurbishing, the theatre reopened as Curzon West End on March 8, 1985, with *Wetherby*. In March 1987, Curzon opened a third theatre, the Curzon Phoenix, which adjoins the Phoenix Theatre (a legitimate house) off the Charing Cross Road. The opening film was *Come and See*.

BIBLIOGRAPHY

Eyles, Allen, and Keith Stone. *London's West End Cinemas*. Sutton, Surrey: Premier Bioscope, 1984.

CYPRUS. The small island nation of Cyprus had only 5 theatres in 1920, but 250 by 1970. The number decreased in later years as video became popular. Film production is limited to the Greek portion of the island, with filmmakers receiving support from the Greek Film Centre* and from the state-funded Cypriot Cinema Consultative Committee (founded in 1983).

Two major Cypriot directors are Andreas Pantzis and Christos Siopachas. The first major production to be filmed on the island was *Cyprus Is an Island,* the production of which is documented in *We Made a Film in Cyprus* by Laurie Lee and Ralph Keene (New York: Longmans, Green, 1947).

CZECHOSLOVAKIA. The Lumière films were first screened in Prague in 1896 by Jan Kříženecký, a Czech who began filming actualities as early as 1898. The first two important production companies to be founded in the country were Kinofa Film, incorporated in 1908 by Anton Pech, and the Asum Film Company, formed a little later by actress Andula Sedláčková and her husband, architect Max Urban. The First World War put an end to production, but after the establishment of the Czech Republic in 1918 a number of companies, including Praga and Weteb, were created. In 1921, the American and Biographia film companies joined forces to build A.B. Film Studios.

Jaroslav Hašek's novel, *The Good Soldier Schweik,* was filmed as early as 1926 by Karel Lamač, with Karel Noll in the title role. It was also filmed in 1931, 1957, and in 1959 by Jiří Trnka as a puppet film.

Czechoslovakia's first talkie, *Tonka Šibenice/Tonka the Gallow's Bird,* was directed by Karel Anton in 1929. A year later, J.S. Kolár's epic *Sv. Václac/St. Wenceslas,* produced in commemoration of the one thousandth anniversary of the Saint's martyrdom, had problems in obtaining a release, because it was a silent feature. In 1932, Gustav Machaty made his first film, *Extase/Ecstasy,* starring Hedy Lamarr, which created a sensation and helped gain the actress a Hollywood contract.

Miloš Havel is generally regarded as the creator of the modern Czech film industry, having built the Barrandov Studios in 1933, and also controlling Lucerna Film. His 1938 feature, *Cech Panen Kutnohorských/The Guild of the Virgins of Kutná Hora,* was a prize winner at the Venice Film Festival*. Havel tried, unsuccessfully, to continue his control of the Barrandov Studios after the Second World War.

In March 1939, Czechoslovakia was occupied by the Nazis. Prag-Film Company was established as part of a German scheme to transfer its productions to Prague as bombing became too great in Germany. Some Czech features continued to be produced.

Within months of the close of the Second World War, the Czech film industry was nationalized, on August 11, 1945, but it was not until 1948 that state control of the cinema became a reality. Few films of importance were produced, with the exceptions of *Siréna/The Strike* (1947), directed by Karel Steklý, and *Předtucha/The Premonition* (1947), directed by Otakar Vávra. Throughout the fifties, the Czech film industry produced little that had impact outside of the country, with the prominent directors being Václav Krška, Vojtěch Jasný, and Ladislav Helge.

A new Czech cinema flowered in the sixties, thanks to directors who were not members of the Communist party and were not concerned with ideologies. Among such figures are Evald Schorm, Věra Chytilová, Ivan Passer, Jan Němec, Jiří Menzel, and, of course, Miloš Forman, who left Czechoslovakia to become a member of the international film community. The films of these and other directors of the period are remarkable in their freshness, originality, and lack of any Communist influence. The "golden age" died in 1968 with the intervention of the Soviet military in Czechoslovakia, and the majority of the directors involved left the country for good. Others, including Schorm, were denied work, while some, such as Menzel and Chytilová simply refused to work until the situation improved.

Films continued to be made in Czechoslovakia—Menzel and Chytilová returned to filmmaking in the late seventies—but they were generally considered insignificant. Features by a new generation of directors, including Karel Smyczek, Jaroslav Soukup, and Zdeněk Troška, are either innocuous entertainment subjects or "safe" party-approved historical dramas.

The export of films from Czechoslovakia is controlled by Czechoslovak Filmexport (Václavské Náméstí 28, 111 45 Prague 1).

BIBLIOGRAPHY

Boček, Jaroslav et al. *Modern Czechoslovak Film, 1945–1965*. Prague: Artia, 1965.

Broz, Jaroslav. *The Path of Fame of the Czechoslovak Film*. Prague: Československý Filmexport, 1967.

Dewey, Langdon. *Outline of Czechoslovakian Cinema*. London: Informatics, 1971.

Hames, Peter. *The Czechoslovak New Wave*. Berkeley: University of California Press, 1985.

Liehm, Antonin J. *Closely Watched Trains: The Czechoslovak Experience*. New York: International Arts and Sciences Press, 1974.

Paul, David W. *Politics, Art, and Commitment in the East European Cinema*. New York: St. Martin's Press, 1983.

Škvorecký, Josef. *All the Bright Young Men and Women*. Toronto: Peter Martin Associates, 1971.

———, "Czechoslovakia," in *World Cinema since 1945*, editor William Luhr. New York: Ungar, 1987, pp. 154–169.

Stoil, Michael Jon. *Cinema beyond the Danube*. Metuchen, N.J.: Scarecrow Press, 1974.

Whyte, Alistair. *New Cinema in Eastern Europe*. New York: Studio Vista/Dutton, 1971.

D

DAIEI COLOR was a name created by the Daiei Motion Picture Co. Ltd.* to describe the color process in which its films were shot and released, a process which was, in reality, Eastman Color.

DAIEI MOTION PICTURE CO. LTD. The Japanese production and distribution company, Daiei began life as Dai-Nikon Eiga (Greater Japanese Motion Picture Company) in 1941, when the Japanese government tried to reorganize the major producers into three companies. Masaichi Nagata, who headed the Shinko Kyoto Studios, was able to persuade the government to form three companies, and through various machinations, one was Daiei, of which Nagata was appointed managing director and president. Following the Second World War, Daiei distributed the productions of Samuel Goldwyn and Walt Disney in Japan, and, in 1950, was able to gain international recognition with its production of Akira Kurosawa's *Rashomon*. Shortly thereafter, Daiei became the first Japanese company actively to produce color features.

Daiei ceased operations in December 1970, but three years later a new organization was formed, with Yasuyoshi Tokuma as its president. It was not until 1983 that Daiei was once again recognized as one of Japan's leading motion picture producers.

Address: 602 Kojima-cho, Chofu City, Tokyo 182, Japan.

BIBLIOGRAPHY

Provinzano, Linda, Howard Besser, Stephanie Boris, and Frank Motofufi. *Films in the Collection of the Pacific Film Archive, Volume I: Daiei Motion Picture Co., Ltd., Japan*. Berkeley, Calif.: University Art Museum, 1979.

THE DANISH FILM INSTITUTE came into being through the Film and Cinema Act of 1982, replacing the old Danish Film Foundation, which had been established in 1965 by the Ministry of Cultural Affairs. Governed by a five-member board and financed by the Danish government and through a cooperative production agreement with Danish television, the Danish Film Institute supports film production either in the form of a guarantee or by direct financing. It provides funding for the importation of films for children and films of artistic merit, promotes Danish films abroad, finances filmmaking workshops, and finances the National Film School of Denmark.

Associated with the Danish Film Institute is the self-supporting, government-owned Danish Film Studio (Blomstervaenget 52, DK-2800 Lyngby, Denmark) and the Danish Film Museum, which shares a building with the Institute, and was founded in 1941. Also associated with the Institute is the Government Film Office/Statens Filmcentral (Vestergade 27, DK-1456, Copenhagen K, Denmark), which produces documentaries and short subjects and also purchases the latter from abroad.

Address: Store Søndervoldstraede, DK-1419 Copenhagen K, Denmark.

BIBLIOGRAPHY

Schmidt, K., ''Sådan fungerer manuskriptstøften,'' *Kosmorama,* vol. XXV, no. 143–144, Winter 1979, pp. 172–176.

DANZIG. The Baltic seaport of Danzig was a free city from 1807 to 1814 and from 1919 to 1939. During the second period of its freedom, it had no film industry, but it did have twenty-four theatres, screening primarily German films during the thirties. American films were shown, but in dubbed German versions. The city is now part of Poland and known as Gdansk.

THE DAVID DI DONATELLO AWARDS are presented each spring in Rome and are the Italian equivalents of the Academy Awards. They take the form of a miniature gold replica of Donatello's statue of David, and are presented in much the same categories as the Oscars, except that a special directorial award is presented in the name of Luchino Visconti.

DEBRIE was one of the best-known names in European cameras for many years. The company was founded in 1900, and in 1908, André Debrie (1880–1967) built the Debrie Parvo camera—''Parvo'' means compact—which was used extensively in Europe, Asia, and South America. A Super Parvo camera was introduced in 1932 for the shooting of sound films. The company continues in existence and is involved in the manufacture of various types of film-related equipment. It received a Technical Achievement Award from the Academy of Motion Picture Arts and Sciences in 1980, ''for the development of a continuous contact, total immersion, additive color, motion picture printer.''

Address: Debrie International, Zone Industrielle des Richardets, 2 rue des Aeorstiers, 93160 Noisy Le Grand, France.

DECLA BIOSCOP was an important German film company, which was created in 1920 by the merger of the Decla and Bioscop organizations. The latter had been formed by Erich Pommer (1889–1966) in 1915, and he became head of the new company, among whose films are *Das Cabinett des Dr. Caligari/The*

Cabinet of Dr. Caligari (1920), *Die Spinnen/The Spiders* (1920), *Genuine* (1920), *Ireende Seelen/Lost Souls* (1920), and *Der Müde Tod/Destiny* (1921). Decla Biscop was merged with Ufa* some three years after its formation, and, as a result, Erich Pommer began a career at Ufa as one of Germany's most prestigious and successful producers.

DÉCOUPAGE is a French cinema term with many meanings, which is somewhat erroneously translated into English as "editing." It can also refer to the shooting script, the visual breakdown of a sequence, or the technique involved in recording a scene on film. It is discussed in detail in Nöel Burch's *Praxis du Cinéma* (Paris: Gallimard, 1969).

DEFA. In May 1946, the Russian occupying forces in East Berlin granted a license to produce films to DEFA (Deutsche Film Aktiengesellschaft/German Film Corporation), which was housed at the former Ufa* studios at Neubabelsberg, with administrative offices in the former Ufa building in the heart of Berlin. DEFA immediately began a production program, which included ten feature films, newsreels, and short subjects. It produced the first postwar German feature, *Die Mörder sind unter uns/The Murderers Are Among Us* (1946), directed by Wolfgang Staudte. This was followed by *Irgendwo in Berlin/Somewhere in Berlin* (1946), *Freies Land/Free Land* (1946), *Razzia/Round-Up* (1947), *Ehe im Schatten/Marriage in the Shadow* (1947), and *Affaire Blum/The Blum Affair* (1947). When the two German states came into being in 1949, DEFA became the official state-run film corporation of the German Democratic Republic. It also controls the export and import of all films into East Germany.

Address: Milastrasse 2, 1058 Berlin, East Germany.

BIBLIOGRAPHY

Manvell, Roger, and Heinrich Fraenkel. *The German Cinema*. New York: Praeger, 1971.

DENHAM STUDIOS was created by Hungarian-born Alexander Korda (1893–1956) as part of his dream that Britain, his adopted country, should have a film industry truly worthy of itself. The site chosen for this "British Hollywood" was an estate near the small village of Denham, north of London. Created by American art director and designer, Jack Okey, it was, at the time, the largest studio in the United Kingdom, with seven stages in 165 acres. It had 118,800 square feet of floor space with eighteen cutting rooms, and was well equipped with its own labs and film vaults and used Western Electric sound. The studios employed some two thousand people and was built mainly with loans from the Prudential Life Assurance Company. The first film to go into production was *Southern Roses* (1936), made by an outsider, Max Schach. Korda's own production company was London Films*, and his first film to go into production at Denham was *Rembrandt* (1936), starring Charles Laughton. Other Korda films made there include *Moscow Nights* (1936), *Things To Come* (1936) and *Knight* *without Armor* (1937). 20th Century-Fox shot Britain's first Technicolor feature, *Wings of the Morning* (1937), there.

By 1939 over fifty feature films had been made at Denham, but the Prudential had grown tired of Korda's extravagance—London Films owed them over $1 million. Rank's Pinewood Studios* had opened in September 1936, and there was cut-throat competition between the two studios. Prudential decided to rid itself of Korda and engineered a merger with Pinewood Studios, enabling control of Denham to pass to J. Arthur Rank. With the outbreak of the Second World War in September 1939, Denham was taken over by various government departments, but films continued to be made on most of the sound stages. Some outstanding productions from the war years are *Gaslight* (1940), *Major Barbara* (1941), *49th Parallel* (U.S. *The Invaders,* 1941), *Hatter's Castle* (1941), and *The Life and Death of Colonel Blimp* (1943). In the postwar years, the Rank Organization* moved into Denham and produced a series of films utilizing its contract stars, including Margaret Lockwood, James Mason, Stewart Granger, and Michael Wilding. Denham's fifteen-year history as a major studio ended with Walt Disney's *Robin Hood* (1952). Rank decided to close Denham in 1952 and to concentrate all production at Pinewood. The U.S. Air Force leased the building for some time, and presently it houses equipment for Rank Xerox (the British division of Xerox Corporation of America).

BIBLIOGRAPHY

Low, Rachael. *Film Making in 1930s Britain*. London: George Allen & Unwin, 1985.

Street, Sarah, "Denham Studios: The Golden Jubilee of Korda's Folly," *Sight & Sound,* vol. LV, no. 2, Spring 1986, pp. 116–122.

DENMARK. In December 1896, Peter Elfert shot the first films in Denmark, six months after the Lumière brothers' films were shown in Copenhagen. Elfert, who later became the Danish court photographer, shot films of the royal family in 1898 and photographed Denmark's first story film *Henrettelsen/The Execution* in 1903.

Nordisk Films Kompagni, which became the world's second largest production company in 1913, was formed in 1906 by cinema owner Ole Olsen, formerly a shepherd, sailor, and barker with a traveling troupe. Its studio in Valby, near Copenhagen, is the oldest studio in the world still operating, and today Nordisk Films is Denmark's leading distributor. Its influence on world cinema began in 1907 with the release of the popular *Løvejagten/The Lion Hunt,* which sold over 250 prints outside of Denmark; it soon opened distribution branches throughout Europe and in New York, where their Great Northern Film Company was established in 1908.

Approximately 560 films were made by Nordisk Films between 1907 and 1910, the year it distributed *Den hvide Slavehandel/The White Slave Traffic,* 706 meters in length, made by their competitor, Fotorama, which was so successful that it influenced Nordisk Films and other companies to make longer films and films about the same subject. Historians relate this trend to the 1913 *Traffic in Souls,* one of the first successful long films in the United States.

Denmark's "Golden Age," 1911–1914, was marked by internationally successful films known for their realistic atmosphere, aristocratic milieu, clear photography, reserved acting by members of the Danish stage, including Asta Nielsen (1883–1972) and Vladimir Psilander, and the skillful direction of August Blom (1869–1947), Benjamin Christensen (1879–1959), Peter Urban Gad (1879–1947), and Holger-Madsen (1878–1943), among others. Nordisk Films made a high percentage of Danish productions; at its peak, the company employed 1,400 full-time employees. Carl-Theodor Dreyer (1889–1968), who began writing scripts for a small Danish company in 1912, joined Nordisk in 1913 and wrote intertitles, cut film, and served as a literary consultant before directing his first film, *Praesidenten/The President* in 1918.

After the European and American markets disappeared during the First World War, in which Denmark was a neutral country, Denmark's production declined drastically (it produced only 8 films in 1920, compared with 123 in 1916 and exported only 55,000 feet of film to the United States in 1923, compared with 1.3 million feet in 1913) and its standing among the leaders of world cinema has not been regained. Historians have suggested that the Danish industry did not pay its people what they could make in other countries, so that once they were established, they left, and that the industry was interested more in product than art, so that some filmmakers, particularly Dreyer, Gad, and Christensen, had to go elsewhere.

After the war, Denmark tried to win back its English and American audience with adaptations by popular director A.W. Sandberg (1887–1938) of works by Charles Dickens and Frederick Marryat, but these failed to capture the flavor of the originals. The only success in the twenties was a series made by Palladium, which was established in 1921, of farcical comedies directed by Lau Lauritzen (1878–1938) with Carl Schenström (1881–1942) and Harald Madsen (1890–1949) appearing as "Fyrtårnet og Bivognen" ("Long and Short" in England), which proved popular around the world except for the United States.

Nordisk Films, which fell behind Palladium in the twenties, was liquidated in 1928 and reorganized by Carl Bauder, a banker who obtained the rights to the sound on disk system developed by Danish engineers Petersen and Poulsen. Sound films, while allowing Danish audiences to hear their own language in films, virtually ended the marketability of Danish films elsewhere. With poor scripts, old-fashioned technique, lack of operating capital, and a hefty 40 percent tax on cinema tickets, producers struggled to make even modest films. (Some films, deemed to be of national importance, were not taxed.) Producers complained that a film costing on the average DKr 150,000 had to be seen by 600,000 people to make a profit. Summing up the thirties, Danish film historian Ib Monty has written, "virtually no Danish film then made is of any interest today except as a document of the popular taste of a bygone era." This taste included comedies, melodramatic literary films, and folksy tales. Nevertheless, the Danish public liked the films, which were exhibited in nearly every theatre, while foreign productions rarely reached the smaller theatres. A U.S. government report noted in 1938, "For the average Danish film fan, attending a domestic film is comparable to looking at the family album." During the thirties a few new companies were created including Minerva, which produced documentaries; Asa Film; and Dansk Filmkompagni. Some films were made at Swedish studios and with Swedish financial interests.

The better films of the decade include *Palo Brudef oerd/Palo's Wedding,* shot in 1931–1933 by the explorer Dr. Knut Rasmussen in East Greenland with Angmagsalik Eskimos; two films by former cameraman George Schneevoigt, *Fredløs* (1936) and *Lajla* (1937), both of which dealt with Lapp life; and two films by Benjamin Christensen, *Skilsmissens Børn/Children of Divorce* (1939) and *Barnet/The Child* (1940), concerning abortion.

Government support for film production began with a law effective April 1, 1933, stipulating that fees collected for censorship would be used to support the distribution and production of Danish cultural and educational films. The Social Democratic party pushed for central government control of production, distribution and importation. The government responded with a new cinema law effective April 15, 1938, which established a Filmsradet (Film Council) to advise the government on all aspects of the film industry and a Film Fund to further the exhibition of educational, cultural, and artistic films with most of its revenue coming from the 40 percent ticket tax. The Fund provided documentary filmmakers the opportunity to subversively produce films to support the national interest during the Nazi occupation, which began in April 1940. Dansk Kulturfilm, formed by the government in 1932 to produce educational and children's films, and Ministeriernes Filmudvalg (Government Film Committee), established in 1941 to make films on behalf of all government departments, were the leading documentary producers. Influenced by the British documentary movement, filmmakers Mogens Skot-Hensen, Theodore Christensen (born 1914), Karl Roos (born 1914), Johan Jacobsen, Bjarne (born 1908) and Astrid Henning-Jensen (born 1914), Ole Palsbo, and others made over 150 documentaries that kept Danes in touch with their culture. After the war, British documentary producer and director Arthur Elton (born 1906) came as an adviser. Documentaries about the resistance were made in the next few years, but as the fifties approached, many documentarists became feature filmmakers. Since the fifties, a number of documentarists, including Jørgen Leth (born 1937), Jon Bang Carlsen, and Franz Ernst have continued producing outstanding works, some of which have expanded the reach of documentary films.

As a whole, the occupation and the war spurred Danish filmmakers to improve the quality of their films. Dreyer returned to filmmaking during the war when Mogens Skot-Hensen, in charge of production at the Government Film Committee, asked him to produce a documentary on the Mother Help Organization which aided married and unwed mothers. In 1943 he directed for Palladium

Vredens Dag/Day of Wrath, his first dramatic film in a decade. Although it received mixed reviews, the film is now considered an artistic masterpiece.

On August 1, 1946, the entertainment tax was raised to 60 percent of the net price of a ticket making it the highest in the world (although ticket prices in Denmark remained the lowest). From this increase, DKr 500,000 was earmarked by the government for production grants to be administered by Udvalget til stotte af Dansk filmproduktion (the Committee for the Support of Danish Film Production). The grants, which only went to exceptional films, were replaced when legislation passed in November 1949 allowed all producers to recoup 25 percent of the entertainment tax and to have cinema licenses.

The productions of the fifties were for the most part undistinguished folksy dramas, popular comedies, and social problem films. Dreyer's *Ordet/The Word,* made in 1955 for Palladium, stood far above anything else and was regarded highly throughout the world.

French "new wave" films, which began in 1960 to be shown in Denmark, inspired a renaissance that elevated personal expression to the fore in the work of filmmakers such as director Palle Kjaerulff-Schmidt and author Klaus Rifberg, who together made *Weekend* in 1962, *To/Two* in 1964 and *Taenk på et tal/Once There Was a War* in 1969, regarded as one of the best Danish films made in that decade. Henning Carlsen (born 1927), a documentarist who turned to features and perhaps became Denmark's most famous director, made *Sult/Hunger* in 1966 and *Man sku' vaere noget ved musikken/Oh, To Be on the Bandwagon!* in 1972. A neorealist movement began in the late sixties with Sven and Lene Grønlykke, who made *Balladen om Carl Henning/The Ballad of Carl-Henning*; Henrik Stangerup; and Franz Ernst. The seventies and eighties saw the impressive continuation of the career of Astrid Henning-Jensen and the first films of Bille August, Erik Clausen, Lars von Trier, whose first film *Forbrydelsens element/The Element of Crime,* made while he was a student at the Danish Film School, won an award at Cannes, and Gabriel Axel, whose *Babette's Feast* was a 1987 nominee for an Academy Award.

The rise in the quality of films was made possible partly by developments in the laws concerning government subsidizing. On January 1, 1965, a new Cinema Act became effective which replaced the entertainment tax, which had dropped to 27 percent, with a levy of 15 percent on the price charged for admissions, most of which was used to support production through the newly created Danish Government Film Foundation, an eight-member board appointed by the Ministry of Cultural Affairs, which was set up in 1961. The Film Foundation, which was also supported by a sliding scale tax on cinema licenses, provided grants to scriptwriters, production loan guarantees, usually amounting to about 50 percent of a film's budget, and awards to films of outstanding quality which were selected by the Film Council, which could also veto the Film Foundation's grants. In addition, the Short Film Committee was set up to support short films, most of which were shown on television.

The Film Foundation was replaced by the Danish Film Institute after the Cinema Act of 1972 took effect. The ticket levy and the cinema license system was abolished, and the Film Institute became financed directly by the Treasury. The Film Institute has since acquired the old Asa Film Studio, now named the Danish Film Studio, which they make available to both foreign and domestic production companies. In 1987, DKr 56.1 million, in addition to DKr 6.5 million from Danish radio (approximately $7 million) was used to provide 70 percent to 80 percent of the budget of eleven feature films. Twenty five percent of the funds available for production are to be used for children's films. Between 1981 and 1984, only one of thirty-four supported features made enough money to start repayment.

The advisory board of the Film Council was replaced according to the 1972 Act (which was amended in 1977 and 1982) by three consultants; the recommendation of one is needed for production grants to be accepted. (One of the consultants only reviews grants for children's films.) In 1987, virtually every Danish film made received government support. The decisions of the consultants, appointed for terms of three years by the Minister of Culture, have been criticized and alternative systems have been studied by the Danish Parliament. At the end of 1987, the passing of a new film law, which would allow films without artistic merit to receive grants if they could be matched, was being debated.

Film censorship, which was conducted by a committee beginning in 1913, was abolished for adults in 1969. Exhibition in Denmark was controlled by the Ministry of Justice since the law of March 17, 1922. Licenses were granted only to Danish citizens, and only one cinema was allowed per person. As of 1938, the licensee had explicit artistic responsibility for the choice of films, and schools and cultural organizations had the right to use cinemas during hours when they were not being used for regular performances. When the license system was abolished in 1972, the regulation restricting chains of cinemas also ended, and some distribution companies acquired cinemas. Because of competition from television, cinema attendance dropped 50 percent between 1948 and 1963. By 1987, when 202 cinemas were operating, a number of cinemas had closed in the small towns as competition from the video market grew. About two-thirds of the films exhibited in Denmark are now imported; half of these are American.

The idea of a national archive was discussed in the late thirties; in November 1941 it was established and run by Dansk Kulturfilm until 1950 when a museum was approved. In 1965, the Danish Film Museum became an independent institution under the Ministry of Cultural Affairs. The Museum now has more than 13,000 films, including nearly 650 Danish features; publishes the journal *Kosmorama;* and is a member of FIAF*.

The Danish National Film School, funded by the Ministry of Cultural Affairs, was opened in September 1966. Located in Christianshavn in Copenhagen, it provides a four-year course of instruction for about twenty-five students.

BIBLIOGRAPHY

Bergsten, Bebe. *The Great Dane and the Great Northern Film Company*. Los Angeles: Locare Research Group, 1973.

Bordwell, David. *The Films of Carl-Theodor Dreyer*. Berkeley: University of California Press, 1981.

"Danish Film Institute Stimulates the Art," *The Hollywood Reporter,* April 16, 1980, pp. S8–S10.

Danish Films. Copenhagen: Danish Film Institute and Ministry of Foreign Affairs of Denmark, 1973.

Engberg, Marguerite, *Den danske stumfilm 1903–1930*. Copenhagen: Det danske Filmmuseum, 1968.

———. *Registrat over danske film 1896–1914*. Copenhagen: Institute for filmvidenskab, 1977.

Film Centre, London. *The Film Industry in Six European Countries*. Paris: UNESCO, 1950.

Hardy, Forsyth. *Scandinavian Film*. London: Falcon Press, 1952.

"I.F.G. Dossier: Scandinavian Cinema Now," in *International Film Guide 1988,* editor Peter Cowie. London: Tantivy Press, 1987, pp. 33–47.

Iverson, Ebbe, "Denmark," in *International Film Guide 1988,* editor Peter Cowie. London: Tantivy Press, 1987, pp. 159–166.

Mottram, Ron. *The Danish Cinema before Dreyer*. Metuchen, N.J.: Scarecrow Press, 1988.

Neergaard, Ebbe, "The Rise, the Fall, and the Rise of Danish Film," *Hollywood Quarterly,* Spring 1950, pp. 217–232.

DEULIG are the initials by which the Deutsche Lichtbildgeselschaft (German Cinematographic Company) is best known. It was founded in November 1916 by Ludwig Klitzsch and Alfred Hugenberg to produce and distribute German films aimed at counteracting Allied film propaganda. The company remained in existence after the end of the First World War, and in 1920 commenced the production of fictional features. It was similar in function to BUFA (Bild-und-Filmamt*/Photographic and Film Office), which was established in January 1917 by the German Supreme Command.

DEUTSCHE FILM- UND FERNSEHAKADEMIE BERLIN GmbH. Opened in September 1966, the Deutsche Film- und Fernsehakademie Berlin was created by the West German government. Among its graduates are Marianne Lüdcke, Wolfgang Petersen, and Christian Ziewer.

Address: Pommernallee 1, D-1000 Berlin 19, West Germany.

DINOCITTA was the name of the studio built by producer Dino De Laurentiis (born 1919) in 1959 on 115 acres of land just outside of Rome. The facility closed in 1972 because of the gradual demise of American films being shot in Italy.

BIBLIOGRAPHY

Werba, Hank, "Not the End but Beginning," *Variety,* July 5, 1972, pp. 23, 25.

THE DIORAMA, a form of precinema entertainment, was invented by Louis Daguerre (1787–1851). It was first seen in Paris in a specially designed building in 1822. It consisted of a series of paintings on transparencies that were viewed by the audience under changing lights as they slowly revolved. Diorama entertainments quickly became popular in other European cities.

BIBLIOGRAPHY

Ceram, C.W. *Archaeology of the Cinema*. New York: Harcourt, Brace & World, undated (1985).

Cook, Olive. *Movement in Two Dimensions*. London: Hutchinson, 1963.

DISCINA was the first major French production company to be formed by André Paulvé (1899–1982). In the forties and fifties, it was responsible for a number of major French features, including *Les visiteurs du soir/The Devil's Envoy* (1942), *Lumière d'été* (1943), *L'eternel retour/The Eternal Return* (1943), *La belle et la bête/Beauty and the Beast* (1946), *Sylvie et le fantôme/Sylvie and the Phantom* (1950), *Orphée/Orpheus* (1950), and *Les vacances de Monsieur Hulot/ Mr. Hulot's Holiday* (1953). Paulvé established an American distribution company, Discina International Film Corporation, that handled the U.S. release of many of his films.

THE "DOCTOR" SERIES. Mild and lightweight, the "doctor" series were popular British comedies, produced between 1954 and 1970. The first three and the fifth film in the series—*Doctor in the House* (1954), *Doctor at Sea* (1955), *Doctor at Large* (1957), and *Doctor in Distress* (1963)—all starred Dirk Bogarde as Dr. Simon Sparrow and James Robertson Justice as Sir Lancelot Spratt. Justice was also featured in the remaining films in the series: *Doctor in Love* (1960), *Doctor in Clover* (1965), and *Doctor in Trouble* (1970). The films were based on characters in the novels of Richard Gordon; all were directed by Ralph Thomas and produced by Betty Box for the Rank Organization*. Dirk Bogarde starred in the 1959 feature, *The Doctor's Dilemma,* but that is based on the play by George Bernard Shaw and has nothing to do with the series.

DOCUMENTO was a major Italian production company, headed by Gianni Hecht Lucari, founded in 1974. It ceased operations in 1974 with debts of between $3 and $10 million. Among the hundred features and 1,200 documentaries with which Documento was involved, the best known is probably Vittorio De Sica's *Il giardino dei Finzi-Contini/The Garden of the Finzi-Continis* (1971).

BIBLIOGRAPHY

"Banks Foreclose Documento, a major Italian Film Prod. Co.," *Variety,* October 23, 1974, pp. 81–82.

THE DOLIMITI FILM PRODUCTION COMPANY was created in Italy in the late thirties by Luciano Emmer, his wife Tatina Granding, and Enrico Gras to produce experimental and avant-garde art films. When its efforts were attacked by the Mussolini government, the company moved to Switzerland, but returned to Italy after the Second World War, where it produced, among others, *Racconto da un affresco/The Story of a Mural* (1946) and *Paradise Terrestre* (1946).

BIBLIOGRAPHY

Margolis, Herbert F., "Luciano Emmer and the Art Film," *Sight & Sound*, vol. XVI, no. 61, Spring 1947, pp. 1–3.

THE DOMINICAN REPUBLIC has a small film industry, primarily devoted to short subjects, and filmmakers include Jean Louis Jorge, José Luis Sáez, Agliberto Meléndez, Winston Vargas, Adelso Cass, Martin López, Max Rodríguez, and Pedro Guzmán. A film school was established in 1979 at the Universidad Autónoma de Santo Domingo. There were 22 theatres in the country in 1937, rising to 150 in 1987, of which 6 are in the capital, Santo Domingo. The biggest exhibitor/distributor is Wometco, followed by Cine-Film S.A. and Cinema Centro. The republic is utilized for some location shooting, following encouragement from the Ministry of Tourism, which led to the filming there of Alberto Lattuada's *Christopher Columbus* (1985).

BIBLIOGRAPHY

Hidalgo, Hildebrando, "Dominican Republic," in *International Film Guide 1986*, editor Peter Cowie. London: Tantivy Press, 1985, p. 122.

THE DREYFUS AFFAIR, involving the court martial of Captain Alfred Dreyfus (1859–1935), which led to Emile Zola's famous 1898 article, "J'Accuse," has been the subject of French films in 1899 (by Georges Méliès), 1908, and 1939 (*J'Accuse*, directed by Abel Gance). It was covered in the 1939 Warner Bros. feature, *The Life of Emile Zola*, and a 1957 M-G-M feature, *I Accuse*, as well as a 1931 British feature and a 1935 German production.

DUBLIN. The capital of the republic of Ireland was seen on American screens as early as 1912 in Vitagraph's *Scenes of Irish Life in Dublin. Ireland in Revolt* (1921) included footage of the devastation in Dublin from the 1916 Easter Rebellion and the later activities of the Black and Tans. The city is often utilized as a stand-in for Belfast, where filmmaking has become increasingly impossible because of the activities of the Irish Republican Army. It was seen to advantage in the Gene Wilder vehicle, *Quackser Fortune Has a Cousin in the Bronx* (1970), and in two James Joyce adaptations, *Finnegan's Wake* (1964) and *Ulysses* (1967).

DUFAYCHROME is a three-color subtractive process, in many respects similar to Technicolor, that had some popularity in the United Kingdom in the thirties and forties. It used a geometrical color-screen or *réseau* imprinted on the film base. Unlike the American Technicolor process, the system required no major changes in the equipment used in its photographing, processing, or projecting. It had its origins in the experiments of French photographer Louis Dufay between 1910 and 1917, and was developed by the British paper manufacturer, Spicers

Ltd., which, in 1932, formed Spicer-Dufay Ltd. A year later, the name of the company was changed to Dufaycolor Ltd. The first major British film to be shot in Dufaycolor was *Radio Parade* (1934). In 1937, the company name was changed, yet again, to Dufay-Chromex Ltd. In 1948, this company took over rights to an earlier British color process, British Tricolour.

Although Dufaychrome was utilized in a number of European countries, India, and South Africa, it made little impact in the United States, where the process was handled by Dufaycolor Company Inc. A complete list of British Dufaycolor and Dufaychrome films may be found in John Huntley's *British Technicolor Films* (London: Skelton Robinson, undated).

BIBLIOGRAPHY

Carson, W.H., "The English Dufaycolor Film Process," *Journal of the Society of Motion Picture Engineers,* vol. XXIII, no. 1, July 1934, pp. 14–20.

Cornwell-Cline, Major Adrian. *Colour Cinematography*. London: Chapman & Hall, 1951.

DUFAYCOLOR. See DUFAYCHROME

DYNAMIC FRAME is a concept advocated by Soviet director Sergei Eisenstein (1898–1948) in an essay, "The Dynamic Square" in *Close-Up* (March-June 1931). Eisenstein argued that filmmakers should not be limited by the standard size of the film frame or by recently introduced widescreen frame sizes. He felt that the frame size should be governed by the subject matter.

E

EADY LEVY. In the late forties, British film producers had the problem of recouping the costs of their films further compounded by a particularly high entertainment tax of approximately 37 percent, which hived off a large percentage of box-office revenue. As a result, the British Production Fund was established in an attempt to ensure that at least some of the box-office revenue would reach the producers who would, in turn, put the money back into filmmaking. The Fund, or Eady Money, as it was generally known after the civil servant Sir Wildred Eady who devised the scheme, was introduced on a voluntary basis in 1950. When theatres proved to be less than enthusiastic about participating, contribution was made compulsory under the Cinematograph Films Act of 1957. The system continued until 1985. With certain minor exceptions, the Levy was paid on every theatre ticket sold, and at the time of its abolition, it was one-twelfth of the ticket price, net of VAT (Value Added Tax).

The Levy was collected each month by Customs and Excise and paid over to the British Film Fund Agency, which was responsible for its administration. After deducting the costs of collecting and administering the Fund, grants were made to the Children's Film and Television Foundation*, the National Film and Television School*, and the British Film Institute's Production Board. The remaining money was divided among eligible British films by placing the amount of money earned in a particular year by a British film against the amount of Eady money available for distribution, and a percentage rate worked out. The producer received payment for an eligible film in proportion to the amount his film earned at the box office. At the end of 1979, a restriction was introduced in that no feature was allowed to earn more than half-a-million pounds.

The method of allocating Eady money was frequently criticized as most of it went to those companies that had already been adequately rewarded at the box office and did not need additional boosting of their profits. Interpretation of the regulations was such that a film made by a foreign company, working through a British registered company and utilizing a British cast, crew, and facilities, was eligible for Eady money. In the late sixties, it was estimated that 80 percent of Eady money actually went to American companies. There was also harsh criticism of the automatic dispersal of money, regardless of the quality of the films; sex-exploitation features, for example, were sizeable earners of Eady money. Indeed, it appeared that those who benefited least were the independent filmmakers trying to make good quality, British films, but unable to obtain wide distribution, and therefore ineligible for Eady money. The government ended the Eady Levy in 1985, with the passing of the 1985 Film Act.

BIBLIOGRAPHY

Wood, Linda, editor. *British Film Industry*. Information Guide No. 1. London: British Film Institute, 1980.

———. *Film/Video Production and Funding*. London: British Film Institute, 1984.

EALING STUDIOS. The construction of Ealing Studios—the first to be custom built for sound in the United Kingdom—began in 1931 under the supervision of Basil Dean, a theatrical producer–turned–film magnate who headed Associated Talking Pictures (ATP). Situated in a leafy suburb of West London, the studios had the air of a family business, with their administrative block, flanked by a rose garden, looking more like a country cottage. During the early and mid-thirties, ATP produced competent versions of plays and popular novels, as well as entertaining comedies starring Gracie Fields and George Formby. Big changes occurred in 1938, when Michael Balcon replaced Dean as head of production, and the name of Associated Talking Pictures was phased out in favor of Ealing Studios. Paternalism was still very much the basis on which the studios were run. Gracie Fields had been lured to Hollywood, and a new kind of realism began to emerge, especially in those films directed by Pen Tennyson. This realism continued through the war years, which saw the production of Pen Tennyson's *Convoy* (1940), Charles Frend's *The Foreman Went to France* (1942), Cavalcanti's *Went the Day Well* (1942), Harry Watt's *Nine Men* (1943), and Charles Crichton's *For Those in Peril* (1944).

At the end of the war, Ealing secured a deal with J. Arthur Rank which gave the company a secure future and a guaranteed release of its films on the Rank circuit. With the postwar years came Ealing's richest period when the famous comedies emerged. Three were produced in 1949: *Passport to Pimlico,* in which the inhabitants of the London district of Pimlico declare themselves an independent state; *Whiskey Galore* (U.S. *Tight Little Island),* in which Hebridean islanders clash over whiskey purloined from a wrecked boat; and *Kind Hearts and Coronets,* in which Dennis Price, a shop clerk, tries to rid himself of eight relatives, all played by Alec Guinness, who stand between him and an earldom. Other perennial Ealing favorites are *The Ladykillers* (1955), in which a bizarre gang of criminals delude their landlady, played by Katie Johnson, that they are musicians rehearsing a Boccherini minuet; and *The Lavender Hill Mob* (1951), in which a mild-mannered bank clerk, Alec Guinness again, thinks he has a fool-proof plan to relieve his employer of £1 million worth of gold bullion. There were also rich human dramas during this same period: *It Always Rains on Sunday* (1947), *The Blue Lamp* (1949), *Pool of London* (1951), *The Cruel Sea* (1952), and *Mandy* (1952).

However, as the fifties progressed, the Ealing formulas began to falter, and, in 1955, the studios were sold to the British Broadcasting Corporation. In 1956, Balcon managed to reestablish Ealing Films at M-G-M's British studios at Boreham Wood, but this arrangement lasted for only three years, after which the Ealing team broke up and went their separate ways.

BIBLIOGRAPHY

Balcon, Michael. *Michael Balcon Presents: A Lifetime of Films*. London: Hutchinson, 1969.

Barr, Charles. *Ealing Studios*. London: David & Charles, 1977.

Brown, George, "Ealing, Your Ealing," *Sight & Sound,* vol. XLVI, no. 3, Summer 1977, pp. 164–176.

Fluegel, Jane, editor. *Michael Balcon: The Pursuit of British Cinema*. New York: Museum of Modern Art, 1984.

Perry, George. *Forever Ealing: A Celebration of the Great British Film Studio*. London: Pavilion/Michael Joseph, 1981.

Pickard, Roy, "The Ealing Story," *Films in Review,* vol. XXVI, no. 2, February 1975, pp. 101–107.

Wilson, David. *Projecting Britain: Ealing Studios Film Posters*. London: British Film Institute, 1982.

ECLAIR. The Société Française des Films et Cinématographes Eclair was founded in 1907 with a capitalization of Fr 500,000 as a modestly sized rival to the leading French companies Pathé* and Gaumont*. With Charles Jourjon as chairman of the board and associate director Marcel Vandal, Eclair took over the small production house of Parnaland et Ventujol, founded in 1896 that made cameras and began producing intermittently in 1904. Eclair purchased the grounds and chateau of the famous eighteenth-century French naturalist Bernard Lacépède at Epinay-sur-Seine, a suburb of Paris, and built a studio amidst the forty acres of parks, terraces, water, forests, and meadows that provided beautiful settings for the many outdoor scenes in Eclair's films.

In April 1907, Victorin Jasset (1868–1913) was hired as artistic director along with his colleague Georges Hatot. Jasset, well known as director of the Hippodrome, was trained as a sculptor and had a varied theatrical career as a fan painter, costume designer, composer of ballets, and director and writer of pantomimes, large festivals, parades, and cavalcades, before directing for many of the other French film companies. Film historian Georges Sadoul called Jasset the best and most intelligent director of 1908.

In September 1908, Eclair released the first series in film history, Jasset's *Nick Carter,* based on the popular American detective novels. Actor Liabel, who played Carter, became a romantic idol around the world even though his name was unknown to his fans. Following the immense success of the series, Eclair opened offices in New York, Berlin, Moscow, Vienna, and Milan and became one of the leading French companies.

Jasset followed with a number of other series including more Nick Carter stories, *Riffle Bill, le roi de la prairie/Rifle Bill* (1909), *Les Dragonnades sous Louis XIV/The Dragonnades under Louis XIV* (1909), *Morgan le Pirate/Morgan the Pirate* (1909), *Meskal le contrabandier* (1909), *Vantour de la Siria* (1909), *Zigomar* (1911), and *Protea* (1913). Eclair became known for their detective series, which helped establish an audience who attended the cinema on a regular basis to see stories featuring characters and actors with whom they were familiar.

After the success of rival Film d'Art's *L'Assassination du Duc de Guise/The Assassination of the Duke de Guise* (1908), an artistic spectacle with eminent stage actors based on a classic play, other French companies set up companies to make similar adaptations of proven stage successes. Eclair formed Théâtre-Film, replaced later by Association des Comédiens et Auteurs Dramatiques (ACAD), whose principal director was Émile Chautard (1881–1934). ACAD produced films based on works by Alfred de Musset, Balzac, and Molière, in addition to scenarios by actors in the troop. Chautard asked his former colleague in the Théâtre de la Renaissance, Maurice Tourneur (1876–1961), to join in 1911.

Eclair's films were acquiring a reputation for their excellent photography, especially those shot outdoors, and high quality. Besides detective stories and ACAD films, Eclair produced comedies with minor French comedian characters Gontran, Gravoche, and Willy; scenic, educational, historical, and dramatic films; the *Eclair Weekly* newsreel; and a group of over six hundred films on science and nature, some using footage shot through a microscope in their "Scientia" series. *The Moving Picture World* (September 12, 1908) noted "the class and quality of 'Eclair' films"; a reviewer of *Pirate's Honor* and *A Gust of Wind* (both 1908) commented that the "photographic quality is good and the action easy and natural, nothing is forced and the effects are well rendered. Both are entirely outdoor productions and the natural scenes are a pleasant departure from the surfeit of studio work to which we have been accustomed." A 1911 reviewer noted about a group of Eclair films that "it was a pleasure to notice a distinct advance in the highest branches of cinematography" (*The Moving Picture World*, January 21, 1911).

In 1911, Eclair built a factory and studio in Fort Lee, New Jersey, to produce, in Jourjon's words, "an American picture made the Eclair way." Chautard was sent to run the studio early in 1912, but because of his poor English, he was replaced by cameraman Étienne Arnaud. Jourjon's goal was to have French directors and technical staff work with American directors, scenarists, and players. Arnaud invited art director Ben Carré (1883–1978), who arrived in November 1912, and animator Émile Cohl (1857–1938), who came in September 1912. Cohl created thirteen cartoons between March 1913 and January 1914 featuring "Baby Snookums" in his *The Newlyweds* series, based on a *New York World* comic strip, which became the first cartoon series with characters appearing regularly. After Chautard suggested that Tourneur, who had acted in some of Jasset's films, assisted Chautard and directed his own films for Eclair, including

Le Mystère de la Chambre Jaune (1913), go to Fort Lee because he spoke English, Tourneur arrived in May 1914, and collaborating with Carré, soon established himself as one of the world's top directors. Other Frenchmen working at Fort Lee included Georges Benoit, Lucien Andriot (b. 1897), and René Guissart. The Americans there included Lawrence McGill, Will S. Rising, Wray Physioc, Barbara Tennant, Oscar Lund, Alec B. Francis (1869–1934), Bert Starkey, Stanley Walpole, and Clara Horton.

Meanwhile in France, Jasset made two films based on the exploits of the infamous Bande à Bonnot, the Bonnot gang of automobile bandits, *L'Auto grise/Auto Bandits of Paris* (1912) and *Hors la loi*. Also in 1912, he began a series of social dramas *Les Battailles de la vie,* which included the realistic drama *Au pays des ténèbres,* inspired by Zola's *Germinal,* and shot in the coal-mining regions of the North, *Redemption* (1912), *Le saboteur* (1913), *La terre:le testament* (1913), *Une campagne de presse* (1913) and others which were on the whole unsuccessful. Jasset returned to the detective series with *Zigomar contre Nick Carter/Zigomar vs. Nick Carter* (1912), *Zigomar peau d'anguille* (1913), and *Protea I,* which he was making when he became ill and died. Hardly any of Jasset's work has survived.

In November 1913, the Fort Lee studio sent a company to Tucson, Arizona, under the direction of Webster Cullison to start a Western studio. After a disastrous fire at the Fort Lee plant in March 1914 which destroyed the factory and many prints and negatives, including all of the American animated films of Émile Cohl who returned to France just before the fire, some of the company, including Tourneur, went to the Peerless studio, also in Fort Lee, while the rest went to Tucson. By 1915, Eclair was located in Hollywood under the direction of general manager Robert Levy, but by October of that year, Levy had reorganized the company and taken it back to Tucson.

In France, before the First World War began, the parent factory, which employed eight hundred people, began manufacturing equipment including cameras, machines for coloring film, a device for continued focusing of objects in motion, a home projector, and a portable laboratory that fit into a two-foot square box. The war halted film production throughout France in August 1914. Eclair continued producing newsreels and sent their technical manager Georges Maurice to join cameramen from Pathé*, Gaumont*, and Eclipse* to form Service photographique et cinématographique de l'armée, created by the Minister of War to produce a weekly newsreel covering the war.

Gérard Bourgeoise, demobilized in 1915, joined Eclair and directed two episodes of *Protea*. Eclair lost its German branch and in August 1917, their studios were used by the American army.

After the war, Eclair gradually ended commercial film production, rented out their studios at Epinay-sur-Seine and concentrated on manufacturing equipment (their 16mm cameras are still being produced), film processing, and production of their newsreel *Eclair-Journal,* on which animator Lortak (Robert Collard) worked. In 1921, Eclair merged with Film d'Art, AGL, and a circuit of cinemas owned by Edmond Benoit-Levy to form the Campagnie Générale de Cinématographie, which produced only one film, *La rêve*.

BIBLIOGRAPHY

Abel, Richard. *French Cinema: the First Wave, 1915–1929*. Princeton, N.J.: Princeton University Press, 1984.

''American Eclair Studio,'' *The Moving Picture World,* October 7, 1911, pp. 24–25.

Bardèche, Maurice, and Robert Brasillach. *The History of Motion Pictures*. New York: Norton, The Museum of Modern Art, 1938.

Bush, W. Stephen, ''The Film in France,'' *The Moving Picture World,* July 12, 1913, pp. 179–181.

Crafton, Donald. *Before Mickey: The Animated Film 1898–1928*. Cambridge, Mass.: MIT Press, 1982.

''Eclair Company Now at Tucson, Arizona,'' *Motography,* October 30, 1915, p. 923.

''Eclair Factory Fire,'' *The Moving Picture World,* April 4, 1914, p. 45.

''Eclair Forces Go To Tucson,'' *The Moving Picture World,* July 25, 1914, p. 575.

''Eclair Players Out,'' *New York Dramatic Mirror,* July 15, 1914, p. 25.

''Eclair 'Scientia' Films,'' *Motography,* July 11, 1914, p. 62.

''Eclair Western Branch,'' *New York Dramatic Mirror,* November 12, 1913, p. 30.

Jourjon, Charles, ''Concerning Eclair Enterprises,'' *The Moving Picture World,* July 11, 1914, p. 207.

''New Eclair Artist,'' *The Moving Picture World,* November 30, 1912, p. 883.

Sadoul, Georges. *Histoire du cinéma mondial; des origines à nos jour*. Paris: Flammarion, 1949.

———. *Histoire générale du cinéma*. Vols. 2 and 3. Paris: Les Editions Denoel, 1947–1952.

''Some Notable Eclair Films,'' *The Moving Picture World,* January 21, 1911, p. 146.

THE ECLIPSE COMPANY was formed in the early years of this century by entrepreneur Charles Urban as an Anglo-French producing organization. It was amalgamated with the London-based Charles Urban Trading Company in 1907, but later became an independent French company, under the leadership of director Louis Mercanton. Eclipse produced a newsreel for release in both the United Kingdom and France. In 1919, it built a new studio at Boulogne-sur-Seine for use as a rental facility. It ceased production in 1920, but continued in existence for a number of years as a distributor of films featuring René Navarre, René Cresté, and Suzanne Grandais.

L'ÉCRAN FRANÇAIS was a French production company, founded in 1943 and active throughout the decade. Its first feature was *Premier de Cordée* (1943), but its best known production was Claude Autant-Lara's *Sylvie et la Fantôme/Sylvie and the Phantom* (1944).

ECUADOR has no feature film industry, but an average of fifteen short subjects a year were produced there in the eighties. These shorts are seen in Ecuadorian theatres through an agreement between the government and the Association of

Filmmakers of Ecuador (ASOCINE), whereby theatres screening the shorts are exempt from municipal taxation.

There were thirty-four theatres in the country in 1937, rising to 190 in 1983, with the majority located in Quito and Guayaquil. Censorship is minimal. Ecuador was the first Latin American country to permit release of *Last Tango in Paris* (1973).

BIBLIOGRAPHY

Attwood, A.W., "The Cinema in Guayaquil," *Sight & Sound,* vol. XVI, no. 61, Spring 1947, p. 14.

"Ecuador's Situation Not Great, But It Could be a Lot Worse," *Variety,* March 30, 1983, p. 36.

THE EDINBURGH FILM GUILD was a film society founded in 1930 by Forsyth Hardy and Norman Wilson. It published the intellectual journal, *Cinema Quarterly,* from 1932 to 1935.

EFFTEE FILM PRODUCTIONS. One of the most important of early Australian sound film producers, Efftee Film Productions was founded in 1931 by F.W. Thring, former managing director of Hoyts Theatres. Its first studios were located at His Majesty's Theatre, Melbourne, with a later studio, Wattle Path, in St. Kildare, Victoria. The company ceased operations in the mid-thirties, largely because the government of the state of Victoria refused to adopt a quota system that would have aided local film production.

The following is a complete list of Efftee's features: *A Co-Respondent's Course* (1931), *Diggers* (1931), *The Haunted Room* (1931), *His Royal Highness* (1932), *The Sentimental Bloke* (1932), *Harmony Row* (1932), *Clara Gibbings* (1934), and *A Ticket in Tatts* (1934).

EGYPT is the only Arab country and, along with South Africa, the only African nation with a substantial film heritage. Films were screened in Egypt as early as 1896, and theatre owners in Alexandria and Cairo produced the country's first short subjects in 1913 and 1915 respectively. The first Egyptian feature was *Laila* (1927), directed by Ahmed Galal and starring stage actress Aziza Emir. The following year, another actress, Assia Dagher, produced and starred in a second feature directed by Galal, and a third feature, produced by and starring Fatma Rouchdi, was also released. Interestingly, both Emir and Dagher remained in the film industry, and, by 1950, Dagher was heading the Lotus Film Company and Emir was head of the Isis Film Company.

The first Egyptian sound on disc film, *Moonlight,* was directed by Shoukri Madi in 1929. The first sound on film features from Egypt were *Song of the Heart,* directed by M. Volpi, and *Sons of Nobility,* directed by Mohamed Karim, both released in 1931. The first Egyptian sound studios were Studios Misr, opened in 1935, and Studio Wahby, opened in 1937.

Important directors of the thirties were Mohamed Karim, Togo Mizrahi, Ibrahim Lama, and Ahmed Galal, while the most popular screen actor was Fawzi El-Gazaierly appearing as the comic character, "Mr. Bahbah." Leading Egyptian directors of the forties include Kamel Selim, Henry Barakat, Ahmed Badrakhan, Youssef Bey Wahby, and Saad Nadim (who specialized in short subjects).

By 1986, it was the Egyptian film industry's proud claim that it had produced some 2,250 feature films.

The government first became involved in the film industry in 1952, with the overthrow of the monarchy, when the Ministry of National Culture and Social Guidance sought to encourage the production of quality films. A State Broadcasting Authority was created in 1960, and, in 1981, the Ministry of Culture established the Egyptian Film Fund to subsidize the production and exhibition of Egyptian films. Government nationalization of sectors of the film industry led to a decline in the number of films produced per year from an average of ninety to fifty (by 1971). The nationalization process began in 1963 with the establishment of six companies in the areas of production and distribution. In 1966, these companies were reformed as two organizations, the Cairo Cinema Company, and the Cairo Distribution Company, with the National Centre for Documentary Films being formed a year later. In 1971, a new body, the Organization of Cinema, Theatre, and Music was created.

By the eighties, the Egyptian film industry was dominating the Arab world, producing an average of seventy features a year, primarily for release on video. (By the mid-eighties only 160 film theatres were operating in the country.) Egypt's leading actor, aside from Omar Sharif, is comedian Adel Imam. Independent production companies are once again flourishing, with women such as Magda El-Sabah, Madiha Kamel, and Faten Farid following in the footsteps of the pioneering female producers of the Egyptian film industry. Leading directors include Daoud Abdel-Sayed, Ashraf Fahmi, Mohamed Khan, Ali Abdel Khalek, Salah Abou Seif, Kamal El Sheikh, and Rafaat El Mini.

Film censorship in Egypt is strictly enforced. The most famous incident of government action came following the 1983 televizing of Columbia Pictures' mini-series, *Sadat*. The Egyptian government objected so strongly to the production that it banned all films produced or distributed by Columbia from January 1984. The ban was partially lifted in September 1986.

BIBLIOGRAPHY

Borsten, Joan, "Egypt Films: Dearth on the Nile," *Los Angeles Times Calendar*, January 6, 1980, pp. 3–4.

———, "Films Lead Egyptian Women out of the Wilderness," *Los Angeles Times Calendar*, February 22, 1981, pp. 1, 6.

"Cairo's Booming Cinema," *News Front*, November 1965, p. 42.

El-Mazzaoui, Farid, "Film in Egypt," *Hollywood Quarterly*, vol. IV, no. 3, Spring 1950, pp. 245–250.

Kamphausen, Hannes, "Cinema in Africa: A Survey," *Cineaste*, vol. V, no. 3, Summer 1972, pp. 29–41.

Tuohy, William, "Egyptian Film Industry Falls on Hard Times—Tries Comeback," *The Journal of the Producers Guild of America,* vol. XIII, no. 2, June 1971, pp. 23–25.

Werba, Hank, "Egypt Pyramids New Hopes for Film Biz," *Variety,* December 30, 1981, pp. 3, 7.

———, "Cairo Hopes to Regain Former Arab World Lead," *Variety,* May 12, 1982, pp. 390, 440.

EIRE. Although films had first been screened in Ireland on April 20, 1896, the country has no great filmmaking tradition, and it is only in recent years that Irish films have achieved any international reputation.

The earliest films to be shot in Ireland were newsreels, with one of the first being of the 1900 visit of Queen Victoria to Dublin. The American Kalem Company first came to Ireland, on a filmmaking trip, in 1910, and since then American and British filmmakers have taken advantage of Irish scenery for films as varied as *Henry V* (1945) and *Ryan's Daughter* (1970). Some of the earliest Irish fictional films are *The Life of St. Patrick* (1913), *In the Days of St. Patrick* (1920), and *Cruiskeen Lawn* (1922). The Film Company of Ireland, formed by Irish-American lawyer, James Mark Sullivan, was active in the late teens, producing *O'Neil of the Glens* (1916), *Widow Malone* (1917), *Knocknagow* (1918), and *Willy Reilly and His Colleen Bawn* (1918), among others.

The Celtic Film Company produced one feature in 1920, *Rosaleen Dhu,* and, in 1924, John Hurley produced *Land of Her Fathers,* whose cast included Barry Fitzgerald and Micheál Mac Liammoir. The last Irish silent feature was *Irish Destiny* (1927), written and directed by Dr. I.J. Eppel.

The first Irish sound film, *The Voice of Ireland,* was produced by Victor Haddick in 1932, but the first major Irish sound feature was *The Dawn,* filmed in Killarney in 1936 by Tom Cooper. Despite isolated filmmaking in the thirties and forties, there was no major development in the Irish film industry until 1958, when Ardmore Studios* were founded.

A new Irish cinema—although there was no such thing as an old Irish cinema—sprang forth in the eighties, with directors such as Pat Murphy, Cathal Black, and, most importantly, Neil Jordan, making features that often dealt with the violence of Northern Ireland and were far removed from the traditional, stereotypical Irish image that the Hollywood film industry had sought to perpetuate.

The Irish government first concerned itself with film production in 1982, with the creation of the Irish Film Board (Bord Scannán n hÉireann or BSÉ). Its only other involvement has been in the form of heavy censorship, which dates back to 1924.

BIBLIOGRAPHY

McIllroy, Brian. *World Cinema 4: Ireland.* Trowbridge, United Kingdom: Flicks Books, 1988.

O Conluain, Proinsias. *Scéal na Scánnan.* Dublin: Oifig an tSoláthair, 1953.

O'Leary, Liam. *A Seat among the Stars: The Cinema and Ireland.* Belfast: Ulster Television, 1984.

Rockett, Kevin, Luke Gibbons, and John Hill. *Cinema and Ireland*. Beckenham, United Kingdom: Croom Helm, 1987.
Slide, Anthony. *The Cinema and Ireland*. Jefferson, N.C.: McFarland, 1988.

EL SALVADOR. See CENTRAL AMERICA

ELSTREE STUDIOS. In the mid-twenties, an enterprising American film executive named J.D. Williams arrived in England with an idea to produce films there. He purchased forty acres of land at Elstree, in Hertfordshire, believing this area of the country to be less prone to fog, a major problem to English film studios. The studios opened in 1926 as British National Studios, with Herbert Wilcox as director-in-chief, and he immediately went into production with *Madame Pompadour* (1928).

Williams departed for the United States following a financial crisis at the studios, which were acquired by distributor John Maxwell, who formed British International Pictures* and renamed the studios BIP. His first production was *The White Sheik* (1928). With the arrival of sound, the four stages at Elstree were redesigned as nine sound-proof stages, and here what is generally considered to be Britain's first "talkie," Alfred Hitchcock's *Blackmail* (1929), was shot. Hitchcock left the studios acrimoniously after the production of *The Skin Game* (1931).

Herbert Wilcox returned to Elstree, renting a couple of the sound stages for his company, British and Dominion Film Corporation. For *Goodnight Vienna* (1932), he signed actress/singer/dancer Anna Neagle, and so commenced a partnership which continued on screen and in private life for forty-five years. When fire swept the British and Dominion stages in February 1936, Wilcox moved his company to Pinewood Studios*.

After the completion of two hundred films at Elstree, the Second World War brought a close to production, and the studio was turned over to the production of camouflage materials and electronic devices for the war effort. It also housed the Garrison Theatre group.

In 1933, Maxwell had formed the Associated British Picture Corporation (ABPC), as a holding company for his business ventures, and following his death in 1940, it had been assumed his family would continue running the company. However, the bulk of the shares were acquired in 1946 by Warner Bros., which modernized the studios, and appointed director Robert Clark to supervise all film production. He fostered young talent and created a stable of actors and actresses at the studio. The first postwar film produced at Elstree was *Man on the Run* (1949), directed by Lawrence Huntington. It was followed by *The Hasty Heart* (1949), starring Richard Todd, and two Hollywood performers brought over for the film, Patricia Neal and Ronald Reagan. *The Dancing Years* (1949), with Dennis Price in the role created on stage by Ivor Novello, was the first musical in color produced at Elstree. The studio's biggest success came in 1954, with *The Dam Busters*. In the fifties and sixties, American and British stars who worked at Elstree included Gregory Peck, Errol Flynn, Diana Dors, Cary Grant, Ingrid Bergman, William Holden, Yvonne Mitchell, Sophia Loren, Laurence Olivier, John Mills, Tommy Steele, Tony Hancock, Warren Beatty, and Bette Davis.

In 1969, following a short, but fierce fight, controlling interest in ABPC was acquired by EMI, one of Britain's biggest and most influential conglomerates, and it brought a new head to the studio, director Bryan Forbes, who was named head of production and managing director. He spent less than two years there, during which time he launched an ambitious program of films which enjoyed only variable success. In 1970, the M-G-M British Studios at Boreham Wood were closed, but the company formed a joint association with EMI, and Elstree Studios were renamed EMI-MGM Elstree Studios Ltd.

Successes filmed there in the early seventies include *The Raging Moon* (U.S. *Long Ago Tomorrow,* 1971), *The Railway Children* (U.S. *The Secret Adventures of the Railway Children,* 1971), *The Boy Friend* (1971), *The Go-Between* (1971), and *Murder on the Orient Express* (1974). In the mid-seventies, it was decided to operate Elstree as a "facility" studio, and Andrew Mitchell was appointed managing director. Among the features filmed there at this time were ITC's *Voyage of the Damned* (1976), 20th Century-Fox's *Star Wars* (1977) and *Julia* (1977), and United Artists' *Valentino* (1977).

In 1979, the electrical giant, Thorn, acquired EMI, resulting in a name change to Thorn-EMI Screen Entertainment*, and a modernization program began at Elstree.

In 1984, Cannon Group acquired the studio, and among the producers working there were Steven Spielberg and George Lucas. Elstree was once again sold, in the summer of 1988, to the British investment consortium, Tranwood Earl, which announced plans to close the studios and develop the real estate potential of the lot. Despite efforts by political and film bodies to preserve the studios, the staff was informed that Elstree would close on October 28, 1988, with the last production to shoot there being Steven Spielberg's *Indiana Jones and the Last Crusade*.

Address: Shenley Road, Boreham Wood, Herts WD6 1JG, United Kingdom

BIBLIOGRAPHY

Banks, Leslie et al. *The Elstree Story: Twenty-One Years of Film-making*. London: Clerke and Cockeran, 1949.

Doyle, Terence, "Space To Dream," *Films and Filming,* no. 391, April 1987, pp. 16–18.

Firth, Vincent, "Elstree's 50 Glorious Years," *Film Review,* vol. XXVI, no. 11, November 1976, pp. 30–33.

———. "Elstree's 50 Glorious Years, Part 2," *Film Review,* vol. XXVI, no. 12, December 1976, pp. 34–37.

Low, Rachael. *Film Making in Britain*. London: George Allen & Unwin, 1985.

Pickard, Roy, "50 Years of 1930s Studios," *Photoplay Film Monthly,* vol. XXVI, no. 11, November 1976, pp. 42–47.

Warren, Patricia. *Elstree: The British Hollywood*. London: Elm Tree Books, 1983.

THE EMPIRE, LEICESTER SQUARE, is probably one of the best known of British theatres. It opened on November 8, 1928, although a theatre had stood on the site as early as 1884. During the Second World War, the theatre was the site of the initial screening of *Gone with the Wind,* a "must" for every serviceman. In the forties, the theatre attempted to model itself after Radio City Music Hall, billing itself as "The Showplace of the Nation," with *The Forsyte Saga* (1949), being the first film there to be presented with a complementary stage show. The Empire closed down on May 28, 1961, with *Ben-Hur,* but reopened as a new theatre and ballroom (in what had been the orchestra section) on December 19, 1962.

Address: Leicester Square, London W.C.2, United Kingdom.

BIBLIOGRAPHY

Eyles, Allen, "Empire Leicester Square," *Focus on Film,* no. 31, November 1978, pp. 48–50.

EMPIRE NEWS BULLETIN was a British newsreel produced from 1926 to 1930. Footage from the series is preserved and controlled by Visnews*.

ENTE AUTONOMO GESTIONE CINEMA (EAGC) is the name of the Italian holding company for Istituto LUCE* and Cinecittà*. The company was restructured in 1983, but in 1986 questions were raised as to whether the government would continue its funding.

Address: via Tuscolana 1055, 00173 Rome, Italy.

EON PRODUCTIONS. See "JAMES BOND" SERIES

E. RANCATI & CO. is Italy's foremost creator of props for both stage and screen. Founded in Milan by Edoardo Rancati in 1860, it began by building all the props for the Teatro alla Scala. It entered the film industry after the Second World War, when Edoardo's son, Angelo, opened an office in Rome.

Address: Via Ghisolfa 87, 20010 Cornaredo (Milan)/Via Luigi Pierantoni 6, 00 146 Rome, Italy.

BIBLIOGRAPHY

Hamblin, Dora Jane, "Make-Believe Can Be Good Business in Milan and Rome," *Smithsonian,* October 1985, pp. 132–142.

ESPERANTO. The universal language devised by L.L. Zamenhof in 1887, Esperanto has been utilized in one feature, *Incubus,* produced by Antony M. Taylor for Daystar, directed and written by Leslie Stevens, starring William Shatner, and first seen at the San Francisco Film Festival in October 1966. *Daily Variety* (October 31, 1966) was highly critical of the production, shot entirely on location in California's Big Sur country, commenting, "It is a pretentious piece of hocus-pocus of evil demons vs. good in the mythical land of Nomen Tuum. . . . Perhaps Esperanto loses something in translation. It sounds like Latin recited in a Brooklyn classroom, which also pretty well describes the performances director-writer Leslie Stevens gets from the cast, who learned their roles by phonetics.''

The film, which was screened with subtitles, was not well received by critics, the public, or Esperantists. Mark Starr, chairman of the Esperanto League for North America, wrote *Variety* (December 14, 1966) pointing out that Esperanto was in the public domain and could be used for any purpose without restriction, and that he and fellow Esperantists ''were distressed by the form as well as the content of the film.''

ESTONIA had limited film production in the twenties and thirties. Eesti Kultuurfilm produced some sixty films, virtually all short subjects, between 1937 and 1938. The number of theatres in the country increased from fifty-nine in 1928 to sixty-two in 1938. All imported films had to be approved for screening by the Estonian Film Inspector. Since the annexation of the country to the USSR in 1940, one studio, Tallinfilm, has been established there, for the production of features, cartoons, popular science subjects, and documentaries. The first Soviet films were made in Estonia in 1948.

ETABLISSEMENTS AUBERT. Headed by Louis Aubert, Etablissements Aubert was an early French distributor of foreign films; it introduced French audiences to the early comedies of Charlie Chaplin and the Italian epic, *Quo Vadis* (1913). In the early twenties, the company began distributing a number of French features, notably Jacques Feyder's *L'Atalantide* (1921). It remained in existence through most of the decade.

THE EUROPEAN ECONOMIC COMMUNITY (also known as the EEC or the Common Market) has adopted a number of regulations relating to the film industry in Europe. The regulations primarily relate to the abolition of quotas as to the numbers of domestic films that must be screened in any one country, government subsidy for theatres devoted exclusively to the screening of domestic films, and the obligation to ''dub'' films.

1988 was declared European Cinema and Television Year by the EEC.

EUROPEAN PARLIAMENT. On May 7, 1981, the European Parliament proposed the adoption of a resolution for ''the promotion of European cinema.'' It called for the establishment of a special organization to promote European cinema, the award of cash prizes for the best European films of the year, the preservation of European films, the defense of the integrity of films against ''editing for television,'' and the free circulation of films throughout Europe.

THE EVERYMAN CINEMA is located off Hampstead High Street in an area of northwest London, popular with artists, intellectuals and pseudointellectuals. It began life as a drill hall for the Hampstead Rifle Volunteers, but in 1920 it became a legitimate theatre, with its best-known production being Nöel Coward's *The Vortex*. The theatre folded in 1931, but on December 26, 1933, Jim Fairfax-Jones, a lawyer-turned-film buff, reopened it as a motion picture theatre, with the first film being René Clair's *Le Million*. Fairfax-Jones continued to run the theatre for the next forty years, hosting British premieres for a number of major foreign-language films, including Jean Vigo's *Zéro de Conduite,* Jean Renoir's *La Règle du Jeu/The Rules of the Game* and Donskoi's Maxim Gorky trilogy. The Everyman Cinema has not been too concerned with the screening of new films, but has operated almost like a film society open to the general public. It has presented seasons of films by Fritz Lang, Frank Capra, G.W. Pabst, and the Marx Brothers (favorites of Fairfax-Jones). The Everyman Cinema is very much a part of the local art scene; Fairfax-Jones' wife has run an art gallery in the foyer (where Paul Klee was given his first public showing), and the theatre participates in local arts festivals, serving as a venue for concerts.

When Fairfax-Jones died in 1972, the family tradition continued with son Martin running the theatre. In 1985, its future was in jeopardy when its lease came to an end and its owner, the Camden City Council, asked for a substantial increase in rent. As a result of a vigorous campaign, the Council granted a thirteen-year lease and, with the British Film Institute*, made it a grant for a new heating system. The Greater London Council gave it £41,500 for a facelift and Channel 4* provided £1,500 for a new screen and sound system.

Address: Holly Bush Vale, London N.W.3, United Kingdom.

BIBLIOGRAPHY

Powell, Dilys, "The Everyman," *Sight & Sound,* Summer 1955, p. 43.

EVE'S FILM REVIEW was the title of a theatrical news magazine produced for the screen by the British Pathé News from 1921–1933, and intended for women filmgoers. Footage from this series is preserved in the Pathé Library at Elstree Studios* (Shenley Road, Boreham Wood, Herts WD6 1JG, United Kingdom).

EXPRESSIONISM as an art form in theatre, music, and literature came into existence in Germany in the early years of the twentieth century. It was promoted, in the teens, by the magazine *Sturm,* and eventually influenced German filmmakers, beginning with Robert Wiene and *Das Cabinett des Dr. Caligari/The Cabinet of Dr. Caligari* (1919), although there are expressionist elements in earlier German features, such as *Homunculus* (1916). Expressionism attempted to outwardly depict man's internal feelings. Objects in films—both the sets and furnishings—were intended to evoke the emotions that they symbolized rather than present a realistic look.

Among the major German directors and films that were part of the expressionist movement are Paul Wegener's *Der Golem/The Golem* (1920), Paul Leni's *Hintertreppe/Backstairs* (1921), F.W. Murnau's *Nosferatu* (1922), and Paul Leni's *Das Waschfigurencabinett/Waxworks* (1924). Expressionism reached its zenith in the German cinema with E.A. Dupont's *Variete/Vaudeville/Variety* (1925). F.W. Murnau and Paul Leni helped popularize expressionism in American features through, respectively, *Sunrise* (1927) and *The Cat and the Canary* (1927). In the late twenties, it was popular with a number of American directors, including John Ford and Josef von Sternberg.

BIBLIOGRAPHY

"Aspects of Expressionism: It Lives Again," *Monthly Film Bulletin*, vol. XLVI, no. 547, August 1979, p. 188.

Eisner, Lotte. *The Haunted Screen*. Berkeley: University of California Press, 1969.

Kracauer, Siegfried. *From Caligari to Hitler*. Princeton, N.J.: Princeton University Press, 1947.

Salt, Barry, "From Caligari to Who?," *Sight & Sound*, vol. XLVIII, no. 2, Spring 1979, pp. 119–123.

F

FAMU is the familiar name by which the Film and Television faculty of the Prague Academy of Music and Dramatic Arts is known. Established in 1947, the school operates seven departments, and among its first graduates who appeared in 1949–1950 are Vojtěch Jasný, Karel Kachyňa, Stanislav Barabáš, and Peter Solan. Later graduates who gained prominence in the Czech film industry include Věra Chytilová, Miloš Forman and Jan Němec. Housed in a building on the Vlatava River, FAMU now offers a four-to-five-year course with an average of 250 full-time students.

Address: Smetanovo Nabřeži 2, Prague 1, Czechoslovakia.

FANTÔMAS. A mysterious, criminal character in a series of novels by Marcel Allain and Pierre Souvestre, Fantômas was first brought to the screen in 1913 by the French director Louis Feuillade (1873–1925). This one film led to Feuillade's directing four other Fantômas productions and to the establishment of the serial film in France. Fantômas was first portrayed by René Navarre. The character has since been revived on screen a number of times, most notably in two films, *Fantômas contre Scotland Yard/Fantomas* (1964) and *Fantômas se déchaine/Fantomas Tears Loose* (1966), in both of which Jean Marais portrayed both the title role and that of the newspaper reporter, Fandor.

FÉDÉRATION FRANÇAISE DES CINÉ-CLUBS. An organization representing the interests of French film societies, Le Fédération Française des Ciné-Clubs was initially founded in 1930 by director Germaine Dulac. It ceased operations with the Second World War, and was reconstituted after the liberation of France on May 9, 1946. It publishes a journal, *Cinéma,* and occasional monographs.

Address: 6 rue Ordener, Paris 75018, France.

FEKS (Fabrika Eksentricheskovo Aktyora/Factory of the Eccentric Actor) was founded as a theatre group in Leningrad in 1921 by Grigori Kozintsev, Ilya Trauberg, and Sergei Yutkevich. As a group, it produced the 1924 comedy,

Pokhozhdeniya Oktyabrini/Adventures of Oktyabrini, which was followed by *Chyortovo koleso/Devil's Wheel* (1926) and *Shinel/The Cloak* (1926). FEKS was influenced by the futurism* movement in its efforts to bring a new freshness to both theatre and film, but, in time, its eccentricity became at odds with social realism, and the group was disbanded in 1929.

FERRANIA COLOR. A three-color, subtractive process, Ferania Color was introduced in Italy in 1952. One of the earliest features to be photographed in Ferrania Color was a screen version of Verdi's opera *Aida* (1953), which was notable for its starring of Sophia Loren with the singing voice of Renata Tebaldi. Ferrania Color first came into usage in the United States in 1964, when the company was acquired by the Minnesota Mining and Manufacturing Co.

BIBLIOGRAPHY

Ryan, Roderick T. *A History of Motion Picture Color Technology*. London and New York: Focal Press, 1977.

FIAF. The Fédération Internationale des Archives du Film/International Federation of Film Archives (FIAF) was founded in 1938, with the declared purpose "to promote the preservation of the film as art and historical document throughout the world and to bring together all organisations devoted to this end; to facilitate the collection and international exchange for the purpose of making them as widely accessible as possible; to develop cooperation between its members; and to promote the development of cinema art and culture." The organization is now involved with television as well as film.

French director Georges Franju has claimed that the idea for FIAF came from director Germaine Dulac, and that the initiators of the organization were himself, Henri Langlois, Olwen Vaughan, and Iris Barry. Langlois was founder of the Cinémathèque Française, Olwen Vaughan was with the British Film Institute, and Iris Barry was founder of the Film Department of the Museum of Modern Art. A fourth organization, the Reichsfilmarchiv, represented by Frank Hensel, also joined the group, whose headquarters were in Paris until 1969, when they moved to Brussels. FIAF's first general assembly was held in New York in 1939, but the Second World War put a halt on its activities until 1946, when FIAF was reestablished without the German Reichsfilmarchiv, which was a victim of the war.

FIAF organizes a general assembly each year in a different country. It also maintains commissions on preservation, cataloging, and documentation. It has produced a number of publications, most notable among which are its annual *International Index to Film Periodicals* (published since 1972) and its *International Index to TV Periodicals* (published since 1979).

Many of the activities of FIAF are confidential, and, to an outsider, it often appears a highly bureaucratic organization, more concerned with politics than with film preservation.

Address: 70 Coudenberg, 1000 Brussels, Belgium.

FICA is the name of a system whereby color films are placed in specially sealed bags for up to seven days while moisture is drawn from them. Once the process is completed, the films can be placed in cold storage, thus preventing the color from fading. The system was conceived in 1979 and developed after consultation with Eastman Kodak and Agfa-Gevaert (see Agfacolor) by Hans-Evert Bloman and Roland Gooes of the Swedish Film Institute*. The FICA cabinet is marketed by AB Film-Teknik (P.O. Box 1328, S-17126 Solna, Sweden).

FIDO. See FILM INDUSTRY DEFENSE FUND

FIJI has no film industry, but it has been utilized as a location site for the shooting of a few features, including *The Drums of Tabu* (1967) and *The Fantastic Plastic Machine* (1969). There are four distributors located in this South Pacific nation, as well as the Fiji Broadcasting Commission (P.O. Box 334, Suva).

FILM ARCHIVES. The following is a listing of major film archives worldwide. Those whose name is followed by (FIAF) are full members of the International Federation of Film Archives (FIAF*).

Albania

Arkivi Shtetëror i Filmit i Republikes Populore Socialiste të Shqipërisë (FIAF)
Rruga Alexandre Moissu Nr-76
Tirana

Algeria

Cinémathèque Algérienne
rue Larbi-Ben-Mhidi 49
16000 Algiers

Angola

Cinemateca Nacional de Angola
Caixa Postal 3512
Largo Luther King 4
Luanda

Argentina

Cinemateca Argentina (FIAF)
Corrientes 2092, piso 3°
1045 Buenos Aires

Australia

National Film and Sound Archive (FIAF)
McCoy Circuit
Acton
Canberra ACT 2601

State Film Archives of Western Australia
Alexander Library Building
Perth Cultural Centre
Perth
Western Australia 6000

Austria

Osterreichisches Filmarchiv (FIAF)
Rauhensteingasse 5
A-1010 Vienna

Osterreichisches Filmmuseum (FIAF)
Augustinerstrasse 1
A-1010 Vienna

Bangladesh

Bangladesh Film Archive
Ministry of Information
Block No. 3, Gano Bhaban
Sher-E-Bangla Nagar
Dhaka-7

Belgium

Cinémathèque Royale (FIAF)
23 Ravenstein
1000 Brussels

Bolivia

Cinemateca Boliviana
Pichincha esq. Indaburo s/n
Casilla 20271
La Paz

Brazil

Cinemateca Brasileira (FIAF)
Caixa Postal 12900
São Paulo

Cinemateca de Museu de Arte Moderna (FIAF)
Caixa Postal 44
20,000 Rio de Janeiro

Bulgaria

Bulgarska Nacionalna Filmoteka (FIAF)
ul Gourko 36
1000 Sofia

Canada

Conservatoire d'Art Cinématographique de Montréal
1455 de Maisonneuve West
Montréal
Québec

La Cinémathèque Québécoise (FIAF)
335 Boulevard de Maisonneuve est
Montréal
Québec H2X 1K1

Moving Image and Sound Archives (FIAF)
395 Wellington Street
Ottawa
Ontario K1A ON3

Ontario Film Institute*
770 Don Mills Road
Don Mills
Ontario M3C 1T3

Chile

Cinemateca Chilena en al Exilio
Padre Xifré 3
Oficin 111
Madrid 2

China

Zhongguo Dianying Ziliaoguan (FIAF)
Xin Wai Dajie 25B
Beijing

Colombia

Cinemateca Distrial
Carrera 7, No. 22–79
Bogota, D.E.

Cuba

Cinemateca de Cuba (FIAF)
Calle 23n 1155
Vedado
Havana

Cyprus

Kypriaki Tainiothiki
P.O. Box 5314
Nicosia

Czechoslovakia

Ceskoslovenský filmový ústav-archive (FIAF)
Národni 40
110 000 Prague 1

Denmark

Det Danske Filmmuseum (FIAF)
Store Søndervoldstraede
DK-1419 Copenhagen K

Ecuador

Cinemateca Nacional del Ecuador
Casilla 3520
Avenue 6 de Diciembre 794 y Tarqui
Quito

Egypt

Al-Archive Al-Kawmy Lil-film
Egyptian Film Center
City of Arts, Pyramids Avenue
Guiza

Finland

Suomen elokuva-arkisto (FIAF)
Pursimiehenkatu 29–31
SF-00150 Helsinki

France

Cinémathèque de Toulouse (FIAF)
3 rue Roquelaine
31000 Toulouse

Cinémathèque Française*
29 rue du Colisée
F-75008 Paris

Cinémathèque Universitaire
U.E.R. d'Art et d'Archéologie
rue Michelet 3
F-75006 Paris

Musée du Cinema de Lyon
rue Jean Jaurès 69
691000 Villeurbanne

Service des Archives de Film de Centre National de la Cinématographie (FIAF)
7 bis rue Alexandre Turpault
78390 Bois D'Arcy

Germany (East)

Staatliches Filmarchiv der Deutschen Demokratischen Republik (FIAF)
Hausvogteiplatz 3–4
1080 Berlin

Germany (West)

Arsenal Kino der Freunde der Deutschen Kinemathek
V, Welserstrasse 25
D-1000 Berlin 30

Bundesarchiv-Filmarchiv (FIAF)
Potsdamer Str. 1
POB 320 D 5400 Koblenz

Deutsches Institut für Filmkunde (FIAF)
Schaumainkai 41
D-6000 Frankfurt am Main 1

Deutsches Institut für Filmkunde
Langenbeckstr. 9
D-6200 Wiesbaden

Münchner Filmmuseum
St-Jakobs-Platz 1
D-8000 Munich 2

Stiftung Deutsches Kinemathek (FIAF)
Pommernallee 1
D-1000 Berlin 19

Greece

Tainiothiki tis Ellados
1 Canari Street
10671 Athens

Hungary

Magyar Filmtudományi Intézet És Filmarchívum (FIAF)
Népstadion út. 97
1143 Budapest XIV

Iceland

Kvikmyndasafn Islands (FIAF)
Laugavegur 24
P.O. Box 320
Revkjavik

India

National Film Archive of India (FIAF)
Ministry of Information and Broadcasting
Law College Road
Poona 411004

Indonesia

Sinematek Indonesia
Pusat Perfilman H. Usmar Ismail
Jalan H.R. Rasuna Said
Jakarta Selatan

Iran

Filmkhaneh Melli Iran
P.O. Box 5158
11365 Tehran

Israel

Israel Film Archive (FIAF)
Jerusalem Film Centre
Hebron Road
P.O. Box 8561
Jerusalem 91083

Italy

Cineteca Italiana (FIAF)
Via Palestro 16
20121 Milano

Cineteca Nazionale (FIAF)
Via Tuscolana N. 1524
00173 Rome

Museo Nazionale del Cinema (FIAF)
Palazzo Chiablese
Piazza S. Giovanni 2
10122 Torino

Japan

National filmcenter
7–6, 3 chrome
Kyobashi

Korea (North)

The National Film Archive of the Democratic People's Republic of Korea (FIAF)
15 Sochangdong
Central District
Pyonyang

Korea (South)

Korean Film Archive (FIAF)
34–5, 3–ka, Namsandong-ku
Seoul 100

Luxembourg

Cinémathèque Municipale de la Ville de Luxembourg
28 place Guillaume
1648 Luxembourg City

Mexico

Cinemateca Luis Buñuel
Calle 5
Oriente 5
Apdo

Cineteca Nacional (FIAF)
Av. México-Coyoacán 389
03330 México City

Filmoteca de la Unam
Apartado Postal 45–002
San Ildefonso 43
06020 México City

Netherlands

Stichting Nederlands Filmmuseum (FIAF)
Vondelpark 3
1071 AA Amsterdam

New Zealand

The New Zealand Film Archive (FIAF)
P.O. Box 9544
Wellington

Nicaragua

Cinemateca de Nicaragua
Apartado Postal 4642
Managua

Norway

Norsk Filminstitutt
Postboks 482, Sentrum
Grev Wedels plass 1–5
0105 Oslo 1

Panama

Cinemateca del GEGU
Apartado 6–1775
Estefeta El Dorado
Panama

Peru

Cinemateca Peruana
Apartado 456
Lima

Philippines

Film Archives of the Philippines
P.O. Box 1394
Manila 2801

Poland

Filmoteka Polska (FIAF)
ul. Pulawaska 61
00–975 Warszawa

Portugal

Cinemateca Portuguesa (FIAF)
Rue Barata Salgueiro 39
1200 Lisboa

Romania

Archiva Nationala de Filme
Bd. G.H. Gheorghiu dej 68/65
Bucharest

South Africa

South African National Film Archives
Private Bag 236
Pretoria 0001

Spain

Filmoteca Española (FIAF)
Carretera de la Dehesa de la Villa s/N
28040 Madrid

Sweden

Cinemateket (FIAF)
Filmhuset
Box 27 126
S-102 52 Stockholm 27

Switzerland

Cinémathèque Suisse (FIAF)
Case Postale 2512
1003 Lausanne

Taiwan

Tien-ying t'u-shu-kuan
4th Floor
7 Ch'ingtao East Road
Taipei

Turkey

Sinema-TV Enstitüsü (FIAF)
Kislaönü-Besiktas
Istanbul

United Kingdom

Imperial War Museum* (FIAF)
Lambeth Road
London SE1 6HZ

National Film Archive (FIAF)
21 Stephen Street
London WIP IPL

Scottish Film Archive
Scottish Film Council
74 Victoria Crescent Road
Downahill
Glasgow G12 9JN

United States of America

Anthology Film Archives
80 Wooster Street
New York, NY 10012

Human Studies Film Archives
National Museum of Natural History
Room E307
Smithsonian Institution
Washington, DC 20560

International Museum of Photography at George Eastman House (FIAF)
900 East Avenue
Rochester, NY 14607

Library of Congress (FIAF)
Motion Picture, Broadcasting, and Recorded Sound Division
Washington, DC 20540

Museum of Modern Art (FIAF)
Department of Film
11 West 53 Street
New York, NY 10019

National Center for Film and Video Preservation
John F. Kennedy Center for the Performing Arts
Washington, DC 20566

UCLA Film and Television Archive (FIAF)
1015 North Cahuenga Boulevard
Los Angeles, CA 90038

Wisconsin Center for Film and Theater Research
816 State Street
Madison, WI 53706

Uruguay

Cinemateca Uruguaya (FIAF)
Lorenzo Carnelli 1311
Casilla de Correo 1170
Montevideo

USSR

Gosfilmofond (FIAF)
Stantsia Byelye Stolby
Moskovskaya oblast 143050

Vatican City

Filmoteca Vaticana
00120 Vatican City

Venezuela

Cinemateca Nacional
Museo de Ciencias Naturales
Edf. Anexo
Plaza Morelos
Los Cacobas, Aptdo. Postal 17045
Caracas 1015-A

Vietnam

Vien Tu Leiu Phim Viet Nam
Hoang Hoa Thám 62
Hanoi

Yugoslavia

Jugoslovenska Kinoteka (FIAF)
Knez Mihailova 19/1
11,000 Belgrade

FILM À THÈSE (literally "Problem Film") is a phrase used to describe films that are anticapitalist and proworker. The best-known example of the genre is Jean Renoir's *Le crime de M. Lange/The Crime of M. Lange* (1935).

FILM AUSTRALIA is the film and audiovisual arm of the Australian Film Commission*, producing films for specific government departments. Its films are available to nontheatrical users throughout the world, and it also maintains a stock footage library with more than three million feet of film on file. In February 1984, a women's production unit was established, becoming the permanent Women's Film Unit in April 1985, to produce films on issues of interest and concern to women.

Prior to its renaming as Film Australia in 1973, the agency was, perhaps, better known as the Commonwealth Film Unit, a highly renowned documentary production agency, whose origins lie in a 1940 visit to Australia by documentary filmmaker John Grierson. The unit was formed in 1940 as the Film Division of the Australian Department of Information. Stanley Hawes was its head from 1946–1970, with one of his first films there being *School in the Mailbox* (1946). In 1956, the agency was renamed the Commonwealth Film Unit, although it never had any real independence until 1975, when it was taken over by the Australian Film Commission, following passage of the Australian Film Commission Act.

Address: 8 West Street, North Sydney, Box 3984, NSW 2001, Australia.

BIBLIOGRAPHY

Lansell, Ross, and Peter Beilby. *The Documentary Film in Australia.* Sydney: Cinema Papers, 1982.

THE FILMBEWERTUNGSSTELLE (Film Evaluation Office) was created in 1951 by the various German states. It is able to rate a film as either ''wertvoll'' (worthy) or ''besonders wertvoll'' (very worthy) and thus provide the producer with a substantial tax benefit.

FILM D'ART. The early French film producer, Le Film d'Art, was established on March 25, 1907, by the Lafitte brothers, to utilize the talents of the Comédie Française in films. The company's first film was *L'Assassinat du Duc de Guise/The Assassination of the Duke de Guise* (1908), co-directed by Charles Le Bargy and written by Henri Lavédan, both of whom were intensely involved in the company's creation. The film is important in that it is the first production to boast a score written by an important contemporary composer, Camille Saint-Saëns, and, curiously, is the only film of the company to have lasting recognition.

Louis Nalpas became production head of Film d'Art in the late teens, and it was he who invited director Abel Gance to join the company (for whom he made his 1918 feature, *La Dixième Symphonie*). Later Jacques de Baroncelli became Film d'Art's artistic director, and he was responsible for *La Rafale* and *Le Secret du Lone Star* (both released in 1920), starring the American actress, Fanny Ward. In 1923, the company financed the production of Germaine Dulac's *La souriante Madame Beudet/The Smiling Madam Beudet.*

In the twenties, Charles Delac, who had taken over the company from the Lafitte brothers, attempted a merger with Eclair* and other companies, to form la Compagnie Générale Français de Cinématographie, but it lasted for only a short time in 1921, and produced only one feature, de Baroncelli's *Le Rêve* (1921). Later, Delac operated the company as an independent producer and as such it survived until the coming of sound.

FILM FESTIVAL AWARDS. The following is a listing of some of the more important film festival awards, with the names of the festivals at which they are presented. The Best Film usually receives a Golden award, and the runners-up receive Silver and Bronze awards.

"Bear" (Berlin)
"Charybdis" (also known as "Golden Horse" or "Cariddi") (Taormina)
"Dove" (Leipzig)
"Hugo" (Chicago)
"Leopard" (Locarno)
"Lion" (Venice)
"Palm" (Cannes)
"Sheaf" (Valladolid)
"Shell" (San Sebastian)
"Toucan" (Rio de Janeiro)

FILM FESTIVALS. In direct contradiction to the argument that the film industry is waning, film festivals have proliferated in recent years, with the major international festivals concerned with both the art of the film and the selling of the film. Berlin and Cannes are as much marketplaces as they are centers for the appreciation of new films. Increasingly, festivals tend to specialize in one particular area of filmmaking, such as documentaries, silent films, short subjects, or comedies. The oldest surviving film festival is Venice, which was first held in 1932.

Useful commentary on film festivals is provided annually in *International Film Guide,* edited by Peter Cowie (London: Tantivy Press/New York: New York Zoetrope), and a "Calendar of Film/TV Festivals & Related Events" is published each spring in *Movie/TV Marketing*. Although outdated, two other useful sources are *Gadney's Guide to 1800 International Contests, Festivals & Grants* by Alan Gadney (Glendale, Calif.: Festival Publications, 1979) and *AIVF Guide to International Film and Video Festivals* (New York: The Association of Independent Video and Filmmakers, 1986). The AIVF's journal, *The Independent,* also includes a monthly "Festival Column." Film festivals are sanctioned, and the dates on which they are held are approved by FIAPF (Federation Internationale des Associations de Producteurs de Films, 33 Champs-Elysées, 75008 Paris, France).

BIBLIOGRAPHY

British Council and British Film Institute. *Directory of International Film and Video Festivals: 1987 and 1988*. London, 1987.

The following is a listing of major international film festivals:

Amiens Marché International du Film
36 rue de Noyon
80000 Amiens
France

Annecy Journeés Internationales du Cinéma d'Animation
21 rue de la Tour d'Auvergne
75009 Paris
France

Anvers Film Festival
Lange brilstraat
2000 Anvers
Belgium

Avoriaz Festival International du Film Fantastique
33 avenue Mac Mahon
75017 Paris
France

Barcelona Setmana Internacional de Cinema
Avinguda Maria cristina
Palau 1
08004 Barcelona
Spain

Bastia Festival des Cultures Mediterranéennes
7 bis rue Imperatrice Eugénie
20200 Bastia
France

Berlin International Film Festival
Budapester Strasse 50
D-1000 Berlin 30
West Germany

Biarritz Festival du Film Iberique et Latino Americain
24 rue Saint Martin
75004 Paris
France

Biarritz Festival National de L'Audiovisuel d'Enterprise
15 bis rue de Marignan
75008 Paris
France

Bilboa International Festival of Documentary and Short Films
Colon de Larreategui 37–4 drcha.
48009 Bilboa
Spain

British Animation Festival
41B Hornsey Lane Gardens
London N6 5NY
United Kingdom

British Industrial and Sponsored Film Festival
26 D'Arblay Street
London W1V 3FH
United Kingdom

Brussels Festival Internationale du Cinema
32 avenue de l'Astronomie
1030 Brussels
Belgium

Cambridge Film Festival
8 Market Passage
Cambridge CB2 3PF
United Kingdom

Cannes International Film Festival*
71 rue de Faubourg St. Honoré
75008 Paris
France

Cartagena International Film Festival
1405 Apart Aéro
40094 Bogota
Colombia

Chambrousse Festival International du Film d'Humour
3 rue Morand
75011 Paris
France

Chicago International Film Festival
415 North Dearborn Street
Chicago, IL 60610
USA

Clermont-Ferrand Festival du Court Metrage
26 rue des Jacobins
63000 Clermont-Ferrand
France

Cognac Festival du Film Policier
33 avenue Mac Mahon
75017 Paris
France

Cork Film Festival
38 MacCurtain Street
Cork
Eire

Cracow Film Festival
Pl. Zwyciestwa 9
P.O. Box 127
00–950 Warsaw
Poland

Creteil Festival International de Films de Femmes
Maison des Arts
Place Salvador Allende
94000 Creteil
France

Damascus Film Festival
BP 7187
Damascus
Syria

Deauville Festival for American Cinema
33 avenue Mac Mahon
75017 Paris
France

Edinburgh Film Festival
The Film House
88 Lothian Road
Edinburgh EH3 9BZ
Scotland

Epinay-sur-Seine Rencontres Cinématographiques
3 rue Mulot
93800 Epinay-sur-Seine
France

European Environmental Film Festival
55 rue de Varenne
75341 Paris
France

Festival dei Popoli
Via Fiume 14
50123 Florence
Italy

Festival des 3 Continents
BP 3306
Nantes
France

Festival du Cinema Italien
3 esplenade Kennedy
06300 Nice
France

Festival du Film Arabe
10 rue Gustave Courbet
75016 Paris
France

Festival Internacional de Cinema de Animačao
rue 62, No. 251–1/Apart. 43
4500 Espinho
Portugal

Festival International du Film de Comédie
Place de la Gare 5
CH-1800 Vevey
Switzerland

Festival International du Film Fantastique et de Science Fiction
9 rue du Midi
92200 Neuilly-sur-Seine
France

Festival International du Film Nature
WWF-Geneva
Ch-1212 Grand-Lancy
Switzerland

Festival International du Film sur l'Ecologie et l'Environment
AFIFEE, Domaine de Grammont
route de Mauguio
34000 Montpellier
France

Festival International du Nouveau Cinéma et de la Vidéo
3724 Boulevard Saint-Laurent
Montreal
Quebec H2X 2V8
Canada

Festival Internazionale Cinema Giovani
Piazza San Carlo 161
10123 Turin
Italy

Festival of Festivals
69 Yorkville Avenue
Suite 206
Toronto
Ontario M5R 1B7
Canada

Festival of the Americas
P.O. Box 56566
Houston, TX 77256
USA

Figueira da Foz
rua Luis de Camões 106
2600 Vila Franca de Zira
Portugal

Filmfest München
Türkenstrasse 93
D-8000 Munich 40
West Germany

Film International
Eendrachtsweg 21
3012 LB Rotterdam
Netherlands

Florence Film Festival
Via Sant'Egidio 21
50122 Florence
Italy

Gand Festival International Cinematographique
Kortrijksesteenweg 1104
9820 Gent
Belgium

Giffoni Valle Piana
84095 Giffoni Valle Piana
Salerno
Italy

Gijon International Film Festival for Children & Young People
Paseo de Begoña 24
Gijon 2
Spain

Göteborg Film Festival
Götabergsgatan 17
S-411 34 Göteborg
Sweden

Grenoble Festival du Court Metrage
6 place Notre-Dame
38000 Grenoble
France

Havana International Film Festival
ICAIC
Calle 23 No. 1155 Vedado
Havana
Cuba

Hong Kong Film Festival
HK Coliseum Annex Building
Parking Deck Floor
KCR Kowloon Station
8 Cheong Wan Road
Kowloon
Hong Kong

Hyeres Festival International du Jeune Cinéma
Villa La Voute
83000 Hyeres
France

Iberoamerican Film Festival
Hotel Tartessos
Huelva
Spain

India International Film Festival
Lok Nayak Bhavan
4th Floor
Khan Market
New Delhi 11003
India

Indonesia Film Festival
Jalan Merdeka Barat no. 9
Jakarta
Indonesia

International Children's Film Festival
Communal Cinema Oulu
Rantakatu 30
SF-90120 Oulu
Finland

Internationale Hofer Filmtage
Posfach 1146
D-8670 Hof.
D-8000 Munich 2
West Germany

Internationales Film-wochenende Würzburg
Gosbertsteig 2
D-8700 Würzburg
West Germany

International Week of the Silent Film
Centro Studi Televisivi
Casella postale 6104
00195 Rome
Italy

Kaleidoscope
Box 2068
S-103 12 Stockholm
Sweden

Karlovy Vary International Film Festival
Jindřiškà 34
110 00 Prague 1
Czechoslovakia

Knokke-Heist International Film Festival
Zeedi jk 581 -- bus 16
Knokke-Heist
Belgium

La Rochelle Festival
26 Rue de Washington
75008 Paris
France

Leipzig Festival
Chodowieckistr. 32
DDR 1055 Berlin
East Germany

Lille International Festival of Short and Documentary Films
26-34 rue Washington
75008 Paris
France

Locarno Festival Internationale del Film
Casella Postale
6601 Locarno
Switzerland

London Film Festival
British Film Institute
21 Stephen Street
London W1P 1PL
United Kingdom

Mannheim International Film Festival
D-6800 Mannheim
Rathaus E5
West Germany

Melbourne International Film Festival
GPO Box 2760EE
Melbourne 3001
Australia

Miami Film Festival
Film Society of Miami
7600 Red Road, Suite 307
Miami, FL 33143
USA

MIFED*
Largo Domodossola 1
20145 Milan
Italy

Montreal World Film Festival
1455 Boulevard de Maisonneuve ouest
Montreal
Quebec H3G 1M8
Canada

Moscow International Film Festival
10 Khokhlovsky pereulak
Moscow 109028
USSR

Mostra Internacional de Cinema
av. Borges de Medeiros 915/7 andar
Pôrto Alegre
Brazil

Mostra Internacional de Cinema
Al. Lorena 937Cj. 302,01424
São Paulo
Brazil

New York Film Festival
Film Society of Lincoln Center
140 West 65 Street
New York, NY 10023
USA

Nordic Film Festival
Kaisaniemenkatu 2B
SF-00100 Helsinki
Finland

Nordische Filmtage
Senat der Hansestadt Lübeck
Amt für Kultur Rathaushof
D-2400 Lübeck 1
West Germany

Norwegian Film Festival
Lille Grensen 3
Oslo 1
Norway

Nyon Festival International de Cinéma
Case postale 98
CH-1260 Nyon
Switzerland

Oberhausen Short Film Festival
Grillostrasse 34
D-4200 Oberhausen 1
West Germany

Odense Film Festival
Vindegade 18
DK-5000 Odense
Denmark

Oesterreichische Film Tage
Columbusgasse 2
A-1100 Vienna
Austria

Ottawa International Festival of Animation
75 Albert Street
Ottawa
Ontario K1P 5E7
Canada

Pesaro Mostra Internazionale del Nuovo Cinema
Via Yser 8
00198 Rome
Italy

Piccadilly Film Festival
197 Piccadilly
London W1V 9LF
United Kingdom

Pordenone Giornate del Cinema Muto
La Cineteca del Friuli
Via Osoppo 26
33014 Gemona (Udine)
Italy

Pula Festival
Marka Laginje 5
52000 Pula
Yugoslavia

Rencontres Internationales du Jeune Cinéma
70 rue Faider
1050 Brussels
Belgium

Rotterdam Film Festival
P.O. Box 21696
3001 AR Rotterdam
Netherlands

San Francisco International Film Festival
3501 California Street
San Francisco, CA 94118
USA

Sanremo Mostra Internazionale del Film d'Autore
Rotonda dei Mille 1
24100 Bergamo
Italy

San Sebastian International Film Festival
Apartado correos 397
20 080 San Sebastian
Spain

Seattle International Film Festival
801 East Pine Street
Seattle, WA 98122
USA

SELB Internationale Grenzlandfilmtage
P.O. Box 307
D-8592 Wunsiedel
West Germany

Semana Internacional de Cine de Autor
Palacio de Congresos
Torremolinos
Malaga
Spain

Settimana Cinematografica Internazionale di Verona
Via S. Mammaso 2
37100 Verona
Italy

Singapore International Film Festival
P.O. Box 3714
Singapore 9057

Soluthurn Filmtage
Postfach 92
CH-4500 Solothurn
Switzerland

Sydney Film Festival
P.O. Box 25
Glebe, NSW 2037
Australia

Taipei International Film Exhibition
7 Ch'ingtao East Road
Taipei
Taiwan

Tampere Film Festival
P.O. Box 305
SF-33101 Tampere
Finland

Taormina International Film Festival
Palazzo Corvaja
Taormina
Sicily

Telluride Film Festival
The National Film Preserve, Ltd.
P.O. Box B1156
Hanover, NH 03755
USA

Tokyo International Film Festival
2–4–19, No. 3 Asano Building
Ginza Chuo-ku
Tokyo 104
Japan

Trieste Festival of Festivals
Cinema Ariston
Trieste
Italy

Trondheim Short Film Festival
Wesselsgt 4
N-0165 Oslo 1
Norway

Tyneside Film Festival
10–12 Pilgrim Street
Newcastle upon Tyne NE1 6QK
United Kingdom

Uppsala Film Festival
Box 1746
S-751 47 Uppsal
Sweden

USA Film Festival
P.O. Box 3105
Dallas, TX 75275
USA

Valencia Mostra of Mediterranean Cinema
Salvador Giner No. 14
46003 Valencia
Spain

Valladolid Semana Internacional de Cine
Apartado de correos 646
47006 Valladolid
Spain

Varna World Festival of Animation
1 Bulgaria Sevare
1414 Sofia
Bulgaria

Venice International Film Festival
Ca. Giustinian, San Marco
30124 Venice
Italy

Wellington Film Festival
P.O. Box 9544
Cortenzy Place
Wellington
New Zealand

Zagreb Festival of World Animation
Zagreb 4100
Yugoslavia

FILMFÖRDERUNGSANSTALT is a West German funding agency, created in 1967 through the passage of the Filmförderungesetz (Film Promotion Law). It is comprised of representatives from the Federal Government, the film and television industries, the press, and the church, and is financed through a "tax" on theatre tickets. Since 1974, the Filmförderungsanstalt has also helped finance films for airing on the two major West German television channels.

Address: P.O. 87, Berlin 301, West Germany.

FILM INDUSTRY DEFENSE FUND. By the late fifties, British exhibitors had become concerned at the competition from films shown on television. In 1958, at the instigation of Cecil Bernstein of the Granada Theatres circuit, the Film Industry Defense Fund (FIDO) was established, which required that a levy of one farthing (one quarter of one penny) be made on each theatre ticket sold in the United Kingdom. The funds raised were utilized to purchase the television rights to British films and thus keep them off British television. In time, producers and distributors realized the potential of television sales, and films ceased to be available for purchase by FIDO. However, a ruling was introduced that was intended to prevent the exhibition of British films on British television until some five years after their initial theatrical release.

FILMKREDITBANK (Film Credit Bank) was established by the financial wing of Joseph Goebbel's Reichskulturkammer (State Chamber of Culture) to subsidize worthwhile film projects during the Nazi era in German history.

"FILMOLOGIE" is a word coined by French film critic Gilbert Cohen-Seat to describe the study by college professors and students of film from a strictly philosophical and psychological viewpoint.

FILM POLSKI was established by government decree on November 13, 1945, as part of the nationalization of the Polish film industry. A state agency, it now functions exclusively as an import and export bureau under the Ministry of Culture and Arts, providing services for filmmakers from abroad working in Poland, acting as an intermediary between Polish technicians and foreign producers, promoting Polish films abroad, and publishing *Polish Film/Film Polonais/Film Polski*.

Address: 6/8 Mazowiecka, 00–048 Warsaw, Poland.

FILMS À CLEF is a French expression referring to fictional features that are based on reality. Obvious examples are *The Great Dictator* (1940, Adolph Hitler), *Citizen Kane* (1941, William Randolph Hearst), *All the King's Men* (1949, Huey Long), and *Call Me Madam* (1953, Perle Mesta). The term has little relevance today, with most features clearly indicating the events upon which they are based and utilizing the names of actual persons.

FILMS AND FILMING was one of the first periodicals to combine both a popular and a serious outlook on the motion picture. It commenced publication in London in October 1954, and soon became noted for the quality of its articles. It ceased publication in June 1980, but was revived in October 1981.

Address: Brevet Publishing Limited, P.O. Box 252, London SW1P 2LD, United Kingdom.

BIBLIOGRAPHY

Slide, Anthony, editor. *International Film, Radio, and Television Journals*. Westport, Conn.: Greenwood Press, 1985.

FILMS D.-H. was a French production company, established in 1916 by one of Europe's first female directors, Germaine Dulac (1882–1942) in association with her husband, Albert, and poet-novelist, Irene Hillel-Erlanger. It produced a number of films, including *Les soeurs ennemies/The Hostile Sisters* (1917), *Géo, le mystérieux* (1917), *Le Bonheur des autres/The Happiness of Others,* and a serial, *Ames de fous* (1918), before its dissolution in 1921.

LES FILMS DE LA PLEÏADE. Formed by French short film producer, Pierre Braunberger, Les Films de la Pleïade was responsible for the first three shorts of director Jean-Luc Godard (born December 3, 1930)—*Tous les garcons s'appellent Patrick/Every Boy Is Called Patrick* (1957), *Charlotte et son Jules/Charlotte and Her Boy Friend* (1958), and *Une Histoire d'eau/A Story of Water* (1958)—as well as one of his early features, *Vivre sa vie/My Life To Live* (1962).
Address: 95 Champs-Elysees, 75008 Paris, France.

LES FILMS DU CARROSSE was founded by French film director François Truffaut and his wife, Madeleine, in 1957. It produced or co-produced virtually all of the director's films: *Les Mistons* (1957), *Les Quatre Cents Coups/The 400 Blows* (1959), *Jules et Jim/Jules and Jim* (1961), *La Peau Douce/The Soft Skin* (1964), *La Mariée Etait en Noir/The Bride Wore Black* (1967), *Baisers Volés/Stolen Kisses* (1968), *La Sirène du Mississippi/Mississippi Mermaid* (1969), *L'Enfant Sauvage/The Wild Child* (1969), *Domicile Conjugal/Bed and Board* (1970), *Les Deux Anglaises et le Continent/Two English Girls* (1971), *Une Belle Fille comme Moi/Such a Gorgeous Kid Like Me* (1972), *La Nuit Américaine/Day for Night* (1973), *L'Histoire d'Adèle H./The Story of Adèle H.* (1975), *L'Argent de Poche/Small Change* (1976), *L'Homme Qui Aimait Les Femmes/The Man Who Loved Women* (1977), *La Chambre Vert/The Green Room* (1978), *L'Amour en Fuite/Love on the Run* (1979), *Le Dernier Métro/The Last Metro* (1981), and *Vivement Dimanche!/Confidentially Yours* (1983).
Address: 5 rue Robert Estienne, 75008 Paris, France.

FILMS DU LOSANGE. Active since 1965, Films du Losange is a French production company responsible for many major features, including *Paris vu par . . .* (1965), *La collectionneuse* (1966), *Ma nuit chez Maud/My Night with Maud* (1969), and *Le genou de Claire/Claire's Knee* (1970).
Address: 26 avenue Pierre lre de Serbie, 75016 Paris, France.

FILMS ERMOLIEFF was a French production company, founded in the early twenties by Russian emigré Joseph Ermolieff. It operated a studio at Montreuil-sous-bois, and produced a number of features, including *L'Angoissante aventure* (1920), *L'ombre du péché* (1922), *Les milles et une nuits* (1922), and *La maison du mystère* (1922). The company was sold in 1922 to Alexandre Kamenka and Noë Bloch and became Films Albatros.

FILM SOCIETIES. Although film societies do exist in the United States and are fostered through the American Federation of Film Societies, they are a non-American creation, more closely associated with Europe. The first film society is believed to have been the Bungei Katsudo Shashin Kai/Literary Motion Picture Society, founded in Tokyo, Japan, in 1912. The first British film society was the Stoll Picture Theatre Club, formed in 1918. The first French film society was Le Ciné-Club, founded by critic Louis Delluc in 1920.

THE FILM SOCIETY. The world's first so-called film society, titled appropriately enough The Film Society, was created in London in 1925. Its executive council consisted of Iris Barry, Sidney L. Bernstein, Adrian Brunel, Frank Dobson, Hugh Miller, Ivor Montagu, and Walter C. Mycroft. Its first secretary was J.M. Harvey, and founding members were Lord Ashfield, Anthony Asquith, G.A. Atkinson, Clare Atwood, Anthony Butts, Lord David Cecil, Aubrey Clark, George Cooper, Edith Craig, H. Fraenkel, Roger Fry, J.B.S. Haldane, Julian Huxley, J. Isaacs, Augustus John, E. McKnight Kauffer, J. Maynard Keynes, Angus MacPhail, Olga Miller, George Pearson, H.F. Rubinstein, Christopher St. John, George Bernard Shaw, J. St. Loe Strachey, Lord Swaythling, Dame Ellen Terry, Ben Webster, and H.G. Wells. It held its first performance at London's New Gallery Kinema, on Regent Street, on October 25, 1925, with the feature presentation being Paul Leni's *Das Waschfigurencabinett/Waxworks* (1924). The Film Society was disbanded in 1939 at the outbreak of the Second World War; it was resurrected in 1945 by Olwen Vaughan as The New London Film Society.

FILM WEEKLY was founded in 1928 and quickly became a popular British fan magazine of the thirties. With the Second World War, it was amalgamated with *Picturegoer** on September 23, 1939.

BIBLIOGRAPHY

Slide, Anthony, editor. *International Film, Radio, and Television Journals*. Westport, Conn.: Greenwood Press, 1985.

FINLAND was an autonomous part of the Russian empire when the Cinématographe Lumière was exhibited there in 1896. The first Finnish films were made in 1904, the year in which Finland's first cinema was established. The first Finnish story film, *Salaviinan polttajat/The Moonshiners,* was made in 1907 by the company Atelier Apollo, which was formed in 1906. By the time of Finland's independence on December 6, 1917, about twenty-five films, mostly farces and romances, had been produced and over one hundred cinemas were in operation. Adams-Filmi Oy, which grew to be Finland's largest distributor, importer, and exporter, was founded in 1912; its leading competitor Oy Kinosto was established in 1920.

Approximately 80 features and 700 newsreels were made between 1896 and 1933. The dominant company during this period, Suomi-Filmi Oy, established in 1919, was run by Teuvo Puro and Erkki Karu (1887–1935). Puro, co-director on *Salaviinan polttajat,* made *Sylvi* in 1913, the earliest Finnish film extant, albeit in fragmentary form, and *Kihlaus/The Betrothal* in 1922, an adaptation of a novel by one of Finland's greatest writers, Aleksis Kivi (1834–1872). Karu, co-director of *Finlandia,* a 1922 feature-length documentary commissioned by the Ministry of Foreign Affairs, directed 18 films including *Koskenlaskijan morsian/The Lumberjack's Bride* and *Nummisuutarit/The Village Shoemaker,* from a novel by Kivi, both made in 1923, and both exemplifying the best in the prevalent type of film made at the time, romance, comedy, or adventure stories set in an agricultural setting.

After Karu left Suomi-Filmi in 1933, Risto Orko (born 1899) became the managing director. Karu formed Suomen Filmiteollisuus (SF) in 1933, and after his death in 1935, Toivo Särkkä (1890–1975) became the general director. Orko and Särkkä, besides being prolific and sometimes notable directors, expanded their companies' output during the next three decades to the point of overproduction, according to some historians who lament the overall poor quality of the films of that period. Finland's production figures rose from an average of four to five films per year from 1930 to 1935, to between twenty and thirty per year from the late thirties until the late fifties, excluding the war years. Six hundred of Finland's seven hundred to eight hundred films were produced between 1933 and 1966.

Finland's most acclaimed filmmaker during the thirties, Nyrki Tapiovaara (1911–1940), died before his fifth film was completed. His films, *Juha, Varastettu kuolema/Sudden Death, Kaksi Vihtoria/Two Victors, Herra Lahtinen lähtee lipettiin/Mr. Lahtinen Takes French Leave* and *Miehen tie/The Way of a Man,* showed a freshness and vitality absent from most other Finnish films. Tapiovaara's influence on succeeding generations of young filmmakers has been strong.

In 1950 a third large production company, Fennada-Filmi Oy, was formed by a merger of Adams-Filmi and Fenno-Filmi. Two Finnish films of the fifties achieved international acclaim: *Valkoinen peura/The White Reindeer,* winner of the prize for cinematography at Cannes, was made in 1952 by Erik Blomberg (born 1913), cameraman for a number of Tapiovaara's films; and *Tuntematon sotilas/The Unknown Solder,* an epic war drama was made in 1955 by Edvin Laine (born 1905). Other filmmakers of interest during this period include Matti Kassila (born 1924) and Jack Witikka (born 1916).

With the spread of television, cinema attendance dropped 54 percent between 1958 and 1964, and the amount of film production greatly declined in the late fifties and reached a low point when a three-year strike by the Union of Stage Actors severely curtailed production in the major companies during the early sixties. A break in the established tradition of farce and melodrama occurred when young filmmakers and amateur actors making films strong in sociological content for small independent companies reflected changes in Finnish society as more and more people moved to urban areas.

Film was not considered an art form in Finland during the period in which most of its films were made, but by the sixties, a growing movement to put pressure on the government to support film as a cultural institution achieved some success. Suomen elokuvakerhojen liitto (The Federation of Finnish Film Societies) was established in 1956 (the first film society, Projektio, was formed in 1937 by Nyrki Tapiovaara, architect Alvar Aalto, and others) and Suomen elokuva-arkisto (The Finnish Film Archive), was founded in 1957 by Jörn Donner, Aito Mäkinen, and others. The first state involvement in production took place in 1961 when, in response to pressure put on the state, monetary prizes were awarded for outstanding achievement. Directors making their first features during this time included Risto Jarva (1934–1977), considered to be Finland's finest director during the sixties and seventies, Jaakko Pakkasvirta (born 1934), Mikko Niskanen (born 1929), and Aito Mäkinen (born 1927). Important films of the early sixties included *Auto-tytöt/Girls of the Highway,* a study of an alienated urban male made in 1960 by Maunu Kurkvaara (born 1926), the first important director who did not rely solely on literature for material for his sources and who in the seventies retired from filmmaking to design boats; Jarva and Pakkasvirta's 1962 *Yö vai päivä/Night or Day,* stylistically influenced by the French New Wave; and Niskanen's *Käpy selän alla/Under Your Skin,* made in 1966, which because of its success at the box office encouraged other young filmmakers.

The governmental prizes, however, failed to halt the crisis in the industry. Suomi Filmilmiteollisuus went bankrupt at the end of 1965, and in 1967, total production declined to three features, Finland's lowest point since 1932. On October 15, 1969, Suomen elokuvasäätiö (The Finnish Film Foundation*) was created by organizations representing cinema owners, distributors and producers. Borrowing features of the Swedish Film Institute* and the Danish Government Film Foundation, the Finnish Film Foundation was originally funded by a 4 percent levy on box office grosses. Today, in addition, the Foundation is supported by a tax on blank video sales, direct allocations from the treasury, and funds from Yleisradio (YLE), the state television company. The Foundation grants loans and subsidies to productions, subsidies for the promotion and export of Finnish films, interest subsidies and loans to theaters, subsidies for the import and screening of artistic films and films for children, and subsidies or grants for research, educational, publishing, training, and informational activities.

The establishment of the Foundation failed initially to revive the industry. The largest companies, Suomi-Filmi and Fennada-Filmi, put their emphasis in importing, distribution and exhibition, as they could import twenty-five to thirty films for the cost of one production. Only seven of the twenty-eight films produced between 1970 and 1972 made profits. In 1974 when the agreement establishing the Foundation expired, only two features were produced, imports had dropped to only conventional films, and many theaters had closed in remote areas so that up to one-third of the population had no access to a cinema. Despite an abundance of criticism, centering on the accusations that the Foundation favored certain filmmakers, and that its limited funds were divided up among too many productions and often went to uncommercial ones, the Foundation's agreement was extended and continues to the present.

Some notable films made during the crisis of the late sixties and early seventies include Rauni Mollberg's (born 1929) first feature *Maa on syntinen laulu/The Earth is a Sinful Song,* made in 1973, which attracted international acclaim and over 700,000 viewers (Finland's population at present is 4.9 million); Pakkasvirta's first film as sole director *Vihreä leski/The Green Widow,* made in 1968;

a number of politically and sociologically oriented films by Jarvo including *Tyomiehen paivakirja/A Worker's Diary,* made in 1967, and *Ruusujen aika/Time of Roses,* made in 1969; and films by Jörn Donner, including *Mustaa valkoisella/Black on White,* made in 1968, and *Anna,* made in 1970, who returned to Finland from Sweden after the success of Niskanen's *Käpy selän alla* to become Finland's best known and most outspoken filmmaker, and the chairman of the Finnish Film Foundation from December 1985 through 1987. In the eighties, a remake of the epic war drama *Tuntematon sotilas/The Unknown Soldier,* by Rauni Mollberg drew critical and popular praise.

Production has increased to between fifteen and seventeen films per year in the mid-eighties. Some filmmakers do not rely on Foundation subsidies, including Spede Pasanen, whose annual farces about the character ''Uuno Turhapuro'' (''Numbskull Emptybrook'') have accounted for four of the top five box-office leaders between 1977 and 1986; Kaj Holmberg; and the prolific and critically acclaimed collective Film-Total, consisting of Villealfa Filmproductions Oy, founded by the brothers Mika (born 1955) and Aki Kaurismäki (born 1957), Anssi Mänttäri's (born 1941) Reppufilmi Oy, and Markku Lehmuskallio's (born 1938) Gironfilm Oy. Film-Total member companies, which share cameras and crew, now also distribute and exhibit films and run the Midnight Sun Film Festival.

In recent years Finland has served as a location for a number of foreign productions including *Reds, Gorky Park, Dr. Zhivago, White Nights,* and *The Fourth Protocol.* More foreign films are made there than in other Scandinavian countries because of the Finnish landscapes that resemble Siberia and city buildings like those in Leningrad.

Exhibition recently has concentrated in the larger cities (35 percent of all theaters are in Helsinki; 80 percent are in the ten largest cities) and in one company, Finnkino Oy*, formed in September 1986 by the merging of Adams-Filmi Oy (which in November 1983 purchased Suomi-Filmi's theater circuit), Oy Kinosto, and Savoy Filmi Oy. Finnkino now controls 40 percent of Finland's cinemas and 53 percent of distribution. Because of this, the Finnish Film Foundation is planning a subsidy program of low-interest loans to two hundred cinemas in remote areas. In addition, since the seventies, municipalities have begun to operate cinemas, and film consultants have been hired by nearly all the country's districts.

Censorship, historically very strict in Finland, has recently been an issue. In 1986, *Born American,* the first international co-production filmed entirely in Finland, was banned for most of the year because of political reasons (it portrays three young Americans who sneak into the Soviet Union for a prank and are hunted and imprisoned before they escape) and for reasons of violence. On January 1, 1988, legislation took effect to prevent the retail selling of home videos that were given an adult rating from the state censorship board; this accounts for about 20 percent of current titles and it is projected that the law will induce piracy.

BIBLIOGRAPHY

Cowie, Peter. *Finnish Cinema.* South Brunswick and New York: A.S. Barnes, 1976.

Film in Finland 1984. Helsinki: The Finnish Film Foundation, 1984.

Hiller, Jim, editor. *Cinema in Finland: An Introduction.* London: British Film Institute, 1975.

———, "Time of Roses? New Cinema in Finland," *Sight & Sound,* Winter 1972/73, pp. 41–43.

"I.F.G. Dossier: Scandinavia," *International Film Guide 1988,* editor Peter Cowie. London: Tantivy Press, 1987, pp. 48–55.

Uusitalo, Karl, "Finland," in *International Film Guide 1988,* editor Peter Cowie. London: Tantivy Press, 1987, pp. 168–179.

THE FINNISH FILM FOUNDATION (Suomen Elokuvasäätiö) was established by the Finnish government in 1969, utilizing a percentage of the income from the sale of theatre tickets to encourage film production, as well as support research and publications on Finnish cinema. Because only a limited amount of its income can be spent on export activities and the sponsorship of Finnish films at film festivals outside of the country, it has not been totally successful in the promotion of the country's film industry.

Finland's best-known film director, Jörn Donner (born February 5, 1933) has been chairman of the Finnish Film Foundation from 1982 to 1983 and from 1985 to the present; he was previously (from 1978 to 1981) managing director of the Swedish Film Institute*.

Address: Pohjoisranta 12, 00170 Helsinki, Finland.

FINNKINO OY was formed in the fall of 1986 through the amalgamation of Finland's three oldest theatres chains, Adams Filmi Oy (founded in 1912), Oy Kinosto (founded in 1920) and Savoy Filmi Oy. The merger was arranged by Oy Kinosto in the wake of a major decrease in theatre attendance in Finland. The new company operates one hundred screens and distributes the films of 20th Century-Fox and Orion Pictures Corporation, among others, in Finland.

Address: Kaisaniemenkatu 2b, 00100 Helsinki, Finland.

FLEAPIT is a British slang expression used, with a certain amount of affection, to refer to a rundown, neighborhood movie theatre where the implication is that the audience might be bitten by fleas. Few, if any, fleapits have survived the closure of many of the United Kingdom's theatres. *The Smallest Show on Earth* (1958), directed by Basil Dearden, written by William Rose and John Eldridge, and starring Bill Travers, Virginia McKenna, Peter Sellers, Margaret Rutherford, and Bernard Miles, is a film tribute to these establishments.

THE FOREIGN LEGION has appealed to filmmakers for many years. The two most popular stories in which the Legion appears are *Beau Geste* (filmed in 1926, 1939, and 1966, and in a 1977 comedic version, *The Last Remake of*

Beau Geste) and *The Desert Song* (filmed in 1929, 1943, and 1953). The French Foreign Legion has provided humor to Abbott and Costello, with *Abbott and Costello in the Foreign Legion* (1950), to Stan Laurel and Oliver Hardy in *Beau Hunks* (1931) and *The Flying Deuces* (1939), and to the British "Carry On" series*, with *Follow That Camel* (1967). Other features that have utilized the Legion are *Under Two Flags* (1922), *Beau Sabreur* (1928), *The Foreign Legion* (1928), *Morocco* (1930), *Beau Ideal* (1931), *The Devil's in Love* (1933), *The Lost Patrol* (1934), *Sons of the Legion* (1938), *Sahara* (1943), *Rogue's Regiment* (1948), *Outpost in Morocco* (1949), *Ten Tall Men* (1951), *Desert Legion* (1953), and *March or Die* (1977).

On television, this division of the French Army was the subject of a 1957 series, *Assignment Foreign Legion,* hosted by Merle Oberon.

FORMALISM is an expression used in connection with silent Soviet films, indicating the emphasis on form, or technique, rather than content. The major directors associated with formalism are Sergei Eisenstein, Dziga Vertov, Vsevolod Pudovkin, Leonid Trauberg, Alexander Dovzhenko, and Grigori Kozintsev, with the major formalist films being Eisenstein's *Staroe i novoe/The Old and the New/The General Line* (1929), Kozintsev and Trauberg's *Novyi Babylon/New Babylon* (1929), Fridrikh Ermler's *Oblomok imperii/Fragment of an Empire* (1929), and Vertov's *Chelovek s kinoapparatom/Man with a Movie Camera* (1929). Formalism in Soviet cinema came under increasing attack from elements within Soviet society, which identified it with bourgeois cinema, and it disappeared in the early thirties, along with the careers of many of Russia's greatest directors who had become too associated with formalism.

The only volume dealing with formalist film theory is *Poetika kino/The Poetics of Cinema,* edited by Boris Eikhenbaum in 1927.

BIBLIOGRAPHY

Youngblood, Denise J. *Soviet Cinema in the Silent Era, 1918–1935*. Ann Arbor, Mich.: UMI Research Press, 1985.

FRANCE. The French film industry had its beginnings in February, 1895 when Louis Lumière (1864–1948) patented his cinématograph machine. In March and June of 1895, he screened the first films he made to different societies. As Roy Armes argues, these films were probably "shot to demonstrate the qualities of the Lumière camera" and not with the idea of exhibiting the films. However, Lumière's aims changed, since on December 28, 1895, he had the first public showing of his films to a paying audience and, early in 1896, he began to train operators to take his camera around the world and have public shows. Lumière refused to sell his cinematograph and attempted to control both production and distribution, only leasing the films his company made.

While Lumière was the most important company, there were rivals challenging its dominance. The best known of the aesthetic rivals was Georges Méliès (1861–1938) whose films offered a fictional world in opposition to the actualities of the Lumières. However, the two people who followed Lumière's business example and later superseded his company were Charles Pathé and Léon Gaumont.

Charles Pathé (1863–1957) had been selling and exhibiting Edison Kinetoscope films and phonographs when he founded Pathé-Freres in 1896. After the success of Lumière's screening, Pathé commissioned a camera/projector that he marketed under his own name. In 1902 he acquired Lumière's patents and commissioned a new camera, which soon grew to dominate the world market. By 1907, when Pathé-Freres began to lease its films instead of selling them, the company sold cinematographic equipment, produced film stock, had a series of foreign exchanges to distribute films, and had its own cinemas to show its films.

Léon Gaumont (1863–1943) had begun by selling photographic equipment but then branched out to sell cinematogaphic equipment. Etablissements Gaumont was never as powerful as Pathé-Freres, though it also sought vertical integration of production, distribution, and exhibition. However, production was never one of Gaumont's main interests and his first films were made by his secretary, Alice Guy (1873–1968) (one of the first woman directors), on the understanding that it would not affect her work as his secretary.

While Pathé and Gaumont were dominant, they did not monopolize the entire industry and there were other companies such as Eclipse*, Eclair*, and Film d'Art* that successfully produced films which the Agence générale cinématographique (AGC) or Etablissements Aubert distributed. By 1907, then, the French industry had become rationalized and attained a state of equilibrium that lasted until the beginning of the First World War.

When the war broke out in August 1914, all the studios immediately ceased operation and did not reopen until November or December. When they did reopen, production was curtailed and this void was filled by both Aubert and Pathé who began releasing American films. By 1917, over 50 percent of the programs in Paris were from the United States. An attempt to win back the market was undertaken in 1918 when Pathé proposed a cartel of manufacturers. This idea was rejected by most distributors and exhibitors with the result that Pathé gave up the hope of competing with American films. In November 1918 Pathé-Cinema was formed from Pathé-Freres and this new company concentrated on distribution and exhibition while, in effect, ignoring production. Gaumont followed Pathé's lead and also turned away from production, except for the serials of Louis Feuillade (1873–1925), to concentrate on distribution.

The postwar industry was radically different in that according to historian Richard Abel, "it became dependent . . . on a cottage industry of small companies and individual producer-directors, on several big studios, and on an increasing number of co-production deals with other European countries." Two of the companies that were formed to fill the gap left by Pathé and Gaumont were Films Louis Nalpas, which produced *La Sultane de L'Amour/The Sultan of Love* (1919) and Germaine Dulac's *La Fête Espagñole/Spanish Festival* (1920), and Films Diamant, which had a great success with Max Linder in *Le Petit Café/*

The Little Cafe (1919). Neither company was strong enough to survive after their initial successes, however.

The independent filmmakers ranged from Abel Gance (1889–1981), who had been making films since 1911, to Jacques Feyder (1888–1948), who had began making comedies during the war, to the critic-turned-filmmaker Louis Delluc (1890–1924), who made his first film in 1919. The success of the independents with such varied films as *La Roue/The Wheel* (1922–1923) and *L'Atlantide* (1921) led Gaumont to fund a group of films called "Series Pax," while Pathé, after reorganizing in 1920 his company into two companies (Pathé-Cinema and Pathé-Consortium), provided funding for *Les Trois Mousquetaires/The Three Musketeers* (1921–1922). The return to producing was short-lived and by 1923 both Gaumont and Pathé-Consortium were basically making only serials.

With no dominant studios in the early twenties, experimental filmmakers began to attract attention. Among the most important of the new guard were: Jean Epstein (1897–1953), René Clair (1898–1980), and Jean Renoir (1894–1979). The films that they, and others, made generally fell under the heading of avant-garde, in that they were concerned not just with a narrative but with atmosphere, psychology, and subjectivity. The experimental avant-garde splintered further as one faction wished to do away with narrative altogether (Fernand Leger's *Ballet Mecanique* [1924] and Marcel Duchamp's *Anemic Cinema* [1926], for example) while another sect, the surrealists, wanted to exploit the cinema's relationship to dream and the unconscious (as in, most famously, *Un Chien Andalou* [1929]).

The commercial cinema, though, was not dead and the Société des Cinéromans, which made serials, formed an alliance with Pathé-Consortium in 1922 and by 1924 had become a vertically integrated company. Yet 1925 was not 1907, and Cinéromans was unable to dominate the market. The French industry was weak and the advent of sound only served to emphasize the point.

The two vertically integrated companies, Pathé-Natan and Gaumont-Franco-Film-Aubert (GFFA), were both thrown into virtual bankruptcy in, respectively, 1936 and 1934. With no major companies to lead the way, production once again devolved into the hands of small, undercapitalized companies. Paradoxically, this meant an increase in production as it, according to critic Roy Armes, "virtually doubled between 1929 and 1930 (rising from 52 to 94 features) and from 1931 onwards remained comfortably above one hundred films a year."

The films being made in the early thirties were thus as different as the companies set up to make them. Ranging from the assault of *L'Age d'or* (1930), to the comedy of *Le Million* (1931), to the anarchy of *Zero de Conduite* (1933) the only thing most of the films had in common was that someone had agreed to spend money to produce the film. This had changed by the middle of the thirties and the bulk of the films being produced were genre pieces; guaranteed not to lose money, if not necessarily to make money. There were exceptions to the rule such as Renoir's *Toni* (1935), but they were infrequent. The reaction to such banality were the films of the Popular Front and, in a different way, the poetic realists.

French society was being split apart in the thirties and as the threat of Hitler grew, so did the right-wing reaction in France. In 1933, a group of left-wing artists formed "Artists and Intellectuals against Fascism" and in 1934 the Popular Front was formed by an alliance of most of the left-wing groups. Films that strove to support the Popular Front included *Le Crime de Monsieur Lange* (1935), *La Marseillaise* (1938), and *La Belle Equippe* (1936). While the films of the poetic realists were not overtly political, such films as *Quai des Brumes/Port of Shadows* (1938) and *Le Jour Se Leve/Daybreak* (1939) indicate the despair and desperation which lay under the cheerfulness of most commercial films.

In 1940 France was occupied by the Nazis, and the film industry had a rebirth since the country was cut off from American films. While production was somewhat curtailed, there was seemingly little attempt by the Nazis to make the French industry a propaganda arm of the occupation. The industry prospered until 1946 when the government signed an agreement allowing thirty-six weeks a year of free competition at the theatres and only sixteen weeks a year for a French film quota. Since the U.S. companies had such a large backlog of films, they dominated the French theatres once again.

For the next ten years, the French films that the industry turned out were ruled by a "tradition of quality." This meant a well-crafted script, psychological realism, attention to detail, commercial considerations, and often, period reconstruction. This tradition was attacked in the fifties by the critics at two magazines: *Cahiers du Cinéma* and *Positif*. The critics at *Cahiers* developed out of the cine-clubs, the Cinémathèque Française,* and under the tutelege of André Bazin. Their criticism of the French film industry was basically apolitical and aesthetic. The critics from *Positif,* on the other hand, attacked the film culture from a left-wing, political position. While both groups of critics would go on to make films, it would be the people associated with *Cahiers* (François Truffaut, Jean-Luc Godard, Eric Rohmer, Jacques Rivette, and Claude Chabrol) who would be called "the New Wave."*

With the appearance of such films as *Les Cousins* (1959), *Les Quatre Cents Coups/The Four Hundred Blows* (1959), *À Bout de Souffle/Breathless* (1960), and *Paris Nous Appartient* (1961) a new style of filmmaking began to dominate the industry and a "New Wave" was proclaimed by critics in other countries. The "New Wave" was not limited to the *Cahiers* group but was expanded to include Alain Resnais, Louis Malle, and Roger Vadim among others. Producers began to fund many first-time directors, but it soon became apparent that the new directors were using a new style (modern settings, jump cuts, inside jokes, and hommages) to tell, in many cases, the same old stories.

While the events of May 1968 politicized some filmmakers (such as Godard) and helped bring about an interest in social issues, by the seventies the industry had become dominated by genres such as the gangster film and pornographic film. While many films were being made, the audience was being lost to television. Events have not improved any in the eighties except that the audience is now being lost to VCRs. In many ways the French industry remains caught in the trap it found itself in after the First World War: an audience that could barely support the native industry prefers foreign (i.e., U.S.) films and this basic instability leads to an instability in production. While such a structure can accommodate many different viewpoints, too often it has led to attempts to play it safe and give the audience the same genres, the same stars, and the same directors that have been popular earlier.

BIBLIOGRAPHY

Abel, Richard. *French Cinema: The First Wave, 1915–1929*. Princeton, N.J.: Princeton University Press, 1984.

Andrew, Dudley. *André Bazin*. New York: Oxford University Press, 1978.

Armes, Roy. *French Film*. New York: Dutton, 1970.

———. *French Cinema since 1946*. Cranbury, N.J.: A.S. Barnes, 1970.

Bandy, Mary Lea, editor. *Rediscovering French Film*. Boston: Little, Brown, 1983.

Bazin, André. *French Cinema of the Occupation and Resistance*. New York: Frederick Ungar, 1981.

Coissac, G.-Michel. *Histoire du Cinématographie*. Paris: Libraire Gauthier-Villars, 1925.

Ehrlich, Evelyn. *Cinema of Paradox: French Filmmaking under the German Occupation*. New York: Columbia University Press, 1985.

Fowler, Roy. *The Film in France*. London: Pendulum, 1946.

Graham, Peter. *The New Wave*. Garden City, N.Y.: Doubleday, 1968.

Lowry, Edward. *The Filmology Movement and Film Study in France*. Ann Arbor, Mich.: UMI Research Press, 1985.

Martin, John W. *The Golden Age of French Cinema, 1929–1959*. Boston: Twayne, 1983.

Martin, Marcel. *France*. New York: A.S. Barnes, 1971.

Michalczyk, John J. *The French Literary Filmmakers*. Philadelphia: The Art Alliance Press, 1980.

Monaco, Paul. *Cinema and Society: France and Germany during the Twenties*. New York: Elsevier Scientific, 1976.

Paris, James Reid. *The Great French Films*. Secaucus, N.J.: Citadel Press, 1983.

Renaitour, M. Jean-Michel. *Ou Va le Cinéma Français?* Paris: Éditions Baudinière, 1937.

Roux, Jean, and René Thevenet. *Industrie et Commerce du Film en France*. Paris: Éditions Scientifiques et Juriques, 1979.

Sadoul, Georges. *French Film*. London: Falcon Press, 1953.

Slide, Anthony. *Fifty Classic French Films: 1912–1982*. New York: Dover, 1987.

Thiher, Allen. *The Cinematic Muse: Critical Studies in the History of French Cinema*. Columbia: University of Missouri Press, 1979.

Védres, Nicole. *Images du Cinéma Français*. Paris: Les Éditions du Chene, 1945.

FRANCITA-REALITA was an additive color system, marketed in France between 1934 and 1938 by the Société de Films en Couleurs Naturelles Francita. In the United Kingdom, it was called British Realita and in the United States, Opticolor*. After the Second World War, the color process was remarketed by the Société Chromofilm of Paris.

BIBLIOGRAPHY
Koshofer, Gert. *Color: Die Farben des Films*. Berlin: Spiess, 1988.

THE FRANCO-AMERICAN CINEMATOGRAPHIC CORPORATION was a French production company founded in the summer of 1921, with financial backing from Henri de Rothschild, André Citroën, and others. Following the arrest of its secretary-general, André Himmel, for embezzlement, the company collapsed without the production of a single film.

FREE CINEMA was the name given to a movement—although it was never as formalized or as obvious as the word implies—to introduce social realism to British films. Its leader was Lindsay Anderson, and its origins lie in the Oxford University critical film journal of the late forties and early fifties, *Sequence*. The title "Free Cinema" was adopted for use in a series of six programs at London's National Film Theatre from 1956–1959. These screenings included all of the documentaries that had helped create the movement: Lindsay Anderson's *O Dreamland* (1953), Tony Richardson and Karel Reisz's *Momma Don't Allow* (1955), Lindsay Anderson's *Every Day except Christmas* (1957), and Karel Reisz's *We Are the Lambeth Boys* (1959). Free Cinema heralded the cycle of social-realist features that commenced with *Room at the Top* (1958), continued with *Look Back in Anger* (1959), *Saturday Night and Sunday Morning* (1960), *A Kind of Loving* (1962), and *The Loneliness of the Long Distance Runner* (1962), and ended with *This Sporting Life* (1963).

The Free Cinema movement was an attack on the old-style of documentary filmmaking, associated with John Grierson. It gained momentum, in part, because it obtained funding for its documentaries from the Experimental Fund of the British Film Institute*, and because Lindsay Anderson and others of its supporters were able to plead their cause in the Institute's journal, *Sight & Sound,* which was edited by an undergraduate colleague of Anderson's, Penelope Houston.

BIBLIOGRAPHY
Ellis, Jack C., "Changing of the Guard: From the Grierson Documentary to Free Cinema," *Quarterly Review of Film Studies,* vol. VII, no. 1, Winter 1982, pp. 23–35.

THE FRENCH REVOLUTION (1789–1799) has been the subject of a number of feature films, including *The Two Orphans* (1911), *The Two Orphans* (1915), *A Tale of Two Cities* (1917), *Orphans of the Storm* (1921), *Madame Sans Gêne* (1925), *Napoléon* (1927), *A Tale of Two Cities* (1936), *La Marseillaise* (1938), *Marie Antoinette* (1938), *Reign of Terror* (1949), *A Tale of Two Cities* (1958), *Start the Revolution without Me* (1970), and *Danton* (1983).

FUGITIVE CINEMA was a cooperative effort aimed at producing and releasing independent films in Belgium, with headquarters in Antwerp. Active through the seventies, it was established in 1964 by poet and art critic Paul De Vree, who was joined in the venture in 1966 by Robbe De Hert. Among the group's productions are *La Bombe* (1966), *S.O.S. Fonske* (1968), *Le Jugement Dernier* (1971), and *Hommage à Don Helder Camara* (1971). A similar group was later formed in the Netherlands.

BIBLIOGRAPHY

Davay, Paul, "Fugitive Cinema," in *International Film Guide 1973*, editor Peter Cowie. London: Tantivy Press, 1972, pp. 106–107.

FUJICOLOR is a three-color, subtractive process that was introduced by Japan's Fuji Photo Film Co. Ltd. in 1955. A number of features have been photographed or released in Fujicolor in the United States, but generally credit has gone to the American laboratory that handled the work, and the color is often identified as De Luxe Color or some other color system. Thanks to aggressive marketing of color film for consumer use, Fujicolor has become a household name in the United States.

BIBLIOGRAPHY

Ryan, Roderick T. *A History of Motion Picture Color Technology*. London and New York: Focal Press, 1977.

FUTURISM is generally conceded to be the creation of Filippo Tommaso Marinetti (1876–1944) in Italy in the early years of this century. The movement rejects all aspects of the past and embraces and glorifies a modern age of technology and machinery. Marinetti perceived of the film as being the natural vehicle of futurism although he rejected what is cited as the first futurist film, Aldo Molinari's *Mondo Baldoria* (1914). Aside from Italy, futurism was an active movement in Russia, where it was embraced by a number of revolutionists. It was more important in Russia in the field of literature, although it did exert some influence on a number of Soviet filmmakers, notably Sergei Eisenstein and Dziga Vertov.

G

GABON. According to a 1966 USIA report, Gabon had only two film theatres. It produced its first feature, *Les Tams-Tams se sont tus,* directed by Philippe Mory, in 1972. The only other Gabonese director is Jean-Marie Dong.

GAELIC. The Dublin-based Gael-Linn organization has sponsored many documentaries narrated in Gaelic, notable among which are George Morrison's *Mise Eire/I Am Ireland* (1959) and *Saoirse?/Freedom?* (1961). The first feature-length film to be shot in Gaelic is *Poitin/Poteen* (1979), directed by Bob Quinn and starring Cyril Cusack as a moonshiner, shot in the Gaelic speaking regions of Connemara in the Republic of Ireland. Quinn founded Cinegael in 1973, and he uses the company to produce Gaelic language films and television programs.

GAINSBOROUGH STUDIOS was founded in 1924 by Michael Balcon and Victor Saville, who purchased the former British studios of Paramount for £14,000. The building, which had started life as a power station supplying electricity for trams, was situated on Poole Street in the North London suburb of Islington. In 1928 Gainsborough was absorbed into the Gaumont-British Picture Corporation*, and when the Gaumont Studio at Shepherds Bush underwent a prolonged process of rebuilding from 1928–1932, Gainsborough served as the production arm of Gaumont-British. Balcon was in charge of production from 1924 to 1936, and his first "international" production, with Emelka Studios, Munich, was *The Pleasure Garden* (1924), which marked Alfred Hitchcock's directorial debut. Other Hitchcock features made at this time were *The Lodger* (1926), *Downhill* (1927), and *Easy Virtue* (1927). When Balcon left to join Metro-Goldwyn-Mayer, he was succeeded by the studio manager, Edward Black. In contrast with the cultured Balcon, Black was a shrewd, down-to-earth man with the common touch. Control of the company was now in the hands of the financiers, the Ostrer Brothers, and Mark Ostrer became executive producer. During the thirties, Black catered to popular tastes with a string of successful comedies which included the Crazy Gang films and seven Will Hay vehicles. *Oh,*

Mr. Porter! (1938), with Hay as the pompous stationmaster, has become a comedy classic. With *Bank Holiday,* directed by Carol Reed in 1938, a new type of heroine—an independent working girl irked by social restraints—emerged with Margaret Lockwood. Alfred Hitchcock directed Lockwood in *The Lady Vanishes* at Gainsborough in 1938.

During the early months of the Second World War, theatres were closed in the United Kingdom, and J. Arthur Rank shrewdly bought up film concerns such as Gainsborough, which he left more or less to its own devices. New ground was broken with the success of the Frank Launder and Sidney Gilliat populist epic, *Millions Like Us* (1943), and the first of the cycle of costume melodramas, *The Man in Grey* (1943). However, disagreements broke out between Black and Ostrer over choice of subjects, and Black resigned in 1943. In 1945, Gainsborough's *The Wicked Lady* was chosen for the Royal Film Performance—a daring choice in the opinion of many who considered the film bawdy and immoral.

In the postwar years, Sydney Box, a successful independent producer, took over as executive producer, and Gainsborough tried to come to terms with contemporary subjects. However, financial realism throughout the Rank Organization* brought about the sale of the studios in 1949. In recent years, the building has been used as a carpet warehouse.

Gainsborough had one asset for which it is uniquely remembered and that is its famous trademark. A smiling woman in a picture hat, based on the Gainsborough painting of actress Sarah Siddons, bows graciously to the audience to the accompaniment of a Mozart minuet. There were at least four different women who smiled on two generations of British filmgoers and introduced some 160 films.

BIBLIOGRAPHY

Aspinall, Sue, and Robert Murphy, editors. *Gainsborough Melodrama.* London: British Film Institute, 1983.

Durgnat, Raymond, "Gainsborough: The Times of Its Time," *Monthly Film Bulletin,* vol. LII, no. 619, August 1985, pp. 259–261.

Low, Rachael. *Film Making in 1930s Britain.* London: George Allen & Unwin, 1985.

Mason, James, "Gainsborough Portrait," (London) *Sunday Times Magazine,* November 1, 1970, pp. 84–85.

Seaton, Ray, and Roy Martin, "Gainsborough," *Films and Filming,* no. 332, May 1982, pp. 8–15.

———, "Gainsborough," *Films and Filming,* no. 333, June 1982, pp. 13–18.

GASPARCOLOR was a subtractive color process invented in Hungary in 1930 by Dr. Bela Gaspar (1899–1973), who came to the United States in 1939. The process was developed in the United Kingdom by Gasparcolor Ltd. (formed in 1934), utilizing special film manufactured by the Belgium Gavaert Company. With the outbreak of the Second World War, the company moved to the United States, with a laboratory in Burbank, California, and film manufactured by the Ansco Division of General Aniline and Film Corporation. In the United States, the process was chiefly utilized for the George Pal Puppetoon short subjects.

BIBLIOGRAPHY
Ryan, Roderick T. *A History of Motion Picture Color Technology*. New York: Focal Press, 1977.

GAUMONT. Gaumont is today the oldest extant film company in the world, having come into existence, initially as La Société Léon Gaumont et Cie in 1895. Its founder Léon Gaumont (1863–1946) was originally involved in photographic work, but, in 1896, appointed his secretary, Alice Guy, as a film director, and entered film production. Alice Guy was not only the world's first female director, but also one of the world's first directors. Gaumont quickly became involved not only in production, but also in distribution and exhibition, and, in 1907, his company was renamed La Société des Etablissements Gaumont (SEG). His company gained an international reputation for its serials of the teens, directed by Louis Feuillade. The early comedies of Gaumont's Jean Durand may well have influenced the American films of Mack Sennett.

In the twenties, Gaumont distributed the American features of M-G-M in France, but the decade also saw the pioneer's resignation from the company he had created, and its merger with Aubert Franco Film to become Gaumont Franco Film Aubert (GFFA). The latter was declared bankrupt in 1934, and four years later, a new company was formed with its merger with Publicité Alsacienne as La Société Nouvelle des Etablissements Gaumont (SNEG). SNEG became simply Gaumont in 1975, when a controlling interest in the company was purchased by Nicolas Seydoux.

The company has maintained its archives of newsreel footage shot between 1900 and 1974, when the newsreel department was disbanded. A documentary on the history of Gaumont, *Mille et une marguerites/A Thousand and One Daisies,* was produced in 1986 by Pierre Philippe, to celebrate the company's ninetieth year as a major part of the French film industry. It was a curious coincidence that the anniversary should have occurred at a time when Gaumont was suffering a number of reversals, and had been forced to sell its Italian subsidiary and scale back its distribution and production activities. It was a far cry from the pre–First World War years when the company had 21,000 employees worldwide, operated a 6,000-seat theatre, the Gaumont-Palace in Paris (opened in 1911), and had the world's largest studio at Buttes-Chaumont.

Address: 30 avenue Charles-de-Gaulle, 92200 Neuilly-sur-Seine, France.

BIBLIOGRAPHY
Alderman, Bruce, "Gaumont: 90 Years Old & Geared toward the Future," *The Hollywood Reporter,* October 21, 1986, p. G-3.
Slide, Anthony, editor. *The Memoirs of Alice Guy Blaché*. Metuchen, N.J.: Scarecrow Press, 1986.

GAUMONT-BRITISH NEWS was a British newsreel produced from 1929 to 1959. Its best-known commentator was E.V.H. Emmett. Footage from the newsreel is preserved and controlled by Visnews*.

GAUMONT-BRITISH PICTURE CORPORATION. In 1922, financier Isidore Ostrer acquired holdings in the Gaumont Company, one of the oldest-established film companies in the United Kingdom, which had started as an agent for the French company of the same name. It had soon expanded into production and distribution, and in 1913 had erected the first purposely built glass studio at Lime Grove, in the Shepherds Bush area of West London. In 1927, a new studio was built, and in 1929, Isidore Ostrer, and his brother Maurice, acquired total control of the company. The Ostrers were also interested in Michael Balcon's production company, Gainsborough Studios*, and floated it as a public company in 1928. It was formally associated with Gaumont-British, but not controlled by it. In 1932, yet another studio was built at Shepherds Bush, and Michael Balcon became director of production there, while still retaining responsibility for production at Gainsborough.

Between 1932 and 1936, the Shepherds Bush studios were working at virtually full capacity, but internal reorganization resulted in Balcon's choosing not to renew his contract in 1936, and by February 1937, the Gaumont-British had an annual debt of half-a-million pounds. The Shepherds Bush studios were closed down, new productions were based at Pinewood* and Islington studios, and the distribution of Gaumont-British films was turned over to General Film Distributors. In August 1939, a deal was arranged between General Film Distributors and Gainsborough, resulting in the reopening of the Gaumont-British studios under C.M. Woolf. In October 1941, Isidore Ostrer resigned from the company, and J. Arthur Rank became chairman. The Shepherds Bush studios were sold in 1948 to the British Broadcasting Corporation for conversion to television studios. The activities of Gaumont-British were gradually absorbed by the Rank, and in 1961 it was totally merged with the Rank Organization*.

The Ostrers were also interested in exhibition, and, in 1928, acquired one of the largest British theatre circuits, Provincial Cinematograph Theatres (PCT). By 1929, Gaumont-British controlled 287 theatres in the United Kingdom, with its chief competitor being ABC, headed by John Maxwell, who tried, unsuccessfully, to merge the two circuits in 1936. Under the chairmanship of J. Arthur Rank, the Gaumont-British and Odeon* circuits were merged, although remaining independent, to form the Circuits Management Association (CMA) in 1947. When theatre-going habits declined in the fifties, the Gaumont-British and Odeon circuits were so thinned out, that in 1958 they were merged into one Rank circuit.

BIBLIOGRAPHY

Allen, Frank, ''The History of British Film Studios: Gaumont (1914–1922) and Gaumont-British (1922–1937),'' *Film Collecting,* no. 7, 1980, p. 19.

Hartog, Simon, ''L'Histoire Exemplaire de la Gaumont British,'' *Filmechange,* no. 13, Winter 1981, pp. 47–62.

Low, Rachael. *Film Making in 1930s Britain.* London: George Allen & Unwin, 1985.

Oakley, Charles. *Where We Came In: The Story of the British Cinematograph Industry.* London: George Allen & Unwin, 1964.

GAUMONT GRAPHIC was a British newsreel produced from 1910 to 1932. Footage from the newsreel is preserved and controlled by Visnews*.

LES GEMEAUX (The Twins) was the first French company to be involved in the full-scale production of animated films. It was founded in 1936, in Paris, by designers André Sarrut and Paul Grimault. All of its productions were in color, with the best known being *Le petit soldat/The Little Soldier* (1947) and *La bergère et le ramoneur/The Shepherdess and the Chimney Sweep* (1953), a feature written by Jacques Prévert.

THE GEORGES DE BEAUREGARD AWARD is presented in France for a released feature, an unreleased feature, and a short. It was first given in 1985.

THE GERMAN LEAGUE FOR THE INDEPENDENT FILM (Deutsche Liga für Unabhängigen Film) was established in 1929 by Hans Richter and others to oppose censorship, to screen films that furthered its aims and which were primarily of Soviet origin.

GERMANY. Unlike most countries where the Lumière productions were the first films to be screened, Germany first saw the motion picture as presented by two brothers, Max (1863–1939) and Emil Skladanowsky (1859–1945) on November 1, 1895. The Lumière films were not seen in Berlin until December 2, 1895. Within months of those screenings, Oskar Messter (1866–1943) had opened a studio, and gradually developed the country's first major production company, whose most important star was Henny Porten (1888–1960). (Messter is also claimed by Germans as the inventor of the Maltese Cross mechanism, permitting intermittent movement in cameras and projectors.)

Aside from Messter, the most important German producer of the early teens was Paul Davidson, who introduced Danish actress Asta Nielsen (1883–1972) to the German cinema in 1911, and also persuaded Max Reinhardt (1873–1943) to be associated with him in a 1913 production, *Eine Venezianische nacht/A Venetian Night*. Trained by Reinhardt, Paul Wegener (1874–1948) developed as one of the country's leading actors in *Der student von Prag/The Student of Prague* (1913) and *Der Golem/The Golem* (1914), which he also co-directed with Henrik Galeen. The pair remade *The Golem* in 1920, and Galeen directed a remake of *The Student of Prague* in 1926.

In 1917, the German government created Universum Film Aktiengesellschaft/Ufa*, into which was merged Messter and Davidson's companies. Ufa was to become the dominant producer of German cinema for the next two decades, with some of the great names associated with the company being Fritz Lang (1890–1976), Ernst Lubitsch (1892–1947), Carl Mayer (1894–1944), F.W. Murnau (1888–1931), Pola Negri (1894–1988), and Erich Pommer (1889–1966).

Expressionism* was introduced to world cinema in 1919 with the production of *Das kabinett des Dr. Caligari/The Cabinet of Dr. Caligari,* written by Carl Mayer, directed by Robert Wiene (1881–1938), and starring Conrad Veidt (1893–1943). Other major German films of the genre include Wiene's *Genuine* (1920), Paul Leni's *Hintertreppe/Backstairs* (1921), and F.W. Murnau's *Schloss Vogelöd/Haunted Castle* (1921) and *Nosferatu* (1922).

The first German sound feature was *Melodie der Welt/World Melody* (1929), directed by Walter Ruttmann (1887–1941). It was the precursor of many lightweight, musical features of the thirties, including *Der Congress Tanzt/Congress Dances,* directed by Erik Charell (1895–1974) and *Zwei Herzen in Dreivierteltakt/Two Hearts in Waltz Time,* directed by Geza von Bolvary (1898–1961), both released in 1931. However, the most famous of early German sound films is unquestionably *Der blaue engel/The Blue Angel* (1930), directed by Josef von Sternberg (1894–1969) and starring Marlene Dietrich (born 1901), who had been in German films since 1923, but here achieved international fame and coincidentally a Hollywood film contract.

Von Sternberg and Dietrich had long departed Germany before the coming to power of the national socialists in 1933. The Nazi regime heralded the end of the "golden age" of German cinema, which had lasted for more than a decade and produced such classics as *Die spinnen/The Spiders* (1920), *Der Müde tod/Destiny* (1921), *Dr. Mabuse, der spieler/Dr. Mabuse, the Gambler* (1922), *Die Nibelungen* (1924), *Die Freüdlose gasse/The Joyless Street* (1925), *Faust* (1926), *Metropolis* (1927), *Spione/The Spy* (1928), *Mädchen in Uniform* (1931), *M* (1931), and *Das testament des Dr. Mabuse/The Last Will of Dr. Mabuse* (1933).

It meant the departure from the country of many of its greatest film personalities, including Elizabeth Bergner, Max Reinhardt, Albert Bassermann, Fritz Lang, Douglas Sirk, Fritz Kortner, and Peter Lorre. The Reichsfilmkammer* was created in 1933, and gradually the film industry came totally under the control of the Nazi Party and its propaganda minister Joseph Goebbels. One major director, G.W. Pabst (1885–1967), remained. Active throughout this period was Leni Riefenstahl (born 1902) who directed what are, despite their political undertones, two of the greatest documentaries of all time, *Triumph des willens/Triumph of the Will* (1934) and *Olympia* (1938). One of the most influential of Nazi filmmakers was Veidt Harlan (1899–1964), who directed the infamous anti-Semitic feature, *Jud Süss* (1940).

Despite the politics and even with the Second World War, entertainment features continued to be produced, with one of the most extraordinary being *Münchhausen/Baron Munchhausen,* filmed in Agfacolor*, directed by Josef von Baky and starring Hans Albers (1892–1960). The film was released in 1943 in celebration of Ufa's twenty-fifth anniversary.

GERMANY—EAST. Following the Second World War, the occupying Soviet forces in what became the German Democratic Republic (or East Germany) centralized the film industry under one state-owned company, DEFA* (Deutsche

Film Aktiengesellschaft), which took over the old Ufa studios. It was the Eastern sector of Berlin that contributed Germany's first postwar feature, *Die Mörder sind unter uns/The Murderers Are Amongst Us* (1946), directed by Wolfgang Staudte (born 1906). The film was an attempt to bring Germans face to face with their immediate past and starred Hildegard Knef/Hildegarde Neff (born 1925).

Producing an average of eighteen features a year after 1949, when the two German republics became a reality, East German cinema concerned itself with working class problems, national heroes, and the country's Nazi past. The films were not as ideological as one might expect, in part because many East German filmmakers lived in West Berlin, and because Stalin's death came relatively soon (in 1953) after the birth of the new republic, before a repressive Soviet influence could become too strong.

Slatan Dudow (1903–1963) had been a member of the Communist Party before fleeing Germany in the thirties, and he returned to East Germany to produce *Unser täglicht brot/Our Daily Bread* (1949) and *Stärker als die nacht/Stronger than the Night* (1954), among other films. Kurt Maetzig (born 1911) attacked anti-Semitism with *Ehe im schatten/Marriage in the Shadows* (1947), and glorified a national hero in the two-part *Ernst Thälmann* (1953 and 1955). In 1954, Konrad Wolf (1915–1982) came to East Germany, and became the country's most important and first internationally known director, thanks to such features as *Lissy* (1957) and *Sterne/Stars* (1958).

With the building of the Berlin Wall in 1961, East German filmmaking became more politicized for a new generation of directors, including Horst Seemann, Rolf Kirsten, and Frank Vogel. A decade later, the climate became somewhat more liberal, with films such as Heiner Carow's *Die legende von Paul und Paula/The Legend of Paul and Paula* (1974) and Egon Günther's *Der Dritte/The Third One* (1971). East German cinema made something of a breakthrough in 1977, when Frank Beyer's *Jakob, der lügner/Jacob the Liar* was nominated for an Academy Award for Best Foreign Language Film.

GERMANY—WEST. Wolfgang Staudte and Helmut Käutner (1908–1980) had both been active during the Nazi era, and both continued to produce films in postwar Germany, but ultimately neither had a major influence on the medium. Indeed, during the years in which Konrad Adenauer was rebuilding West Germany—basically from the late forties through the early sixties—German cinema had little impact outside of the country. One major genre during this period was Heimatfilm*/Homeland Film, concerned with the new image of German society. Robert Siodmak returned to Germany in the mid-fifties, as did Fritz Lang a few years later (to end his career where it had began), but neither man made films of any importance. One returning emigré, Peter Lorre, had some success in 1951 with *Der Verlorene/The Lost Man*.

A few German actors—Horst Buchholz, Curd Jürgens/Curt Jurgens, Romy Schneider, Maximilian Schell—gained fame outside of the country, but their talents could not hide the reality that West German films were dull and uninspired. As a revolt against these productions, a group of young filmmakers, led by Alexander Kluge (born 1932), issued the so-called Oberhausen Manifesto* in 1962, declaring their intention to create a new German cinema. A funding agency, Kuratorium Junger Deutscher Film* (Board of Curators of Young German Film) was created in 1965, and the German cinema was reborn, when *Der junge Törless/Young Törless,* directed by Volker Schlöndorff (born 1939) won the International Prize at the 1966 Cannes Film Festival*. Following Schlöndorff's success, there came films from Jean-Marie Straub (born 1933), Rainer Werner Fassbinder (1946–1982), Peter Schamoni, Wim Wenders, and Werner Herzog (born 1942). By the seventies, the German cinema had once again received worldwide recognition, and a new "golden age" was underway.

As of 1987, there were 3,297 theatres in operation in West Germany and West Berlin.

BIBLIOGRAPHY

Barlow, John D. *German Expressionist Film*. Boston: Twayne, 1982.

Bucher, Felix. *Germany: An Illustrated Guide*. New York: A.S. Barnes, 1970.

Collier, Jo Leslie. *From Wagner to Murnau*. Ann Arbor, Mich.: UMI Research Press, 1988.

Collins, Richard, and Vincent Porter. *WDR and the Arbeiterfilm*. London: British Film Institute, 1981.

Corrigan, Timothy. *New German Film: The Displaced Image*. Austin: University of Texas Press, 1983.

Eisner, Lotte H. *The Haunted Screen*. London: Thames and Hudson, 1969.

Fischer, Robert. *Der neue Deutsche film 1960–1980*. Munich: Goldmann Verlag, 1981.

Franklin, James. *New German Cinema: From Oberhausen to Hamburg*. Boston: Twayne, 1983.

Helt, Richard C., and Marie E. Helt. *West German Cinema since 1945: A Reference Guide*. Metuchen, N.J.: Scarecrow Press, 1987.

Hembus, Joe, and Christa Bandmann. *Klassiker des Deutschen Tonfilms 1930–1960*. Munich: Goldmann Verlag, 1980.

Hull, David Stewart. *Film in the Third Reich*. Berkeley: University of California Press, 1969.

Jansen, Peter W., and Wolfram Schütte. *Film in der DDR*. Munich: Hanser, 1977.

Kluge, Alexander, editor. *Bestandsaufnahme: Utopie Film*. Frankfurt: Zweitausendeins, 1983.

Kracauer, Siegfried. *From Caligari to Hitler*. Princeton, N.J.: Princeton University Press, 1947.

Kreimeier, Klaus. *Kino und filmindustrie in der BRD: Ideologieproduktion und klassenwirklichkeit nach 1945*. Kronberg: Scriptor, 1973.

Leiser, Erwin. *Nazi Cinema*. New York: Macmillan, 1974.

Manvell, Roger, and Heinrich Fraenkel. *The German Cinema*. New York: Praeger, 1971.

Monaco, Paul. *Cinema & Society: France and Germany during the Twenties*. New York: Elsevier Scientific Publishing Co., 1976.

Ott, Frederick W. *The Great German Films*. Secaucus, N.J.: Citadel Press, 1986.

Petley, Julian. *Capital and Culture: German Cinema 1930–1945*. London: British Film Institute, 1979.

Pflaum, Hans Günther, and Hans Helmut Prinzler. *Cinema in the Federal Republic of Germany*. Bonn: Inter Nationes, 1983.
Phillips, Klaus, editor. *New German Filmmakers: From Oberhausen through the 1970s*. New York: Frederick Ungar, 1984.
Rentschler, Eric. *West German Film in the Course of Time*. Bedford Hills, N.Y.: Redgrave, 1984.
Sandford, John. *The New German Cinema*. New York: Da Capo, 1980.
Wollenberg, Hans H. *Fifty Years of German Film*. London: Falcon Press, 1948.

GEVA FILMS was a major Israeli production company of the fifties and sixties. Founded in 1950, it was headed by Mordecai Navon and maintained studios in Givatayim.

THE GHANA FILM UNIT (formerly known as the Gold Coast Film Unit) was a government-sponsored documentary group, active in the forties and fifties, under the supervision of Sean Graham. Among its productions are *The Boy from Kumasenu* (1951), *Mr. Mensa Builds a House* (1955), and *Jaguar* (1957).

GIBRALTAR has no film industry, although it was utilized for location shooting of features such as *The Clue of the Missing Ape* (1962), *Seven Days in May* (1964), and *The Living Daylights* (1987). There have been three theatres on the rock since the thirties. There is one distributor, Venus Enterprises Ltd., 4 Ocean Heights, P.O. Box 153. Entertainment is chiefly the responsibility of the Gibraltar Broadcasting Corporation (18 South Barrack Road).

GLASGOW. Scotland's largest city, Glasgow, probably first became familiar to American filmgoers with the 1984 Universal release of *Comfort and Joy,* starring Bill Patterson and written and directed by Bill Forsyth. The latter had also been responsible for two earlier features with Glasgow backgrounds, *That Sinking Feeling* (1980) and *Gregory's Girl* (1981). One of the first features with a Glasgow location, although it was, in reality, filmed in London by New World, was *The Gorbals Story* (1949), directed by David MacKane and featuring members of the Glasgow Unity Theatre.

BIBLIOGRAPHY

McArthur, Colin, editor. *Scotch Reels*. London: British Film Institute, 1982.

GODZILLA. A stereotypical prehistoric monster, usually played by a man in a rubber suit, Godzilla has proved to be one of the most enduring of horror creations. He was introduced by the Japanese Toho Company in 1954 in *Godzilla, King of the Monsters/Gojira*. Raymond Burr was the human star, assuring the film an American release (by Embassy in 1956). Godzilla was revived because of nuclear radiation in the South Pacific, and virtually all of the Godzilla films make antinuclear statements. In trying to assess Godzilla's appeal, Vincent Price and V.B. Price wrote in *Monsters* (New York: Grosset & Dunlap, 1981), "Old

Godzilla still comes through as a lumbering but well meaning lout—sort of an overgrown version of Steinbeck's Lennie put into animation.''

The Godzilla films are: *Godzilla, King of the Monsters/Gojira* (1954), *Gigantis the Fire Monster/Gojira No Gyakushyu* (1955), *King Kong vs. Godzilla/Kingu Kongu Tai Gojira* (1962), *Godzilla vs. the Thing/Mosura Tai Gojira* (1964), *Gidrah, the Three-Headed Monster/Sandai Kaiju Chikyu Saidai No Kessan* (1964), *Monster Zero/Kaiju Daisenso* (1965, reissued in 1970 as *Invasion of the Astro-Monsters), Godzilla vs. the Sea Monster/Nankai No Dai Ketto* (1966), *Son of Godzilla/Gojira No Musuku* (1968), *Destroy All Monsters/Kaiju Soshingeki* (1968), *Godzilla's Revenge/Oru Jaiju Daisingeki* (1969), *Godzilla vs. the Smog Monster/Gojira Tai Hedora* (1971), *Godzilla on Monster Island/Gojira Tai Gaigan* (1971), *Godzilla vs. Megalon/Gojira Tai Megaro* (1973), *Godzilla vs. the Bionic Monster/Gojira Tai Mekagojira* (1974), *Terror of Godzilla/Mekagojira No Gyakushu* (1975), and *Godzilla 1985* (1985). Godzilla also appeared in a dream sequence in Paramount's *The Bad News Bears Go to Japan* (1978), and the name was used in the documentary, *Godzilla Meets Mona Lisa* (1984).

Godzilla, or as he is known in Japan, Gojira, has spawned a number of other Japanese monsters, including Rodan, Spiga, Manda, Mothra, Ghidrah, and his son, Minya. Most of the films were produced by Tomoyuki Tanaka, and the directors most closely associated with the series are Inoshiro Honda and Jun Fukuda.

U.S. rights to the Godzilla character are controlled by Henry G. Saperstein, and the monster has been utilized to endorse products as varied as Dr. Pepper and Hallmark Greeting Cards.

BIBLIOGRAPHY

Kogan, Rick, ''It Was a Long Time Coming, But Godzilla, 'This Is Your Life,' '' *Chicago Tribune*, Section 13, September 15, 1985, pp. 15–16.

Kwitny, Jonathan, ''He Says 'AARGHH!' Or Else 'YOWWLL!' And Makes Millions,'' *Wall Street Journal*, July 19, 1977, pp. 1, 21.

Leerhsen, Charles, ''Going Gaga for Godzilla,'' *Newsweek*, July 28, 1986, p. 60.

Newsom, Ted, ''A Silver Anniversary Tribute to Godzilla,'' *Oui*, June 1981, pp. 93–97.

GOFILEX FILM B.V. is short for Goede Film Exploitatie (Good Film Exploitation), a Dutch distributor specializing in quality films suitable for Catholic tastes. Founded in March 1939, it is one of the oldest extant Dutch film companies.

Address: Postbus 421, 3430 AH Nieuwegein, Netherlands.

BIBLIOGRAPHY

''Gofilex: From Shaky Beginnings to International Prominence,'' *The Hollywood Reporter*, March 13, 1984, pp. S1–S6.

THE GOFTA AWARD was first presented by the New Zealand Guild of Film and Television Arts in 1986.

THE GOLD BUG AWARDS are presented annually by the Swedish Film Institute*. The multicolored ceramic "bugs" are usually presented in only five categories and limited to Swedish films and personalities. They were first awarded in 1984, when the winner for Best Direction was Ingmar Bergman.

GOLDCREST FILMS AND TELEVISION LTD. One of the most important and influential British producing and releasing companies of the last two decades, Goldcrest was founded in 1977 by Jake Eberts, with financial assistance from the Pearson-Longman Publishing Group. The chairman of the latter, Lord Blakenham, is also chairman of the Royal Society of Birds, and so, perhaps appropriately, Goldcrest is named in honor of a British bird which is a member of the wren family.

Jake Eberts left the company in 1983, following a restructuring, but he returned in 1985, at which time Sir Richard Attenborough became a figurehead chairman of the board, replacing James Lee as the company's chief executive. Sandy Lieberson was production chief at Goldcrest from 1984 to 1985, but the producer most associated with the company is board member David Puttnam.

Among the features with which Goldcrest is associated are *Chariots of Fire* (1981), *Gandhi* (1982), *The Killing Fields* (1984), *The Mission* (1985), *Absolute Beginners* (1985), *A Room with a View* (1986), *Sid and Nancy* (1986), and *Maurice* (1987).

Because of its involvement with the disastrous epic of the American war of independence, *Revolution* (1985), the company suffered a $15 million loss. Its television arm had been producing films for Channel 4*, but these activities were put on hold. After a bidding war, which began the previous year, Goldcrest was acquired in 1987 by Brent Walker.

Address: Waverly House, 7/12 Noel Street, London W1V 3PB, United Kingdom.

BIBLIOGRAPHY

"Embattled Goldcrest: Sir Richard to the Rescue," *Variety*, October 29, 1985, pp. 172–173, 175.

Feder, Barnaby J., "Goldcrest: New Star of British Film," *New York Times*, November 25, 1984, pp. F8–F9.

"Goldcrest's Touch," *Forbes*, May 23, 1983, p. 166.

Greenberg, James, "Special-Event, Mid-Range Films with a Difference Parameters for Goldcrest," *Daily Variety*, March 29, 1985, pp. 1, 39.

GOSKINO. Formed in 1923, the Moscow-based Goskino was an important Soviet production company of the twenties. Among its features are Lev Kuleshov's *Neobychainiye priklucheniya Mistera Vesta v stranye bolshevikov/The Extraordinary Adventures of Mr. West in the Land of the Bolsheviks* (1924), Dziga Vertov's *Kino-glaz/Kino-Eye* (1924), Lev Kuleshov's *Luch smerti/The Death Ray* (1925), Sergei Eisenstein's *Bronenosets Potemkin/Potemkin* (1925), and Sergei Eisentein's *Stachka/Strike* (1925).

THE GOYA AWARDS are the Spanish equivalents of the ''Oscars'' and are presented by the Academia de las Artes y las Ciencias Cinematograficas (Academy of Motion Picture Arts and Sciences) (c/ General Oráa, 68-5 Dcha, 28006, Madrid). They were first awarded in April 1987, when the winners were Fernando Fernan-Gomes (Best Picture and Best Screenplay for *Viaje a ningana parte/Voyage to Nowhere,* and Best Actor for *Mambru se fue a la guerre/Mambru Went to War*), Amparoro Rivellas (Best Actress for *Hay que deschacer la casa*), and Teo Escamilla (Best Cinematography for *El Amor brujo*).

GRANDSCOPE was the first Japanese anamorphic widescreen system, similar to CinemaScope. It was created by the Shochiku Company* and first used for *Rebyu Tanjo/Birth of a Revue* (1955).

GRANDS FILM INDEPENDENTS was a French production company, founded by Jacques Feyder and Max Linder, with financial backing from Dimitri de Zoubaloff and François Porcher. It ceased operations in 1925, with its last film being *Visages d'enfants*.

GREECE. Greek cinema did not come into its own until the fifties. The earliest known Greek film is a 1906 short on the revival of the Olympic Games. The first Greek filmmaker was, in actuality, a Hungarian named Joseph Hepp. He, along with others, was responsible for the meagre forty-seven features produced in the country prior to 1940, a country with 150 theatres (in 1937) and no film studio. The forties witnessed little progress in the Greek film industry; the Second World War and the civil war severely limited filmmaking to less than 20 features in the decade.

The number of features increased in the fifties, a decade that saw the emergence of the country's best-known director, Michael Cacoyannis (born 1922) whose first feature was *Karikatiko Xipnima/Windfall in Athens* (1954). Cacoyannis' second feature, *Stella* (1955), introduced actress Melina Mercouri (born 1923) to the screen, and she, like Cacoyannis, went on to enjoy international fame (and to become Minister of Culture following the 1981 election of Andreas Papandreou as prime minister). Other directors of importance in the fifties were Grigoris Grigoriou, Nikos Koundouros, and George Tzavellas. The first two were later to become instructors at the Stavrakos Film School in Athens, of which they were graduates.

The following decade saw more international success for the Greek cinema with Cacoyannis' *Zorba the Greek* (1965) and Jules Dassin's *Never on Sunday* (1960). The former helped draw world attention to the music of Mikis Theodorakis. Greek writer Vasili Vasilikos provided the novel upon which Greek-born director Costa-Gavras' film, *Z* (1968) was based. In 1960, Greece gained its own international film festival, with the creation of the Thessaloniki Film Festival.

The sixties decade ended with the 1967 right-wing takeover of the country, which, surprisingly, did not hurt Greek cinema. In 1970, a total of eighty-eight features were produced. Theodore Angelopoulos, who is considered by many the most important of "new" Greek directors, made his debut in 1970 with *Anapatastassi/ Reconstruction* (1970). The film paved the way for the New Greek Cinema, which worked within the system created by the country's military dictatorship, producing films primarily concerned with a reexamination of Greek history. Directors, many of whom were also screenwriters, who emerged during this period include Alexis Damianos, Pandelis Voulgaris, Pavlos Tassio, Tonia Marketaki, Dimitris Mavrikios, and Nikos Panayiotopoulos. The establishment of the Greek Film Centre*, although its workings were often criticized, helped the promotion of Greek cinema abroad.

On the negative side, the introduction of television in the early seventies hurt the industry, with the number of features produced dropping from sixty-three in 1973 to thirty-eight in 1974.

With the return to democracy in 1981, the Greek film industry flourished, with films dealing with topics as controversial as aging and death (*To taxidi toy melitos/Honeymoon,* director George Panaussopoulos, 1979), homosexuality (*Angelos/Angel,* director George Katakouzinos, 1982), and alcoholism (*Enas isichos thanatos/A Quiet Death,* director Frieda Liappa, 1987) receiving wide praise.

In 1986, the Thessaloniki Film Festival was reorganized, and the government introduced a new cinema law that required the return of the levy on theatre admissions to producers and distributors, together with a difficult-to-enforce arrangement whereby theatre owners were required to screen a certain number of Greek productions. With only thirty-six Greek features released in the 1985–1986 season there is obviously insufficient product for such a law. Censorship has been abolished, except with regard to children under seventeen. No children under five may be admitted to any of the country's two hundred indoor and four hundred outdoor theatres.

BIBLIOGRAPHY

Carter, Syndey, "Greek Films," *Sight & Sound,* vol. XV, no. 60, Winter 1946–47, pp. 133–134.

Dallas, Athena, "Michael Cacoyannis," *Film Comment,* vol. I, no. 6, Fall 1963, pp. 44–45.

Georgakas, Dan, "The Bacchae on Broadway: A Conversation with Michael Cacoyannis and Irene Pappas," *Greek Accent,* October 1980, pp. 32–35.

———, "Greece," in *World Cinema since 1945,* editor William Luhr. New York: Ungar, 1987, pp. 273–286.

Safilos-Rothschild, C., " 'Good' and 'Bad' Girls in Modern Greek Movies," *Journal of Marriage and Family,* August 1968, pp. 527–531.

Schuster, Mel. *The Contemporary Greek Cinema.* Metuchen, N.J.: Scarecrow Press, 1979.

THE GREEK FILM CENTRE was created as a subsidiary of the government-controlled Hellenic Industrial Development Bank. Founded in 1970, it is one of the primary producers of Greek films—through the issuance of grants—and it is also responsible for the promotion of Greek films. During its first decade of existence, the Centre was highly criticized as a bureaucratic organization with little understanding of filmmaking, but in recent years it has gained in stature and support from Greek producers and directors. Michalis Koutouzis became its director in 1986, replacing Pavlos Zannas, and he organized Hellas Film as a branch of the Centre for the promotion and sale of Greek films abroad.

Address: 10 Panepistimou Avenue, Athens 134, Greece.

GREENLAND has been the subject of two major documentary features. In 1922, Pathé released Robert Flaherty's study of Eskimo life, *Nanook of the North*. In 1985, a Swedish feature, *Iughuit: The People at the Navel of the World,* directed by Staffan and Ylva Julen, dealt with the Eskimos of Upper Thule. See also NORTH POLE.

GREENWICH FILM. Active from 1967, Greenwich Film has long been associated with director Luis Buñuel and producer Serge Silberman. It has produced or co-produced *La voie lactée/The Milky Way* (1968), *Le charme discrét de la bourgeoisie/The Discreet Charm of the Bourgeoisie* (1972), *Le fantôme de la liberté/The Phantom of Liberty* (1974), and *Cet obscur object du désir/That Obscure Object of Desire* (1977), all directed by Buñuel, as well as the immensely popular French feature, *Diva* (1980).

Address: 72 Champs-Elysees, 75008 Paris, France.

GROUPE OCTOBRE was a radical French theatre group active from 1933 to 1936. None of its members were particularly well known, but the group, as a whole, did have an influence on French films of the late thirties, notably those of Jean Renoir.

GROUP 3 was established in 1951 by the National Film Finance Corporation* (NFFC) to provide opportunities for young directors and actors in the British film industry. John Grierson was executive producer; John Baxter, an experienced feature director, was production controller; and Michael Balcon was chairman. Coming from documentary filmmaking, Grierson was slow in organizing scripts, and so the first feature was directed by Baxter at Southall Studios. This was *Judgment Deferred* (1952), a simple thriller set in Dorset against the background of modern-day drug trafficking. It served to initiate less experienced members of the studio and, incidentally, introduced Joan Collins to the film public. The next three projects that went into production in 1952 were typical of the twin pulses driving the group—Grierson's documentary tradition and Balcon's Ealing* comedies. They were *Brandy for the Parson,* directed by John Eldridge (previously known for his documentaries) and starring Kenneth More; *You're Only*

Young Twice, on which another documentary filmmaker, Terry Bishop, made his somewhat unsuccessful feature film debut; and *Time Gentlemen Please,* directed by Lewis Gilbert and introducing a young Irish actor, Eddie Byrne. The most praised and best remembered of the early Group 3 productions was *The Brave Don't Cry* (1952), a dramatic reconstruction of a true mining disaster, directed by Philip Leacock and starring John Gregson. The most commercially successful film was, ironically, a documentary, *The Conquest of Everest* (1953), for which Group 3 had taken the foresighted decision to pay the cost of getting whatever footage was possible without knowing the outcome of the expedition.

However, the life of Group 3 was to be short—it was closed down in 1955. It had lost Grierson as executive producer in 1952, due to illness, and Balcon resigned in 1954, feeling that he was involved in too many overlapping activities. During the time that Grierson, Balcon, and Baxter had been together there had been many struggles due to their strong, differing personalities. Within the industry, the Rank Organization*, independent producers, and executives of the British Film Producers' Association were opposed to the existence of Group 3. Unfriendly exhibitors saw to it that these government-subsidized films appeared mainly on the lower half of double bills and until the final year, they received only a demeaning flat fee at the box office.

During its existence, Group 3 completed twenty-two films, with average budgets of £50 thousand. In 1969, the British Broadcasting Corporation purchased the entire library from the NFFC, and the Group 3 films are still seen, from time to time, on British television.

BIBLIOGRAPHY

MacCann, Richard Dyer, "Subsidy for the Screen: Grierson and Group 3," *Sight & Sound,* vol. XLVI, no. 3, Summer 1977, pp. 169–173.

GUAM has no film industry, but there is one distributor active, Con Ros Inc. (P.O. Box 8696, Tamuning, Guam 96911), and there are two broadcasters, Guam Educational Telecommunications Corporation (P.O. Box 21449, Guam 96921) and Pacific Broadcasting Corporation/Guam Television (P.O. Box 368, Agana, Guam 96910).

GUATEMALA See CENTRAL AMERICA

H

HAGGAR AND SONS. Between 1899 and 1907, William Haggar and his son, Walter, toured the fairgrounds of South Wales exhibiting films that they had produced themselves. The best known of the Haggar productions is *The Life of Charles Peace* (1905), which is considered a sophisticated British film of the period.

BIBLIOGRAPHY

Low, Rachael, and Roger Manvell. *The History of the British Film: 1896–1906*. London: George Allen & Unwin, 1948.

Slide, Anthony, "William Haggar," *Cinema Studies,* vol. II, no. 4, June 1967, p. 65.

HAITI has almost no film production history, despite former-president Jean-Claude Duvalier's attempts in 1976 to encourage a film industry there and the government's surprising lack of control with regard to censorship, exhibition, or distribution. The country has no appeal for location shooting, and, not surprisingly, the 1967 film version of Graham Greene's Haitian novel, *The Comedians,* was shot elsewhere. There were seven theatres in the country in 1937, with the number rising to eighteen by 1949. There is one major distributor, Airport-Cine (3 boulevard Jn. Jacques Dessaline, Port-au-Prince).

The first self-proclaimed Haitian feature, *Haitian Corner* (1987), directed by Raoul Peck, was shot in New York and concerned with the life of exiled Haitians there.

HALAS AND BATCHELOR CARTOON FILMS LTD. Two of the best-known and most highly respected of British animators are John Halas and Joy Batchelor. The former immigrated to the United Kingdom from his native Hungary in 1936, and, in 1940, joined forces with Joy Batchelor to form Halas and Batchelor Films Ltd. In the forties, the couple were primarily involved in the production of propaganda and informational cartoons. International recognition came in 1954 with their somewhat pedantic feature-length animated film of George Orwell's *Animal Farm,* the first British cartoon feature. Other films that are widely known include *The Owl and the Pussy Cat* (1953), *The History of the Cinema* (1956), and *Ruddigore* (1966). The company was eventually taken over by Tyne Tees Television, and Halas and Batchelor reorganized as the Educational Film Centre.

Address: John Halas & Joy Batchelor Educational Film Centre, 3/7 Kean Street, London W.C.2, United Kingdom.

HAMMER FILM PRODUCTIONS LTD. has the distinction of being the least critically acclaimed company, but the most financially successful in British film-making history. It is internationally renowned for its production of low-budget horror films, although these are, by no means, its only output.

The company's origins go back to 1935, when Enrique Carreras, owner of a theatre circuit, formed a distribution company, Exclusive Films, and a film production company, Hammer Productions, with William Hinds, a vaudeville performer who had worked under the name of Will Hammer. Carreras and Hinds reformed the company in 1947 with their sons, James Carreras and Anthony Hinds. That same year, it began production of a series of films based on popular radio serials, such as "PC49," "Dick Barton," "The Lyon Family," and "The Man in Black." After several moves, the company settled at Bray Studios in Berkshire, where it remained until 1968.

Hammer's first major success came in 1955, when it adapted the television series, *The Quatermass Experiment* (U.S. *The Shock*) for £48 thousand and made a profit of more than £1 one million. This success continued in 1958 with *Dracula* (U.S. *House of Dracula*), starring Christopher Lee and directed by Terence Fisher and established the company's reputation for horror films. During the next decade, Hammer concentrated on producing versions of Dracula and Frankenstein and popular classics such as *The Hound of the Baskervilles* and *Dr. Jekyll and Mr. Hyde*. Werewolves and mummies also received the Hammer treatment. Christopher Lee continued as Count Dracula, and Peter Cushing was introduced as Baron Frankenstein. Among the distinguished actors who have appeared in Hammer horror films are Bette Davis, Tallulah Bankhead, Cesar Romero, Ursula Andress, Jack Palance, and Ben Lyon. Joseph Losey directed *The Damned* (1962, U.S. *These Are the Damned*) for Hammer, but it is Terence Fisher who has provided the company with its distinctive Gothic style.

In 1966, to celebrate its one-hundredth film, Hammer made its first and most successful prehistoric epic, *One Million Years B.C.*, starring Raquel Welch. In 1968 the company was awarded the Queen's Award for Industry in recognition of its earnings of foreign currency. The company's commercial success continued into the seventies with a series of films based on popular television series, such as "On the Buses," "Love Thy Neighbour," and "Nearest and Dearest." However, late in the decade, the company was on the verge of bankruptcy, from which it was rescued by Brian Lawrence and Roy Skeggs, who have, in the eighties, revitalized Hammer with the production of a series of made for television movies, "Hammer House of Mystery and Suspense."

Address: EMI Elstree Studios, Boreham Wood, Herts WD6 1JG, United Kingdom.

BIBLIOGRAPHY

Castell, David, "The Rise of the House of Hammer," *Films Illustrated*, December 1972, pp. 20–25.

Eyles, Allen, Robert Adkinson, and Nicholas Fry. *The House of Horror: The Story of Hammer Films*. London: Lorrimer, 1973.

Marrero, Robert. *Vampires: Hammer Style*. Key West, Fla.: RGM Publications, 1982.

Pirie, David. *Hammer: A Cinema Case Study*. London: British Film Institute, 1980.

Smith, Trevor, "The Hammer Story," *Film Collecting*, no. 3, 1977, pp. 4–9.

HANDMADE FILMS. A low profile production company, primarily known for its comedies, Handmade Films was hailed (in the August 2, 1986, edition of *Screen International*) as "one of the UK's most successful." Also in 1986, it received a special award at the London Standard Film Awards for "Outstanding Contributions to British Cinema." Handmade Films, whose logo consists of a hand and camera molded together, was founded in 1978 by U.S. businessman Denis O'Brien and former Beatle George Harrison. Its films have all been well received in the United States, both critically and at the box office, with some of its more important productions being *Life of Brian* (1979), *The Long Good Friday* (1980), *Time Bandits* (1981), *Privates on Parade* (1983), *A Private Function* (1984), *Mona Lisa* (1986), and *Withnail and I* (1987).

Address: 26 Cadogan Square, London SW1X OJP, United Kingdom.

HEIMAT (Homeland) was a German film genre of the fifties, presenting a bright picture of Germany and German society. A typical example of such films is Hans Deppe's *Schwarzwaldmädel/Black Forest Girl* (1950), the first German feature to be shot in color after the Second World War.

HEPWORTH MANUFACTURING COMPANY. Cecil Hepworth (1874–1953) was one of the most important pioneers, and certainly one of the best-known names, in the British film industry. The son of a famous magic lantern lecturer, he set up a film printing laboratory at Walton-on-Thames, just outside of London, in 1898, making developing and processing available to any film producer in the United Kingdom. When business was not as profitable as he had hoped, Hepworth turned to making films, fifty feet in length, of simple subjects such as rough seas, comic cycle races, and phantom railroad rides. By the turn of the century, the Hepworth Manufacturing Company was producing one hundred films a year. In 1905, it produced one of the most popular films of the period, *Rescued by Rover,* written by Hepworth's wife and telling the story of an infant (Hepworth's baby), who is kidnapped by a gypsy and rescued by the family dog (Hepworth's dog). Rather than use titles, the film utilized low angle and panning shots and innovative editing to convey the narrative. It sold nearly four hundred copies, causing the negative to wear out so that the production had to be twice refilmed.

Hepworth's next achievement was the Vivaphone system, a rather primitive sound process involving synchronization of film with a phonograph. In 1907, disaster struck when fire swept the studios. Both the film trade and Hepworth's own staff, in whom he inspired great loyalty, rallied around, and recovery was slowly made, with the producer building a bigger and better glass-house studio alongside his original one. One of the company's biggest successes at this time was the Tilly Girls series of one-reel films, directed by Lewin Fizhamon and starring Chrissie White and Alma Taylor.

Of the principal companies at the outbreak of the First World War, only Hepworth continued in operation. Larry Trimble, who had come over from the United States to produce films starring American Florence Turner, under the brand name of "Turner Films," returned to the States in 1916, and his place as director was taken by Henry Edwards, who specialized in tender, sentimental dramas, in which he often starred.

In 1920, Hepworth made its most commercially successful feature, *Alf's Button,* starring Leslie Henson, and it was followed two years later by the company's best known film, *Comin' thro' the Rye*. Hepworth decided to expand from two to six studios, and to generate his own electrical power, a decision that proved to be a costly error. A public company, Hepworth Picture Plays Limited was formed, but it was badly undersubscribed, and went bankrupt in 1924. The studios were acquired by Nettlefold Film Productions, and the Hepworth negatives were disposed of by an obtuse receiver as "junk."

BIBLIOGRAPHY

Hepworth, Cecil M. *Came the Dawn: Memories of a Film Pioneer*. London: Phoenix House, 1951.

Honri, Baynham, "Cecil M. Hepworth: His Studios and Techniques," *British Journal of Photography,* January 15, 1971, pp. 48–51, 60.

———, "Cecil M. Hepworth: His Studios and Techniques, Part 2," *British Journal of Photography,* January 22, 1971, pp. 74–79.

If It Moves—Film It: A History of Film-Making in Walton-on-Thames 1900–1939, Commemorating the Work of Cecil Hepworth and Clifford Sapin. Weybridge, Surrey: Weybridge Museum, 1973.

Low, Rachael. *The History of the British Film: 1906–1914*. London: George Allen & Unwin, 1949.

———. *The History of the British Film: 1914–1918*. London: George Allen & Unwin, 1950.

———. *The History of the British Film: 1918–1929*. London: George Allen & Unwin, 1971.

Low, Rachael, and Roger Manvell. *The History of the British Film: 1896–1906*. London: George Allen & Unwin, 1948.

THE HERKOMER FILM COMPANY was founded in March 1913 by Sir Hubert von Herkomer, a member of the Royal Academy, and utilized a small amateur theatre in the garden of the painter's home, Lululand, in Bushey, just North of London, as its studio. Between 1913 and 1914, the company produced a number of films, including *The Old Wood Carver* (1913), *The White Witch* (1913), *His Choice* (1914), and *Grit of a Dandy* (1914). From 1914 to 1920, the studios were occupied by British Actors Film Co. Ltd., and they survive to the present as Bushey Studios, for many years owned by Alfred and Gilbert Church of Ambassador Film Productions Ltd.

BIBLIOGRAPHY

Pritchard, Michael. *Sir Hubert von Herkomer and His Film Making in Bushey, 1912–1914*. Bushey: ALLM Books and the Bushey Museum Trust, 1987.

HOCHSCHULE FÜR FERNSEHEN UND FILM. The regional government of Bavaria established the Hochschule für Fernsehen und film, and it opened officially in November 1967. One of the two most important film schools in Germany, its graduates include Alexander von Eschwege, Peter Heller, Ilse Hofmann, and Wim Wenders.

Address: Ohmstrasse 11, D-8000 Munich 40, West Germany.

HONDURAS. See CENTRAL AMERICA

HONG KONG. Filmmaking in the British Crown Colony of Hong Kong dates back to 1913, but production on a major scale did not commence until the thirties, when some fifty companies were active. In 1940, ninety feature films were produced in Hong Kong, with an average budget of—unbelievably—$2,730. After the Second World War, refugees from throughout Asia poured into Hong Kong, and the industry was revitalized in 1950 with the arrival of Chinese filmmakers from Shanghai. The Hong Kong film industry is dominated by martial arts films and Cantonese comedies. The majority of films are produced primarily in Mandarin Chinese, and the minority in Cantonese (considered a dying language), and intended for Chinese-speaking audiences throughout Asia.

An average of two hundred feature films a year were produced in the fifties. Production reached its peak in the early sixties, when the number went over three hundred. In the eighties, the average is 125 films a year.

The three major production companies in Hong Kong are the Shaw Brothers*, Golden Harvest (HK) Ltd., and Cinema City Co. Ltd. Golden Harvest was founded in 1970 by Raymond Chow, who had earlier worked for the Shaw Brothers, and in 1971 he took over the Cathay Studios. Here, he produced an average of fifteen features a year, including a number starring Bruce Lee. Cinema City was founded in 1980 by Karl Maka, Dean Shek, and Raymond Wong, and is noted for its comedies. Between 1982 and 1984, it distributed the top grossing Hong Kong films: *Aces Go Places, Aces Go Places II,* and *Aces Go Places III*.

Hong Kong–produced films had had little impact in the West until the late sixties, when the industry realized it needed more markets and that some co-production with other countries was necessary. The major breakthrough came at the 1972 Cannes Film Festival*, where both the Shaw Brothers and Golden Harvest were able to persuade American distributors that there was an audience outside of Asia for Kung Fu movies. A year later, the first Hong Kong–American co-production, *Enter the Dragon,* was released.

Kung Fu movies and Cantonese comedies continued to dominate Hong Kong film production until 1979, when new, younger directors with talent, including Yim Ho, Tam Ka Ming, Wong Kah-Kei, Alex Cheung Kwok-Min, Ronnie Yu, Hark Tsui, Leung Po-Chi, Peter Yung, and Fong Yuk Ping, emerged, and began making modern social dramas.

In 1978, the Hong Kong Film Culture Centre was established to provide film study courses, research the history of Hong Kong production, and work toward the establishment of a film archive. Since 1982, the Hong Kong Film Awards, sponsored by Eastman Kodak and organized by *Film Biweekly,* have been presented to Chinese language films released in Hong Kong.

BIBLIOGRAPHY

Coward, Rosalind, and John Ellis, "Hong Kong—China 1981," *Screen,* vol. XXII, no. 4, 1981, pp. 91–100.

Elley, Derek, "Distorted Impressions," *Films and Filming,* vol. XXVI, no. 4, January 1980, pp. 46–47.

Glaessner, Verina. *Kung Fu: Cinema of Vengeance.* New York: Bounty Books, 1974.

———, "Chinese Cinema," *Cinema Papers,* no. 14, October 1977, pp. 107–110.

———, "Hong Kong Centre," *Sight & Sound,* vol. XLVII, no. 2, Spring 1978, p. 84.

Lightman, Herb A., "Films in the Far East . . . and Down Under: Hong Kong," *American Cinematographer,* vol. LI, no. 6, June 1970, pp. 544–545, 548–549, 555.

Rayns, Tony, "Threads through the Labyrinth: Hong Kong Movies," *Sight & Sound,* vol. XLIII, no. 3, Summer 1974, pp. 138–141.

HUNGAROFILM was founded in February 1956 to handle the export of all films from Hungary and to act as a representative of the Hungarian film industry with the Western world. Additionally, Hungarofilm persuades outside filmmakers to use Hungarian studio facilities and organizes tributes and screenings of Hungarian features and short subjects at film festivals worldwide. The most successful of the Eastern European, government-sponsored film agencies, Hungarofilm was headed from the late fifties through 1984 by Istvan Dosai.

Address: 1050 Budapest, V Bathori 4, Hungary.

BIBLIOGRAPHY

Fainaru, Edna, "Hungarofilm, at 30, a Model for Gov't Pic Organizations," *Daily Variety,* February 25, 1986, p. 42.

HUNGARY. The Lumière films were first seen in Hungary, in Budapest, on May 10, 1896. Within two years, Mór Ungerleider and József Neumann had formed the country's first film company, Projectograph, to produce actualities and newsreels. Hungary's first studio was built in 1911, and a year later the first fictional film, *Ma és holnap/Today and Tomorrow,* was produced. It was probably directed by Mihály Kertész, who later changed his name to Michael Curtiz (1888–1962), and enjoyed a substantial career in Hollywood. Among the fourteen other directors active in Hungary in the teens was Sándor Korda, who later became

Alexander Korda (1893–1956), and who had been responsible for some nineteen Hungarian productions prior to 1918.

The film industry was briefly nationalized in March 1919 by the Hungarian Republic of Councils, and during this four month period some thirty-one films were made. Both Korda and Curtiz left Hungary in the twenties, a decade during which the industry stagnated. One major director did appear, Pál Fējos, but he also emigrated from Hungary, moving eventually to the United States, where he was known as Paul Fejos (1897–1963). Between 1925 and 1929 only thirteen films were produced.

Sound film were first seen in Budapest in 1929, but it was not until 1931 that the first Hungarian talkies were produced: *A kék bálvány/The Blue Idol* and *Hyppolit a lakáj/Hyppolit the Butler*. City Studios was founded by Sándor Winter in 1933, and it enjoyed some success later that year with the production of Rákóczi-induló/The Rákóczi March. However, within a year, the company was bankrupt. A second company, Hajdú, was also formed in 1933, and it produced fourteen features. In 1936, István Erdélyi founded Kárpát Films. Among the directors active in Hungary in the thirties were Steve Sekely and Andre de Toth, both of whom went on to successful careers in Hollywood.

The Second World War had little impact on the Hungarian film industry. Features continued to be made at the Hunnia Studios*. Twenty-eight features were produced in the country in 1939; thirty-eight in 1940; forty-one in 1941; forty-five in 1942; and fifty-three in 1943. The most important feature from this period is *Emberek a havason/People of the Alps* (1942), directed by István Szőts.

Following the war, there were 280 theatres open in Hungary—10 more than in 1912—with two production companies, Hunnia and MAFIRT, and a major distributor (primarily of American films), MOPEX. The first films to be made in the country after liberation were Márton Keleti's *A tanítónő/The School Mistress* and Ákos Ráthonyi's *Aranyóra/The Gold Watch,* both released in 1945.

The Hungarian film industry was nationalized for a second, and final time, on March 21, 1948, with the Communist takeover of the country. The first feature under the new regime was Frigyes Bán's *Talpalatnyi föld/The Soil under Your Feet* (1948), which depicted the poverty of the peasants immediately following the Second World War.

Less than one hundred features were produced in Hungary in the fifties, with the most important being those directed by Zoltán Fábri (born 1917). Directors of importance who emerged in the sixties, and gained an international reputation for the Hungarian film industry, include István Gaál (born 1933), István Szabó (born 1938), Péter Bascó (born 1928), and Miklós Jancsó (born 1921).

Production in Hungary is supervised by Mafilm, while the export and import of films is handled by Hungarofilm*. Since the sixties, an average of twenty features a year are produced.

Hungary is also notable not only for having contributed a considerable number of celebrities to the Hollywood film industry (Adolph Zukor, Vilma Banky,

Victor Varconi), but also at least two major film theorists. Béla Balázs (1884–1949) is Hungarian, and best known for his 1945 volume, *Theory of Film*. Also Hungarian is László Moholy-Nagy.

BIBLIOGRAPHY

Hibbin, Nina. *Eastern Europe: An Illustrated Guide*. New York: A.S. Barnes, 1969.

Hungarian Film Directors: 1948–1983. Budapest: Interpress, 1984.

Liehm, Mira, and Antonin J. Liehm. *The Most Important Art: Eastern European Film after 1945*. Berkeley: University of California Press, 1977.

Mosier, John, "Hungary," in *World Cinema since 1945*, editor William Luhr. New York: Ungar, 1987, pp. 287–300.

Nemeskurty, Istvan. *Word and Image: A History of the Hungarian Cinema*. Budapest: Corvina Press, 1968.

———. *A Short History of the Hungarian Cinema*. Budapest: Egyetemi, 1980.

Passek, Jean-Louis, Jacqueline Brisbois, and Philippe Haudiquet. *Le cinéma hongrois*. Paris: Centre Georges Pompidou, 1979.

Paul, David W., editor. *Politics, Art, and Commitment in the East European Cinema*. New York: St. Martin's, 1983.

Petrie, Graham. *History Must Answer to Man: The Contemporary Hungarian Cinema*. Budapest: Corvina Kiado, 1978.

Stoil, Jon Michael. *Cinema beyond the Danube*. Metuchen, N.J.: Scarecrow Press, 1974.

White, Alistair. *New Cinema in Eastern Europe*. New York: Dutton, 1971.

HUNNIA was the preeminent, pre–Second World War Hungarian film studio, producing an average of twenty-six features a year. It was founded in 1929 and occupies a lot previously operated as the Corvin Studios (which failed in 1925). Following the Second World War, the studio was reorganized and, eventually, nationalized.

Address: Lumumba ú. 174, Budapest 14, Hungary.

I

ICELAND. With a population of approximately one-quarter-of-a-million, Iceland boasts an annual cinema attendance of two-and-a-half million. Theatre ticket prices are governed by the state, with 40 percent going in taxes. The first theatre opened in Iceland's capital, Reykjavík, in 1906, and today the city has some fourteen theatres. Foreign films are sold directly to exhibitors, while one organization, Icelandic Films, handles the sale of native product abroad; it was established by the country's leading film and television (introduced in 1966) producers.

The first feature film to be shot in Iceland was *Borgaroettin/The Saga of the Borg Family,* based on the novel by Icelandic author Gunnar Gunnarsson, and produced by a Danish company in 1919. British director A.E. Coleby filmed some of his 1923 version of *The Prodigal Son* in Iceland. The first Icelandic film was a short comedy, directed by Loftur Guđmundsson in 1923. He also directed Iceland's first sound feature, shot in 16mm, *Milli fjalls offjöru/Between Mountain and Sea,* in 1948. Iceland's 1944 independence from Denmark was celebrated by filmmaker Óskar Gíslason with a documentary in 16mm. Gíslason's later documentaries gained him a reputation outside of Iceland, and he remains the country's best known filmmaker, with an award presented annually in his honor by the Association of Icelandic Producers.

Gíslason made his first fictional feature, *Siđasti boerinn i dalnum/The Last Farm in the Valley,* in 1949. His first major documentary was *Björgunarafrekiđ viđ Látrabjarg/Rescue at Látrabjarg* (1946), concerned with the salvage of an English trawler and its crew. Other Icelandic documentary filmmakers are Osvaldur Knudsen, noted for his films of the Hekla and Surtsey volcanoes, and Reynir Oddson, who has produced a two-part documentary on Iceland's occupation during the Second World War, *Hernámsárin/Years of Occupation* (1966–1968).

In 1954, Edda Film was established in Reykjavík, and its first feature was an Icelandic-Swedish co-production, *Salka Valka* (1954), based on a story by the Icelandic Nobel Prize winner, Halldór Laxnes. It was also responsible for a 1962 Danish-Icelandic co-production, *Taxi Nr. 79,* directed by Erik Balling, and a

1966 Danish-Icelandic co-production, *Rauđa skikkjan/The Red Mantle,* directed by Gabriel Axel.

The modern Icelandic film industry is generally dated from 1979, when the National Film Fund and the National Film Archive was established. Ágúst Guđmundsson and Þorstein Jónsson, graduates from foreign film schools, returned to Iceland, and in 1980 the former released the country's first 35mm feature production, *Land og Synir/Land and Sons*. It was financed by Iceland's largest film producer, ISFILM, and cost $150,000 to make. As a result of this rebirth of Icelandic cinema, New York's Museum of Modern Art presented a tribute to the country's films in October 1980.

BIBLIOGRAPHY

Hollinger, Hy, "Iceland No Paradise for Pic Industry," *Daily Variety*, November 7, 1980, p. 7.

Icelandic Films, 1980–1983. Rekjavík: The Icelandic Film Fund and the Icelandic Film Archive, 1983.

"Icelandic Folk Tilt to the Capital Where 7 Cinemas Pack Them In," *Variety,* October 22, 1986, p. 361.

Kardish, Larry, "Journal from Reykjavik," *Film Comment,* vol. XVI, no. 5, September-October 1980, pp. 6, 8, 78.

Odermatt, Urs, "Still To Be Discovered: Iceland's Viking Cinema, An Essay Interview," *New Orleans Review,* Winter 1982, pp. 45–48.

"State Handing Over a Little More for Iceland's Feature Production," *Variety,* October 16, 1985, pp. 335, 408.

IDHEC (Institut des Hautes Études Cinématographiques) is one of the best-known film schools in the world. It was founded in 1943 by director Marcel L'Herbier and based on the Centre Artistique et Technique des Jeunes de l'Écran (CATJE), which was organized in Nice in 1941. Funded by the French Ministry of Information, IDHEC's best-known director (from 1951 to 1968) was Rémy Tessonneau. Student unrest in 1968 led to the eventual reorganization of the school in 1970.

Address: 4 avenue de l'Europe, 94360 Bry-sur-Marne, France.

BIBLIOGRAPHY

Rose, Ernest D. *World Film & TV Study Resources*. Bonn-Bad Godesberg: Friedrich-Ebert-Stiftung, 1974.

IMPÉRIA FILMS was the French distributor of the first two features directed by Jean-Luc Godard (born 1930): *À bout de souffle/Breathless* (1959) and *Le petit soldat/The Little Soldier* (1960).

IMPERIAL WAR MUSEUM. Britain's Imperial War Museum was founded in 1917, and two years later it began collecting motion pictures, when unedited film shot by the various official camera units during the First World War was handed over. Since then, the Museum has acquired not only British government footage, but any variety of film dealing with military or war activities. Among the fifty million feet of film in its archives are British newsreels from the First and Second World Wars, as well as German and Soviet newsreels from the Second World War. All of the film may, in principle, be viewed, and much of it is available for commercial use.

Address: Department of Film, Imperial War Museum, Lambeth Road, London SE1 6HZ, United Kingdom.

THE INDEPENDENT FILM AND VIDEO MAKERS' ASSOCIATION was founded in 1974 to represent the interests of independent British filmmakers. It became involved in video ten years later.

Address: 79 Wardour Street, London W1V 3PH, United Kingdom.

THE INDEPENDENT FILM DISTRIBUTORS' ASSOCIATION is an organization of specialist film distributors, founded in the United Kingdom in 1973.

Address: 55 Greek Street, London W1V 6DB, United Kingdom.

"INDEPENDENT PRODUCERS" was an umbrella title utilized by British producer and distributor J. Arthur Rank for various companies, such as Cineguild, Ltd.* and the Archers*, that were active within his organization. The following features come under this heading: *The Great Mr. Handel* (1942), *Secret Mission* (1942), *The Silver Fleet* (1943), *The Life and Death of Colonel Blimp* (U.S. *Colonel Blimp,* 1943), *They Met in the Dark* (1943), *On Approval* (1944), *A Canterbury Tale* (1944), *They Knew Mr. Knight* (1945), *I Know Where I'm Going* (1945), *Brief Encounter* (1945), *The Rake's Progress* (U.S. *Notorious Gentleman,* 1945), *Caesar and Cleopatra* (1946), *I See a Stranger* (U.S. *The Adventuress,* 1946), *A Matter of Life and Death* (U.S. *Stairway to Heaven,* 1946), *Green for Danger* (1946), *Great Expectations* (1946), *Black Narcissus* (1947), *Take My Life* (1947), *Captain Boycott* (1947), *The End of the River* (1947), *The Woman in the Hall* (1947), *Blanche Fury* (1948), *Oliver Twist* (1948), *The Red Shoes* (1948), and *Esther Waters* (1948).

INDIA produces more films than any other nation—912 features in 1985—and yet only one of its directors, Satyajit Ray, has name recognition outside of the country, and none of its stars are known in the Western world. Most of the country's films cannot be regarded as quality entertainment, and yet they have tremendous influence on Indian society and their actors and actresses have followings envied by many Hollywood personalities.

Indian stars have long been active in politics and used their influence accordingly. Actor-producer-politician Sunil Dutt made a 1987 peace march from Bombay to Amritsar, urging an end to civil unrest in the Punjab. Actress Shabana Azmi went on a hunger strike on behalf of the homeless and formed a committee to end the dowry system in India. Three Hindi stars are members of Rajiv Gandhi's government: Sunil Dutt, Vijayantimala, and Amitabh Bachchan. Bachchan, who specializes in angry young men roles, came to prominence in the early seventies, and is regarded as the biggest star, in terms of fans, not only in India but in the world. Among the top stars from the forties onwards are Ashok Kumar, Raj Kapoor, Dilip Kumar, Dev Anand, Shammi Kapoor, Raaj Kumar, Rajendra Kumar, Shashi Kapoor, Nargis, Madhybala, Meena Kumari, Geeta Bali, and Waheeda Rehman.

Indian films are produced in sixteen languages—including Hindi, Teluga, Tamil, Malayam, Kannada, Gujarati, and Marathi—with major filmmaking centers located in Bangalore, Bombay, Calcutta, Hyderabad, Madras, and Trivandrum. Films produced in Hindi have the widest circulation outside of the country and until the seventies were the most popular within India. Eleven distributors handle Hindi films internally. English-language films are screened in most major cities. The most important markets for Indian films abroad are the United Kingdom, Singapore, Dubai, Indonesia, Mauritius, Fiji, and Kenya (all of which have substantial Indian populations).

There are more than twelve thousand theatres on the subcontinent. Censorship is based on the British system and conducted by the Central Board of Film Certification (formerly known as the Board of Film Censors), which grants "A" (adult) or "U" (unrestricted) certificates. In the mid-eighties, the government asked the Board to be more restrictive in its censorship activities.

Films were first seen in India on July 7, 1986, when the Lumière shorts were screened at Watson's Hotel, Bombay, by a Lumière representative, Maurice Sestier, on his way to Australia. The first Indian to produce films was Harischandra Sakharam Bhatvedekar, who filmed a number of actualities as early as 1897. In 1907, J.F. Madan opened his first theatre in Calcutta, which became the basis for the cinema chain of Madan Theatres of Calcutta. By the twenties, Madan was the major operator of theatres in India and had also become involved in film production.

The first feature-length film to be produced in India was *Rajah Harischandra,* directed by Dadasaheb Phalke, who had become so fascinated with the cinema that he traveled to Europe to study the technique of filmmaking. Both *Rajah Harischandra,* and Phalke's second feature, *Bhasmasur Mohini,* were released in 1913. Prior to the production of the latter, no actress had appeared in an Indian film. Phalke founded the Hindustan Film Company in 1917, which paved the way for other production companies, including the Lotus Film Company in Hyderabad (formed in 1922) and the Prabhat Film Company in Kolhapur (formed in 1929).

The most important Indian film of the silent era was *The Light of Asia,* produced by Himansu Rai as a German-Indian co-venture in 1925. Based on the life of Gautama Buddha, the film was shot in Lahore. *The Light of Asia* opened in London at the Philharmonic Hall to widespread critical acclaim. The *Times* (March 29, 1926) remarked that it "lacks nothing in magnificence," while *Sphere* (March 4, 1926) called it "a revelation."

Sound films were first seen in India in 1929, but it was not until 1931 that the first Indian talkie, *Alam Ara/Beauty of the World,* produced by Ardeshir Irani, was released in Hindi. The thirties saw the demise of the Madan production and exhibition empire, but it also witnessed the rise of new companies, such as Wadia Movietone (formed in 1933) and Vauhini Pictures (formed in 1939). Founded in 1934, Bombay Talkies was the most important of sound film producers in India, with its first release being Himansu Rai's *Karma,* starring Devika Rani. A major breakthrough against old taboos came in 1936 with the production, in Tamil, of *Balayogini/Child Saint,* starring a Brahmin widow as a Brahmin widow.

During the war, the government set up an advisory board to encourage the production of films for the war effort, but most producers supported the independence movement that denied Indian involvement in a war for a freedom that was denied to her. Despite the 1942 censorship of photographs of Gandhi and Nehru, producers found subtle ways in which to introduce independence motifs into their films.

Among the directors who emerged in the postwar years are Raj Kapoor (born 1924), Guru Dutt (1925–1964), Ritwik Ghatak (1925–1976), and Mrinal Sen (born 1923). Sen is, aside from Satyajit Ray, one of the few Indian filmmakers to gain any sort of reputation outside of his own country. He is noted for the experimental nature of many of his features, beginning with *Bhuvan Shome/Mr. Shome* (1969) and including the "Calcutta trilogy" (1971–1973).

In 1950, French director Jean Renoir came to India to film his version of Rumer Godden's *The River,* in Bengal. It was Renoir who encouraged Satyajit Ray (born 1921) to begin making films. Ray, along with Chidananda Das Gupta, had founded the Calcutta Film Society in 1947. In 1955, he made his first feature, *Pather Panchali,* which was screened at the Cannes Film Festival, and first brought Indian cinema to international attention. The film was the first of the "Apu trilogy," with the other two films being *Aparajito* (1956) and *Apur sansar/The World of Apu* (1959). Later Ray features include *Devi/The Goddess* (1960) and *Pratiwandi/The Adversary* (1970). All of Ray's films prior to 1977 were filmed in Bengali, but in that year he made *Shantranj ke khilari/The Chess Players,* his first Hindi production.

The last of the major Indian studios, the Prabhat Film Company ceased operations in 1953. Its studios in Poona became the home of the Film Institute of India (created in 1961).

In 1960, the Film Finance Corporation was established as the first government agency concerned with the funding of Indian films. It had its first major success in 1968 with Mrinal Sen's *Bhuvan Shome/Mr. Shome*. A Directorate of Film Festivals was created in 1974, responsible for the Panorama of New Indian Cinema, and, in 1980, the National Film Development Corporation* was established.

India has been used as a backdrop for many British and American features, including *The Young Rajah* (1922), *The Green Goddess* (1923), *The Black Watch*

(1929), *The Green Goddess* (1930), *Elephant Boy* (1937), *The Rains Came* (1939), *Black Narcissus* (1947), *Kim* (1950), *The Rains of Ranchipur* (1955), *Nine Hours to Rhama* (1962), *Gandhi* (1983), *Far Pavilions* (1984), *A Passage to India* (1985), and *The Razor's Edge* (1985). An animated view of India was provided by Walt Disney in *The Jungle Book* (1967).

BIBLIOGRAPHY

Allen, William D., "World's Second Biggest Film Maker," *Films in Review,* February 1950, pp. 6–10.

Banerjee, S., editor. *New Indian Cinema.* New Delhi: NFDC, 1982.

Barnouw, Erik, and S. Krishnaswamy. *Indian Film.* New York: Oxford University Press, 1982.

Fazalbhoy, Y.A. *The Indian Film: A Review.* Bombay: Bombay Radio Press, 1939.

Fifty Years of Indian Talkies. Bombay: Indian Academy of Motion Picture Arts and Sciences, 1981.

Gorga, B.D., "Background to the Indian Film," *Sight & Sound,* January-March 1954, pp. 158–169.

"Hollywood in the East," *Newsweek,* August 5, 1957, pp. 44–45.

Mahmoud, Hameeduddin. *The Kaleidoscope of Indian Cinema.* New Delhi: Affiliated East-West Press, 1974.

Murthy, K.K., "Conditions in India," *Sight & Sound,* vol. IX, no. 34, Summer 1940, pp. 33–34.

Parrain, Philippe. *Regards sur le cinéma indien.* Paris: Le Cerf, 1969.

Passek, J-L, editor. *Le cinéma indien.* Paris: L'Equerre, 1983.

Patel, Baburao, "Stardom in India," *Films in Review,* January 1951, pp. 32–36.

Rahim, N.K., "The Film in India," *Penguin Film Review,* no. 4, October 1947, pp. 69–75.

Ramachandran, T.M. *70 Years of Indian Cinema.* Bombay: Cinema India-International, 1985.

Rama-Rau, S., "Letter from Bombay," *New Yorker,* May 3, 1952, pp. 89–90.

Rangoonwalla, F. *Pictorial History of Indian Cinema.* London: Hamlyn, 1979.

———. *Indian Cinema Past and Present.* New Delhi: Clarion, 1983.

Seton, Marie. *Portrait of a Director: Satyajit Ray.* London: Dobson, 1971.

Shah, Panna. *The Indian Film.* Bombay: Motion Picture Society of India, 1950.

Thomas, Rosie, "India," in *World Cinema since 1945,* editor William Luhr. New York: Ungar, 1987, pp. 301–329.

Willeman, Paul, and B. Gandhy, editors. *Indian Cinema.* London: British Film Institute, 1982.

THE INDIAN MOTION PICTURE PRODUCERS ASSOCIATION is the oldest and most important of Indian film trade organizations. It was founded on May 15, 1936, and has more than 1,200 members.

Address: Sandhurst Building, S.V.P. Road, Bombay 4, India.

INDIVIDUAL PICTURES LTD. was established by British screenwriters Frank Launder and Sidney Gilliat to produce feature films for release through the "Independent Producers"* program of the Rank Organization*. The following are its films: *The Rake's Progress* (U.S. *Notorious Gentleman,* 1945), *I See a Dark Stranger* (U.S. *The Adventuress,* 1946), *Green for Danger* (1946), *Captain Boycott* (1947), *London Belongs to Me* (U.S. *Dulcimer Street,* 1948), *The Blue Lagoon* (1949), and *The Happiest Days of Your Life* (1950).

INDONESIA. Filmmaking in Indonesia dates back to 1910, when the country was still a Dutch colony. The first Indonesian feature film was *Loetoenn Kasaroeng,* directed in 1926 by G. Kruger. He was also involved with F. Carli in the production of the most important Indonesian feature of the thirties, *Terang Bulan/The Moonlight* (1937), inspired by the 1936 Paramount feature, *Jungle Princess,* starring Dorothy Lamour.

Following independence in 1949, two nationalistic production companies were created, Persari Studio, founded by Djamaluddin Malik, and Perfini Studio, founded by Usmar Ismail. The latter was a major figure in Indonesian cinema. In the fifties, the Persari Studio was criticized for producing Indian films with Indian technicians in Indonesia, rather than encouraging local production.

The industry faltered in the sixties, and the Ministry of Information established a National Film Production Board, which levied a tax on imported films to help pay for local production. (Asian filmmakers have long criticized Indonesia for its efforts to restrict imports.) The feature that is generally credited with reviving the Indonesian industry is *Bernafas Dalam Lumpur/Survival in the Mud* (1970). In the seventies, new figures entering the film industry included theatre director Teguh Karya, film academician Syuman Djaya, and modern theatre proponent Arifin C. Noer.

There are approximately 1,800 theatres in Indonesia. Production centers are located in Surabaya, Jawa Tengah, and Bandung. Indonesian films are seen outside of the country in Malaysia and Singapore, but seldom elsewhere. The country is little used for location shooting by foreign companies. Major directors include Arifin C. Noer, Teguh Karya, Slamet Rahardjo, and Wim Umboh.

BIBLIOGRAPHY

Biran, H. Misbach Yusa, "The Cinema in Indonesia," *Cinema India-International,* vol. IV, no. 1, 1987, pp. 89–90.

"Indonesia's Unique in Way It Exhibits and Distribs Films," *Variety,* October 22, 1986, pp. 443, 446.

INSPIRATION FILMS was founded in the United Kingdom in the thirties by Horace Shepherd to produce series of short subjects under titles such as *This England* and *Romance of England.*

THE INTERNATIONAL FEDERATION OF FILM SOCIETIES was founded in 1947 and held its first annual meeting that year in Cannes. The Federation is concerned with the promotion of the work of film societies throughout the world and the free circulation of films for its members' use. The following is a listing of major film society organizations that are members of the Federation:

Aktion "der gute Film"
P.O. Box 208
Vienna
Austria

Association des professeurs pour l'éducation cinématographique
73 avenue des Coccinelles
1070 Brussels
Belgium

Fédération Socialiste des Ciné-Clubs
Boulevard de l'Empereur 15
bte 6
1000 Brussels
Belgium

Socialist Federation of Film Klubs
Dorpstraat 73
B-8340
Damme-Sijselle
Belgium

Bulgarian Film Clubs
Boulevard Rusky 8A
Sofia
Bulgaria

Film Club of the Canary Islands
17 Tomas Miller
Las Palmas de Gran Canaria
Canary Islands

Cyprus Film Club
P.O. Box 5314
Nicosia
Cyprus

Ceskoslovensky Filmovy Ustav Prag
Narodni 40
11000 Prague 1
Czechoslovakia

Sammenslutningen Af Danske Filmklubber
Parkhalle 7
8000 Aarhus C
Denmark

Suomen Elokuvakerhojen liitto SEKL ry
Yrjönkatu 11 A 5
SF-00120 Helsinki
Finland

Fédération Française des Ciné-Clubs
6 rue Ordener
F-75018 Paris
France

Fédération Jean Vigo
8 rue Lamarck
F-75018 Paris
France

UFOLEIS, Ligue Française de l'enseignement et de l'éducation permanente
3 rue Récamier
F-75341 Paris
France

Zentrale Arbeitsgemeinschaft Filmklubs der DDR
Otto-Nuschke-Strasse 51
108 Berlin
East Germany

Arbeitsgemeinschaft für DeutschenJugend Filmclubs
Melatenerstrasse 106
51 Aachen
West Germany

Gibraltar Film Societies
P.O. Box 327
Gibraltar

Tainiothiki tis Ellados
1 Kanari Street
Athens 138
Greece

Hungarian Federation of Film Clubs
Nepstadion ut 97
Budapest 15
Hungary

Fjalakötturinn
P.O. Box 1347
121 Reykjavík
Iceland

Federation of Irish Film Societies
c/o Project Theatre
39 East Essex Street
Dublin 2
Republic of Ireland

Federazione Italiana del Circolo del Cinema
Piazza dei Caprettari 70
00186 Rome
Italy

Centre de diffusion et d'animation cinématographique
23 avenue Gaston-Diderich
Luxembourg

Film Appreciation Centre
New University
Msida
Malta

Norsk Filmklubbforbund
Teatergt 3
Oslo 1
Norway

Polska Federacja Dyskusyjnch Klubow Filmowych
Skrt. Pocst 120
UI. Polna 40
PL-00950 Warsaw
Poland

Federaçao Portuguesa de Cine-Clubes
Centro de Apoio
Rua de Camoes 777-4° Dto.
4000 Porto
Portugal

Commission of Film Clubs ACIN
Bd. Gh. Georghiu Dej. No. 65
Bucharest
Romania

Federación de Cine-Clubs
Paseo de la Castellana No. 210-5° Madrid 16
Spain

Swedish Federation of Film Societies
Box 27126 S
S-10252 Stockholm
Sweden

Cinélibre
Postfach
CH-4005 Basel
Switzerland

British Federation of Film Societies
21 Stephen Street
London W1P 1PL
United Kingdom

Kinoklubs des Verbandes der Filmschaffenden der USSR
Wassiljewskaja 13
D56 Moscow
USSR

Filmklubs der Arbeiteruniversitat Split Radnicko sveuciliste "Dur Salaj"
Centar za Kulturu
Dioklecijanova 7
58000 Split
Yugoslavia

Filmski Klub "Mosa Pijade"
Centar za Kultur
Ul. Proleterski Brigada 68
Zagreb
Yugoslavia

The address of the International Federation of Film Societies (Federation Internationale des Cine-Clubs) is Case Postale CH-2301, La Chaux-de-Fonds, Switzerland.

BIBLIOGRAPHY

Brossard, Jean-Pierre, editor. *Film and Film Societies in Europe*. Lisbon: International Federation of Film Societies, 1981.

INTERNATIONAL FILM GUIDE is unquestionably the most important source for contemporary information on world cinema, with its sections on filmmaking in individual countries, film festivals, animation, educational films, film schools, archives, bookshops, and periodicals. The book has been published annually since 1963—it is always dated for the year ahead of publication—by the Tantivy Press, and was founded and is edited by Peter Cowie.

Address: 2 Bedford Gardens, London W8 7EH, United Kingdom.

THE INTERNATIONAL SHORT FILM CONFERENCE was founded as a worldwide organization in 1970, with the purpose of promoting the distribution and exhibition of short films. It held its first meeting in September 1970 at the Cork Film Festival, at which time Asa Briggs was appointed its first chairman. It has published an occasional bulletin as well as various editions of *List of Recent Best Short and Documentary Films*.

IRAN. It is believed that the first film to be shot in Iran was by Ibrahim-Khan Akkasbashi in 1901. A number of actualities were shot by Khan-Baba Motazadi from 1920 onward, including the coronation of Reza Khan in 1925. The first Iranian feature film was a silent production, *Abbi and Rabbi,* directed in 1929 by Avaness Ohanian, who made a second feature, *Haji-Agha/The Film Actor,* the following year. The first Persian sound film was *The Daughter of Lor,* directed by Abdolhossein Sepanta and Ardeshi Irani in 1931. It was, however, filmed in India with Iranian actors and was followed by four more features directed by Sepanta between 1931 and 1937.

No films were produced between 1937 and 1948, but in the latter year Ismail Kushan produced and photographed *The Tempest of Life,* which is often credited as the first Iranian sound feature. It was directed by Ali Darya Beigi.

In 1968, the government agreed to invest some $5 million in a major film production centre in Tehran, through the efforts of two brothers, Mostafa and Morteza Akavan, who controlled a leading Iranian theatre circuit and also owned Moulin Rouge Productions. The sixty-five-acre site included two sound stages, and complete editing, sound, and film processing units. The first film to be shot there was *The Invincible Six* (1970), directed by Jean Negulesco.

New Iranian cinema dates from 1970, when the first film festival was held in Tehran and the magazine, *Film-Va-Honar,* was established. *Film-Va-Honar* presented the Sepass Awards, the equivalents of the American Oscars. The Ministry of Culture and Arts began to sponsor film production. The first Tehran International Film Festival was held in April 1972. The directors of the new Iranian cinema include Bahran Beizai, Dariush Mehrjui, Massood Kimia'ie, and Parviz Kimiavi.

In the mid-seventies, a number of new companies were formed, including Telefilm, owned by National Radio-Television, New Film Group Cooperatiur, and Société Anonyme Cinématographique de l'Iran. The last entered into a co-production deal with Italian filmmaker Carlo Ponti and is probably best remembered for its financing of two Orson Welles projects, *F for Fake* and *The Other Side of the Wind.* So successful had the Iranian film industry become that an Iranian Film Week was held at the 1975 Cannes Film Festival.

The 1979 Islamic Revolution had an initial negative effect on the film industry. Most filmmakers fled the country, and from a high of 120 films a year, production dropped to 12. However, as the situation stabilized in Iran, film production increased to 60 features in 1984, down to 33 in 1986, but then up to 60 in 1987 (a quite remarkable number considering the country was primarily involved in a long-running war with Iraq). In order to aid production and to raise the standards of Iranian films, the government created the Farabi Cinema Foundation (No. 55 Si-e-tir Avenue, Tehran) in 1983. It is also responsible for the export, import, and distribution of films. Independent production still exists, indeed flourishes, in Iran through companies such as Pakshiran Corp., and with directors such as Darioush Mehrjui and Massoud Jafari Jozani (whose careers predate the revolution).

BIBLIOGRAPHY

"Iran Builds Production Center," *Hollywood Reporter,* November 4, 1968, p. 1.

Omid, Jamil, "The Cinema in Iran," *Cinema India-International,* vol. IV, no. 1, 1987, pp. 91–92.

"Tehran's Film City Paves Way for Iranian Film Industry 'Comeback,' " *Screen International,* April 26, 1986, p. 18.

ISKUSSTVO KINO. The most important of Soviet film journals, *Iskusstvo Kino* was first published in January 1936, although it has its origins in *Sovetskii Ekran,* first published in January 1925. In October 1945, it became the official organ of the Soviet Ministry of Cinematography.

Address: Soiuz kinematografistov SSSR, 125319 Moscow, A-319, Ul. Usievich 9, USSR.

BIBLIOGRAPHY

Slide, Anthony, editor. *International Film, Radio, and Television Journals*. Westport, Conn.: Greenwood Press, 1985.

ISRAEL. Although Jewish films had been produced in what became Israel prior to its independence in 1948, the Israeli film industry as such did not commence until the fifties. Two studios, Geva and Herzeliyya, opened in 1950 and 1951 respectively, and in 1955 British filmmaker Thorold Dickson directed the first Israeli film to have any impact abroad, *Giva 24 eina ona/Hill 24 Does Not Answer*. Like so many Israeli features that were to follow, it was Zionist in content, so typical of later films that glorified the creation of the Israeli state and the victory of the Jews over the Arabs.

Many critics choose to date the Israeli film industry from the sixties, during which some eighty features were produced and Israelis were the most prolific filmgoing nation in the world. In 1968, television was introduced, and obviously had a negative effect on filmmaking. To offset such an impact, the government founded the Israel Film Centre of the Ministry of Commerce (P.O. Box 299, Jerusalem) in 1969, with the aim of encouraging outside filmmakers to come to Israel.

In the seventies, features continued to appear that were highly insular in content. *Kazablan* (1973), directed by Menahem Golan, was a musical concerned with tensions between the Ashkenazim and the Sephardim. *Or min ha'hefker/Light Out of Nowhere* (1973), directed by Nissim Dayan, dealt with crime among Sephardic Jews. Both *Ani ohev otach Rosa/I Love You Rosa* (1972) and *Ha'bait be'rechov Chlouch/The House on Chlouch Street* (1973), directed by Moshe Mizrahi, concern themselves with relationships between Arabs and Jews.

A major change came over the Israeli film industry in the late seventies. *Lemon Popsicle* (1978), co-written and directed by Boaz Davidson, was the first feature in a decade-and-a-half to gain international recognition. It helped the career of its producer Menahem Golan and showed Israeli filmmakers that there was a non-Jewish audience for their films. As a result, fewer and fewer features were made in Hebrew, and films are now made with the international market in mind. Additionally, the late seventies saw a number of new directors coming on the scene, graduates from film schools, such as Avraham Hefner, Judd Ne'eman, and Igal Burstein. In 1980, a Fund for the Promotion of Quality Films was created, and through its investments, Israeli features did improve. Initially, it invested some $400,000 a year, but by the mid-eighties could only provide three-quarters of that amount.

A new director with a highly personal approach to filmmaking was Dan Wohlman, who emerged in the seventies with films such as *Ha'timhoni/The Dreamer* (1971) and *Michael sheli/My Michael* (1975).

By the eighties, two of the most famous figures in Israeli cinema, Menahem Golan and Yoram Globus were concerned with film production abroad. Popular directors of the decade include Renen Schorr, Rafi Bukaee, and Daniel Waxman. Actress Michael Bat-Adam also enjoyed some success as a director.

There are more than two hundred theatres in Israel, together with a further six hundred locations, mostly kibutzim, at which films released on 16mm are screened.

See also PALESTINE.

BIBLIOGRAPHY

Arzooni, Ora Gloria Jacob. *The Israeli Film: Social and Cultural Influences, 1912–1973*. New York: Garland, 1983.

Klausner, Margot. *The Dream Industry: Memories and Facts*. Tel Aviv: Israel Publishing, 1974.

Shohat, Ella, "Israel," in *World Cinema since 1945*, editor William Luhr. New York: Ungar, 1987, pp. 330–346.

THE ISTITUTO LUCE (L'Union Cinematografica Educativa) was founded in Rome, under Benito Mussolini, as a newsreel and film archive in 1926. It has close ties with the Cinecittà* studios, on whose lot it is housed, and it is financed through the same holding company, Ente Autonomo Gestione Cinema*. The Istituto maintains its archives and operates today as a specialized theatrical and non-theatrical distributor.

Address: via Tuscolana 1055, 00173 Rome, Italy.

ITALA FILM. The Turin-based Itala Film was founded in 1908 by Giovanni Pastrone (1883–1959), and remained in existence until 1919, when it merged with Unione Cinematografica Italiana. The company is best remembered for its production of *Cabiria* (1914), for the "Maciste"* series of films beginning with *Maciste* (1915), and for the 1909–1911 comedies of André Deed, a French comedian who was dubbed "Cretinetti" by Itala and known in France during that period as "Gribouille."

ITALNOLEGGIO was created through a 1966 Italian law as a major film distributor. It commenced operations in the spring of 1967, under the presidency of Mario Gallo and with a capitalization of $3 million. Its initial release program of some twenty features began with *Everyman is My Enemy*. Italnoleggio was eventually merged with Istituto LUCE*

ITALY. The Lumière cinematograph was first presented in Turin in February 1896, and shortly thereafter a music hall performer named Leopoldo Fregoli arranged for the Lumière films to be screened as part of his act. The earliest film company to be formed in Italy was created in Rome, also in 1896, by Luigi Topo, Ezio Crisofari, and others, initially to exploit the Edison Kinetoscope and later, in 1900, to produce a "passion play." Filmmaking commenced almost simultaneously in Turin, where Roberto Omegno (1876–1948) shot the first newsreels. Meanwhile, in Rome, in 1905, Filoteo Alberini—who had earlier invented a cinematograph machine—produced what is generally regarded as Italy's first important film, *La presa di Roma,* featuring Carlo Rosaspina.

Filmmaking was concentrated in Rome and Turin until 1908, when what became Milano Film was established in Milan by Luca Comerio. Other companies sprang up, including Cines* and Charles Pathé's Film d'Arte Italiano, until by 1909, the Italian film industry was producing an average of five hundred short subjects a year.

In the teens, Italy produced several major screen comedians notably André Deed (who acted at Cines under the name of Cretinetti, or Little Cretin) and Fernand Guillaume (who was known initially as Tontolini, but gained wider fame, at Pasquali, under the name of Polidor). However, it was for epic features that the Italian film industry gained an international reputation, with *Quo Vadis?* (1912), directed by Mario Caserini and Enrico Guazzoni; *Cabiria* (1913), directed by Giovanni Pastrone; *Gli ultimi giorni di Pompei/The Last Days of Pompeii* (1913), directed by Mario Caserini and Enrico Vidal; *Nerone Agrippina/ Nero and Agrippina* (1913), directed by Mario Caserini; *Christus!* (1915), directed by Giulio Antamoro; and, of course, the dramas featuring strong man Maciste*. Competing with these costume epics were the so-called Commedia Brillante* and melodramas, starring Francesca Bertini, Lyda Borelli, and Lina Cavalieri. Febo Mari directed the great stage actress Eleonora Duse in *Cenere* (1916) on location in Sardinia, and, in Naples, Nino Martoglio filmed *Sperduti nel Buio/Lost in Darkness* (1914), which critic Pierre Leprohon sees as one of the first examples of Neo-Realism*.

The Italian film industry was considered of international importance, with a ready market for its films not only in Europe, but also in the United States, but it fell rapidly into decline with the First World War. There were occasional bright spots, such as the production of *Frate Sole* (1917), directed by Mario Corsi for a Roman company named Tespi, one of whose founders was Luigi Pirandello; and the 1925 production of *Quo Vadis?,* starring Emil Jannings as Nero. However, on the whole, little happened to Italian cinema in the twenties, except that in 1924 Benito Mussolini came to power, and it was he who was to save the Italian film industry through the creation of a new era of fascist cinema.

Fascist filmmaking in Italy is generally dated from 1930–1943. One of the first directors to come to prominence during this period was Alessandro Blasetti (born 1900), who founded the film cooperative, Augustus, and, in 1929, made his first film, *Sole*. His career, which survived fascism, includes such films as *1860* (1934), *Vecchia Guardia/The Old Guard* (1935), *La corona di ferro* (1940), *Quattro passi fra le nuvole* (1942), *Fabiola* (1948), and *Simon Bolivar* (1969).

Mussolini, whose son, Vittorio, was increasingly involved in the film industry, founded the Centro Sperimentale di Cinematografia*, the Cinecitta* studio complex, and the Istituto LUCE*. Important features from the Mussolini era include Carmine Gallone's *Scipione l'Africano* (1937), Augusto Genina's *L'Assedio* *dell'Alcazar/The Siege of Alcazar* (1940), and the patriotic films of Alessandrini Goffredo (born 1904): *Luciano Serra, Pilota* (1937), *Caravaggio* (1940), and *Noi Vivi* (1942).

Following the Second World War, the Neo-Realist movement began in Italy with *Roma città aperta/Rome, Open City* (1945), directed by Roberto Rossellini (1906–1977), who had earlier made two propaganda films during the war for Mussolini. *Rome, Open City* deals with life in Italy under the German occupation in a realistic, semidocumentary style. It paved the way for later films of Neo-Realism, including Rossellini's *Paisà/Paisan* (1946), Luigi Zampa's *Vivere in pace/To Live in Peace* (1946), Vittorio De Sica's *Ladri di biciclette/Bicycle Thief* (1948), Luchino Visconti's *La terra trema/The Earth Trembles* (1948), Alberto Lattuada's *Senza pietà/Without Pity* (1948), and Giuseppe De Santis' *Riso amaro/Bitter Rice* (1948).

The last starred Silvana Mangano (born 1930), who exuded an eroticism with which a number of later Italian actresses, such as Sophia Loren (born 1934), and Gina Lollobrigida (born 1927) were endowed, to the benefit of themselves and the international cinema.

While the Neo-Realists were presenting a bleak vision of Italy, Renato Castellani, (born 1913) who had been active since 1941 when he made *Un colpo di pistola,* began producing a series of features full of vitality and humorous observation, beginning with *Sotto il sole di Roma* (1948) and *E Primavera/Springtime* (1949). It was films such as these that the Italian government rewarded with substantial grants as a result of a December 29, 1949, law aimed at supporting Italian cinema against the importation of American films.

The result of this law was, in part, that Americans came to Italy to produce features, beginning with *Prince of Foxes,* produced by 20th Century-Fox in 1949, and continuing with *Roman Holiday* (1953), *Ulysses* (1954), *War and Peace* (1956), *Ben-Hur* (1959), and *Cleopatra* (1963). Rome quickly gained the appellation of "Hollywood on the Tiber" (so bestowed by a writer for *The Hollywood Reporter*). Two producers took advantage of the international interest in Italy to launch themselves on international careers: Carlo Ponti (born 1910) and Dino De Laurentiis (born 1919), who at one time had their own joint production company.

These two men helped establish the career of Federico Fellini (born 1920) with *La Strada* (1954). Fellini had been active as a director since 1950 and achieved worldwide success with films usually starring his wife, Giulietta Masina (born 1920), whom he had married in 1943.

Other directors who came to prominence in the fifties are Michelangelo Antonioni (born 1912), Pier Paolo Pasolini (1922–1975), Ermanno Olmi (born 1931), and Ettore Scola (born 1931). With the exception of Pasolini, who died a homicide victim, these men continue to dominate Italian cinema to the present, joined in the sixties by Elio Petri (born 1929), Paolo Taviani (born 1931), and Vittorio Taviani (born 1929), and Lina Wertmuller (born 1928). Sergio Leone (born 1921), the best-known exponent of the Spaghetti Western* genre, also came to prominence in the sixties.

The number of theatres in Italy has grown in tandem with the strength of the film industry. There were 4,013 in 1938; rising to 5,236 in 1942; 6,551 in 1948; 7,896 in 1950; 8,625 in 1951; 8,988 in 1952; and 9,502 in 1953. Film production has steadily dropped, from 103 features in 1981 to 89 in 1985. The leading studios in Rome are Dear (with five sound stages), Centro Sperimentale (with three), Cinecittà (with fourteen), Istituto LUCE (with two), De Paolis (with nine), Titanus (with six), ATC Grottaferrata (with two), Elios (with two), and Vides (with two). Other major studios are Cosmopolitan (with four sound stages) in Tirrenia, ICET-De Paolis (with four) in Milan, Fert (with three) in Turin, and Bertolazzi (with two) in Peschiera.

BIBLIOGRAPHY

Armes, Roy. *Patterns of Realism*. South Brunswick, N.J.: A.S. Barnes, 1971.

Barzini, Luigi, Jr., "The Motion Picture Industry," *Atlantic*, December 1958, pp. 178–181.

Bondanella, Peter. *Italian Cinema: From Neorealism to the Present*. New York: Frederick Ungar, 1983.

Brunetta, Gian Piero, "The Conversion of the Italian Cinema to Fascism in the 1920's," *The Journal of Italian History*, vol. I, 1978, pp. 432–454.

Frayling, Christopher. *Spaghetti Westerns: Cowboys and Europeans from Karl May to Sergio Leone*. Boston: Routledge and Kegan Paul, 1981.

Hay, James. *Popular Film Culture in Fascist Italy: The Passing of the Rex*. Bloomington: Indiana University Press, 1987.

"Hollywood on the Tiber," *Time*, August 16, 1954, pp. 54–56.

Incontri Internazionali d'Arte Roma. *The Fabulous Thirties: Italian Cinema, 1929–1944*. Milan: Electra, 1979.

"Italian Movies, the Last Act?," *US News & World Report*, August 17, 1956, pp. 82–84.

Jarratt, Vernon. *The Italian Cinema*. London: Falcon Press, 1951.

Leprohon, Pierre. *The Italian Cinema*. New York: Praeger, 1972.

Liehm, Mira. *Passion and Defiance: Film in Italy from 1942 to the Present*. Berkeley: University of California Press, 1984.

Malerba, Luigi, and Carmine Siniscalco, editors. *Fifty Years of Italian Cinema*. Rome: C. Bestetti, 1955.

Mancini, Elaine. *Struggles of the Italian Film Industry during Fascism, 1930–1935*. Ann Arbor, Mich.: UMI Research Press, 1985.

Marcus, Millicent. *Italian Film in the Light of Neorealism*. Princeton, N.J.: Princeton University Press, 1986.

Overby, David, editor. *Springtime in Italy: A Reader on Neorealism*. Hamden, Conn.: Archon Books, 1979.

Rondi, Gian Luigi. *Italian Cinema Today, 1952–1965*. New York: Hill and Wang, 1966.

Staig, Lawrence, and Tony Williams. *Italian Western: The Opera of Violence*. London: Odeon, 1975.

Witcombe, R.T. *The New Italian Cinema: Studies in Dance and Despair*. New York: Oxford University Press, 1982.

IVORY COAST. Perhaps because it has more theatres than most African nations—a reported fifty in 1966—the Ivory Coast has maintained a small, yet vital film industry. Important features include Henri Ouparc's *Abusuan/The Family* (1973) and Kitia Touré's *Comedie Exotique/Exotic Comedy* (1984). Other directors active in the Ivory Coast include Timité Bassori, Desiré Ecaré, M'Bala Roger Gnoan, Vodio Etienne Ndabian, Jean-Louis Koula, Moussa Dosso, and Fadika Kramo-Lanciné. A national production agency, Société Ivoirienne de Cinéma, was created in 1962, but gave little help to the burgeoning film industry, and was dissolved in 1979.

The 1976 Academy Award winner for Best Foreign Language Film was *Noir et blancs en couleur/Black and White in Color,* which was a co-production of Arthur Cohn and Société Ivoirienne de Cinéma, and the official entry from the Ivory Coast. This was the first and only time that an African film has received an Oscar.

BIBLIOGRAPHY

Brachy, Victor. *Le Cinéma en Côte D'Ivoire*. Brussels: OCIC, 1982.

J

"JACK THE RIPPER," the nineteenth-century mass murderer who terrorized the East End of London, has been the subject of a number of feature films, including *The Lodger* (1926, 1932, and 1944), *The Man in the Attic* (1953), *Jack the Ripper* (1958), *A Study in Terror* (1965), *Jack the Ripper* (1971), *Hands of the Ripper* (1971), *The Ruling Class* (1972), *Time after Time* (1979), and *Murder by Decree* (1979).

JAMAICA is primarily known as a film location rather than a film producer. The eleven producers on the island are basically concerned with offering support facilities for foreign producers and in the making of commercials and music videos. Prime Minister Edward Seaga tried to encourage film production, and, in 1982, the Motion Picture Industry Encouragement Act was passed, which offered tax incentives for those wishing to establish production companies, but did not help in the actual production process.

Although the number of theatres on the island has increased from the fifteen operating in 1937, there is not enough local support to make Jamaican film production financially viable. Jamaican films seem unable to find an audience either in the United States or Western Europe. Notwithstanding, there are Jamaican filmmakers whose works are concerned with native life and culture including Perry Henzell and *The Harder They Come* (1972), Lennie Little-White and *Children of Babylon* (1980), Barbara Blake-Hanna and *Race, Rhetoric and Rastafari* (1982), and Dickey Jobson and *Countryman* (1983).

BIBLIOGRAPHY

Marshall, Victoria M, " 'Likkle but Tallawah': Small but Aggressive Describes the Jamaican Film Industry," *Black Film Review*, vol. III, no. 1, Winter 86/87, pp. 7, 23.

"JAMES BOND" SERIES. It is arguable that, on film, the exploits of the fictional British spy, James Bond, have far exceeded his popularity in the novels of his creator, Ian Fleming (1908–1964), who selected the name James Bond for his hero because a gentleman of that name had authored *Birds of the West Indies,* which Fleming was currently reading. James Bond made his first appearance outside the pages of a book on October 21, 1954, in the Climax Mystery Theater production of *Casino Royale* on CBS, with Barry Nelson as Bond.

Twenty-five James Bond features have been produced by Albert R. "Cubby" Broccoli, with the first nine (up to and including *The Man with the Golden Gun*) co-produced with Harry Saltzman. The first eleven features (up to and including *Moonraker*) were made by the London-based Eon Productions. All twenty-five features were released in the United States by United Artists. Sean Connery was the first James Bond in *Dr. No* (1962), *From Russia with Love* (1963), *Goldfinger* (1964), *Thunderball* (1965), *You Only Live Twice* (1967), and *Diamonds Are Forever* (1971). Connery was replaced by George Lazenby in *On Her Majesty's Secret Service* (1969). Roger Moore played James Bond in *The Man with the Golden Gun* (1974), *The Spy Who Loved Me* (1977), *Moonraker* (1979), *For Your Eyes Only* (1981), *Octopussy* (1983), and *A View to a Kill* (1985). Moore was replaced in *The Living Daylights* (1987) by a new James Bond, Timothy Dalton.

Aside from the Broccoli series, Charles K. Feldman produced a James Bond spoof, *Casino Royale,* in 1967, with David Niven as the spy, released by Columbia. In 1983, Jack Schwartzman produced *Never Say Never Again* for Taliafilm (released by Warner Bros.), with Sean Connery as Bond.

BIBLIOGRAPHY

Benson, Raymond. *The James Bond Bedside Companion.* New York: Dodd, Mead & Company, 1984.

Brosnan, John. *James Bond in the Cinema.* San Diego: A.S. Barnes, 1981.

Rubin, Steven Jay. *The James Bond Films.* New York: Arlington House, 1983.

JAPAN. In 1896, two years after the Edison Kinetoscope was first exhibited publicly in New York, a number of Kinetoscopes were imported into Japan and proved to be very popular. The next year both the Lumière Cinématographe and Edison Vitascope were exhibited within the same week in Japan. Emperor Taisho's publicized presence at a Vitascope presentation probably accounted for that machine's greater popularity among Japanese audiences.

The first films produced in Japan were shot in 1898 by Tsunekichi Shibata of the Mitsukoshi Department Store. In 1899, Shibata persuaded Danjuro Ichikawa, the leading Kabuki actor of the time, to appear in *Momijigari/Maple Viewing,* the earliest Japanese film still in existence. The first Japanese newsreels were shot in 1900 during the Boxer Rebellion in China. The first permanent movie theatre in Japan opened in 1903 in Asakusa, Tokyo's amusement district.

The early Japanese film was influenced heavily by Japanese theatre and borrowed such elements as the benshi*, or narrator, and oyama, female impersonators. The oyama, males playing female roles, a practice that developed in traditional Japanese theatre, acquired prestige and power and thus kept the industry from using actresses. After the first women stars appeared in the early twenties, the oyama began to disappear and a strike by them in 1922, led by Teinosuke Kinugasa (1896–1982), who later became an important director, was on the whole ineffectual.

Besides the institutions of the benshi and oyama, Japanese film felt the influence of the theatre in the overwhelming use of plays as source material and in the types of heroes borrowed. The different types of theatre became the basis for the different types of film. Kabuki, a rigidly formalistic tradition developed in the feudalistic Tokugawa period, were always set in that period. Shimpa, originally part of the Meiji revolt against feudalistic ways, used contemporary settings, but soon became as rigid in its romanticism as Kabuki was in its formalism. Shingeki, or new drama, began in the mid-1900s and embraced realism during World War I. Two types of heroes from Kabuki pervade the history of Japanese film: tateyaku, the main lead who played noble, wise samurai and always placed loyalty above romantic love; and nimaime, the second billed male who easily fell in love and would sometimes die with the heroine because of this love.

Japan's first film star was Matsunosake Onoe (born 1875), a Kabuki actor who, with director Shozo Makino (born 1878), made 168 films for the Yokota Company between 1909 and 1911. Onoe continued to be Japan's only star for ten years.

In 1911, the major companies, including Yokota, Yoshizawa, M. Pathé (which borrowed its name from the French company but was not connected with it) and the Fukuhodo theatre chain, formed Dai Nippon Fuirumu Kikai Seizo (The Greater Japan Film Equipment Manufacturing Company, Ltd.) a trust patterned after the Motion Picture Patents Company, which was formed two years earlier to monopolize the American industry. In 1912, the trust became Nippon Katsudo Shashin (Japan Motion Picture Company, Ltd.), later shortened to Nikkatsu*.

Tennenshoku Katsudo Shashin (Natural Color Moving Picture Company), shortened to Tenkatsu, was formed in 1914 to rival Nikkatsu and used the British Kinemacolor process until the cost proved prohibitive during the First World War. In 1917, Norimasa Kaeriyama (born 1893) joined Tenkatsu and started a movement to encourage the use of film techniques common in America and the West, realistic acting, actresses instead of oyama, and intertitles instead of benshi. Although Eizo Tanaka at Nikkatsu directed *Ikeru Shikabane/The Living Corpse* (1917), based on a work by Tolstoy, using some of the new principles, while retaining some of the old (Kinugasa played the heroine), the new techniques were considered foreign and did not become popular until the formation in 1920 of Taisho Katsuei, shortened to Taikatsu, and the entrance into production of the Shochiku* Cinema Company, a theatrical monopoly established in 1896. Taikatsu hired Thomas Kurihara, formerly an actor in the United States with Thomas H. Ince (to direct, along with author Junichiro Tanizaki [born 1886], influenced at the time by European writers, to write scripts), and arranged for actors to be schooled in the techniques of realistic acting. Shochiku set up the

Shochiku Cinema Institute, a research center run by Kaoru Osanai, a founder of Shingeki, and tried to hire Sessue Hayakawa (1889–1973), then one of Hollywood's top stars, but settled for Henry Kotani, a cameraman from Famous Players-Lasky. Shochiku used no oyama and developed Japan's earliest female stars including Sumiko Kurishima (born 1903). The great Kanto earthquake of September 1923 also facilitated the changeover in method as it caused a complete reorganization of the industry.

The twenties saw the development of a new type of hero, beginning with *Ukiyoe-shi—Murasaki Zukin/Woodcut Artist,* made in 1923, in a series of films with alienated, nihilistic, and violent samurai heroes. Influenced by American action films and new developments in Japanese theatre and literature, these films responded in the late twenties to the upheavals in society due to the end of the Taisho era, the depression, labor unrest, and the growth of the military's influence in government. The best were directed by Daisuke Ito (1898–1981) and Masahiro Makino, son of Shozo Makino, and starred Tsumasaburo Bando.

Also in the twenties, the genre gendai-geki, or films about contemporary life (after 1868, the beginning of the Meiji era) gained popularity due to the efforts of Shiro Kido, head of Shochiku's Kamata studios, and director Minoru Murata, who with Kaoru Osanai made *Rojo no Reikon/Souls of the Road* (1921), which interwove two stories, one of which was based on Gorki's *The Lower Depths.* Traditionally, gendai-geki have been filmed in Tokyo, while the period films (set before 1868), or jidai-geki, have been made in Kyoto studios. By the late twenties jidai-geki accounted for 60 percent of Japanese films.

In 1925, the top four companies, Nikkatsu, Shochiku, Teikine (established in 1920 as Teikoku Cinema Geijutsu/Imperial Cinema Art Company), and Toa Cinema formed the Japan Motion Picture Producers Association to try to force out the independent companies. In response to this, many of the top period stars left the majors and formed their own production companies during the late twenties.

The last new genres of the silent era were shomin-geki, or drama about ordinary people, developed by Yasujiro Shimazu (born 1897), Kenji Mizoguchi (1898–1956), Yasujiro Ozu (1903–1963), and Heinosuke Gosho (1902–1981); the tendency film, which thrived between 1929 and 1931 and was concerned with social problems; nansensu-mono or nonsense comedies, which developed into erotic comedies; and rumpen-mono, dramas about the lower classes. Notable films of the period include Marata's antiwar film *Seisaku no Tsuma/Seisaku's Wife* (1924), Kinugasa's *Kurutta Ippeiji/A Crazy Page* or *Page of Madness* (1926), an impressionist film about insanity in a mental institution, written with novelist Yasunari Kawabata (born 1899), and *Jujiro/Crossroads* or *Shadows of the Yoshiwara,* directed by Kinugasa in 1928, which received critical acclaim in Europe.

Sound was introduced gradually in Japan during the thirties. In 1929, Nikkatsu made two features with a sound-on-disc system. After these and a number of other unsuccessful sound features, Shochiku, with a sound-on-film system, produced the first successful talkie, Gosho's *Madamu to Nyobo/The Neighbor's Wife* *and Mine* (1931). The film, a comedy with a jazz score, won the 1931 *Kinema Jumpo* (Best One) award, an annual prize given by a leading film magazine beginning in 1926. It wasn't until 1935 that more sound films were produced than silent ones. Although Nikkatsu acquired the best sound system, Western Electric, in 1933, labor tensions, infighting, and violence marked the next few years of fierce competition between Shochiku and Nikkatsu (Teikine had been transformed into the Shinko Company, supported with secret Shochiku capital, and Toa stopped production around 1930), during which Photo Chemical Laboratories (PCL), originally established as a lab and rental studio in 1929, began production. In 1935, PCL was taken over by Ichizo Kobayashi, a railroad magnate who created Toho Motion Picture Distribution Corporation* in 1936 to distribute product from PCL and the J.O. Company. PCL hired actors from vaudeville and Shingeki and in 1935 instituted examinations to hire young talent, whereby Akira Kurosawa (born 1910) began his career as an assistant director. PCL's young directors, including Kajiro Yamamoto (1902–1974), Mikio Naruse (1905–1969), Sotoji Kimura, and Shu Fushimizu, were, in Kurosawa's words, "progressive and energetic." Although Shochiku forced Nikkatsu to join a producers' association to make theatres boycott Toho's product, the popularity of Toho's films, especially the period ones, convinced owners to disregard the boycott. By the end of the decade, after Toho lured away top star Kazuo Hasegawa (born 1908) and gained control of various small independent companies, including the acclaimed Tokyo Hassei, they were Japan's leading company.

Production during the thirties ranged from 413 to 583 features per year, a drop from an average 700 to 800 per year at the end of the twenties. Although the U.S. Bureau of Foreign and Domestic Commerce, which published yearly analyses of foreign film industries, considered the Japanese product juvenile in plot, poorly directed, and geared toward the masses, and noted that Japanese intelligentsia preferred foreign films, the period beginning in 1932 has been called the first golden age of Japanese cinema by Japan's leading film critic Tadao Sato. The decade saw outstanding films in a variety of genres: period films made by Kinugasa, Hiroshi Inagaki (1905–1980), Mansaku Itami, and Sadao Yamanaka, considered by some as the greatest period director, who was killed fighting in China in 1938; shomin-geki by Yasujiro Shimazu, Tomotaka Tasaka (born 1902), Mikio Naruse, Gosho and Kajiro Yamamoto; nonsense comedy by Yasujiro Ozu and Enjiro Saito; realistic drama by Mizoguchi and Tomu Uchida (1898–1970); adaptations of contemporary literature by Shiro Toyoda (1906–1973) and Kimisaburo Yoshimura (born 1911); and children's films by Hiroshi Shimizu.

Coinciding with the military buildup and involvement in China, government interference in the industry increased. Although a central censorship bureau had been established on July 1, 1925, under the Department of Home Affairs, censorship was moderate until 1937, except for a period in the late twenties and early thirties when certain tendency films were suppressed because of their political content. In 1937, a code was introduced that called for the censorship and suppression of films thought to trivialize the military, lower morale, and portray pleasure seeking or individualism. Films that promoted the Japanese family and sacrifice for the nation were encouraged. From September 1937 until October 1938, American film imports were prohibited, although this was considered more an economic dispute than an ideological one.

On April 5, 1939, a motion picture law went into effect that placed the film industry under the control of the government, specifically the Ministry of Home Affairs and the Media Section of the Imperial Army. Scenarios were to be approved by the government, actors and directors had to be licensed, the showing of educational films in theatres was made mandatory, and the distribution and exhibition of foreign films was restricted. Subsequently laws took effect that greatly restricted subject matter and sought to promote government propaganda. Kokusaku eiga, or national policy films, dominated the industry and stressed the importance of the war effort, Japanese nationalism, sacrifice of the individual, and the importance of the home front, while prohibiting eroticism, Western influence, and most comedy. War films, which began to be made in large numbers in 1938, became a prevalent genre led by Kajiro Yamamoto, who made *Hawai-Marei Oki Kaisen/The War at Sea from Hawaii to Malaya* in 1942, an expensive reconstruction of the Pearl Harbor attack and the preceding naval buildup, and Yutaka Abe, who in the teens acted in American films. According to critic Tadao Sato, the war films stressed the human side of the Japanese soldier, treated war as a kind of spiritual training, and delineated the enemy only vaguely. Historical films were encouraged to dramatize Japanese greatness and documentaries flourished.

To establish further control over production, the government in 1942 forced the ten major companies to consolidate into three companies led by Shochiku, Toho, and Shinko. The third company, Dai-Nihon Eiga (The Greater Japan Motion Picture Company), later known as Daiei*, became a power in the postwar industry. Nikkatsu, although larger than Shinko, was deliberately kept from becoming the dominant company of Daiei because of their objection to the scheme.

The end of the war brought the end of the censorship bureau in October 1945. The next month, General Headquarters, Supreme Command for the Allied Powers (SCAP) issued a list of prohibited subjects and a list of themes to be encouraged to inculcate democratic content and suppress militarism, nationalism, and feudalistic tendencies. In March 1946, a unit in the Civil Information and Education Section (CI&E) of SCAP was created to censor subjects and issue seals of approval to completed films.

Although filmmakers during the Occupation were again faced with censorship and limitations (the period film was almost completely suppressed because of its feudalistic setting), many thrived during this period. Akira Kurosawa wrote about the American censors, "Not a single one among them treated us as criminals, the way the Japanese censors had." Kurosawa, who began as an assistant director for Kajiro Yamamoto and others in the late thirties and directed some scenes in Yamamoto's 1941 film *Uma/Horse,* wrote scripts during the war years and directed his first film, *Sugata Sanshiro/Sanshiro Sugata,* about a judo expert in 1943. After the war, with such films as *Waga Seishun ni Kuinashi/No Regrets for Our Youth* (1946), *Subarashiki Nichiyobi/One Wonderful Sunday* (1947), *Yoidore Tenshi/Drunken Angel* (1948), his first film with actor Toshiro Mifune (born 1920), *Shizukanaru Ketto/The Quiet Duel* (1949), and *Nora Inu/Stray Dog* (1949), Kurosawa exhibited great power, creativity, and independence. Other young directors who developed during the Occupation included Keisuke Kinoshita (born 1912) and Kimisaburo Yoshimura. Older directors seemed to have little difficulty adjusting from national policy to democratic content films. During this time, gangster films became popular, possibly because of the suppression of period films; the number of children's films and youth pictures increased dramatically; and kissing scenes, which formerly were prohibited and in fact cut from foreign films exhibited in Japan, were introduced and encouraged by the Americans.

In 1949, Eiga Rinri Kitel, or Eirin, the Motion Picture Ethics Regulation and Control Committee, was created for self-regulation of censorship within the industry. Eirin, which was reorganized in 1957 to include representatives from outside the industry, remains at present the censoring body for films.

After some leaders of the industry were purged as war criminals by Occupation forces from a list drawn up by the Japan Motion Picture and Drama Employees Union, which was communistic, the power of labor unions grew dramatically. Labor disputes pervaded the Occupation period, particularly at Toho, which in three years fell from being the leading producer to abandoning production in 1949 because of three divisive strikes that gave the union great power in studio management. During the second strike in October-December 1946, ten leading stars of Toho along with about 450 other employees formed a separate union and began production at the abandoned Tokyo Hassei studios. In 1947, this studio formed the Shintoho Company*. The third strike, lasting from April until October 1948, ended when 20,000 police and the U.S. Army, using cavalry, airplanes, and tanks, surrounded the studio, which had been taken over by the union. The Army's involvement was seen as a warning against other communist-inspired action, both in Japan and the United States.

During the late forties many independent companies arose for short periods of time, the most prestigious being Eiga Geijutsu Kyokai (Film Art Association), founded in 1948 by directors Kajiro Yamamoto, Mikio Naruse, Taniguchi Senkichi, and Akira Kurosawa. After the expulsion of the Toho labor leaders, many of whom were members of the Communist Party, and purges of the communists by SCAP in 1950 from Toho, Shochiku, and Daiei, many leftists formed their own independent companies. When the Occupation ended in 1952, a number of anti-American films, some financed by the left-wing Japan Teachers' Union, were produced, including *Genbaku no Ko/Children of the Atom Bomb* (1952), *Hiroshima* (1953), and *Akasen Kichi/Red-Light Bases.*

The fifties saw the fruition of a second "golden age" with masterpieces by Kurosawa, Ozu, Mizoguchi, and Naruse. Kurosawa's *Rashomon* (1950) won the Grand Prix at the Venice Film Festival in 1951 and brought the Japanese cinema to world attention. In the following years, a number of Japanese films won prizes at international festivals including Yoshimura's *Genji Monogatari/A Tale of Genji* (1952); Mizoguchi's *Ugetsu Monogatari/Ugetsu* (1953) and *Sansho Dayo/Sansho the Bailiff* (1954); Kinugasa's *Jigokumon/Gate of Hell* (1953), widely praised for its use of color; and Kurosawa's *Shichinin no Samurai/Seven Samurai* (1954).

By 1953, the five major companies, Shochiku, Toho, Nikkatsu, Daiei, and Toei (the Tokyo Motion Picture Distribution Company, formed in 1951 from the Toyoko and Yoshimoto-Oizumi companies) controlled about 90 percent of the production, distribution, and exhibition in Japan. Shintoho, after losing its stars, cut back production and gambled with Japan's first widescreen film, *Meiji Tenno to Nichi-Ro Daisenso/The Emperor Meiji and the Great Russo-Japanese War,* which was successful. Nikkatsu, which ceased production when Daiei was formed, concentrating instead on its lucrative theatre chain, resumed production and attracted stars from the other companies. Double-features became the norm, and when Toei and Shochiku increased production to two films per week, a production race began which brought block-booking to most theatres and an increase to triple features in 60 percent of the theatres by 1960. The expansion reached a peak in 1958 when attendance of over 1 billion represented an average of twelve to thirteen films seen per person per year.

It wasn't until 1962 that color, which was first used in a feature in the 1951 *Karumen Kokyo ni Kaeru/Carmen Comes Home,* directed by Kinoshita, was used in more features during a year than black and white. Widescreen was introduced in the mid-fifties, and by 1958, three-quarters of all features made in Japan were in some form of widescreen.

During the fifties, a number of new types of film became popular. Youth films continued and dealt increasingly with teenage sex, particularly in the taiyozoku (sun tribe) films beginning in the summer of 1956. Based on the novels of Shintaro Ishihara, these films portrayed rebellious youth in conflict with the older generation and the law. In the mid-fifties female nudity was introduced, the gangster film thrived, and the period film, buoyed by the international success of *Rashomon,* became popular again. In 1956, 35 percent of the films made in Japan were period films. Popular new genres included ghost stories and science-fiction monster films. The revival of shomin-geki in the work of Ozu, Naruse, and Gosho brought new masterpieces to international attention.

With the rise of television (the number of sets in Japan rose from nine hundred in February 1953 to 13 million in December 1962) and an increase in other leisure activities, attendance at cinemas dropped drastically in the early sixties, and with the introduction of video cassette players in the seventies and eighties, a continued fall has not been overcome. In 1987, attendance reached its lowest point since World War II at about 143 million. The average person at present sees only one or two films per year, and many prefer imports. In 1976 revenue from imported films exceeded that from domestic product for the first time. Although much of the Japanese economy has thrived in the past twenty-five years, the film industry has not been able to recover from the loss to television. The major companies, which resorted first to spectaculars and later to sex and action films, have survived only by diversifying into unrelated fields, renting their studios, and producing for television. By 1987, only Toei and Shochiku among the majors were still producing. Shintoho fell in 1961; Daiei went bankrupt in 1971; Toho built a real estate empire and ceased production; and Nikkatsu, which still distributes, survived only by distributing and producing soft-core erotic films in the seventies.

The decline in attendance has been matched by a decline in quality, which some filmmakers and critics have blamed on the majors' refusal to let young directors emerge, their reliance on low to moderately budgeted "safe" films that proved to be unpopular, and the stranglehold on the exhibition circuits by the majors that made it difficult for independent films to get decent exhibition. Although independent companies were producing more than half of the films in Japan by 1970, most of these were erotic films that the majors distributed to survive. Young directors had little opportunity to develop their talents other than in the erotic field, since banks refused to loan money to back independent films. There were some exceptions to this bleak situation. Shochiku, following the success of the French New Wave films in Japan, allowed their young assistant directors Nagisa Oshima (born 1932), Masahiro Shinoda (born 1931), and Yoshishige Yoshida (born 1933) to direct; and the Art Theatre Guild (ATG), a small exhibition circuit, provided an alternative to the major exhibition chains and also provided partial financing for some independents.

In the sixties and early seventies, some in the industry called for government involvement. In 1967 low-interest loans were provided to a small extent (later it came out that some of the money was used to finance non-film activities), and in 1973 an incentive award program was instituted to provide prize money after a film's completion, but these solutions did little to revitalize the industry.

As for the erotic films, two types became prevalent, the pinku eiga ("pink" films) films of the sixties, which had little plot, and the roman poruno eiga ("roman" porn films) of the seventies that added a dramatic element to the sex scenes. Some of the latter type were critically acclaimed, as were many of the more serious films by Oshima, Shohei Imamura (born 1926), Shinoda, and others that were quite frank and probing in their sexual content.

The yakusa film, that was similar in many ways to the period film (that was rarely made any longer), but took place in a contemporary setting, was very popular between 1963 and 1973. Animation became big business with production shipped first to South Korea and later to Taiwan (with the Philippines currently being considered) because of rising labor costs. The first Japanese 70mm film *Shaka/Buddha* (1961) was very successful as was the "Tora-san" series of Yoji Yamada, the only continually successful filmmaker of the seventies and eighties who also has earned critical acclaim. The series, which stars Kiyoshi Atsumi, helped save Shochiku from bankruptcy, and after thirty-seven installments, is the longest in film history. The largest independent producer, publisher Haruki Kadowaka, has made some fifty films since 1977, nearly all of them successful. In 1986 he produced Japan's most expensive film, the $18 million epic *Ten to Chi to/Heaven and Earth*.

Many of the great directors from the fifties and earlier died or retired in the past three decades, including Gosho, Ozu, Mizoguchi, Toyoda, Naruse, Kinoshita, and Yoshimura. Kurosawa has made only five films since 1965 and has had to rely on foreign financing for the last three. A few directors of the next generation, including Oshima, Shinoda, Imamura, Yoshida, Susumu Hani (born 1928), Kaneto Shindo (born 1912), and Shuji Terayama (born 1936) have survived to produce compelling films.

BIBLIOGRAPHY

Anderson, Joseph L., and Donald Richie. *The Japanese Film: Art and Industry*, expanded edition. Princeton, N.J.: Princeton University Press, 1982.

Bock, Audie. *Japanese Film Directors*. New York: Kodansha International for the Japan Society, 1978.

Burch, Noel. *To the Distant Observer: Form and Meaning in the Japanese Cinema*. Berkeley: University of California Press, 1979.

McDonald, Keiko I. *Cinema East: A Critical Study of Major Japanese Film*. Rutherford, N.J.: Fairleigh Dickinson University Press, 1983.

Mellen, Joan. *Voices from the Japanese Cinema*. New York: Liveright, 1975.

———. *The Waves at Genji's Door: Japan Through Its Cinema*. New York: Pantheon Books, 1976.

Richie, Donald. *Japanese Cinema: Film Style and National Character*. Garden City, N.Y.: Doubleday, 1971.

———. *The Japanese Movie: An Illustrated History*. Tokyo, New York, and San Francisco: Kodansha International, 1982.

Sato, Tadeo. *Currents in Japanese Cinema*. Tokyo, New York, and San Francisco: Kodansha International, 1982.

Svensson, Arne. *Japan: An Illustrated Guide*. New York: A.S. Barnes, 1971.

Tucker, Richard Neil. *Japan: Film Image*. London: Studio Vista, 1973.

UniJapan Quarterly. Tokyo: UniJapan Film, 1958–1965.

JÖRN DONNER PRODUCTIONS. Jörn Donner (born February 5, 1933) is considered the most precocious, as well as the best known of Finnish filmmakers. He is co-founder of the Finnish Film Archive, a film critic, a founder of many Finnish Film societies, a politician, and, since 1951, a professional writer. After directing four features in Sweden (1962–1967), he returned to Finland, and there, in 1968, he founded his own production company. Its first feature was *Mustaa Valkoisella/Black on White* (1968), which was followed by *Sixtynine* (1969), *Naisenkuvia/Portraits of Women* (1970), and *Anna* (1970), which starred Harriet Andersson, and was the first Finnish film by the director to gain international recognition. Aside from films directed by its founder, Jörn Donner Productions has also been responsible for features by other directors, including Jotaarkka Pennanen, Erkko Kivikoski, and Rauni Mollberg. After acquisition of FJ-Filmi, Jörn Donner Productions also began marketing its films abroad.

Address: Pohjoisranta 12, 00170 Helsinki, Finland.

THE JUSSI AWARDS are the most important of Finnish film awards, the country's equivalent of America's Academy Awards. Consisting of a statue designed by sculptor Ben Renvall, the Jussis are also the oldest of Finnish film awards, and named after the principal male character in the play, *Pohjalaisia,* which was filmed in 1925 and 1936.

The Jussis were first presented on November 16, 1944, by Elokuvajournalistit ry (an association of film journalists founded on September 16, 1944), and primarily honored best performances by actors and actresses. In the mid-fifties foreign performers also were honored, and, later, certificates of honor for best foreign films of the year were also presented. Because of disputes within the organization, a new group, Filmiaura ry was formed and registered on November 17, 1962. The majority of its members are not journalists but members of the film community. It has presented the Jussi awards since 1963 in the areas of both film and television, and it also awards certificates of honor for both Finnish and foreign films.

K

KACHUSHA-MONO is a genre in Japanese cinema in which the heroine is self-sacrificing. It takes its name from the heroine of Tolstoy's *Resurrection*.

KAMMERSPIELFILM (or Chamber Film) has its origins in the intimate theatre (Kammerspiele) created by Max Reinhardt in Germany in the mid-teens. As described by Heinz Herald, "If an actor needs to lift his whole arm at the Grosses Schauspielhaus, he need only move his hand at the Deutsches Theater; and at the Kammerspiele it's enough if he moves a finger."

Translated to the screen, Kammerspiele not only offered an intimacy, generally through the use of close-ups, but also required a minimum use of subtitles (particularly narrative titles), sets, and characters (who are referred to not by name but by the part they are playing). Kammerspielfilm has close links to Expressionism*. The most important of the films in this genre were scripted by Carl Mayer (1894–1944): *Hintertreppe/Backstairs* (1921), *Scherben/Shattered* (1921), *Sylvester/New Year's Eve* (1923), and *Der Letzte Mann/The Last Laugh* (1924). Another important film in the genre is *Nju* (1924), written and directed by Paul Czinner, and starring his wife, Elizabeth Bergner, who was considered by contemporary critics to be a superb exponent of Kammerspielfilm.

BIBLIOGRAPHY

Barlow, John D. *German Expressionist Film*. Boston: Twayne, 1982.

Eisner, Lotte H. *The Haunted Screen*. Berkeley: University of California Press, 1969.

THE KINEMATOGRAPH WEEKLY, once the most important of British film trade periodicals, began life on June 15, 1889, as *Optical Magic Lantern Journal and Photographic Enlarger*. It merged in September 1971 with *Today's Cinema*, and through much of its life was affectionately known as *Kine Weekly*.

BIBLIOGRAPHY

Slide, Anthony, editor. *International Film, Radio, and Television Journals*. Westport, Conn.: Greenwood Press, 1985.

THE KINEOPTICON was the name of Britain's first cinema, opened by film pioneer Birt Acres (1854–1918) at the intersection of London's Piccadilly Circus and Shaftesbury Avenue on March 21, 1896. After only a few weeks of existence, the facility was destroyed by fire.

KINO FILMS (1935) LTD. was founded in England in 1935 by Ivor Montagu (1904–1984) for the purpose of producing socialist films. Probably the most interesting of films that it released was Norman McLaren's pacifist production of *Hell Unlimited* (1936). Montagu and Kino were also responsible for the establishment of the Progressive Film Institute, that produced *In Defence of Madrid* (1936), made in Spain by Montagu and McLaren.

KINO-PRAVDA (Film Truth) was the name given to twenty-three newsreels produced by Soviet filmmaker Dziga Vertov (1896–1954) between 1922 and 1925. Pravda is the Russian word for truth, but it is also the name of the Soviet newspaper founded by Lenin, and it may well be that Dziga Vertov chose the name both as a tribute to the father of the Russian Revolution and because his newsreel was intended as a film version of *Pravda*. A popular record of Soviet life, Kino-Pravda introduced experimental ideas in the use of the candid camera and montage, and had a profound effect not only on Dziga Vertov's later work, but also on the work of many documentary filmmakers.

BIBLIOGRAPHY

Michelson, Annette, editor, and Kevin O'Brien, translator. *Kino-Eye: The Writings of Dziga Vertov*. Berkeley: University of California Press, 1984.

KINOREFORMBEWEGUNG was a 1912 Cinema Reform Movement in Germany that denounced films for corrupting the youth of the country.

KLANGFILM was established in 1928 by Siemens and Halske A.G. and Allgemeine Elektrizitäts Gesellschaft (AEG), two of Germany's largest electrical companies, in order to protect and promote their interests in electrical sound recording on film. Following a legal battle with Tobis* over the Tri-Ergon* patents, Klangfilm merged with Tobis in March 1929.

KOMMUNALES KINO (Communal Cinemas) is the name of a movement in West Germany in the seventies, whereby "communal cinemas" were created, subsidized by local communities, to ensure that German productions and worthwhile features from abroad could be seen by the public. The movement was particularly strong in the cities of Frankfurt and Hamburg.

KONICOLOR was a Japanese color system, similar to Fujicolor, marketed by the Konishiroku Photo Industry Co. Ltd. from 1949 to 1959.

BIBLIOGRAPHY

Koshofer, Gert. *Color: Die Farben des Films*. Berlin: Spiess, 1988.

KOREA. Films were first screened in Korea in 1903, and films have been produced in the country since 1919. The most active of Korean producers in the twenties and thirties was Ra Un-gyu, two of whose films, *Arirang* (1926) and *Pungana/Man of Rough Life* (1927), were rediscovered in 1982.

Following the Second World War, North Korea established the National Film Studio in 1947, producing its first feature film some two years later. In 1959, a second studio, the February 8th Studio, was also established. North Korea has an active program for the education of workers in the film field through the Pyongyang University of Cinematography, founded in November 1953. North Korean films are seldom seen outside of the country and in other Communist countries. The first North Korean International Film Festival was held in September 1987.

In South Korea, the film industry took longer to establish itself after the Second World War. Only three production companies were active in the forties, the Korea Motion Picture Company, Chosun Yun Wha Sa, and Lee Productions, which by 1949 had produced a total of fifty films. The government controlled the studios utilized by Chosun Yun Wha Sa. Ninety-eight theatres were in operation, and a 30 percent tax on admission was levied. Censorship by the Motion Picture Section of the Department of Public Information of the U.S. Army Military Government was very light and was mainly concerned with preventing the exhibition of films that might offend Korean sensibilities or criticize the United States.

The admission tax was revoked in 1955. Production soared in the fifties and sixties, from ninety-two features in 1958 to 212 in 1968. In 1958, the government of the Republic of Korea established the Korean Film Unit to make films promoting official policies, and it turns out an average of one hundred documentary subjects a year, most of which are dubbed into English, French, German, Japanese, Arabic, and Spanish.

Government interference in the film industry has increased steadily since the early sixties. A report in the *New York Times* (February 11, 1968) indicated that the South Korean Central Intelligence Agency paid close attention to native productions. Any films that depicted South Korea in a sordid light, showed any sympathy toward communism, or displayed any positive attitude toward North Korea were subject to censorship. One director was indicted and spent two months in jail for portraying a Communist officer as "a warm human being."

Because the government restricted the import of foreign films, it has been able in the past to force producers only to release films of which it approves. Those whose films are acceptable to the government were granted import licenses that had a value equivalent to half the cost of producing a feature. The government's restrictions on the import of foreign films, the prohibition on American film companies from establishing local offices, and the heavy cash payments required for the import of films garnered much criticism from the United States. Eventually the South Korean government was forced to change its rulings, and a new motion picture code was implemented on January 1, 1987, revoking most of the earlier restrictions.

The advent of television has seriously affected the South Korean film industry, and only eighty-five features were produced in 1986. Unfortunately, production has decreased at a time when government censorship has started to lift. Film producers are no longer required, as of 1987, to submit scripts for approval to the Korean Ethics Committee for Public Performance. Major Korean directors include Kim Soo-Yong, Chung Jin-Woo, Bae Chang Ho, and Lee Doo Young.

BIBLIOGRAPHY

Lukas, J. Anthony, "Seoul Is Vigilant on Film Industry," *New York Times,* February 11, 1968, Section L, p. 10.

Marshall, Fred, "The Cinema in the Republic of Korea," *Cinema India-International,* vol. IV, no. 1, 1987, pp. 108–109.

Pagano, Penny, "Studios Ask U.S. to Fight Trade Curbs," *Los Angeles Times,* September 11, 1985, Part VI, p. 4.

"U.S. Majors, Indies Eyeing S. Korea as Newest Big Market," *Variety,* October 28, 1987, pp. 6, 9.

KOSMORAMA. The oldest and largest of Danish film journals, *Kosmorama* was founded in October 1954 as an official publication of the Danish Film Museum. Although primarily concerned with native film production, it does devote space to international cinema.

Address: Det Danske Filmmuseum, St. Søndervoldstraede, 1419 Copenhagen K, Denmark.

BIBLIOGRAPHY

Slide, Anthony, editor. *International Film, Radio, and Television Journals.* Westport, Conn.: Greenwood Press, 1985.

KUNSTLICHTATELIER is the German name for "artificial light studio," the first of which was opened by Oskar Messter (1866–1943) in 1896.

KURATORIUM JUNGER DEUTSCHER FILM (Board of Curators of Young German Cinema) was created in 1965 by the West German government, thanks to the efforts of various young filmmakers led by Alexander Kluge (born 1932). It made interest-free loans, averaging DM 300,000 to help produce films by some of the country's new, young directors.

KUWAIT. Although most of its citizens watch films on video rather than in theatres, film piracy is rife, Kuwait does have a small film industry, thanks largely to the efforts of the former assistant undersecretary in the Ministry of Information, Mohammed Sanoussi. Through his efforts, the Ministry opened its own film studios in 1981. Aside from Sanoussi, the best-known name there is Khalid Siddik, a director who first came to prominence in 1972, and has been described by *Screen International* (September 10, 1983) as "Kuwait's one man film industry." Kuwait is one of the few Arab countries that does not actively discriminate against films with Jewish connections, and, therefore, a number of American features are imported into the country, as well as films from France, Italy, and the United Kingdom, through the Kuwait Cinema Company, that operates less than a dozen theatres in this oil-rich state. As of 1982, 52 percent of all households in Kuwait had video facilities, and viewed an average of twelve features a month.

BIBLIOGRAPHY

Borsten, Joan, ''Drilling for Dollars in Movie-Mad Kuwait,'' *Los Angeles Times*, Calendar, March 11, 1984, pp. 20–21.

L

LAPP. The only feature to be made in the Lapp language is the Norwegian production, *The Pathfinder,* based on a twelfth-century legend, and directed by Nils Gaup in 1987.

LATERNA MAGICA was a Czechoslovakian creation that combined film with live theatre and ballet. Performers would interact with the images on screen and actors would appear to step off screen onto the stage and vice versa. Laterna Magica was first seen at the Brussels World's Fair in the summer of 1958 and was first presented in the United States, relatively unsuccessfully, at New York's Carnegie Hall in August 1964.

BIBLIOGRAPHY

"Czech Mate," *Newsweek,* August 17, 1964, p. 76.

LATIN. The only feature film to be shot in Latin is *Sebastiane,* a British production directed, in 1976, by Derek Jarman and Paul Humfress, written by Jarman and James Waley, with Latin translation by Jack Welch. A decidedly homosexual view of the life of St. Sebastian, the film is noted for its subtitles which render Latin in the vernacular; thus Oedipus is translated as "Motherfucker."

BIBLIOGRAPHY

Jarman, Derek. *Dancing Ledge.* London: Quartet Books, 1984.

Rayns, Tony, "Sebastiane," *Monthly Film Bulletin,* vol. XLIII, no. 514, November 1976, pp. 235–236.

LATVIA boasted two production companies (making shorts and newsreels) and three film distributors in the twenties and thirties. There were sixty-nine theatres in 1928, and one hundred by 1938. Censorship of all films was undertaken by the Film Control Board of the Ministry of Public Relations. Since its annexation to the USSR in 1940, one studio has been established in the capital, Riga, for the production of features, cartoons, popular science subjects, and documentaries. The first Soviet films were made in Latvia in 1946.

LAVENDER PRINT was a term in use in the United Kingdom from the twenties through the forties (and still occasionally used) to describe fine grain prints (from which duplicate negatives can be manufactured). The name refers to the lavender tint of the film stock.

LEAGUE OF NATIONS. As with its successor the United Nations*, the League of Nations (1919–1946) had some involvement with film. As early as 1925, it sponsored a documentary titled *The Star of Hope,* and a year later it was responsible for Hans Nieter's *The World War and After,* which was reissued in revised versions for a number of years. Two other important League of Nations–sponsored documentaries, both from 1937, are Alberto Cavalcanti's *Message from Geneva* and Stuart Legg's *The League at Work.*

The League maintained a Commission on Cultural and Educational Films, and in October 1933 adopted a Convention for Facilitating the International Circulation of Educational Films, that eventually lapsed because of problems countries such as the United Kingdom had in accepting so-called educational films from fascist Italy. One curious aspect of the League's film-related activities was sponsorship of an international institute of educational cinema, that was financed by the government of Benito Mussolini and that closed in 1937, following complaints from the United Kingdom that its main function was the propagation of fascist films. The idea for such an Institute was first mooted in the July 1929 issue of the Rome-based *The International Review of Educational Cinematography,* which also seems to have close ties to the League of Nations.

LEBANON. Prior to the civil war, Lebanon imported an average of four hundred feature films a year from the United States, the United Kingdom, France, Italy, and Egypt, and filmgoing was more popular than in any other Arab country. Since 1952, when it moved from Cairo, the Motion Picture Export Association of America has made its Arab headquarters in Lebanon. George Haddad opened the first cinema in the country in 1919; he imported the first talkie in 1931; and, today, his sons continue in business, calling themselves, appropriately, Sons of George Haddad. The first Lebanese-produced feature was a 1929 silent comedy, *Adventures of Elias Mabrouk,* made by Jordano Pidutti. The country was little regarded for the quality or quantity of its film productions until 1962, when Mohamed Selmane's *Hello, Love!* enjoyed some success in Africa, Asia, South America, and the other Arab countries. There was a revival of interest in filmmaking in the early seventies when a number of young, European-trained directors, including George Shamshum, Samir Khoury, Samir Ghoseini, Burhan Alawiya, Rafik Hajjar, and George Nasser, became active. These directors generally worked on Lebanese-Syrian co-productions through the government-supported Syrian Cinema Centre.

BIBLIOGRAPHY
Borsten, Joan, "The Show Goes on—under the Gun," *Los Angeles Times* Calendar, July 15, 1984, pp. 3–4.
Khoury, Lucienne et al., "Film in Lebanon," *CTVD Cinema TV Digest*, no. 16, Winter (1966) 1967, pp. 5–7.
"Live from Beirut," *Hollywood Reporter*, August 28, 1984, unpaged supplement.

LENFILM. Active in the Soviet Union from the thirties onwards, Lenfilm's productions include Sergei and Georgy Vasiliev's *Chapayev* (1934) and Grigori Kozintsev and Leonid Trauberg's *Vyborgskaya storona/The Vyborg Side* (1939).

LIBYA. Prior to 1962, there was no film production in Libya. The country's thirty-five theatres screened an average of 750 films a year, imported primarily from the United States, Egypt, and Italy. When Muammar el-Qaddafi became military leader in 1969, he displayed some interest in production, and helped finance two large-scale features, with international stars, *Mohammad: Messenger of God* (1976) and *Lion of the Desert* (1981), both directed by Moustapha Akkad.

LITHUANIA produced no films except for newsreels during its years of independence. There were approximately seventy-three theatres in the country, of which nine, as late as 1938, were still not capable of screening sound films. Censorship of all films was handled initially by the Ministry of the Interior and later by the Public Activity Administration. Since its annexation by the USSR in 1940, one studio, the Lithuanian Film Studio, has been established in the capital, Vilna, for the production of features, cartoons, popular science subjects, and documentaries. The first Lithuanian feature to be produced after the Soviet takeover was *Marite* (1947), directed by Vera Stroyeva.

THE LLOYDS BANK SCREENWRITING COMPETITION has been organized annually in the United Kingdom since 1984 by the Oxford Film Foundation.

LODZ FILM SCHOOL. Although it is generally known as the Lodz Film School, the correct name of this world-renowned Polish institution, situated in an industrial city some sixty miles from Warsaw, is Pańswowa Wyzsa Szkova Filmowa, Telwizyjna i Teatralna, im Leona Schillera (Leon Schiller National School of Film, Television and Theatre). Government-funded, the school was founded in 1947, and its best-known graduates are directors Roman Polanski, Andrzej Wajda, Andrzej Munk, and Jerzy Skolimowski. It combines both technical training and aesthetic study, and its four-year programs are based on earlier programs in theoretical studies held in Cracow.

Address: ul. Targova 61, Łódż, Poland.

BIBLIOGRAPHY
Rose, Ernest D. *World Film & TV Study Resources*. Bonn-Bad Godesberg: Friedrich-Ebert-Stiftung, 1974.

LONDON. Among the many films that have utilized London as a historical backdrop are *Black Beauty* (1921), *The Road to London* (1921), *Sherlock Holmes* (1922), *The Glorious Adventure* (1922), *Lady Windermere's Fan* (1925), *Nell Gwyn* (1934), *The Barretts of Wimpole Street* (1934), *Lloyds of London* (1937), *Victoria the Great* (1937), *Sixty Glorious Years* (U.S. *Queen of Destiny,* 1938), *The Private Lives of Elizabeth and Essex* (1939), *Tower of London* (1939), *Henry V* (1945), *Forever Amber* (1947), *The Mudlark* (1950), *Tower of London* (1962), *Mary Poppins* (1964), *Cromwell* (1970), *The Missionary* (1983), and *Young Sherlock Holmes* (1986). The "Sherlock Holmes" series of features, starring Basil Rathbone and Nigel Bruce, might also be mentioned here, although many of the films are set in a time that is neither historical nor contemporary.

Pygmalion (1938), and its musical adaptation, *My Fair Lady* (1964), both utilize London as a background, from their openings at Covent Garden Market. *It Happened Here* (1964) is both historical and futuristic in its depiction of a London and a United Kingdom subjugated by Nazi Germany.

From Alfred Hitchcock's *Blackmail* in 1929, there have been countless British sound features set in London. Among the more memorable are *Britannia of Billingsgate* (1933), *My Old Dutch* (1934), *Hyde Park Corner* (1935), *The Man Who Knew Too Much* (1935), *The Thirty-Nine Steps* (1935), *Sabotage* (U.S. *A Woman Alone,* 1936), *St. Martin's Lane* (U.S. *Sidewalks of London,* 1938), *So This Is London* (1939), *Murder in Soho* (1939), *Waterloo Road* (1944), *London Town* (U.S. *My Heart Goes Crazy,* 1946), *It Always Rains on Sundays* (1947), *London Belongs to Me* (U.S. *Dulcimer Street,* 1948), *Britannia Mews* (1949), *Passport to Pimlico* (1949), *Night and the City* (1950), *Seven Days to Noon* (1950), *The Blue Lamp* (1950), *Stage Fright* (1950), *Pool of London* (1951), *The Lavender Hill Mob* (1951), *A Kid for Two Farthings* (1955), *The Ladykillers* (1955), *Gideon's Day* (1958), *The Day the Earth Caught Fire* (1961), *The Day of the Triffids* (1962), *The L-Shaped Room* (1962), *I Could Go on Singing* (1963), *The Servant* (1963), *Sparrows Can't Sing* (1963), *The Pumpkin Eater* (1964), *A Hard Day's Night* (1964), *Three Hats for Lisa* (1965), *Repulsion* (1965), *The Knack . . . and How To Get It* (1965), *Alfie* (1966), *Tonite Let's All Make Love in London* (1967), *To Sir, with Love* (1967), *The Killing of Sister George* (1968), *Up the Junction* (1968), *Poor Cow* (1968), *The Best House in London* (1969), *Battle of Britain* (1969), *10 Rillington Place* (1970), *The Long Good Friday* (1983), *Dance with a Stranger* (1984), *Betrayal* (1984), and *28 Up* (1984).

Honorable mention must also be made of the series of films, named after areas of London, directed by Herbert Wilcox and starring his wife, Anna Neagle: *I Live in Grosvenor Square* (U.S. *A Yank in London,* 1945), *Piccadilly Incident* (1946), *The Courtneys of Curzon Street* (1947), *Spring in Park Lane* (1948), and *Maytime in Mayfair* (1949).

There have been fewer American productions with London settings. Among the more important are *My Old Dutch* (1926), *Twinkletoes* (1926), *The Sorrows of Satan* (1926), *While London Sleeps* (1926), *London after Midnight* (1927), *Scotland Yard* (1930), *So This Is London* (1930), *London* (1930), *Waterloo*

Bridge (1931), *Foreign Correspondent* (1940), *Waterloo Bridge* (1940), *Mrs. Miniver* (1941), *Journey for Margaret* (1942), *Gaslight* (1944), *To Each His Own* (1946), *Royal Wedding* (1951), *Dial M For Murder* (1954), *Knock on Wood* (1954), *23 Paces to Baker Street* (1956), *Indiscreet* (1958), *Star!* (1968), *Frenzy* (1972), and *An American Werewolf in London* (1982).

The city is also the site of the London Film Festival (British Film Institute, 21 Stephen Street, London W1P 1PL).

THE LONDON EVENING STANDARD AWARDS, also known as the British Film Awards, are sponsored by the English newspaper of that name. From 1973, when they were first presented, through 1979, the Awards were called The Evening News Awards, after that London newspaper. When the Evening News was combined with the London Evening Standard, the Awards were taken over by the latter and renamed. They are presented only for British films, with categories including Best Actor, Best Actress, Best Film, Best Screenplay, Technical Achievement, Most Promising Newcomer(s), and Special Award. A Best Comedy award has been presented since the Awards inception, but since 1980 it has been known as the Peter Sellers Award for Comedy and has been awarded to an individual rather than a film.

LONDON FILMS, with its ''Big Ben'' logo, was founded in 1932 by Alexander Korda (1893–1956). It achieved international fame with its 1933 production of *The Private Life of Henry VIII,* starring Charles Laughton, one of the first British sound films to achieve considerable box-office success in the United States. The company's next two ''private life'' films, *The Private Life of Don Juan* and *Catherine the Great* (both released in 1934) were not as successful, but *The Scarlet Pimpernel* (1934) helped redress the balance. An additional thirty prestigious feature films were to follow.

Korda's productions needed immense financial investment, and the producer was an expert at manipulating financiers. The finance for London Films came from two sources, the Prudential Assurance Company and United Artists. It was the former that financed the building of Denham Studios*, but it was also the Prudential that first grew tired of Korda's extravagances.

In 1939, London Films was dissolved, and Korda went to Hollywood. He returned in 1943, and spent two frustrating years trying to set up the merger of M-G-M-British and London Film Productions, from which he resigned after having directed only one film, *Perfect Strangers* (1945). In 1946, London Films was reformed, and Korda was able to attract a number of independent filmmakers to the company, including Carol Reed, David Lean, Frank Launder and Sidney Gilliat, and Michael Powell and Emerich Pressburger. As a distribution outlet, Korda gained control of British Lion* and he rebuilt Shepperton Studios* as a production base. He obtained the first government loan to the film industry through the National Film Finance Corporation*, but when, in 1954, the loan amounting to £3 million had not been repaid, Korda's second empire collapsed. The company ceased production with Korda's death in 1956.

In 1978, financial control of the company was acquired by Mark Shelmerdine, who had been its managing director for a number of years. He was interested in reviving London as a production entity and appointed David Conroy as managing director of London Films International. Conroy arranged co-production with the British Broadcasting Corporation of a number of highly popular series, including *I Claudius, Poldark, Testament of Youth,* and *Thérèse Raquin* (all of which have been seen in the United States on "Masterpiece Theatre"). London Films also co-produced *The Country Girls* with Channel 4* and *Kim* with CBS.

In 1985, the company announced plans to expand its production operations, with Mark Shelmerdine moving to a newly opened Los Angeles office. A year later, the sale of the film library to Britain's Central Television was announced "for a substantial seven figure sum" (according to *Television Today,* November 10, 1986).

Address: London Film Productions Ltd., 44a Floral Street, London WC2E 9DA, United Kingdom.

BIBLIOGRAPHY

British Film Academy Journal, Spring 1956, special issue, "Sir Alexander Korda, 1893–1956."

Korda, Michael. *Charmed Lives: A Family Romance.* New York: Random House, 1979.

Kulik, Karol. *Alexander Korda: The Man Who Could Work Miracles.* London: W.H. Allen, 1975.

Petley, Julian, "Carry On London," *Stills,* April-May 1984, pp. 48–50.

Street, Sarah, "Alexander Korda, Prudential Assurance and British Film Finance in the 1930s," *Historical Journal of Film, Radio, and Television,* vol. VI, no. 2, 1986, pp. 161–179.

———, "Denham Studios: The Golden Jubilee of Korda's Folly," *Sight & Sound,* vol. LV, no. 2, Spring 1986, pp. 116–122.

Tabori, Paul. *Alexander Korda: A Biography.* London: Oldbourne, 1959.

Thompson, Kenneth, "Looking Back," *Films Illustrated,* vol. IX, no. 103, March 1980, pp. 276–277.

THE LONDON INTERNATIONAL FILM SCHOOL was founded in 1956 by Gilmore Roberts as an independent, non-profit organization. Its initial location was in Brixton, where it was known as the London School of Film Technique. In the mid-sixties, it moved to a converted warehouse in Covent Garden. A non-profit company, whose students are its stockholders, the school provides a two-year course in various aspects of film production.

Address: 24 Shelton Street, London WC2H 9HP, United Kingdom.

BIBLIOGRAPHY

Mottram, Phil, "The London International Film School: Thirty Years of Training Film-Makers," in *International Film Guide 1988,* editor Peter Cowie. New York: New York Zoetrope, 1987.

THE LONDON UNDERGROUND has been the subject of a silent feature film, *Underground,* directed by Anthony Asquith, and starring Elissa Landi and Brian Aherne. It has also been seen in a number of feature films, including *Bulldog Jack* (U.S. *Alias Bulldog Drummond,* 1935), *Waterloo Road* (1945), *Passport to Pimlico* (1949), *Three Hats for Lisa* (1965), and *Rotten to the Core* (1965). London Transport, which is responsible for the management of the underground, has sponsored a number of documentary films.

LOOK AT LIFE was an interest magazine produced for British filmgoers by British Movietone News from 1959 to 1969. Footage from the series is preserved and controlled by the British Movietone Library (North Orbital Road, Denham, Uxbridge, Middlesex UB9, 5UQ United Kingdom).

THE LOUMA REMOTE CONTROL CAMERA PLATFORM, with a 360° pan and tilt capability was developed by David Samuelson and Derek Lee, from a concept by Jean-Marie Lavalou and Alain Masseron. It was first used on the British feature, *Moonraker,* and the American feature, *1941,* both released in 1979. Its creators received the 1980 Scientific and Engineering Award from the Academy of Motion Picture Arts and Science.

THE LUMIÈRE CINÉMATOGRAPHE is the name of the most famous of early film screenings, presented by the pioneer French brothers, Louis (1864–1948) and Auguste (1862–1954) Lumière. The presentation was first given, privately, at the Societé d'Encouragement à l'Industrie Nationale in Paris on March 22, 1895. It was first presented before a paying audience at what is generally claimed to be the world's first motion picture theatre (also called the Lumière Cinématographe) in the Grand Café, 14 Boulevard des Capucines, Paris, on December 28, 1895. The Lumière cinématographe was first presented in London at the Regent Street Polytechnic on February 20, 1896. It was first seen in New York, simultaneously, at Keith's Union Square Theatre and the Eden Musée on 23rd Street, on June 29, 1896.

Among the films in the Lumière cinématographe presentation were *La Mer/The Sea, La sortie des ouvriers de l'usine Lumière/Workers Leaving the Lumière Factory, L'arrivée d'un train en gare/The Arrival of the Mail Train,* and *L'Arroseur arrosé/The Sprinkler Sprinkled* (which is generally regarded as the first screen comedy).

LUMINA FILMS was a French production company, active in the late teens and early twenties, that was established immediately after the First World War by director Jacques de Baroncelli (1881–1951).

LUXEMBOURG. The Grand Duchy of Luxembourg has its own film archive, approximately fifty theatres, but no significant film industry. Prior to 1980, only documentary films had been produced in the country, but in that year Paul Scheuer directed the feature, *Wât huet e gesôt/What Did He Say* for AFO-Film (7 route d'Eppeldorf, L-9353 Bettendorf), a company that three years later was responsible for *Congré fir e mord/The Murderer Takes a Day Off*. In 1987, Luxembourg produced its most important feature to date, *Die reise das land,* directed by Frank Hoffman and Paul Kieffer. It cost one quarter of a million dollars to make, and was produced by Samsa Film Productions (P.O. Box 316, L-4004 Esh-sur-Alzette).

A government commission on film and television was established in 1987. The government is also involved in motion pictures through a ratings agency, Commission de Surveillance des Cinémas (17 rue Pierre Frieden, L-4448 Soleuvre), that has been in existence since 1922.

BIBLIOGRAPHY

Thilges, Jean Pierre, "Luxembourg," in *International Film Guide 1988,* editor Peter Cowie. London: Tantivy Press, 1987, pp. 257–259.

M

"MACISTE" SERIES. Gabriele d'Annunzio's script for *Cabiria,* produced and directed in Italy by Giovanni Pastrone, and released in 1914, called for a magnificent strong man character, called Maciste. A dock worker named Bartolomeo Pagano was selected for the role, and as a result of his success in this feature, he changed his name to Maciste and starred in a series of features during the rest of the decade. The Maciste character was very much an Italian version of Tarzan, who could overcome any obstacle with the use of brute strength.

The character was revived in 1960 with Carlo Campogalliani's *Maciste nella dei re/The Son of Samson,* with Mark Forest, and the following year five further Maciste features were produced.

THE "MAD MAX" SERIES consists of three features, starring Mel Gibson as a former highway patrolman in a post–Third World War Australia, where oil is the most precious commodity. Directed by George Miller and produced by Byron Kennedy, *Mad Max* was released in 1979. A sequel, *Mad Max II* (U.S. *The Road Warrior*) was released in 1981. A third feature, *Mad Max beyond Thunderdrome,* directed by Miller and George Ogilvie, and co-starring Tina Turner, was released in 1985. Although far from the best of the new Australian features, the films are certainly the best known of that country's output.

BIBLIOGRAPHY

Chute, David, "The Ayatollah of the Movies," *Film Comment,* vol. XVIII, no. 4, July-August 1982, pp. 26–31.

Williams, Mark. *Road Movies.* New York: Proteus, 1982.

MALAYSIA. The Malayan film industry dates from 1933, when the first feature, *Laila Majnun,* was directed by two Indian nationals in Singapore (prior to its independence). Singapore was the first home of the Malayan film industry, and here a number of films were produced, featuring members of the Bangsawan (Malay Opera) stock company. The Shaw Brothers* began their careers here, importing equipment from China and taking the first steps into exhibition. The Second World War ended Malayan film production, but it was revived in 1947, when the Shaw Brothers established Malay Film Productions Ltd., which was soon in competition with another new company, Cathay-Keris Productions (created through the merger of Keris Film Productions and Cathay Productions). Both companies enjoyed tremendous successes in the fifties, but eventually ceased production; Malay in 1967 and Cathay-Keris in 1972.

The Shaw Brothers remained active in Malaysia, taking over the Studio Merdeka in Kuala Lumpur—it closed in 1975. The company's biggest star was P. Ramlee (1928–1973), who had a major influence on Malaysian cinema, not only as an actor, but also as a writer and director.

A new breed of independent filmmakers, known as Bumiputeras, became active in the seventies, with one of the first of the "new wave" features being *Keluarga Comat,* produced by Deddy M. Borhan. "Older" directors such as Jins Shamsudin and Aziz Jaafar remain active, while newer directors include Othman Hafsham, Rahim Razali, Zarul Hisham Al-Bakri, Nasir Jani, Meor Hashim Manaf, Kamarul Ariffin, Azmil Mustapha, and Johari Ibrahim.

Government film censorship was introduced in 1972 and is fairly strict; in 1977, board chairman, Haji Hassan Haji Mohammed Noor, told *Variety* that grounds for proscriptions included "excessive violence, lurid sexual and immoral scenes, propagation of communism, or other delicate political themes." FINAS or National Film Development Corporation was founded in 1981, but it remained inactive for a couple of years before helping to refurbish and reopen the Merdeka Studios. FINAS levies a 25 percent entertainment tax on all theatre tickets, which is used to help subsidize production. With the advent of video, theatres have been closing at a steady pace, with little over one hundred left in 1988, compared to seven times that number in 1978. The government-controlled Filem Negara (P.O. Box 214 Kuala Lumpur) produces an average of sixty documentary films a year.

BIBLIOGRAPHY

Latif, Baharudin A., "The Cinema in Malaysia," *Cinema India—International,* vol. IV, no. 1, 1987, pp. 98–99.

MALI. According to a 1966 USIA report, Mali had sixteen theatres, with a weekly attendance of 71,000. Newsreels have been produced in this African republic since 1966, and four years earlier a national film office, Office Cinématographique National du Mali (P.O. Box 197, Bamako, Mali) was established, primarily for the production of documentaries. The first fictional short subject, *Bambo,* was produced in 1968 by members of the Camera Club of the Bamako Technical School. Film directors active in Mali include Alkaly Kaba, Falaba Issatraore, Sega Coulibaly, and Souleymane Cissé.

MALTA. The former British colony of Malta was first prominently used for location shooting in 1953, when Brian Desmond Hurst made *The Malta Story* there, starring Alec Guinness and Jack Hawkins. The government has actively encouraged outside production, and in 1964 Malta Film Facilities was set up to provide a special water tank for filming of underwater sequences. *Casino Royale* (1967) is just one of the many features to make use of this facility.

Satadema Films Ltd., formed in 1973, is one of the major producers on the island, concentrating primarily on television commercials until 1983, when it embarked on feature film production. There are some thirty theatres on Malta.

BIBLIOGRAPHY

Grima, Joseph G., "Malta as Isle for Production," *Variety,* May 12, 1965, pp. 54, 76.

MANCUNIAN FILM CORPORATION. Established by John E. Blakeley, with studios in Manchester, Mancunian was active in the thirties and forties as a producer of films for unsophisticated North of England audiences; its productions were never intended for screening in London's West End. It concentrated primarily on films featuring popular British Music Hall* performers, among which are *The Penny Pool* (1937), with Duggie Wakefield; *Demobbed* (1944), with Norman Evans and Nat Jackley; *Under New Management* (1946), with Norman Evans and Nat Jackley; *Cup-Tie Honeymoon* (1948), with Sandy Powell; *Holidays with Pay* (1948), with Tessie O'Shea; and *What a Carry On!* (1949), with Jimmy Jewel and Ben Warriss. It also produced *Love—Mirth—Melody* (1934), with Nöel Coward's leading man, Graham Payne, and *Dodging the Dole* (1936), with popular British leading man, Barry K. Barnes, in one of his first screen appearances. Perhaps the most popular series of features produced by Mancunian was the "Somewhere" group of films starring Frank Randle. The company also has the distinction of producing George Formby's first two sound films: *Boots! Boots!* (1934) and *Off the Dole* (1935). Mancunian films were usually released through Butcher's Film Service, Ltd. (Townsend House, 22-25 Dean Street, London W1V 5AL, United Kingdom).

MARIANNE PRODUCTIONS was a French company, active from 1961 to 1975, among whose productions or co-productions are *Compartiment Tueurs/The Sleeping Car Murders* (1964), *Barbarella* (1967), and *Une femme douce/A Gentle Woman* (1968).

THE "MARIUS" TRILOGY consists of three self-contained French features, all written and produced by Marcel Pagnol and starring Pierre Fresnay in the title role. The three films are each set in Marseilles and notable for the performance of Raimu. The films in the series are *Marius* (1931, released in the United States in 1933), *Fanny* (1932, released in the United States in 1948), and *César* (1936, released in the United States in 1949).

MAY-FILM was the German production company of director Joe May (1880–1954), active in the teens and early twenties. Among its features are *Veritas Vincit* (1919), *Die Herrin der Welt/The Mistress of the World* (1919) and *Das Indische Grabmal/The Indian Tomb* (1921).

MAYFLOWER PICTURES CORPORATION, LTD. Actor Charles Laughton decided to form his own production company after the abortive fiasco of the feature *I Claudius*. German producer Erich Pommer, who had been forced out of his own country by Hitler, joined Laughton as a partner, and the other two directors of the newly formed company, Mayflower Pictures Corporation, Ltd., were John Maxwell and F.M. Guedalla. The company was named after the ship that brought the pilgrims to the United States, because both Laughton and Pommer were determined that the company should produce British films for the American market and possibly even branch out into American production.

Utilizing the Elstree Studios* of Associated British Pictures, Mayflower produced only three features: *The Vessel of Wrath* (U.S. *The Beachcomber,* 1938), directed by Erich Pommer and starring Laughton and his wife Elsa Lanchester; *St. Martin's Lane* (U.S. *Sidewalks of London,* 1938), directed by Tim Whelan and starring Laughton and Vivien Leigh; and *Jamaica Inn* (1939), directed by Alfred Hitchcock and starring Laughton and Maureen O'Hara.

MEDUSA DISTRIBUZIONE is a major Italian distributor and some-time producer, founded in 1964 by Franco Poccioni (1921–1988) and Felice Colaiacomo. (The former was the company's president until his death.) Medusa became an international distributor in 1966 with *The Poppy Is Also a Flower,* and has also co-produced a number of Italian features, notably Lina Wertmuller's *Mare d'agosto/Swept Away* (1974) and *Pasqualino Settebellezze/Seven Beauties* (1976).

MEMORIAL FILMS LTD. is a British production company, formed in 1965 by actor Albert Finney, utilizing his percentage profits from *Tom Jones*, and facetiously named after the Albert Memorial in London's Hyde Park. To head the company, Finney chose his close friend and fellow actor, Michael Medwin. Concerned with all areas of entertainment, Memorial's first activity was the presentation of two stage plays, *Spring and Port Wine* and *A Day in the Death of Joe Egg*. Memorial's first film was *Charlie Bubbles* (1967), of which Finney was both director and star, and that was financed by Jay Kanter at Universal Pictures. It was not particularly successful. The company's next production was Lindsay Anderson's *If* . . . (1969), financed at the last moment by Paramount, which won the Grand Prix at the 1969 Cannes Film Festival.

In the early seventies, Memorial was responsible for Anthony Scott's *Loving Memory* (1970), Mike Leigh's *Bleak Moments* (1972), Stephen Frears' *Gumshoe* (1971), and Lindsay Anderson's *O Lucky Man!* (1973). Considering itself a little too parochial, in 1974, Memorial decided to produce an international film, Ivan Passer's *Law and Disorder,* which was shot in the United States. Since then, Memorial has announced various projects, but none of them have come to fruition. Albert Finney has continued his acting career, and Michael Medwin has returned to the stage.

Address: 6e Ladbroke Square, London W.11, United Kingdom.

MERCHANT-IVORY PRODUCTIONS was formed early in 1961, in India, by director James Ivory (born 1928) and producer Ismail Merchant (born 1936) with the initial aim of producing English language films in India for international audiences. Since then, the company has been active in both Europe and the United States, although it remains, in the words of John Pym, "an independent outfit," which "exists on its wits." Merchant-Ivory's first feature was *The Housekeeper,* with a screenplay based on her own novel by Ruth Prawer Jhabvala, who remains closely associated with the company.

Thanks to the success of *A Room with a View* (1986), Merchant-Ivory has become familiar to the average filmgoer as much as the film buff. Its other features include *Shakespeare Wallah* (1965), *Bombay Talkie* (1970), *The Wild Party* (1974), *The Europeans* (1979), and *The Courtesans of Bombay* (1983).

Address: 46 Lexington Street, London WIR 3CE, United Kingdom.

BIBLIOGRAPHY

Gillett, John, "Merchant-Ivory," *Sight & Sound,* vol. XLII, no. 2, Spring 1973, pp. 95–97.

Pym, John. *The Wandering Company*. London: British Film Institute/New York: Museum of Modern Art, 1987.

Trojan, Judith, "The Merchant-Ivory Synthesizer," *Take One,* vol. IV, no. 9, May 1975, pp. 14–17.

MEXICO. The Mexican cinema, first heralded by the bourgeoisie as a sign of the country's progress, and subsequently transformed into an instrument of pleasure for the popular classes, was one of the few Latin American national cinemas to develop successfully on an industrial basis.

Introduced by Lumière representatives in 1896, the cinema was quickly taken up by local filmmakers like Salvador Toscano, Jorge Stahl, and Enrique Rosas, whose films aimed to record public life. For the most part intended to bolster the thirty-year-old regime of president Porfirio Díaz, these films took as their subject matter "official" and rather staid events—military parades, speeches and the visits of foreign dignitaries. But the Mexican Revolution that ripped convulsively through all spheres of Mexican life in 1910 also revolutionized the cinema. Cinematographers left the cities and went to the contested countryside to follow the exploits of revolutionary leaders like Madero, Zapata, and Pancho Villa, bringing back lively footage that was eagerly consumed by the public. The pioneer documentary work of Salvador Toscano and Jesús H. Abitia was later compiled into features, respectively *Memorias de un Mexicano* (1950) and *Epopeyas de la Revolución Mexicana* (1963).

Although the first decade of the Mexican cinema was dominated by artisanal, documentary production, the decade beginning in 1917, coinciding with the end of the revolution and the triumph of constitutionalism, was characterized by the ascendance of the fictional cinema and the first efforts to develop an industrial mode of production. Over one hundred films were released between 1917 and 1930 by producers who, although deluded by dreams of industrial grandeur, rarely managed more than four or five consecutive productions. Haphazardly financed and with uncertain distribution and exhibition possibilities (given the strong presence of European and, later, Hollywood films in the market), even successful individual films such as *La Luz/The Light* (1927) (the first fictional feature), or a series of films, like Azteca Film's five melodramas of 1917 or director/producer German Camus' literary adaptations of 1920, could not sufficiently stimulate industrial development.

El Automóvil Gris (1919), directed by Enrique Rosas, Joaquín Coss, and Juan Canals, is considered the most important and ambitious film of this first "golden era" of the Mexican cinema. This fifteen-part semi-documentary serial (dealing with the rash of hold-ups of rich families by uniformed bandits riding grey automobiles who were then terrorizing the middle classes) was successful, not only because of the broad appeal and currency of its topic, but also because of its excellent camerawork and innovative blending of documentary and fictional material. It inspired another popular serial, *La Banda del Autómovil Gris/The Grey Car Gang* (1919), directed by Ernesto Vollrath.

The release of *El Automóvil Gris* and *La Banda del Autómovil Gris* as serials was the first sign of Hollywood's growing influence on the Mexican cinema. Slowly displacing the European cinema, Hollywood films took the Mexican market for its own in the twenties and made sustained Mexican production increasingly more difficult. Throughout the twenties production declined steadily, not picking up again until after the coming of sound.

The introduction of sound cinematography coincided with the emergence and eventual election to power in 1929 of a new political party with strong nationalist tendencies, the Partido Revolucionario Instituciónal (PRI). The same impetus that fostered a strong nationalist, public art in painting (Orozco, Siqueiros, Rivera) also prompted a hostile reaction to "talkies" from Hollywood: it was feared that they would facilitate a "peaceful" invasion by the United States, and that the English language would replace Spanish shortly thereafter. Rejecting also Hollywood's Spanish-language productions (over eighty films between 1930 and 1940) because of their insensitive handling of the dialect differences among Spain and the Latin American nations, Mexican producers attempted national sound production with, at first, little success. The first sound feature, *Santa* (Antonio Moreno, 1931), was a box-office hit, but only five other films were produced that year. By 1933, however, annual production totaled twenty-one films, making Mexico the most active Spanish-language producer despite precarious production conditions, the absence of top-quality directors, the lack of an innovative thematic focus or aesthetic, and almost non-existent international distribution networks.

Nevertheless, the feverish pace of production continued in 1934, when twenty-four films were released, among them *Redas/The Wave* (Fred Zinnemann and Emilio Gomez) and *Janitzio* (Carlos Navarro), long considered the models for a cinema of social criticism. This was the year that cinema workers, allied with the increasingly leftist policies of the government, formed a union (UTECM) in association with the national workers' union. And this was also the year that the government guaranteed a loan to build the first modern film studio in Mexico City (CLASA: Cinematografa Latino Americana S.A.). From this point on, the Mexican state would be closely linked to the national cinema, developing a unique system blending state protectionism and nationalization with private development that, although troublesome in its first years (1935–1936), would later catapult the national cinema to Latin American prominence.

The crucial year was 1936. Of the twenty-five films produced, the success of three was greater than that of all the others combined: Gabriel Soria's *Ora Ponciano,* Roberto O'Quigles' *Cielito Lindo,* and especially, Fernando de Fuentes' *Allá en el Rancho Grande/Out at Big Ranch.* These *comedias rancheras* (comedies of peasant/country life with musical numbers) proved that Latin American audiences appreciated, above all, the depiction of the most idiosyncratic aspects of Mexican life. The spectacular success of *Allá en el Rancho Grande/Out at Big Ranch,* in particular, opened up the Latin American markets to Mexican films, permanently transforming the industry while garnering Mexico its first international film award (best cinematography at the Venice festival), and led to dozens of *comedias rancheras* in subsequent years (over twenty in 1937). The development of this genre made realistic depictions of country life obsolete, requiring the invention of an idyllic, apolitical countryside—where ranch hands suddenly burst into song to make love to virginal *rancheritas*—which became the stereotypical international image of Mexican life.

The golden years of the Mexican cinema were 1937 to 1949, with production climbing steadily to more than one hundred films per year. Given the interruption of Spanish production caused by the Spanish Civil War, the weakening of the Argentine industry (especially after the Second World War), the aid received from the Hollywood industry during the Second World War, and continued state protection (the Banco Nacional Cinematográfico founded in 1947), Mexican films were able to completely take over the Latin American market (the coup de grace came with the creation of Pelmex, the largest Latin American distributor, founded by a group of producers in 1947).

Among the most important directors of this golden era were Emilio "el Indio" Fernández (*Flor Silvestre/Wild Flower* and *María Candelaria,* both 1943), Alejandro Galindo (*Refugiados en Madrid/Refugees in Madrid* 1938; *Esquina Bajan!/Corner, Getting Off!* 1948, *Doña Perfecta,* 1950), and Ismael Rodríguez (*Los Tres García/The Three Garcias,* 1946, *Nosotros los Pobres/We Poor Folks,* 1947). While Fernández perfected the rules of the *ranchera* genre, Galindo and Rodríguez developed its urban counterpart, neighborhood melodramas filled with poor but hard-working individuals struggling against the forces of greed and moral perdition.

Another important genre of this period was the *cabaretera* that evolved from the urban melodramas, always focusing on the prostitute with the heart of gold. Director Alberto Gout, the specialist of this genre, was responsible for catapulting the dancer Ninón Sevilla to stardom. Other great "stars" (several of whom did double-duty in Hollywood films) were also created by the Mexican industry: Cantinflas, Tin Tan, Jorge Negrete, Pedro Infante, Dolores del Rio, María Félix, Katy Jurado.

Although Mexican production remained strong throughout the fifties (1,052 films in comparison to Argentina's 352 or Spain's 587), its hold on the Latin American market gradually declined. The fifties were years of transition for Mexico—growing industrialization, urbanization, class differentiation, and "americanization"—and, for the cinema industry, years of stagnation. Unwilling to risk change, most of the films produced simply repeated the formulas of the established genres; when television (introduced in 1950) began to make inroads into the national audience and the industry's unions limited entry to the trade, the industry itself was pushed to expensive and unsuccessful excesses.

The most interesting work of the fifties took place on the margins of the industry. Manuel Barbachano Ponce, one of Mexico's most courageous producers, released two films without precedent in the history of the industry: Benito Alazraki's *Raíces/Roots* (1953), a film about the Indian heritage, and Carlos Velo's *Torero* (1956), a realistic exploration of the bullfighting world. And, within the industry but working alone and according to different models, the Spanish surrealist artist Luis Buñuel directed a series of films between 1946 and 1965 that would later be heralded as some of the greatest achievements of the cinema of the period, although at the time no one within the industry heeded them (*Los Olvidados/The Young and the Damned* [1950], *Él/This Strange Passion* [1952], *Nazarín* (1958), *El Ángel Exterminador/The Exterminating Angel* [1962], *Simón del Desierto/Simon of the Desert* [1965]).

The disastrous trends of the fifties continued in the sixties and developed, by the end of the decade, into a real domestic and international crisis for the Mexican cinema. There were however encouraging signs as the state began the process of nationalizing part of the exhibition sector (1960), an important critical establishment emerged around the journals *La Revista de la Universidad* and *Nuevo Cine,* and the efforts of avant-garde and independent filmmakers became increasingly more visible. The first experimental film festival/contest was held in 1965.

In the aftermath of the political chaos of 1968 (which put into question the undisturbed power of the PRI party and forced it to reinvent itself to remain in power) and the dire economic and aesthetic crisis of the industry (with annual production down to less than eighty films), the state began to take an even more active role in the national cinema. The president of the Banco Nacional Cinematográfico proposed a project to restructure the industry that included, among other less-significant proposals, permission for new directors to enter the directors' union. These new directors (Jorge Fons, Felipe Cazals, Mauricio Wallerstein, Jaime Humberto Hermosillo, Arturo Ripstein, and others), young, accustomed to working independently, and trained in film schools rather than within the industry, formed the core of the New Cinema of the seventies.

Unlike the "new" cinemas of Brazil, Cuba, and Argentina—already by this time recognized as a New Latin American Cinema—the Mexican New Cinema did not attempt to develop new cinematic forms, either aesthetically or economically. Working within the production constraints of the established industry, and with only superficial thematic innovations, the New Cinema was not a radical break from prior practices, but, rather, the result of the sudden influx of new directorial talent into a stale, aesthetically decadent, and closed group. The New Cinema was, simply, a cinéma d'auteurs. In the best of cases, the new directors finally assimilated the lessons of Buñuel and introduced other frames of reference, which were renovatory given the decrepit state of the industry: *Reed, México Insurgente/Reed, Insurgent Mexico* (Paul Leduc, 1971), *Los Dias del Amor* (Alberto Isaac, 1971), *El Castillo de la Pureza/Castle of Purity* (Arturo Ripstein, 1972), *Caridad* (Jorge Fons, 1972), *La Pasión Según Berenice/The Passion According to Berenice* (Jaime Humberto Hermosillo, 1975), *Canoa* (Felipe Cazals, 1975), *Los Indolentes* (José Estrada, 1977).

In the eighties, the state continued to attempt to renovate the national industry, although the country's dire economic problems, exacerbated by severe aesthetic bankruptcy and marketing stagnation within the industry (although annual production has been steady at an average ninety films) have not allowed extensive intervention. In 1983, the government created IMCINE, the Mexican Film Institute, and appointed director Alberto Issac as its head. In control of eleven para-state institutions (ranging from the government-run production companies CONACITE, the two national film studios, and the national and international distributors, to the national film school), IMCINE initiated an extensive program that included the promotion of experimental works, co-productions with national and international producers (including TV), strict enforcement of the national film screen quota (50 percent) for all exhibitors including the national exhibition chain, and innovative pedagogical use of video in the film school. However, after three unsuccessful years, Isaac resigned his directorship in 1986 and IMCINE has become yet another inefficient official agency in Mexico's bureaucratic governmental maze.

The crisis of the Mexican cinema worsens each year. With its national economic base constantly eroding (theater tickets, at fifty cents, are the lowest in the continent), its national audience disappearing due to inflation and television, its international market limited to the highly contested U.S.–Latino areas, and its most consistent revenues derived from home video sales, the industry seems doomed to more years of crisis.

In the interstices of the crisis, however, there is some interesting filmmaking taking place, most notably the production of Paul Leduc's *Frida* (1985), a breathtaking account of the life and work of Frida Kahlo (brilliant painter, wife of muralist Diego Rivera, and close friend of Leon Trotsky) produced by the still courageous Manuel Barbachano Ponce, and Arturo Ripstein's *El Imperio de la Fortuna/The Empire of Fortune,* a surrealist adaptation of Juan Rulfo's script, "El Gallo de Oro." Both national and international successes, these films signal that even within the current dire crisis of the industry there are still some spaces left open for innovation and achievement.

BIBLIOGRAPHY

Askenazy, Natalia, "The Two Kinds of Mexican Movies," *Films in Review*, May 1951, pp. 35–39.

Burton, Julianne, compiler. *The New Latin American Cinema: An Annotated Bibliography of English-Language Sources, 1960–1976*. New York: Cineaste, 1976.

del Castillo, Ramon, "Mexican Cinema," *Sight & Sound*, vol. XIII, no. 51, October 1944, pp. 55–57.

———, "Religious Films of Mexico," *Sight & Sound*, vol. XVI, no. 64, Winter 1947–48, pp. 155–157.

Michel, Manuel, "Mexican Cinema: A Panoramic View," *Film Quarterly*, vol. XVIII, no. 4, Summer 1965, pp. 46–55.

Mora, Carl J. *Mexican Cinema: Reflections of a Society, 1896–1980*. Berkeley: University of California Press, 1982.

Nicholson, Irene, "Mexican Films: Their Past and Their Future," *Quarterly Review of Film, Radio, and Television*, vol. X, no. 3, Spring 1956, pp. 248–252.

Oliver, Maria Rosa, "The Native Films of Mexico," *Penguin Film Review*, no. 6, April 1948, pp. 73–79.

Reyes Nevares, Beatrice. *The Mexican Cinema*. Albuquerque: University of New Mexico Press, 1976.

Wollenberg, H.H., "Mexican Screen Art," *Sight & Sound*, Spring 1949, pp. 27–28.

"MID-ATLANTIC PICTURES" was a term coined in the fifties to refer to nominally British films, which were produced with American money and, usually, with Americans in key production positions. Two obvious examples of "mid-Atlantic pictures" are *The Bridge on the River Kwai* (1957) and *The Key* (1958).

MIFED is the acronym for Mercato Internazionale del Film del TVfilm e del Documentario. A major trade show at which films and television programs are bought and sold, MIFED first opened on April 12, 1960, and was a biannual event—each spring and fall—through 1985. Since 1986, it has been held once a year in late October/early November. An offshoot of the Milan Fair, MIFED was founded by Michele Guido Franchi.

Address: Largo Domodossola 1, 20145 Milan, Italy.

MILAN. The best known of Italian features set in Milan is Vittorio De Sica's *Miracolo a Milano/Miracle in Milan* (1951). Other major Italian features utilizing the city as a background are Luchino Visconti's *Rocco e i suoi fratelli/Rocco and His Brothers* (1961), Michelangelo Antonioni's *La Notte/The Night* (1962), and Pier Paolo Pasolini's *Teorema* (1969). In 1983, Ermanno Olmi directed a feature-length, 16mm documentary on the city titled *Milano '83*.

MINERVA FILMS was formed in London in April 1920 with the idea of "demonstrating that it was possible to be funny without being vulgar, and that a two-reel comedy need not be a knock-about farce in order to be entertaining" (according to a contemporary trade paper report). Its original board members included Adrian Brunel, Leslie Howard, A.A. Milne, Nigel Playfair, and C. Aubrey Smith. In October 1920, it presented four two-reel comedies, *Bookworms, The Bump, £5 Reward,* and *Twice Two,* all directed by Brunel, starring Howard and Smith, and written by A.A. Milne. In 1921, Minerva Films produced a three-reel comedy, *A Temporary Lady,* starring Annette Benson and Miles Mander, and shortly thereafter the company ceased operations.

MINING REVIEW (later known as simply *Review*) was a news and interest magazine produced for British filmgoers by the National Coal Board from 1947 to 1972. It was seen in only some theatres and so boring was it considered by filmgoers that every effort would be made to avoid those theatres. Footage from the series is preserved and controlled by the Film Production Library of the National Coal Board (Hobart House, Grosvenor Place, London SW1X 7AE, United Kingdom).

MOLDAVIA had no film industry prior to its formation as a republic within the USSR in 1940. A documentary and newsreel production studio, Moldovafilm, was founded in the capital, Kishinev, in 1952, with the first important films from the area coming in 1957.

MONTY PYTHON. The popular British comedy group, Monty Python, consists of six members, Michael Palin, Terry Jones, Terry Gilliam (an American), John Cleese, Graham Chapman, and Eric Idle. They first came to prominence in the British Broadcasting Corporation television series, *Monty Python's Flying Circus* (1969–1974), which was subsequently aired in the United States on public television. They have also starred in five feature films: *And Now for Something Completely Different* (1971), *Monty Python and the Holy Grail* (1974), *Monty Python's Life of Brian* (1979), *Monty Python Live at the Hollywood Bowl* (1982), and *Monty Python's Meaning of Life* (1983). As individuals, members of the group have also been involved in television series and feature films, most notably *Fawlty Towers* (1975 and 1979, TV series with John Cleese), *Ripping Yarns* (1977 and 1979, TV series with Michael Palin, written by Palin and Terry Jones), *Time Bandits* (1981, feature directed by Terry Gilliam, and written by Gilliam and Michael Palin), *The Missionary* (1982, feature film co-produced by and starring Michael Palin), *Yellowbeard* (1983 feature film, co-scripted by Graham Chapman, and starring Chapman, John Cleese and Eric Idle), and *A Fish Called Wanda* (1988, feature written by and starring John Cleese, with Michael Palin).

BIBLIOGRAPHY

Perry, George. *The Life of Python.* Boston: Little, Brown, 1983.

MOROCCO. Since its independence in 1956, Morocco has produced more than fifty feature films, with the majority being made after 1980, when the government began to support the film industry. The country boasts studios in Casablanca*, Rabat, and Marrakech, with laboratory facilities available in Tangier. As of 1975, there were 250 theatres in Morocco, with the largest number concentrated in Casablanca.

Most filmmaking activities—including import and export—are administered through the Centre Cinématographique Marocaine (85 Shari Moulay Ismail, B.P. 421, Rabat, Morocco). Leading directors include Latif Lahlou, Akim Noury, Ahmed al Maanouni, Souhel Ben Barka, Abdou Achouba, Mohamed Abderrahman Jazi, Moumen Smihi, Ahmed Yashfine, and Tayeb Saddiki.

BIBLIOGRAPHY

Malkmus, Lizbeth, "Morocco," in *International Film Guide 1986,* editor Peter Cowie. London: Tantivy Press, 1985, pp. 231–233.

MOSCOW. The capital of the USSR has been utilized as a backdrop for a number of features (although such features have been filmed elsewhere, in recent years primarily in Helsinki). Among these films are *Moscow Nights* (U.S. *I Stand Condemned,* 1935), *Mission to Moscow* (1943), *War and Peace* (1956), *Doctor Zhivago* (1965), *The Kremlin Letter* (1970), *The Twelve Chairs* (1970), *Gorky Park* (1983), and *Moscow on the Hudson* (1984). The most important Soviet films set in Moscow, one a costume drama and the other relatively contemporary, are Mikhail Kalatozov's *Letyat Zhuravli/The Cranes Are Flying* (1957) and Sergei Bondarchuk's *Volny i mir/War and Peace* (1968).

The city is also the site of the Moscow International Film Festival (10 Khokhlovsky pereulak, Moscow 109028).

MOSFILM. Active in the Soviet Union from the thirties onward, Mosfilm's productions include Mikhail Romm's *Trinadtstat/The Thirteen* (1937) and *Lenin v Okyabre/Lenin in October* (1937), Sergei Eisenstein's *Alexander Nevsky* (1938) and *Ivan Grosny/Ivan the Terrible Part Two* (1946), and Sergei Yutkevich's *Othello* (1956).

MOUNTAIN FILMS (or Bergfilm) was a German genre of the twenties and early thirties, in which the snow-covered Alps played a crucial role. The genre was dominated by two directors, Dr. Arnold Fanck (1889–1974) and Leni Riefenstahl (born 1902), and the actor most associated with the films is Luis Trenker. The genre is generally dated from 1924 when Fanck made *Der berg des schicksals/The Mountain of Fate/The Peak of Destiny,* featuring Trenker. Leni Riefenstahl played opposite Trenker in Fanck's *Der heilige berg/The Sacred Mountain/Wrath of the Gods* (1924), and is the leading lady in the best-known film of the genre, *Die weisse hölle vom Piz Palü/The White Hell of Pitz Palu* (1929), co-directed by Fanck and G.W. Pabst. In 1931, Riefenstahl directed and starred in one of the most visually impressive of all mountains films, *Das blaue licht/The Blue Light*.

BIBLIOGRAPHY

Trace, Maurice, ''Upon That Mountain,'' *The Silent Picture*, no. 14, Spring 1972, pp. 31–37.

N

NARROW GAUGE (or substandard film) refers to a film of a width other than 35mm, which is the width of films used for theatrical production and exhibition. This field has been dominated for many years by 16mm and 8mm, both of which were introduced in the United States by Eastman Kodak. However, the first narrow-gauge films came from the Pathé Company in France. 17.5mm was introduced in 1899; 28mm in 1912, and 9.5mm in 1923. 28mm did not survive the silent era, but 9.5mm has been kept alive by a small band of enthusiasts in Europe, and 17.5mm had a brief resurgence of interest in the thirties.

THE NATIONAL FILM AND TELEVISION SCHOOL is the official British school for the film and television industries, funded in part by the government, through the Office of Arts and Libraries, and partly through voluntary contributions from the industry. It is nonprofit and autonomous. Its origins date from August 5, 1965, when then joint parliamentary under-secretary of the Department of Education and Science, Jennie Lee, announced the appointment of an independent committee to enquire fully into the need for a National Film School.

The committee, under the chairmanship of Lord Lloyd of Hampstead, was appointed in October 1965, and published its findings in 1967. A planning committee was appointed in 1969, and one year later, Colin Young was named as the school's first director. He continues as the school's director, and Lord Lloyd of Hampstead is the chairman of the Board of Governors. In 1971, the school purchased the Beaconsfield Film Studios, and in the fall of that year, the first group of twenty-five students were admitted. The average number of students is seventy-five, who pay tuition fees of approximately $3,000 a year. The school offers a three-year course, with the emphasis on creative ability and personal motivation. The school works closely with the British film and television union, the Association of Cinematograph, Television and Allied Technicians*, and graduates automatically gain membership upon graduation and gaining employment in the industry.

In celebration of the school's tenth anniversary, a fellowship program was announced, with the first two awards going to David Lean and Ossie Morris. In 1984, Colin Young received the Michael Balcon Award from the British Academy of Film and Television Arts* "for an outstanding contribution to British Film and Television."

Address: Beaconsfield Studios, Station Road, Beaconsfield, Bucks HP9 1LG, United Kingdom.

NATIONAL FILM BOARD OF CANADA. There can be no doubt that the National Film Board of Canada is the preeminent documentary film producer, and has been such since its creation in 1939.

The man responsible for the Board's inception and its basic philosophy was documentary film pioneer John Grierson (1898–1972). He developed a plan for the agency that resulted in the Canadian government's passing the National Film Act in May 1939, "to initiate and promote the production and distribution of films in the national interest and in particular . . . to interpret Canada to Canadians and to other countries." Grierson was offered and accepted the appointment as the Board's first film commissioner and chairman. He promised, "The National Film Board will be the eyes of Canada. It will, through a national use of cinema see Canada and see it whole . . . its people and its purpose. The documentary film is the creative treatment of actuality. It is important not for what it teaches but for the manner of its illumination." (Grierson left the National Film Board in 1945.)

The National Film Board quickly became involved in the production of films for the war effort. It commenced two series, "Canada Carries On"* and "World in Action"*, and its 1941 documentary, *Churchill's Island,* received an Academy Award, and was the first Canadian film so to do. In 1942, it began sending out traveling projectionists to present films in rural Canadian areas out of reach of the commercial cinema. A year later, it opened offices, for the 16mm distribution of its films, in London, Chicago, and New York.

The Board commenced its work with a staff of three, advancing to ten by 1940. In 1941, the filmmaker most associated with the National Film Board, Norman McLaren (1914–1987), became a member of the staff and established the animation studio. McLaren was one of the first animators to experiment with optical printing and drawing directly on film. His best known work for the Board is the classic parable, *Neighbors,* released in 1953. The first animators to work with McLaren at the Board were René Jodoin and Jean-Paul Ladouceur, and they were followed, through the years by Colin Low, George Dunning, Grant Munro, Wolf Koenig, Evelyn Lambart, Robert Verrall, and Jim McKay.

After the Second World War, the concept of traveling projectionists was replaced by regional distribution offices throughout Canada. The Board began producing films for television in 1953, and was also involved in a number of series, including "On the Spot," "Perspective," and "Passe-Partout." Colin Low's 1957 documentary, *City of Gold,* helped revive interest in the work of the Board, which gained further international acclaim in 1961 with Roman Kroitor's and Wolf Koenig's documentary on Paul Anka, *Lonely Boy*.

In 1963, the Board produced the first of more than thirty feature-length films that it has made, *Drylanders* and *Pour la suite du monde*. Two French-language features from the Board have been particularly well-received abroad, *Mon Oncle Antoine/My Uncle Antoine* (1971), directed by Claude Jutra, and *J.A. Martin, Photographe/J.A. Martin, Photographer* (1977), directed by Jean Beaudin. Since the fifties, the Board has been active in the production of French as well as English-language films.

The National Film Board of Canada is governed by a board of eight members with the film commissioner as their chairman. All are appointed by the government, with three selected from the civil service and five from the public at large. Initially headquartered in Ottawa, since 1956, the Board's offices, laboratory and production facilities have been located in Montreal. It has a staff of over one thousand.

The Board has operated a women's unit since 1974 under the name "Studio D." "Studio G" is the name of the division that produces educational filmstrips and other audiovisual aids.

It continues to live up to the words of John Grierson, spoken at the end of his tenure with the National Film Board of Canada.

> We have followed along the perspective of modern life and sought to find themes which gave a new significance to the terms of ordinary living. Sometimes we have approached the task on a journalistic level or poetic level or analytical level or more dramatic level, but always we have been concerned to bridge a gap between the citizen and the world about him and always we have been concerned to find a degree of beauty in the process and make our own contribution to the spectacle of democracy at work.

Address: P.O. Box 6100, Station A, Montréal, Quebec H3C 3H5, Canada.

BIBLIOGRAPHY

Canemaker, John, "Canada's National Film Board: What's Old and What's New," *Millimeter,* May 1977, pp. 12, 72–73.

Dworkin, Sol, "Life at the Early N.F.B.," *Take One,* vol. IV, no. 5, September 1974, pp. 31–33.

Handling, Piers, "Censorship and Scares: The National Film Board of Canada, 1940–52," *Cinema Canada,* no. 56, June-July 1979, pp. 25–31.

Harcourt, Peter, "The Innocent Eye," *Sight & Sound,* vol. XXXIV, no. 1, Winter 1964–65, pp. 19–23.

Herrick, D., "The Canadian Connection: John Grierson," *Cinema Canada,* No. 49–50, September-October 1978, pp. 28–32.

Irwin, Arthur, "A View from the Top," *Cinema Canada,* No. 56, June-July 1979, pp. 37–41.

Junker, Howard, "The National Film Board of Canada: After a Quarter Century," *Film Quarterly,* vol. XVIII, no. 2, Winter 1964–65, pp. 22–29.

Morris, Peter, editor. *The National Film Board of Canada: The War Years*. Ottawa: Canadian Film Institute, 1971.

Starr, Cecile, "For Canada and the World," *Saturday Review,* November 10, 1956, pp. 26–27.

THE NATIONAL FILM DEVELOPMENT CORPORATION is the official Indian government film agency, founded in 1980. It was the latest in a number of government organizations concerned with film, among which were the Film Finance Corporation (created in 1960) and the Directorate of Film Festivals (established in 1974). The Corporation finances the production of an average of one dozen films a year, imports and exports films, organizes film festivals, and publishes a quarterly magazine, *Cinema in India*. It is also involved in co-productions, with its first effort being Richard Attenborough's *Gandhi* (1982).

Address: 5/6/7 Floor, Discovery of India Nehru Centre, Dr. Annie Besant Road, Worli, Bombay 400 018, India.

THE NATIONAL FILM FINANCE CORPORATION (NFFC) was set up in 1949 by Harold Wilson, then president of the British government department, the Board of Trade. It was empowered to make loans to independent producers (meaning those not linked with large theatre circuits or American parent companies) without security other than the revenues arising from the films being financed. In its early days, it was principally the provider of "end money"—usually amounting to one-third of the necessary finance—with the other two thirds—"front money"—being provided by the distributor. "Front money" is repaid before "end money" from the film's receipts. Between 1950 and 1959, the NFFC helped finance 483 films.

A major incident in the history of the NFFC was when it became involved in the fortunes of British Lion*, lending it, under government orders, £3 million. When this money was not repaid, a receiver was appointed in 1954; a new company was formed and the government, through the NFFC, put up a capital of approximately £600,000. From the late fifties, film audiences declined steadily and the subsequent reduction in the level of profits flowing back into the industry resulted in far fewer films being made. By the early seventies, the NFFC's funds had been depleted, and this lack of finance seriously curtailed its ability to provide an effective stimulus to British production during the decade.

Up to 1980, the Corporation was funded through interest-bearing loans made by the government. However, the Cinematograph Films Act of that year instituted a number of changes. Instead of government advances, it received an annual income from the British Film Fund Agency (also known as the Eady Levy*) or £1.5 million or 20 percent, whichever was the greater. The Corporation was also empowered to borrow up to £5 million from nongovernment sources. It financed script development and preproduction work through the National Film Development Fund. The Corporation only financed films that were made for theatrical exhibition. Although the government had never set guidelines as to what sort of films should be made, there existed a tacit understanding that the

Corporation would invest only in films that in some way reflect British life and manners.

In 1986, the Conservative Government of Margaret Thatcher decided to "privatize" the NFFC. It was renamed British Screen, with Simon Relph as its manager and received limited funding from the Treasury plus private contributions (initially from the Rank Organization* and the Cannon Group). British Screen's announced policy is to encourage "original, high quality, British work, especially from younger, less established producers and directors," and in its first year it was able to contribute £3 million toward the production budgets of seven features.

Address: 22 Southampton Place, London WC1A, 2BP, United Kingdom.

BIBLIOGRAPHY

Kelly, Terence, with Graham Norton and George Perry. *A Competitive Cinema*. London: Institute of Economic Affairs, 1966.

Walker, Alexander. *Hollywood England: The British Film Industry in the Sixties*. London: Michael Joseph, 1974.

———. *National Heroes: British Cinema in the Seventies and Eighties*. London: Harrap, 1985.

Wood, Linda, editor. *Film/Video Funding*. London: British Film Institute Library Services, 1984.

NEDERLANDSE BIOSCOOPBOND is an organization of Dutch distributors and exhibitors, regulating the film industry on a voluntary basis, founded in 1918.

Address: Jan Luykenstraat 2, 1071 CM Amsterdam, Netherlands.

NEO-REALISM is the term used to describe Italian feature films made immediately after the Second World War, from 1945–1951, in the making of which their directors took their cameras out into the streets, rejecting the conventionality of studio-produced films. Neo-Realism in Italian cinema represented the rejection of Calligraphism* and the fascism that had dominated the country's filmmaking since the early thirties. Director Pier Paolo Pasolini (quoted in *Patterns of Realism*) described Neo-Realism as "the product of a cultural and democratic reaction to the standstill of the spirit during the Fascist period."

The major films of Neo-Realism are *Roma, Città Aperta/Rome, Open City* (1945), *Paisà/Paisan* (1946), *Sciuscià/Shoe Shine* (1946), *Le Terra Trema* (1947), *Ladri Biciclette/Bicycle Thief* (1948), *Riso Amaro/Bitter Rice* (1948), *Senza Pietà/Without Pity* (1948), *Miracolo a Milano/Miracle in Milan* (1950), *Bellissima* (1951), and *Umberto D* (1951). The directors most closely associated with the genre are Roberto Rossellini, Alberto Lattuado, Vittorio De Sica, Luigi Zampa, Giuseppe De Santis, Renato Castellani, Luchino Visconti, and Pietro Germi.

BIBLIOGRAPHY

Armes, Roy. *Patterns of Realism*. South Brunswick, N.J.: A.S. Barnes, 1971.

Bondanella, Peter. *Italian Cinema: From Neorealism to the Present*. New York: Frederick Ungar, 1983.

Borde, Raymond, and André Bouissy. *Le Néo-réalisme Italien*. Lausanne: Clairefontaine, 1960.

Castello, Giulio Cesare. *Il cinema neorealistico italiano*. Milan: Scwarz, 1958.

Nowell-Smith, Geoffrey, "Cinema Nuovo and Neo-Realism," *Screen,* vol. XVII, no. 4, Winter 1976/77, pp. 111–117.

Perry, Ted, "The Road to Neorealism," *Film Comment,* vol. XV, no. 6, November-December 1978, pp. 7–13.

Ranvaud, Don, "Neo-Realism—The Second Coming," *Monthly Film Bulletin,* vol. XLVIII, no. 566, March 1981, p. 60.

Verdone, Mario, "A Discussion of Neo-Realism," *Screen,* vol. XIV, no. 4, Winter 1973/74, pp. 69–77.

Walsh, Martin, "Open City: The Rise to Power of Louis XIV," *Jump Cut,* no. 15, 1977, pp. 13–15.

NEPAL has a small film industry, supported to a large extent by the Royal Nepal Film Corporation, created by the government in 1971. It has produced some half-a-dozen feature films, as well as a number of co-productions with Jaya Ajima Films, Pragati Films, and others. The first Nepalese film was *Raja Harishchandra,* which was actually photographed in India in 1952; the first Nepalese film to be shot in Nepal was *Amma/Mother* (1960). Both films were directed by Hira Singh.

NERO-FILM A.G. Co-founded by Richard Oswald and Seymour Nebenzahl (1898–1961) in 1924, it was the latter who was responsible for the success of the Berlin-based Nero-Film until its demise in 1933. The company produced or co-produced five features directed by G.W. Pabst: *Die Büchse der Pandora/ Pandora's Box/Lulu* (1929), *Westfront 1918* (1930), *Kameradschaft/Comradeship* (1931), *Dreigroschenoper/The Three Penny Opera* (1931), and *L'Atlantide* (1932). It also produced Fritz Lang's last two prewar German features: *M* (1931) and *Das Testament des Dr. Mabuse/The Last Will of Dr. Mabuse* (1933).

NETHERLANDS. The Edison Kinetoscope was first presented in the Netherlands, in Amsterdam, on December 27, 1894, by Karel van Egmond and H.F. Degens. The Lumière Cinematograaf (the Dutch spelling) was first seen, also in Amsterdam, on March 12, 1896, presented by Camille Cerf. As early as 1897, there were three producers of actualities active in the Netherlands: M.H. Laddé, Franz Anton Nöggerath, Sr., and De Nederlandsche Biograaf-en Mutoscope-Maatschappij (the Dutch subsidiary of the American Mutoscope and Biograph Company). The first fiction film to be produced in the Netherlands was *A Souvenir of the Late King William III Riding in His Carriage through the Vondel Park, Amsterdam,* dating from 1899. The earliest surviving Dutch fictional film is *Mesaventure van een Fransch Heertje zonder Pantalon op get Strand te Zandvoort/The (Mis)Adventures of a French Dandy without His Trousers on the Beach at Zandvoort*. It was produced in 1905 by Albert and Willy Mullens, who operated a mobile cinema and called themselves Alberts Frères.

Among the major production companies of the teens were Johann Gildemeijer's Rembrandt-Film, active from 1911 to 1913; Theo Frenkel, Sr.'s, Amsterdam-Film, active from 1916 to 1921; and Mauritz H. Binger's Hollandia Filmfabriek, active from 1912 to 1923. The last developed the first major Dutch star, Annie Bos. Two important producers of the twenties were the Dutch Film Co., active from 1923 to 1926 and Alex Benno's Actueel-Film, active from 1921 to 1927.

The first sound feature to be completely shot in the Netherlands was *William the Silent,* directed by Jan Teunissen, produced during 1933 and released in January 1934. Two important Dutch features of the thirties are Gerald Rutten's *Dood Water/Dead Water* (1934) and Charles Huguenot van der Linden's *Jonge Harten/Young Hearts* (1936). Two major continental directors, Max Ophüls and Ludwig Berger visited the Netherlands in the mid-thirties to direct *Komedie on Geld/A Comedy about Money* (1936), which was produced by Cinetone Studios, shortly thereafter taken over by Ufa*.

Production in the thirties was very limited. For example, only three Dutch features were released in 1937, one of which was a screen adaptation of George Bernard Shaw's *Pygmalion*. It was directed by Ludwig Berger for Filmex and starred Lily Bouwmeester as Eliza Doolittle and Johan de Meester as Professor Higgins.

The Netherlands has had a long tradition of documentary filmmaking, which generally is dated from 1927, when Joris Ivens (born 1898) made *The Bridge*. However, Ivens must be regarded as an international rather than a Dutch filmmaker. The most influential and important of postwar Dutch documentary filmmakers is Bert Haanstra, who first gained international attention in 1951 with *Spiegel van Holland/Mirror of Holland*. His 1958 documentary short, *Glas/Glass,* received an Academy Award. Haanstra has made an occasional fictional feature, such as *Doctor Pulder Zaait Papavers/When the Poppies Bloom Again* (1975), but he is primarily known both at home and abroad for his documentaries. Other documentary filmmakers of note include Jan Hulsker, Nico Crama, Fons Grasveld, Theo van Haren, and John Ferno. Documentaries, shorts, and non-commerical features can receive government funding, up to the total cost of the production, from the Film Fund. Similar funding is available for features, but only for less than 60 percent of the production costs, through the Production Fund. The latter was created in 1956 by the Ministry of Cultural Affairs, Recreation, and Social Welfare.

The only Dutch director to enjoy a successful career both in the pre- and postwar years was Charles Huguenot van der Linden, who discovered Audrey Hepburn with his feature, *Nederlands in Zeven Lessen/Dutch in Seven Lessons,* produced in the autumn of 1947 and released in May 1948.

The first major postwar Dutch director was Fons Rademakers (born 1920), who made his first feature, *Dorp aan de Rivier/Village on the River,* in 1958. Rademakers' best-known works are *Mira* (1971) and *Max Havelaar* (1976). In 1987, he received an Academy Award for *De Aanslag/The Assault.* A new Dutch cinema emerged thanks to the work of Rademakers, Paul Verhoeven, Rob Houwer, Pim de la Parra, and Wim Verstappen. Verhoeven has received international attention with *Spetters* (1980) and *Die Vierde Man/The Fourth Man* (1983). Aside from its filmmakers, one actor, Rutger Hauer, has achieved worldwide recognition, after earlier native success in Verhoeven's *Cathy Tippel/Keetje Tippel* and Herbert Curiel's *Het Jaar van de Kruft/Year of the Cancer,* both released in 1975.

Several new Dutch filmmakers have emerged from the Netherlands Film Academy, created in 1958. Its graduates founded the journal, *Skoop,* in 1964—the only other prominent film magazine is *Skrien.* Directors who emerged from the school include Rene Daalder, Ja Vrijman, Franz Weisz, and Nikolai van der Heyde.

There were 487 theatres in 1987, compared to 297 in 1937. The two major theatre circuits, Tuschinski and City, were acquired by the Cannon Group in 1984. The largest distributor is Concorde Film (Lange Voorhout 35, 's-Gravenhage 2514 EC). Censorship was introduced through a 1926 law that classified films and permitted any municipality the right to ban a specific production. At the present time, there is no film censorship in the Netherlands, but films remain classified for audiences over twelve and over sixteen, and pornographic films may only be screened for those eighteen or older. An average of between ten and twenty features are produced annually in the Netherlands—there were thirteen films in 1986, compared to sixteen the previous year. They must compete with almost three hundred other feature films released annually each year in the Netherlands, of which two-thirds are American.

BIBLIOGRAPHY

Cowie, Peter, "Dutch Film," *Film Quarterly,* vol. XIX, no. 2, Winter 1965–66, pp. 41–46.

———, "Where Are We Going Now?" *Film,* no. 59, Summer 1970, pp. 4–8.

———. *Dutch Cinema: An Illustrated History.* New York: A.S. Barnes, 1979.

De Vaal, Jan, "Film Research in the Netherlands," *Cinema Studies,* vol. I, no. 1, March 1960, pp. 9–12.

Holmes, Winifred, "Forty Years," *Sight & Sound,* vol. VII, no. 26, Summer 1938, pp. 57–59.

Hulsker, T., "News Out of Holland," *Cinema Journal,* vol. I, no. 1, Autumn 1932, pp. 26–27.

Mancini, Elaine, "The Netherlands," in *World Cinema since 1945,* editor William Luhr. New York: Ungar, 1987, pp. 466–475.

Stephenson, Ralph, "Films from Holland," *Film,* no. 44, Winter 1965–66, pp. 34–36.

THE NETHERLANDS ANTILLES, with its favorable tax treaties with the United States (dating from 1948) and other countries has become a tax haven for a number of major film producers. Two producers that have registered companies here are Cannon and Dino De Laurentiis, with the result that a number of their features, including *Orca* (1977), *Hurricane* (1979), *Bolero* (1984), and *Death Wish 3* (1985), are legally Netherlands Antilles productions.

THE NEUBABELSBERG STUDIOS were created in 1911 by the German film company, Deutsche Bioscop, but gained international prominence from 1923 onward as the production headquarters for Ufa*. Between 1938 and 1940, a film school functioned on the studio grounds. Following the Second World War, the studios became the headquarters for the East German production company, DEFA*.

THE NEVILLE WRAN AWARD FOR EXCELLENCE was first presented in 1986 by the New South Wales Film Corporation*.

NEW CALEDONIA was the location for the filming of the 1964 feature, *McHale's Navy*. There is one distributor on the island, Société d'Exploitation des Cinémas Hickson (18 rue de la Somme, Noumea).

THE NEWMAN SINCLAIR CAMERA, that was initially hand-cranked and later utilized a clockwork mechanism (for the "Auto Kine" model introduced in 1926) was a popular tool with silent filmmakers in the United Kingdom and, later, was in general use by documentary and newsreel cinematographers. A Newman Sinclair camera was utilized by Robert Flaherty to photograph *Man of Aran* (1933). More than one thousand cameras, none of which were completely alike, were produced between 1911 and 1963 by the London-based Newman and Sinclair Ltd. James A. Sinclair was responsible for financing and marketing the camera, while Arthur S. Newman (1861–1943) was the inventor and engineer.

BIBLIOGRAPHY

"All Our Yesterdays: Tales of the Newman Sinclair Camera," in program for "British Film Institute: A Celebratory Banquet at Guildhall on the Occasion of the Institute's 50th Anniversary, the Presentation of a Royal Charter, and the Award of Its First Fellowships," October 5, 1983, pp. 19–31.

THE NEWS AND SPECIALISED THEATRE ASSOCIATION OF GREAT BRITAIN AND NORTHERN IRELAND. A trade organization established to promote the interests of its members, the News and Specialised Theatre Association of Great Britain and Northern Ireland remained in existence from 1939 to 1951.

THE NEW SOUTH WALES FILM CORPORATION is a statutory authority established under the New South Wales Film Corporation Act of 1977. It fosters the development of the Australian film industry through the funding of both features and documentaries. In the latter area, according to the Act, the New South Wales Film Corporation has "sole responsibility for the making, promotion, distribution and exhibition of short films and documentary films for all government departments and statutory bodies.'' Among the feature films from the New South Wales Film Corporation that have received international recognition are *Careful He Might Hear You, My Brilliant Career* (the first Australian feature to be nominated for an Academy Award), and *Newsfront.*

In June 1988, a bill was passed by the New South Wales government, abolishing the Corporation.

Address: 4th Floor, 45 Macquarie Street, Sydney, NSW 2000, Australia.

BIBLIOGRAPHY

Murdoch, Blake, ''NSW Pic Corp Replacement Org Still a Questionmark,'' *Daily Variety,* June 22, 1988, p. 8.

NEWSREEL ASSOCIATION OF GREAT BRITAIN AND IRELAND LTD. According to the 1942 edition of the *Kinematograph Year Book,* the Newsreel Association of Great Britain and Ireland Ltd. was established ''To promote and protect the interests, welfare and business of associates engaged in the production and distribution of cinematograph films depicting current events, known as Newsreels, and to bring about and maintain co-operation between them.'' The Association was incorporated on October 31, 1937, and it remained active through 1959. The Association's records are deposited with British Movietone News Ltd. (North Orbital Road, Denham, Uxbridge, Middlesex UB9 5HQ, United Kingdom).

NEW WAVE. The French New Wave or Nouvelle Vague was, as noted by critic Peter Graham, ''less a movement than a useful journalistic catchphrase,'' that described a new group of directors making their feature film debuts in 1958–1959. The directors in question were François Truffaut, Claude Chabrol, Eric Rohmer, Jean-Luc Godard, Jacques Rivette, and Jacques Doniol-Valcroze, many of whom had been critics for *Cahiers du Cinéma.* They had denounced the French cinema of the past (with the honorable exception of Jean Renoir) for its lack of a personal viewpoint, and admired the American cinema as exemplified by the directorial style of Alfred Hitchcock.

Thanks to the political climate of the times and the problems within the French film industry, these New Wave filmmakers were able to make low-budget productions that drew favorable critical response, beginning with Chabrol's *Le Beau Serge/Bitter Reunion* (1958). The New Wave gained international attention with the successes of Truffaut's *Les Quatres Cents Coups/The 400 Blows* and Alain Resnais' *Hiroshima Mon Amour/Hiroshima My Love* at the 1959 Cannes Film Festival*. In fact, so great was their success that the New Wave directors of 1958 and 1959, with the exception of Godard, went on to become some of France's leading commercial filmmakers.

In the late fifties, critic Robert Benayoun was not exaggerating when he wrote in *Positif* that foreign countries were jealous of France because of two things: De Gaulle and Nouvelle Vague.

BIBLIOGRAPHY
Borde, Raymond et al. *Nouvelle Vague*. Lyons: SERDOC, 1962.
Burch, Nöel, "Qu'est-ce que la Nouvelle Vague," *Film Quarterly*, vol. XIII, no. 2, Winter 1959, pp. 16–30.
Butcher, Maryvonne, "France's Film Renascence," *Commonweal*, January 8, 1960, pp. 414–416.
Durgnat, Raymond. *Nouvelle Vague: The First Decade*. London: Motion Publications, 1963.
Gary, Romain, "The Foamy Edge of the Wave," *Show*, April 1964, pp. 75–76.
Graham, Peter. *The New Wave*. Garden City, N.Y.: Doubleday, 1968.
Holland, Norman N., "How New? How Vague?" *Hudson Review*, Summer 1960, pp. 270–277.
Jacob, Gilles, "Nouvelle Vague or Jeune Cinéma," *Sight & Sound*, Winter 1964–65, pp. 4–8.
Labarthe, André S. *Essai sur le jeune cinéma Française*. Paris: Le Terraine Vague, 1960.
Monaco, James. *The New Wave: Truffaut, Godard, Chabrol, Rohmer, Rivette*. New York: Oxford University Press, 1976.
Sadoul, Georges, "Notes on a New Generation," *Sight & Sound*, vol. XXVIII, nos, 3-4, Summer-Autumn 1959, pp. 111–117.
Siclier, Jacques, "New Wave and French Cinema," *Sight & Sound*, vol. XXX, no. 3 Summer 1961, pp. 116–120.
Weightman, J.G., "New Wave in French Culture," *Commentary*, September 1960, pp. 230–240.

NEW ZEALAND. Moving pictures were first screened in New Zealand in 1896, and two years later the first known films were shot there. A film record of the 1901 visit of the Duke and Duchess of Cornwall and York is the oldest material that has so far been found and preserved in the New Zealand Film Archive. The first feature shot in New Zealand was *Hinemoa* (1914), which no longer survives, and the few filmmakers working in the country prior to 1920 concentrated on news films or scenics.

New Zealand's earliest pioneer filmmaker was Rudall Hayward, who died in 1972. In the twenties and thirties, he produced six features and a large number of one and two-reel short subjects, with the first feature being *My Lady of the Cave* (1922) and the last *To Love a Maori* (1972). Gaston Méliès was the first foreign producer to use New Zealand as a location, making two one-reel films for American distribution in 1912. Australian producers, including Raymond Longford and Beaumont Smith, made features in New Zealand in the twenties.

Utilizing equipment of his own design, Edwin Coubray was the first New Zealander to make sound films. The first New Zealand sound feature was *Down on the Farm*, produced by Stewart Pitt and Lee Hill in 1935. In the period from 1940 to 1970, only three features were made, all produced and directed by John O'Shea of Pacific Films in Wellington: *Broken Barrier* (co-directed by Roger Mirams, 1952), *Runaway* (1964) and *Don't Let It Get You* (1966). John O'Shea has since produced four features in the eighties, including *Ngati* (directed by Barry Barclay), which was selected for the Critics' Week at Cannes in 1987.

A resurgence of filmmaking began in the mid-seventies, as filmmakers observed the revival of the Australian film industry, with key features being Tony Williams' *Solo* and Roger Donaldson's *Sleeping Dogs,* both made in 1977. The following year, after a lengthy and fervent campaign by filmmakers, the government established the New Zealand Film Commission*.

Sixty features have been made since the Film Commission was established, and the Commission has invested in more than thirty of them. Some of the most interesting features of this extraordinarily productive ten years have included three by Geoff Murphy: the comedy/road movie *Goodbye Pork Pie* (1980), the historical epic, *Utu* (1983), and the science-fiction drama, *The Quiet Earth* (1985). Roger Donaldson's *Smash Palace* (1981) led him to a career in Hollywood. Sam Pillsbury, with *The Scarecrow,* became the first New Zealander to have a feature chosen for the Directors' Fortnight at Cannes. Vincent Ward's *Vigil* (1984) was the first New Zealand feature chosen for the Cannes Film Festival* competition, and in 1988 he completed his second feature, *The Navigator*.

In spite of an initial resistance to the idea of American features using New Zealand locations, in the late eighties, New Zealanders worked on several high-budget Hollywood productions being shot in the Southern Alps.

The most successful New Zealand feature at the box office is the full-length animated cartoon, *Footrot Flats,* directed by Murray Ball and based on his daily syndicated newspaper cartoon strip. Its New Zealand gross was over $2.5 million New Zealand, almost double the previous record set by *Goodbye Pork Pie* (with $1.4 million New Zealand) in 1981.

Since 1985, the New Zealand film industry has had an annual awards competition organized by the Guild of Film and Television Arts. The main industry organization is the New Zealand Independent Producers' and Directors' Guild; the Motion Picture Academy and the Film and Video Technicians Guild represent technicians, and Actors Equity represents performers.

Exhibition in New Zealand is dominated by the Kerridge Odeon chain, until recently 50 percent owned by the British Rank Organization*, and the Amalgamated chain, until recently 100 percent owned by the American 20th Century-Fox. Both organizations are now 100 percent New Zealand owned, in each case by companies specializing in property redevelopment.

BIBLIOGRAPHY

Bromby, Robin, "New Zealand," *Sight & Sound,* vol. XLVII, no. 2, Spring 1978, pp. 82–83.

"The New Zealand Film Industry," special supplement to *Cinema Papers,* June-July 1980, pp. 5–47.

Reid, Russell, "New Zealand's Film Production," *Films in Review,* vol. II, no. 8, October 1951, pp. 36–37.

Roddick, Nick, "New Zealand: Taking Off?" *Films and Filming,* June 1982, pp. 7–12.

Sowry, Clive. *Film Making in New Zealand: A Brief Historical Survey*. Wellington: The New Zealand Film Archive and Friends of the Film Archive, 1984.

THE NEW ZEALAND FILM COMMISSION was established by a 1978 Act of Parliament "To encourage and also to participate and assist in the making, promotion, distribution, and exhibition of films," "To encourage and promote cohesion within the New Zealand film industry," "To encourage and promote the exchange of information among persons engaged in the film industry," and "To encourage and promote employment in the New Zealand film industry, and the productivity of that industry." The Commission consists of the secretary for internal affairs and between three and six members appointed by the minister for the arts. It can make advances, grants, awards of money, purchase stock, act as an agent, give or receive guarantees or indemnities, and participate in the management of companies producing films that have a significant New Zealand content.

Thanks to its efforts, New Zealand feature films have received recognition throughout the world. Among the films that it has supported are *Skin Deep* (1978), *Smash Palace* (1981), *The Scarecrow* (U.S. *Klynham Summer,* 1982), *Patu!* (1983), *Utu* (1983), *Other Halves* (1984), *Leave All Fair* (1985), *Mr. Wrong* (U.S. *Dark of the Night,* 1985), and *Bridge to Nowhere* (1986).

Address: P.O. Box 11-546, Wellington, New Zealand.

BIBLIOGRAPHY

"The New Zealand Film Commission," *Cinema Papers,* no. 27, June-July 1980, pp. 21–47.

THE NEW ZEALAND NATIONAL FILM UNIT is the government's film production agency, consisting of six main units: Production, Laboratory, Technical Services, Video, Marketing, and Administration. The New Zealand government first became involved in filmmaking in 1901, but it was not until 1923 that film production was organized on a regular basis by the Government Publicity Office. In 1928, the Miramar Film Studios were built by Filmcraft Ltd., the contractor for government film processing and printing. In 1936, the studios were leased by the Tourist Department, which bought out Filmcraft's interest in 1938. The Studios were renamed the Government Film Studios, and following a reorganization in 1941, they became the home of the New Zealand National Film Unit.

Stanhope Andrews, who produced *Countrylads* (1941), took up his appointment as first producer of the Unit in August 1941. Under Andrews, the Unit produced its newsreel, *Weekly Review,* which continued until August 1950, six months after Andrews resigned. In the late forties, questions arose as to the Unit's being a propaganda tool of the Labour Party, and, with a change of government, the National Film Unit was forced to become more commercial, with series such as *New Zealand Now, New Zealand Mirror,* and *Pictorial Parade*. Among the more important of the Unit's later films are *1950 British Empire Games* (1950), *Journey for Three* (1950), *Royal New Zealand Journey* (1954), *Snows of Aorangi* (1955, nominated for a 1958 Academy Award), *One Hundred and Forty Days under the World* (1964, nominated for an Academy

Award), *This Is New Zealand* (1970), *Games 74* (1974), *War Years* (1983), and *The Frog, the Dog and the Devil* (1986, nominated for an Academy Award).

On October 18, 1978, the National Film Unit's new studio complex was officially opened at Lower Hutt.

Address: Fairway Drive, P.O. Box 46-002, Lower Hutt, New Zealand.

BIBLIOGRAPHY

Hugham, Oxley, "National Film Unit," *New Zealand's Heritage,* vol. VII, part 93, 1973, pp. 2577–2582.

"The New Zealand National Film Unit," *American Cinematographer,* vol. LX, no. 3, March 1979, pp. 252–253, 299–301.

NICARAGUA. A large but sparsely populated nation, Nicaragua was, until 1979, completely in the hands of one family, the Somozas, who controlled its political, economic, and cultural life with the aid of the United States. Thus the history of the Nicaraguan cinema is synonymous with the history of Nicaragua's struggle against the Somoza and the Sandinista movement (FSLN, Frente Sandinista de Liberacion Nacional).

After a late introduction, the cinema developed slowly in Nicaragua, with only a few amateur documentaries produced in the twenties and no production at all for the next three decades. Production did not resume until 1970, when Somoza himself founded Producine and the company began to produce occasional newsreels aggrandizing the family, short films for the training of his military, and TV commercials for Somoza-manufactured goods.

In the late seventies, as the FSLN intensified its armed struggle against Somoza's forces, its efforts drew the attention of European and Latin American militant filmmakers who shot documentaries among the guerrillas—*Nicaragua, September 1978* (Octavio Cortes, 1978), *Nicaragua: Loes Que Haran la Libertad* (Berta Navarro, 1978)—as well as one fictional feature about the conflict (Lourdes Portillo and Nina Serrano's *Después del Terremoto,* 1978).

Approximately a year before Somoza's fall, the FSLN decided to set up its own film and video unit—the Leonel Rugama Film Brigade and/or War Correspondent Corps—to document wartime activities. Crews trained in Mexico were sent to different parts of the country, managing to film over 25,000 meters of footage that would later serve as the archival infrastructure of the new Nicaraguan cinema.

Shortly after coming to power in July 1979, the Sandinista government offered members of the Corps the task of coordinating, as a branch of the Ministry of Culture, a Nicaraguan Film Institute (INCINE). Corps filmmakers Ramiro Lacayo, Carlos Ibarra, and Franklin Caldera became the directors of the new Institute, housed in the abandoned Producine studios.

Under very primitive conditions—twelve cameras without sync sound and limited editing capabilities—INCINE set out to produce periodic (eight per year) ten-minute newsreels, utilizing footage obtained during the war and the archival footage left behind in the old Somoza studios. These films, more like documentary shorts than newsreels, quickly developed a unique form of their own, and became as well an important training ground for new filmmakers. Tightly edited and with unconventional combinations of visual and aural elements, these films provided the structural basis for the development of a Nicaraguan film culture. Although well received by the public, these newsreels were still fundamentally flawed—the absence of labs in Nicaragua necessitated processing abroad (mostly in Cuba) and had a crippling impact on their timeliness.

After the fiftieth edition of the *Noticiarios Incine,* the Institute redirected its energies toward single-topic, longer documentaries and, shortly thereafter, toward fictional filmmaking. Between 1984 and 1986, it produced four fictional shorts, *Manuel* (Rafael Vargas), *Nunca nos Rendiremos* (Fernando Somarriba), *Esbozo de Daniel* (Mariano Marin), and *El Center Fielder* (Ramiro Lacayo). Nicaragua's first fictional feature (sixty minutes) was *Mujeres de la Frontera,* directed by Ivan Arguello in 1986.

INCINE has also developed a "special projects" section to handle co-productions and/or liaisons with foreign filmmakers and collaborations with other government agencies. Many Latin American and European filmmakers have filmed in Nicaragua in the last decade, directly or indirectly helping to train the INCINE crews: Helena Solberg Ladd (*Nicaragua from the Ashes,* 1980), Peter Lilienthal (*The Insurrection,* 1980), Berta Navarro (*Victoria de un Pueblo en Armas,* 1980). INCINE has also participated in a number of international and Latin American co-productions, for example Miguel Littin's Oscar-nominated *Alsino y el Condor* (1983) with Costa Rica, Mexico, and Cuba; Manuel Octavio Gomez's *El Señor Presidente* (1983) with Cuba and France; and Alex Cox's U.S. independent production, *Walker* (1983). Its latest co-production, with Spain, Mexico, and Cuba, is a big-budget ($750,000) feature entitled *El Espectro de la Guerra* (1987), directed by INCINE director Ramiro Lacayo.

In addition to its production activities, INCINE also changed the distribution and exhibition sectors in Nicaragua, formerly controlled by either the Somoza family or U.S. representatives. INCINE's distribution arm, Enidiec, is in charge of selling national films abroad and of buying international films for domestic distribution in 125 national theatres. Of these, INCINE runs the formerly Somoza-owned Cines Rap chain of 25 theatres. It has also developed a mobile-cinema program (following the Cuban ICAIC model), consisting of fifty units that travel throughout the country.

After only a decade, INCINE is experiencing a vigorous growth which, although hampered by economic problems and political pressures, bodes well for the future of the Nicaraguan cinema. Although it has centralized film-related activities, INCINE has not taken over all of the national cinema, as is evidenced by the 1980 film-video *Sandino Vive* produced by the armed forces and Sandinista Television Network (SSTV). Furthermore, its open distribution and exhibition policies seem to promise the continued growth of the critical cinematic audiences necessary for the development of a national cinema.

BIBLIOGRAPHY
Burton, Julianne, "Central America: Political Economies of Scale," in *World Cinema since 1945,* editor William Luhr. New York: Ungar, 1987, pp. 443–446.
Dagron, Alfonso Gumicio, "Nicaragua," *International Film Guide 1981,* editor Peter Cowie. London: Tantivy Press, 1980, pp. 247–248.

NIGER. In 1966, Niger boasted nine theatres with a weekly attendance of 21,000, but by 1986 less than six theatres were operative in this African republic. The country's three major directors are Mustapha Alassane (who produced his first film in 1962), Oumarou Ganda (who produced his first film in 1969), and Bakabe Mahamane.

NIGERIA is black Africa's leading film production nation, with more than thirty feature films to its credit since 1971. It also has the largest number of theatres of any African nation—more than 500—and the highest weekly attendance rate (over half-a-million). The majority of films are produced in the English language, but since 1975 a number of features have been released in native languages. Major Nigerian directors include Sanya Dosunmu, Jab Adu, Eddie Ugbomah, Adamu Halilu (who specializes in documentaries), and Ola Balogun (who is considered the continent's most prolific director). American and Indian films are the most popular with Nigerian audiences.

BIBLIOGRAPHY
Armes, Roy, "Nigeria," in *International Film Guide 1986,* editor Peter Cowie. London: Tantivy Press, 1985, pp. 259–261.
Balogun, Françoise. *Le cinéma au Nigeria.* Brussels: OCIC/Paris: L'Harmattan, 1984.
Bower, Roger, "Nigeria Upgrades Pic Biz," *Variety,* May 4, 1966, p. 159.
Landry, Robert J., "Nigeria's Theaters & U.S. Encouragement," *Variety,* July 26, 1978, pp. 7, 39.

NIKKATSU. The oldest of Japanese film companies, Nikkatsu was founded in 1911 as Nippon Katsudo Sashin (Japan Cinematograph Company), with four studios and 70 percent of all theatres in the country. It made an uneasy transition to sound in 1932 (after earlier attempts at sound films in 1929), and lost many of its top personnel because of the company's failure to grasp the new medium. It suffered further reversals during the Second World War, when government reorganization of the film industry led to its loss of production facilities. Nikkatsu made no attempt to resume production in the forties, concerning itself only with exhibition and distribution until the early fifties. In recent years, the company has been involved in the production of soft-core sex films for internal and Hong Kong consumption, and the production of children's films for Eastern European countries.

Address: 9-6-24 Akasaka, Minato-ku, Tokyo, Japan.

NOAH FILMS LTD. is the best known of Israeli film companies, thanks to the international success of its two owners, Menahem Golan and Yoram Globus, who head the Cannon Group. The company was founded in 1963 by Golan—his cousin, Globus—joined in 1966, and Noah's first production was *El Dorado* (1963), starring Haim Topol. Noah Films was the first Israeli company to produce non-Zionist features and thus gain an international audience for its product. It is presently associated with Golan-Globus Productions Ltd. and GG Israel Studios Jerusalem Ltd.

Address: 32 Allenby Street, Tel Aviv, Israel.

NORDISK FILM (whose correct name is A/S Nordisk Films Kompagni) is the oldest extant film company in Scandinavia, and maintains the oldest, operating, film studio in the world. It was founded on November 6, 1906, by Danish businessman Ole Olsen, who built a studio in the Copenhagen suburb of Valby. For his trademark, he chose a polar bear astride the world, which remains the company's logo. Olsen was able to expand his operation to the United States, and in 1908, he opened an office in New York, calling himself the Great Northern Film Company. The office closed in 1917, and Olsen was forced into retirement in 1924.

Nordisk Film was responsible for Denmark's first sound feature, in 1931, and its first color feature, in 1956. Director Carl Theodor Dreyer (1889–1968) was closely associated with the company during most of his career. In recent years, Nordisk Film achieved some international success with a series of "Olsen Gang" comedies that broke all box-office records in Denmark.

The organization is made up of a variety of subsidiary companies, that operate under the banner of Nordisk Film. Nordisk Films Video (NFV) is the largest distributor of videotapes in Scandinavia. Nordisk Films Distribution (NFD) is the largest film distributor in Denmark. Nordisk Film Cinemas (NFC) operates fifty-nine screens in Denmark; the flagship is Palads in Copenhagen, which opened in 1981 and has 2,040 seats and eighteen screens. Nordisk Film TV (NFTV) is involved in all aspects of television production. Nordisk Film Studios operates the two sound stages of the Valby studios. Johan Ankerstjerne is a film laboratory. International Film Teknik A/S handles the subtitling of films.

Address: 7 Axeltorv, DK-1609 Copenhagen V, Denmark.

BIBLIOGRAPHY

Bergsten, Bebe. *The Great Dane*. Los Angeles: Locare Research Group, 1973.

Keller, J.R. Keith, "Denmark's Nordisk Film Marks Off Its 80th Year Calm, Cool & Collected," *Variety*, November 12, 1986, pp. 7, 90.

"Nordisk: Many-Sided Co.; World's Oldest Studios," *Variety*, May 13, 1981, p. 306.

NORSK FILM A/S is Norway's leading film producer, a limited company of which the Norwegian government owns two-thirds of the shares. (The National Association of Municipal Cinemas/Kommunale Kinematografers Landsforfund owns the remaining one-third of the shares of the company.) The company was established in 1932, built its first sound stage in 1935, and released its first feature in 1937. One of Norsk's first important films was *Fant/The Gypsy* (1937), directed by the country's most influential director of the period, Tancred Ibsen, and starring Alfred Maurstad.

Presently Norsk Film A/S operates Norway's most modern studio in an Oslo suburb, with two sound stages and ancillary facilities. In the past fifty years, it has produced more than fifty features and innumerable shorts and documentaries.

Address: Wedel Jarlsbergs vei 36, P.O. Box 4, 1342 Jar, Norway.

NORTH POLE. As the home of Santa Claus, the North Pole has been featured in many films, as varied as Walt Disney's *Santa's Workshop* (1932) and *The Christmas That Almost Wasn't* (1966). The earliest film to deal with the North Pole is probably *The Truth about the Pole* (1911), which is an attack on the claim (later verified) by Robert E. Perry that he discovered the North Pole in 1909. The film claims that it was F.A. Cook who should have received the credit.

Other films set in the region of the North Pole include Georges Méliès' fantasy, *À la conquête du pole/The Conquest of the Pole* (1912), *Uncharted Seas* (1921), and *Ice Station Zebra* (1968). See also GREENLAND.

NORWAY. The first presentation of motion pictures in Scandinavia was the Bioskop-shop of Max and Emil Skladanowsky at a music hall in Kristiania (now Oslo) on April 6, 1896, five months after its Berlin opening. Only traveling shows were given throughout the next decade, and it was not until 1904 that the first cinema opened in Kristiania. Cinemas spread and their popularity occasioned a fierce public debate in 1910 concerning the possible harmful effect of film viewing on children. The controversy culminated in the Film Theatres' Act of July 25, 1913, that established the Statens Filmkontroll, or Board of Film Censors (until recently, censorship in Norway has been much stricter than in the other Scandinavian countries), and empowered the various municipal councils, which traditionally were quite powerful, to license all exnibitors within their areas.

The councils built their own theatres beginning in 1915 and took over theatres when licenses expired. In 1917, after distributors, feeling threatened, increased rental fees to the municipal cinemas, the Kommunale Kinematografers Landsforbund (KKL) or National Association of Municipal Cinemas (NAMC), was formed. Responding to a boycott by the distributors, NAMC formed their own distribution company, Kommunenes Filmcentral A/S (KF), in 1919, acquired Fotorama, a large distribution company, and soon had control of one-third of the country's rentals.

NAMC grew during the twenties to control half of Norway's theatres and nearly 90 percent of the market, percentages that continue to the present day. American imports decreased from nearly 85 percent to around 60 percent in the late twenties due to NAMC and KF. Norwegian films were shown at the height of the season, while imports were held back.

In 1970, NAMC created Norsk kino- og filmfond, or Norwegian Cinema and Film Foundation (NCFF). Working with a 2.6 percent levy on box-office grosses, NCFF is responsible for improving and maintaining the municipal cinemas, as well as promoting film as a cultural institution, which includes supporting film clubs, traveling cinemas, children's film exhibition, presentations abroad and the Norwegian Film Festival, which began in 1972. With the creation of NCFF, NAMC has assumed a larger political role as lobbyist and negotiator for a concerted media policy.

On January 1, 1988, the new Film and Video Act which replaced the 1913 Film Theatres' Act, took effect. It includes a more relaxed censorship law and requirements for video dealers to be licensed and taxed. The new act aims to "safeguard and maintain the current diversified and extended cinema structure in Norway."

Municipal ownership, which in 1986 accounted for 170 of the 336 theaters in Norway, has allowed the smaller localities to show a diverse number of quality films. With no theatre chains in existence, the appointed directors of the cinemas have a free hand in choosing their programs, and as a result, the level of quality in Norwegian programming is considered unique in Europe. Although the cinemas often lose money, they are looked upon as important local institutions for culture and are strongly subsidized. With the defeat of the Labor Party in the fall 1987 elections, the Conservatives vowed to allow any private entrepreneur the opportunity to become an exhibitor. It remains to be seen how the promised competition will affect the municipal cinemas.

Film production has been limited in Norway in comparison with its neighbors Denmark, Finland, and Sweden. Systematic production did not begin until the late 1910s and only proceeded at the average rate of three to four films per year until the fifties. Only about one hundred films were produced during the first thirty-five years; four hundred films had been made by the early eighties. Norway currently produces eight to ten features per year, some of which attract international attention.

Fiskerlivets farer/The Perils of a Fisherman, shot in 1907 in Kristiania harbor, is considered to be the first Norwegian story film. The producer, Hugo Hermansen, who in 1905 and 1906 had footage shot of Haakon VII on his coronation tour, established a cinema empire, but soon suffered a stroke and abandoned production. Between 1907 and 1920, nineteen other films were made, nine by Peter Lykke-Seest, the only Norwegian filmmaker of that era considered to have artistic ambitions. His company, Christiania Film Compagni A/S, failed after trying to break into the U.S. market. Today only one film by Lykke-Seest, the 1919 *Historien om en gut/The Story of a Boy,* is known to exist.

Since 1920, the problematic financial situation of filmmaking has insured the limited quantity and quality of Norwegian productions. Government taxation in the early years limited profitability. Lykke-Seest stopped in 1919 because of the great financial risks involved. In 1937, a U.S. government report quoted in *The 1937 Film Daily Year Book of Motion Pictures* noted, "Because of the difficulty in raising the funds needed, and due to the small amount allowed for each picture (approximately Kr. 100,000 in comparison with Swedish films costing from Kr. 150,000 to Kr. 200,000), a Norwegian picture, has little, if any, chance of becoming wholly satisfactory." The same organization concluded in 1938, "The Norwegian product may still be said to be in its infancy" (*The 1938 Film Daily Year Book of Motion Pictures*).

Although the municipalities of Norway became involved in the governance of cinemas in 1913, funds for production were not forthright in coming. From 1920 through 1923, five films were made by Kommunenes Filmcentral A/S, but because of the postwar depression, most filmmakers were forced to spend more time and energy financing their films than producing them. The only government incentive to promote production was the reduction of the exhibition tax by 5 percent for films made in Norway.

When the government did not accede to filmmakers' and NAMC's wishes to establish a national film company, fifty-two municipal cinemas in 1932 established Norsk Film A/S* which opened its studio at Jar outside Oslo in 1935. Norsk produced two hits in the late thirties: *Fant* in 1936 and *To levende og en død/Two Living and One Dead,* both of which were directed by Tancred Ibsen, grandson of Bjørnson and Henrik Ibsen, and Norway's most prominent director of what is now known as the "Golden Age." Other important directors of that period include Rasmus Breistein, who in 1920 made Norway's first full-length feature, *Fante-Anne/Gypsy Anne,* and Leif Sinding. The thirties saw a number of films produced in Sweden with Norwegian actors and directors, and co-productions with both Norwegian and Swedish versions of the same film.

During the Nazi occupation which began in 1940, the idea of government funding for film production finally took hold. Attendance rose even though American imports, which in 1939 accounted for 62 percent of films exhibited in Norway, were stopped. The Norwegian industry, run by Nazis and Quisling collaborators, produced up to six features per year of mostly escapist farces.

Faced with more urgent rebuilding tasks after the war, the government did not actively begin aiding production until the "Support Scheme" of 1950, which was modified in 1955 and 1963. Initially the government provided a premium after a film's completion; in 1955, government loan guarantees and direct subsidies for 45 percent (later 55 percent) of ticket sales, became available. Today nearly every film produced, except for commercial comedies, receives government subsidies and guarantees of up to 90 percent of production costs. Production figures rose to 92 films from 1950 to 1960, but with the introduction of television in the late fifties, attendance (which hit its peak in 1956 at 35 million, or ten per capita, compared with 2.7 in 1986) fell.

During the early sixties, young filmmakers opposed the administrative leadership of Norsk, which they said did not promote creative work. Norsk, which produced only two films between 1962 and 1968, was reorganized, and in 1971, the government, which had become a minority shareholder in 1948, took over two-thirds interest in the company. Some filmmakers during this period organized their own small companies, while other production was carried on by organizing a company when a film was to be made, a practice dating from the thirties.

Today Norsk remains Norway's biggest producer. Teamfilm A/S, which produced the popular "Olsen Gang" series* between 1969 and 1981, and Norsk have made more than 100 of the 400 Norwegian films produced by the early eighties, while the remaining 300 films were made by 118 separate companies. Norway's film history also shows an abundance of directors. While the ten most prolific have made 137 films, the remaining 252 films were made by 134 directors.

With the discovery of North Sea oil in the early eighties, foreign productions turned to Norway for investment and locations. Coincident with this, some Norwegian films received international acclaim, including Norway's biggest box office attraction *Orions belte/Orion's Belt, Hard asfalt/Hard Asphalt, X,* the winner of the Silver Lion at Venice, and *Hud/The Wild One,* official selection for Cannes' "Un Certain Regard."

In 1987, a fund was established by the state-operated broadcasting corporation, NRK/TV, and the government for productions that could be exhibited both theatrically and on television. Also looming on the horizon is a bill for production funding to come from fees placed on video rentals, which are booming.

Directors of note following the Second World War included Nils R. Müller, one of Norway's most prolific directors; Arne Skouen, who made seventeen films beginning in 1949 before becoming a columnist in the late sixties; and Per Hoest, an outstanding documentarist who captured the life of the Lapp people. Other are: Knut Bohwim, Knut Anderson, Anja Breien, Per Blom, Oddvar Bull Tuhus, Oddvar Einarson (born 1949), Lasse Glomm (born 1944), Ola Solum (born 1943), Vibeke Løkkeberg (born 1945), Bredo Greve, the team of Svend Wam and Petter Vennerød, Nicole Macé and Laila Mikkelson. Since the late sixties, directors tended toward "personal" films, women directors have made a significant impact, and children's films have been produced in abundance.

BIBLIOGRAPHY

Bakke, Hallvard, "Statement of Policy," in *International Film Guide 1988,* editor Peter Cowie. London: Tantivy Press, 1987, pp. 64–65.

Bech, Leif-Erik, *Norsk Filmografi 1908–1979*. Oslo: Norsk Kinoog Filmfond, 1980.

Cowie, Peter, "Tackling the Issues," in *International Film Guide 1988,* editor Peter Cowie. London: Tantivy Press, 1987, pp. 66–68.

Film Centre, London. *The Film Industry in Six European Countries*. Paris: UNESCO, 1950.

Hardy, Forsyth. *Scandinavian Film*. London: Falcon Press, 1952.

Helgeland, Axel, "International Adventures," in *International Film Guide 1988,* editor Peter Cowie. London: Tantivy Press, 1987, pp. 65–66.

Holst, Jan Erik, "Norway," in *International Film Guide 1988,* editor Peter Cowie. London: Tantivy Press, 1987, pp. 287–296.

Keller, J. R. Keith, "Oslo's New Solons Open Door for Private Exhibitors to Enter," *Variety,* November 18, 1987, p. 27.

Klevjer Aas, Nils A., "Cinema in Norway: 70 Years of a Singular System," in *International Film Guide 1988,* editor Peter Cowie. London: Tantivy Press, 1987, pp. 64–65.

———, "75 Years of Norwegian Film Production," *Screen International,* August 20, 1983, pp. ii–x.

Norwegian Film Council, *Norwegian Films 1984*. Oslo, 1984.

Norwegian Film Institute, *Norwegian Films 1981*. Oslo, 1981.

LA NOUVELLE EDITION FRANÇAISE (NEF) was created by French film director Jean Renoir (1894–1979) in 1939 for the production of *La règle du jeu/The Rules of the Game* (1939), after his previous film, *La bête humaine/The Human Beast* had been cut against Renoir's wishes by its producer.

NOUVELLE EDITIONS DE FILMS. Active from 1956 to 1981, Nouvelle Editions de Films was responsible for the production or co-production of a number of major French features, including *Un condamné à mort s'est echappé/A Man Escaped* (1956), *Zazie dan le Métro* (1960), *Le Feu Follet/The Fire Within* (1963), *Viva Maria* (1965), *Le Voleur/The Thief of Paris* (1966), *Calcutta* (1968), *Lacombe Lucien* (1973), and *L'Inde fantôme/Phantom India* (1975).

O

THE OBERHAUSEN MANIFESTO was a declaration by young German filmmakers, influenced by the French New Wave* and the British Free Cinema*. It was signed on February 28, 1962, by twenty-six filmmakers present at the Oberhausen Short Film Festival, among whom were Edgar Reitz, Haro Senft, Peter Schamoni, Herbert Vesely, Heinz Tichawsky, Hans-Jürgen Pohland, and Alexander Kluge (who was the most influential of the group and the only one to make a lasting impact on German cinema). The following is a translation of the Oberhausen Manifesto in its entirety:

> The collapse of the conventional German film at long last deprives an intellectual attitude which we reject of its economic foundation. Thus, the new film has a chance of coming to life.
>
> In recent years, German short films, made by young writers, directors, and producers, have won a large number of prizes at international festivals and attracted the attention of critics from other countries. These films and their successes demonstrate that the future of German cinema lies with those who have shown that they speak a new cinematic language.
>
> As in other countries, the short film in Germany has become both a training ground and an area of experimentation for the feature film.
>
> We declare that our ambition is to create a new German feature film.
>
> This new film requires new freedoms. Freedom from the usual conventions of filmmaking. Freedom from commercial interests. Freedom from the domination of special interest groups.
>
> We have realistic intellectual, structural, and economic ideas about production of the new German film. We are jointly ready to take economic risks.
>
> The old film is dead. We believe in the new film.

BIBLIOGRAPHY

Pflaum, Hans Günther, and Hans Helmut Prinzler. *Cinema in the Federal Republic of Germany*. Bonn: Inter Nationes, 1983.

"OCKER" COMEDIES are Australian films from the seventies that glory in the vulgarity of the "ocker" or Australian working man. The first film in the genre is generally credited to have been Tim Burstall's *Stork* (1971). The best-known "Ocker" films are those featuring the characters of "Alvin Purple" and "Barry Mackenzie." The most important, and serious, film of the genre is Bruce Beresford's *Don's Party* (1976).

ODEON CIRCUIT. The best known of British theatre chains, the Odeon circuit was founded by Oscar Deutsch (1893–1941), who had first become involved in the film industry with two other Birmingham-born film personalities, Michael Balcon and Victor Saville. He owned a number of theatres in the twenties, but it was not until August 4, 1930, that he opened the first Odeon theatre, the Odeon, Perry Barr, Birmingham (which closed as a theatre in 1969, to reopen as a bingo parlor). He chose the name Odeon from the Greek (already the basis for the French name of concert halls and the American nickelodeon), because it began with his first two initials. His wife always claimed that the "on" was added because Oscar Deutsch was always "on."

The Odeon circuit, as such, did not come into being until 1935, by which time more than twenty distinctive, art deco–style Odeon theatres were operational. Architects principally involved in the design of the Odeon theatres were Harry Weedon, Cecil Clavering, George Coles, and Andrew Mather. On November 2, 1937, the best-known theatre in the chain, the Odeon, Leicester Square, London, opened. Deutsch expanded his theatre chain to Canada in 1938. Following Deutsch's death, the Odeon circuit was acquired by the Rank Organization*.

BIBLIOGRAPHY

Eyles, Allen, "Oscar and the Odeons," *Focus on Film,* no. 22, Autumn 1975, pp. 38–57.

THE "OLD MOTHER RILEY" SERIES featured a British Music Hall* comedian, Arthur Lucan, in the guise of an Irish washerwoman, Old Mother Riley, living with her daughter, played by Lucan's wife Kitty McShane. Lucan (1887–1954), whose real name was Arthur Towle, had first introduced the character in 1913, and it remained immensely popular with less-sophisticated British audiences. The following is a complete list of films in the series: *Old Mother Riley* (1937), *Old Mother Riley in Paris* (1938), *Old Mother Riley M.P.* (1939), *Old Mother Riley Joins Up* (1939), *Old Mother Riley in Business* (1940), *Old Mother Riley's Ghosts* (1941), *Old Mother Riley's Circus* (1941), *Old Mother Riley Detective* (1943), *Old Mother Riley Overseas* (1944), *Old Mother Riley at Home* (1945), *Old Mother Riley's New Venture* (1949), *Old Mother Riley Headmistress* (1950), *Old Mother Riley's Jungle Treasure* (1951), and *Mother Riley Meets the Vampire* (U.S. *Vampire over London,* 1952). The last co-starred Bela Lugosi and was the only film in which Kitty McShane did not also appear.

BIBLIOGRAPHY

Slide, Anthony. *Great Pretenders.* Lombard, Ill.: Wallace-Homestead, 1986.

THE "OLSEN GANG" SERIES. Produced between 1968 and 1981 by Nordisk Film*, the "Olsen Gang" was immensely popular in Denmark, and even generated a Swedish version, the Jönsson Gang. The films were created by screenwriter Henning Bahs and co-writer and director Erik Balling. They feature Ove Sprogøe as Egon Olsen, with Morten Grunwald and Poul Bundgaard as his sidekicks, Benny and Kjeld. The hero of these gangster comedies is usually shown at the commencement of each film leaving prison, and he usually ends the film back in jail.

Among the thirteen films in the series are *Olsen-Banden/The Olsen Gang* (1968), *Olsen-Banden pa spanden/The Olsen Gang in Trouble* (1970), *Olsen-Banden i Jylland/The Olsen Gang in Jutland* (1971), *Olsen-Banden's store kup/The Olsen Gang's Big Heist* (1972), *Olsen-Banden gaar amok/The Olsen Gang Goes Wild* (1973), *Olsen-Banden's sidste bedrifter/Exploits of the Olsen Gang* (1974), *Olsen-Banden paa sporet/The Olsen Gang on the Track* (1975), *Olsen-Banden ser roedt/The Olsen Gang Sees Red* (1976), *Olsen-Banden deruda'/The Olsen Gang Outta Sight* (1977), *Olsen-Banden gaar i krig/The Olsen Gang Goes to War* (1978), and *Olsen-Bandens flugt over plankevaerket/The Olsen Gang Jumps the Fence* (1981).

Because the humor in the series is typically Danish, the films have had only limited release outside of Scandinavia. They have, however, often been submitted for Academy Award consideration for Best Foreign Language Film as the official Danish entries, but have never won an Oscar or even been nominated.

OLYMPIA-FILM GmbH was the name of a company created by the Propaganda Ministry in Nazi Germany, with an estimated DM 1.5 from the Reich Ministry of Finance, for the production of Leni Riefenstahl's film of the 1936 Olympic Games in Berlin, *Olympia*.

BIBLIOGRAPHY

Graham, Cooper C. *Leni Riefenstahl and Olympia*. Metuchen, N.J.: Scarecrow Press, 1986.

THE ONTARIO FILM DEVELOPMENT CORPORATION was created in 1986 to provide financial assistance to the Ontario, Canada–based film and television industry. Among the important films that it has helped finance are *I've Heard the Mermaids Sing* and *Too Outrageous,* both released in 1987. The Corporation is also involved in location promotion and location services, and is an agency of the Ontario Ministry of Citizenship and Culture.

Address: 81 Wellesley Street East, Toronto, Ontario M4Y lH6, Canada.

ONTARIO FILM INSTITUTE. Part of the Ontario Science Centre, the Ontario Film Institute was founded in 1969, "to encourage the development of the art of the film and to foster public appreciation and study of film history, origins and accomplishments." It also serves as a clearinghouse for all information relating to film in the Canadian province of Ontario.

The Ontario Film Institute has three divisions: a reference and information centre, the Ontario Film Archive (which serves chiefly as a repository for government-produced films), and the Ontario Film Theatre, with regular screenings in its 482-seat theatre. The Institute publishes a newsletter, *film news,* and, since 1980, has presented an Award for Excellence in Canadian Cinema (with the first recipient being Christopher Chapman).

It cooperates with similar organizations in Canada: the Cinematheque Québecois and the Conservatory of Cinema Art, both in Montreal, the National Film Theatres of Edmonton and Kingston, and the Pacific Cinematheque in Vancouver.

Address: Ontario Science Centre, 770 Don Mills Road, Toronto, Ontario M3C 1T3, Canada.

OPTICOLOR was an additive color process developed in Germany by Siemens & Halske of Berlin and Otto Perutz of Munich, utilizing the earlier Berthon/Keller-Dorian patents. It was initially known as the Berthon-Siemens color system (after Rodolphe Berthon and Siemens & Halske). The process was first seen in the 1936 feature, *Das Schonheitsfleckchen/The Beauty Spot* (1936), and its experimental use was ended in 1938 when Josef Goebbels decided to supercede it with Agfacolor*. Opticolor was also the American name for the Francita-Realita* color system.

BIBLIOGRAPHY

Koshofer, Gert. *Color: Die Farben des Films*. Berlin: Spiess, 1988.

THE ORSON WELLES MOTION PICTURE DIRECTORIAL ACHIEVEMENT AWARD was first presented at the Cannes Film Festival in 1987.

THE OSKAR GISLASON AWARD was first presented in 1987 by the Association of Icelandic Film Producers.

OSPK, the Society of Builders of Proletariat Cinema/Obshchestvo Stroitelei Proletarskogo Kino, was founded in Leningrad in September 1924. Active in the Soviet film industry of the twenties, its philosophy (according to Denise J. Youngblood) was that proletarian cinema should not be a "source of entertainment, enrichment, refined debauchery, and stupefication of the masses," but "a weapon of organization, education, enlightenment of the worker-peasant masses" in the struggle for communism and against the West. It was soon replaced by ODSK (Society of Friends of Soviet Cinema/Obshchestvo Druzei Sovetskogo Kino).

BIBLIOGRAPHY

Youngblood, Denise J. *Soviet Cinema in the Silent Era, 1918–1935*. Ann Arbor, Mich.: UMI Research Press, 1985.

OUIMETOSCOPE was the name of the theatre in Montreal's Klondike Hotel, which Canadian film pioneer, Léo Ernest Ouimet (1877–1972) opened January 1, 1906. He subsequently purchased the site on which the theatre stood, and there, on August 31, 1907, he opened his new Ouimetoscope, the first major film theatre in the world. It had seating for 1,200, with a seven-piece orchestra, a bar, and even its own magazine, *Le Ouimetoscope*. Competition forced Ouimet to rent out the facility in 1915, and it closed permanently in 1926.

BIBLIOGRAPHY

Morris, Peter. *Embattled Shadows: A History of Canadian Cinema 1895–1939*. Montreal: McGill-Queen's University Press, 1978.

P

PAKISTAN. Filmmaking in Pakistan predates independence in 1947, with some six studios functioning in Lahore. The first Pakistani film was *Teri Yaad,* released in 1948, and directed by Dawood Chand. The first important Pakistani feature is considered to be *Pheerey* (1949). The most important director of the fifties was Anwar Kemal Pasha, all of whose features were commercially successful. Khalil Qaiser and Riaz Shahid gained a reputation in the sixties for films of a more serious nature. Color photography was not widely used until the mid-sixties, with the first major color feature being *Naila* (1965), directed by Sharif Nayyar.

Censorship is Pakistan is strict, and was tightened in 1985 by a Censor Code that paid closer attention to Islamic laws. "Vulgar" and violent films are barred, and between 1962 and 1966, the Central Board of Film Censors banned some 772 foreign films. As a result of censorship, Pakistan has a thriving black market in videotapes, which has resulted in major problems for the country's producers and more than seven hundred theatres. The import of Indian films was restricted between 1947 and 1965, and following the 1965 war between the two countries, all Indian films have been banned.

A National Film Development Corporation (56-F, Blue Area, Islamabad) was created in 1973; a state film authority took over some of its activities in 1975. The Corporation imports films, helps finance production, and issues permits to local producers. Without registration by the Ministry of Culture, producers are unable to function in Pakistan, and the Ministry tends to favor older, established producers. Lahore is the centre for the production of films in Punjabi and Urdu, while films in Urdu and Sindhi are produced in Karachi.

Major contemporary directors include Javed Fazil, Irfan Khoosat, Nazaral Islam, and Mumtaz Ali Khan. However, it is stars rather than directors to whom Pakistani audiences are loyal. Films remain highly commercial in orientation, with most containing at least half-a-dozen musical numbers.

BIBLIOGRAPHY

Gul, Ijaz, "The Cinema in Pakistan," *Cinema India-International,* vol. IV, no. 1, 1987, pp. 102–104.

PALESTINE. Prior to the establishment of the state of Israel in 1948, a modest film industry existed in Palestine. The first film to be shot there was of the British entry into Jerusalem in December 1917, by Ben-Dov. Nathan Akselrod began film production in 1927, and among his releases are *And It Was in the Days of—* (1931), *Oded the Wanderer* (1932), *Above the Ruins* (1937), and a newsreel, *Moledet/The Motherland* (first issued in 1927, and, in 1935, changing its name to *Carmel Film*).

In 1946, Americans Herbert Kline and Meyer Levin came to Palestine to film *My Father's House* (1948), and, after completion of the feature, they left their equipment for use by Norman Luria's Palestine Film Productions. Virtually all Palestinian films emanated from the country's Jewish community (with many sponsored by bodies such as the Jewish Agency, the Jewish Foundation Fund, and the Jewish National Fund), although the British Public Information Office did sponsor some Arabic shorts.

BIBLIOGRAPHY

Harris, E., ''Film Production Problems and Activities in Palestine,'' in *The Penguin Film Review,* editor Roger Manvell. London and New York: Penguin Books, 1948, pp. 36–41.

PANAMA. Filmmaking in Panama did not start until 1971, when the country's dictator, General Omar Torrijos, established a Motion Picture Division within his government to promote the use of Panama for location shooting and to encourage film projects and co-productions. One of the first 35mm documentary films to be produced in Panama was *An mar tule/We the People* (1971), made by American filmmaker Richard C. Levy, with a script by Wolf Mankowitz and narration by Laurence Harvey. In 1972, Torrijos helped create the Grupo Experimental de Cine Universitario/Experimental Cinema Group of the University of Panama, also known as GECU (Apartado 60-1775, Estafeta El Dorado, Panama). Since its formation, GECU has made more than thirty documentaries, but has suffered from a lack of support since the overthrow of Torrijos.

The number of theatres in Panama has increased from thirty-two in 1940 (with a further thirty in the Panama Canal Zone) to sixty in 1986, serving a population of 2 million. There are an additional six theatres in the Canal Zone. More than 25 percent of the entire profits made by the American film industry in Central American comes from the distribution of films in Panama.

PANNONIA FILMSTUDIO. The primary centre of animated film production in Hungary is the Pannonia Filmstudio, which came into being in 1950 following the breakup of Magyar Filmgyártó Vállalat/Hungarian Film Productions (which had been formed in 1948). The first head of Pannonia was Gyula Mackássy, who directed the studio's first cartoons: *A kiskakas gyémánt félkrajcárja/The Little Cock's Diamond Coin* (1951), *Erdei sportverseny/Forest Sports Compe-*

tition (1952), and *Kutyakötelesség/Moral Obligation* (1953). The studio's 1974 short, *Sisyphus/Sisiphus,* was nominated for an Academy Award.

Address: Vörös Hadesereg útja 64, Budapest 11, Hungary.

BIBLIOGRAPHY

"30 Years of Pannonia Film Studio," special edition of *Hungarofilm Bulletin,* no. 3, 1980.

PAPUA/NEW GUINEA has been a favorite location for ethnographic filmmakers, from Frank Hurley in the twenties—and films such as *Head Hunters of Papua*—to Australian documentary producer, Dennis O'Rourke, in the seventies and eighties, with films such as *Yumi Yet* (1977) and *Ileksen* (1978). In 1972, French director Barbet Schroeder made a feature in Papua/New Guinea titled *La Vallee/The Valley Obscured by Clouds,* about a Frenchwoman deserting civilization for primitive society. Bulle Ogier was the star, with music by the Pink Floyd and cinematography by Nestor Almendros. The tourist attraction of the country's cannibals was the subject of Dennis O'Rourke's *Cannibal Tours* (1987).

PARAGUAY has no film industry, although three production companies were established in 1948 to produce documentaries and newsreels. There were fourteen theatres in the country in 1937, twenty-six in 1948 and one hundred in 1987. Censorship is slight, and film distribution is handled through Argentinian companies.

PARIS. The many films that have utilized Paris as a historical backdrop, from the middle ages to the Second World War, include: *Trilby* (1913), *The Two Orphans* (1915), *Camille* (1915), *Camille* (1917), *A Tale of Two Cities* (1917), *A Tale of Two Cities* (1921), *Camille* (1921), *The Three Musketeers* (1921), *The Four Horsemen of the Apocalypse* (1921), *Orphans of the Storm* (1922), *The Three Must-Get-Theres* (1922), *Scaramouche* (1923), *Trilby* (1923), *Zaza* (1923), *The Hunchback of Notre Dame* (1923), *The Phantom of the Opera* (1925), *Madame Sans-Gêne* (1925), *La Bohème* (1926), *Beloved Rogue* (1927), *Napoleon* (1927), *Camille* (1927), *Marie Antoinette* (1929), *Du Barry, Woman of Passion* (1930), *Svengali* (1931), *The Scarlet Pimpernel* (1935), *A Tale of Two Cities* (1935), *Return of the Scarlet Pimpernel* (1937), *Camille* (1937), *Marie Antoinette* (1938), *La Marseillaise* (1938), *The Three Musketeers* (1939), *The Hunchback of Notre Dame* (1939), *The Moon and Sixpence* (1942), *The Phantom of the Opera* (1943), *Les enfants du paradis/Children of Paradise* (1945), *Bel Ami* (1947), *The Three Musketeers* (1948), *Moulin Rouge* (1952), *French Cancan/Only the French Can* (1955), *The Hunchback of Notre Dame* (1957), *A Tale of Two Cities* (1958), *The Phantom of the Opera* (1962), *The Four Horsemen of the Apocalypse* (1962), *Jules et Jim/Jules and Jim* (1962), *Those Magnificent Men in Their Flying Machines* (1965), *The Great Race* (1965), *La Bohème* (1965), *Is Paris Burning?* (1966), *The Madwoman of Chaillot* (1969), *The Three*

Musketeers (1973), *Le Dernier Métro/The Last Métro* (1981), and *Swann in Love* (1985).

The 1922 British feature, *Squibs Wins the Calcutta Sweep,* reaches its climax in Paris. Also set in Paris are the three British silent features—*The Rat* (1925), *The Triumph of the Rat* (1926), and *The Return of the Rat* (1929)—featuring Ivor Novello as the apache of the title—and the one British sound film—*The Rat* (1937)—with Anton Walbrook as the same character. Other British films that utilize a Paris background include *Paris Plane* (1934), *It Happened in Paris* (1935), *Old Mother Riley in Paris* (1938), *This Was Paris* (1942), *Idol of Paris* (1948), *Innocents in Paris* (1953), *The Lyons in Paris* (1955), and *To Paris with Love* (1955).

The British film industry has generally taken a jaundiced look at Paris and the French. The French themselves adopted a similar approach in the 1955 feature *Les carnets du Major Thompson/The French They Are a Funny Race*. American filmmakers have viewed Paris more as a city of romance, and among the dozens of American features with a Parisian backdrop are *A Woman of Paris* (1923), *Young April* (1923), *While Paris Sleeps* (1923), *Open All Night* (1924), *The King of Main Street* (1925), *Kiki,* (1926), *Paris* (1926), *Paris at Midnight* (1926), *A Gentleman of Paris* (1927), *7th Heaven* (1927), *The Cohens and Kellys in Paris* (1928), *Gentlemen Prefer Blondes* (1928), *The Battle of Paris* (1929), *Lady of the Pavements* (1929), *The Love Parade* (1929), *Paris* (1929), *Remember the Night* (1932), *Love Me Tonight* (1932), *Paris Interlude* (1934), *Paris in Spring* (1935), *History Is Made at Night* (1937), *Ninotchka* (1939), *Paris Underground* (1945), *Arch of Triumph* (1948), *An American in Paris* (1951), *April in Paris* (1952), *The Last Time I Saw Paris* (1954), *Funny Face* (1957), *Paris Does Strange Things* (1957), *Love in the Afternoon* (1957), *A Certain Smile* (1958), *Can-Can* (1960), *Paris Blues* (1961), *Gigot* (1962), *Gay Pur-ree* (1962), *What a Way to Go!* (1962), *Irma La Douce* (1963), *Charade*(1963), *Paris When It Sizzles* (1964), *What's New Pussycat?* (1965), *Boeing Boeing* (1965), *How to Steal a Million* (1966), *Two for the Road* (1967), *Topaz* (1969), and *The Aristocats* (1970).

As far as French filmmakers are concerned, no one has shown Paris more perfectly on screen than René Clair in such films as *Paris qui dort/The Crazy Ray* (1924), *Sous les toits de Paris/Under the Bridges of Paris* (1930), *Le Million/The Million* (1931), *À Nous la liberté* (1931), *Quatorze Juillet/July 14th* (1933), and *Porte des lilas/Gates of Paris* (1957). Other memorable French films set in Paris include *Boudu sauvé des eaux/Boudu Saved from Drowning* (1932), *L'Atalante* (1934), *Rififi* (1955), *Le ballon rouge/The Red Balloon* (1956), *Mon Oncle/My Uncle* (1958), *Les quatre cents coups/The Four Hundred Blows* (1959), *Zazie dans le mêtro* (1960), *Cleo de 5 à 7/Cleo from 5 to 7* (1961), *Belle de Jour* (1967), *Playtime* (1968), *La vie devant soi/Madame Rosa* (1977), and *Diva* (1981).

The Italian film industry's best-known contribution to Parisian films is, of course, *Ultimo tango a Parigi/Last Tango in Paris* (1972).

THE **PATHÉ** rooster was first seen on screen on December 16, 1902—it was not registered for trade mark protection in the United States until 1927—and soon became a familiar symbol throughout the world, not just for the French company by whom it was first used, but for newsreels in the United Kingdom and the United States, a major production company in the United States, and a film laboratory in Canada. Pathé and its rooster had as much, if not more, household recognition as M-G-M and its lion.

The company's origins can be traced back to 1893, when Charles Pathé (1863–1957) went into business for himself, providing customers at fairgrounds with the opportunity to listen to the newly invented phonograph. A year later, he expanded his business with the addition of a motion picture "peepshow." He even began producing a few films, beginning with *L'Arrivée d'un Train en Gare de Vincennes* (1898). In 1899, with his brothers, Émile and Théophile, Pathé formed La Société Pathé Frères, which in the years preceding the First World War developed into the largest film company in the world.

It opened branches in cities as varied as Budapest, Singapore, St. Petersburg, and Calcutta, and sent cameramen around the world to shoot footage that would be included in what became the first newsreels. Ferdinand Zecca (1864–1947) joined Pathé in 1901; he headed production at the company's studios in Vincennes specializing in "trick" films in every way as impressive as those produced by rival Georges Méliès. Max Linder (1883–1925), the great French comedian, to whom Chaplin has always acknowledged a debt, made his debut with Pathé in 1905. Pathé was the first company to introduce standard renting contracts, forbidding exhibitors from rerenting, selling, or copying its films. It opened an American studio, which produced its first film in 1910, and produced the first American newsreel a year later.

By 1913, it was claimed that Pathé controlled 98 percent of the films projected throughout the world. It employed a total staff, worldwide, of 6,500, and boasted profits of $8 million. Historian Georges Sadoul quite rightly calls Charles Pathé the "Napoleon of the Cinema."

Unfortunately, the First World War had a devastating effect on Pathé. It reduced the company's market, while allowing the American film companies to expand their operations. It led Charles Pathé to reorganize his company, phasing out production he considered risky in comparison to such "safe" activities as the manufacture of film stock and equipment.

In 1920, the company was split into two. Pathé Cinéma was involved in nontheatrical film equipment and film processing, introducing the various substandard film gauges—9.5mm, 17.5mm, and 28mm—with which Pathé's name is closely linked in Europe, although such gauges never gained much attention in the United States. Pathé-Consortium handled the exhibition and distribution of film. (At this time, the company operated approximately fifty theatres in France, Belgium, the Netherlands, and Algiers, with the most important being Pathé-Cinéma in Paris.)

In 1929, Pathé-Consortium was taken over by Bernard Natan, and he is generally considered to be responsible for the company's financial failure of the thirties, which led to bankruptcy. The company was reorganized as La Société Nouvelle Pathé during the Second World War, with its most important film from this period being *Les Enfants du Paradis/The Children of Paradise* (1945). Charles Pathé was invited to return to the company he had created and was named honorary Chairman of the Board.

By the eighties, the company, now known as Pathé Cinema, had become primarily a theatre chain, with more than four hundred screens in France. It is currently controlled by an investment company, Groupe Rivaud. The Pathé name continues to be used in Canada by two linked companies, Pathé Sound and Post Production Centre (121 St-Patrick Street, Toronto, Ontario M5T 1V3) and Astral Bellevue Pathé (175 Montpellier Boulevard, Montreal, Quebec H4N 2G5).

Address: 6 rue Francoeur, 75018 Paris, France.

BIBLIOGRAPHY

"Charles Pathé, Film Publisher," *The Moving Picture World,* vol. XXII, no. 7, November 14, 1914, pp. 904–905.

"Charles Pathé—World Promoter of the Photoplay," *The Film Index,* vol. VII, no. 3, January 21, 1911, p. 1.

La Cinématographie Française, no. 1239, 1947, special issue devoted to Pathé.

Pathé, Charles. *De Pathé Frères à Pathé Cinéma.* Lyons: Premier Plan/SERDOC, 1970.

"Pathé Freres," *Views and Film Index,* vol. I, no. 4, May 19, 1906, p. 8.

Sadoul, Georges, "Napoleon of the Cinema," *Sight & Sound,* Spring 1958, p. 183.

PATHÉCOLOR was the best known of hand-coloring methods used for films during the silent era. Because it utilized a stencil process, there were no problems with color registration, as occurred with more primitive methods of hand-coloring. The process was undertaken by Pathé at its French studios at Vincennes. The following description is given by cinematographer Arthur Kingston in *The Parade's Gone By* by Kevin Brownlow (New York: Alfred A. Knopf, 1968):

> Pathe employed about three hundred women. Each worker sat at a bench. On her right was a ground-glass projection screen and a handle. Each turn of the handle moved one frame of the film to be tinted. The frame was enlarged to 6 by 9 inches. On her left was another copy of the same film, which was to be the stencil. In front of her was a pantograph and a ten-to-one reduction, to which an electro-magnetic vibrating needle was attached. This was fed by a fifty-cycle supply, and it cut the stencil for each section. There were never more than three sections. One woman would work on the blue, another on the red, another on the yellow. To add more color, the release print would be specially toned. Then the three stencils would be lined up in synchronization on a special machine, and rollers would spread the dye.

PATHÉ NEWS was a British newsreel produced from 1946 to 1970. It began life as *Pathé Animated Gazette* in February 1910, later becoming *Pathé Super Sound Gazette, Pathé Super Gazette,* and *Pathé Gazette,* which was last produced in 1945. Footage from these series is preserved in the Pathé Library at Elstree Studios* (Shenley Road, Boreham Wood, Herts WD6 1JG, United Kingdom).

BIBLIOGRAPHY

Cave, G. Clement, "Newsreels Must Find a New Policy," *Penguin Film Review,* No. 7, 1948, pp. 50–54.

PATHÉ PICTORIAL was an interest magazine produced for British filmgoers by Pathé News from March 1918 to March 1969. Footage from the series is preserved in the Pathé Library at Elstree Studios* (Shenley Road, Boreham Wood, Herts WD6 1JG, United Kingdom).

PATHÉTONE WEEKLY was an interest magazine produced for British filmgoers by Pathé News on a weekly basis from 1930 to 1941. Footage from the series is preserved in the Pathé Library at Elstree Studios* (Shenley Road, Boreham Wood, Herts WD6 1JG, United Kingdom).

PENGUIN FILM REVIEW came about through the enthusiasm of Sir Allan Lane, originator of Penguin Books, and critic Roger Manvell. It was published on a quarterly basis from August 1946 to May 1949; a reprint edition was published by Rowman and Littlefield in 1978.

BIBLIOGRAPHY

Slide, Anthony, editor. *International Film, Radio, and Television Journals.* Westport, Conn.: Greenwood Press, 1985.

PERU. In this Andean nation, where the effects of underdevelopment and extreme social and ethnic differences are only too visible, the national cinema has always had a fragile existence. Given a small national market (less than three hundred screens) controlled by international distributors and the impossibility of foreign distribution (given the strength of the Argentine and Mexican cinemas), the Peruvian cinema has been unable to sustain regular production or to develop an industry. Its history is primarily one of isolated efforts, failed experiments, and, often, lackluster profit-seeking.

This barrenness was particularly true in the silent period. Although different intellectuals and entrepeneurs experimented with the medium only a few years after the cinema's arrival in Lima (March, 1897), their efforts were always isolated and rarely successful: Federico Blume's *Negocio al Agua* (1913, the first fictional short) and *Del Manicomio al Matrimonio* (1914) and Enrique Cornejo Villanueva's *Luis Pardo* (1927, the first feature).

Although the coming of sound did not immediately spur national production (the first sound feature, *Buscando Olvido,* 1937, was produced by an Argentine radio technician), it did lead to a brief filmmaking renaissance led by Felipe Vasela La Rosa, Ricardo Villaran, and Manuel Trillan, and their company, Amauta Films. Amauta Films' productions, beginning with their 1937 *La Bailarina Loca,* capitalized on the popularity of local radio personalities and singers and, designed to serve as a complement to that new medium (radio was introduced in 1925), were well received by the public. Alongside a number of smaller producers, Amauta Films was active from 1937 to 1940, a period in which Peruvian production totalled a never-to-be matched eighteen feature films.

This boom was cut short by the Second World War: the United States eliminated Peru's quota of celluloid and national producers were paralyzed so completely that, even when normal trade relations with the United States were resumed after the war, neither Amauta nor any other producer was able to continue making feature films. Between 1943 and 1956, notwithstanding the imposition of a ten-cent tax on tickets to encourage national production, the Peruvian cinema was limited to a couple of unsuccessful features and commercial or government-sponsored newsreels.

The only exciting cinematic activity of the fifties took place far from Lima, in the Andean city of Cuzco. In 1955, architect Manuel Chambi and his brother Victor founded the Cine-Club de Cuzco and began to shoot ethnographic documentaries of regional festivals and ceremonies. After serving a practical apprenticeship working on the shoot of Italian director Enrico Gras' *El Imperio del Sol/The Empire of the Sun* in 1957, the members of the cine-club produced a series of internationally acclaimed documentaries and became known as "the Cuzco school." Manuel Chambi's 16mm shorts—*Carnaval de Kanas/Carnival in Kanas* and *Lucero de Nieve* (both 1957)—were favorably received at international festivals while *Kukuli* (1960), a 35mm documentary feature that represented the apogee of the school, was even a great commercial success domestically. Unfortunately, *Jarawi* (1965), the sequel to *Kukuli,* was a critical and commercial failure and the last film of the school.

In the sixties, there were isolated pockets of cinematic activity. In Lima, there was a renewed interest in cinema culture evidenced by a number of new cine-clubs, the foundation of the University Cinematheque by Miguel Reynal, and the appearance of a film journal, *Hablemos de Cine*. As with radio, the introduction of television in the late fifties also had repercussions on the national cinema, even stimulating the production of a few films featuring TV personalities as well as a number of co-productions. However, most important was the emergence in this era of a new filmmaker, Armando Robles Godoy.

A former film critic, Robles Godoy began making shorts in the early sixties, but quickly moved to feature filmmaking. His first film, *Ganaras el Pan* (1965), a documentary, was followed by *En La Selva no Hay Estrellas* (1966), a fictional feature that won a prize at the Moscow Film Festival and was very well-received at home. *La Muralla Verde/The Great Wall* (1970) was his most succesful effort, drawing a large national audience and winning a number of prizes at international festivals. Characterized by their technical fluidity and skillful cinematography, Robles Godoy's works were films *d'auteur,* closely modeled on their European counterparts, and quite unsuitable for Peru given the dire economic conditions of national filmmaking. Unable to recoup their high costs nationally or to be widely distributed internationally, his films, especially his last feature, *Espejismo*

(1973), were dismal financial failures, and, since the mid-seventies, Robles Godoy has dedicated himself to the production of *telenovelas* (TV soap operas) and to teaching occasional courses in cinematography.

Fomented by new government legislation—Ley #19377 (1972)—that imposed a surcharge on tickets to finance national films, established obligatory exhibition for national products, and set up an official agency, COPROCI, to implement these changes, the seventies witnessed a surge of filmmaking activity. As in Colombia, where a similar law also promoted the production of "quota-quickies," the mid-seventies were dominated by the production of shorts: between 1972 and 1977 more than two hundred shorts, mostly dealing with archeological and/or tourist themes, were approved by COPROCI. Although many of these shorts were lacking in quality and/or ambition, some important documentarists emerged from the boom in production: Nora de Izcue, Mario Jacob, Nelson Garcia, and Mario Tejada. In 1983, twenty-five independent production companies, with the help of COPROCI, produced seventy documentaries. Although Ley #19377 has not been as favorable to national feature filmmaking, a number of features were produced in the late seventies and early eighties. In 1977, the release of *Los Perros Hambrientos* (Luis Figueroa), *Muerte al Amanecer/Death at Dawn* (Francisco Lombardi, the only feature to recoup its production costs in the history of the national cinema), and *Kuntur Wachana* (Federico Garcia), marked an important first step in the development of a national cinema. Since then, other filmmakers schooled in documentary shorts have also been able to complete their first features, often through international co-production agreements (Nora de Izcue's *El Viento del Ayahuasca,* in co-production with Cuba [1982], for example). Although it has yet to produce great international hits in the eighties, the Peruvian cinema, with steady short and feature film production, seems to have taken its first steps toward becoming a cinema of national consequence.

BIBLIOGRAPHY

Dew, Edward, "A Letter from Peru," *Film Comment,* vol. III, no. 3, Summer 1965, p. 40.

THE PHANTASMAGORIA was the name of a popular magic lantern entertainment introduced in France in the late 1700s by a Belgian entertainer, Étienne Gaspard Robert (1763–1837), who went by the name of Robertson.

THE PHENAKISTISCOPE, an optical toy that proved the persistence of vision, was invented by the Belgian J.A.F. Plateau in 1832.

PHILIPPINES. The film industry in the Philippines has always been a fairly active one. The first theatre screening motion pictures was opened in Manilla by two Swiss businessmen on August 11, 1897. The first Filipino film, *Vida de Rizal,* was produced by an American named Edward M. Gross in 1912. The country's first film company, Malayan Movies, was founded in Manilla in 1917 by Jose Nepomuceno, who made his first film, *Dalagang Bukid* some two years later. Another major company was established by Vicente Salumbides in 1925, with his first production being *Miracles of Love*.

The first Filipino sound film, *Punyal na Ginto,* was made by Nepomuceno in 1932. The most important of companies to be formed in the sound era was LVN Pictures, which was founded by Doña Narcisa Buencamino de Leon in 1934. It produced the first film with a color sequence, *Ibong Adarva* (1941); the first postwar film, *Orasang Ginto* (1946); and the first all-color film, *Batalyon XIII* (1949). LVN ceased production in 1961, but continued as a postproduction facility. It recommenced production in 1977 with *Kung Mangarap Ka't Magising/If You Dream and Wake Up,* directed by the founder's grandson, Mike de Leon. In all, LVN Pictures produced some 350 films.

Aside from LVN, the other two major contemporary production companies were Premiere Productions and Sampaguita Pictures, both of which ceased operations by the seventies. That decade marked the ascendancy of the independent producer, with new directors including Lino Brocka, Ishmael Bernal, and Eddie Romero. Filipino films have received little critical attention outside of the country and are generally noted for the sexual and violent nature of their content.

In 1981, former president Ferdinand Marcos created the Filipino Motion Picture Film Board to oversee the activities of the Film Fund, the Film Archives, and the Board of Standards (which is responsible for film censorship). A year later, the organization was superseded by the Experimental Cinema of the Philippines. On January 19, 1982, the first Manilla International Film Festival opened, through the organization of Imelda Marcos. It ran for two years. The film industry and the Marcos regime were closely linked, with movie stars campaigning for the deposed president and theatres lowering prices in his support.

The major Filipino feature of the eighties is *The Sultan and the Emperor,* a co-production with the People's Republic of China, which Eddie Romero directed in 1987.

More than one hundred features a year are produced in the Philippines with a shooting schedule for each of between two weeks and four months. The industry is very highly taxed. There are more than nine hundred theatres in the country, and a quota law requires that 10 percent of all films screened be Filipino.

BIBLIOGRAPHY

Cruz, Isagani R. *Movie Times.* Manilla: National Book Store, 1984.

Guerrero, Rafael Ma. *Readings in Philippine Cinema.* Manilla: Experimental Cinema of the Philippines, 1983.

PHOENIX FILM COMPANY was a Budapest (Hungary) production company of the silent era, which made three features in 1917–1918 starring Bela Lugosi. The first, *Az Ezredes/The Colonel* (1917), was directed by Mihaily Kertész, who was to come to the United States and change his name to Michael Curtiz.

PHONO-CINÉ THÉÂTRE was the name of an entertainment, presented at the 1900 Paris Exposition, whereby great entertainment figures of the day, including Sarah Bernhardt, Coquelin, and Little Tich, were both seen and heard through the synchronization of film with sound on cylinders.

PHOTOSONOR was a French production company of the thirties and forties, with studios at Courbevoie. The company was founded in 1932, and its first feature production was *La Maternelle* (1933), directed by Jean Benoit-Levy.

THE PICTUREGOER, one of the most popular of all British fan magazines, was published from May 30, 1931, through April 23, 1960. However, it had commenced life as *Pictures and the Picturegoer* in 1911. Its only major competitors were *Film Weekly**, which merged with it in 1939, and *Picture Show**.

BIBLIOGRAPHY
Slide, Anthony, editor. *International Film, Radio, and Television Journals.* Westport, Conn.: Greenwood Press, 1985.

PICTURE SHOW was a popular British fan magazine from 1919 through 1960. Like its competitor, *Picturegoer**, it was published on a weekly basis.

BIBLIOGRAPHY
Slide, Anthony, editor. *International Film, Radio, and Television Journals.* Westport, Conn.: Greenwood Press, 1985.

PINEWOOD STUDIOS. In an effort to create a British studio to rival the best of Hollywood, a builder named Charles Boot acquired Heatherden Hall, with its one hundred acres of grounds at Iver Heath, twenty miles west of London, in May 1935. J. Arthur Rank, also interested in raising the status of British films, joined Boot in the venture. The name Pinewood was chosen by Boot in a conscious effort to imitate Hollywood. Nine months after the first brick had been laid, Pinewood Studios were officially opened on September 30, 1936. The first film on the floor of what was described as the most modern studio complex in the world was Herbert Wilcox's *London Melody* (1937), which had been started at Elstree Studios*. The first production to be completely filmed at Pinewood was Carol Reed's *Talk of the Devil* (1936), which had commenced shooting under the title of *A Man with Your Voice.*

The studios were continually active until the Second World War, when they were requisitioned by the government, and served as a factory for the Royal Mint, offices for Lloyds of London, and as a base for the Royal Air Force and Crown Film Units*. On April 4, 1946, the studios were officially reopened. The first production was Frank Launder and Sidney Gilliat's *Green for Danger* (1946). In 1947, two classic British films were shot there, Michael Powell and Emeric Pressburger's *The Red Shoes* and David Lean's *Oliver Twist.*

In the forties, all of the major production companies with links to the Rank Organization* shot at Pinewood, and in 1949, following a major reorganization of the latter, all Rank film production was concentrated there. In 1960, 20th Century-Fox hired Pinewood's full-service facilities for the production of *Cleopatra,* but because of Elizabeth Taylor's illness and particularly foul weather, the film was eventually shot in Italy. Pinewood did, however, serve as the site for the production of the 1964 comedy, *Carry on Cleo*. In 1962, Pinewood began a long association with the production of the James Bond* films. In May 1987, the studios became a strictly rental facility, offering no ancillary production offices.

Address: Iver Heath, Bucks SL0 0NH, United Kingdom.

BIBLIOGRAPHY

Low, Rachael. *Film Making in 1930s Britain*. London: George Allen & Unwin, 1985.

Perry, George. *Movies from the Mansion: A History of Pinewood Studios*. London: Elm Tree, 1982.

Pulleine, Tim, "Home-Counties Hollywood," *Stills,* no. 9, November-December 1983, pp. 76–78.

"Special 66-page Section Celebrating the 50th Anniversary of Pinewood Studios," *Screen International,* no. 567, October 9, 1986.

Whitehead, David, "Pinewood's Progress," *Movie Maker,* vol. XVI, no. 7, July 1982, pp. 408–409.

PLAN SÉQUENCE (Shot Sequence) is a French expression used to describe a scene with only one shot. Director Miklós Janscó is noted for this approach to filmmaking, although the French usually use the term with reference to the films of Jean Renoir.

POLAND. Films were first screened in Poland in Cracow on November 14, 1896, and the country's first cinematographer, Boleslaw Matuszewski, filmed actualities for the Lumière brothers between 1896 and 1898. National film production dates from 1910, when a number of companies were formed. The country had a considerable number of production companies—more than 120 active between 1919 and 1929—but the majority produced only one or two features during their existence. One major star emerged in Poland in the teens, Pola Negri (1894–1988), who began her screen career in 1914. However, such was her fame that she abandoned Polish cinema for Germany and later Hollywood.

Poland's most important director of the twenties was Aleksander Hertz, whose *Strzał/The Shot* (1921) helped bring success to actress Jadwiga Smosarska. Other major directors of the twenties were Wiktor Biegański, Henryk Szaro, Leon Trystan, and Jośef Lejtes. Michael Waszyński directed the country's first talkie, *Kult Ciała/The Cult of Flesh* in 1929.

Aleksander Ford (born 1908), a director whose career was to last well into the seventies, made his debut in the late twenties and directed his first feature in 1930. Ford's first sound feature, *Legion Ulicky/Legion of the Street* proved to be the most popular feature released in Poland in 1932. In 1943, Ford helped organize the Polish Army Film Command in the USSR, in association with Jerzy Bossak.

Generally, Poland produced an average of twenty features a year in the thirties. In a typical year, 1936, the total number of Polish films released was 124, of which 23 were features. There were 741 theatres operational in Poland in 1937. The Polish film industry was almost totally destroyed during the Second World War, although cameramen risked their lives during the war, covertly filming such events as the 1944 uprising in Warsaw. At the close of the Second World War, only one theatre was extant, along with one makeshift studio in Łódż.

Between 1946 and 1956, only forty features were produced, but in the late fifties Polish cinema began to blossom and quickly gained international recognition thanks largely to the work of Andzej Munk (1921–1961) and Andrzej Wajda (born 1926). Munk, who was killed in a car accident, began directing features in the mid fifties; he is best remembered for *Eroica* (1957) and *Pasażerka/The Passenger* (1963), which was completed after his death with the use of still photographs.

Andrzej Wajda heralded the new Polish cinema in 1954 with his first feature film, *Pokolenie/Generation*. He followed it with two other major productions, *Kanal* (1957) and *Popiól i diament/Ashes and Diamonds* (1958). The star of *Generation* and *Ashes and Diamonds* was Zbigniew Cybulski (1927–1967), who died in a railway accident at the height of his fame. He personified the young Polish people of his generation, and he gained international acclaim as an actor in the mold of James Dean or Marlon Brando.

In the sixties, two new directors who emerged were Jerzy Kawalerowicz and Wojciech Has, both of whom directed major epics, with which the Polish cinema became fixated during the decade. The former directed *Faraon/Pharaoh* (1965), while Has was responsible for *Rękopis znaleziony w Saragossie/The Saragossa Manuscript* (1965). Kawalerowicz also gained critical and commercial success with *Matka Joanna od Aniołów/Mother Joan of the Angels* (1961).

Poland's directors were notable for their ability—in a Communist country—to work elsewhere. Wajda spent most of the sixties outside of the country, and, indeed, when he does return to Poland, as with *Kronika wypadkow milosnych/A Chronicle of Amorous Accidents* (1985), it is a cause for celebration in the industry. Other Polish directors of note who left the country in the sixties include Jerzy Skolimowski, animator Walerian Borowczyk, and Poland's most famous emigré, Roman Polanski.

Among the Polish directors who made names for themselves in the seventies are Krzysztof Zanussi and Krzyysztof Kieslowski.

The Polish cinema encourages independent production through the formation of "Creative Groups," financed by the state but run by a creative group of director, writer, etc. For example, Wajda heads the "X" Unit. Initially responsible for all aspects of production, the business side was taken away from the groups in 1969.

Since the sixties, an average of thirty features a year have been produced in studios in Łódż, Warsaw, and Wroclaw, together with some four hundred short subjects and a newsreel, produced at six smaller studios. There are three animation studios, Featurette, in Warsaw, SE-MA-FOR Łódż and Cartoon Film Studio in Bielsko-Biala. The number of theatres, all state-run, has remained at around three thousand since the sixties, and these theatres are complemented by screenings at some two hundred film societies. The export and import of films is controlled by Film Polski*.

BIBLIOGRAPHY

Banaszkiewicz, Wladyslaw. *Contemporary Polish Cinematography*. Warsaw: Polonia, 1962.

Bukowiecki, Leon, "Polish Cinema after World War II," *Film Culture,* vol. IV, no. 16, 1958, pp. 7–10.

Coates, Paul. *The Story of the Lost Reflection*. London: Verso, 1985.

Fuksiewicz, Jacek. *Film and Television in Poland*. Warsaw: Interpress, 1976.

Hibbin, Nina. *Eastern Europe: An Illustrated Guide*. New York: A.S. Barnes, 1969.

Liehm, Mira. *The Most Important Art*. Berkeley: University of California Press, 1977.

Michalek, Boleslaw, "The Polish Drama," *Sight & Sound,* vol. XXIX, no. 4, Autumn 1960, pp. 198–200.

Moskowitz, Gene, "The Uneasy East," *Sight & Sound*, vol. XXVII, no. 3, Winter 1957–58, pp. 136–140.

Paul, David W., editor. *Politics, Art, and Commitment in the East European Cinema*. New York: St. Martin's Press, 1983.

Stoil, Jon Michael. *Cinema beyond the Danube*. Metuchen, N.J.: Scarecrow Press, 1974.

Sulik, Boleslaw. *A Change of Tack*. London: British Film Institute, 1976.

Whyte, Alistair. *New Cinema in Eastern Europe*. New York: Studio Vista, 1971.

POLITIQUE DES AUTEURS. See AUTEUR THEORY

POLYVISION. Similar to Cinerama, Polyvision was created by Abel Gance (1889–1981) for the climactic sequences of his feature *Napoléon,* which received its world premiere on April 7, 1927, at the Paris Opéra. Polyvision consisted of three screens, sometimes with one image stretching across all screens, sometimes with complementary images on each screen, projected from three synchronized projectors. A special Tryptich camera, invented by Gance and built by André Debrie, was used to photograph the sequences. The system was christened Polyvision by critic Émile Vuillermoz, and later renamed Magirama.

BIBLIOGRAPHY

Brownlow, Kevin. *Napoleon*. New York: Alfred A. Knopf, 1983.

PORTUGAL. The Portuguese film industry has never been a major one; approximately one hundred features have been produced in the country and less than four hundred theatres are in operation. The first fictional short to be made in Portugal was *Os crimes de Diogo Alves/The Crimes of Diogo Alves,* directed in 1911 by João Correia. The most important figure in Portuguese film history is José Leitaõ de Barros (1896–1967), who established the first major film company in Portugal, Lusitañia Film, in 1918, and made the country's first sound feature, *A Severa/The Severe Woman* in 1931. (The sound was actually dubbed in France, and the first sound film to be completely made in Portugal was de Barros' 1933 production, *A Cançâo de Lisboa/Song from Lisbon.*)

With the advent of fascism in Portugal, through the creation of a corporate state in 1933, and the strengthening of the power of dictator Antonio de Oliveira Salazar, the film industry concentrated on political subjects such as *A Revoluçâo de Maio/The May Revolution* (1937) and *Feitiço do Império/Imperial Spell* (1940). De Barros established Tobis Studios in 1937, named after the German company and with backing from the Nazis. A major director from this period was António Lopes Ribeibo.

Following the Second World War, during which Portugal remained neutral, the film industry concentrated on escapist fare, such as costume dramas, rural melodramas, and comedies. Directors active at this time include Arthur Duarte, Henrique Campos, Perdicão Queiroga, Manoel Guimarães, and Fernando Garcia.

It has been claimed by some critics that the new Portuguese cinema dates back to 1959, when new film magazines and directors first became active, and Italian Neo-realism* began to have an impact on Portuguese filmmakers. Certainly there was a new type of Portuguese feature to be seen in the sixties and early seventies, such as Manoel de Oliveira's *O acto da primavera/Spring Mystery Play* (1963) and *O passado e o presente/The Past and the Present* (1971); Paulo Rocha's *Os anos verdes/The Green Years* (1963); Fernando Lopes' *Belarmino* (1964); and António da Cunha Telles' *O cerco/Surrounded* (1970).

However it was the 1974 overthrow of Salazar that set Portuguese cinema free. The film industry was nationalized, censorship ceased, and the Portuguese Film Institute (Rua de S. Pedro de Alcantra, 45–1°, Lisbon 2) was created to produce, import, and export films. The government attempted to break up the distribution monopoly of two companies, Luso-Mundo and Intercine.

A number of documentaries of a political nature were produced, notably *As armas e o povo/Arms and the People* (1975), *Deus, Pátria, Autoridade/God, Country, Authority* (1975) and *A lei da terra/Law of the Earth* (1977). The feature that is generally credited with introducing postrevolutionary Portuguese cinema is Alberto Seixas Santos' *Brandos costumes/Sweet Customs* (1975), which is a combination of drama, musical revue, and documentary footage. (Santos utilized the same concept for a 1982 feature, *Gestos e fragmentos/Gestures and Fragments.*)

One director who continued to remain active, producing highly personal films at a slow pace was Manoel de Oliveira, who has made only six features in a career that dates back to 1931. His 1942 feature, *Aniki-Bobo,* was highly praised for its use of the conflicts of children as a metaphor for a world and society at war, but it was his features from the fifties and sixties that gained him an international reputation.

Following initial communistic enthusiasm, the country turned somewhat conservative by 1977, as did the film industry, which had gained in maturity but suffered from overlegislation. Twenty features were produced in 1977, but in later years the average was six. Portuguese films were overshadowed at the country's box office by films from the United States and United Kingdom. Co-productions with France and Germany were encouraged, and funding for films also came from Portuguese television. The 1974 revolution set the Portuguese film industry free, but it also created problems that the country has yet to resolve and that may leave the industry without any major hope of international success in the years ahead.

BIBLIOGRAPHY

Bessas, Peter, "Teetering on Brink of Ruin," *Daily Variety*, October 10, 1975, pp. 1, 6.

———, "Austerity Pains Exhibs, Distribs," *Variety*, March 23, 1977, pp. 7, 38.

———, "Portugal Vies for Its Film Identity," *Variety*, August 26, 1987, pp. 65, 72, 73.

Passek, Jean-Loup. *Le Cinéma Portugais*. Paris: Centre Georges Pompidou/L'Equerre, 1982.

Viera, Joao Luiz, and Robert Stam, "Portugal: Redeeming the Past," in *World Cinema since 1945*, editor William Luhr. New York: Ungar, 1987, pp. 490–498.

PRAESENS-FILM AG, the oldest extant film company in Switzerland, was founded in Zurich by Lazare Wechsler and Walter Mittelholzer in 1924. It is generally known to American audiences thanks to two 1945 features, directed by Leopold Lindtberg, *Die Letzte Chance/The Last Chance* and *Marie-Louise*. For the latter, Richard Schweizer, who was closely associated with the company, received an Academy Award for Best Writing (Original Screenplay).

Address: Munchhaldenstrasse 10, 8034 Zurich, Switzerland.

BIBLIOGRAPHY

Buache, Freddy. *Le Cinéma Suisse*. Lausanne: L'Age d'Homme, 1974.

THE PREVOST CAMERA, manufactured by the Attilio Prevost Company in Italy, was first introduced in 1922. It was a popular 35mm camera in pre–Second World War Europe.

THE PRIX FRANCE-CANADA is a biannual award, first presented in 1986, to two individuals who have been involved in official Franco-Canadian co-productions.

PRODUCTION NATAN was regarded as one of France's leading film producers in the late twenties. It was founded in 1926 by Bernard Natan, with its first two feature films being *La Châtelaine du Liban* (1926) and *Education de Prince* (1927). The latter starred Charlie Chaplin's leading lady, Edna Purviance. Prior to its demise in the thirties, the company was linked to Pathé*. It operated two studios: at Epinay and the Studio Réunis in Montmartre.

PRODUCTIONS ARTISTES ASSOCIÉS. Active from 1963, Productions Artistes Associés has co-produced films as varied as *Moonraker* (1978) in the "James Bond" series* and *La Cage aux Folles* (1978), the most successful foreign film

to be released in the United States. It has had a long association with director François Truffaut, having co-produced *La Mariée était en noir/The Bride Wore Black* (1967), *Baisers Volés/Stolen Kisses* (1968), *La Sirène du Mississippi/Mississippi Mermaid* (1969), *L'enfant sauvage/The Wild Child* (1969), *L'histoire d'Adèle H./The Story of Adèle H.* (1975), *L'homme qui aimait les femmes/The Man Who Loved Women* (1977), and *La chambre vert/The Green Room* (1978).
Address: 25/27 rue d'Astorg, 75008 Paris, France.

PROJEKTIONS-A.G.-UNION was formed in Germany in 1907, and constitutes the earliest attempt to gather theatres together into a single distribution network.

PROMETHEUS-FILM-GmbH was created in Germany in 1926 to distribute and screen Soviet films.

PUBLIC SCHOOLS. The British public school is often likened to the American private school, but it is far more rigid and tradition-bound than its American counterpart. Thomas Hughes' novel, *Tom Brown's Schooldays* is the quintessential story of an English public school, and it has been filmed in 1919 and 1951. James Hilton's novel, *Goodbye, Mr. Chips,* has had two screen incarnations, in 1939 with Robert Donat in the title role and in 1970 with Peter O'Toole. Ian Hays' play, *Bachelor Born,* was filmed as *Housemaster* in 1938. A far more cynical view of public school life was presented by Lindsay Anderson and David Storey in *If . . .* (1968), which was actually filmed at a British public school, Cheltenham College.

PUERTO RICO. There is little native filmmaking in Puerto Rico. Guastella Film Producers, Inc. is the largest producer on the island, specializing in television commercials, and it was founded by Roberto Guastella, who arrived penniless from Cuba in 1960. Documentaries are produced on a fairly regular basis, and, in 1986 three feature films were produced: *Reflejo de un desco/Reflection of a Desire, Nicholás y los demás/Nicholas and the Others,* and *La gran fiesta/The Big Party*. Directors in Puerto Rico include Ivonne María Soto, Jacobo Morales, Noel Quiñones, and Ramón Almódovar. Marcos Zurinaga's *Tango Bar* (1987), considered the definitive portrait on film of the tango, is a Puerto Rico/Argentinia co-production.

A 1918 fan magazine writer, Eugenia Keleher, commented that "It seems strange that thus far the advantages of Puerto Rico as the setting for scenarios have been unrecognized. For nowhere else could be found a land where mountains, sea and dense tropical vegetation combine to form a more ideally beautiful spot than in this romantic little continent of enchantment." In an effort to encourage the use of Puerto Rico for location shooting, the Puerto Rico Film Institute (G.P.O. Box 2350, San Juan 00936) has been established.

There are approximately 150 theatres on the island, and American films, subtitled in Spanish, are the most popular.

BIBLIOGRAPHY

Keleher, Eugenia, "The Movies in Puerto Rico," *Motion Picture Magazine,* January 1918, pp. 130–131.

Torres, José Artemio, "Puerto Rico," in *International Film Guide 1988,* editor Peter Cowie. London: Tantivy Press, 1987, pp. 304–305.

Q

QUEBEC PRODUCTIONS CORPORATION was formed in July 1946 by Paul L'Anglais and others. Based in Montreal, Canada, its first production was *La Forteresse/Whispering City* (1946), directed by Russian Fedor Ozep, and shot simultaneously in French and English. It later specialized in films of interest to Quebec audiences, and also embarked on a co-production with France, *Son copain/The Unknown from Montreal* (1950), directed by Jean Devaivre. The corporation ceased operations in the early fifties.

BIBLIOGRAPHY

Véronneau, Pierre, "The First Wave of Quebec Feature Films: 1944–1953," in *Self Portrait,* editor Pierre Véronneau. Ottawa: Canadian Film Institute, 1980.

"QUOTA QUICKIES." The term "Quota Quickies" entered the English language as a result of the passing of the 1927 Cinematograph Films Act in the United Kingdom. The Act, which remained in force for ten years, aimed at keeping British production alive in the face of American competition by building up a healthy British industry. In the twenties, the renting subsidiaries of American producers had forced British exhibitors to block book a large number of films in order to acquire one desirable feature. With the passing of the act, distributors were obliged to offer and exhibitors to screen a proportion or "quota" of British film footage, which had risen in annual steps to 20 percent by 1938. Block booking was not made illegal, but advance and blind booking were restricted. Seventy-five percent of the salaries of those engaged in the production of any film was to go to British subjects, and the screenwriter was to be British. Importers of foreign films found themselves in need of a large number of British features, and soon they were making, sponsoring, or acquiring films made solely for the quota, with the aim less to make a profit than to make as small a loss as possible.

It was maintained that the total cost of manufacturing quota quickies was no more than £1 per foot of released film. Quota Quickies provided a final refuge for many who had once been active in the making of silent films, but could no longer find employment. West End theatres rather than be forced to screen Quota Quickies for minimal audiences during peak hours would book the films, but screen them only in the mornings to empty houses.

British production expanded, but not as the government had intended. When the act came up for renewal in 1938, a government committee under Lord Moyne met to reconsider the quota. A new act was finally passed, but the committee that had framed the legislation attempted to ensure higher quality in British films by insisting that production costs should reach a certain minimum, and it was this minimum cost clause that effectively killed off cheap Quota Quickies. How effective the act might have been remains subject to argument, as the outbreak of the Second World War a year later brought major change to the industry.

BIBLIOGRAPHY

Low, Rachael. *Film Making in 1930s Britain*. London: George Allen & Unwin, 1985.

R

THE RANK ORGANIZATION, which celebrated its fiftieth anniversary in 1985, was founded by J. Arthur Rank (1888–1972), a British flour magnate and devout Methodist, who first became interested in the motion picture as a means of promoting his religious beliefs. In 1935, he joined forces with C.M. Woolf, formerly of Gaumont-British Corporation*, to form General Film Distributors (GFD), and in August of the same year, Rank became joint owner of Pinewood Studios*. When Alexander Korda's London Films* ran into financial problems in 1938, a consortium, headed by J. Arthur Rank, acquired its Denham Studios*. Also in 1939, Rank acquired Amalgamated Studios at Elstree, and moved into the exhibition field by becoming a board member of the Odeon Theatres* circuit. During the Second World War, fellow film magnates John Maxwell, Oscar Deutsch, and C.M. Woolf died, and thus Rank became chairman of Gaumont-British and Odeon Cinemas, and *the* undisputed major force in the British film industry.

In the postwar years, Rank did not fare as well. In 1947, a Labor government devised the ad valorum duty to deal with the hard currency shortage, and this put a limit on the profit revenue that could go to the United States. The major American producers and distributors retaliated by refusing to send any more films to the United Kingdom. With filmgoing at a peak, Rank and other British filmmakers were forced to produce more films, but, unknown to them, the Board of Trade was working out an agreement with the Americans to permit some money to leave the country and the remainder to be invested in British film production. The release of held-up American films flooded the country just as the British productions were ready, and by 1949, Rank had a bank debt of £16 million.

The company was saved by John Davis, who had joined Rank in 1939, and became managing director in 1948. He slashed production budgets, and regrouped production at Pinewood under the banner of J. Arthur Rank Production Ltd. Film production at Pinewood remained steady in the fifties, with the major successes being comedies starring Norman Wisdom, the "Carry On" series*, the "Doctor"* series, and the ever-endearing *Genevieve* (1954). In the mid-fifties, the more unprofitable theatres were closed, and by 1958, the Odeon and Gaumont circuits were so thinned that they could be merged into the Rank Circuit without public outcry or comment. John Davis expanded Rank's interests into bingo, electronics, catering, and television. Profits for 1960 were £7 million. In the sixties, Rank embarked on a series of co-productions with major American companies, and began a ten-year association with 20th Century-Fox, first as joint owners of the company and for the latter five years as sales agents.

Today, the Rank Organization includes many diverse companies involved in vacations and recreation, hotels and catering, precision industry and lighting, as well as film and television services. The subsidiary film and television companies comprise Pinewood Studios Ltd., Rank Advertising Films Ltd., Rank Audio Visual Ltd., Rank Film Distributors Ltd., Rank Film Laboratories Ltd., Rank Theatres Ltd., and Rank Video Services Ltd. Their turnover in 1986 was £137.9 million.

Address: 6 Connaught Place, London W2 2E2, United Kingdom.

BIBLIOGRAPHY

Falk, Quentin. *The Golden Gong: Fifty Years of the Rank Organization, Its Films and Its Stars*. London: Columbus Books, 1987.

Low, Rachael. *Film Making in 1930s Britain*. London: George Allen & Unwin, 1985.

Oakley, Charles. *Where We Came In: The Story of the British Cinematograph Industry*. London: George Allen & Unwin, 1964.

PEP (Political & Economic Planning). *The British Film Industry: A Report on Its History and Present Organization with Special Reference to the Economic Problems of British Feature Film Production*. London: PEP, 1952.

Perry, George. *Movies from the Mansion: A History of Pinewood Studios*. London: Elm Tree Books, 1982.

Sellers, Maurice et al. *Best of British: A Celebration of Rank Film Classics*. London: Sphere, 1987.

Spaos, John. *The Decline of the Cinema*. London: George Allen & Unwin, 1962.

"Special Supplement to Celebrate the 50th Anniversary of Rank Film Distributors," *Screen International*, no. 492, April 13–20, 1985, pp. 17–62.

Walker, Alexander. *Hollywood England: The British Film Industry in the Sixties*. London: Michael Joseph, 1974.

———. *National Heroes: British Cinema in the Seventies and Eighties*. London: Harrap, 1985.

Wood, Alan. *Mr. Rank: A Study of J. Arthur Rank and British Films*. London: Hodder & Stoughton, 1952.

REGANNE FILMS is a French producer, active since 1961, and best known for its co-production of two major features by Costa-Gavras: *Z* (1968) and *État de Siège/State of Siege* (1972).

Address: 14 rue de Chateau, 92250 La Garenne Colombes, France.

THE REICHSFILMKAMMER (or Chamber of Commerce) was created in the newly Nazi-dominated Germany on September 22, 1933, by minister of propaganda Joseph Goebbels. It was to control all aspects of film production in

Germany: economic, political, administrative, and artistic. Although it had little effect at first, by 1934 its power was being felt as German films were censored, subjects rejected as unsuitable for production, Jews hounded out of all aspects of German film production and distribution, and foreign films subjected to close scrutiny as to content and religion of those involved. Dr. Fritz Scheuermann was the first president of the Reichsfilmkammer. He was replaced in 1935 by Dr. Oswald Lehnich.

BIBLIOGRAPHY

Hull, David Stewart. *Film in the Third Reich.* Berkeley: University of California Press, 1969.

Leiser, Erwin. *Nazi Cinema.* New York: Macmillan, 1974.

RENAISSANCE FILMS DISTRIBUTION (RFD) was founded in Montréal, Canada, on April 25, 1945, by Joseph-Alexandre DeSève. It was a successor to the earlier Renaissance Films, created in 1944 by Charles Philipp. The latter had commenced production on *Le Père Chopin,* directed by the Russian filmmaker, Fedor Ozep. With financial backing from French investors, DeSève was able to build a studio in Montreal, but he was forced out of the company, which was renamed Les Productions Renaissance. Prior to its closure in 1950, Les Productions Renaissance produced *Docteur Le Gros Bill* (1949) and *Les lumières de ma ville* (1950), and also co-produced (with France) *Docteur Louise* (1949).

Aside from his involvement with Renaissance Film Distribution, DeSève was also associated with France Film, the sister company of Compagnie Cinématographique Canadienne (founded in 1930), which distributed French-speaking films in Quebec.

BIBLIOGRAPHY

Véronneau, Pierre, "The First Wave of Quebec Feature Films: 1944–1953," in *Self Portrait,* editor Pierre Véronneau. Ottawa: Canadian Film Institute, 1980, pp. 54–63.

RENTER is a generally obsolete term used in the United Kingdom for a distributor.

REVELATION FILMS was a British producer of industrial shorts and cartoons in the thirties. It later changed its name to Cartoon Films.

RIO DE JANEIRO has served as a backdrop for a handful of American features, including *The Girl from Rio* (1927), *Flying Down to Rio* (1934), *Carnival of Crime* (1964), and *Blame It on Rio* (1984). Its carnival atmosphere was well captured in the 1959 French-Italian-Brazilian co-production, *Orfeu Negro/Black Orpheus,* which received the Academy Award for Best Foreign Language Film.

ROBERT AWARDS. One of Denmark's two film awards—the other is the Bodil*—the Robert Awards were established by the Danmarks Film Akademi (The Danish Film Academy) (c/o Advokat Michael Rostock,Vestagervej 5, DK

2100 Copenhagen Ø) on March 10, 1984. The Danish Film Academy has been in existence since November 15, 1982, with its members consisting of producers, directors, screenwriters and others active in the film industry.

The award, which is named after Robert Jacobsen, who created the sculpture, is presented in the following categories: Danish Feature, Foreign Feature, Short Documentary, Short Fictional Film, Set Decoration, Costume Design, Special Effects/Lighting, Editing, Film Score, Screenplay, Cinematography, Supporting Actor, Supporting Actress, Actor, and Actress.

THE ROBERTO ROSSELINI AWARD was first presented at the Cannes Film Festival in 1987.

ROBIN HOOD. The legend of the English outlaw who robbed from the rich to give to the poor is found in literature dating from 1377. The first film to feature the outlaw is believed to be *Robin Hood and His Merry Men,* produced in the United Kingdom in 1909. The major films on the subject are *Robin Hood* (produced in the United States in 1921/1922, with Douglas Fairbanks in the title role), *The Adventures of Robin Hood* (produced in the United States in 1938, with Errol Flynn in the title role), and *The Story of Robin Hood* (an American production filmed in England in 1952, with Richard Todd in the title role). Richard Greene starred in the popular British television series, *The Adventures of Robin Hood,* which was seen on CBS from 1955 to 1958.

BIBLIOGRAPHY

Behlmer, Rudy, "Robin Hood on the Screen," *Films in Review,* vol. XVI, no. 2, February 1965, pp. 91–102.

ROMANIA. The first films were screened in Bucharest on May 27, 1896, and within a year the country's first newsreels were produced by Romanian film pioneer Paul Menu (1896–1973). The first custom-designed film theatre, the Carmen Sylva, opened in Bucharest in 1910, around which time the country's first major production company, Romania Film, was being formed by Constantin T. Theodorescu.

There was little production during the silent era, and by 1930, when the first talkie, *Ecaterina Teodoroiu,* was produced by Ion Niculescu Brună, there were 279 theatres in Romania. The number rose to 325 by 1937. Eighteen distributors were active in Bucharest prior to the Second World War, and there was strict censorship.

In 1934, the National Cinematograph Office was created, as part of the National Tourist Office, and it produced newsreels and documentaries. In all, some fifty features were made in Romania in the prewar years, and important early directors were Grigore Brezeaunu, Jean Mihail, and Jean Georgescu.

The film industry was nationalized following the Second World War, and three studios were created. Bucurşti Studios, at Buftea near Bucharest, is responsible for the production of features, while short subjects are made at the

Alexandru Sahia and Animafilm studios. An average of fifteen features a year were produced in the late sixties and early seventies, rising to twenty-five annually when the industry was decentralized into five autonomous companies in 1972 as part of an effort to stimulate production. Film production courses have been offered since the early fifties at the Institute of Theatrical and Cinematic Art in Bucharest.

As of 1987, 630 theatres were open in Romania, and there were many 16mm projection facilities serving rural areas. The import and export of film is handled by Romania Film (25 Julius Fucik Street, Bucharest).

BIBLIOGRAPHY

Cernat, Mauela. *A Concise History of the Romanian Film*. Bucharest: Editura Stiintifica si Enciclopedica, 1982.

Hibbin, Nina. *Eastern Europe: An Illustrated Guide*. New York: A.S. Barnes, 1969.

Liehm, Mira. *The Most Important Art: Eastern Europe Film after 1945*. Berkeley: University of California Press, 1977.

Paul, David W., editor. *Politics, Art, and Commitment in the East European Cinema*. New York: St. Martin's Press, 1983.

Stoil, Michael Jon. *Balkan Cinema*. Ann Arbor, Mich.: UMI Research Press, 1982.

ROME has served as a backdrop for probably more historical dramas than any other city. Among the more important are *The Roman* (1910), *Quo Vadis* (1912), *Nerone e Agrippina* (1913), *Nero* (1922), *Quo Vadis* (1923), *Ben-Hur* (1926), *Don Juan* (1926), *The Sign of the Cross* (1932), *Cleopatra* (1934), *Quo Vadis* (1951), *Androcles and the Lion* (1953), *Ben-Hur* (1969), *Spartacus* (1960), *Cleopatra* (1963), *The Fall of Rome* (1963), *The Fall of the Roman Empire* (1964), *The Agony and the Ecstasy* (1965), and *Fellini Satyricon*. Rome has also served as a location for at least four historical comedies: *Roman Scandals* (1933), *Fiddlers Three* (1944), *Carry on Cleo* (1964), and *A Funny Thing Happened on the Way to the Forum* (1966).

Italian features in which the city has played an important part include *Roma, città aperta/Rome Open City* (1945), *Sciuscià/Shoeshine* (1946), *Paisà/Paisan* (1946), *Ladri di biciclette/The Bicycle Thief* (1948), *Umberto D* (1952), *Lo sceicco bianco/The White Sheik* (1952), *La notti di Cabiria/The Nights of Cabiria* (1957), *La ciociara/Two Women* (1960), *Il gobbo/The Hunchback of Rome* (1960), *La dolce vita* (1960), *Il conformista/The Conformist* (1970), *Roma* (1972), and *Scherzo del destino agguato dietro l'angelo come un brigante di strada/A Joke of Destiny* (1983).

Among the American features that have utilized Rome are *The Eternal City* (1915), *The Eternal City* (1923), *One Night in Rome* (1924), *Never Take No for an Answer* (1952), *Roman Holiday* (1953), *Three Coins in the Fountain* (1954), *Seven Hills of Rome* (1958), *The Roman Spring of Mrs. Stone* (1961), *Two Weeks in Another Town* (1962), *The Pigeon That Took Rome* (1962), *Light in the Piazza* (1962), and *Gidget Goes to Rome* (1963).

ROUXCOLOR was a curious four-color system, developed by Armand and Lucien Roux in France between 1932 and 1934. It utilized four identical images on each frame of film. When the film was processed these four images were combined to form a color print which was, because of the size of the original images, somewhat ''fuzzy.'' The system was used for a short while after the Second World War, with the first feature in Rouxcolor being *La belle meuniere/The Miller's Beautiful Daughter,* directed by Marcel Pagnol in 1948 as a vehicle for his wife, Jacqueline Bouvier.

BIBLIOGRAPHY

Koshofer, Gert. *Color: Die Farben des Films.* Berlin: Spiess, 1988.

ROYAL COMMAND FILM PERFORMANCES date back in the United Kingdom to July 21, 1896, when film pioneer Birt Acres (1854–1918) screened a program of films, including footage of the Prince of Wales at the Cardiff Exhibition, at Marlborough House. The first performance before a British monarch took place on November 23, 1896, at Windsor Castle, before Queen Victoria. Royal Command Performances, presented to benefit various charities, at London theatres became an annual event from November 1, 1946, when King George VI saw *A Matter of Life and Death* (U.S. *Stairway to Heaven,* 1946) at the Empire Theatre, Leicester Square.

ROY EXPORT COMPANY ESTABLISHMENT was the name of the company created by Charles Chaplin (1889–1977) to distribute all of the films still controlled by the comedian in the fifties. The name came from Chaplin's mispronunciation of the French word for King, ''Roi,'' in reference to the French title for *A King in New York/Un Roi à New York.*

RUGBY. A game that originated on the playing fields of the English public school of the same name in 1823, rugby is popular not only in the United Kingdom and countries of the former British Empire, but also in many European communities.

It has been the subject of surprisingly few films, notably *Allez France/The Counterfeit Constable* (1966) and *This Sporting Life* (1967).

RURITANIA was a European country created by Anthony Hope (1863–1933) as the setting for his 1894 novel, *Prisoner of Zenda* (which was filmed in 1922, 1937, 1952, and 1979). Mythical kingdoms, such as Ruritania, have fascinated filmmakers, and among the features set in Ruritania-like surroundings are *The Merry Widow* (1925 and 1934), *Million Dollar Legs* (1932), *The Mouse That Roared* (1959), *Romanoff and Juliet* (1961), and *The Slipper and the Rose* (1976).

The Marx Brothers invented their own kingdom, Freedonia, for their 1932 classic, *Duck Soup*.

RUSHES is the British term for the unedited film footage shot each day and printed up for immediate viewing purposes. It translates into American film terminology as "dailies."

S

"ST. TRINIAN'S" COMEDIES. Ronald Searle had first introduced the pupils and staff of the English public (i.e., American private) school for girls, St. Trinian's, in a series of cartoon drawings for the British humor magazine, *Punch*. The cartoons were transferred to the screen by the producing-directing team of Frank Launder and Sidney Gilliat in four feature films: *The Belles of St. Trinian's* (1955), *Blue Murder at St. Trinian's* (1958), *The Pure Hell of St. Trinian's* (1961), and *The Great St. Trinian's Train Robbery* (1966). Actor George Cole was featured in each film as "Flash" Harry. The films proved so popular in the United States that there was talk of a 1978 CBS television series to be based on them.

SAMUELSON GROUP plc. The Samuelson family has long been an integral part of the British film industry. G.B. "Bertie" Samuelson (1888–1947) had entered the film industry in 1906 and by 1913 was responsible for an ambitious feature film on the life of Queen Victoria, *Sixty Years a Queen*. He hired George Pearson as his director, and, in 1914, opened the Worton Hall Studios at Isleworth, Middlesex, where his first production was an adaptation of Arthur Conan Doyle's *A Study in Scarlet* (1914). For the next six years, he produced an average of ten features a year at Worton Hall. In 1920, this extraordinary entrepreneur went to Hollywood, where he rented space at Universal Studios and produced two features.

Back at Worton Hall, Samuelson continued to produce features, and also turned to directing (which he continued to do through 1934). Unfortunately, Samuelson's career floundered with the coming of sound, and he turned, unsuccessfully, to new endeavors, including a mobile fish-and-chips service.

Three of Samuelson's four sons, Sydney, David, and Michael, followed their father into the film industry, gaining reputations as free-lance cameramen. Realizing the need for a rental source offering film equipment, the three brothers founded Samuelson Film Service Ltd. in the late fifties. A fourth brother, Anthony, joined the business later. The first feature the company serviced was *Tom*

Jones (1963), and shortly thereafter, Sydney Samuelson was able to arrange for his company to become exclusive European agent for the American Panavision cameras.

Today, as the multinational company, Samuelson Group plc, the company continues to rent film cameras and ancillary equipment through Samuelson Film Service. It also controls Samuelson Lighting, Cine-Europe, Cinevideo, Samuelson Communications, Theatre Projects Services, Zenith Lighting, Samuelson Vari-Lite, Sam-Cine Sales, Samuelson Video Equipment Sales, Samcine Cases, Samfreight, and Bray Film Studios Ltd. In France, it controls Samuelson Alga; and in Australia, Samuelson Film Service, John Barry Group, and Jands. In April 1986, it made its first move into the United States with the acquisition of Victor Duncan, which has the exclusive franchise for Panavision in Texas, Illinois, Michigan, and Georgia.

In 1986, the Michael Balcon Award was presented to Sydney Samuelson by the British Academy of Film and Television Arts* "for Outstanding British Contribution to Cinema."

Address: 303–315 Cricklewood Broadway, London NW2 6PQ, United Kingdom.

BIBLIOGRAPHY

Harden, Fred, "David Samuelson," *Cinema Papers,* no. 37, April 1982, pp. 149–150.

Henderson, Scott, "The Samuelson Story," *American Cinematographer,* vol. LX, no. 7, July 1979. pp. 694–700, 708–709 and 719–721.

Honri, Baynham, "The Samuelson Saga," *The Silent Picture,* no. 5, Winter 1969/70, pp. 2–7.

SANDREW FILM & TEATER AB has been a major force in the Swedish film industry for more than fifty years. Its origins lie in the arrival of a fourteen-year-old farmer's son, named Anders Andersson, in Stockholm in 1901. With an elder brother, he decided to establish his own grocery store. Because another company was already named Andersson Brothers, Anders adopted the name of Sandrew after seeing it on a bottle of "Sandrews Port." The company flourished and became involved in real estate in the twenties, eventually, in 1926, acquiring the Metropol theatre in Stockholm.

While continuing to work in his grocery shop, Anders Sandrew acquired more theatres, and, in 1937, his company officially became AB Sandrew-Biograferna. That same year, Sandrew entered film production, and took over a Stockholm film studio in 1948. His first international success came in 1951 with the production of *Miss Julie,* directed by Alf Sjöberg. The company was equally involved in theatrical production, and entered the television field in 1954.

Anders Sandrew died in 1957, but by the terms of his will, his company became a non-profit foundation, whose earnings go for scholarships to young individuals in the arts and to provide financial assistance for elderly actors and actresses.

By the eighties, Sandrew Film & Teater AB was operating three legitimate theatres, eighty-six screens in twenty-three Swedish communities, one of the largest video companies in Sweden, a major film importing organization, and a production entity.

Address: Box 5612, 114 86 Stockholm, Sweden.

SASCHA-WIEN FILM was the amalgamation of two Austrian film companies, Sascha-Film GmbH and Wien-Film Gesellschaft mbH. The former was founded circa 1910 by Graf Alexander "Sascha" Kolowrat-Krakovsky and was the most important of early Austrian film producers. Wien-Film was established in 1938, following the Nazi occupation of Austria, and was noted for its wartime productions by Karl Hartl. The two companies were revitalized following Austrian independence in 1955, under the direction of Heinz Lazek and Dr. Arthur Klausberger, and began producing films for the German-speaking market. The company was further revitalized through foreign co-production arrangements, with its best known "international" features being *A Little Night Music* (1977) and *The Fifth Musketeer* (1979). It ceased operations in 1986.

BIBLIOGRAPHY

"Sascha-Wien Centerfold of Austrian Breakout from Limited Appeal," *Variety*, May 18, 1977, p. 70.

THE SCHÜFFTAN PROCESS combines live action with a painted background on a single frame of film. A large mirror is placed in front of the camera, reflecting the painting into its field of view. A portion of the mirror's reflective surface is removed in order that the live action may be seen through the mirrored glass, and the sequence is then filmed. The process is named after its inventor, Eugen Schüfftan (born 1893), who was a major cinematographer from the twenties through the fifties, active in Germany, France, the United States, and elsewhere. The Schüfftan process is believed to have been first used in the production of *Metropolis* (1927).

SCORPIO VERSTAPPEN FILMS N.V. Founded in 1965 as Scorpio Films N.V. by Pim de la Parra (born 1940) and Wim Verstappen (born 1937), this company was highly influential in the creation of the new Dutch cinema, producing a popular series of features and short subjects, which often bordered on exploitation, but which were well received by the critics. Its early successes include *Obsessions* (1969), *Blue Movie* (1971), and *Alicia* (1975).

Address: Nicolas Maesstraat 68, 1071 RC Amsterdam, Netherlands.

THE SCOTTISH FILM COUNCIL was created in 1934 as a voluntary organization, concerned primarily with the promotion of the use of film in education, and associated with the British Film Institute*. It sponsored the Scottish Central Film Library, and was a major supplier of audiovisual aids to Scottish schools. In the mid-sixties, a new director, Ronnie Macluskie, was appointed, and he expanded the activities of the organization in the educational technology field to such an extent that it was renamed, in 1974, the Scottish Council for Educational Technology. The cultural aspects of the organization were continued under the old name of the Scottish Film Council, which operates as a division of the Scottish Council for Educational Technology, but which may, in the future, be given independent status.

With a grant of almost half-a-million pounds a year, the Scottish Film Council is active in a number of areas. In 1976, it established the Scottish Film Archive, which has more than seven thousand titles on file and is a major resource for archival film relating to Scotland. The Scottish Archive Film for Education (SAFE) project, created in 1985, produces compilations of historical footage primarily for classroom use. Since 1982, the Scottish Film Production Fund has provided production and completion grants for more than sixty film and television projects, both documentary and fictional. The Scottish Training Trust has been active since 1985 in providing grants to full- and part-time film and television students. Regional theatres have been established and supported by the Scottish Film Council in Glasgow, Edinburgh, Stirling, Inverness, Dundee, Kirkcaldy, and Dumfries.

Funding for the Scottish Film Council is provided by the Scottish Education Department, and the organization is governed by a board, appointed by the Secretary of State for Scotland, the Convention of Scottish Local Authorities, and the Scottish Education Department.

Address: Dowanhill, 74 Victoria Crescent Road, Glasgow, G12 9JN, Scotland.

SCREEN INTERNATIONAL. The last major British trade paper, *Screen International* began life on September 6, 1975, and has been published ever since on a weekly basis. It has its origins in a number of other trade papers, including *Kinematograph Weekly**, *Daily Film Renter, The Cinema, The Daily Cinema,* and *Today's Cinema*. It is edited by popular British journalist, Peter Noble.

Address: Kingston House, 6–7 Great Chapel Street, London W1V 4BR, United Kingdom.

BIBLIOGRAPHY

Slide, Anthony, editor. *International Film, Radio, and Television Journals*. Westport, Conn.: Greenwood Press, 1985.

SENEGAL. A small African nation, which became independent of France in 1960, Senegal has one of the best-known film industries on the continent, and enjoyed a major tribute at New York's Museum of Modern Art in 1978. Ousmane Sembene is Senegal's most important director, with his films including *Borom Sarret* (1963), *Niaye* (1965), *Black Girl* (1966), *Taw* (1970), *Emitai* (1971), *Xala* (1974), and *Ceddo* (1977). Other Senegalese directors include Cheikh Tidiane Aw, Moussa Bathilly, Ben Diogaye Beye, Yves Badara Diagne, Djibril Diop-Mambety, Abdou Fari Faye, Ababacar Samb-Makharam, Blaise Senghor,

Momar Thiam, Mahama Johnson Traore, Paulin Soumanou Vieyra, and one female director, Safi Faye.

Curiously since its initial public recognition in the late seventies, little has been written on the country's film industry. Senegalese documentary filmmaker Baidy Dia announced plans for Senegalese-American co-production in 1981, but nothing appears to have come of the project.

BIBLIOGRAPHY

Gabriel, Teshome H. *Third Cinema in the Third World*. Ann Arbor, Mich.: UMI Research Press, 1982.

Perry, G.M., and Patrick McGilligan, "Ousmane Sembene: An Interview," *Film Quarterly*, Spring 1973, pp. 36–42.

"Senegal: Fifteen Years of an African Cinema: 1962–1977," 1978 Museum of Modern Art (New York) brochure.

SEQUENCE. Founded in 1946 by a group of film enthusiasts at England's Oxford University, *Sequence* published the first writings of Lindsay Anderson, Penelope Houston, and Gavin Lambert. Initially published by the Oxford University Film Society, the journal was later published, until its demise in 1952, in London.

BIBLIOGRAPHY

Slide, Anthony, editor. *International Film, Radio, and Television Journals*. Westport, Conn.: Greenwood Press, 1985.

SÉRIES PAX was the title given to a group of French films produced between 1920 and 1923, financed by Gaumont*, with Edgar Costil as executive producer and Léon Poirier as artistic director. Among the films in the series are Léon Poirier's *Le penseur* (1920) and Marcel L'Herbier's *El Dorado* (1921).

SERVICE PHOTOGRAPHIQUE ET CINÉMATOGRAPHIQUE DE L'ARMÉE was established in February 1915 by the French government to produce films on the French First World War effort. It was responsible for *La bataille de Verdun* (1916), *La guerre Anglaise* (1917), and a weekly newsreel, *Annales de la guerre*.

SHADOW PLAYS have an obvious relationship to the motion picture, and are generally considered under the heading of "precinema." They utilize jointed puppets whose shadows are projected on to a screen, and were popular entertainments in China, Java, and Turkey. When first introduced into Europe in the eighteenth century, they were usually described as *Ombres Chinoises*.

BIBLIOGRAPHY

Ceram, C.W. *Archaeology of the Cinema*. New York: Harcourt, Brace & World, undated (1985).

Cook, Olive. *Movement in Two Dimensions*. London: Hutchinson, 1963.

SHAKAI-MONO is a genre in Japanese cinema in which the films make social commentaries.

SHAW BROTHERS (HONG KONG) LTD. The most successful of Asian producers and exhibitors and the company most associated with Kung Fu movies is Shaw Brothers. The company maintains a major studio complex, Shaw's Movie Town, on Hong Kong's Clearwater Bay, with ten sound stages, a laboratory, editing facilities, and music scoring building. It operates theatre chains in Hong Kong, Taiwan, Malaysia, and Singapore. The present company was established in 1958 and became public in 1971.

The man responsible for the success of Shaw Brothers is Sir Run Run Shaw (he was knighted in 1977), the son of a wealthy Shanghai textile factory owner. Run Run, with his brother Run Me (died 1985) had become involved with motion pictures in the early twenties, operating a theatre in Shanghai and producing at least one film. The brothers moved to Singapore, and built up a successful operation there prior to the Japanese invasion.

Although Shaw Brothers is primarily known for its commercial productions intended for Asian audiences, it has produced a number of artistic features, including *Ch'ing Kuo Ch'ing Ch'eng/The Empress Dowager* (1975), *Hong Kong, Hong Kong* (1983), and *Love in a Fallen City* (U.S. *Reigning Beauty,* 1984). In 1966, Shaw Brothers purchased the Europa Theatre on Beverly Boulevard in Los Angeles, to introduce its films to American audiences, and subsequently the company also became involved in exhibition in the United Kingdom. Until the early eighties, Shaw Brothers had produced an average of forty features a year, but production was severely curtailed by the middle of the decade, and late in 1986 there were rumors that it was considering ceasing production.

Address: Lot 220, Clearwater Bay Road/P.O. Box 5638, Kowloon, Hong Kong.

BIBLIOGRAPHY

Birns, Jack, "The Golden Claw of Run Run Shaw," *Los Angeles Times* Calendar, January 8, 1978, pp. 1, 20, 23.

Greenfeld, Josh, "A Czar Rises in the East," *Oui,* April 1974, pp. 55–56, 103–106.

"Shaw Bros. in Perennial Bloom," *Variety,* May 14, 1975, p. 75.

Tobias, Mel, "Shaw Bros. Keeps Pace with S.E. Asia's Tastes," *Variety,* October 24, 1984, pp. 295, 372.

SHEFFIELD PHOTO CO. Founded in 1882 as a photographic concern by Frank Mottershaw, the Sheffield Photo Co., located in the Northern British city of the same name, was active as a film producer from 1900 to 1909. Its most important film was *A Daring Daylight Robbery,* released in 1903.

BIBLIOGRAPHY

Low, Rachael, and Roger Manvell. *The History of the British Film: 1896–1906*. London: George Allen & Unwin, 1948.

Sutherland, Allan T., "The Yorkshire Pioneers," *Sight & Sound,* vol. XLVI, no. 1, Winter 1976/77, pp. 48–51.

SHELL FILM UNIT. Synonymous with the terms "sponsored film" or "industrial film" is the British Shell Film Unit. In 1933, the Shell Oil Group began to study what were then new concepts in public relations and public information, and invited John Grierson to make a report on the use of films. From this the Shell Film Unit was established, and Edgar Anstey was engaged as its first producer early in 1934. The Unit's first film was *Airport,* a day at Croydon Airport, released in 1935. Begun at the same time but delayed by difficulties in production was *Power Unit,* which was a significant example of the Shell style. It uses animated diagrams prepared by Francis Rodker, an engineering draftsman, to explain the principles of the internal combustion engine. Rodker's animation work was to be featured in many subsequent Shell productions.

Meanwhile, it had been decided that while members of the Unit would be an integral part of Shell staff, creative direction would be engaged from outside on a consultancy basis through the Associated Realist Film Producers Group. The first appointment was Arthur Elton, and this system of external producers certainly helped to achieve the variety and wider circulation of Shell films. The Unit's tenth film, released in 1939, was Geoffrey Bell's *Transfer of Power,* which received a rare tribute for a documentary, a rave review from film critic Dilys Powell in the London *Sunday Times.*

During the Second World War, the Unit was turned over to the Ministry of Information, for which it made films on civil defense training, and the Admiralty, for which it made detailed instructional films on radar and Asdic. In the mid-fifties, Shell followed the general trend of moving into color, and produced its first spectacular, *The Rival World,* directed by Bert Hanstraa. It shows the plundering by insects of man's crops and remains one of the most popular items in the Shell Library. The Unit still thrives today, with nine or ten films in various stages of production at one time. The films are used internally by Shell companies around the world, but are also available on free loan to the public from the Shell Film Library as part of a continuing public relations exercise. The Library handles forty thousand bookings a year, with an average audience of seventy-five for each booking, thus reaching an audience annually of some three million, of which more than two-thirds are children or students.

Address: Shell Center, PAC/11, London SE1 2NA, United Kingdom.

BIBLIOGRAPHY

Legg, Suart, "Shell Film Unit: Twenty-One Years," *Sight & Sound,* vol. XXIII, no. 4, April-June 1954, pp. 209–212.

Thomas, Dora, "The Shell Film Unit," *Eyepiece,* vol. IV, no. 2, March/April 1983, pp. 48–49.

Thompson, Mike, "Global Film-Aware Shell," *Audio Visual,* no. 129, September 1982, p. 30.

SHEPPERTON STUDIOS came into being thanks to a young Scotsman named Norman Loudon, who ran a successful company producing a novelty item called "Flicker Books." Deciding to enter film production, he purchased a sixty-acre estate and mansion at Littleton Park, Shepperton, southwest of London. The ballroom was immediately converted into a sound stage and a second stage created in another part of the mansion. In February 1932, the opening of Sound City Film Producing and Recording Studios was announced, and production began that summer. Like other studios, it was initially involved in the production of "Quota Quickies*." The first nine films made there were all shot in the mansion.

By the late thirties, Loudon had built four large sound stages and two smaller ones, making a total number of eight stages, which were available for rental. Changes in the quota system threatened the future of the studio, but with the outbreak of the Second World War, it was occupied by the Air Ministry.

The first feature film made at Shepperton after the War was *London Town* (U.S. *My Heart Goes Crazy,* 1946), starring Sid Field, and directed by American Wesley Ruggles. Loudon then sold his interest in the studio to British Lion*, which Korda had recently acquired. The latter reestablished London Films* at Shepperton with an adaptation of Oscar Wilde's *An Ideal Husband* (1948), directed by Korda and costumed by Cecil Beaton. In 1953, another sound stage was added, and in 1958 British Lion carried out reconstruction of the four main stages, making Shepperton the largest production center in Europe.

In 1964, the British government decided to dispose of British Lion, but with the right to veto the selling off of Shepperton Studios except under well-defined circumstances. This eliminated the property speculators and control passed to a consortium headed by Michael Balcon. During the boom years of the sixties, Shepperton broke even, but as early as 1969, it was incurring escalating losses. In 1972, "take-over tycoon" Jim Bentley made a bid for British Lion, including Shepperton Studios. His intention was to sell part of the lot for property development, but before this happened, his company was taken over. A very unsettled period followed until the studio was acquired by Mills & Allen, which operated it as a strictly rental facility. In turn, Mills & Allen sold the studios in 1984 to Lee Electric (Lighting) Ltd., billed as the world's largest film and TV lighting hirers. Lee had interesting expansion plans for Shepperton, but these were delayed until late 1985, when the government made over the gold-controlled share to them.

Recent productions at Shepperton have included Neil Jordan's *The Company of Wolves* (1985), David Lean's *A Passage to India* (1984), the musical *Absolute Beginners* (1985), and the television mini-series, *Ellis Island* (1984).

Address: Studios Road, Shepperton, Middlesex, TW17 OQD, United Kingdom.

BIBLIOGRAPHY

Glaessner, Verina, "British Lion Sellout," *Time Out,* no. 122, June 16–22, 1972, p. 9.

Leader, Raymond, "Shepperton Comes of Age," *ABC Film Review,* February 1954, pp. 10–11.

Low, Rachael. *Film Making in 1930s Britain*. London: George Allen & Unwin, 1985.

Walker, Alexander. *National Heroes: British Cinema in the Seventies and Eighties*. London: Harrap, 1985.

SHINTOHO (literally "New Toho") was founded in the spring of 1947 as a breakaway from its parent company, Toho*, following a major strike there. It occupied the Tokyo Hasei Studios, and its first film, *Toho Senichi-ya/A Thousand and One Nights with Toho,* was also the first film of director Kon Ichikawa.

In the early fifties, it experienced financial difficulties, and began producing quickly and cheaply made films under its chairman of the board, Munehide Tanabe, who had close ties to Toho. Heavier losses in 1955 resulted in Mitsugu Okura's becoming head of the company. He introduced a policy of producing films for mass audiences, and was responsible for the widescreen epic, *Meiji tenno to nich-ro Daisenso/The Empress Meiji and the Great Russo-Japanese War*. He also was responsible for "nude" films, starring Michiko Maeda.

SHOCHIKU CO. LTD. One of Japan's three major entertainment companies, involved in film, video, and the legitimate theatre, Shochiku can trace its beginnings back to 1896, when it was founded by twin brothers, Matsujiro Shirai and Takejiro Otani to produce and present Kabuki theatre (which it still does). The company entered film production in 1920; built studios at Kamata, on the outskirts of Tokyo; and subsidized the Shochiku Cinema Institute, to train young filmmakers. It attempted American-style productions, beginning with *Shima no Onna/Island Woman* (1920), directed by Henry Kotani, who was brought over from the United States, but stayed only a couple of years with the company. Shochiku had really wanted to sign the best-known Japanese star of American films, Sessue Hayakawa.

In 1936, it closed the Kamata studios, and opened new ones at Ofuna. Throughout the decade, the company was involved in intense rivalry with Toho*, and no sooner was that settled than it was in trouble with the Japanese government during the Second World War for its failure to produce a sufficient number of nationalistic films.

In the mid-fifties, Shochiku was the first Japanese company to produce widescreen films. Long associated with directors such as Kenji Mizoguchi, Yasujiro Ozu, Nagisa Oshima, and Akira Kurosawa, the company has proudly described itself as "the studio of the director." Long a major importer of films through its wholly owned subsidiary, Fuji Pictures Corp., Shochiku changed the name of that division to Shochiku-Fuji on April 1, 1983. In August 1986, it formalized its ties with Warner Bros., whose films it has released in Japan for many years.

The company's logo embraces bamboo and pine, both of which are nationalistic Japanese symbols. It adopted these symbols because of the names of the founders of the company; Matsu means pine and Take means bamboo. The Chinese letters from Matsu can be pronounced Sho, and, similarly, the Chinese letters for Take can be pronounced Chiku.

Address: 13-5 Tsukiji 1 Chrome, Chuo-Ku, Tokyo 104, Japan.

BIBLIOGRAPHY

"Okuyama on the Shochiku Strategy," *Variety,* March 4, 1987, pp. 51, 60.

Tanaka, Koki, "Shochiku, Its Great Directors and I," *Variety,* March 4, 1987, p. 56.

Thomas, Kevin, "Shochiku—Thy Name Is Diversity," *Los Angeles Times* Calendar, August 12, 1979, pp. 34, 36.

SINGAPORE. Although a few films have been made in the island republic since 1960, Singapore has no film industry, and has held little appeal as a location for foreign filmmakers. Filmgoing, once very popular, has been affected by the introduction of video, and the numbers of theatres has been cut in half from over eighty in the early eighties to around forty by 1987. The majority of the theatres are controlled by the Shaw Brothers* and the Cathay Organization. Censorship of films, particularly with regard to sex and violence, is very rigid through the Ministry for Culture, Science, and Technology.

The main body concerned with film as an art form is the Singapore Film Society (Maxwell Road, P.O. Box 3714, Singapore 9057), which was founded in 1959. The first Singapore International Film Festival was held in February-March 1987.

Singapore has long been regarded as a major center for film, video, and recording piracy, but in 1987 passed a copyright law designed to stamp out such activity.

BIBLIOGRAPHY

Marshall, Fred, "The Cinema in Singapore," *Cinema India-International*, vol. IV, no. 1, 1987, p. 110.

THE 16mm FILM EXHIBITORS' GUILD was a short-lived British organization, founded in 1948, to represent the interests of mobile 16mm exhibitors, primarily in the west of England. It was particularly concerned with improving the standard of 16mm screenings in rural areas.

THE SLADE FILM HISTORY REGISTER was created in 1969 at the suggestion of former director Thorold Dickinson, who was then professor of film at the Slade School of Fine Art at London's University College. It was, and is, intended to serve as a national register of film materials. In June 1975, funding for the project was no longer available, and its assets were transferred from the Slade School to the British Universities Film Council, which continues the project, in a limited fashion. A 1976 working party reviewing the Register's work recommended the addition of television materials.

Issue sheets for the various British newsreels, gathered together by the Slade History Register, have been issued on microfiche by Graphic Data Publishing (197–213 Lyham Road, London SW2 5PY, United Kingdom).

Address: British Universities Film and Video Council, 55 Greek Street, London W1V 5LR, United Kingdom.

SOCCER, the most popular game in the world (outside of the United States), has been the subject of countless feature films from countries as varied as the United Kingdom, Japan, Italy, Germany, Argentina, Czechoslovakia, Portugal,

USSR, Romania, Yugoslavia, Spain, Israel, Austria, Korea, India, Bulgaria, and Sweden. Among the more important features are *Adventures of a Football* (1914), *The Cup Final Mystery* (1914), *The Winning Goal* (1920), *The Great Game* (1930), *Goal!* (1936), *The Arsenal Stadium Mystery* (1939), *Cup-Tie Honeymoon* (1947), *Up for the Cup* (1950), *The Great Game* (1953), *Small Town Story* (1953), *Rattle of a Simple Man* (1964), *Goal!* (1966), *Yesterday's Hero* (1979), *The Club* (1980), *Coup de tête/The Hothead* (1980), *Victory* (1981), and *Gregory's Girl* (1982).

BIBLIOGRAPHY

Robertson, Patrick, "Soccer Filmography," in *Movie Facts and Feats*. New York: Sterling, 1980, pp. 81–82.

Zucker, Harvey Marc, and Laurence J. Babich. *Sports Films: A Complete Reference*. Jefferson, N.C.: McFarland, 1987.

SOCIÉTÉ CINÉMATOGRAPHIQUE DES AUTEURS ET GENS DES LETTRES (SCAGL). A subsidiary of Pathé*, SCAGL was established by Pierre Decourcelle and Eugene Guggenheim, from an idea by Edmond Benoît, and was an active French film producer in the teens and early twenties. It was created primarily to produce literary classics, to be directed by André Capellani, and two of its first successes were Capellani's *Les Miserables* (1912) and Gérard Bourgeois' *Les Victimes de l'alcool* (1911). André Antoine, a major theatrical figure in France, joined the company as a director in 1914.

SOCIÉTÉ DES CINÉROMANS was a French production company, founded in the late teens by Jean Durand and René Navarre. In 1922, it was taken over by Jean Sapène, and commenced production of a series of popular serials, produced by Louis Nalpas, beginning with *Rouletabille ches les Bohemiens* (1922). Other of its serials are *Vidocq* (1923), *Tao* (1923), *Mandarin* (1923), and *Surcouf* (1925). Later in the decade, it entered feature film production, most notably co-producing Marcel L'Herbier's *L'Argent/Gold* (1929).

SOCIÉTÉ DES FILMS HISTORIQUES was founded in Paris in 1923 by Henry Dupuy-Mazuel and Jean-José Frappé to produce films of major French historical subjects. Its first production was Raymond Bernard's magnificent *Le miracle des loups/Miracle of the Wolves* (1924). Bernard's second feature for the company was *Joueur d'échecs,* released in 1927. Société des Films Historiques remained active through 1929, with its last productions including Henry Roussel's *Valse de l'adieu* (1928) and Jean Renoir's *Le tournoi dans la cité* and *Le bled* (both 1929). The last was produced with financial backing from the French government, and glorified French colonization of Algeria.

LA SOCIÉTÉ DES FILMS MARCEL PAGNOL was the name of the French company in the thirties, which produced the features of Marcel Pagnol (1895–1974), including *Fanny* (1932), *César* (1936) and *La femme du boulanger/The Baker's Wife* (1938).

SOCIÉTÉ DES FILMS SACHA GORDINE was a prominent French producer of the forties and fifties, whose features include Georges Lampin's *L'Idiot* (1946) and Max Ophüls' *La Ronde* (1950).

SOCIÉTÉ DES FILMS SONORES TOBIS was the French subsidiary of the German Tobis* that produced a number of major features in the early thirties, including *Sous les toits de Paris/Under the Roofs of Paris* (1930), *Le Million* (1931), *À Nous la Liberté* (1931), and *La Kermesse Héroïque* (1935).

LA SOCIÉTÉ EDIC (Edition et Diffusion Cinématographiques) was a French production company, founded in December 1938, and active through the forties. Its first feature was *Le Président Haudecoeur* (1939), directed by Jean Dréville.

SOCIÉTÉ GÉNÉRALE DE FILMS (SGF) was created in 1925 by Jacques Grinieff, a Russian emigré living in Paris, who was interested in film production. He took over a small company, Rodina, that had been formed in Paris in 1924 by other Russian exiles, and named Henri de Cazotte as president (succeeding Rodina's former president, Alexander d'Arbeloff). The company was to produce two of the French cinema's greatest silent classics, Abel Gance's *Napoléon* (1927) and Carl Theodor Dreyer's *La Passion de Jeanne d'Arc/The Passion of Joan of Arc* (1928). It was declared bankrupt in the early thirties.

SOCIÉTÉ GÉNÉRALE DU CINÉMA DU QUÉBEC. Aimed at the French-speaking Canadian filmmaker, the Société Générale du Cinéma du Québec was established in 1983, to provide financing of up to 60 percent of the total budget for feature and short film production. It does not fund television production, and offers grants of up to $500,000 for feature films, $75,000 for short subjects, and $150,000 for documentaries. One of the first major features supported by the Société Générale du Cinéma du Québec was Denys Arcand's *Le déclin de l'empire Américain/The Decline of the American Empire* (1986), which was nominated for an Academy Award as Best Foreign Language Film.

Address: 80 rue de Brésoles, Montréal, Québec H2Y 1U5, Canada.

BIBLIOGRAPHY

McCarthy, Todd, "Quebec Seeks Higher Int'l Film Profile," *Daily Variety,* November 11, 1987, pp. 6, 12.

"The SGC—Seeing Success," in *International Film Guide 1987,* editor Peter Cowie. London: Tantivy Press, 1986, pp. 39–42.

SOCIÉTÉ IVOIRIENNE DE CINÉMA, located in Abidjan, Ivory Coast, gained fleeting recognition in 1976, for its co-production of *La victoire en chantant/Black and White in Color,* the first feature to be directed by Jean-Jacques Annaud (born 1944), which received the Academy Award for Best Foreign Film. It was the first film from a black African nation to be so honored, although the reality was that all the other co-producers of the feature were European.

SOCIETY FOR CINEMA STUDIES. The British organization, the Society for Cinema Studies was formed in January 1959 at the initiative of Ernest Lindgren, then curator of the National Film Archive, "with the object of encouraging historical research into all aspects of the cinematograph, both in the British Isles and abroad." Its membership was small, and the Society never made much of an impact, aside from publication of a journal, *Cinema Studies,* from 1960 to 1967. The three honorary secretaries of the Society were Rosemary Heaword, Anthony Slide, and David Francis. Its papers are housed at the British Film Institute*.

THE SOCIETY FOR EDUCATION IN FILM AND TELEVISION (SEFT) began life in the United Kingdom on October 28, 1950, as the Society of Film Teachers. Closely associated with the British Film Institute*, the Society is, as its name suggests, concerned with the promotion and furtherance of education in film and television. Between 1959 and 1968, it published a journal titled *Screen Education,* and since 1969, it has published a sister journal, *Screen,* concerned primarily with film theory. The Society became a limited company in April 1978.

Address: 29 Old Compton Street, London W1V 5PL, United Kingdom.

SOCIETY OF FILM DISTRIBUTORS. Founded in 1915, the Society of Film Distributors is a major British trade organization that promotes the interests of its members (including all the major distributors) as they affect other film organizations and government agencies. It began life as the Kinematograph Renters Society, whose initial aims were "mutual protection of trade interest; to cooperate with other branches of the trade for the protection of mutual interests; to confer with County Councils, Local Boards and other public bodies on matters affecting the trade; to arrange and promote the adoption of legal and equitable forms of contracts and other documents used in the trade; to encourage and promote the settlement of disputes by conciliation and arbitration; the suppression of piracy or duplication of the films; to protect members from any unfair or illegitimate methods of business; to watch the interests of members in regard to any proposed restrictive legislation." The name was changed in the summer of 1979, because, as the Society's president, Percy Livingstone, indicated (in *Screen International,* June 16–23, 1979), "the new name would give a more immediate indication of the Society's composition and work."

Address: Royalty House, 72–73 Dean Street, London W1V 5HB, United Kingdom.

THE SOLOMON ISLANDS has no film industry, but there are two theatres in the capital, Honiara. The islands are also the site of Guadalcanal, immortalized on film in 1943 by 20th Century-Fox in *Guadalcanal Diary,* directed by Lewis Seiler, and starring Preston Foster, Lloyd Nolan, and William Bendix.

SOUTH AFRICA. It is, perhaps, not surprising that of all African countries, only South Africa has a substantial heritage of filmmaking. Motion pictures were first screened in Johannesburg in April 1895, and in 1898, Joseph Rosenthal filmed a number of actuality subjects there. Rosenthal, along with others, was actively filming the Boer War from 1899 to 1902. The country's first permanent film theatre, the Electric Theatre, opened in Durban on July 29, 1909, and a couple of years later, the country's first production company, African Film Productions Ltd., was formed.

South Africa's first feature-length production was a comedy titled *An Artist's Inspiration,* released in 1916, and it was quickly followed the same year by the nation's first dramatic feature, *A Zulu's Devotion*. Newsreels were first filmed in 1912, and a year later the first regular newsreel, *African Mirror,* was produced and continued to be released through the sixties. The most important of South African silent films were *De Voortrekkers* (1916) and *Symbol of Sacrifice* (1918).

The first synchronized South African sound film was *Moedertjie,* released in 1931, and shot in Afrikaans. A 1937 government-sponsored film, *Die Bou Van Nasie/They Built a Nation,* was released in both English and Afrikaans versions. African Film Productions Ltd. was revived after the Second World War, and, in 1959, its name was changed to South African Screen Productions Ltd.

The *New York Times* (October 2, 1949) reported that only a third of South Africa's black population had ever seen a motion picture, but by the eighties that had changed to the extent that the majority of filmgoers were black. In 1970, Bantu Film Bank began financing, producing, and distributing films for black audiences, not only in South Africa, but in other African countries. However, it was not until 1975 that the first two major films intended for all-black South African audiences, *U-deliwe/The Little One* and *Inkedama/The Orphan,* were produced by Heyns Films of Pretoria. The most important of black South African filmmakers is Nana Mahomo, who established his own company, Morena Films, in London, with a staff consisting of South African exiles. He has filmed clandestinely in South Africa *Phela Ndaba: End of the Dialogue* (1970) and *Last Grave at Dimbaza* (1974).

The South African government's primary involvement in film is in the area of censorship, through the Publications Control Board (PCB), which would automatically ban films such as *Guess Who's Coming to Dinner, In the Heat of the Night,* or any other film starring Sidney Poitier. In recent years, it has become somewhat liberalized (at least by South African standards). Since the early seventies, the government has also commenced the sponsoring of some film production through grants.

The best known of South African filmmakers is Jamie Uys, whose 1978 comedy, *The Gods Must Be Crazy,* opened in the United States in 1984 to widespread critical praise and was an instant box-office success. Despite the political unrest in South Africa and the introduction of television in 1976, the film industry is relatively active, producing upwards of twelve feature films a year. As late as 1985, a new studio, Midrand Film Studio, opened in Johannesburg. Hotel owner and entrepreneur Sol Kerzner controls much of the South African film industry through the Satbel Group, in which he acquired a controlling interest in 1984. Aside from being the country's largest producer and distributor, Satbel owns South Africa's largest theatre chain, Ster Kinekor, Northview Film and Video, and Irene Laboratories, the only processing plant in the country.

In 1985, American filmmakers, led by Woody Allen, began insisting that their films not be screened in South Africa. In 1987, American distributors refused to permit their releases to be shown in segregated theatres, and, as a result, Ster Kinekor announced that there would be no segregation in any of its theatres or drive-ins.

BIBLIOGRAPHY

Anthony, David H. III, "Clandestine Filming in South Africa: An Interview with Nana Mahomo," *Cineaste,* vol. VII, no. 3, Fall 1976, pp. 18–19, 50.

Hay, Rod, "Political Unrest, Money Shortages—SA's Film Industry Feels the Pinch," *Screen International,* May 3, 1986, pp. 230–234.

Howes, E.C., "The History of Films in South Africa," *Journal of the SMPTE,* vol. LXXII, no. 11, November 1963, pp. 882–885.

Levison, Evelyn, "White, Coloured and Hindu Theatres Boom; South Africa Important Distribution Point," *Variety,* April 26, 1961, p. 109.

Liknaitzky, Eric, "Letter from South Africa: Censored," *Take One,* vol. V, no. 12, November 1977, pp. 38–39.

Robb, David, "S. Africa Filming Boom," *Daily Variety,* June 20, 1988, pp. 13, 65, 68, 70, 72, 74.

THE SOUTH AUSTRALIAN FILM CORPORATION was created in 1972 by the State Government of South Australia. It was founded with the intention to establish a viable film industry in Adelaide and to produce both features and documentaries. Its first feature-length production, *Sunday Too Far Away,* was released in 1975, and the Corporation enjoyed its greatest success with *Gallipoli* in 1980. It first became involved in television production in the late seventies, with a number of made-for-television movies and the 1979 mini-series, *Sara Dane,* and in recent years its chief concern has been with television. The South Australian Film Corporation also operates the Hendon Studios, on whose lot it has its headquarters.

Address: 113 Tapleys Hill Road, Hendon, South Australia 5014.

THE SOUTH PACIFIC has served as a location for three classic American feature films: Robert Flaherty's *Moana* (1926), W.S. Van Dyke's *White Shadows in the South Seas* (1928), and F.W. Murnau's *Tabu* (1931). It has also served as a backdrop for many other films, including *The Idol Dancer* (1920), *The Love Flower* (1920), *South Sea Love* (1923), *Soul-Fire* (1925), *Typhoon Love* (1926), *Sadie Thompson* (1928), *South Seas* (1930), *Hurricane* (1930), *Rain* (1932), *Mutiny on the Bounty* (1935), *Island Captives* (1937), *Wallaby Jim of the Islands* (1937), *The Hurricane* (1937), *Vessel of Wrath* (U.S. *The Beachcomber*, 1938), *The Tuttles of Tahiti* (1942), *Another Shore* (1948), *Blue Lagoon* (1949), *Mutiny on the Bounty* (1962), *Donovan's Reef* (1963), *Father Goose* (1964), *Hurricane* (1979), and *The Blue Lagoon* (1980).

SOVCOLOR is the color film process generally in use in the USSR. It was developed in the late forties and onward after the allied seizure of the Agfa plant in Wolfen, Germany, and its subsequent placement in Soviet-occupied Germany.

SOVEXPORTFILM. The All-Union Corporation V/O Sovexportfilm claims to be the largest exporter of feature films in the world. The international sale of all Soviet films is handled by Sovexportfilm, and the company is also responsible for the import to the Soviet Union of all foreign features and short subjects. Prior to the creation of Sovexportfilm in 1951, the Soviet Union exported and imported films through the New York–based Amkino Corporation, which was established in 1926. Amkino was dissolved in 1940 and became Artkino. The export and import of Soviet films in Europe was handled through Intorgkino, which had offices in Berlin (closed in the early thirties) and London. Intorgkino's name was changed in February 1933 to Soyuzintorgkino.

Address: Kalashny pereulok 14, Moscow 103009, USSR.

SOVKINO was created following the May 13, 1924, meeting of the Council of People's Commissars of the USSR to control the entire Soviet film industry. It was operated rather like a stock company or a syndicate, with various Soviet studios holding shares. Sovkino's first chairman was Leonid Krasin. The organization first came under attack in 1927 for exhibiting too many non-Soviet films in Moscow. In 1928, it was urged by the Commissariat of Education "to create films which stand the test ideologically, present themes of actual life and at the same time constitute works of art." Eventually, in May of 1930, Sovkino was replaced by the new All-Union Combine of the Movie-Photo Industry, Soyuzkino*.

BIBLIOGRAPHY

Babitsky, Paul, and John Rimberg. *The Soviet Film Industry*. New York: Research Program on the USSR and Frederick A. Praeger, 1955.

SOYUZKINO. The All-Union Combine of the Movie-Photo Industry, or Soyuzkino, was established by Soviet decree in May 1930 to replace Sovkino*. Boris Zakharovich Shumyatski was appointed chairman and Vladimir A. Sutyrin secretary of the organization, which operated as a trust primarily concerned with distribution. Soyuzkino's charter was revoked on May 27, 1933, and it was replaced by a group of bodies: the Trust for Production of Movie Apparatus (Kino-Mekh-Prom), the Trust for Production of Art Feature Films (Soyuzfilm), and the Trust for the Production of Newsreel and Documentary Films (Soyuzkinokhronika).

BIBLIOGRAPHY

Babitsky, Paul, and John Rimberg. *The Soviet Film Industry*. New York: Research Program on the USSR and Frederick A. Praeger, 1955.

SPAGHETTI WESTERNS is a term used to describe Western features produced in Italy, among the most popular of which are *Il Buono, Il Brutto, Il Cattivo/The Good, the Bad, and the Ugly* (1966), *C'Era una volta il West/Once upon a Time in the West,* (1968) and *Lo chiamanvano Trinità/They call Me Trinity* (1970). The films are notable for their violence and for the antiheroic stance and manner of the central character. The genre first came to international prominence in 1964, when Sergio Leone, using the pseudonym of Bob Robertson, directed *Per un pugno di dollari/For a Fistful of Dollars*. It was the first of a series of features, directed by Leone, and starring Clint Eastwood as "The Man with No Name." The following year, of the entire Italian film output, some twenty-four features were Westerns.

Aside from Sergio Leone, other Italian directors who have worked in the genre utilizing "American" names are Giorgio Stegani (George Finlay) and Carlo Lizzani (Lee W. Beaver). Among the American actors most closely associated with the Spaghetti Western are Clint Eastwood, Cameron Mitchell, and Lee Van Cleef. Although the genre appears to have lost much of its popularity in the eighties, it has generated a magazine devoted exclusively to the subject: *Spaghetti Cinema,* published by William Connolly (6635 DeLongpre Avenue, Suite 4, Hollywood, CA 90028).

BIBLIOGRAPHY

Cumbow, Robert C. *Once upon a Time: The Films of Sergio Leone*. Metuchen, N.J.: Scarecrow Press, 1987.

Frayling, Christopher. *Spaghetti Westerns: Cowboys and Europeans from Karl May to Sergio Leone*. London: Routledge and Kegan Paul, 1981.

Staig, Laurence, and Tony Williams. *Italian Western: The Opera of Violence*. London: Odeon, 1975.

SPAIN witnessed its first films, a program of Lumière subjects, presented by a Mr. Promio in Madrid on May 15, 1896. Within a few years, a Spanish film industry had grown up, but it was a very insular affair, producing an average of twenty films a year in the twenties and ten a year in the thirties for screening at the country's theatres, which grew from a staggering 2,062 in 1928 to an even more staggering number of 2,600 in 1935.

Spanish cinema was dominated by General Francisco Franco from 1936 until his death in 1976. He wrote the official film version of the Spanish Civil War, *Raza/The Cause,* directed by Primo de Rivera in 1941, and he imposed strict censorship that prohibited the depiction of many subjects—some as commonplace as divorce. The only newsreels and documentaries screened were those of the state-run No-Do (Noticiarios-Documentales).

Some freedom became evident in the Spanish film industry in the fifties, with the production of *Surcos/Furrows* (1951) and *El ultimo cuple/The Last Couplet* (1957), and in the commencement of the career of director Luis Garcia Berlanga (born 1921). Considered an expert in the direction of broad comedy, Berlanga's best known feature is *El verdugo/The Executioner* (1963). In 1961, Uninci, a production company controlled by Juan Antonio Bardem, invited Luis Buñuel (1900–1983), who had made only one film in his native land, *Las hurdes/Land without Bread* (1932), to return to Spain and direct *Viridiana* (1961). Despite the film's international success, it was banned in Spain because of its anti-Catholic stance. However, Buñuel returned yet again to Spain, one final time, in 1969 to direct *Tristana*.

After Buñuel, Spain's greatest director is Carlos Saura (born 1932), whose films—some of which feature his wife, Geraldine Chaplin—include *La Caza/The Hunt* (1965), *El jardin de las delicias/Garden of Delights* (1970), *Cría cuervos/Cría* (1975), and *Mama cumple 100 anos/Mama Turns 100* (1979). A new Spanish cinema emerged following the death of Franco, but its directors, who include Basilio Martin Patino, Gonzalo Herralde, and Manuel Gutiérrez Aragón, have gained little commercial success out of their own country, despite considerable critical praise. An exception is Victor Erice and *El espíritu de la colmena/Spirit of the Beehive* (1974), starring Ana Torrent as a young girl entranced by a screening of the 1931 *Frankenstein* feature.

A self-proclaimed "School of Barcelona" filmmakers developed in the seventies, and it is dominated by Catalan Films (Diputacio 279, 08004 Barcelona).

In 1984, the Miro Law, named after Pilar Miro, director general of cinematography at the Ministry of Culture, encouraged production through the grant of up to 50 percent of a film's budget. Miro is a well-known director in her own right. Although the number of theatres is dwindling, there were still more than three thousand open in the mid-eighties. There is no censorship in Spain—it was abolished in 1977—but films are classified by the Junta de Clasificación on an advisory basis.

BIBLIOGRAPHY

"Boom in Spain," *Time,* June 6, 1955, p. 106.

Clouzot, Claire, "The Young Turks of Spain," *Sight & Sound,* Spring 1966, pp. 68–69.

Higginbotham, Virginia, "Spain," in *World Cinema since 1945,* editor William Luhr. New York: Ungar, 1987, pp. 499–513.

Marti-Rom, J.R., "Le cinéma Espagnol après Franco: de la politisation au désenchantement," *La Revue du Cinéma,* May 1981, pp. 79–97.

Moris, Cyril Brian. *This Loving Darkness*. London: Oxford University Press for University of Hull, 1980.

Mouna-Foix, Vicente. *New Cinema in Spain*. London: British Film Institute, 1977.

Patmore, Derek, "A Newsletter from Madrid," *Films in Review,* July-August 1950, pp. 5–6.

"The Reign of Spain," *Time,* February 26, 1965, pp. 60–61.
Ross, Walter S., "Something for Everyone," *Saturday Review,* December 25, 1965, pp. 18–20.
Schickel, Richard, "Spanish Films: Paradoxes and Hopes," *Harper's,* September 1967, pp. 127–129.
Schwartz, Ronald. *Spanish Film Directors (1950–1985).* Metuchen, N.J.: Scarecrow Press, 1986.
Valleau, Marjorie A. *The Spanish Civil War in American and European Films.* Ann Arbor, Mich.: UMI Research Press, 1981.

THE SPANISH CIVIL WAR (1936–1939) has been the subject of a number of feature films, including *The Last Train from Madrid* (1937), *Blockade* (1938), *For Whom the Bell Tolls* (1943), *The Angel Wore Red* (1960), and *Behold a Pale Horse* (1964), as well as the 1965 documentary *To Die in Madrid.*

Because it was the first major conflict, aside from the First World War, to be the subject of major newsreel coverage, there have been a number of analyses of the extant footage of the Spanish Civil War indicating a profascist bias by the newsreel companies.

BIBLIOGRAPHY

Aldgate, Anthony, "British Newsreels and the Spanish Civil War," *Film & History,* vol. III, no. 1, February 1973, pp. 1–8, 16.
———, "Covering Civil War: The Bombing of Guernica and the British Cinema Newsreels," *The Media Reporter,* vol. II, no. 4, December 1978, pp. 22–23.
———. *Cinema & History: British Newsreels and the Spanish Civil War.* London: Scolar Press, 1979.
Butler, Richard, "Newsreel Man in the Firing Line: The Adventures and Misadventures of Richard Butler, Pathé Cameraman in Search of Newsreel Pictures on the Aragon Front," *World Film News,* vol. II, no. 12, March 1938, pp. 6–8.
Calder-Marshall, Arthur, "Propaganda in Films," *Life and Letters To-Day,* vol. XV, no. 6, Winter 1936–37, pp. 151–161.
Crosthwaite, Brian, "Newsreels Show Bias: Editing of Spanish War Scenes Discloses Partisan Views," *World Film News,* vol. I, no. 7, October 1936, p. 41.
Romeiser, John B., "The Spanish Civil War and Fox Movietone News, 1936–1939," *New Orleans Review,* Spring 1978, pp. 25–30.

SPECTRUM FILM is a major documentary film producer, established in Amsterdam in 1950 by Louis Van Gasteren (born 1922).

Address: Kloveniersburgwal 49, 1011 JX Amsterdam, Netherlands.

THE "SQUIBS" SERIES of silent comedy-dramas featured British actress Betty Balfour as a cockney flower-seller. The three features in the series, all of which were directed by George Pearson, are *Squibs Wins the Calcutta Sweep* (1922), *Squibs M.P.* (1923), and *Squibs' Honeymoon* (1923).

BIBLIOGRAPHY
Pearson, George. *Flashback*. London: George Allen & Unwin, 1957.
Slide, Anthony, "George Pearson's Squibs Wins the Calcutta Sweep," *The Silent Picture*, no. 5, Winter 1969/70, pp. 11–12.

SRI LANKA. In 1972, the year in which the island of Ceylon became the Republic of Sri Lanka, the former British colony celebrated the twenty-fifth anniversary of its film industry. At that time an estimated 250 films had been produced in the Sinhalese language. However, between 1947 and 1956, all of those so-called Sinhalese features had, in reality, been filmed not in Ceylon, but in Indian studios in Bombay and Madras.

The most influential of Sinhalese filmmakers is Lester James Peries (born 1921), a leading figure in Third World Cinema*, whose first feature was *Rekawa/The Line of Destiny* (1956). His other films, which have been well received at film festivals and the subject of a Museum of Art (New York) retrospective, include *Sandesaya/The Message* (1960), *Delovak Athara/Between Two Worlds* (1966), *Ran Salu/The Yellow Robe* (1967), and *Nidhanaya/The Treasure* (1971).

Prior to 1973, the major Sinhalese distributors were Ceylon Theatres Ltd., Cinemas Ltd., and Ceylon Entertainments Ltd., but in that year the State Film Corporation (224 Baudhaloka Mawatha, Colombo 7) was created, and it has attempted the takeover of all foreign film importation. The State Film Corporation also makes available credit and technical facilities, provides subsidized raw stock, and tries to train new, young filmmakers. In 1975, the Corporation announced plans to produce more films in the Tamil language, catering to Sri Lanka's 19 percent minority population. (Of the forty films produced in 1975, only two were in the Tamil language.) An important film dealing with the relationship between Sinhalese and the Tamils, on a personal level, is *Adara Kathawa/A Love Story* (1985), directed by Chandran Rutnam.

Chandran Rutnam is the head of Sri Lanka Film Location Services Ltd. (35/3 Guildford Crescent, Colombo 7), which has helped promote the use of Sri Lanka as a location for many international productions, including *Indiana Jones and the Temple of Doom* and the Bo Derek vehicle, *Tarzan the Ape Man*. Earlier films shot on location in Sri Lanka include *Elephant Walk, Outcast of the Islands, Bridge on the River Kwai,* and, of course, the classic documentary, *The Song of Ceylon*.

Aside from Lester James Peries and Chandran Rutnam, other Sinhalese directors include P. Hettiarachi (who is closely associated with the Government Film Unit), K.A.W. Perera, Dharmasena Pathirajah, Manik Sandrasagara, Titus Thotawatte, and Amarnath Jayatilaka. The last is highly regarded in his native country as a film critic and scholar, whose 1984 feature, *Arunata Pera/Before the Dawn,* was screened at the London Film Festival.

BIBLIOGRAPHY
Burton, Geoff, "Sri Lankan Cinema," *Cinema Papers,* no. 15, January 1978, pp. 232–234.

STAATSAUFTRAGSFILME is the collective name given to the ninety-six films commissioned by the Nazi Propaganda Ministry between 1933 and 1945. The most important of the group are *Hitlerjunge Quex/Hitler Youth Quex* (1933, Hans Steinhoff), *Morgenrot/Dawn* (1933, Gustav Ucicky), *S.A.-Mann Brand* (1933, Franz Seitz), *Bismarck* (1940, Wolfgang Liebeneiner), *Jud Süss/Jew Süss* (1940, Veit Harlan), *Ohm Krüger* (1941, Hans Steinhoff), and *Kolberg* (1945, Veit Harlan).

A complete listing of all the Staatsauftragsfilme, with credits, appears in Jeffrey Richards' *Visions of Yesterday* (Boston: Routledge & Kegan Paul, 1973, pp. 369–376).

STAR FILM was the company created by French film pioneer Georges Méliès (1861–1938), under whose name he produced some five hundred "trick" films between 1896 and 1912. The first of these films was *Un Partie de cartes/Playing Cards* (released in May 1896), and among the best known are *L'Homme à la tête de Caoutchouc/The Man with the Rubber Head* (1902), *Le Voyage dans la Lune/A Trip to the Moon* (1902), *Le Voyage à travers l'Impossible/An Impossible Voyage* (1904), *L'Éclipse du soleil en pleine lune/The Eclipse* (1907), and *À la Conquête du Pôle/Conquest of the Pole* (1912).

The trademark of the company was a star containing the initials "M" for Méliès and "R" for Lucien Reulos, who was a businessman and Méliès' associate. Because of American duplication and piracy of his films, Georges Méliès sent his brother Gaston to New York to form an American branch of the company, active from 1904 to 1913. In 1911, Charles Pathé became involved with Star Film as both a distributor and a financial backer, and when Méliès was unable to refund Pathé's advances, he lost his assets, including Star Film, in 1913.

Star Film is believed to be the earliest brand name and trademark in film history.

BIBLIOGRAPHY

Hammond, Paul. *Marvellous Méliès*. New York: St. Martin's Press, 1975.
Malthête-Méliès, Madeleine. *Méliès: L'Enchanteur*. Paris: Hachette, 1973.
Sadoul, Georges. *Georges Méliès*. Paris: Éditions Seghers, 1962.

STAR FILM COMPANY was a Hungarian production company from the silent era, notable for having made six features with Bela Lugosi (then known as Arisztid Olt), all directed by Alfréd Deésy, and including the actor's first film, *A Léopard/The Leopard* (1917).

START (Society of the Devotees of the Artistic Film) was a film society, founded in Poland in 1930 by a group of students: Eugeniusz Cękalski, Mieczysław Choynowski, Wanda Jakubowska, Tadeusz Kowalski, Stanisław Wohl, and Jerzy Zarzycki. It attempted to raise the standards of Polish film production, to encourage filmmaking among its members, and to advance the art of the film. Among its members, whose influence extended beyond the group's life, were

Jerzy Bossak, Aleksander Ford, Ludwik Perski, and Jerzy Toeplitz. START was disbanded in 1935, but its ideas were continued through the Cooperative of Film Authors (Spółdzielnia Autorów Filmowych), founded in 1937. The latter produced a full-length feature film, *Strachy/Ghosts* in 1938, directed by E. Cękalski and K. Szołowski.

BIBLIOGRAPHY

Contemporary Polish Cinematography. Warsaw: Polonia, 1962.

STATENS FILMCENTRAL (Danish Government Film Office) has been distributing short films of all types since 1939. It is also a producer of an average of thirty short subjects a year.

Address: Vestergade 27, DK-1456 Copenhagen-K, Denmark.

STATENS FILMSENTRAL (State Film Central) was established in 1948 and is Norway's largest non-theatrical film distributor. It also operates touring cinemas and a 16mm laboratory.

Address: Kongens Gate 15, Oslo 1, Norway.

STEENBECK is the best known name in flatbed editing equipment, and like the American company Moviola, the name has become a generic term for editing apparatus. W. Steenbeck & Co. was founded in Hamburg, Germany, in 1931, by Eng. Wilhelm Steenbeck as a manufacturer of fine precision mechanical and electrical parts. It manufactured its first flatbed editing machine, a 16mm model designed in collaboration with local German television stations, in 1953. Eng. Wilhelm Steenbeck died in 1975, but a year earlier Hildegard McCall had become managing director, and in 1985, she became chairman of the board. Steenbeck opened a factory in California in 1979.

Aside from its 35mm and 16mm film editing tables, Steenbeck also produces video sound postproduction equipment, a film-to-video transfer system for use with its editing tables, a computerized dialogue replacement system, magnetic film recorders, high-speed studio projectors, and multiformat high-speed motor rewind tables.

Address: Hammer Steindamm 27-29, 2000 Hamburg 76, West Germany.

STERN-FILM was a German production company of the twenties, responsible for at least four major features directed by Karl Grune (1890–1962), *Der graf von Charolais/The Count of Charolais* (1922), *Die Strasse/The Street* (1923), *Komödianten/Actors* (1924), and *Eifersucht/Jealousy* (1925).

STIMMUNG (or Mood) was very important in films from the "Golden Age" of German cinema. Historian and critic Lotte Eisner has suggested that "the 'vibrations of the soul' is linked to the use of light. In fact this *Stimmung* hovers around objects as well as people: it is a 'metaphysical' accord, a mystical and singular harmony amid the chaos of things, a kind of sorrowful nostalgia which, for the German, is mixed with well-being, an imprecise nuance of nostalgia, languor coloured with desire, lust of body and soul.''

Among the German films in which Stimmung is a very important factor are *Der Letzte Mann/The Last Laugh* (1924), *Orlacs Hände/The Hands of Orlac* (1924), *Die Chronik von Grieshuus/The Chronicle of the Grey House* (1925), *Varieté/Variety/Vaudeville* (1925), *Der Student von Prag/The Student of Prague* (1926), and *Alraune/Unholy Love* (1928).

BIBLIOGRAPHY

Eisner, Lotte. *The Haunted Screen*. Berkeley: University of California Press, 1969.

STOCK FOOTAGE LIBRARIES. The following is a listing of major stock footage libraries outside of the United States:

Australia

Cinesound Movietone
541A Darling Street
Rozelle, N.S.W. 2039

Film Australia Eton Road
Lindfield, N.S.W. 2070

Film Search Australia Pty Ltd.
24 Carlotta Street
Artarmon, N.S.W. 2064

Canada

Fabulous Footage Inc.
12 Mercer Street
Toronto, Ontario M5V 1H5

Jack Chisholm Film Productions Ltd.
229 Niagara Street
Toronto, Ontario M6J 2L5

France

Cinémathèque Gaumont
1 quai Gabriel Peri
94340 Joinville

New Zealand

Air New Zealand Film Library
105 Federal Street
P.O. Box 6190
Auckland

New Zealand National Film Unit
P.O. Box 46-002
Lower Hutt

Switzerland

World Life Films (Pty) Ltd.
Postfach 6586
CH-8023 Zurich

United Kingdom

BBC Film & Video Tape Library
BBC Enterprises
Windmill Road
Brentford, Middlesex

British Movietone News Ltd.
North Orbital Road
Denham, Uxbridge, Middlesex UB9 5HQ

Granada Television Film Library
Manchester M60 9EA

Rank Audio Visual
P.O. Box 70
Great West Road
Brentwood, Middlesex, TW8 9HR

Visnews Ltd.
Cumberland Avenue
London NW10 7EH

World Backgrounds
Imperial Studios
Maxwell Road
Boreham Wood, Herts WD6 1WE

STOCKHOLM. Although featured in almost all Swedish films, Stockholm has held little interest for filmmakers from other countries. It has been seen in *The Prize* (1963), *I'll Take Sweden* (1965), *Torn Curtain* (1966), *Gorky Park* (1983), and the Shirley MacLaine mini-series (for ABC), *Out on a Limb* (1986).

STUDIO DES URSULINES was established in Paris in 1925 by actors Armand Tallier and Laurence Myrga for the exhibition of contemporary avant-garde films, with its initial presentation including G.W. Pabst's *Die freudlose gasse/Joyless Street* (1925) and René Clair's *Entr'acte* (1924). Other important films shown here include Germaine Dulac's *La coquille et le clergyman/The Seashell and the Clergyman* (1928) and Man Ray's *L'Étoile de mer* (1929).

STUDIO 45 was formed at the end of the Second World War in West Germany by Ernst Hasselbach. It was granted a production license by the British occupying forces in July 1946, with its earliest features being *Zugvögel/Birds of Migration* (1946) and *Sag die Wahreit/Tell the Truth* (1946).

STUDIO 28 was established in Paris in 1928 by Jean Mauclaire for the exhibition of contemporary avant-garde films, and it opened with Abram Room's *Bed and Sofa* (1927). Other films screened there include Luis Buñuel's *Un chien andalou* (1928) and *L'âge d'or* (1930), and Jean Cocteau's *Le sang d'un poète/The Blood of a Poet* (1930).

SUOMI-FILMI OY. The oldest of Finnish production companies, Suomi-Filmi Oy was founded in 1918 by Teuvo Puro and Erkki Karu. The latter was a prominent Finnish director (who was to found a rival company, Oy Suomen Filmiteollisuus, in 1933), who was responsible for three silent classics, *Koskenlaskijan morsian/The Logroller's Bride* (1923), *Nummisuutarit/The Village Shoemakers* (1923), and *Meidan poikame/Our Boys* (1929). The figure most associated with the company is Risto Orko, who joined Suomi-Filmi Oy in 1933 as a director and production manager, was its managing director from 1945 to 1976, and continues as chairman of the board. The company's present managing director is Kare Orko.

Suomi-Filmi Oy operates 16mm and 35mm film laboratories, a sound studio, a theatrical distribution organization, and a short film section, involved with newsreels, commercials and documentaries. Since its formation, it has produced more than 150 features and 2,000 short subjects. At the height of its importance, from 1930 to 1950, when it was one of the two major production companies in Finland, it boasted a staff of approximately three hundred, down now to around ninety.

Address: Bulevardi 12, Helsinki, Finland.

SURREALISM is a twentieth-century art movement concerned with the workings of the subconscious mind, or, as Paul Hammond so aptly put it (in *Sight & Sound,* Summer 1978), in its relationship to the motion picture, "the eye that looks out on to the world but also behind itself, so to speak, towards the interior model." Such a description quickly reminds one of perhaps the most famous of moments in all surrealist films, the slicing of the human eye in Luis Buñuel's 1928 classic, *Un Chien Andalou.*

The first surrealist text, *Les champs magnetiques,* was written by André Breton and Philippe Soupault in France in 1919. It recognized a number of films—the serials of Pearl White and *Das Kabinett des Dr. Caligari/The Cabinet of Dr. Caligari* (1919)—as surrealist in outlook. The first important surrealist film, conceived as such, is René Clair and Francis Picabia's *Entr'acte* (1924). It was followed by Marcel Duchamp's *Anémic Cinéma* (1926), Germaine Dulac's *La Coquille et le clergyman/The Seashell and the Clergyman* (1927), Man Ray's *L'Étoile de mer* (1928),and Luis Buñuel's *L'Age d'Or* (1930).

As a movement or a genre of the motion picture, surrealism is, by its very nature, hard to classify. Among the films that scholars and historians have endorsed as surrealist are the comedies of Laurel and Hardy and the musicals of Busby Berkeley, along with such features as Tod Browning's *Freaks* (1932),

Leo McCarey's *Duck Soup* (1933), Otto Preminger's *Laura* (1944), John Cromwell's *The Enchanted Cottage* (1945), Joseph H. Lewis' *Gun Crazy* (1949), and Charles Laughton's *The Night of the Hunter* (1955). Hans Richter, associated with the movement in the twenties, is responsible for *Dreams That Money Can Buy* (1946), that recalls the "golden age" of surrealism in the twenties. As late as 1977, Marty Feldman's *The Last Remake of Beau Geste* has been hailed as surrealist.

In 1963, surrealist philosopher and poet, Gérard Legrand, commented that "Nobody sees the same film." Thus surrealism can and does survive within the motion picture, long after the original movement in Paris from 1923 to 1930 has passed into history.

BIBLIOGRAPHY

Ahrens, Julie, "Getting What You Need and That Obscure Object of Desire," *Movietone News,* No. 58–59, August 14, 1978, pp. 17–21.

Caws, M.A., "For a Cinema of the Central Eye," *Millenium,* vol. I, no. 1, Winter 1977–78, pp. 25–37.

Dale, R.C., "Rene Clair's *Entr'acte,* or Motion Victorious," *Wide Angle,* vol. II, no. 2, 1978, pp. 38–43.

Delamater, Jerome, "Busby Berkeley: An American Surrealist," *Wide Angle,* vol. I, no. 1, 1979, pp. 24–29.

Gould, Michael. *Surrealism and the Cinema.* Cranbury, N.J.: A.S. Barnes, 1976.

Hammond, Paul, "Poetic Justice," *Sight & Sound,* vol. XLVII, no. 3, Summer 1978, pp. 178–182.

Kovacs, Steven. *From Enchantment to Rape: The Story of Surrealist Cinema.* Rutherford, N.J.: Fairleigh Dickinson University Press, 1980.

Kyrou, Ado. *Le Surrealisme au Cinéma.* Paris: Le Terrain Vague, 1963.

Lawder, Standish D. *The Cubist Cinema.* New York: New York University Press, 1975.

Liebman, Stuart, and D. Shapiro, "Surrealism and Cinema," *Millenium,* vol. I, no. 1, Winter 1977–78, pp. 52–59.

Matthews, J.H. *Surrealism and Film.* Ann Arbor: University of Michigan Press, 1971.

Ringel, Harry, "*Blackmail:* The Opening of Hitchcock's Surrealist Eye," *Film Heritage,* vol. LX, no. 2, Winter 1973–74, pp. 17–23.

Thiher, Allen, "Surrealism's Enduring Bite: *Un Chien Andalou,*" *Literature/Film Quarterly,* vol. V, no. 1, Winter 1977, pp. 38–49.

SVENSKA BIO (or to give its full name, Svenska Biografteatern) was founded in 1907 in the Swedish town of Kristianstad; it moved its headquarters to Stockholm in 1911. The company is important, both to Swedish and international cinema, in that, in 1912, it hired the two most important figures in early Swedish filmmaking, directors Victor Sjöström and Mauritz Stiller, and here the two men produced their first early successes. Svenska Bio merged with Filmindustribolaget Skandia in 1919 to form Svensk Filmindustri*.

SVENSK FILMINDUSTRI. The leading film distributor and exhibitor in Sweden, AB Svensk Filmindustri can trace its origins to 1907, when Svenska Bio* was formed. In 1919, Svenska Bio and AB Skandia, a rival company, were merged to form Aktiebolaget Svensk Filmindustri, with eighty-six theatres and its own production studio. The major figure behind the company was Charles Magnusson, who had joined Svenska Bio in 1909 and remained with Svensk Filmindustri until his retirement in 1928. He brought Greta Garbo to Svensk Filmindustri, along with directors Mauritz Stiller and Victor Sjöström.

With the coming of sound, Svensk Filmindustri lost much of its international regard, and it was not until Carl Anders Dymling became head of production (from 1942 to 1961) that the company's fortunes improved. Dymling built a new studio in the forties at Stocksund, replacing the earlier studio at Lindingo. Thanks to Dymling, Ingmar Bergman began his career at Svensk Filmindustri.

Svensk Filmindustri continues to produce films—it had a major international success in 1985 with *My Life as a Dog*—but its primary concerns in the eighties are distribution and exhibition. It has pioneered the building of multiplex theatres in Sweden. In December 1985, the company began publication of what became Sweden's largest film magazine, *Filmjournalen*.

As of 1986, it was Svenska Filmindustri's proud boast that it had produced more than one thousand films.

Address: Söder Mälarstrand 27 S-117 88 Stockholm, Sweden.

SWEDEN. The first exhibition of films in Sweden was on June 28, 1896, when the Cinématographe Lumière came to Malmö. Later that year, Max Skladanowsky, the German film pioneer, took what are believed to be the first motion pictures in Sweden, and in 1897 the first Sweden film company, Numa Petersons Handels & Fabriks AB was established. One-reel films with sound supplied by phonograph records, called Biophon Films, may have been made in Sweden as early as 1903. Historians conjecture that approximately three hundred of these films, primarily of singers, were made by 1911 when production stopped, presumably because of the lack of adequate loudspeaker systems in theatres.

Svensk Filmindustri*, Sweden's oldest and at present one of its most important companies, had as its earliest precursor Kristianstads Biograf-Teatern, established in Kristianstad on September 5, 1905, by Nils Hansson Nylander (1856–1940) and Gustaf A. Björkman (1881–1945). On February 16, 1907, AB Svenska Biografteatern (Svenska Bio*) took over the former company, and in 1909 hired Charles Magnusson (1878–1948), a cameraman who in 1905 shot the entry of Norwegian King Haakon into Kristiania (now Oslo), as managing director and Julius Jaenzon (1885–1961), who shot footage of Theodore Roosevelt in 1907 and the first Norwegian story film *Fiskelivets faror/The Perils of a Fisherman*. Jaenzon became Sweden's leading cameraman during the silent era. The company moved to Stockholm in 1911, and the next year, Magnusson, whom historians credit with starting the Swedish tradition of giving directors artistic control of their productions, hired actors Mauritz Stiller (1883–1928) and Victor Sjöström (1879–1960), who, as directors during the next decade, made about forty films each and were largely responsible for Sweden's rise to international recognition. Magnusson also acquired the rights to the works of novelist Selma Lagerlöf

(1858–1940), which Stiller and Sjöström adapted for many of their best films. Stiller's films include *Herr Arnes pengar/Sir Arne's Treasure,* made in 1919, *Erotikon,* made in 1920, *Gunnar Hedes saga,* made in 1922, and *Gösta Berlings saga/The Atonement of Gosta Berlin,* made in 1923 starring Greta Garbo (born 1905) and Lars Hanson (1886–1965), both of whom went with Stiller to Hollywood in 1925. Sjöström, who acted in most of his films, made the 1913 *Ingeborg Holm, Terje Vigen* in 1916, *Tösen från Stormyrtorpet/A Girl From the March Croft,* made in 1917 which was chosen in 1919 as one of the best films released that year in the United States, and *Körkarlan/The Phantom Carriage,* made in 1920. He went to Hollywood in 1923 and changed his name to Seastrom.

During the First World War, the Swedish film industry survived while most other European production was halted. On December 27, 1919, Svenska Biografteatern merged with Filmindustri AB Skandia, itself an amalgamation formed on May 17, 1918 of Hasselbladfilm, formed in 1915, and some other concerns, to form Svensk Filmindustri AB. Although Magnusson became the head of Svensk Filmindustri and remained so until 1928, and in March 1926 the company made a deal with the German company Ufa* to make joint productions, the Swedish film industry went through a decline in the twenties as competition from the American and German industries overtook them in the international market. Notable filmmakers during the twenties include John W. Brunius (1884–1937); Ivan Hedqvist (1880–1935); Gustaf Molander (1880–1973), who wrote for both Stiller and Sjöstrom and became Sweden's most prolific director, having made sixty- four films; Gustaf Edgren (1895–1954); and the Danes Benjamin Christensen (1879–1959) and Carl-Theodor Dreyer (1889–1968).

In the thirties production increased from seven to twelve films per year to twenty to thirty films per year. Europa Film AB, founded in 1930, and Sandrews-Bauman (later Sandrew Film & Teater AB*), which produced its first film in 1937, became Svensk Filmindustri's greatest rivals during the next few decades. An attempt was made to regain the international interest in Swedish films by producing simultaneous foreign language versions of some of the films, but apart from a few significant works such as Molander's *En natt/One Night,* made in 1931 and the 1936 *Intermezzo,* whose international success brought Ingrid Bergman (1915–1982) to prominence, the bulk of Swedish production, mainly comedies, farces, and operettas based on stage plays, was of low quality and of little interest to other countries. Concerned authors, civic leaders, and social workers met in Stockholm in 1936 to protest the decline.

As the forties began, a revitalization of the industry began with filmmakers such as Anders Henrikson (1896–1965), whose *Ett brott/A Crime* made in 1940 exhibited psychological realism; Alf Sjöberg (1903–1980), who, absent since his 1929 critically acclaimed *Den starkaste/The Strongest,* in 1939 made *Med livet som insats/They Staked Their Lives,* praised for its expressive visual style; and short filmmaker Arne Sucksdorff (born 1917), whose lyrical documentary shorts about animals, cultures, and subcultures fascinated international audiences. Production reached an all-time high in the forties (forty-four features were made in 1947) as films dealing with naturalism and mysticism, concerns neglected since the silent films of Stiller and Sjöström, and war films replaced the staid films from the thirties.

Sjöberg's 1944 film *Hets/Frenzy,* about a tormented student rebelling against an older generation, marked the first screen credit of Ingmar Bergman (born 1918), who wrote the screenplay. Bergman, Sweden's premier director until his retirement from cinema in 1982, took filmmaking in new directions as he explored his characters' lives in terms of their religious, philosophic, aesthetic, and psychological dilemmas with a power and visual flair equalled by few other filmmakers. In addition, Bergman wrote screenplays that stimulated other directors, including Molander, to greater achievements. Bergman's films and Sjöberg's *Fröken Julie/Miss Julie* (that shared the top award at Cannes in 1951) brought a renewed Swedish cinema to international attention. Other Swedish directors of interest in the late forties include Hasse Ekman (born 1915), Arne Mattsson (born 1919), Erik "Hampe" Faustman (1919–1961), and comedian Nils Poppe (born 1908).

Although the quality of Swedish films increased, by the late forties they were losing money. On February 8, 1948, the government instituted a hefty increase in the entertainment tax raising it from 15 percent to 30 percent for tickets costing up to Kr 1.0, and from 35 percent to 40 percent for tickets costing more than Kr 1.0. This hurt production companies not only because less money per ticket returned to the producer, but also because of Sweden's limited market, production companies had also become distributors and theatre chain owners. It was estimated that an average costing film had to be seen by nearly 800,000 people to recoup its costs and that the average film was losing $20,000. Although experts were appointed to study how the industry could be helped by government involvement without sacrificing companies' independence, no solution was offered.

On January 1, 1951, producers protested the tax increase by stopping production. Nine months later an agreement was reached that for a certain number of films, 20 percent of the tax would be returned to the producer. In addition, the cinema owners association agreed that a small percentage of box-office revenues would go directly to producers, but these steps failed to prevent decreasing production throughout the fifties.

As the result of negotiations between the government and the industry, on July 1, 1963, the entertainment tax was abolished and the Swedish Film Institute*/ Svenska Filminstitutet* was established to be financed by 10 percent of box-office receipts. Sixty-five percent of the Institute's funds were to be used to support production; half in proportion to box-office receipts, the rest as quality grants to be determined by an independent jury. The plan, devised in large part by Harry Schein, an industrialist who headed the Institute for the next decade, was a compromise between the government, that wanted to subsidize only films of superior artistic quality, and the industry, that wanted the marketplace to determine which films should be encouraged by subsidies. The agreement allowed no advance subsidies.

The establishment of the Institute revitalized the industry in the sixties. Production figures doubled, co-productions with other countries were encouraged, and a new generation of filmmakers were given the chance to direct; in the next decade two-thirds of the films produced were made by directors who made their first film after 1963, the most important of whom were Bo Widerberg (born 1930), Jörn Donner (born 1933), Vilgot Sjöman (born 1924), Jan Troell (born 1931), Jan Halldoff, Mai Zetterling (born 1925), Kjell Grede (born 1936), and Tage Danielsson.

Competition from television continued to threaten the industry as cinema attendance dropped from 80 million in 1956 to 20 million in 1982. The Film Institute funding, coming as it did as a reward for artistic or box-office success, was not enough for producers reluctant to take risks without some preproduction guarantees. To keep production at the desired rate of twenty to twenty-five films per year, the government revised the Institute's agreement on July 1, 1972, changing the allocation of the 65 percent of Institute funds for production to 10 percent for quality grants for films already produced; 10 percent for the Institute's own productions; 15 percent as a guarantee against losses of up to 15 percent of a film's production costs up to Kr. 300,000; and 30 percent to be granted as production guarantees of up to 50 percent of production costs for films with artistic ambitions to be distributed by two boards, one with four of its five members representing the industry, the other with four of its five members representing creative filmmakers.

Swedish films of the sixties developed an international reputation for their frank treatment of sex, beginning with Bergman's *Jungfrukällan/The Virgin Spring* (1959) and *Tystnaden/The Silence* (1963), Sjöman's *491* (1963), Lars-Magnus Lindgren's *Käre John/Dear John* (1964), and culminating with Sjöman's *Jag är nyfiken-gul/I am Curious-Yellow* (1967). Censorship, which was instituted on the state level on September 4, 1911, (Sweden was the first country to have state censorship) with the establishment of Statens Biografbyrå (The State Censorship Board) after police censorship beginning in 1905 proved chaotic for the industry, has been motivated throughout the century by the desire to keep "coarsening or harmfully exciting" films or sequences from the screen. The fact that all exhibited film must have a certificate from the censorship board has been noted to be at odds with Sweden's tradition of freedom of the press, dating from 1809, and the abolishment of censorship in theatre in 1872. Since the sixties, pornography has, for the most part, been allowed, while violence has been banned or excised from prints. At present, the board rates films according to five classes depending on age.

The Swedish Film Institute and the Swedish Broadcasting Corporation entered into an agreement in February 1975 to establish a fund for the production of films to be exhibited first in theatres and later on television. In the late seventies as video sales and rentals soared, film attendance dropped and the Film Institute had to be supported by direct government grants. The 1982 Film Agreement sought to help the Institute by adding a surcharge on video sales and rentals to be paid to the Institute for production, but by the late eighties the video boom seemed to be over while production costs were still rising and attendance declining. The Institute was criticized in the early eighties when under the leadership of Jörn Donner, it funded two expensive projects, Bergman's final film *Fanny och Alexander/Fanny and Alexander* and Troell's *Ingenjör Andrées luftfärd/The Flight of the Eagle,* in preference to a number of more modestly budgeted films, but the films were well-received internationally.

At present, very few films are produced in Sweden without support from the Institute. In addition to supporting production, the Institute, which has over 150 full-time employees, produces and distributes film, runs a theatre, operates a studio and lab, promotes the country's films abroad, runs an archive, restores and preserves films, and publishes books, pamphlets and the respected film journal *Chaplin.*

By the late eighties, two companies, Svensk Filmindustri AB, owned by the large newspaper group Bonnier and having merged with the near bankrupt Europa Film in 1983, and Sandrew Film & Teater AB dominate the industry. Most independent producers get partial to near total financing from the two large companies or the Swedish Film Institute.

In the seventies and eighties a number of promising filmmakers began careers including Lasse Hallström (born 1946), Stefan Jarl (born 1941), Gunnel Lindblom (born 1931), and Suzanne Osten (born 1944). A number of distinguished foreign filmmakers produced films in Sweden in association with the Swedish Film Institute including Susan Sontag, Dusan Makavejev, and Andrei Tarkovsky.

BIBLIOGRAPHY

Bjorkman, Stig. *Film in Sweden: The New Directors.* South Brunswick, N.J. and New York: A.S. Barnes in association with the Swedish Film Institute and the Swedish Institute, 1977

Cowie, Peter. *Swedish Cinema.* New York: A.S. Barnes, 1966.

———. *Sweden 2.* New York: A.S. Barnes, 1970.

———. *Film in Sweden: Stars and Players.* South Brunswick, N.J., and New York: A.S. Barnes in collaboration with the Swedish Film Institute, 1977.

———, "Sweden," in *International Film Guide 1988,* editor Peter Cowie. London: Tantivy Press, 1987, pp. 314–322.

Cowie, Peter, in collaboration with Arne Svensson, *Sweden 1.* New York: A.S. Barnes, 1970.

"Dossier: Scandinavia," in *International Film Guide 1988,* editor Peter Cowie. London: Tantivy Press, 1987, pp. 73–85.

Film Centre, London. *The Film Industry in Six European Countries.* Paris: UNESCO, 1950.

Hardy, Forsyth. *Scandinavian Film.* London: Falcon Press, 1952.

Lawrence, Eric, "The Motion Picture Industry in Sweden," *Hollywood Quarterly,* Winter 1950, pp. 182–188.

Sundgren, Nils Petter. *The New Swedish Cinema.* Stockholm: Swedish Institute for Cultural Relations with Foreign Countries, 1970.

Winquist, Sven G. *Swedish Silent Pictures 1896–1931 and Their Directors*. Stockholm: Swedish Film Institute, 1967.

THE SWEDISH FILM INSTITUTE (Svenska Filminstitutet) is involved in both film production and film culture. It co-produces more than three-quarters of all the films produced annually in Sweden, providing, on an average, one-third of the budget for each feature film. The filmhuset (Film House), in which the Institute is housed, offers full studio facilities, with two sound stages, editing rooms, makeup rooms, dressing rooms, a prop room, and a metal and paint shop. Filmhuset also houses the nonproduction side of the Institute's work, including a library, clippings archives, still photograph and poster archives, two theatres (with nightly screenings), a film archive, and publication offices for two journals, *TM* and *Chaplin*. Outside of Stockholm, the Swedish Film Institute operates a full-service laboratory, handling not only its film preservation work, but also general work for film productions.

The Institute was founded in 1963, but has its origins in the Swedish Film Club, founded in October 1933. It is run by a board of directors, appointed by the Swedish government, and by an executive director, appointed by the board. It is funded through a 10 percent levy on the gross box-office receipts from all Swedish cinemas and from a tax on all home video cassette sales.

Address: Filmhuset, Borgvägen 1-5, S-115 26 Stockholm, Sweden.

BIBLIOGRAPHY

Slide, Anthony, "Sweden's Unique Film Institute," *American Cinematographer*, vol. LXVIII, no. 3, March 1987, pp. 80–84.

SWITZERLAND. To many, it would appear that there was no Swiss cinema until the sixties, but, in reality, Swiss filmmaking dates back to the early years of this century and the Swiss film industry gained mild attention in the early forties.

Films were first seen in Switzerland, in Geneva, in 1896. In 1905, the Lumière brothers filmed *Le fête des vignerons/The Winegrowers' Festival* at Vevey, but it was not until 1920 that the first prominent Swiss film, *Une heureuse invention/A Happy Invention,* directed by Léon Tombert, was released. Prewar features were usually produced in association with foreign companies. During the Second World War, a number of filmmakers worked in Switzerland, notably Jacques Feyder. In 1945, two features directed by Leopold Lindtberg for Praesens-Film*, received considerable attention in the United States: *Die Letzte Chance/The Last Chance* and *Marie-Louise*.

Filmmaking in Switzerland was dominated by the German-speaking community until the late sixties, when a New Swiss Cinema emerged, thanks to a production unit called Groupe 5, which was financed in part by Suisse Romande TV. Among the directors associated with this unit are Michel Soutter, Yves Yersin, Jean-Louis Roy, and Claude Goretta. However, it was another member, Alain Tanner (born 1929) who really brought Swiss filmmaking to international attention with films such as *Charles mort ou vif/Charles Dead or Alive* (1969), *La Salamandre/The Salamander* (1971), *Le milieu du monde/The Middle of the World* (1974), and *Jonas qui aura vingt-cinq ans en an 2000/Jonah Who Will Be 25 in the Year 2000* (1976). Jean-Luc Godard (born 1930) was educated in Switzerland and made his first short film there; in 1980 he returned to direct the feature *Suave qui peut/Every Man for Himself,* a Swiss-French co-production as were two of Godard's later features, *Passion* (1982) and *Je vous salue Marie/Hail Mary* (1984).

The Schweizer Filmzentrum/Swiss Film Centre (Münstergasse 18, CH-8001 Zurich) was formed in the early seventies to help fund production from monies made available by local municipalities. However, the cantons subsequently refused to finance the Centre, and it operates now as a distribution organization and as a promoter of Swiss films. The government agency concerned with the film industry is the Federal Bureau of Culture—Film Section (Thunstrasse 20, 3000 Berne 6), which heads the Secretary of the National Commission on Films.

There were 437 theatres in operation in the late eighties. There is no censorship in Switzerland, but Catholic and Protestant organizations classify films rather as did the Legion of Decency in the United States. Local authorities do have the power to censor films, but many cantons and cities have abolished such ability.

BIBLIOGRAPHY

Barron, Fred, "Letter from Switzerland," *Take One,* vol. IV, no. 11, May-June 1974, pp. 36–37.

Buache, Freddy. *Le cinéma Suisse*. Lausanne: L'age d'homme, 1974.

Mancini, Elaine, "Switzerland," in *World Cinema since 1945,* editor William Luhr. New York: Ungar, 1987, pp. 542–549.

Schenk, Rolf, "Is There a Swiss Film Industry?" *Film Society Review,* October 1967, pp. 36–37.

Wollenberg, H.H., "The Scene in Switzerland," *Sight & Sound,* vol. XVI, no. 64, Winter 1947–48, pp. 144–147.

SYDNEY. The best known of Australian cities has been seen in relatively few films with international appeal: *The Siege of Pinchgut* (1959), *Summer of the Seventeenth Doll* (1959), and *They're a Weird Mob* (1966). Among the Australian films that have utilized the city for their stories are *The Cheaters* (1929), *Caddie* (1976), *The Last Wave* (1976), *Newsfront* (1978), *Money Movers* (1978), *The Best of Friends* (1981), *Heatwave* (1981), *The Killing of Angel Street* (1981), *Dead Easy* (1982), *Going Down* (1982), *Kiss the Night* (1982), *Starstruck* (1982), *Fast Talking* (1983), *The City's Edge* (1983), *The Empty Beach* (1985), and *Dangerous Game* (1988).

The city is also the home of the Sydney Film Festival (P.O. Box 25, Glebe, NSW 2037, Australia).

BIBLIOGRAPHY

Stratton, David, "Camera-Shy Sydney Hopes Producers Will Sit Up and Take Notice," *Daily Variety,* September 2, 1988, p. 9.

SYRIA. Filmmaking in Syria dates from 1928, when the country's first production, *The Accused Innocent,* was released. In 1963, the government established the National Film Organization (Rawda al Takriti, Damascus, Syria), but it was not until 1968 that it produced its first film, *The Truck Driver,* directed by a Yugoslavian, Boško Foćinić. That same year, the comedy team of Douraid and Nouhad—they were compared to Laurel and Hardy—became popular with Syrian filmgoers. The National Film Organization failed to make much of an impact until the seventies, during which decade it produced a considerable number of features and documentary shorts. Among important Syrian features of the eighties are Samir Zikra's *Haditha al nasf metr./Half Meter Incident* (1983), Mohamed Malass' *Ahlam al madina/Dreams of the City* (1984), Doreid Lahum's *Hudud/Borders* (1984), and Mohamed Shahine's *Shams fi yaum ghaim/Sun on a Cloudy Day* (1985).

BIBLIOGRAPHY

"Before War, Syria Updated Film Biz," *Variety,* October 17, 1973, pp. 1, 47.

Malkmus, Lizbeth, "Syria," in *International Film Guide 1987,* editor Peter Cowie. London: Tantivy Press, 1986, pp. 315–316.

T

TACHYSCOPE. A sophisticated version of the Zoetrope*, the Tachyscope was invented in 1887 by the German photographer Ottomar Anschütz (1846–1907). The device was manufactured by Siemens and presented throughout the world.

TAIWAN. Although the Taiwan film industry is usually discussed in connection with Hong Kong* cinema, the island does have an industry which is very much its own. It has its origins in mainland China's film industry and was founded by refugees from Shanghai and elsewhere, including Li Hsing, Sung Ts'unshou, and Pai Ching-jui. The government established three studios, Zhong Ying, Zhong Zi, and Tai Zhi, and films were made for the Central Motion Picture Corporation, which continues to provide production assistance.

Because the Shaw Brothers* dominated the Taiwan film industry, a close relationship developed with Hong Kong cinema as directors and performers worked in both industries, with Taiwan producing features in either Mandarin or Taiwanese. Through the seventies, the bulk of the films produced were martial arts costume dramas and teenage melodramas.

A so-called "New Wave" swept the Taiwanese film industry in the eighties, as new directors such as Hou Xiaoxian, Yang Dechang, and others began producing films of a more personal nature. However, by the mid-eighties, the "New Wave" was considered largely dead. A number of filmmakers and critics began calling for less government supervision of the industry—there is heavy censorship in Taiwan—and a need for recognition of the motion picture as a serious force for social and cultural change. Many critics looked to filmmakers in 8mm and 16mm to produce an alternative Taiwanese cinema.

There are more than 450 theatres on the island. With an average feature film costing under $100,000 to produce, the number of Taiwanese features a year has dropped from 250 in the early eighties to under 150 in the latter part of the decade. For many years Japanese films were banned as a result of that country's breaking off diplomatic relations with Taiwan.

BIBLIOGRAPHY

Eberhard, Wolfram. *The Chinese Silver Screen: Hong Kong and Taiwanese Motion Pictures in the 1960's*. Taipei: Orient Cultural Service, 1972.

Elley, Derek, "Taiwan," in *International Film Guide 1988*, editor Peter Cowie. London: Tantivy Press, 1987, pp. 328–333.

TEAMFILM A/S operates one of Norway's three film studios. Established in 1962 by Knut Andersen, Knut Bohwin, and Mattis Mathiesen, the company's features include *Brent Jord/Scorched Earth* (1969) and *Karjolsteinen/The Turn of the Road* (1977).

Address: Kersersgt 1, N-0165 Oslo 1, Norway.

TELEFILM CANADA was founded by the Canadian government in 1967 as the Canadian Film Development Corporation (CFDC) "to foster and promote the development of a feature film industry in Canada." Telefilm Canada does not produce or distribute films, but works closely with individual producers and distributors. It also offers a script development program, an interim financing program (that permits producers to commence production in advance of total financing), the equity investment program (encouraging the production of films of a strictly Canadian nature), the promotion and advertising program (supporting the marketing of films), and the test marketing program. A special Canadian Broadcast Program Development Fund was established by the Canadian government on July 1, 1983, to encourage an increase in quality television production, and this is also coordinated by Telefilm Canada.

Address: 600 de la Gauchetiere Street West, 25th Floor, Montréal, Québec H3B 4L2, Canada.

TELERECORDING is the British name for a kinescope, being a film record made by photographing an image directly from the television monitor.

TERRA-FILM Akt. Ges. An important German production company of the twenties and thirties, Terra-Film produced what is considered the first German anti-Semitic feature, *Robert und Bertram* (1935). It was absorbed by Ufa*, which distributed its films, in 1938, and a new company with the same name was organized in the summer of that year.

THAILAND. In 1976, *Variety* hailed the Thai film industry as "one of the fastest growing" in South East Asia. An average of seventy features a year are produced for budgets of under $100,000 each, and are seen throughout the region (but never dubbed into English for the Western market). The government did little to encourage native production with a theatre admission tax that was as high as 50 percent. The government also began the imposition, in 1977, of an import tax on films, initially aimed at keeping out cheaply produced films from

Japan, India, Indonesia, and Hong Kong, but also resulting in a decrease in American features (which are the most popular in Thailand).

The first film to be made in what was then known as Siam was *Suvarna of Siam,* directed by American filmmaker Henry McRae in 1923, under the sponsorship of the Railway System of Siam. In 1932, Sri Krung, the country's first major film production company established under the patronage of the royal family, made the country's first sound film, *Going Astray*. In 1938, the Thai Film Company was created, but it produced only four films before its bankruptcy and the taking over of its studios by the Royal Siamese Air Force. By the forties, Sri Krung had also ceased production—the last film made at the studio was in 1943—and it was subsequently converted to a publishing house for two newspapers and a theatre. An important feature, released in 1940, was *The King of the White Elephants,* directed by politician Pridi Panomyong, in English, and screened in a number of Western countries.

After the Second World War, for economy reasons, most films were made in 16mm, often without sound. Live sound was provided by actors located behind the screen. (This same practice continues to a certain extent today with foreign-language films that are too expensive to dub, and that are seen with live translations.) The industry enjoyed a revival in the fifties. A new company, Hanumarn Film, was founded in 1953, with its first feature being *Santi Weena,* scripted by Vichit Kounavudhi, who has since made more than thirty films and is regarded as one of the most influential figures in recent Thai cinema. Following the founding of Hanumarn Film, two other companies were created by members of the Thai royal family; Prince Bhanu established Aswin Film and Prince Anusorn was resonsible for Lavo Film.

Production has been declining since 1980, when one hundred features were produced. Since then the number of films produced has been dropping by ten or more each year to a low of sixty in 1983. In the late seventies, the American film industry placed a ban on the export of all films to Thailand to protest the import tax, but the ban was lifted in 1981. The country is occasionally used for location shooting, most notably for *The Ugly American,* starring Marlon Brando, in 1963. Leading directors include Prince Chatri Chalerm, Permphol Chucaroon, Eouthana Mukdasanit, and Somdej Santipracha.

BIBLIOGRAPHY

Cacnio, Paul, "New Tax on Foreign Pix Perils Imports in Thailand & Booms Native Industry to Peak Level," *Variety,* December 22, 1977, p. 35.

Dome, Sukwongs, and Knit Kounavudhi, "The Cinema in Thailand," *Cinema India-International,* vol. IV, no. 1, 1987, pp. 116–117.

Marshall, Fred, "Thailand," *Variety,* May 2, 1979, pp. 375, 404.

THE THAUMATROPE, an optical toy illustrating the persistence of vision, was invented by Englishman Dr. John Ayrton Paris in 1825.

THÉÂTRE DU VIEUX-COLOMBIER. The legitimate Paris theatre, Vieux-Colombier, was acquired by Jean Tedesco, and opened on November 14, 1924, as a theatre specializing in the presentation of avant-garde films, with André Savage's *La traversé du Crepon,* Marcel Silver's *L'horlage,* and Charlie Chaplin's *Sunnyside* (1921). It screened revivals of many earlier silent features, and introduced a series of Saturday lectures during 1925–1926. Behind the theatre, a small studio was built, and here Tedesco and Jean Renoir made *La petite marchande d'allumettes/The Little Match Seller* (1928).

THEATROGRAPH. British film pioneer, R.W. (Robert William) Paul (1869–1943) used the name of "Theatrograph" to describe his original camera and projector, films from and on which were first seen at London's Royal Institute on February 28, 1896. He was actively involved in producing films for screening at Britain's variety theatres through the turn of the Century. A number of his films involved trick photography, and C.W. Ceram has suggested that he might be described as "the English Méliès."

BIBLIOGRAPHY

Ceram, C.W. *Archaeology of the Cinema*. New York: Harcourt, Brace & World, undated (1985).

THIRD WORLD CINEMA is a term utilized to describe filmmaking in countries of the Third World (Africa, Asia, and Latin America) from the sixties onward. The film movement in these countries, aimed at depicting the struggles for freedom and national identity—for which the motion picture has become a political weapon—has come to be called "Third Cinema." Main themes in Third World Cinema are armed struggles, class, culture, religion, and sexism. The films of Third World Cinema are generally produced outside of commercial filmmaking, which is usually associated with the established film industry.

Some of the earliest films of Third World Cinema are Glauber Rocha's *Barravento* (1962) from Brazil, Lester James Peries' *Rekawa* (1963) from Sri Lanka, Ahmed Rachedi's *The Dawn of the Damned* (1965) from Algeria, and the collective effort, *The East Is Red* (1965) from China. There are some films that predate the Third World Cinema movement, such as Lester James Peries' *Gamperaliya* (1956) from Ceylon and Satyajit Ray's *Pather Panchali* (1956) from India.

BIBLIOGRAPHY

Cyr, Helen W. *A Filmography of the Third World.* Metuchen, N.J.: Scarecrow Press, 1976.

———. *A Filmography of the Third World, 1976–1983*. Metuchen, N.J.: Scarecrow Press, 1985.

Gabriel, Teshome H. *Third Cinema in the Third World: The Aesthetics of Liberation.* Ann Arbor, Mich.: UMI Research Press, 1982.

THORN-EMI SCREEN ENTERTAINMENT (TESE) came into being in September 1983, when chairman and chief executive Gary Dartnall announced the reorganization of Thorn-EMI, resulting in the amalgamation of Thorn-EMI Cinemas, Thorn-EMI Films, and Thorn-EMI Video into one company. The origins of the company go back to 1969, when EMI, one of Britain's largest and most influential conglomerates, acquired the Associated British Pictures Corporation, and, with it, Elstree Studios*. In 1979, when EMI was in financial difficulties, Thorn, the British electrical giant, offered £169 million for the company, which became Thorn-EMI.

For the next eighteen months, the parent company witnessed EMI Films running at a loss, with Allan Carr's *Can't Stop the Music* (1980) and John Schlesinger's *Honky Tonk Freeway* (1981) unmitigated box-office failures. When, in July 1982, EMI Films showed a £10 million loss, reorganization commenced, with Verity Lambert appointed director of production, the Los Angeles staff cut to four, the departure of the chairman and chief executive officer Barry Spikings, and the appointment of Gary Dartnall, a former executive of British Lion* and EMI's American distribution company and then head of VHD development at Thorn. Thus was TESE established.

One of TESE's first tangible actions was to revitalize the ailing ABC Cinema Circuit, through guaranteed, regularly spaced playdates, Friday changeovers in programs, fixed starting times, a premium pricing policy, use of smaller screens to provide more choice, and refurbishment of theatres. Cable projects included the development of a music cable service, Musicbox, the setting up of the Premiere film channel, and a children's channel. TESE acquired for the world, excluding the United States and Canada, productions from Silver Screen, HBO's feature film production arm. Dartnall also tried stimulating British film production with the announcement of a series of deals with independent producers. TESE would establish a revolving project development fund, to be drawn upon by producers who would also receive a contribution toward their running overheads. In return, TESE would have first option on investment in future projects. Among the films produced in this manner were *A Passage to India* (1984), *Comfort and Joy* (1984), *Morons from Outer Space* (1985), *Dreamchild* (1985), and *Restless Natives* (1986).

However, TESE's existence was short-lived. In October 1985, Thorn-EMI put up for sale its film and television interests in a cash-raising exercise to help the parent company. An attempted management buy-out by Gary Dartnall, assisted by Australian tycoon Alan Bond, failed. In May 1986, the Cannon Group acquired Screen Entertainment, and it continues under the name of its new owner.

Address: Cannon Group, 167–169 Wardour Street, London W1V 3TA, United Kingdom.

BIBLIOGRAPHY

Auty, Chris, "Thorn EMI: The Business of Entertainment," *Stills,* no. 10, February/March 1984, pp. 46–49.

Park, James, "The Nervous Summer of the British Film Industry," *Sight & Sound,* vol. LV, no. 1, Winter 1985/86, pp. 8–13.

Snoddy, Raymond, "Screen Entertainment Faces Instant Hard Times," *Stills,* no. 24, February 1986, p. 7.

Willmott, Nigel, "A Thorn Outside the British Film Industry," *Broadcast,* May 16, 1986, p. 21.

TITANUS spa. Italy's oldest surviving film company, Titanus has its origins in Naples, where founder Gustavo Lombardo opened an office in 1904 for the purchase and sale of films. He started a production company, Lombardo Film, there in 1914, and kept his headquarters in Naples until a 1929 move to Rome. Lombardo's son, Goffredo, took over as head of the company in 1951, and remained its head after a 1963 merger with the Angelo Rizzoli company, Cineriz. Active in both production and distribution, Titanus was chiefly concerned with the latter in recent years up to its acquisition, in 1986, by the Italian finance group, Acqua Marci-Bastogi, headed by industrialist Vincenzo Romagnoli.

Address: via Sommacampagna 28, 00185 Rome, Italy.

BIBLIOGRAPHY

Hammond, Margo, "Titanus Spans Italian Film History," *Variety,* May 2, 1979, pp. 51, 79.

"Naples: Titanus' Birthplace Is Home of a Pix Genre," *Variety,* May 2, 1979, p. 50.

TOBAGO was the location for the filming of the 1960 Walt Disney feature, *Swiss Family Robinson,* directed by Ken Annakin, and starring John Mills, Dorothy McGuire, and James MacArthur.

TOBIS is the name by which the German production company of Tonbild Syndikat A.G. is generally known. It was formed in 1928 by the Swiss company Triergon-Musik A.G., the German company, Deutsche Tonfilm A.G., the Dutch company Küchenmeister Kommendit Gesellschaft, and the German company Messter Ton. It was able to acquire the rights to the Tri-Ergon* sound-on-film system, and, in 1929, merged with Klangfilm, to become Tobis-Klangfilm, with headquarters in Amsterdam. Its first sound feature was Walter Ruttmann's *Melodie der welt/World Melody* (1929), and its first international success was G.W. Pabst's *Die Dreigroschenoper/The Three Penny Opera* (1931). It produced many films outside of Germany, some through a French subsidiary, Société des Films Sonores Tobis*, and others in the United Kingdom. It also maintained an American distribution company, Tobis Forenfilms, Inc., which released all of the Tobis productions, including the two 1931 French classics directed by René Clair, *Le Million* and *À Nous la Liberté.*

As the only major competitor to Ufa* in Germany, Tobis formed subsidiary production companies, Tobis Syndikat, Tobis Rota, and Tobis Magna, as well as a distribution company, Tobis Europa, and an export division, Tobis Cinema. On December 1, 1937, the company became fully owned by the German government, although the Dutch parent company still retained control of the various sound patents. The company's activities ceased with the German surrender at the end of the Second World War.

TOEI is the name by which the Tokyo Motion Picture Distribution Company is best known. It was formed in 1953 from two earlier production companies, Toyoko and Oizumi, with Hiroshi Okawa as its head. It was initially known for the production of cheap features designed to fill the lower half of a double bill. However, in 1957, it became the first Japanese company to commence major production of widescreen features—using the term Toeiscope—beginning with *Otori-jo no hanayone/Bride of Otori Castle*.

Address: Toei Co. Ltd., 2-17, 3 Chome, Ginza, Chuo-Ku, Tokyo 104, Japan.

TOHO CO., LTD. is a Japanese entertainment giant, involved in film and television production, film distribution, film importation, and film exhibition. It was founded on August 12, 1932, when real estate entrepreneur Ichizo Kobayashi organized the Tokyo Takarazuka Theatre Corporation. Toho, itself, was formed on August 16, 1937, and the two companies were merged on December 10, 1943. A major labor strike erupted at the Toho studios in August 1948, and the U.S. occupation forces in Japan were required to bring the situation under control.

In the fifties, Toho gained worldwide recognition for its productions, thanks to the work of two of its directors, Akira Kurosawa and Hiroshi Inagaki. It became active in the United States in the sixties, opening a theatre in Los Angeles on August 3, 1960, a theatre in New York on January 22, 1963, and a theatre chain in Hawaii in July 1964.

Address: 1-2-1 Yuraku-Cho, Chioyoda-Ku, Tokyo, Japan.

BIBLIOGRAPHY

"Toho at 50 years; Nothing Comparable in the U.S.," *Variety,* May 12, 1982, p. 325.
"Toho Topper—Japan No Monopoly," *Variety,* May 4, 1983, p. 339.

TOKYO. Aside from being a favorite city for Godzilla*, Tokyo has also been seen in *Blood on the Sun* (1945), *Tokyo Rose* (1946), *Tokyo Joe* (1949), *A Majority of One* (1961), *My Geisha* (1962), and *Walk, Don't Run* (1966). During the Second World War, it was the subject of *Thirty Seconds over Tokyo* (1944). The first American feature to be shot in its entirety in Japan after the war was *Tokyo File 212* (1951). The 18th Olympiad, held in Tokyo, was the subject of Kon Ichikawa's *Tokyo Olympiad* (1965).

TOPICAL BUDGET was a British newsreel produced from 1911 to 1932. During the First World War, the British government took over the stock of the company that produced the newsreel, Topical Budget Film Company, and produced the newsreel as a propaganda vehicle.

TRANSIT-FILM is a company exclusively owned by the Federal Republic of Germany and governed by a board of trustees. It was established on January 18, 1966, to market documentary films and newsreels produced between 1914 and 1945, the copyright in which is controlled by the West German government.

In 1966, the Friedrich-Wilhelm-Murnau-Stiftung was founded to handle similarly the approximately 1,100 feature films produced by Ufa*, Terra, Tobis*, and Bavaria prior to 1962 and now under the control of the government. On November 11, 1967, the distribution of these films was taken over by Transit-Film from Friedrich-Wilhelm-Murnau-Stiftung, and the features are marketed under the package heading of "Klassicher Deutscher Film" (Classic German Films).

Although Transit-Film claims ownership of all classic German films throughout the world, it appears that many of the titles in its catalog are, in fact, in the public domain in the United States. A complete title listing of all films claimed by Transit-Film appeared in *Daily Variety,* October 7, 1986, pages 13–14.

Address: Transit-Film-Gesellschaft MBH, Dachauer Strasse 35, 8000 München 2, West Germany.

TRENTON STUDIOS. Located in the Ontario, Canada, town of Trenton, the Trenton Studios were important to early Canadian filmmaking. The studios were opened in 1916 by George Brownridge and his Canadian National Features. They closed in 1919, but reopened in 1923, after purchase by the Ontario Motion Picture Bureau, and remained in use until their permanent closure in 1934. The closure of the studios coincided with the October 1934 closure of the Bureau, which had been established in May 1917.

BIBLIOGRAPHY

Morris, Peter. *Embattled Shadows: A History of Canadian Cinema 1895–1939*. Montreal: McGill-Queen's University Press, 1978.

TRI-ERGON was a sound-on-film system, utilizing a photocell, that was developed as early as 1918 by three Swiss-German inventors, Josef Engl, Joseph Massolle and Hans Vogt. The trio named their process Tri-Ergon because it was "the work of three." The system was publicly demonstrated in Berlin on September 17, 1922, and acquired by a Swiss company, Ton-F. Zweke, Glimmlampe für Licht-Tonaufnahme, which subsequently sold the rights to Ufa*. The rights were later obtained by Tobis*. American rights to Tri-Ergon were acquired by William Fox in 1925, and as a result he was able to initiate law suits against most sound systems operative in the United States. However, in 1935, the Supreme Court ruled that "in the public interest" the Tri-Ergon patents were invalid.

TRINIDAD had a short-lived film industry in the thirties, when a local newsreel and a number of short subjects were produced. Distribution to the Island's twenty-one theatres was regulated by a Film Board, formed in Port of Spain in July 1937. In the eighties, there are nine distributors active in Trinidad and Tobago.

"TRÜMMERFILME" is the name given to films produced in both East and West Germany immediately following the Second World War. Literally, it means films of the ruins.

TSUMA-MONO is a genre in Japanese cinema, in which the wife is the central character.

TUNISIA has long been popular as a location site for filmmakers as varied as the Monty Python* troupe, George Lucas, Franco Zeffirelli, and Steven Spielberg. One of the first international filmmakers to "discover" the country was Italian Roberto Rossellini, who came there in 1975 to commence filming of his *Il Messia/The Messiah* (1978). Thanks to Rossellini, a young Tunisian named Tarak ben Ammar realized the potential for a Tunisian film industry; he established Carthago Films and by 1986 had become producer of such major films as Roman Polanski's *Pirates*. The producer also operates studios at Port El Kantaoui and Monastir and owns many theatres.

In 1957, the Tunisian government established SATPEC (Société Anonyme Tunisienne de Production et d'Expansion Cinématographique, 10 rue Ibn Khaldun, Tunis, Tunisia). It is involved primarily in production, with limited interests in distribution. In 1967, SATPEC created the major film complex at Gammarth, which includes a film laboratory, editing suites, a sound stage, viewing rooms, and mobile film units. Major Tunisian film directors include Tayeb Louichi, Mahmoud Ben Mahmoud, Ridhi Behi, Nacir Khemir, Abdeuatif Ben Ammar, Moncef Dhouib, and Lotfi Essid.

Tunisia is also important in the Arab and African film world as the site of Journées Cinématographiques de Carthage (Carthage Film Days), a biennial event at which African and Arab films are screened and filmmakers have the opportunity to meet and discuss common concerns. It has been held, with funding provided in large part by the Tunisian government, since 1976.

BIBLIOGRAPHY

Borsten, Joan, "Tunisia—An Oasis of Western Culture," *Los Angeles Times* Calendar, November 21, 1982, pp. 4–5.

Malmus, Lizbeth, "Tunisia," *International Film Guide 1986,* editor Peter Cowie. London: Tantivy Press, 1985, pp. 333–335.

McCarthy, Todd, "Ben Ammar Plans Huge Soundstage for Tunisia plus 100 New Cinemas," *Variety,* June 19, 1985, pp. 45, 47.

Werba, Hank, "Tunisia in Bid for Int'l Film-TV Role," *Variety,* October 22, 1980, pp. 41, 54.

TURKEY. The Turkish film industry has had a long life, dating from 1914, when Fuat Uzkinay (who was later involved in the Army Cinema Department, created in 1917) made the documentary, *The Destruction of the Russian Monument in Agia Stefanos*. Films had first been screened in Turkey as early as 1897, and the first motion picture theatre was built in 1908.

From 1923 to 1939, Turkish cinema went through a "theatre period," when stage directors and actors, such as Muhsin Ertugrul, dominated the industry, making films during the off-season from the theatre. The first Turkish sound film was *Istanbul's Streets,* made in 1932 by Ipek Film Studio Company, which was to produce six sound films in the 1932–1933 period. Ipek, along with Halil Kamil operated the two major pre–Second World War Turkish studios, which supplied product for the country's 155 theatres.

During the Second World War, European films were not screened in Turkey, and Egyptian cinema was dominant. However, in the postwar years, Egyptian films were banned, and the Turkish film industry grew from eight production companies in 1948 to twenty in 1959. Similarly, the number of Turkish films proliferated, from sixteen in 1949 to twenty-three in 1959. By the seventies the country was producing an average of two hundred features a year, and its seven hundred and fifty winter theatres and two thousand summer theatres constituted an important market for American films. By the eighties the situation had deteriorated through the advent of television, and the country's film output was largely limited to sex-oriented productions.

Censorship has been strictly enforced in the Turkish film industry since 1936. The winner of the Golden Bear award at the Berlin Film festival, *Susz Yaz/The Dry Summer* (1965), directed by Metin Erksan, had to be smuggled out of the country because of censorship problems.

"Young Turkish Cinema" was a movement within the industry from 1961 onwards, and among the directors associated with it are Ertem Görec, Ömer Kavur, Ali Ozgentürk, and Yilmal Güney. The last had been an actor and he continued making films from political imprisonment until his death in 1985; his memorable features are *Umut/Hope* (1971) and *Yol* (1983), which was written in prison by Güney and directed by Şerif Göen.

BIBLIOGRAPHY

Borsten, Joan, "In Istanbul, a Thirst for Movies," *Los Angeles Times* Calendar, December 13, 1981, pp. 3–4.

———, "Turkish Cinema Prosperous on the Bosporus," *Los Angeles Times,* Part VI, December 29, 1981, p. 5.

Dorsay, Atilla, "Growing in Quality and Quantity, Turk Films Find Place in the Sun," *Variety,* February 25, 1987, pp. 356, 378.

Evren, Burçak. *Türk Sinema Sanatçilari Ansiklopedisi.* Istanbul: Film-San Vakfi Yayinlari, 1983.

Franko, Ayse, "Turkey" in *World Cinema since 1945,* editor William Luhr. New York: Ungar, 1987, pp. 550–557.

Manus, Willard, "Turkish Troubles," *Sight & Sound,* vol. XLVI, no. 3, Summer 1977, pp. 152–153.

Nijat, Özön. *Türk Sinemast Tarihi.* Istanbul: Artist, 1977.

Pertan, Ersin, "Turkish Cinema through the Years," *The Hollywood Reporter,* October 25, 1983, pp. M20–M22.

TWICKENHAM FILM STUDIOS. Located in a West London suburb, Twickenham is the oldest working studio in the United Kingdom. Formerly a skating rink, it was opened by the London Film Company in 1912 under the directorship of R.T. Jupp. The London Film Company produced films there from 1913 to 1921. It had a variety of owners in the twenties, but in the following decade was under the control of Julius Hagen, a colorful film producer, who made dozens of "quota quickies"* there until the outbreak of the Second World War.

The studios were requisitioned by the government during the Second World War, but reopened in 1944 as the Alliance Film Studios, part of a conglomerate that also included studios at Southall and Riverside, formed by Alfred Shipman. Humphries Holding Group acquired Twickenham in 1972, and it changed hands again in 1977, when it was taken over by Film Location Facilities.

Twickenham Film Studios has three sound stages, dubbing facilities and the usual production offices. Producer-director Richard Lester maintains offices there and has made some eighteen films in the last twenty years at Twickenham. It was here that the Beatles made their first two features in 1964, *A Hard Day's Night* and *Help!* Other recent features that were at Twickenham include *Isadora* (1967), *Yanks* (1978), *Reds* (1979), *The French Lieutenant's Woman* (1980), *Wetherby* (1984), and *Murder on the Orient Express* (1985).

Address: The Barons, St. Margarets, Twickenham, Middlesex TW1 2AW.

BIBLIOGRAPHY

"Little Studio—Big Heart," *Screen International,* October 18, 1986, pp. 68–84.

TWO CITIES FILMS, LTD. was a British production company set up in the late thirties, with the two cities in question being London and Rome. It was formed by producer Ludovic Toeplitz in 1937, and had links with the Italian company, Pisorno. By August 1938, Two Cities had an entirely new board of directors, that included the Italian banker, Filippo del Guidice, who had arrived in England some years previously as a refugee from Mussolini's Italy. The capital was £40,000, and the original intention was to make Anglo-Italian, bilingual films at Shepperton Studios and in Rome.

Two Cities' first film was *French without Tears* (1939), directed by Anthony Asquith, and based on a play by Terence Rattigan. Asquith was a director particularly associated with the company, later making *The Demi-Paradise* (1943), *The Way to the Stars* (1945), *The Importance of Being Earnest* (1952), and *The Net* (1953). Del Giudice's greatest achievement, however, was persuading Nöel Coward to write, direct, and star in *In Which We Serve* (1942), which became one of Britain's most successful war films, earning £300,000 at British theatre box offices and $2 million in the United States. With an established reputation, Del Giudice was approached by the British Ministry of Information to produce a film about the ATS (Auxiliary Territorial Service/British Women's Service), to be called *The Gentle Sex*. J. Arthur Rank provided some of the financing, and an association formed between the two men. A wonderful group of films followed, including *This Happy Breed* (1945), *Blithe Spirit* (1945), *Brief Encounter* (1945), all combining the talents of Nöel Coward and David Lean; Carol Reed's *The Way Ahead* (1944) and *Odd Man Out* (1947); and Laurence Olivier's *Henry V* (1945) and *Hamlet* (1949). Unfortunately, Del Giudice was prone to extravagance—it was part of his philosophy of filmmaking—and *Henry V* went way over budget. The feature was rescued by Rank, who financed it in return for control of Two Cities.

When the Rank Organization* began to have its own financial problems, drastic measures were taken by managing director John Davis. Del Giudice left Two Cities, and the company, along with Pinewood Films and Gainsborough* became part of J. Arthur Rank Productions, Ltd.

U

UBU. Australia's first major avant-garde film production group, Ubu, was formed in 1965 by David Perry, Aggy Read, John Clark, and Albie Thomas. It was named for Alfred Jarry's 1962 stageplay, *Ubu Roi,* and had its headquarters in Sydney. The group's films, which include *Man and His World* (1966), *Puncture* (1966), and *Boobs a Lot* (1968), were distributed by its self-created Sydney Filmmakers' Cooperative. Ubu ceased its activities in 1971.

BIBLIOGRAPHY

Thoms, Albie, "The Australian Avant-Garde," in *An Australian Film Reader,* editors Albert Moran and Tom O'Regan. Sydney, Australia: Currency Press, 1985, pp. 279–287.

UFA (Universum film Aktiengesellschaft) is the best known of all German production companies, associated with the "Golden Age" of German cinema, and the work of F.W. Murnau, E.A. Dupont, Erich Pommer, Ernst Lubitsch, Paul Leni, and others. Its stars included Emil Jannings and Pola Negri, and its influence was felt as far away as Hollywood, where such directors as Murnau and Leni introduced the Ufa style to American cinema, affecting the work of such steadfastly American filmmakers as John Ford.

The company was created in 1917, during the First World War, by the German government, with an initial capital of DM8 million. It was established through the merger of Davidsons Union, Messter Film, Bild-Und Filmaten (BUFA)*, and others, with the intent to promote German culture and improve the nation's image abroad. Its initial incarnation was short-lived, and in 1918 the government's control in the Ufa was taken over by the Deutsche Bank, that initiated a policy of producing strictly commercial features, including costume pictures. It was one of the latter, *Madame Dubarry/Passion* (1919), directed by Ernst Lubitsch and starring Pola Negri, that opened Ufa's new Berlin theatre, the massive Film Palast am Zoo.

In 1923, Erich Pommer became production head of the company, and he was responsible for many of its classic films, including *Der Letzte Mann/The Last*

Laugh (1924) and *Metropolis* (1927). He also established a documentary production unit at Ufa in 1925, with its first effort being *Wege zur kraft und schönheit/ Ways to Strength and Beauty* (1925).

During this same period, Ufa became associated with Paramount and M-G-M—adopting the name Parafumet—and producing many films in the Hollywood style. The company was taken over in 1927 by Alfred Hugenberg, a right-wing publishing mogol, who politicized Ufa to a certain extent, although it was still able to produce such important films as *Der Blaue Engel/The Blue Angel* (1930) and *Der Kongress Tanzt/Congress Dances* (1931).

Hugenberg had close ties to Hitler—he became the head of the Nazi Department of Economics for a short time in 1933—and he turned the company toward the production of Nazi propaganda films, beginning with *Morgenrot/Dawn* (1933) and *Hitlerjunge Quex/Hitler Youth Quex* (1933). However, it should not be assumed that Ufa's productions in the thirties were entirely Nazi-oriented; it was still producing entertainment films, providing a glossy view of reality, what critic Lotte Eisner has called "The Ufa Style."

In March 1937, the German government was able to acquire majority shares in Ufa, forced its board of directors to resign, and created a new board, including actors Eugen Klöpfer and Paul Hartmann and directors Carl Froelich and Karl Ritter. Ufa was now completely under the control of propaganda minister Joseph Goebbels. He created a new Ufa star in Zarah Leander, intended as a substitute for Marlene Dietrich.

Ufa remained active throughout the Second World War. In 1941, it produced the first feature in Agfacolor*, *Frauen sind doch bessere diplomaten/ Women Are the Best Diplomats,* directed by Georg Jacoby. A year later, director Wolfgang Lieberneiner became head of production. In 1943, to celebrate its twenty-fifth anniversary, Ufa produced its last great film, *Münchhausen,* directed by Josef von Baky, shot in Agfacolor, and starring Hans Albers in the title role.

Production ceased in 1945, and the studios at Neubabelsberg* which had suffered little damage during the war were taken over by DEFA*.

Rights to all Ufa films are now controlled by Transit-Film*. The initials Ufa are still utilized in West Germany today by a theatre chain and by a brand of candy available for sale in theatres.

BIBLIOGRAPHY

Ford, Charles, "Grandeur and Decadence of Ufa," *Films in Review,* June-July 1953, pp. 266–268.

"ULTUS" SERIES. In the mid-teens, the British office of the French Gaumont* company sought to make a series of films modelled after the popular French serials of Louis Feuillade. Gaumont's director, George Pearson, conceived of a character named Ultus (from the Latin Ultor, an avenger), to be portrayed by Aurele Sydney, a Frenchman of Australian ancestry. Four features were produced: *Ultus, the Man from the Dead* (1915), *Ultus and the Grey Lady,* (1915),

Ultus and the Secret of the Night (1916), and *Ultus and the Three-Button Mystery* (1916).

BIBLIOGRAPHY

Pearson, George. *Flashback*. London: George Allen & Unwin, 1957.

UNIFRANCE FILM is the popular name by which the Association Nationale pour la Diffusion du Film Français à l'Étranger is known. Founded in 1949, it is responsible for the promotion of the French film industry abroad, and maintains offices in Argentina, Brazil, West Germany, Italy, Japan, Mexico, Spain, and the United States.

Address: 114 Champs-Elysées, 75008 Paris, France.

UNIJAPAN FILM is the familiar name by which the Association for the Diffusion of Japanese Films Abroad is known. As the name suggests, the organization is concerned with the promotion of Japanese films throughout the world, initially through *Unijapan Film Quarterly,* first published in July 1958, and later through a *Bulletin* and *Film News*. Founded in 1958, Unijapan Film has given the impression of being somewhat inactive in recent years.

Address: 5-9-23 Ginza, Chuo-Ku, Tokyo 104, Japan.

UNION GÉNÉRALE CINÉMATOGRAPHIQUE (UGC) has been a major French exhibitor and distributor since the end of the Second World War. In more recent years, it has also taken an interest in production. UGC owns 300 screens, of which 130 are in Paris, and it controls some 400 films in partnership with Paribas Bank. It is also associated with publisher, Calmann-Levy, and with the Polygram record company, and is involved in publication of a popular film magazine, *Studio* (founded in 1987).

Address: 24 avenue Charles de Gaulle, Paris 92200, France.

UNITALIA was formed in 1950 by the Italian film industry for the promotion of Italian films abroad. Lack of government funding forced Unitalia to cease operations in 1977.

UNITED KINGDOM. The British film industry has long and rightfully been obsessed with its own colonization by American economic interests. This has led to innumerable crises of finances and faith. It has also contributed to the throwing up of hands on the part of critics, who constantly measure the British fiction film against the specious "standards" established by the country's noted documentary movement. The result has been to make the British cinema an international whipping boy, economically and critically. Indeed, except for a brief "Golden Age" in the mid-forties, the British industry since the early twenties has teetered on the brink of either extinction or nationalization. Yet it has also produced remarkable auteurs (Alfred Hitchcock, Carol Reed, and Michael Powell), great studio styles (Ealing*, Gainsborough*, Hammer*), and great genres and movements (the British music hall* film, the "Angry Young Man"* cycle). In fact, the chaotic nature of the British industry accounts for a tradition of pluralism absent from its American overseers' work.

Demonstrations by photographer-inventor William Friese-Greene (1855–1921) in 1886 before the Royal Photographic Society are considered by many to be the earliest attempts to synthesize various optical illusions with projection in front of a live audience to achieve the ingredients of the motion picture experience. But Friese-Greene was not a promoter, and he had difficulty marketing his invention, even as he continued to improve it. His attempts to refine and distribute his apparatus evaporated in financial mismanagement, personal problems, and technical debates in the pages of professional journals.

Most Britons received their first exposure to projected motion pictures at fairs and through other exhibitions given by itinerant showmen. Some of these entrepreneurs used the experience and capital thus earned to start chains of nickelodeons. British producers in the period 1896–1905 were able to attract viewers with "actualities" such as footage of Queen Victoria's funeral and film from around the Empire. Production shifted to primitive studios such as that constructed by Cecil Hepworth in 1898–1899, which consisted of a sixty-foot square wooden platform with uprights against which painted flats could be stood. Early trick films gave way to fictional works such as *Rescued by Rover* (1905), Hepworth's early story film in which he first employed paid actors, and *The Life of Charles Peace* (1905) noted for its length (over 800 feet).

The introduction of the long film presaged the consolidation of the British industry after 1908. The industry was served by a burgeoning trade press (most notably *The Bioscope**) and a trade organization, the Kinematograph Manufacturers Association, formed in 1906. Shortly thereafter, the nation's first trade union, the National Association of Cinematograph Operators, was created. In 1910, the Incorporated Association of Film Renters was formed, which showed the increasing importance of distribution in the industry and demonstrated the intent of some interests in the industry to restrain trade. By this time, the practice of renting or hiring films rather than selling them outright had made distribution the keystone of the industry. While most cinema showings took place in "town hall" settings, The Daily Bioscope, a redesigned shop seating one hundred people which opened in 1904 in Bishopsgate Street, London, showed that films had a future in venues of their own, though the presence of films on a variety program, with musical and comedy acts, illustrated the dependence film still had on other popular arts for its sustenance. By 1908, the first buildings designed as film theatres, featuring raked floors and discreet, fireproof projection booths, were opening in cities away from London. And, finally, cinema chains were developing, the most notable of which were the Albany Ward circuit and the Provincial Cinematograph Theatres (PCT). PCT began a producing subsidiary, London Films Company, with up-to-date studios at Twickenham. Thus, by 1914, all the elements neccessary for the advancement of the industry into a monopolistic period of intense centralization of capital were in place, in at least rudimentary form.

But by 1910, in an era when worldwide distribution channels were opening, British films were losing their own market. In 1910, for example, when it was estimated that there were 1,600 theatres in the country, British films accounted for only 15 percent of screen time, less in the important London market. In that year, 36 percent of the films shown in Britain were of French origin, 28 percent were American-made, and 17 percent were Italian. Germany and Holland each had 2 percent of the British market. The reasons for this failure to compete are many, but one legitimate explanation lies in the weakness of production values as expressed through the out-moded, artisanal system of production still in use at that time. George Pearson's London Pathé studio staff, for example, numbered only five: a cameraman, an electrician, a carpenter, a scene painter, and a handyman. Comparatively epic values of American and Italian films, as well as their exotic location photography and genre material, accounted for a good measure of the British industry's early subordination.

In this same period, the British embarked on genuine feature film production. Reginald Barker's *Henry VIII* (1910) heavily advertised its production costs and utilized spectacular production values. Barker recruited noted Shakespearean actor Herbert Beerbohm Tree to play the lead, establishing a crucial link with the West End stage. But although Barker used a discriminatory pricing system when marketing his film to exhibitors, his example does not seem to have been widely copied. And, in any case, there was little attempt, beyond the PCT-London Films Company example, to aspire toward vertical integration in the industry. However, the Cinematograph Act of 1909, the first active government intervention in the industry, while it dealt directly only with design and safety standards in the theatre buildings, does seem to have encouraged greater amalgamation of exhibitors into chains. But, unlike its American counterpart, the British industry remained fragmented on the eve of the First World War.

The war dealt a mortal blow to British hopes of being a world power in motion pictures. By the end of 1914, though the number of cinemas had more than doubled since 1910, the British share of screen time had decreased substantially. In the last quarter of that year, in the wake of curtailed British and French production and the end of German imports, the American share of the British market had risen to 60 percent. By the middle of the War, the Americans had thoroughly colonized British screens. As an example, in January 1916, only 53 of the 528 films released in Britain were British-produced. In spite of high import tariffs and the threat of submarine warfare, the American share of the market grew steadily and with it the much discussed preference for American films which would both dog and embarrass industry activists like Michael Balcon who argued for a distinctively "national" cinema in the postwar years.

The core of American power in Britain was its distributorships, set up to negotiate with British exhibition chains. From these points, the Americans could exercise control over British houses while British producers had no such outlets in the United States. And from London, American companies established distributorships in neutral countries in order to export directly to these smaller but still lucrative markets. This reversed a trend begun in the earliest days of the cinema that had placed London as the informal international trading and export exchange for Asia, Africa, and, especially Western Europe. The Americans could avail themselves not only of a unified industry operating far from any semblance of armed conflict, but also of a national government that, through the agency of George Creel's Committee for Public Information, avidly sought the dissemination of "American values" abroad through the medium of the motion picture and utilized diplomatic channels to effect this distribution. The British simply could not compete.

During the twenties, two responses were explored: private competition and public confrontation. Neither had the intended effect. In the private sector, the American model of centralization and vertical integration was followed, after a fashion. But when the British possessed only one modern studio, and when the largest British circuit PCT controlled only sixty-eight theatres (while the largest American chain, First National, controlled 639 houses in the United States) America could afford *not* to compete. After making their initial investments back in the lucrative U.S. market, American producers "dumped" their films in Britain at discount prices, making them attractive to exhibitors too busy competing with one another to resist the tactic and too fragmented to have any effect if they did. British bankers, despite courtship by industry leaders, were leery of investment in British production.

American investments reached directly into all sectors of the British industry by the mid twenties. Fourteen companies handled 84 percent of all films distributed in Britain, and 44 percent of all films were American. The three largest distributors handled 33 percent of the total number of films and were American-owned outlets for the American majors, strongly prejudiced against British films. This prejudice took the form of blind booking, block selling, and advance selling of eighteen months or even more, so that locally financed production would have to wait years before recouping any of its investments. One American magnate smugly claimed in 1923 that British producers eventually would have to distribute in Britain exclusively through American distributors. Several initiatives at beefing up Britain's export film market, most notably that of Lord Rothermere's purchase of Pathé's British interests, were essentially moribund by the end of 1924. In November 1924, even as the industry was advertising a "British Film Week," every British studio was dark; not a single foot of film was exposed. Clearly competition had been unsuccessful.

Industry advisers convinced the government to try a second, more confrontational approach. After much contemplation, the Cinematograph Films Bill of 1927 was passed (the infamous Quota Law), and it was misdirected from its inception. It struck not at distribution, the heart of the Americans' power, but at the rather helpless exhibitor. The law restricted advance booking to six months and outlawed blind selling, requiring distributors to provide 7.5 percent of British films for the exhibitor to choose from; the exhibitor in turn would screen 5 percent of British films yearly. Both quotas were intended to rise to 20 percent by 1935; the law would expire in 1938. In the short term, production money *did* flow to the major British producers, now assured of exhibition outlets. This aided greatly in the development of the first genuinely "major" (that is, along American lines) British producers—Gaumont-British Picture Corporation* and Associated British Picture Corporation. Exhibition capital was then used to outfit studios and plan large production programs. The law also helped producers unaffiliated with exhibitors, such as British Lion (1927), British and Dominion (1928), and Associated Talking Pictures (1929), also to secure capital to upgrade or build studio facilities.

But the law did not specify the production values that constituted a feature film, only its length (3,000 feet). Immediately, American distributors bankrolled tiny British producers, using the resulting films to satisfy the letter, but clearly not the intent, of the quota. Called "quota quickies"*, the films would have meant certain death to an exhibitor who used them regularly. As a result, they were programmed at odd times or occasionally "booked" but never actually shown. This process further eroded the image of British films with conservative city investors. These films, however—like their American counterparts, the "B" Westerns of the period—did provide employment for many figures who later became significant in the British industry, most notably Michael Powell. The coming of the sound film, although clearly on the horizon during the drafting of the quota law, was not factored into its design.

For a moment, British filmmaking revived. British accents were now marketable, or at least, appealing to the eminently bourgeois American moguls. Actors such as Ronald Colman were suddenly greatly prized, and any Briton with a West End accent was quickly drafted. By extension, reasoned British producers, British films themselves would find ready acceptance in America. Gaumont-British more or less stabilized by 1932 and began an ambitious program of filmmaking in 1933. And when Alexander Korda's *The Private Life of Henry VIII* succeeded in cracking the American market in 1933, it appeared that a renaissance was at hand.

In fact, Korda had succeeded in large part because of his United Artists financing and playdates, not because of any essential "British" character of his film. Korda had had a checkered career as a producer and director in Hungary and the United States, but his charismatic personality and glibness convinced all that a new day had dawned for the British film. British studio space increased to four times the number of stages existing in 1927; there were now seventy stages available. Yearly production of British films rose to 288 by 1938, also a new high.

Apart from Korda's immediate circle of influence, but benefiting from it nonetheless, was Oscar Deutsch's Odeon* Theatres circuit. However, when United Artists purchased a 50 percent interest in Odeon in 1936, a new era of even closer cooperation with the Americans was obviously at hand.

Expansion had been too quick and growth outstripped demand. The entire industry had become hugely debt-financed. City investors had become as imprudent after *Henry VIII*'s success as they had been cautious before it. Revenues were nowhere near expectations, and by 1938, the boom was at an end. An investigation revealed, essentially, a gigantic, unwitting pyramid scheme involving the Prudential Assurance Corporation and other city bankers and brokers. Korda's London Films was reorganized, studios at Twickenham went into receivership, and other studios went dark. The reasons for the crash were again complex, but it was clearer than ever that American films had a stranglehold on the world market. An American film released in 1938—*any* American film—was likely to make four times the gross of any British film.

Again, a moment of catastrophe for the British meant opportunity for the Americans. Production at American-owned studios in England, set up originally to sidestep quota laws, began to swing into higher gear. Warner's Teddington studios, Fox's Wembley studios, and M-G-M's British facility began to service location needs of American films, taking advantage of the large pool of unemployed British technicians in the process. With the production of *A Yank at Oxford, The Citadel,* and *Goodbye, Mr. Chips* (1938–1939), the prospect of a British industry operated as a subsidiary of the American majors seemed depressingly at hand.

At the outbreak of the Second World War, concerns about theatres as potential targets for German bombers led to severe early closing laws and in some cases, theatres were shut down altogether. Secondarily, production was greatly affected. Studios were heavily requisitioned; Pinewood, Elstree, Amalgamated, and the small Sound City studio were all removed from production (some for purposes as mundane as use for storage space). All told, 444,000 square feet of studio space was taken from the industry. Actors were called up for National Service without the special status accorded American Hollywood draftees, and shortages and rationing exerted further pressures.

Amidst apparent famine, however, there was plenty. Cinema closings ended by November 4, 1939, and an 11:00 P.M. closing time was instituted nationally. Average weekly attendance increased from 19 million per week in 1939 to 30 million per week in 1945, and box-office receipts tripled. The closing of studios effected a scaling-down of production to feasible levels. Under the auspices of the Ministry of Information, filmmaking interests acted collectively to rationalize production, share resources, and fix a system of group censorship. In effect, they acted monopolistically, producing not only short films, as in the United States, but a successful feature film, *The 49th Parallel* (1941). A tentative truce was enacted between the documentary movement and the fictional film industry. Dozens of films showed the influence of documentarists Alberto Cavalcanti, Harry Watt, Pat Jackson, and others from the documentary field involved in feature film production during the war.

Because of their propaganda value and because American distributors needed films to fill exhibition needs expanded by the War, British films did remarkably well in the United States. Nöel Coward's *In Which We Serve* (1942) might in fact be said to have established the tradition of the British "prestige picture." United Artists also released a number of Ealing features, including *Ships With Wings* (1941) and *The Foreman Went to France* (1941) that filled screen time before the appearance of American war films. American films suffered, conversely, a backlash of public opinion in Britain for what was perceived as a frivolous attitude toward Britain's participation in the war. This condition reached its height in the banning of *Objective, Burma* (1945) for its denigration of British participation in that campaign.

The war saw the rise to power of two men in the British industry with competing ideas of how to attain a position of eminence for the industry. Their figures and philosophies have haunted the industry up to forty-five years later. The first, Michael Balcon (1896–1977), had been active in production since the mid-twenties. He embarked on a program of war-oriented melodramas, produced on modest budgets by a collaborative creative process. Films such as *Went the Day Well?* (1942), *The Next Of Kin* (1942), and *San Demetrio, London* (1943) exemplified the use of a realist aesthetic to express what Balcon felt were British national characteristics—a certain stodginess, good humor, and determination. The films and Balcon's system of organization at Ealing studios proved very profitable. As the war ended. Balcon embarked on the production of a series of comedies culminating in *Kind Hearts and Coronets* (1949) that proved extraordinarily successful in the growing U.S. art theatre market, as well as making good returns in Britain.

Balcon's antithesis was J. Arthur Rank (1888–1972), who cast a long shadow over production, distribution, and exhibition during the war years and after. Originally a flour magnate, Rank had been a major investor in British National Pictures in 1934. In the wake of Korda's success, he had financed the building of Pinewood Studios*. In 1936, Rank purchased a substantial interest in Universal and developed the General Cinema Finance Corporation. General Film Distributors was also an early but crucial part of the Rank "empire" as it was already being called. Rank purchased Gaumont-British in 1937 and took over Denham Studios* from the suddenly impoverished Korda in 1938. In 1939, he purchased Elstree and Amalgamated Studios, and, in 1941, the Odeon and Gaumont-British theatre chains fell under his sway as well. By this time, Rank directly owned much of the industry. Unlike Balcon who concentrated only on quality production, Rank's strategy was more far-reaching. He now controlled financing, production, distribution, and exhibition in England and was enlarging his investments in America with an eye to gaining economic leverage for his films there.

Production for Rank meant diversity with a system of independent units. When he announced the formation of Eagle-Lion Films in March 1944 as a worldwide distribution organization and agressively purchased interests in theatre chains in the Dominions, Rank made it clear that he had international, indeed, unlimited ambitions. The war gave Rank a controlled domestic market in which to incubate his empire and, by the end of the war, capitalized at over £200 million. Rank's organization was fully vertically integrated and had guaranteed exhibition outlets in the United States through Rank's agreements with Universal and United Artists. The dream of British power in international motion picture finance seemed to be on the verge of becoming a reality.

Corporate mismanagement at United Artists was the first of Rank's many impediments. The exhibition campaign of *The Life and Death of Colonel Blimp* (U.S. *Colonel Blimp)* was disastrously bungled in the United States, alienating many theatre owners; the film was cut to fit double-bill status. Universal was equally confused by such films as *A Matter of Life And Death* (U.S. *Stairway to Heaven*) in the immediate postwar period; the film, which had been the first to be selected for a Royal Command Film Performances* in Britain, was one among many Rank films that was poorly received in the years 1945–1947. Only the Gainsborough melodramas, such as *Bedelia* (1945) and *The Wicked Lady* (1945), and films styled after them, such as *The Seventh Veil* (1945), were genuine hits. When distributors exerted themselves and sold films in unique road-show settings (*Henry V*) or in art houses (*I Know Where I'm Going,* 1945), the results were favorable. But Rank was not the savior for a troubled American industry, as both he and the American trade had hoped. In fact, Rank's personal visits to the United States produced an almost messianic response from the American trade press—even as a commission was empaneled in Britain to investigate his control of the industry.

The Labour Government in 1945 ended laissez-faire expansion and brought renewed concern over whether Rank would open British screens to his American friends in even greater volume than before the war. The result was a 75 percent ad valorem tax on American films entering Britain and the freezing of American earnings in Britain. These measures were not intended as draconian, but the response to them was. The American Motion Picture Export Association announced a boycott by member studios as a way of protesting the ''Dalton Duty,'' named after the official who conceived it. Bookings of British films in the United States were seriously compromised. Rank's films suffered in competition with American films for crucial playdates. The lifting of the tax did little good, for it generated a flood of backlogged American films onto British screens which, because Rank had been unable to meet his grandiose production plans, had been stagnating with few new releases.

The Rank empire fell as quickly as had Korda's before it. By February 1949, Rank's losses were over £4.5 million. Rank studios at Islington, Sheperds Bush, and Denham were shuttered. Government studies during this period, especially the Plant, Palache, Gater, and Film Studios Reports (1944–1949), demonstrated the precariousness of an entire industry based on either a personality cult (Korda) or a highly monopolized combine (Rank). The Board of Trade took steps that included raising the quota and finally stabilizing it at 30 percent in 1950; setting up the National Film Development Council, the first advisory board since the Ministry of Information ''roundtable'' during the war; establishing the National

Film Finance Corporation (NFFC)*, "films bank" set up to provide essential "end money" for films in production; and devising the Eady Levy*, conceived by a Treasury officer as a tax on exhibitors that was parcelled out as matching funds grants to producers, based on their takings at the box office.

The Anglo-American Films Agreement, signed in 1948, formalized relations between the two countries, allowing considerable American investment in British filmmaking and paving the way for an era of co-productions in the sixties.

The period 1950–1958 was one in which the industry sought its level as a partially nationalized institution. This involved various measures of austerity. For example, the Rank interests, now centralized at Pinewood, experimented in low-budget shooting with the "Independent Frame" concept. The NFFC was crippled in its early years by a £3 million loan to a disastrous Korda project, a new British Lion* company, and, as a result, much British production in the decade was involved with ongoing, profitable comedy series which were clear offshoots of the music-hall cinema of the late thirties. Also, British audiences were being sapped by television, making large independent production risky. Between 1950 and 1960, nearly 1,500 theatres closed down, over a third of the total number. British producers focused on selling their backlogs of old films to the Americans (Korda's early films were some of the very first seen on American television), thus achieving a kind of "last laugh" at the expense of their tormentors. In the specialized market situations that grew up in the United States after the war, British films such as the Ealing comedies continued to do well in "art house" releases, and *The Red Shoes* (1948) became the largest grossing British film ever in the United States. Hammer Films emerged under the direction of James Carreras to carve out a niche as a producer of low-budget films with strong distribution in the United States, often luring fading American stars such as Zachary Scott, Paul Henreid, and Brian Donlevy to appear in their films, giving them a specious "marquee value." Hammer was one of the earliest companies to subsist on a steady diet of funds from the NFFC.

By 1952, even Balcon's Ealing was borrowing money from the NFFC to stay afloat, and he was forced to sell it in 1955. Independence of the Ealing brand was no longer possible, and the flat fees paid to British producers for their films on art house circuits in the United States were not as lucrative as the use of British facilities for joint productions, which would then be marketed in the United States as American films. Columbia, Fox, and M-G-M made use of studios at Boreham Wood for such films as *Bhowani Junction* (1956) and *Ivanhoe* (1952), while Warner Bros., Disney, and RKO used the Elstree studios for spectaculars such as *Moby Dick* (1956) and *Rob Roy* (1953). In 1957, the Rank Organization mounted another campaign in the United States, based on the success of its war epics such as *The Battle of the River Plate* (1956), opening a system of exchanges and buying large theatres to showcase the films. The experiment proved as unsuccessful as Rank's invasion ten years previous, and the industry seemed ready to suffer another crisis of confidence.

An economic lift, as well as a hugely important massaging of national ego, was provided by the so-called British New Wave, sometimes called the ''Angry Young Men''* films or ''Kitchen Sink Films.'' While exhibition interests were still controlled in Britain by the Rank Organization (which amalgamated the Gaumont and Odeon circuits in 1958 and thus with ABC theatres had a near lock on first-run theatres in Britain) production was still relatively open to investment. Rank and ABPC were the dominant British producers, but Rank's interests were then in diversification, and independent production was thus encouraged by an availability of rentable studio space. Like the American move into independent production in the mid-forties, and like their contemporaries in the French New Wave*, the result was a bewildering number of small, independent companies, many of whom never actually produced a film. Others, such as the Allied Film Makers group constituted in 1959, brought together established filmmakers such as Richard Attenborough, Basil Dearden, and Michael Relph for more or less the same economic reasons that had engendered the American independent movement.

The NFFC had by this time become a major instrument providing, between 1950 and 1961, loans for 366 of the 730 British films released as first features. Yet it continued to have to be renewed periodically, most notably in 1960. As the idea of massive government support was anathema to Conservative governments, the NFFC led a constantly imperiled life. Because it provided the 30 percent or so monies used for the completion of a film (a very real and important service) it could not serve as a genuine force for change, for it was not in a position to provide seed money or ''above-the-line'' costs. American interests, chiefly in the guise of British subsidiaries of American distribution companies, still controlled large-scale financing of British films made away from (and sometimes including) Rank and ABPC-Elstree interest.

Perhaps because of this, the ''Angry Young Men'' movement, if movement it was, died young. Directors such as Tony Richardson, Karel Reisz, and Jack Clayton either emigrated to the United States temporarily or became involved in costly Anglo-American co-productions.

Ironically, American money attracted to British production by the success and international reputation of directors such as John Schlesinger, Jack Clayton, Lindsay Anderson, and others helped block further experimentation in the vein of *Saturday Night and Sunday Morning*. By 1967, American financing was behind 75 percent of British ''A'' films; by 1968, the £31.3 million represented the highest level of American investment in British filmmaking ever. Certain additional resources were also available. The British Film Institute's Experimental Film Fund began functioning in 1952, but the fund was not heavily capitalized enough to make a serious mark on the industry. As the production pipeline began to fill, it became increasingly harder for films not produced by the American studio affiliates or the Rank/ABPC producers to gain access to the theatres of Rank and ABPC. In fact, even during the early sixties, genuinely independent films had difficulty finding access to the major circuits. Sidney

Furie's *The Leather Boys* was delivered to its distributor in March 1963 but had to wait eleven months for a general release with ABPC. By that time, an additional £8,000 had been added in interest charges to the film's original (loaned) cost of £107,000. In addition, producers associated with Rank in particular had begun to release "youth oriented" films of their own, such as *Flame In The Streets* (1961), thus taking much of the high ground from individuals such as Balcon who had an earnest desire to see social realism in the hands of well-minded producers. Not surprisingly, his Bryanston* group, and the AFM group as well, gave up their work in the mid- to late sixties.

In the years 1960–1970, power continued to concentrate in the hands of the two major, vertically integrated British combines. During that decade, their theatre holdings went from 25.7 percent of the total to 31.5 percent, including a far greater proportion of first-run and large capacity houses in choice locations. Meanwhile, audiences declined precipitously, falling from 501 million a year to 193 million a year during the decade. Total box-office receipts, however, declined much less. Clearly, fewer people were going to see films. Those who did go had fewer to choose from, and those films tended to be Anglo-American co-productions, such as the immensely successful "James Bond" series*, or epics such as *The Great Escape* (1963).

Independents and their advocates in Parliament argued for greater state intervention in production, beyond the NFFC and the "matching funds" system of the Eady Levy. One of the agencies chosen was the British Film Institute (BFI)* and longtime opposition to major BFI funding was finally overcome in 1966; the Experimental Film Fund was replaced by the British Film Institute Production Board, now more heavily capitalized than its predecessor. Available funds began to accrue through investments to £100,000 by 1974 and £600,000 by 1980. The sources for this money were various and included Channel 4*. With revenues from American releases of genuinely British titles being seen in the late seventies and early eighties, and with the strength of British titles in the video market, yet another renaissance was at hand, according to some optimists within the industry.

But because of the close linkage between attitudes toward subsidy and changes in government, the question is, as ever, in doubt. In 1984, the Thatcher government announced the end of an important tax shelter, which had been the chief enabling device behind the making of *Chariots Of Fire* (1981), the most economically significant of the new British films. In addition, it was announced that the Eady Levy and the NFFC were to be essentially abolished. In their place was a semiprivate consortium called British Screen. This organization is made up of Channel 4, video trade groups, the Rank Organization, and Thorn-EMI, the inheritor of much of the ABPC holdings. Though *Prick up Your Ears* (1986) and other productions have combined solid art house success with major circuit breakthroughs in the United States, fears about the viability of British Screen persist, due to its undercapitalization. The future of production financing was also made more precarious by the imposition of higher taxes on foreign producers working in England, which seemed to hurt rather than help the industry's transition to genuine independence. The result of this rewriting of policy is that Britain is now the only major national cinema actively attempting to export its films, without the active support of its government, in the form of large subsidies.

Recent successes, contrary to government claims, seem to be tied to the savvy of individual producers rather than to the "hands-off" system favored by officials. The Cannon Group, for instance, had established itself as a modern vertically integrated corporation with its base in England, on the basis of earnings from an innovative, inexpensive production program on an international front. Several independents, having split off from the major trade organization to form their own group (David Puttnam, Alan Parker, Clive Parsons, Davina Belling, and Simon Perry), were able to act adventurously in the late seventies and early eighties. Their task, then and now, has been to attract new sources of investment in their work, investment that would ordinarily come from distributors. One fashion, as mentioned, was to highlight tax advantages. Don Boyd's were companies in the late seventies was successful at this, as were others of less note. Other techniques have been employed by other producers. Handmade Films*, set up in 1978 by George Harrison, has made a practice of carefully reinvesting the profits of early successes such as *The Life of Brian* (1979) and *Time Bandits* (1981).

Smaller companies, such as Lewis Gilbert's Acorn Pictures (*Educating Rita,* 1983) and larger ones, such as Thorn-EMI (*A Room with a View,* 1986) have shown that the art house market in the United States is capable of returning great profits and, just as important, providing the "display window" for a successful video release. Major circuit releases in this period have brought American distributors around full circle, and American investment in British-controlled filmmaking had been on the rise before the conservative crackdown. The aftereffects of successful releases and prudent management are still providing much of the steam in British filmmaking. In 1987–1988 Hemdale, for example, was a major player on the international scene. In the wake of *Platoon* (1986), it announced plans for an $80 million production schedule in 1988. Goldcrest Films and Television*, in spite of the loss of David Puttnam to America's Columbia Pictures (as a producer, he had shepherded *Chariots of Fire*), continued to be a production company on the level of the American majors, as did Handmade, J&M Film Sales, Thorn-EMI, and even Rank, which has renewed its interest in production by putting up $130 million for a production program in exchange for all North American rights of all kinds on the films it distributes for its normal 30 percent of the gross.

But Rank has since the fifties been the harbinger of conservatism in the industry, illustrating the direction British filmmaking may take in a government-inspired new age of austerity. Of the thirty companies financing films in 1983, only seven were active in 1988. Those companies which remain, such as Goldcrest, Virgin, and others, are following Rank's lead, focusing on territorial and ancillary rights as much as production itself. By so doing, they are charting a more narrow course in production philosophy.

Two events have focused attention on the state that British filmmaking finds itself in. The Cannon Group, in the face of overextension, was forced to sell Elstree studios in 1987 and allow control of its nearly 40 percent share of British theatres to shift to Warner Bros. as it began concentrating production away from Britain. The parallels between this imminent collapse and that of the Rank operations in the late forties are made even more chilling by the second event: the change in status of Pinewood Studios in May 1987. At that time, the studio that J. Arthur Rank himself had built ceased to function as an independent, fully staffed studio and began a new, lesser life as a simple rental facility. Staff reductions of over 50 percent made Pinewood a symbol of the grandiose dreams and somber realities that British production has had to face in the past and may yet have to face in the future. Whether the current high standards of British production can succeed in the wake of decreased subsidy is unclear. If not, the fact that production has become discreet from distribution interests in many cases may help to cushion the industry from the precipitous declines of 1938 and 1947–1949. But if production standards can be maintained and if distribution channels remain open around the world, the British cinema may no longer be a whipping boy, but a figure to be emulated.

BIBLIOGRAPHY

Aldgate, Anthony, and Jeffrey Richards. *Britain Can Take It: The British Cinema in the Second World War*. New York: Basil Blackwell, 1986.

Armes, Roy. *A Critical History of British Cinema*. New York: Oxford University Press, 1978.

Balcon, Michael, Ernest Lindgren, and Forsyth Hardy. *Twenty Years of British Film, 1925–1945*. London: Falcon Press, 1947.

Barnes, John. *The Beginnings of the Cinema in England*. New York: Barnes & Noble, 1976.

Chanan, Michael. *The Dream that Kicks*. Boston: Routledge & Kegan Paul, 1980.

Curran, James, and Vincent Porter, editors. *British Cinema History*. Totowa, N.J.: Barnes & Noble, 1983.

Durgnat, Raymond. *A Mirror for England*. New York: Praeger, 1971.

Gifford, Denis. *The Illustrated Who's Who in British Films*. London: Batsford, 1978.

———. *British Film Catalogue, 1895–1985*. New York: Facts on File, 1986.

———. *British Animated Films, 1895–1985*. Jefferson, N.C.: McFarland, 1987.

Low, Rachael. *The History of the British Film, 1906–1914*. London: George Allen & Unwin, 1949.

———. *The History of the British Film, 1914–1918*. London: George Allen & Unwin, 1950.

———. *The History of the British Film, 1918–1929*. London: George Allen & Unwin, 1971.

———. *The History of the British Film, 1929–1939: Documentary and Educational Films of the 1930s*. New York: R.R. Bowker, 1979.

———. *The History of the British Film, 1929–1939: Films of Comment and Persuasion of the 1930s*. New York: R.R. Bowker, 1979.

Low, Rachael, and Roger Manvell. *The History of the British Film, 1896–1906*. London: George Allen & Unwin, 1948.

Park, James. *Learning to Dance: The New British Cinema*. Boston: Faber and Faber, 1984.

Perry, George. *The Great British Picture Show*. Boston: Little, Brown, 1985.

Richards, Jeffrey, and Anthony Aldgate. *British Cinema and Society, 1930–1970*. Totowa, N.J.: Barnes & Noble, 1983.

Slide, Anthony. *Fifty Classic British Films: 1932–1982*. New York: Dover, 1987.

Walker, Alexander. *Hollywood UK*. New York: Stein & Day, 1974.

———. *National Heroes*. London: Harrap, 1988.

Walker, John. *The Once and Future Film*. London: Methuen, 1985.

Wood, Alan. *Mr. Rank*. London: Hodder and Stoughton, 1952.

UNITED NATIONS. Like its predecessor, the League of Nations*, the United Nations (UN) has considerable involvement in film. It has utilized personalities such as Audrey Hepburn, Danny Kaye, and Liv Ullman to promote its work. As early as the late spring and early summer of 1945, a United Nations Theatre was screening films on San Francisco's O'Farrell Street as part of the San Francisco World Security Conference. A Film Division was established in 1949, and that same year a Hollywood liaison officer, the Danish Mogens Skot-Hansen, was appointed to provide information to the Hollywood community on the work of the UN and to encourage film producers to feature the organization in their films. In 1950, the U.S. delegate Mrs. Leo Spitz asked for greater recognition for the film medium, and a year later a UN Film Conference was held to study utilization of film for educational and cultural purposes.

Film production at the UN is usually associated with UNESCO, of which John Grierson became director of mass-communications in 1947. Although Grierson quit the organization a year later, he continued to be associated with UNESCO on a voluntary basis, and his work there had tremendous influence on documentary film production throughout the world. Perhaps the two most important documentaries associated with UNESCO are Basil Wright's *World without End* (1953) and Thorold Dickinson's *Power among Men* (1958).

Although film production is usually associated with UNESCO, the first agency of the UN to sponsor films was the Relief and Reconstruction Administration in 1946, under the directorship of Jean Benoit-Lévy. Films have also been sponsored by the Food and Agriculture Organization, the International Labor Office, the South Pacific Commission, the Technical Aids Commission, and the World Health Organization.

Among the many film-related publications issued from the Paris office of UNESCO are: *The Use of Mobile Cinema and Radio Vans in Fundamental Education* (1949), *International Rules for the Cataloguing of Educational, Scientific and Cultural Films and Filmstrips* (1956), *Developing Mass Media in Asia* (1960), *Film-making on a Low Budget* (1960), *The Influence of the Cinema on Children and Adolescents* (1961), *World Film Directory* (1962), *Screen Ed-*

ucation (1964), *Ten Years of Film on Ballet and Classical Dance, 1956–1965* (1968).

UNITED STUDIOS OF ISRAEL LTD. is the largest film and television studio in the country and the only one with its own processing laboratory. It was formed in April 1978, as a limited partnership, with the merger of the Herzliya Studios (controlled by Miriam Spielman and Amos Mokadi) and the Berkey Pathe Humphries Laboratories. Control of the studios was taken over by the Long Beach, California, Elrina Investment Group in the summer of 1988.

Address: Hakessem Street, Herzliya, Israel.

UPPER VOLTA. Although it is a country with which few are familiar, the former French colony of Upper Volta is a leader in black African filmmaking. It hosts the biennial Festival Panafricain du Cinéma de Ougadougou (B.P. 2505, Ougadougou, Upper Volta), which is the most important festival of black African cinema. Established in 1969, the festival is held in the Upper Volta capital of Ougadougou, which is also the headquarters for a film distribution consortium known as CIDIC, a production organization called CIPROFILMS, and FEPACI, the PanAfrican Federation of Filmmakers.

In 1970, the government of Upper Volta nationalized film distribution and exhibition, and established the Société Nationale Voltaïque de Cinéma (B.P. 206, Ougadougou, Upper Volta), to oversee film activities in the country. The first Upper Volta feature films were Djim Mamadou Kola's *Le sang des parias* and René Bernard Yonly's *Sur le chemin de la réconciliation,* both released in 1973.

BIBLIOGRAPHY

Armes, Roy, "Upper Volta," in *International Film Guide 1984,* editor Peter Cowie. London: Tantivy Press, 1983, pp. 328–329.

URUGUAY. Although until 1973 it boasted of a long and stable democratic tradition (meriting it the nickname of the Switzerland of the Americas), Uruguay was never able to sustain much film production. Its geographical proximity to Argentina meant that it was the first export market for that nation's active producers, and its primarily urban, literate, and centralized population made it an ideal market for Hollywood's products as well.

There were, however, some efforts in the silent era to develop a national cinema. After the first screenings of Lumière shorts in July of 1896, a number of artist-entrepreneurs recorded events of national importance. The first Uruguayan film, Feliz Oliver's *Una Carrera de Ciclismo en el Velodromo de Arroyo Seco* (1898), was followed by a number of shorts in the 1900s and 1910s, and by the first feature film, Edmundo Figari's *Punos y Nobleza,* in 1919. As was the case in most medium and small film markets throughout Latin America, the coming of sound interrupted local production: there were no films made between 1931 and 1936.

Although the first sound film was made in 1936—*Dos Destinos* (director unknown)—little other filmmaking took place until the late forties: Jaime Prades' *Los Tres Mosqueteros* (produced with Argentine actors and financial backing) was released in 1946, Adolfo Fabregat's *Detective a Contramano* in 1949. At this time of production stagnation, however, exhibition flourished: there were approximately 88 movie theaters in Montevideo and 177 in the entire nation (for a population of 2.5 million). At the height of the Korean War boom (1953), there were nineteen screenings per year for each inhabitant of Montevideo. The cinema existed in Uruguay, but only as an imported phenomenon.

However, even though the creation of a national cinema was economically impossible and was not intellectually perceived as an imperative, cinematic culture developed extremely early in Uruguay. Specialized film journals, ciné-clubs and cinémathèques, a number of serious critics, an early boom in amateur filmmaking, and a variety of film festivals both stimulated and were a product of the high cine-literacy of the Uruguayan public.

Among the film festivals, the earliest was the annual International Festival of Documentary and Experimental Films (sponsored by SODRE, the national radio-electric society), an event that provided the first meeting-ground on Latin American soil for Latin American filmmakers and served as an important stimulus for the development of the New Latin American Cinema.

Nationally, the exhibition of several Uruguayan shorts at the SODRE festivals and the pioneering work in alternative distribution by individuals like Walter Achugar and Edgardo Palleres (Cine Club Marcha, la Cinemateca del Tercer Mundo) stimulated the development of an Uruguayan documentary movement that was influential throughout the hemisphere. Among these significant films, Alberto Miller's *Cantegrilis* (1958) was the first. This eight-minute short, an exploration of the slums surrounding the elegant resort town of Punta del Este, was, unlike other amateur efforts, direct and sober in its treatment of an existing social reality. Another important short was Ugo Ulive's *Como el Uruguay no hay/There's No Place like Uruguay* (1960), an eight-minutes satire of Uruguayan politics.

Although faced with tremendous material constraints—including the lack of proper sound mixing and editing equipment—a small group of dedicated documentarists emerged in the mid-sixties and managed to sustain innovative production and distribution activities until the coup d'etat of 1973. Essentially an artisanal cinema, their *cine urgente* (urgent cinema) focused on the most pressing issues of national life and was extremely politicized, sparking similar movements in other Latin American countries.

The most important filmmaker of this movement (and of all the Uruguayan cinema) was Mario Handler. His *Carlos: Cineretrato de un Caminante/Carlos: Film Portrait of a Vagabond* (1965), a portrait of an urban homeless man, was enthusiastically received by critics and public alike. In collaboration with Ugo Ulive, Handler also worked on *Elecciones* (1965), a biting indictment of the Uruguayan electoral system and, according to many, the best Uruguayan film to date. In 1968, Handler produced his most famous work: a five-minute short entitled *Me Gustan los Estudiantes/I Like Students*. Probably the most widely exhibited Latin American documentary, *Me Gustan los Estudiantes* consists of footage of student demonstrations and police violence after Lyndon Johnson's visit to Punta del Este. At its first screening, at the Cine Club Marcha 1968 festival, spectators emerged so enraged that they spontaneously demonstrated, setting up barricades, throwing rocks, and singing the Violeta Parra song that gave the film its title.

Handler made two other short films in Uruguay—*Uruguay 69: El Problema de la Carne/Uruguay 1969: The Meat Problem* (1969) and *Liber-Arce/Liberate Yourself* (1970)—but, like other Uruguayan artists and intellectuals, was forced into exile by the dangerous political instability of the nation. The growing power of the military in the seventies—well evidenced by the arrest and imprisonment of alternative film distributor/exhibitor Walter Achugar—led to a mass exodus in the wake of the 1973 coup de'etat.

The exiled Uruguayan filmmakers, unlike their Chilean counterparts, did not produce an Uruguayan cinema of exile. Instead, they assimilated in different countries: Peru, Venezuela, Argentina. After their departure, the continuing repressive government and steadily deteriorating economic conditions made national film production impossible. In fact, even national cinema attendance has dropped, and there are less than one hundred theatres still open. In the eighties there has been no film production in Uruguay.

BIBLIOGRAPHY

Carrill, M. Martinez, "The Uruguayan Cinema—Slow Death," *CTVD Digest*, Fall 1970, pp. 8–9.

USSR. The words of Lenin, "Of all the arts, cinema is the most important for us," are often quoted as an indication of the strength of the motion picture industry in the Soviet Union. It is easy to forget that the cinema was an important industry and art form long before the 1917 Revolution.

The Lumière films were first seen in Moscow on May 17, 1896. Some days earlier, the Lumière cameramen had filmed the coronation of Czar Nikolai II. Those films were initially screened in a makeshift theatre at 46 Nevsky Prospect; the first film theatres were opened in Moscow in 1903 by I.A. Gutzman. (Jay Ledya reports that when Gutzman opened a theatre in Riga, the audience included a little boy named Sergei Mikhailovich Eisenstein.)

A number of foreign companies, notably Pathé* and Gaumont*, filmed actualities and newsreels in Russia in the early years of the century, and it was not until 1907 that the first Russian film studio was opened in Moscow by Alexander Drankov. One of his first films was a brief glimpse of Tolstoy. In 1908, Drankov began producing fictional shorts, beginning with *Stenka Razin*. So successful was he that a rival company was established by Alexander Kranzhonkov, and foreign producers also began to open studios in Russia. The cinema expanded rapidly, gaining in popularity to such an extent that by 1910, in St.

Petersburg alone there were forty-eight theatres in operation, with fifteen studios, primarily in Moscow, producing "Russian" films. In the early teens, production expanded to St. Petersburg, where three studios were opened.

The first great Russian screen actress was Vera Kholodnaya, who made her debut in 1915. The most important of Russian actors was Ivan Mozhukkin/Ivan Mosjoukine (1889–1939), who had commenced his career with Khanzhonkov in 1911. Mosjoukine enjoyed an immensely successful career in France in the twenties in films such as *Kean/Edmund Kean—Prince of Lovers* (1924), *Feu Mathias Pascal/The Late Mathias Pascal* (1925), and *Casanova/The Loves of Casanova* (1927), and was also starred in one American feature, *Surrender* (1927).

The 1917 Revolution brought a close to the first "golden age" of Russian cinema, with most of the pioneers, including Mosjoukine, fleeing to France, where they were to be influential in the cinema for the next decade. The first Soviet government, the Council of People's Commissars, created the first Soviet film agency on November 9, 1917, as a subsection, kinopodotdel, of the State Commission on Education.

The cinema was totally nationalized in 1919, coming under the control of the People's Commissariat of Education. It was Stalin rather than Lenin who elevated the cinema to equal status with other art forms. In 1924, following Lenin's death, a new commission, headed by Leonid Krassin, formed Sovkino*, to supervise the industry.

Outside of Russia, film industries developed in the other republics forming the Soviet Union. Filmmaking in Georgia dates from 1910, and the first feature there, *Christinae,* was made in 1919 by Alexander Tsutsunava. Uzbeck cinema dates from the late teens, although films were screened in the republic as early as 1897. Filmmaking in Azerbaijan began in 1916. The film organization, Vostokkino, began production in Kazakh in 1928. Kirghiz cinema dates from the late thirties. In Tajik, the first film was made in 1929, but production did not get seriously under way until the Second World War, when filmmakers from Soyuzdetfilm were evacuated to Dushanbe. Filmmaking in Byelorussia dates from 1919 and in Turkmenia from 1929.

The second "Golden Age" of Russian cinema is the twenties, when the directors most associated with the medium were at work. The film that introduced Soviet filmmaking to the world was *Bronenosets "Potyomkin"/Potemkin* (1925), and its director, Sergei Mikhailovich Eisenstein (1898–1948) is the best known of all Soviet directors. *Potemkin* was only his second feature, preceded by *Stachka/Strike* (1925). It was followed by *October/Ten Days That Shook the World* (1928) and *Staroye i novoye/Old and New* (1929). He made an abortive trip to Mexico in 1931 in an attempt to film *Que Viva Mexico!,* and was out of favor in the Soviet Union for many years in both the thirties and forties. Despite this, Eisenstein managed to film *Alexander Nevsky* (1938), and a two-part *Ivan Grozny/Ivan the Terrible* (1945 and 1946).

The other major directors from this period are Abram Room (1894–1976), whose best known feature is *Tretya Meshchanskaya/Bed and Sofa* (1927); Alexander Dovzhenko (1894–1956), whose first major film was *Zvenigora* (1928); Dziga Vertov (1896–1954), whose most important feature is *Chelovek s kinoapparatom/Man with Movie Camera* (1929); and Lev Kuleshov (1899–1970) and Vesvolod Pudovkin (1893–1953), who collaborated on *Neobychainiye priklucheniya Mistera Vesta v stranye bolshevikov/The Extraordinary Adventures of Mr. West in the Land of the Bolsheviks* (1924).

Sound was introduced to the Soviet cinema by two Russian pioneers, P.G. Tager in Moscow and A.F. Shorin in Leningrad, and their respective systems went into commercial use in 1929. The first Soviet sound film was Abram Room's *Plan velikikh rabot/Plan of Great Works* (1930), which included music by Rimsky-Korsakov.

Among the important Soviet films of the thirties are *Zemlya/Earth* (1930), directed by Dovzhenko; *Tri pesni o Leninye/Three Songs of Lenin* (1934), directed by Dziga Vertov; *Chapayev* (1934), directed by Sergei and Georgy Vasiliev; *Yunost Maksima/The Youth of Maxim Gorky* (1935), directed by Grigori Kozintsev and Leonid Trauberg; *Novyi Gulliver/A New Gulliver* (1935), directed by Alexander Ptushko; *Lenin v Oktyabre/Lenin in October* (1937), directed by Mikhail Romm; *Detstvo Gorkovo/Childhood of Gorky* (1938), directed by Mark Donskoy; and *Vyborgskaya storona/The Vyborg Side* (1939), directed by Grigori Kozintsev and Leonid Trauberg.

Following the outbreak of the Second World War, and the Soviet-German pact, all antifascist films were hastily removed from circulation. In 1941, with the German invasion of Russia, the films were put back in distribution. The administration of the film industry was moved from Moscow to Novosibirsk—it moved back in 1942. The system of tight control over the subject matter in films was temporarily dropped, and any filmmaker with a good idea that could be produced quickly was encouraged in his work.

Following the Second World War, a new era of repression began in the Soviet Union, with the Stalin regime keeping an even tighter and more careful control of the film industry. Some of the greatest of Soviet filmmakers found their careers at an end. Eisenstein's *Ivan Groznyi/Ivan the Terrible Part 2* (1946), was suppressed, because of the obvious, close similarities between the film's leading character and Stalin. The production was not seen in the Soviet Union until 1958, and then in a censored version. Dovzhenko's last film, *Zhisn v tsvetu/Life in Bloom* (1946) was censored. Pudovkin was attacked by the government and ended his career making films that toed the party line. Soviet films declined in both quality and quantity as their subject matters were limited to "safe" areas such as Russian victories in the Second World War and Soviet heroes. Stalin had a protégé in director Mikhail Chiaureli, who produced a series of films on the Russian leader's political career.

There was little improvement in the quality of Soviet features following Stalin's death in 1953. In 1951, the production of black-and-white films had been almost curtailed in favor of color, but filmmakers were able to return to black-and-white, with which they seemed more at ease. In time a few major features appeared: Mikhail Kalatozov's *Letiat zhuravli/The Cranes Are Flying* (1957), Grigorii Chukhrai's *Ballada o soldate/Ballad of a Soldier* (1958), and Andrei Tarkovskii's *Andrei Rublev* (1969) and *Solaris* (1971). The Soviet cinema also discovered Shakespeare, and seemed comfortable in the production of features such as Sergei Iutkevich's *Othello* (1955) and Grigorii Kozintsev's *Don Quixote* (1957) and *Hamlet* (1964).

Sergei Bondarhcuk (born 1920) directed a couple of major epics of the seventies—*Oni srazhalis za rodinu/They Fought for Their Motherland* (1974) and *Waterloo* (1970)—in a decade that was noted for its historical dramas largely dealing with the Second World War.

In 1975, the Best Foreign Language Film Award from the Academy of Motion Picture Arts and Sciences went to *Dersu Uzala,* produced by Mosfilm Studios, and directed by Akira Kurosawa. The USSR was again a winner in 1980 with *Moscow Does Not Believe in Tears,* also from Mosfilm Studios.

In the eighties, a certain freedom became detectable in Soviet films, even before Gorbachev's promise of "glasnost." In 1984, Vladimir Bortko directed *Blondinka za uglom/The Blonde around the Country,* that dealt with bribery, corruption and the black market in the Soviet Union. Aleksandr Stefanovich's *Nachat s nachala/Begin at the Beginning,* released early in 1986, deals with the country's dissident musicians and poets.

Elem Klimov has gained considerable attention in the West as an example of the new Soviet film bureaucrat, and the first Russian member of the Academy of Motion Picture Arts and Sciences. His late wife was Larissa Scheptiko, who gained fame in the West as a filmmaker of the eighties.

Film studios are located throughout the Soviet Union as follows:

Moscow: Mosfilm, Maxim Gorki (formerly Soyuzdetfilm and Mezhrabpomfilm), Tsentrnauchfilm, Central Documentary Films, and Soyuzmultfilm

Leningrad: Lenfilm and Lennauchfilm

Kiev: Alexander Dovzhenko (formerly Kiev), Kievnauchfilm, and Ukrainian Documentary Films

Odessa: Odessa

Minsk: Belarusfilm (formerly Belgoskino and Sovetskaya Belarus)

Tbilisi: Gruziyafilm (formerly Goskinprom-Gruziya) and Georgian Studios of Popular Science and Documentary Films

Erevan: Amo Bek-Nazarov

Baku: Dzhafar Dzharbli

Alma-Ata: Kazakhfilm

Tashkent: Uzbekfilm and Uzbek Popular Science and Documentary Films

Ashkhabad: Turkmenfilm

Vilnius: Lithuanian

Riga: Riga

Frunze: Kirghizfilm

Kishinev: Moldovafilm

Tallin: Tallinfilm

Dushanbe: Tadzhikfilm

An average of 150 features are produced each year in the Soviet Union for the country's 153,000 theatres. The export and import of all films is handled by Sovexportfilm*.

BIBLIOGRAPHY

Babitsky, Paul, and John Rimberg. *The Soviet Film Industry*. New York: Praeger for Research Program on the USSR, 1955.

Birkos, Alexander S. *Soviet Cinema: Directors and Films*. Hamden, Conn.: Archon Books, 1976.

Bryher. *Film Problems of Soviet Russia*. Territet, Switzerland: Riant, 1929.

Carter, Huntley. *The New Theatre and Cinema of Soviet Russia*. London: Chapman and Dodd, 1924.

Cohen, Louis H. *The Cultural-Political Traditions and Developments of the Soviet Cinema 1917–1972*. New York: Arno Press, 1974.

Dickinson, Thorold, and Catherine de la Roche. *Soviet Cinema*. New York: Arno Press, 1972.

Leyda, Jay. *Kino: A History of Russian and Soviet Film*. New York: Collier, 1973.

Liehm, Mira, and Antonin Liehm. *The Most Important Art: Soviet and East European Cinema after 1945*. Berkeley: University of California Press, 1977.

Moussinac, Leon. *Le cinéma sovietique*. Paris: Gallimard, 1928.

Passek, Jean-Loup. *Le cinéma russe et soviétique*. Paris: Centre Georges Pompidou/L'Equerre, 1981.

Rimberg, John. *The Motion Picture in the Soviet Union*. New York: Arno Press, 1974.

Schnitzer, Luda, editor. *Cinema in Revolution: The Heroic Era of the Soviet Film*. New York: Hill and Wang, 1973.

Stoil, Michael Jon. *Cinema beyond the Danube*. Metuchen, N.J.: Scarecrow Press, 1974.

Taylor, Richard. *The Politics of the Soviet Cinema, 1917–1929*. Cambridge, U.K.: Cambridge University Press, 1979.

Vronskaya, Jeanne. *Young Soviet Film Makers*. London: Allen and Unwin, 1972.

Youngblood, Denise J. *Soviet Cinema in the Silent Era, 1918–1935*. Ann Arbor, Mich.: UMI Research Press, 1985.

V

VENEZUELA. Although approximately eighty years old, the Venezuelan cinema was largely unsuccessful, plagued by insurmountable technological and financial problems until the seventies. Like most other intermediate-sized film markets in Latin America, Venezuela found it nearly impossible to maintain continuous film production on an industrial basis because of stiff competition from the United States, European, Argentine, and Mexican imports.

From the first film *Carnaval en Caracas* (1909), to the last silent feature, *El Relicario de la Abuelita* (1933), the Venezuelan silent cinema suffered, on the one hand, from inadequate capitalization, technology, and market control and, on the other, from excessive reliance upon foreign models. Only the name of producer/director/cinematographer/projectionist Amabilis Cordero stands out among the many who attempted to make films in this period. Cordero, recognized as the pioneer of the national cinema, was prolific, innovative, *and* commercially successful with films such as *La Cruz del Angel* (1930) and *Rosita La del Valle* (1931), but the coming of sound—and several unsuccessful films—prematurely ended his career.

Convinced that the arrival of sound would make possible the development of a national cinematic industry, the government invested in sound equipment and established a National Film Lab. The employees of the lab—many former silent directors—produced the first sound film in 1937: *Taboga*. This short film, based on a popular melody of the same name, was successful and the labs immediately embarked upon the production of the first sound feature, *El Rompimiento* (1939). Although at first promising, sound was not, however, the magic cure for the Venezuelan cinema. Most of the films produced in the forties, fifties, and sixties (at an average rate of two per year) were mediocre melodramas that exploited *criollismos* and the more folkloric aspects of Venezuelan life.

Several production companies were founded in this period, but the experiences of two diametrically opposed companies—Avila Films and Bolivar Films—were most characteristic. Avila Films was founded in 1941 as a cooperative venture by the Venezuelan novelist Romulo Gallegos and a number of partners.

A cinephile, Gallegos aspired to adapt his own famous epic novel, *Doña Barbara,* to the screen. Instead, Avila's first feature was *Juan de la Calle* (1941, directed by Rafeal Rivero), the first Venezuelan film to have been written specifically for the cinema by a novelist of the stature of Gallegos. Critically hailed, the film was also popularly liked and gave new hopes to the dreams of a national Venezuelan cinema. Unfortunately, however, Avila films ran into insurmountable financial difficulties—*Juan de la Calle* was very poorly distributed—and went out of business the following year.

Bolivar films, on the other hand, appeared and consolidated its activities as a successful commercial enterprise between 1944–1948. With a contract from the government for documentary shorts and newsreels assuring it a steady income, Bolivar Films took over national feature production for a number of years. Although its first few films were not particularly accomplished, its 1949 *La Balandra Isabel* was the most popular and talked-about film of the era. Inspired by a Guillermo Meneses story, the film was also successful abroad, and was awarded for best cinematography at the 1950 Cannes Film Festival*. Steadily producing more or less successful commercial features and weekly newsreels (*Noticiario Nacional*), Bolivar Films is still in existence and is today among the strongest producers.

The fifties and sixties were particularly lean years, with the introduction of TV strongly affecting an already weak national cinema, but two significant events took place in the late fifties: Margot Benecerraf finished her feature-length documentary *Araya* (1958), winning the Critic's Prize in Cannes, and Roman Chalbaud finished his *opera prima, Cain Adolescente* (1959), the first serious effort to produce a formally and intellectually rigorous national film.

Always starting from scratch, producers managed to release a respectable number of films in the sixties—thirty-five in total—although, overall, they lacked quality. The best films of this period—*Entre Sabado y Domingo* (Daniel Oropeza, 1965) and *Los Dias Duros* (Julio Cesar Marmol, 1970)—are technically superior to earlier Venezuelan efforts, but they are nevertheless largely imitative of other foreign cinemas.

In the late sixties and early seventies, newsreels, documentaries, and militant films served as a training ground for new cineastes: Carlos Rebolledo, Jesus Enrique Guedez, Alfredo Lugo, Luis Armando Roche, Alfredo Anzola, and Ugo Ulive. The 1967 Latin American Film Festival in Vina del Mar, Chile, initiated a political cinema movement of great importance that had, among Venezuelan documentarists, some of its most important practicioners. This militant cinema was the most representative of the period, since most commercial features failed due to the strictures of production and the limitations of the market. The development of this movement was also fueled by three other events: the production and release of *Imagenes de Caracas* (1968), a compilation film of social criticism in which many new cineastes debuted; the 1969 Meeting of Latin American Filmmakers that took place in the city of Merida; and the foundation of the Cinema Department at the Universidad de los Andes in 1969.

The late seventies, however, were of great importance for the development of the national cinema. Suddenly, after sixty-six years of indifference, the Venezuelan government shook off its cultural lethargy and, in 1975, introduced a credit program to encourage and help finance national production. This initial investment of a few million bolivares initiated a chain of significant cultural events, at a time when Venezuela, swept by waves of petrodollar nationalism, was most responsive to efforts to establish cinematographic policies. Together with subsequent measures—attempts to regulate the import, distribution, and exhibition of foreign films; legislation controlling the processing of prints of foreign films; and limits on distributors' "take" of box-office receipts—state protectionism generated the production of twenty-nine films between 1975 and 1980. Most important among these films were Mauricio Wallerstein's *La Empresa Perdona un Momento de Locura/The Company Excuses a Moment of Insanity* (1978), Roman Chalbaud's *El Pez que Fuma/The Fish that Smokes* (1977), Carlos Rebolledo's *Alias, el Rey del Joropo/Alias the Joropo King* (1978), and Ivan Feo's *País Portátil/Portable Country* (1978). These, and many other of the national films of this period, were spectacularly successful at the box office, regularly out-grossing North American films.

Although in 1980 the national industry seemed to be booming, a freeze on state funding allocations began to delay and/or suspend production projects. Caused by a jurisdictional struggle among two state agencies seeking to control the national cinema (the Ministry of Development and the Ministry of Tourism), the funding freeze and the debates that followed weakened the national cinema. However, the ensuing debates of a National Cinema Law prompted an ongoing discussion of Venezuelan national culture that had deep cultural repercussions. Together with the success of the independent documentary films of the Film Department of the Universidad de los Andes (in 1981, three of its documentaries were blown up to 35mm and successfully distributed theatrically), these debates led to the establishment of a Film Fund (in 1982) that distributes a tax on box-office receipts to producers.

Although production figures for the mid-eighties have been high—fifteen features in 1987, for example—whether the Venezuelan cinema will ever become a national cinema, reflecting national characteristics and problems *and* success at the box office still remains to be seen.

VENICE. Among the Italian features set in Venice are *Senso* (1955), *Il leone di San Marco/The Lion of St. Mark* (1964), *Amanti/A Place for Lovers* (1968), *Morte a Venezia/Death in Venice* (1971), *Casanova/Fellini's Casanova* (1976), and *Dimenticare Venezia/To Forget Venice* (1979). American features that have used Venice as a backdrop include *Venus of Venice* (1927), *Venice* (1930), *The Venetian Affair* (1967), *Blume in Love* (1973), and *Don't Look Now* (1973). British films with sequences in Venice include *Carnival* (U.S. *Venetian Nights,* 1931), *For Love of You* (1933), and *Betrayal* (1983), while the most important French feature set in Venice is *Les Amours de Casanova/Casanova* (1927).

The city is also the site of the Venice International Film Festival (Ca. Giustinian, San Marco, 30124 Venice).

THE VENICE FILM FESTIVAL is the oldest film festival in the world, having first been held as part of the Venice Biennale in 1932. Although it is administered through the Biennale, with the political and bureaucratic problems that that creates, the Festival is considered an entity in its own right, and has been regarded as such since 1934. Unlike Cannes, with which it was somewhat competitive in the forties, it is not a festival at which films are bought and sold, but is a competitive gathering, at which the major prize is the Leone d'oro/Golden Lion. The festival is held annually in the early fall, but did not take place in 1943, 1944, 1945, 1973, and 1974.

Address: Ca. Giustinian, San Marco, 30124 Venice, Italy.

BIBLIOGRAPHY

Castello, Giulio Cesare, and Claudio Bertieri. *Venezia 1932–1939*. Rome: Bianco e Nero, 1959.

Twenty Years of Cinema in Venice. Rome: Ateneo, 1952.

VGIK stands for Vsesoyuznyi Gosudarstvenyi Institut Kinematografi (The All-Union State Institute of Cinematography). It was established in Moscow in 1919, following Lenin's nationalization of the Russian film industry in August of that year, and is the world's oldest extant film school. One of the first prominent Russian filmmakers to teach there was Lev Kuleshov (who joined the school in 1920). Other teachers have included Vsevolod Pudovkin, Sergei Eisenstein, Alexander Dovzhenko, and Grigori Kozintsev.

Courses vary in years according to the subjects undertaken. Designers study for six years, directors for five years, and cameramen, actors, writers, and critics for four years. The emphasis is on the practical side of filmmaking, and 80 percent of all filmmakers in the Soviet Union are graduates of VGIK.

Address: Tretij Selskokhozjstvenni Proeld No. 3, Moscow, USSR.

VICTORINE STUDIOS. Located in a western suburb of Nice, the Victorine Studios were built in 1917 by Louis Nalpas on the site of what had once been the estate of General Massena and which was at that time a market garden. The studios were named after the hill on which they stand. Robert Boudrioz' *L'Atre* was the first film to be shot there. In 1924, American director Rex Ingram took over the then-derelict studios, and here he filmed *Mare Nostrum* (1926), *The Magician* (1926), *The Garden of Allah* (1927), *The Three Passions* (1929), and *Baroud* (1932). Other films made at the Victorine Studios in the twenties include *Morgane la Sirène* (1927), *Roses of Picardy* (1927), *Venus* (1928), and *Scheherezade* (1928). It was a popular studio for both French and British filmmakers, and among the stars who worked there in the twenties were Rex Ingram's wife Alice Terry, Constance Talmadge, Betty Balfour, and Ricardo Cortez.

Rex Ingram lost control of the studios in 1929, when the ownership passed to Edouard Corniglion-Molinier's company, Franco Films, which had been making features there since 1927. The studio had a checkered history, with its ownership passing through many hands, including those of the municipality of Nice. Among the famous films shot there in whole or part are *Les Enfants du Paradis/Children of Paradise* (1945), *Lola Montez* (1955), *Et Dieu . . . Créa la Femme/And God Created Woman* (1957), *Mon Oncle/My Uncle* (1958), and *La Nuit Américaine/Day for Night* (1973), which provides the viewer with a unique opportunity to watch filmmaking at the Victorine Studios.

Address: 16 avenue Edouard Grinda, 06200 Nice, France.

BIBLIOGRAPHY

O'Leary, Liam. *Rex Ingram: Master of the Silent Cinema.* New York: Barnes & Noble, 1980.

VIENNA. Among the feature films that utilize the Austrian capital as a backdrop are *Merry-Go-Round* (1923), *The Marriage Circle* (1924), *The Enemy* (1927), *Love Me and the World Is Mine* (1928), *The Wedding March* (1928), *Viennese Nights* (1930), *Liebelei* (1932), *The Great Waltz* (1938), *Spring Parade* (1940), *The Third Man* (1949), *Freud* (1962), *Mayerling* (1968), *The Great Waltz* (1972), *Colonel Redl* (1984), and *Amadeus* (1985).

The city is also the site of the Viennale (Künstlerhaus, Karlsplatz 5, A-1010 Vienna).

VIETNAM. Filmmaking in Vietnam dates back to when the country was known as French Indochina. As early as 1940, there had been a number of attempts at film production, but these were limited by both a lack of technical knowledge and a lack of capital. Film distribution was handled by French companies, which imported between 150 to 200 features a year for the approximately one hundred theatres in the country.

The North Vietnamese government sponsored limited production of features and animated films beginning in the late fifties, and a number of the films received awards at Eastern European film festivals. Since the "liberation" of South Vietnam, the country has produced an average of fifteen films a year. Although now under government control, the film industry in the South remains pretty much intact, although filmmaking is concentrated in Hanoi at the Hanoi Feature Film Studio. Feature films are produced in black-and-white and under the supervision of the Ministry of Culture. The country's leading director is Ho Quong Minh (born 1949), who returned to Vietnam from Switzerland in 1981, and gained international recognition with his 1986 feature, *Karma*. In 1987, the Vietnamese film industry announced its interest in co-productions with other countries, including the United States.

BIBLIOGRAPHY

Hampe, Barry, "Vietnam Seeks Co-Prod'n Deals," *The Hollywood Reporter,* December 3, 1987, pp. 1, 18.

Marshall, Fred, "People's Republic of Vietnam," *Variety,* May 2, 1979, p. 404.
Thu, Nguyen, "The Cinema in Vietnam," *Cinema India-International,* vol. IV, no. 1, 1987, p. 118.

VIETNAM WAR. The earliest feature film to deal with the war in Vietnam (1964–1973) is Allied Artists' *A Yank in Vietnam* (1964). The origins of the Vietnam War, namely the French actions in Indochina, are the subject of the French/Vietnamese co-production, *Poussière d'Empire/Dust of Empire* (1983). Among the feature films concerned with Vietnam are *To the Shores of Hell* (1966), *The Green Berets* (1968), *The Losers* (1970), *Hoa Binh* (1971), *Limbo* (1972), *Two People* (1973), *Heroes* (1977), *Rolling Thunder* (1977), *Go Tell the Spartans* (1978), *The Boys in Company C* (1978), *The Deer Hunter* (1978), *Coming Home* (1978), *Who'll Stop the Rain* (1978), *Apocalypse Now* (1979), *Purple Hearts* (1984), *Missing in Action* (1984), *Rambo: First Blood Part II* (1985), *Missing in Action 2: The Beginning* (1985), *Cease Fire* (1985), *Platoon* (1986), and *Full Metal Jacket* (1987).

Among the documentaries on the Vietnam War are *Vietnam: War without Fronts* (1967), *The Anderson Platoon* (1967), *Far from Vietnam* (1968), *17th Parallel: Vietnam in War* (1968), *Vietnam Journey* (1974), *Hearts and Minds* (1975), *Vietnam: An American Journey* (1979), *The War at Home* (1980), *Vietnam Requiem* (1983), and *Soldiers in Hiding* (1985).

BIBLIOGRAPHY

Adair, Gilbert. *Vietnam on Film.* New York: Proteus Books, 1981.

VISATONE was a British sound system from the early thirties, rights to the use of which were purchased by the GPO Film Unit in 1934.

VISNEWS LTD. is an international news agency that gathers news footage on a daily basis from around the world and makes it available to various clients, including the British, Canadian, Australian, and New Zealand broadcasting corporations. It also maintains major archival holdings of Gaumont Graphic News (1913–1925), Gaumont-British News (1934–1959), Empire News Bulletin (1926–1932), the British edition of Universal News (1930–1956), and British Paramount News (1931–1957).

The company was founded in 1957 as British Commonwealth International Newsfilm Agency by the British Broadcasting Corporation, the Rank Organization*, the Australian Broadcasting Corporation, and the Canadian Broadcasting Corporation. In 1960, Reuters became a minority shareholder, and, in 1968, acquired the shares of the Rank Organization. In 1985, it became the majority shareholder after purchasing some of the BBC's shares, and today the latter, along with the Canadian, Australian, and New Zealand broadcasting corporations all own 11 1/4 percent of the capital, with the rest in the hands of Reuters. The name was changed to Visnews (the company's telegraphic address) in 1964.

Visnews began news gathering via satellites in 1975, and, in 1983, set up the BrightStar satellite system with Western Union.

Address: Cumberland Avenue, London NW10 7EH, United Kingdom.

BIBLIOGRAPHY

Stanbrook, Alan, "Today's News Today," *Sight & Sound,* vol. LVI, no. 1, Winter 1986/87, pp. 24–29.

VISONOR EDUCATIONAL FILMS was a British producer of the thirties, specializing, as its name suggests, in documentary, educational, and sponsored films.

VITA-FILM was a German production company with studios in Vienna, where it made three major "French" features: *Salammbô* (1925), Max Linder's *Le roi du cirque/King of the Circus* (1925), and Jacques Feyder's *L'Image* (1926). After a year in existence, the company was declared bankrupt in 1926.

VOLKSVERBAND FÜR FILMKUNST (Popular Association for Film Art) was founded in Germany in 1928 by Heinrich Mann, G.W. Pabst, Karl Freund, Erwin Piscator, and others for the popularization of "artistically progressive films" (*Close Up,* May 1928, p. 71).

VUFKU. With a studio in the Ukrainian city of Kharkov, VUFKU was active from 1923 to 1930. Among its productions are Alexander Dovzhenko's *Zvenigora* (1928), Dziga Vertov's *Chelovek s kinoapparatom/Man with a Movie Camera* (1929), and Alexander Dovzhenko's *Arsenal* (1929) and *Zemlya/Earth* (1930). From December 1925, it also published a monthly film magazine titled *Kino*.

W

THE WARNER BROS. FUND FOR DEVELOPMENT OF SCRIPT WRITING IN ISRAEL was created in 1982 to provide financial assistance to an Israeli citizen while he or she works on a screenplay. It is administered by the Israel Film Centre (30 Gershon Agron Street, P.O. Box 299, Jerusalem 94190).

THE WARWICK TRADING COMPANY was formed in 1898 by Charles Urban, an American film entrepreneur active in the United Kingdom. One of the major British companies from the early years of this century, Warwick joined forces with the Autoscope Company (founded in 1896) in January 1906, and at that time Will Barker became its new head—Charles Urban had left the company in 1903 (when he formed the Charles Urban Trading Company). Under Barker, the Warwick Trading Company enjoyed considerable success, until he left, in August 1909 to form his own company, Barker Motion Photography Ltd. The Warwick Trading Company folded in 1916, when its assets were acquired by Cherry Kearton.

BIBLIOGRAPHY

Low, Rachael, and Roger Manvell. *The History of the British Film: 1896–1906*. London: George Allen & Unwin, 1948.

THE WATERSIDE WORKERS' FEDERATION FILM UNIT was a union-created production group active in Sydney, Australia from 1953 to 1958. Its members, whose first of nine films was *Pensions for Veterans* (1953), were Norma Disher, Keith Gow, and Jerome Levy. The Unit was the subject of a 1981 documentary, *Framework*.

BIBLIOGRAPHY

Hughes, John, and Brett Levy, "The Waterside Workers' Federation Film Unit, 1953–1958: An Interview with Norma Disher, Keith Gow, and Jerome Levy," in *An Australian Film Reader*, editor Albert Moran and Tom O'Regan. Sydney, Australia: Currency Press, 1985, pp. 365–373.

WELSH. The Welsh language has been heard in two features. *Boy Soldier* (1986) was written and directed by Karl Francis and starred Richard Lynch and Daffyd Howell in a story of an unemployed teenager who joins the Welsh Guard. It received its world premiere at the Chapter Arts Centre in Cardiff, but gained little international recognition. *Rhosyn a Rhith/Coming Up Roses* (1986) was released in the United States by Skouras Pictures. It is the story of the efforts of two former employees to keep the Rex Theatre in Aberdare from demolition and to reopen it. It was directed by Stephen Bayly, written by Ruth Carter, and starred Daffyd Hywel and Iola Gregory. Described as "modest, gentle, unassuming and quite charming" by *Variety* (May 21, 1986), *Rhosyn a Rhith* was produced by Red Rooster and S4C (Sinael 4 Cymru/Channel 4 Wales) at a cost of $390,000.

WELSH, PEARSON & CO., LTD. was formed in January 1918, when its partners, T.A. Welsh and George Pearson left the employ of the British office of Gaumont*. Here, director George Pearson produced some of the most important British feature films of the period, including *The Better 'Ole* (1918), one of the first British films to gain a wide audience in the United States, *Nothing Else Matters* (1920), *Love, Life and Laughter* (1923), *Reveille* (1924), *The Little People* (1925), and the Squibs series*, starring Betty Balfour. In 1928, the company became Welsh-Pearson-Elder, with the addition to its main shareholders of T.C. Elder, a businessman. The "new" company was involved in one major co-production, that of *Journey's End* (1930), which Pearson supervised, but which was directed, in Hollywood, by James Whale. By 1934, Welsh-Pearson-Elder had ceased production.

BIBLIOGRAPHY

Pearson, George. *Flashback*. London: George Allen & Unwin, 1957.

WELTFILM was a workers' organization, created in Germany in 1927, to produce and distribute leftist and Communist films.

WELT IM FILM was an Anglo-American newsreel produced in German, for exhibition in occupied Germany from 1945 to 1950. The newsreel is preserved in the Imperial War Museum*, from whom a microfiche of its issue sheets is available.

WESSEX PRODUCTIONS was established by British producer Ian Dalrymple to make feature films for release through the Independent Producers* program of the Rank Organization*. Its productions are: *The Woman in the Hall* (1947), *Esther Waters* (1948) *Once a Jolly Swagman* (U.S. *Maniacs on Wheels,* 1948), *All Over Town* (1949), *Dear Mr. Prohack* (1949), and *The Wooden Horse* (1950).

THE WHITE MAN'S BURDEN, as poet Rudyard Kipling referred to the onerous task of governing portions of the British Empire* has been the subject of a number of British and American features. The most famous of Empire administrators was Commissioner Sanders, created by novelist Edgar Wallace, and seen on screen in *Sanders of the River* (1935), *Death Drums along the River* (1963), and *Coast of Skeletons* (1964). The character is also parodied in *Old Bones of the River* (1938). Other films dealing with colonial service in Africa include *The Sun Never Sets* (1940), *Sundown* (1941), *Tarzan and the Mermaids* (1948), *Tarzan's Peril* (1951), and *The Scarlet Spear* (1953). *Pacific Destiny* (1956) is concerned with service in the South Pacific, while Indian service is the subject of *The Drum* (1929), *King of the Khyber Rifles* (1929), *Charge of the Light Brigade* (1936), *Wee Willie Winkie* (1937), and *The Charge of the Light Brigade* (1968), among others.

BIBLIOGRAPHY

Richards, Jeffrey. *Visions of Yesterday*. Boston: Routledge & Kegan Paul, 1973.

WHITE TELEPHONE FILMS (or Telefoni Bianchi) is a genre unique to the Italian cinema, under fascism, in the thirties, when the industry was under the control of director general of cinematography, Luigi Freddi. White telephone films are primarily comedies, usually concerned with sexual mores, recognizable by their lavish settings and the wealthy and glamorous life-styles that they evoke. In general, they are about people who could afford white telephones. Typical examples of white telephone films, from each end of the era in which they were popular, are Mario Camerini's *Figaro e la sua gran giornata/Figaro's Big Day* (1931) and Alessandro Blasetti's *La contessa di Parma/The Countess of Parma* (1937).

THE WILL DAY COLLECTION. Gathered together by British showman Will Day (1873–1936), the Will Day Collection was a well-known group of items—primarily equipment but also papers—relating to the early history of the motion picture and its antecedents. Once on display in part at London's Science Museum, the entire collection was first offered for sale, accompanied by a fifty-four page catalog, in 1930. It was eventually sold in 1961 to the Cinémathèque Française*.

BIBLIOGRAPHY

Coe, Brian, "The Will Day Collection," *Cinema Studies,* vol. I, no. 5, Spring 1962, pp. 91–94.

THE WOMEN'S FILM, TELEVISION, AND VIDEO NETWORK was founded in 1981 to protect the interests of women in the industry at all levels of British production.

Address: 23 Frith Street, London WIV 5TS, United Kingdom.

WOODFALL FILM PRODUCTIONS LTD. was formed by Tony Richardson and John Osborne in order to make the screen version of the latter's play, *Look Back in Anger*. The entrepreneur behind the British company was producer Harry

Saltzmann, who raised financing from Warner Bros. and Associated British-Pathé. The ultimate film, released in 1959, received good reviews, but was a box-office failure. Financing for Woodfall's second feature, *The Entertainer* (1960), in which Laurence Olivier recreated his stage role of Archie Rice, came from Bryanston Films*, but this also was a box-office flop. Disappointed by two failures, Richardson declined to direct Woodfall's third film, *Saturday Night and Sunday Morning* (1960), and Karel Reisz enjoyed the success of the film, which was financed by Bryanston and the National Film Finance Corporation*.

In part because of temperamental differences between him and Richardson, Saltzmann left the company after production of *Saturday Night and Sunday Morning,* and his place on the board was taken by Oscar Lewenstein, a West End theatrical entrepreneur who had Albert Finney under contract. Woodfall's next film was a screen adaptation of Shelagh Delaney's play, *A Taste of Honey* (1961), which Richardson directed on location. It was followed by *The Loneliness of the Long Distance Runner* (1962), but by this time public interest in working class heroes had declined.

Woodfall had difficulty in raising funding for *Tom Jones* (1963), starring Albert Finney in the title role, but eventually 100 percent financing was provided by United Artists. The film was such a success that its director, Tony Richardson, was invited to Hollywood (where he directed the 1963 cult favorite, *The Loved One*). Surprisingly, Woodfall next produced three low-budget features: *The Girl with Green Eyes* (1964), *One-Way Pendulum* (1964), and *The Knack . . . And How to Get It* (1965). Woodfall's decline came in 1968 when Osborne and Richardson were to have collaborated on *The Charge of the Light Brigade*. Their friendship became badly frayed with disagreements over the script and Osborne withdrew from the production. His and Richardson's creative partnership came to an end and with it Woodfall Film Productions, Ltd.

BIBLIOGRAPHY

Walker, Alexander. *Hollywood England: The British Film Industry in the Sixties*. London: Michael Joseph, 1974.

THE WORLD IN ACTION. A newsreel compilation aimed at a general audience, *The World in Action* was produced by the National Film Board of Canada* and supervised and written by Stuart Legg. Released on a monthly basis from 1941–1945, the series was intended for audiences throughout the world (with an American release by United Artists). The first film in the series, *Churchill's Island,* received a 1941 Special Documentary Award from the Academy of Motion Picture Arts and Sciences.

THE WORLD UNION OF DOCUMENTARY, was a short-lived organization, founded in Brussels in 1947, with Basil Wright as its first president. At its initial meeting, the organization issued a declaration defining the word "Documentary," and continuing:

The indispensable role of documentary in the fields of information and education and in the communication of ideas makes it necessary for the documentary workers, not only to state the problems exactly, but also to guide the public towards the solution of these problems.

In this task, it is the responsibility of every documentary worker to master the technique and artistic potentials of the documentary film, so that art and technique are fused with the social purpose of documentary.

The documentary film has established itself as a form of film art. It has a profound influence on feature films in all countries. This influence will certainly continue. In particular, documentary film workers should engage in all activities designed to secure the full and unfettered expression of social, economic and cultural life through the medium of film.

The principal tasks confronting documentary workers are as follows: the fight against the enemies of peace and democracy; national, racial and economic oppression and religious intolerance; poverty and disease, illiteracy, ignorance and other social evils; and the fight for peace and reconstruction; independence of subject peoples; free intellectual and cultural expression; dissemination of knowledge, not at present available to all.

Documentary film workers will collaborate with all international organizations working for the principles enumerated above.

The establishment of this organization is discussed in *Documentary Film News*, August 1948, p. 89.

Y

YAP is a small Micronesian island, to which television was introduced in 1980, with a subsequent subversion to U.S. culture. The result of that induction is chronicled in Dennis O'Rourke's 1980 fifty-four-minute documentary, *Yap . . . How Did You Know We'd Like TV*.

YIDDISH FILMS, films produced in Yiddish for Jewish audiences, can be traced back even before the coming of sound, when a few silent features, including *Mazel Tov* (1924) and *Yiskor* (1924), had Yiddish subtitles. However Yiddish cinema is generally dated from 1929, when director Sidney M. Goldin (also responsible for the earlier silent films) made *Ad Musae/The Eternal Prayer* and *East Side Sadie*. Goldin was one of the pioneers of Yiddish filmmaking in the United States, with his other films including *The Feast of Passover* (1931), *Shulamith* (1931), and *Uncle Moses* (1932). Aside from Goldin, American Yiddish filmmaking is dominated by Joseph Seiden, who began as an assistant to Goldin and whose films date from 1930, and Edgar G. Ullmer, a cult director whose first Yiddish feature was *Green Fields* (1937), co-directed by Jacob Ben-Ami, and whose cast included Herschel Bernardi. Two major Yiddish American films from the late thirties are Ullmer's *The Singing Blacksmith,* starring Moishe Oysher, and released in 1938, and *Tevya,* released in 1939, and directed by and starring Maurice Schwartz.

Members of New York's Yiddish theatre community on Second Avenue who appeared in Yiddish films include Molly Picon, Boris Tomashefsky, Celia Adler, and Jacob Ben-Ami.

Outside the United States, Poland was the centre for Yiddish filmmaking, with Polish-born Joseph Green its primary producer. He made *Yidl mitn Fidl/ Yiddle with His Fiddle* (1936), starring Molly Picon, followed by *Der Purimshpiler* (1936), *Mamele* (1938), and *A Brivele der Mamen* (1938). Michael Waszkynsky made a version of *The Dybbuk* in Poland in 1938. Yiddish films were also made in the Soviet Union, Rumania, and Hungary.

The Second World War quite obviously ended European production of Yiddish films, but the genre continued in the United States into the fifties, with some of the last Yiddish films being *Got, Mentsh un Tayvl/God, Man and Devil* (1950), *Monticello, Here We Come* (1950), and *Three Daughters* (1961), all directed by Joseph Seiden. A 1969 documentary, *The Golden Age of Second Avenue,* includes clips from many Yiddish films.

BIBLIOGRAPHY

Cohen, Sarah Blacher, editor. *From Hester Street to Hollywood: The Jewish-American Stage and Screen.* Bloomington: Indiana University Press, 1983.

Edelman, Rob, "Yiddish Cinema," *Films in Review,* vol. XXIX, no. 6, June-July 1978, pp. 331–344.

Erens, Patricia, "Mentshlekhkayt Conquers All: The Yiddish Cinema in America," *Film Quarterly,* January-February 1976, pp. 48–53.

Golden, Herb, "Negro and Yiddish Film Boom," *Variety,* January 3, 1940, p. 36.

Goldman, Eric A. *Visions, Images and Dreams: Yiddish Film Past and Present.* Ann Arbor, Mich.: UMI Research Press, 1983.

Hoberman, J., "Yiddish Transit," *Film Comment,* vol. XVII, no. 4, July-August 1981, pp. 36–38.

YOKOTA. Active from the late 1890s through 1912, the Yokota Company, named after its founder Einosuke Yokota, was a pioneering Japanese film enterprise. Initially, it filmed the various Shimpa dramatic companies, but it also introduced one of Japan's first important directors, Shozo Makino, and one of the country's first screen stars, Matsunosuke Onoue. Yokota merged with the Nippon Katsudo Shashin/Japan Cinematograph Company, which became known as Nikkatsu*.

YOSHIZAWA, one of Japan's pioneering film companies, was established in the late 1890s by Kenichi Kawaura. It imported the Lumière cinématographe and the Méliès films from France and in the early years of this century was also exhibiting its own films in Europe and the United States. The company built studios, in 1908, in the Meguro section of Tokyo, and was primarily involved in the production of films for the Shimpa dramatic companies. It merged, in 1912, with the Nippon Katsudo Shashin/Japan Cinematograph Company, which became known as Nikkatsu*.

YUGOSLAVIA is a richly divergent country, with many ethnic, religious, and linguistic groups, organized around a unique form of "market socialism" overseen by the Communist party. The film industry necessarily echoes the benefits and complexity of the nation as a whole. With more than twenty-four production houses scattered throughout six republics and two autonomous provinces, the Yugoslav film industry is the most active cinema of the socialist countries in the Balkans and Eastern Europe.

No systematic film production existed in Yugoslavia until 1945 when the State Film Enterprise was set up under the new Communist leadership. Ambitions at first drifted toward developing a Hollywood-like Studio City in Belgrade, known as Koshutnyak, with the goal of turning out fifty films a year. This dream never came true even though the studio was built. Such dreams did not take into consideration either the need for regional film production or the trend away from studio production that began with the influence of Italian Neo-Realism* after the Second World War.

Decentralization became official by 1956, when the Film Law established that each republic should develop its own film industry. By that time production units already existed in Belgrade, Zagreb, Ljublana, Skopje, Sarajevo, Montenegro, Novi Sad, and the predominately Albanian-speaking province of Kosovo.

Unlike filmmaking in the Warsaw-block Communist nations or the Soviet Union, the Yugoslav film production houses are able to function under ''workers' self management,'' as relatively autonomous businesses. Financing of films, for instance, is a patchwork of income generated from film distribution (since many of the production houses also distribute), from ''awards'' from the various cultural committees of each Republic, from television co-productions, and from foreign investment. Budgets vary, but many of the best feature films of 1987 were made for amounts between $100,000 to $300,000.

There is, in other words, no Central Committee carving up the money and the projects each year. This means that each production house is free to negotiate its own productions both within Yugoslavia and with foreign production companies, either to make their own films or to facilitate foreign production.

While many of the production houses are quite small or specialized (for example, one is set up by the Yugoslav Army to make documentaries and training films), Yugoslavia, nevertheless, manages to produce between twenty and thirty feature films, and several hundred documentaries (not to mention a large volume of television productions) each year, which receive their premieres each July at the Pula Film Festival. In recent years, Yugoslav films have begun to attract much international attention at festivals and through distribution. In 1986, Yugoslav cinema was honored with major retrospectives in London (at the British Film Institute*) and in Paris (with one hundred films shown at the Georges Pompidou Centre).

Foreign producers have been attracted over the years to Yugoslavia because of the high quality of the technical help available (including actors and actresses), the low cost of production, and the impressive variety of locations for shooting. A country that offers Alps (Slovenia), a Mediterranean coastline (Croatia), New England rolling hills (Macedonia), Kansas wheat fields (Voivodina), as well as cities with Old World charm (Zagreb, Ljubljana, Novi Sad) is clearly a haven for filmmakers. Thus both film and television productions ranging from quality features, such as *Sophie's Choice, The Tin Drum,* and *Winds of War,* to low-budget productions by Cannon and others, such as *King Solomon's Mines* and *Transylvania 6500,* have been made in Yugoslavia.

One of the major production houses is Jadran Film (Oporovecka 12, Dubrava, 41041 Zagreb), which has a long history of co-productions, including *Fiddler on the Roof, Sacco and Venzetti,* Orson Welles' *The Trial,* and a number of Westerns. Jadran upgraded its studios in 1987.

Centar Film (Borisa Kidrica 71, Belgrade 11000) is the major production house in Belgrade, the capital of Yugoslavia and of the Republic of Serbia, and also the center for the majority of Yugoslav film production. Centar has made and distributed numerous award-winning Yugoslav films, including documentaries, such as *The Last Oasis* and the 1985 Cannes Film Festival* winner by Emir Kusturica, *When Father Was Away on Business* (distribution only). It also has foreign co-production experience.

Other important companies include Art Film 80 (Knez Mihailova 48, Belgrade 11000), which has a particularly good reputation for encouraging new talent in low-budget films. Viba Film (Zrinjskega 9, Ljubljana) and Vesa Film (Miklosiceva cesta 38, Ljubljana) represent useful contacts in the northern republic of Slovenia, which includes both Italian-like coastlines and Alpine locations.

Yugoslavs are also world-class makers of imaginative animation. The so-called ''Zagreb School'' of animation (reduced line animation) has captured numerous awards, including an Oscar in 1961 for Dušan Vukotić's *Ersatz/ Surrogate.* A variety of production houses—Croatia Film, Viba Film, Avala Film, Jadran Film, Neoplanta Film, and others—provide excellent animation services.

Yugoslavia Film (Knez Mihailova 19, Belgrade 11000) provides information on Yugoslav film production and publishes a newsletter, *Yugoslavia Film News.*

BIBLIOGRAPHY

Goulding, Daniel J. *Liberated Cinema: The Yugoslav Experience.* Bloomington: Indiana University Press, 1985.

Hibbin, Nina. *Eastern Europe: An Illustrated Guide.* New York: A.S. Barnes, 1969.

Horton, Andrew, ''Satire and Sympathy: A New Wave of Yugoslavian Filmmakers,'' *Cineaste,* vol. XI, no. 2, 1981, pp. 18–22.

———, ''The New Serbo-Creationism,'' *American Film,* vol. XI, no. 4, January-February 1986, pp. 24–28, 30.

Liehm, Mira. *The Most Important Art: Eastern European Film after 1945.* Berkeley: University of California Press, 1977.

Stoil, Michael Jon. *Cinema beyond the Danube.* Metuchen, N.J.: Scarecrow Press, 1974.

Z

ZAGREB. The Yugoslav city of Zagreb is noted for its animated film production, considered the most diverse and exciting in Eastern Europe, and highly regarded in the Western world. As early as 1922, animator Sergei Tagatz came to work in Zagreb, but it was not until 1956 that Zagreb Film actively sponsored an animation studio. In 1961, the Zagreb short, *Ersatz/The Substitute,* directed, designed, and animated by Dušan Vukotić, became the first non-American film to win the Academy Award for Best Short Subject (Cartoon).

Among the major animators associated with Zagreb are Milan Blažeković, Zlatko Bourek, Borivoj Dovniković, Nedeljko Dragić, Zdenko Gašparović, Zlatko Grgić, Vladimir Jutriša, Boris Kolar, Vjekoslav Kostanjšek, Nikola Kostelac, Vladimir Kristl, Zvonimir Lončarić, Aleksandar Marks, Vatroslav Mimica, Pavao Štalter, Dušan Vukotić, Dragutin Vunak, and Ante Zaninović.

Address: Zagreb Film, Vlaska 70, 4100 Zagreb, Yugoslavia.

BIBLIOGRAPHY

Holloway, Ronald. *Z Is for Zagreb.* South Brunswick, N.J. and New York: A.S. Barnes, 1972.

ZENIFILMS was a British distributor in the thirties of educational films, chiefly those of Christopher Radley and Eric Spear.

THE ZENKOREN (OR GOLDEN GROSS) AWARD has been presented since 1986 by the Federation of Motion Picture Exhibitors to the best film of the year exhibited in Japan.

THE ZOETROPE, an optical toy that proved the persistence of vision, was invented by Englishman W.G. Horner in 1834. Consisting of a metal drum with slits, through which the viewer looks at a series of drawings on a disc, that appear to move as the drum moves, the Zoetrope was improved upon by Frenchman Emile Reynaud in the mid-1870s, and renamed the Praxinoscope. Reynaud was later able to expand his concept to a theatrical entertainment, Théâtre Optique, which is beautifully recreated in the 1947 French documentary, *Naissance du Cinéma*.

BIBLIOGRAPHY

Ceram, C.W. *Archaeology of the Cinema*. New York: Harcourt, Brace & World, undated (1985).

General Bibliography

Bardeche, Maurice, and Robert Brasillach. *The History of Motion Pictures*. Translated by Iris Barry. New York: Norton and the Museum of Modern Art, 1938.

Bawden, Liz-Anne, editor. *The Oxford Companion to Film*. New York: Oxford University Press, 1976.

Bohn, Thomas W., and Richard L. Stromgren, with Daniel H. Johnson. *Light and Shadows: A History of Motion Pictures*. Washington, N.Y.: Alfred Publishing, 1975.

Bond, Otto F. *Fifty Foreign Films*. Chicago: University of Chicago Press, 1939.

Carter, Huntly. *The New Spirit in the Cinema*. London: Harold Shaylor, 1930.

Cook, David A. *A History of Narrative Film*. New York: Norton, 1981.

Cowie, Peter, editor. *International Film Guide*. London: Tantivy Press, 1964 to present.

———. *Seventy Years of Cinema*. New York: A.S. Barnes, 1969.

———. *A Concise History of the Cinema*. New York: A.S. Barnes, 1971.

Fell, John L. *A History of Films*. New York: Holt, Rinehart and Winston, 1979.

Fulton, A.R. *Motion Pictures*. Norman: University of Oklahoma Press, 1960.

Garbicz, Adam, and Jacek Klinowski. *Cinema, the Magic Vehicle*. Metuchen, N.J.: Scarecrow, 1975.

Guback, Thomas H. *The International Film Industry: Western Europe and America since 1945*. Bloomington: Indiana University Press, 1969.

Halliwell, Leslie. *Halliwell's Filmgoer's Companion*. New York: Scribner's, 1984.

Houston, Penelope. *The Contemporary Cinema*. Baltimore, Md.: Penguin, 1963.

Kemps International Film & Television Year Book. London: Kemps Group, 1955 to present.

Knight, Arthur. *The Liveliest Art*. New York: Macmillan, 1978.

Lacalomita, Michele, editor. *Filmlexicon degli autori e delle opere*. Rome: Edizioni di Bianco e Nero, 1958.

Lejeune, C.A. *Cinema*. London: Alexander Maclehose, 1931.

Limbacher, James. *Four Aspects of the Film*. New York: Brussel & Brussel, 1969.

Luhr, William, editor. *World Cinema since 1945*. New York: Ungar, 1987.

Magill, Frank N., editor. *Magill's Survey of Cinema: Foreign Language Films*. Englewood Cliffs, N.J.: Salem, 1985.

Manvell, Roger, editor. *The International Encyclopedia of Film*. New York: Crown, 1972.

Mast, Gerald. *A Short History of the Movies*. Chicago: University of Chicago Press, 1981.

Mayer, Michael F. *Foreign Films on American Screens*. New York: Arco, 1965.

Montagu, Ivor. *Film World: A Guide to Cinema*. Baltimore, Md.: Penguin, 1964.

Rhode, Eric. *A History of the Cinema: From Its Origins to 1970*. New York: Hill and Wang, 1976.

Robertson, Patrick. *Guinness Film Facts and Feats*. London: Guinness Books, 1985.

Robinson, David. *The History of World Cinema*. New York: Stein and Day, 1981.

Roth, William David. *Technology, Film and the Body Politic*. Berkeley: University of California Press, 1970.

Rotha, Paul, and Roger Manvell. *Movie Parade 1888–1949: A Pictorial Survey of World Cinema*. London: Studio, 1950.

Rotha, Paul, with Richard Griffith. *The Film Till Now*. New York: Twayne, 1960.

Roud, Richard, editor. *Cinema: A Critical Dictionary*. New York: Viking, 1980.

Shipman, David. *The Story of Cinema*. New York: St. Martin's, 1982.

Slide, Anthony, editor. *Selected Film Criticism: Foreign Films 1930–1950*. Metuchen, N.J.: Scarecrow, 1984.

Smith, John M., and Tim Cawkwell, editors. *The World Encyclopedia of the Film*. New York: World, 1972.

Tyler, Parker. *Classics of the Foreign Film*. New York: Citadel, 1962.

Wolf, William, with Lillian Kramer Wolf. *Landmark Films: The Cinema and Our Century*. New York: Paddington, 1979.

Wright, Basil. *The Long View*. New York: Knopf, 1974.

Index

ABC Circuit, 349
A.B. Company, 29
A.B. Film Studios, 102
ABPC, 49
Academia de las Artes y las Ciencias Cinematograficas, 184
Academy Cinema, 1–2
Academy of Canadian Cinema and Television, 2
Ace Films, 2
Acevedo and Sons, 91
Acorn Pictures, 370
Acqua Marci-Bastogas, 350
Acres, Birt, 228
ACT Films Ltd., 18
Actors Equity of Australia, 21
ACTT, 17–18
Actueel-Film, 261
Adams Filmi Oy, 165
Adanac Producing Company, 3
Afghan Films, 3
Afghanistan, 3
AFO-Film, 240
Africa, 3–4, 5. *See also* individual countries
Africa Film, 5
Africa Film Productions Ltd., 324
AGC, 4
Agence Générale Cinématographique, 4
Agfacolor, 4
Agfa Filmfrabrik, 4
Agfa-Gevaert, N.V., 4
Agitaki, 5
Agit-Prop, 5
Aires Cinematografíca, 13
AJYM, 5
Akerman, Chantal, 30
Akkad, Moustapha, 235
Aktiebolaget Svensk Filmindustri, 337
Albania, 5
Alberini, Filoteo, 211
Algeria, 5–6
Allan, Jules and Jay, 58
Allegemeine Elekrizitäts Gesellschaft, 228
Alliance Entertainment Corporation, 6–7
Alliance Film Studios, 355
Alliance of Canadian Cinema, Television, and Radio Artists, 2
All-Red Feature Company, 7
All-Union Combine of the Movie-Photo Industry, 326–27
All-Union Corporation V/O Sovexportfilm, 326
All-Union State Institute of Cinematography, 384
Alonso, Manuel, 98
Amanda Awards, 7
Amauta Films, 289–90
Amkino Corporation, 326
Amsterdam-Film, 261
Ancinex, 7
Andersen, Knut, 346
Anderson, Anders, 312

Anderson, Lindsay, 171
Andes Film, 34
Andrews, Stanhope, 267
Anglia Films Ltd., 8
Anglo-Amalgamated Film Distributors Ltd., 8
Anglo-American Film Agreement, 8
Anglo-EMI, 8
Angola, 9
"Angry Young Men," 9
ANICA, 9
Anouchka Films, 9–10
Anschütz, Ottomar, 345
Ansco Color, 4
Anstey, Edgar, 317
Antarctica, 10
Antin, Manuel, 14
Antoine, André, 321
A–1 Films, 55
Aparsin Films, 3
Archers, the, 10
Archives, 135–44
Ardmore Studios, 10
Argentina, 10–14
Argentina Sono Films, 11
Argui Films, 14
Ariane Films, 15
ARK, 15
Armenia, 15
Arnold, Dr. August, 15
Arnold & Richter Cine Technik, 15–16
Arriflex, 15–16
Art Film, 80, 398
Arthurian cinema, 16
Artkino, 326
Arts Council of Great Britain, 16
Aryama Films, 3
Askania camera, 16
Askania Werke A.G., 16
A/S Nordisk Films Kompagni, 271
ASOCINE, 123
Asquith, Anthony, 18
Associated British Picture Corporation, 49, 126, 349
Associated Realist Film Producers, 16, 317
Associated Screen News of Canada Ltd., 17
Associated Talking Pictures, 118
L'Association des Auteurs de Films, 17
Association des Comédiens et Auteurs Dramatiques, 120
Association for the Diffusion of Japanese Films Abroad, 359
Association Nationale pour la Diffusion du Film Français a l'Étranger, 359
Association of Cinematograph, Television, and Allied Technicians, 17–18
Association of Independent Producers Ltd., 18–19
Association of Revolutionary Cinematography, 15
Association of Women Film Workers, 19
Associazone Nazionale Industrie Cinematografiche Affini, 9
Assotsiatsiia Revoliutsionnoi Kinematografii, 15
Asum Film Company, 102
Aswin Film, 347
Atelier Apollo, 161
Atlantic-Film Ltd., 19
Atlantida Cinematografica, 38
Atlas Film Co. Ltd., 19
Atlas International Film GmbH, 19
ATP, 118
Attenborough, Sir Richard, 47, 183
Attica, 19
Attilio Prevost Company, 298
Aubert, Louis, 129
Aubert Franco Film, 175
Augustus, 211
Australasian Films Productions, 89
Australia, 19–22, 89–90, 123, 144–45, 241, 263, 325, 343, 357, 389
Australian Film Commission, 22
Australian Film Development Corporation, 22
Australian Film, Television, and Radio School, 22–23
Australian Theatrical & Amusement Employees Association, 21
Australian Writers Guild, 21
Australia Screen Directors Association, 21
Austria, 23–24, 313, 385
Austrian Film Fund, 23

Auteur theory, 24–25
Autoscope Company, 389
Avila Films, 381–82

BAFTA, 41
Bahamas, 27
Bahs, Henning, 279
Balcon, Michael, 51, 52, 118, 173, 186, 318, 365
Balfour, Betty, 329
Balling, Erik, 279
Bamforth, James, 27
Bamforth and Co. Ltd., 27
Banca Nazionale del Lavoro, 27
Banco Nacional Cinematográfico, 247
B&C, 42
Bangladesh, 28
Bangladesh Film Development Corporation, 28
Bantu Educational Cinema Experiment, 3
Bantu Film Bank, 324
Barbados, 28
Barcelona Manifesto, 28
Barclay Securities, 51
Bardem, Juan Antonio, 328
Barker, Will, 389
Barnes, John, 28
Barnes Museum of Cinematography, 28–29
Barrandov Film Studios, 29
Barry, Iris, 134
Batchelor, Joy, 189
Baxter, John, 186
Bayard Press, 31
Bazin, André, 57
BBFC, 43
Beaconsfield Studios, 97, 225
Beijing Film Academy, 81
Beirut Agreement, 29
Béla Bálazs Studio, 29
Belfast, 29–30
Belgium, 4, 30–31, 171–72
Belize, 72–74
Bell, Oliver, 45
Bellevue-Pathé, 65
Belokapi, 31
Benno, Alex, 261
Benoît, Edmond, 321
Benoit-Levy, Edmond, 122
Benshi, 31–32
Bentley, John, 51
Bergfilm, 252–53
Berlin, 32
Berthon-Siemens, 280
BFI, 46–47
Bianco e Nero, 32
Bild-und Filmamt, 32, 257
Billancourt Studios, 32–33
Binger, Mauritz H., 261
Biophon, 33, 337
The Bioscope, 33
Bioskop, 33
BIP, 49
Birri, Fernando, 13
Bishop, Kenneth, 74
BKSTS, 50
Black, Edward, 173, 174
Black independent filmmaking in the United Kingdom, 33
Blakeley, John E., 243
Blakenham, Lord, 183
Blasetti, Alessandro, 211
Bloman, Hans Evert, 135
Board of Curators of Young German Cinema, 230
Bodil Awards, 33–34
Bohwin, Knut, 346
Bolivia, 34–36
Bolivia Films, 35
Bolivian Film Institute, 35
Bombay Talkies, 201
Bond, Ralph, 19
Boot, Charles, 293
Bord Scannán n hÉireann, 125
Borneo, 36
Box, Sydney, 174
Bramwell Productions, 27
Brasil Vita Filme, 38
Brazil, 36–41, 85, 305
Braunberger, Pierre, 160
"Brighton School," 41
British Academy of Film and Television Arts, 41–42
British Actors Film Co. Ltd., 193
British American Film Company, 42

British and Colonial Kinematograph Company, 42
British Board of Film Censors, 43–44
British Board of Film Classification, 43–44
British Burma Company, 54
British Columbia Film, 44
British Empire, 44–45
British Empire Films, 45
British Federation of Film Societies, 45
British Film and Television Producers' Association, 45–46
British Film Awards, 237
British Film Designers Guild Ltd., 46
British Film Fund Agency, 117
British Film Institute, 46–47
British Film Year, 47–48
British International Pictures, 49
British Instructional Films, 48–49
British Kinematograph, Sound and Television Society, 50
British Lion, 50–51
British Movietone News, 51–52, 239
British Music Hall, 52
British National Studios, 126
British Production Fund, 117
British Screen, 259
British Universities Film and Video Council, 320
Brodsky, Ben, 82
Brownridge, George, 3, 352
Bryanston Films, 52–53
Bucurşti Studios, 306
Budapest, 53
BUFA, 32
Bulgaria, 53–54
Bundesministerium des Innern, 54
Bungei Katsudo Shashin Kai, 160
Buñuel, Luis, 186, 248, 328
Burma, 54–55
Bushey Studios, 192–93

Cahiers du Cinéma, 57
Cairo Cinema Company, 124
Cairo Distribution Company, 124
Calligraphism, 57
Cambodia, 57–58
Cameroon, 58
Canada, 2, 3, 6–7, 17, 42, 44, 45, 58–70, 74–75, 88–89, 94–95, 256–58, 279–80, 281, 301, 305, 322, 346, 352, 392
"Canada Carries On", 70
Canadian Association for Adult Education, 2
Canadian Bioscope Company, 70
Canadian Cooperation Project, 62, 70
Canadian Film Development Corporation, 346
Canadian International Films, 45
Canadian National Features, 352
Canadian Odeon Theatres Ltd., 88
Canadian Pacific Railway, 17
Canadian Photoplays Ltd., 70
Canary Islands, 70
Cannes Film Festival, 71
Cannon Group, 349–50
Capital and Provincial News Theatres, 90
Captain Kettle Film Company, 71
Cargin, Peter, 45
Carlton Communications PLC, 71–72
Carreras, Enrique, 190
Carreras, James, 190
Carrick Films, 72
"Carry On" Series, 72
Carthage Film Days, 353
Carthago Films, 353
Cartoon Films, 305
Casablanca, 72
Casbah Films, 5
Castellani, Renato, 212
Castillo, Luis, 34
Catalan Films, 328
Cathay-Keris Productions, 242
Cathay Productions, 242
Cathay Studios, 193
CCC, 72
CEA, 87
Cecchi, Emilio, 89
Celor Films, 72
Celtic Film Company, 125
Centar Film, 398
Central African Film Unit, 72
Central America, 72–74. *See also* Nicaragua
Central Cinema Company, 72

Central Film Library, 75
Central Films, 74–75
Central Information Bureau for Educational Films, 75
Central Office of Information: Films and Television Division, 75
Centre Artistique et Technique des Jeunes de l'Ecran, 198
Centre Cinématographique Marocaine, 252
Centre International de Liaison des Écoles, 83
Centre National de la Cinématographie, 75
Centro Costarricense de Production Cinematografica, 74
Centro Sperimentale di Cinematografie, 75
César Awards, 75–76
Ceylon Entertainment Ltd., 330
Ceylon Theatres Ltd., 330
CFL Vision, 75
Chabrol, Claude, 5
Chambara, 76
Chamber Film, 227
Channel 4, 76–77
Chaplin, 77
Chaplin, Charles, 19, 308
Chapman, Graham, 251
Charles Urban Trading Company, 122
Chautard, Émile, 120
Chauvel, Charles, 20
Chesterton Properties PLC, 102
Children's Film and Television Foundation Ltd., 77
Chile, 77–80
Chile Films, 78–79
Chimicolor, 80
China, 80–82
China Cinema Company Ltd., 82–83
China Film Company, 81
Chow, Raymond, 193
Christiana Film Compagni A/S, 273
Chronophotograph, 83
CILECT, 83
Cinéastes Associés, 83
Cinecittà Spa, 83–84
Ciné-Club, 160
Cine Club de Cuzco, 290
Cine Club Vinna del Mar, 79
Cinédia Studios, 37
Cine-Film S. A., 115
Cinegael, 173
Cinégraphic, 84
Cineguild, Ltd., 84–85
Ciné Liberté, 85
Cinema Centro, 115
Cinema City Co. Ltd., 193
Cinéma Djidid, 6
Cinéma Maudjahid, 6
Cinema Novo, 38–40, 85
Cinémathèque Française, 85–87
Cinematografe Latino Americana S. A., 247
Cinematograph Exhibitors' Association of Great Britain and Ireland, 87
Cinematograph Films Council, 87
Cinema-Ye-Azade-Iran, 87
Cineorama, 87–88
Cineplex Odeon Corporation, 67, 88–89
Cine Rebelde, 99
Cineriz, 350
Ciné-Roman, 89
Cines, 89
Cines-Pittaluga, 83
Cines Rap Chain, 269
Cinesound, 89–90
Cinetone Studios, 261
Cinetyp, 90
Circuits Management Association, 176
Citra Awards, 90
Citroën, André, 171
City Studios, 195
Clarendon Film Company, 90
Clark, John, 357
Clarke, Col. W. F., 45
Clarke, Frederick Colburn, 7
Classic Cinemas, 90–91
Cleese, John, 251
Cocinor, 91
Cohen, Elsie, 1
Cohen, Nat, 8
Cohen-Seat, Gilbert, 159
Colaiacomo, Felice, 244
Collins, A. Esme, 41
Colombia, 91–93

Colonial Film Unit, 93
Comerio, Luca, 211
Commedia Brillante, 94
Commercial and Educational Films, 94
Commission on Cultural and Educational Films, 234
Commission Supérieure Technique du Cinéma Française, 94
Commonwealth Film Unit, 145
Commonwealth Productions, 74
Compagne Cinématographique Canadienne, 305
Compagnie Générale Française de Cinématographie, 94, 145
CONACITE, 249
Concorde Film, 262
Congo, People's Republic of, 94
Congrès des Dupes, 94
Conness, Luke Edwin, 94
Conness Till Film Company, 94–95
Conroy, David, 238
Continental Gesellschaft, 95
Cook Islands, 95
Coopératio, 95
COPROCI, 291
Cordero, Amabilis, 381
CORFO, 78
Corniglion-Molinier, Edouard, 385
Corvin Studios, 196
Costa Rica, 72–74
Costa Rican Centre of Film Production, 74
Costil, Edgar, 315
Council of Europe, 96
Coward, Nöel, 84
Cowie, Peter, 207
Cravenne, Georges, 75
Cricket, 96
Cricks, G. H., 96
Cricks and Martin, 96
Cricks and Sharp, 96
Cristofari, Ezio, 210
Crown Film Unit, 96–97
Cuba, 97–101
Cunliffe, Mitzi, 42
Curzon Cinema, 101–2
Cypriot Cinema Consultative Committee, 102
Cyprus, 102
Czechoslovak Filmexport, 104
Czechoslovakia, 29, 102–4, 133, 233

Dagher, Assia, 123
Daguerre, Louis, 114
Dahl, Gustavo, 40
Daiei Color, 105
Daiei Motion Picture Co. Ltd., 105
Dai-Nikon Eiga, 105
Dalrymple, Ian, 97, 390
Dalton, Emmet, 10
Danish Film Academy, 305–6
Danish Film Institute, 105–6
Danish Film Studio, 106
Danish Government Film Office, 332
Danmarks Film Akademi, 305–6
Dansk Kulturfilm, 110
Danzig, 106
d'Arbeloff, Alexander, 322
Darling, Alfred, 41
Dartnall, Gary, 349
David Di Donatello Awards, 106
Davidsons Union, 357
Davis, J. Merle, 3
Davis, John, 303, 304
Day, Will, 391
Dean, Basil, 118
de Baroncelli, Jacques, 145, 239
de Barros, José Leitaõ, 296
Debrie, André, 106
Debrie Parvo camera, 106
de Casa Maury, Marquis, 101
de Cazotte, Henri, 322
Decla Bioscop, 106–7
Découpage, 107
Decourcelle, Pierre, 321
Deed, André, 210
DEFA, 107
De Hert, Robert, 172
Delac, Charles, 145
de la Parra, Pim, 313
De Laurentiis, Dino, 113, 212, 263
del Giudice, Filippo, 355
Delluc, Louis, 160
Delvaux, André, 30
Demeny, Georges, 83
Denham Studios, 107–8

Denmark, 33–34, 105–6, 108–13, 230, 279, 305, 332
de Noialles, Vicomte, 84
de Rothschild, Henri, 171
De Santis, Guiseppe, 57
DeSève, Joseph-Alexandre, 305
DEULIG, 113
Deutsch, Oscar, 278
Deutsche Film Aktiengesellschaft, 107
Deutsche Filmpreise, 54
Deutsche Film- und Fernsehakademie Berlin GmbH, 113
Deutsche Lichtbildgeselschaft, 113
Deutsche Ligs für Unabhängigen Film, 177
Deutsche Tonfilm A. G., 350
De Vree, Paul, 172
de Zoubaloff, Dimitri, 184
Diamant-Berger, Henri, 32
Dickinson, Thorold, 320
Di Domenico Brothers, 91
Dinocitta, 113
Diorama, 114
Discina, 114
Disher, Norma, 389
"Doctor" Series, 114
Documento, 114
Dolimiti Film Production Company, 114–15
Dominican Republic, 115
Doniol-Valcroze, Jacques, 57
Donner, Jörn, 165, 224–25
Drabinsky, Garth, 67, 88
Drankov, Alexander, 375
Dreyfus Affair, 115
Dublin, 115
Dufay, Louis, 115
Dufaychrome, 115–16
Dufay-Chromex Ltd., 116
Dufaycolor, 116
Dulac, Germaine, 133, 134, 159
Dupuy-Mazuel, Henry, 321
Durand, Jean, 321
Dutch Film Co., 261
Duvivier, Julien, 72
Dyer, Anson, 8
Dymling, Carl Anders, 337
Dynamic frame, 116
Eady, Sir Wildred, 117
Eady Levy, 117–18
Ealing Studios, 118–19
Ebberts, Jack, 183
Eclair, 119–22
Eclipse Company, 122
L'Écran, Français, 122
Ecuador, 122–23
Edda Film, 197
Edinburgh Film Guild, 123
Éditions Mondiales, 15
Eesti Kultuurfilm, 129
Efftee Film Productions, 123
Egger, George, 90
Egypt, 123–25
Eiga Rinri Kitel, 221
Eire, 10, 115, 125–26, 173
Eirin, 221
Eisenstein, Sergei, 116
Eisner, Lotte, 86
Elder, T. C., 390
Elfert, Peter, 108
Elliman, Louis, 10
Elokuvajournalistit ry, 225
El Salvador, 72–74
Elstree Studios, 126–27
Elton, Arthur, 317
Elvin, George, 18
Embrafilme, 40
EMI, 349
EMI Films, 51
EMI-MGM Elstree Studios Ltd., 127
Emir, Aziza, 123
Emmer, Luciano, 114
Emmett, E. V. H., 175
Empire Library, 75
Empire Marketing Board Film Unit, 96
Empire News Bulletin, 128
Empire Theatre, Leicester Square, 128
ENCINE, 9
Engl, Josef, 352
England. *See* United Kingdom
Ente Autonomo Gestione Cinema, 84, 128
Eon Productions, 216
Epstein, Marie, 86
E. Rancati & Co., 128
Ermolieff, Joseph, 160

Esperanto, 128–29
Espinosa, Julio García, 99
Estonia, 129
Etablissements Aubert, 129
Europa Film, 341
Europa Film AB, 338
European Economic Community, 129
European Parliament, 129
Evening News Awards, 237
Everyman Cinema, 129–30
Eve's Film Review, 130
Experimental Cinema Group of the University of Panama, 284
Experimental Film Fund, 47
Expressionism, 130–31

Fabrika Eksentricheskovo Aktyora, 133–34
Factory of the Eccentric Actor, 133–34
Fairfax-Jones, Jim, 130
Famous Players Canada, 63, 64, 66
FAMU, 133
Fanck, Dr. Arnold, 252
Fantômas, 133
Farabi Cinema Foundation, 208
Farabundo Marti National Liberation Front, 74
Farias, Roberto, 40
Fédération Française des Ciné-Clubs, 133
Fédération Internationale des Archives du Film, 134
Federation of British Filmmakers, 45
FEKS, 133–34
Fenelon, Moacyr, 38
Fennada-Filmi Oy, 162
Ferrania Color, 134
Ferreyra, José Augustin, 11–12
Festival Awards, 145–46
Festival Panafricain du Cinéma de Ouagadougou, 373
Festivals, 146–58
Feuillade, Louis, 133
Feyder, Jacques, 184
FIAF, 134
FICA, 135
FIDO, 158–59
Fiji, 135
Filem Negara, 242
Filipino Motion Picture Board, 292
Film archives, 135–44
Film à Thèse, 144
Film Australia, 144–45
Filmbewertungsstelle, 145
Filmbulgaria, 54
Film Company of Ireland, 125
Filmcraft Ltd., 267
Film Credit Bank, 159
Film d'Art, 145
Film Defense Fund, 158–59
Film Evaluation Office, 145
Filmex, 261
Film festival awards, 145–46
Film festivals, 146–58
Filmförderungsanstalt, 158
Filmiaura ry, 225
Film industry defense fund, 158–59
Filmkreditbank, 159
Film Location Facilities, 355
Filmmedarbejderforeningen, 33
"Filmologie," 159
Filmové Studio Barrandov, 29
Film Polski, 159
Film Promotion Law, 158
Films à Clef, 159
Films and Filming, 159
Films Ariane, 15
Films de la Pleïade, 160
Films D.-H, 159
Films du Carrosse, 160
Films du Losange, 160
Films Ermolieff, 160
Film societies, 160, 161, 203–7
Film Society, 161
Film Weekly, 161
FINAS, 242
Finland, 161–65, 224, 225, 335
Finney, Albert, 244
Finnish Film Foundation, 165
Finnkino oy, 165
Fleapit, 165
FMLN, 74
FOCINE, 92–93
Forbes, Bryan, 127
Ford, Aleksander, 294
Foreign Legion, 165–66
Forest, Mark, 241

Forgeot, Jacques, 83
Formalism, 166
Forslund, Bengt, 77
Fotorama, 272
France, 4, 5, 7, 9, 14, 17, 31, 32–33, 57, 71, 72, 75, 76, 80, 83, 84, 85–87, 89, 91, 94, 106, 107, 114, 119–22, 129, 133, 145, 159, 160, 165, 166–70, 171, 175, 177, 184, 186, 198, 239, 243, 264–65, 285–86, 287–88, 291, 293, 294, 296, 298, 304, 306, 308, 315, 321, 322, 331, 334, 335, 348, 359, 384–85
France Film, 305
Franchi, Michele Guido, 250
Francis, David, 47, 323
Francita-Realita, 170–71
Franco-American Cinematographic Corporation, 171
Franco Films, 385
Franju, Georges, 85, 134
Frappe, Jean-José, 321
Freddi, Luigi, 83, 391
Free Cinema, 171
Free Cinema of Iran, 87
French Revolution, 171
Frenkel, Theo, Sr., 261
Freund, Karl, 387
Friedrich-Wilhelm-Murnau-Stiftung, 352
Friese-Greene, William, 360
Fugitive Cinema, 171–72
Fujicolor, 172
Fuji Film Co. Ltd., 172
Fuji Pictures Corp., 319
Futurism, 172

Gabon, 173
Gaelic, 173
Gael-Linn, 173
Gainsborough Studios, 173–74
Gallegos, Romulo, 381
Gallo, Mario, 210
Gance, Abel, 296
Gaspar, Dr. Bela, 174
Gasparcolor, 174–75
Gasteren, Louis van, 329
Gaumont, 175
Gaumont, Léon, 167, 175
Gaumont-British News, 175
Gaumont-British Picture Corporation, 176
Gaumont Franco Film Aubert, 175
Gaumont Graphic, 177
Gavaert Company, 174
GECU, 73
Gemeaux, 2
Gemeaux, Les, 177
Geminis, 2
Gendai-Geki Film, 218
Genies, 2
Georges de Beauregard Award, 177
German Cinematograph Company, 133
German League for the Independent Film, 177
Germany, 4, 15, 16, 19, 32, 33, 54, 72, 106, 107, 113, 145, 158, 159, 177–81, 191, 193, 227, 228, 230, 243, 252–53, 260, 263, 277–78, 279, 280, 299, 304, 313, 331, 332, 333, 334, 345, 346, 350, 351, 352, 353, 357–58, 387, 390; Germany–East, 178–79; Germany–West, 179–81
Gevaert Photo-Producten N. V., 4
Geva Films, 181
GG Israel Studios, 271
Ghana Film Unit, 181
Gibraltar, 181
Gibson, Mel, 241
Gildemeijer, Johann, 261
Gilliam, Terry, 251
Gilliat, Sidney, 311
Glasgow, 181
Globus, Yoram, 271
Glucksman, Max, 10
Godard, Jean-Luc, 9, 160, 198
Godzilla, 181–82
Goede Film Exploitatie, 182
Gofilex Film B. V., 182
GOFTA Award, 182
Gojira, 181–82
Golan, Menahem, 209, 210, 271
Golan-Globus Productions, Ltd., 271
Gold Bug Awards, 183
Gold Coast Film Unit, 181
Goldcrest Films and Television Ltd., 183
Golden Gross Award, 399
Golden Harvest (HK) Ltd., 193

Goldin, Sidney M., 395
Gonzaga, Adhemar, 37
Gooes, Roland, 135
Goskino, 183
Gow, Keith, 389
Goya Awards, 184
Graham, Sean, 181
Granding, Tatina, 114
Grandscope, 184
Grands Film Independents, 184
Gras, Enrico, 114
Great Britain. *See* United Kingdom
Greater J. D. Williams Amusement Company, 19
Greater Union Film Distributors, 20
Greater Union Theatres, 19
Great Northern Film Company, 271
Greece, 184–85, 186
Greek Film Centre, 186
Green, John C., 58
Green, Joseph, 395
Greenberg, Harold, 65
Greenland, 186
Greenwich Film, 186
Grierson, John, 75, 96, 97, 145, 186, 256, 317, 372
Grimault, Paul, 177
Grimoin-Sanson, Raoul, 87
Grinieff, Jacques, 322
Gross, Edward M., 291
Groupe Octobre, 186
Groupe Rivaud, 288
Group 3, 186–87
Grune, Karl, 332
Grupo Cine Liberacion, 13
Grupo Experimental de Cine Universitario, 284
Grupo Ukamau, 35–36
Guam, 187
Guastella, Roberto, 299
Guatemala, 72–74
Guggenheim, Eugene, 321
Guild of Film Art Directors, 46
Guild of Television Producers and Directors, 42
Gulistan Films, 3
Gutzman, J. A., 375
Haddad, George, 234
Hagen, Julius, 355
Haggar, Walter, 189
Haggar, William, 189
Haggar and Sons, 189
Haiti, 189
Halas, John, 189
Halas and Batchelor Cartoon Films Ltd., 189–90
Halifax Films, 70
Hall, Ken G., 89–90
Halton, Fiona, 48
Hammer Film Productions Ltd., 190–91
Hancock, Margaret, 45
Handmade Films, 191
Hanumarn Film, 347
Hardy, Forsyth, 45, 123
Harle, Paul-Auguste, 85
Harrison, George, 191
Hasselbach, Ernst, 334
Hasselbladfilm, 338
Havel, Mioš, 103
Hawes, Stanley, 145
Heaword, Rosemary, 323
Heimat, 191
Helstern, Peter and Martin, 19
Hemdale, 370
Hepp, Joseph, 184
Hepworth, Cecil, 191–92
Hepworth Manufacturing Company, 191–92
Herkomer, Hubert von, 192
Herkomer Film Company, 192–93
Heroux, Denis, 6
Hertz, Carl, 19
Herzliya Studios, 209, 373
Heyns Films, 384
Hibbert, Henry, 71
Hillel-Erlanger, Irene, 159
Himmel, André, 171
Hinds, Anthony, 190
Hinds, William, 190
Hindustan Film Company, 200
Hochschule für Fernsehen und Film, 193
Hoellering, George, 1
Holland, Captain H. H. B., 70
Holland, George and Andrew, 58
Hollandia Filmfabriek, 261

Honduras, 72–74
Hong Kong, 193–94
Hong Kong Film Culture Centre, 194
Horner, W. G., 399
Howard-Gwynne, Francis, 45
Hoyts Distribution, 20
Hoyts Theatres, 20
Hugenberg, Alfred, 113, 358
Hungarian Film Productions, 284
Hungarofilm, 194
Hungary, 29, 53, 174, 194–96, 284–85, 292, 331
Hunnia, 195, 196
Hurley, Frank, 89

ICAIC, 98–101
Iceland, 197–98, 280
Icelandic Films, 197
IDHEC, 198
Idle, Eric, 251
IMCINE, 249
Impéria Films, 198
Imperial Cinema Art Company, 218
Imperial War Museum, 198–99
INCINE, 268, 269
Independent Film and Video Makers' Association, 199
Independent Film Distributors' Association, 199
"Independent Producers," 199
India, 199–202, 245, 258
Indian Motion Picture Producers Association, 202
Individual Pictures Ltd., 202–3
Indonesia, 90, 203
Ingram, Rex, 384
Inspiration Films, 203
Institut de Hautes Études Cinématographiques, 198
Instituto Angolano de Cinema, 9
Instituto Cinematográfico Boliviano, 35
Instituto Cubano de Arte e Industria Cinematográfica, 98–101
International Federation of Film Archives, 134
International Federation of Film Societies, 203–7
International Film Guide, 207
International Short Film Conference, 207
Intorgkino, 326
Iran, 87, 207–8
Ireland. *See* Eire
Irish Film Board, 125
Isis Film Company, 123
Iskusstvo Kino, 208–9
Ismael, Usmar, 203
Israel, 181, 209–10, 271, 373, 389
Israel Film Center, 209
Istituto Luce, 210
Itala Film, 210
Italnoleggio, 210
Italy, 9, 27, 32, 57, 75, 83–84, 89, 94, 106, 113, 114, 128, 134, 172, 210–13, 241, 244, 250, 259–60, 298, 307, 327, 350, 359, 384–85, 391
Ivory, James, 245
Ivory Coast, 214

"Jack the Ripper," 215
Jadran Film, 397–98
Jamaica, 215
"James Bond" Series, 215–26
Japan, 31, 76, 105, 172, 181–82, 184, 216–24, 228, 270, 316, 319–20, 351, 353, 359, 396, 399
Japan Cinematograph Company, 270
Japan Motion Picture Producers Association, 218
Jarosy, Ivo, 1–2
J. Arthur Rank Productions, Ltd., 303, 356
Jasset, Victorin, 119–20
Jhabvala, Ruth Prawar, 245
Johnson, Martin and Osa, 3, 36
Jones, Terry, 251
Jörn Donner Productions, 224–25
Jourjon, Charles, 119
Journées Cinématographiques de Carthage, 353
Jupp, R. T., 355
Jussi Awards, 225

Kachusha-Mono, 227
Kael, Pauline, 24
Kammerspielfilm, 227
Karina, Anna, 9

Kawaura, Kenichi, 396
Kemeny, John, 6
Kennedy, Byron, 241
Keris Film Productions, 242
Kerridge Odeon Chain, 266
Kerzner, Sol, 325
Kinematograph Renters Society, 323
The Kinematograph Weekly, 227
Kineopticon, 228
Kingsley, David, 51
Kinofa Film, 102
Kino Films (1935) Ltd., 228
Kino-Pravda, 228
Kinoreformbewegung, 228
Klangfilm, 228
Klausberger, Dr. Arthur, 313
Klimov, Elem, 378
Kluge, Alexander, 230
Kobayashi, Ichizo, 351
Kolm, Anton, 23
Kolowrat-Krakovsky, Graf Alexander "Sascha," 23, 313
Kommunale Kinematografers Landsforfund, 271
Kommunales Kino, 228
Kommunenes Filmcentral A/S, 272
Konicolor, 228
Konishiroku Photo Industry Co. Ltd., 228
Korda, Alexander, 51, 107–8, 194–95, 237, 318
Korea, 229–30
Kosmorama, 230
Kozintsev, Grigori, 133
Kranzhonkov, Alexander, 375
Krasin, Leonid, 326
Kristianstads Biograf-Teatern, 337
Křížnecký, Jan, 102
Küchenmeister Kommendit Gesellschaft, 350
Kunstlichtatelier, 230
Kuratorium Junger Deutscher Film, 230
Kutzsch, Ludwig, 113
Kuwait, 230–31
Kuwait Cinema Company, 231

Lafitte Brothers, 145
Lane, Sir Allan, 289
L'Anglais, Paul, 301
Langlois, Henri, 85–87, 134
Lantos, Robert, 6
Lapp, 233
Laterna Magica, 233
Latin, 233
Latin American Film Festival, 382
Latvia, 233–34
Laughton, Charles, 244
Launder, Frank, 311
Lavalou, Jean Marie, 239
Lavender print, 234
Lavo Film, 347
Lawley, H. V., 90
Lawson, Hannah, 45
Lazak, Heinz, 313
League of Nations, 234
Lean, David, 84
Lebanon, 234–35
Lee, Derek, 239
Lee, James, 183
Lee Electric (Lighting) Ltd., 318
Lee Productions, 229
Legg, Stuart, 70, 392
Lehnich, Dr. Oswald, 305
Lenfilm, 235
Leonel Rugama Film Brigade, 268
Leon Schiller National School of Film, Television and Theatre, 235
Lepage, Henri, 10
Levy, Jerome, 389
Levy, Stuart, 8
L'Herbier, Marcel, 84, 198
Libya, 235
Lieberneiner, Wolfgang, 358
Lieberson, Sandy, 183
Linder, Max, 184, 287
Literary Motion Picture Society, 160
Lithuania, 235
Lithuanian Film Studio, 235
Lloyds Bank Screenwriting Competition, 235
Lodz Film School, 235
Lombardo, Gustavo, 350
Lombardo Film, 350
London, 236–37
London Evening Standard Awards, 237
London Films, 237–38

London International Film School, 238
London School of Film Technique, 238
London Underground, 239
Look at Life, 239
Lotus Film Company, 123, 200
Loudon, Norman, 317
Louma Remote Control Camera Platform, 239
Lucan, Arthur, 278
Lucari, Gianni Hecht, 114
Lucerna Film, 103
Lugosi, Bela, 292, 331
Lumière, Louis and Auguste, 166, 239
Lumière Cinematographe, 36, 97, 102, 108, 161, 166, 177, 194, 200, 210, 216, 239, 245, 260, 294, 327, 337, 342, 373, 375
Lumina Films, 239
Luna Film, 54
Luria, Norman, 284
Lusitañia Film, 296
Luxembourg, 239–40
LVN Pictures, 292
Lykke-Seest, Peter, 273

"Maciste" Series, 241
Mackássy, Gyula, 184
McLaren, Norman, 228, 256
McShane, Kitty, 278
Madan, J. F., 200
Madan, J. F., 200
"Mad Max" Series, 241
Mafilm, 195
MAFIRT, 195
Magirama, 296
Magnusson, Charles, 337
Magyar Filmgyártó Vállalat, 284
Mahomo, Nana, 324
Malayan Movies, 291
Malay Film Productions Ltd., 242
Malaysia, 241–42
Mali, 242
Malik, Djamaluddin, 203
Malta, 242–43
Malta Film Facilities, 243
Mancunian Film Corporation, 243
Mann, Heinrich, 387
Manvell, Roger, 42, 289
Marey, Étienne-Jules, 83
Marianne Productions, 243
Marinetti, Filippo Tommaso, 172
"Marius" Trilogy, 243
Martin, J. H., 96
Masseron, Alain, 239
Massolle, Joseph, 352
Mathiesen, Mattis, 346
Matuszewski, Boleslaw, 294
Mauclaire, Jean, 335
Maxwell, John, 49, 126
May, Joe, 243
May-Film, 243
Mayflower Pictures Corporation, Ltd., 244
Medusa Distribuzione, 244
Medwin, Michael, 244
Meerson, Mary, 86
Melbourne Directors Guild, 21
Méliès, Georges, 166, 331
Memorial Films Ltd., 244
Mentasti, Angel, 11
Menu, Paul, 306
Menz, Dieter, 19
Mercanton, Louis, 122
Mercato Internazionale del Film del TV film e del Documentario, 250
Merchant, Ismail, 245
Merchant-Ivory Productions, 245
Messter, Oskar, 33, 177, 230
Messter Film, 357
Messter Ton, 350
Mexico, 245–50
"Mid-Atlantic Pictures," 250
Midrand Film Studios, 325
MIFED, 250
Milan, 250
Milano Film, 211
Miller, George, 241
Mills & Allen, 318
Minerva Films, 251
Mingxing Film Company, 81
Mining Review, 251
Miramar Film Studios, 267
Miro, Pilar, 328
Mitry, Jean, 85
Mittelholzer, Walter, 298
Mokadi, Amos, 373

Moldavia, 251
Moldovafilm, 251
Montagu, Ivor, 228
Monty Python, 251
MOPEX, 195
Morena Films, 324
Morocco, 252
Moscow, 252
Mosfilm, 252
Mosjoukine, Ivan, 376
Mottershaw, Frank, 316
Mountain Films, 252–53
Moving Picture Co., 71
Munk, Andzej, 295
Museum of the Moving Image, 47
Myrga, Laurence, 334

Nagata, Masaichi, 105
Nalpas, Louis, 145, 384
Narrow Gauge films, 255
Nash Circuit, 58
Natan, Bernard, 288, 298
Nathanson, N. L., 60, 63
National Association of Municipal Cinemas, 271
National Coal Board, 251
National Film and Television School, 255–56
National Film Board of Canada, 61, 70, 256–58, 392
National Film Development Corporation, 258
National Film Finance Corporation, 258–59
National Film Theatre, 47
Natural Color Moving Picture Company, 217
Navarre, René, 321
Navon, Mordecai, 181
Nazir Films, 3
Nebenzahl, Seymour, 260
Nederlandse Bioscoopbond, 259
Neo-Realism, 259–60
Nepal, 260
Nepomuceno, Jose, 292
Nero-Film A.G., 260
Netherlands, 182, 259, 260–62, 313, 329
Netherlands Antilles, 262
Nettlefold Film Productions, 192
Neubabelsberg Studios, 263, 358
Neumann, József, 194
Neville Wran Award for Excellence, 263
New Brunswick Films, 70
New Burma Films, 55
New Caledonia, 263
Newfoundland Films, 70
Newman, Arthur S., 263
Newman and Sinclair Ltd., 263
Newman Sinclair camera, 263
News and Specialised Theatre Association of Great Britain and Northern Ireland, 263
New South Wales Film Corporation, 263–64
Newsreel Association of Great Britain and Ireland Ltd., 264
Newsreels, 5, 17, 51–52, 70, 128, 130, 175, 177, 228, 251, 263, 264, 288, 289, 320, 351, 386–87, 390
New Wave, 169, 264–65
New Zealand, 182, 265–66
New Zealand Film Commission, 267
New Zealand National Film Unit, 267–68
NFFC, 258–59
Nicaragua, 268–70
Niger, 270
Nigeria, 270
Nikkatsu, 270
Nippon Katsudo Sashin, 270
Noah Films Ltd., 271
Noble, Peter, 314
No-Do, 328
Nordisk Film, 271
Norrish, Bernard E., 17
Norsk Film A/S, 271–72
Norsk Kino- og Filmfond, 7, 273
North Korean International Film Festival, 229
North Pole, 272
Norway, 7, 271, 272–76, 332
Norwegian Cinema and Film Foundation, 7, 273
Notcutt, Major L. A., 3
"Noticiario CMQ-Cristal," 98
Noticiarios-Documentales, 328
Nounez, Jacques-Louis, 14

La Nouvelle Edition Française, 276
Nouvelle Editions de Films, 276
Nouvelle Vague, 264–65
Numa Petersons Handels & Fabriks AB, 337

Oberhausen Manifesto, 277
O'Brien, Denis, 191
Obshchestvo Druzei Sovetskogo Kino, 280
Obshchestvo Stroitelei Proletarskogo Kino, 280
"Ocker" comedies, 277–78
Odeon circuit, 278
Office Cinematographique National du Mali, 242
Oizumi, 351
Okawa, Hiroshi, 351
Okey, Jack, 107
Okura, Mitsugu, 319
"Old Mother Riley" Series, 278
Oliver, H. T., 70
Olsen, Ole, 271
"Olsen Gang" Series, 279
Olympia-Film GmbH, 279
Ombres Chinoises, 315
Omegno, Roberto, 211
Ontario Film Development Corporation, 279
Ontario Film Institute, 279–80
Ontario Motion Picture Bureau, 352
Opticolor, 280
Orko, Risto, 162, 335
Orr, J. Russell, 75
Orson Welles Motion Picture Directional Achievement Award, 280
Orwocolor, 4
Osborne, John, 391–92
Oskar Gislason Award, 280
OSPK, 280
Ostrer, Isadore, 176
Ostrer Brothers, 173, 174
Österreichischer Filmförderungsfond, 23
Oswald, Richard, 260
Otani, Takejiro, 319
Ottawa Film Productions, 70
Ouimet, Léo Ernest, 281
Ouimetoscope, 281
Oxford Film Foundation, 235
Oy Kinosto, 165
Oy Suomen Filmiteollisuus, 335

Pabst, G. W., 387
Pagano, Bartolomeo, 241
Pagnol, Marcel, 243, 321
Painlevé, Jean, 94
Pakistan, 283
Pakshiran Corp., 208
Palestine, 284
Palestine Film Productions, 284
Palin, Michael, 251
Palladium, 109, 110
Panama, 72–74, 284
Pannonia Filmstudio, 284–85
Papua/NewGuinea, 285
Parafumet, 358
Paraguay, 285
Paris, 285–86
Paris, Dr. John Ayrton, 347
Pastrone, Giovanni, 210
Pathé, 287–88
Pathé, Charles, 167, 287, 288
Pathé Cinema, 287
Pathécolor, 288
Pathé-Consortium, 287
Pathé News, 288–89
Pathé Pictorial, 289
Pathétone Weekly, 289
Paul, R. W., 348
Paulvé, André, 114
Pearson, George, 41, 93, 311, 329, 358, 390
Pech, Anton, 102
Pelmex, 247
Penguin Film Review, 289
Perfini Studio, 203
Peries, Lester James, 330
Perry, David, 357
Persari Studio, 203
Peru, 289–91
Perutz, Otto, 280
Petkov, Vladimir, 53
Phalke, Dadasaheb, 200
Phantasmagoria, 291
Phenakistiscope, 291
Philippines, 291–92

Phoenix Film Company, 292
Phono-Ciné Théâtre, 293
Phonoscope, 83
Photosonor, 293
Pichon, Nicole, 31
The Picturegoer, 293
Pictures and the Picturegoer, 293
Picture Show, 293
Pinewood Studios, 293–94
Pirandello, Luigi, 211
Piscator, Erwin, 387
Pittaluga, Stefano, 89
Plan Séquence, 294
Plateau, J. A. F., 291
Poccioni, Franco, 244
Poirier, Léon, 315
Poland, 159, 235, 294–96, 331–32, 395
Polish Army Film Command, 294
Polyvision, 296
Pommer, Erich, 106–7, 244, 357–58
Ponti, Carlo, 208, 212
Popular Association for Film Art, 387
Porcher, François, 184
Portugal, 296–98
Portuguese Film Institute, 297
Powell, Michael, 10
Prabhat Film Company, 200, 201
Praesens-Film AG, 298
Prag-Film Company, 103
Praxinoscope, 399–400
Premiere Productions, 292
Pressburger, Emeric, 10
Prevost camera, 298
Prince Edward Island Films, 70
Prix France-Canada, 298
Producciones Angel, 13
Producers & Directors Guild of Australia, 21
Producine, 268
Production Natan, 298
Productions Artistes Associés, 298–99
Projectograph, 194
Projektions-A. G.-Union, 299
Prometheus-Film-GmbH, 299
Provincial Cinematograph Theatres, 176
Prudential Life Assurance Company, 107–8, 237
Public schools, 299
Puerto Rico, 299–300
Puro, Teuvo, 161, 335
Puttnam, David, 183
Py, Eugene, 10
Pyongyang University of Cinematography, 229

Quebec Productions Corporation, 62, 64, 301
Queensway Studios, 62
Quinn, Bob, 173
"Quota Quickies," 301–2

Ramlee, P., 242
Rancati, Edoardo, 128
Rank, J. Arthur, 108, 118, 174, 176, 199, 303–4, 355, 356, 365–66
Rank circuit, 176
Rank Organization, 174, 278, 293, 303–4, 356
Read, Aggy, 357
Reganne Films, 304
Reichsfilmkammer, 304–5
Reinhardt, Max, 227
Relph, Simon, 259
Rembrandt-Film, 261
Renaissance Films Distribution, 305
Renoir, Jean, 276
Renter, 305
Reulos, Lucien, 331
Revelation Films, 305
Reynaud, Emile, 399–400
Rhodes, Eric, 90
Richardson, Tony, 391–92
Richter, Hans, 177
Richter, Robert, 15
Riefenstahl, Leni, 252, 279
Rio de Janeiro, 305
Roadshow, 20
Robert, Étienne Gaspard, 291
Robert Awards, 305–6
Roberto Rosselini Award, 306
Roberts, Gilmore, 238
Robin Hood, 306
Roca, Augusto, 35
Rodina, 322
Rodker, Francis, 317
Rogers, Peter, 72

Romania, 306–7
Romania Film, 306
Rome, 307
Roncoroni, Carlo, 83
Rosenthal, Joseph, 324
Roux, Armand and Lucien, 308
Rouxcolor, 308
Royal Command Film Performances, 308
Royal Nepal Film Corporation, 260
Roy Export Company Establishment, 308
Rugby, 308
Ruiz, Jorge, 35
Ruritania, 308–9
Rushes, 309
Russia. *See* USSR
Rutnam, Chandran, 330

"St. Trinian's" Comedies, 311
Saltzmann, Harry, 391–92
Salumbides, Vicente, 292
Sampaguita Pictures, 292
Samsa Film Productions, 240
Samuelson, David, 239, 311
Samuelson, G. B. "Bertie," 311
Samuelson, Michael, 311
Samuelson, Sydney, 311, 312
Samuelson Film Service Ltd., 311–12
Samuelson Group plc., 311–12
Sandrew Film & Teater AB, 312–13
Sanjinés, Jorge, 35
Sanoussi, Mohammed, 230
Sapper, Alan, 18
Särkkä, Toivo, 162
Sarris, Andrew, 24
Sarrut, André, 177
Sascha-Film GmbH, 313
Sascha-Wien Film, 313
Satadema Films Ltd., 243
Satbel Group, 325
SATPEC, 353
Sault Ste. Marie Films, 70
Saura, Carlos, 328
Saville, Victor, 173
Savoy Filmi oy, 165
SCAGL, 321
Scheuermann, Dr. Fritz, 305
Schuberg, John Albert, 58
Schüfftan, Eugen, 313
Schüfftan process, 313
Schweizer Filmzentrum, 343
Scorpio Verstappen Films N.V., 313
Scottish Central Film Library, 313
Scottish Federation of Film Societies, 45
Scottish Film Council, 313–14
Screen International, 314
Screen Productions Association of Australia, 21
Sedláčková, Andula, 102
SEFT, 323
Segreto, Paschoal and Affonso, 36
Seiden, Joseph, 395
Sellers, William, 93
Sembene, Ousmane, 314
Senegal, 314–15
Sequence, 315
Séries Pax, 315
Service Photographique et Cinématographique de l'Armée, 315
Sestier, Maurice, 200
Setton, Maxwell, 52
Seven Arts Productions U.K., 53
Shadow plays, 315
Shafaq Films, 3
Shakai-Mono, 316
Sharp, H. M., 96
Shaw, Run Me, 241–42, 316, 345
Shaw, Sir Run Run, 241–42, 316, 345
Shaw Brothers (Hong Kong) Ltd., 316
Sheffield Photo Co., 316
Shell Film Unit, 317
Shelmerdine, Mark, 238
Shepherd, Horace, 203
Shepherds Bush Studios, 176
Shepperton Studios, 317–18
Shibata, Tsunekichi, 216
Shields, Ronald, 45
Shinko Kyoto Studios, 105
Shintoho, 319
Shipman, Ernest, 60, 70
Shirai, Matsujiro, 319
Shochiku Co. Ltd., 319–20
Shochiku-Fuji, 31
Shomin-Geki Films, 218
Shumyatski, Boris Zakharovich, 326
Siemens & Halske A.G., 228, 280
Sihanouk, Prince Norodom, 57

Silberman, Serge, 186
Sinclair, James A., 263
Singapore, 320
Singapore Film Society, 320
16mm Film Exhibitors' Guild, 320
Skladanowsky, Max and Emil, 33, 177, 272, 337
Skot-Hanse, Mogens, 372
Slade Film History Register, 320
Slide, Anthony, 323
Smith, G. Albert, 41
Smith, Samuel Woolf, 50
SNEG, 175
Soccer, 320–21
Sociedad Cultural Nuestro Tiempo, 98
Société Anonyme Cinématographique de l'Iran, 208
Société Anonyme Tunisienne de Production et d'Expansion Cinématographique, 353
Société Chromofilm, 170
Société Cinématographique des Auteurs et Gens des Lettres, 321
Société de Films en Couleurs Naturelles Francita, 170
Société des Cinéromans, 321
Société des Établissements Gaumont, 175
Société des Films Historiques, 321
Société des Films Marcel Pagnol, 321
Société des Films Sacha Gordine, 322
Société des Films Sonores Tobis, 322
Société EDIC, 322
Société Française des Films et Cinématographes Eclair, 119–22
Société Générale de Films, 322
Société Générale du Cinéma du Québec, 322
Société Ivoirienne de Cinéma, 322–23
Société Léon Gaumont et Cie, 175
Société Nationale Voltäique de Cinéma, 373
Société Nouvelle des Etablissements Gaumont, 175
Society for Cinema Studies, 323
Society for Education in Film and Television, 323
Society of British Art Directors and Designers, 46
Society of Builders of Proletariat Cinema, 280
Society of Film and Television Arts, 42
Society of Film Distributors, 323
Society of Friends of Soviet Cinema, 280
Society of the Devotees of the Artistic Film, 331–32
SODRE, 374
Solomon Islands, 324
Sons of George Haddad, 234
South Africa, 324–25
South African Screen Productions Ltd., 324
South Australian Film Corporation, 325
South Pacific, 325–26
Sovcolor, 4, 326
Sovexportfilm, 326
Sovkino, 326
Soyuzkino, 326–27
Spaghetti Westerns, 327
Spain, 28, 184, 327–29
Spanish Civil War, 329
Spectrum Film, 329
Spencer's Pictures Ltd., 19
Spicer-Dufay Ltd., 116
Spielman, Miriam, 373
Spitz, Mrs. Leo, 372
"Squibs" Series, 329–30
Sri Krung, 347
Sri Lanka, 330
Sri Lanka Film Location Services Ltd., 330
Staattsauftragsfilme, 331
Staikov, Lyudmil, 54
Star Film, 331
Star Film Company, 331
START, 331–32
Statens Filmcentral, 332
Statens Filmsentral, 332
Steenbeck, 332
Stern-Film, 332
Stimmung, 332–33
Stock footage libraries, 333–34
Stockholm, 334
Stoll Picture Theatre Club, 160
Storck, Henri, 30
Stow, Percy, 90
Strausfeld, Peter, 1

"Studio D," 257
Studio des Ursulines, 334
Studio 45, 334
"Studio G," 257
Studio Merdeka, 242
Studios Misr, 123
Studio 28, 335
Studio Wahby, 123
Suomen Elokuvakerhojen Liitto, 162
Suomen Elokuvasäätio, 165
Suomen Filmiteollisuus, 162, 163
Suomi-Filmi oy, 335
Surrealism, 335–36
Sutyrin, Vladimir, 326
Svenska Bio, 336
Svenska Filminstitutet, 342
Svensk Filmindustri, 336–37
Sweden, 77, 135, 183, 312–13, 334, 336, 337–42
Swedish Film Institute, 342
Swiss Film Centre, 343
Switzerland, 19, 90, 298, 342–43
Sydney, 343
Sydney, Aurele, 358
Sydney Filmmakers' Cooperative, 357
Sylvia, Carmen, 306
Syndicat de la Cinématographe des Couleurs, 80
Syria, 344

Tachyscope, 345
Taikatsu, 217
Taisho Katsuei, 217
Taiwan, 345–46
Tallents, Sir Stephen, 96
Tallier, Armand, 334
Tanabe, Munehide, 319
Tapiovaara, Nyrki, 162
Teamfilm A/S, 275, 346
Tedesco, Jean, 348
Tehran International Film Festival, 208
Teikine, 218
Teikoku Cinema Geijutsu, 218
Telefilm Canada, 346
Telerecording, 346
Tenkatsu, 217
Tennenshoku Katsudo Shashin, 217
Terra-Film Akt. Ges., 346
Tespi, 211
Thailand, 346–47
Thaumatrope, 347
Théâtre du Vieux-Colombier, 348
Théâtre-Film, 120
Theatrograph, 348
Theodorescu, Constantin T., 306
Thessaloniki Film Festival, 184, 185
Third World Cinema, 348. *See also countries individual*
Thomas, Gerald, 72
Thorn-EMI Screen Entertainment, 349–50
Thring, F. W., 123
Tigon Group, 90
Till, Louis A., 94
Titanus spa, 350
Toa Cinema, 218
Tobago, 350
Tobis, 350
Tobis Studios, 297
Toei, 351
Toeiscope, 351
Toeplitz, Ludovic, 355
Toho Co., Ltd., 181, 351
Tokuma Yasuyoshi, 105
Tokyo, 351
Tokyo Hasei Studios, 319
Tokyo Motion Picture Distribution Company, 351
Tokyo Takarazuka Theatre Corporation, 351
Tonbild Syndikat A.G., 350
Topical Budget, 351
Töplitz, Jersy, 23
Topo, Luigi, 210Tourneur, Maurice, 120
Toyoko, 351
Transit-Film, 351–52
Tranwood Earl, 127
Trauberg, Ilya, 133
Trenker, Luis, 252
Trenton Studios, 352
Tri-Ergon, 352
Triergon-Musik A.G., 350
Trinidad, 352
Truffaut, François, 160
"Trümmerfilme," 353
Tsuma-Mono, 353
Tunisia, 353

Turkey, 353
Twickenham Film Studios, 355
Two Cities Films, Ltd., 355–56

UBU, 357
Ufa, 357–58
UGC, 359
"Ultus" Series, 358–59
UNESCO, 372
Ungerleider, Mór, 194
Unifrance Film, 359
Unijapan Film, 359
Uninci, 328
L'Union Cinematografica Educativa, 210
Union Générale Cinématographique, 359
Unitalia, 359
United Kingdom, 1–2, 8, 9, 10, 16, 17–18, 19, 27, 28–29, 33, 41, 42, 43, 44, 45, 46, 47, 48, 49, 50, 51, 52–53, 71, 72, 75, 76–77, 84, 85, 87, 90, 91, 93, 94, 96–97, 100–101, 107–8, 114, 115–16, 117, 118, 119, 122, 123, 126–27, 128, 129–30, 158–59, 161, 165, 171, 173–74, 175, 176, 177, 181, 183, 186–87, 189–90, 191–92, 198–99, 202–3, 207, 215–16, 227, 228, 234, 235, 236, 237, 238, 239, 243, 244, 250, 251, 255–56, 258–59, 263, 264, 278, 279, 288, 289, 293–94, 299, 301–2, 303–4, 305, 306, 308, 309, 311–12, 313–14, 315, 316, 317, 318, 320, 321, 323, 329–30, 346, 348, 349–50, 351, 355–56, 358, 359–72, 387, 388, 389, 390, 391, 392, 399
United Nations, 372–73
United Studios of Israel Ltd., 373
Universum film Aktiengesellschaft, 357–58
Upper Volta, 373
Urban, Charles, 122, 389
Urban, Max, 102
Uruguay, 373–75
USSR, 5, 15, 133–34, 166, 183, 208–9, 228, 235, 251, 252, 280, 326–27, 375–79, 384, 387
Uzbeck Cinema, 376
Uzkinay, Fuat, 353

Vandal, Marcel, 119
Varvasseur, J. H., 51
Vaughan, Olwen, 134
Vauhini Pictures, 201
Venezuela, 381–83
Venice, 383–84
Venice Film Festival, 384
Vera Cruz Studios, 38
Verband der Filmarbeiterinnen, 19
Verstappen, Wim, 313
Vertov, Dziga, 228
Vesa Film, 398
Veyre, Gabriel, 97
VGIK, 384
Viba Film, 398
Victorine Studios, 384–85
Vienna, 385
Vietnam, 385–86
Vietnam War, 386
Vigo, Jean, 14
Village Theatres, 20
Visatone, 386
Visnews Ltd., 386
Visonor Educational Films, 387
Vita-Film, 387
Vivaphone, 192
Vogt, Hans, 352
Volksverband für Filmkunst, 387
Vostakkino, 376
Vsesoyuznyi Gosudartvenyi Institut Kinematografi, 384
VUFKU, 387

Wadia Movietone, 201
Wajda, Andrzej, 295
Walker, Brent, 183
Wardour Films, 49
Warner Bros. Fund for Development of Script Writing in Israel, 389
Warwick Trading Company, 389
Waterside Workers' Federation Film Unit, 389
Weber, H. and J., 90
Wechsler, Lazare, 298
Welsh, Pearson & Co., Ltd., 390
Welsh, T. A., 390
Welsh language, 390
Welsh-Pearson-Elder, 390

Weltfilm, 390
Welt im Film, 390
Wessex Productions, 390
West, T. J., 19
West's Amalgamated Pictures, 19
White man's burden, 391
White Telephone Films, 391
Wien-Film Gesellschaft mbH, 313
Wilcox, Herbert, 126, 236
Will Day Collection, 391
Williams, D. J., 126
Williamson, James, 41
Wilson, Norman, 123
Winnipeg Productions, 60
Winter, Sándor, 195
Women's Film, Television, and Video Network, 391
Wometco, 115
Woodfall Film Productions Ltd., 391–92
Woolf, C. M., 176, 303
Woolf, Henry Bruce, 49
The World in Action, 392
World Union of Documentary, 392–93
Worton Hall Studios, 311
Wright, Basil, 392
W. Steenbeck & Co., 332

Yakusa Films, 223
Yap, 395
Yiddish films, 395–96
Yokota, 396
Yokota, Einosuke, 396
Yoshizawa, 396
Young, Colin, 255, 256
Yugoslavia, 396–98
Yutkevich, Sergei, 133

Zagreb, 398, 399
Zecca, Ferdinand, 287
Zenifilms, 399
Zenkoren Award, 399
Zoetrope, 399–400

About the Author

As the author or editor of more than thirty-five books on the history of popular entertainment, Anthony Slide has been described by the *Los Angeles Times* as "a one-man publishing phenomenon." Among his books are *Early American Cinema* (1970), *The Films of D.W. Griffith,* with Edward Wagenknecht (1975), *Early Women Directors* (1977), *The Vaudevillians* (1981), *International Film, Radio, and Television Journals* (Greenwood, 1985), and *The American Film Industry: A Historical Dictionary* (Greenwood, 1986). In addition, to his writing, he is a lecturer and filmmaker. He has held executive positions with the American Film Institute and the Academy of Motion Picture Arts and Sciences and is co-owner of Producers Library Service, one of the two oldest and largest independent stock footage libraries in the United States.